AMERICAN PHOTOGRAPHY SHOWCASE

VOLUME 10

American Showcase, Inc.
New York

President and Publisher:
Ira Shapiro

Vice President
Advertising Sales:
Julia Martin Morris

Vice-President
Operations:
Wendl Kornfeld

Associate Publisher:
Chris Curtis

Production Manager:
Kyla Kanz

Administration

Executive Assistant:
Connie Grunwald
Controller:
Ronald Durr
Accounting Assistant:
Soraya Acosta

Marketing

Book Sales Manager:
Ann Middlebrook
Promotion/Publicity Manager:
Deborah Lovell

Advertising Sales

Assistant to V.P. Sales/Mail Service Manager:
Lisa Wilker
Sales Representatives:
New York:
**John Bergstrom, Deborah Darr,
Donna Levinstone, Barbara Preminger,
Wendy Saunders**
Midwest:
Carol Grobman
Rocky Mountain:
Kate Hoffman
West Coast:
**Bob Courtman
Ralph Redpath**

Production

Production Coordinator:
Stephanie Sherman
Grey Pages/Distribution Manager:
Scott Holden
Traffic:
Chuck Rosenow

Published by:
American Showcase, Inc.
724 Fifth Avenue, 10th Floor
New York, New York 10019
Telephone: (212) 245-0981
Telex: 880356 AMSHOW P

American Photography Showcase 10
0931144-44-2 (Softback)
0931144-45-0 (Hardback)

ISSN 0742-9975

Book Design and Mechanical Production:
Downey, Weeks & Toomey, Inc., NYC

Freelance Production and Printing:
Fiona L'Estrange

Grey Pages Mechanical Production:
The Mike Saltzman Group, NYC

Typesetting:
**Ultra Typographic Service, Inc., NYC
Automatech Graphics Corporation, NYC**

Color Separation, Printing and Binding:
Dai Nippon Printing Co. Ltd., Tokyo, Japan

Cover Credits:

Cover Design: Downey Weeks & Toomey, Inc., NYC

Front Cover Photograph: Bill Stettner

Title Page Photograph: Carl Fischer

U.S. Book Trade Publication:
Watson-Guptill Publications
1515 Broadway, New York, New York 10036
(212) 764-7300

For Sales Outside U.S.:
Rotovision S.A.
10 Rue De L'Arquebuse
Case Postal 434
1211 Geneve 11, Switzerland
Telephone: (22) 212121
Telex: 421479 ROVI

AMERICAN PHOTOGRAPHY SHOWCASE

VOLUME 10

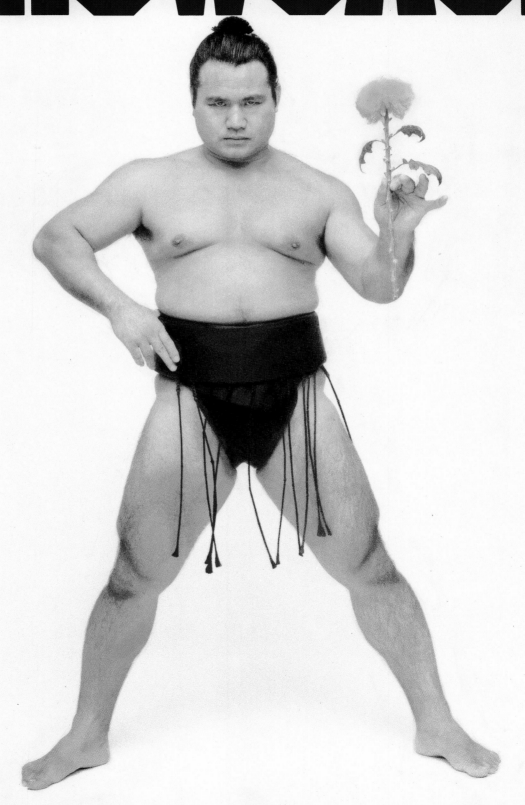

CONTENTS

VIEWPOINTS

GRAPHIC ARTS ORGANIZATIONS

GREY PAGES

Contents

INDEX

ALPHABETICAL LISTING
Photographers

ALPHABETICAL LISTING

continued on next page

ALPHABETICAL LISTING
Photographers

continued from previous page

AMERICAN SHOWCASE 10

An excellent source for ideas, as well as a visual inspiration, American Photography Showcase 10 gives you America's best, most exciting advertising photography at the turn of a page—product shots, portraits, special effects, technical photography, still-life, fashion and much, much more!

This 10th Anniversary Edition is the largest volume of American Photography Showcase ever published! Inside you'll find:

• More than 380 magnificently produced, full-color art pages, representing this country's top commercial photographers with over 1500 photographs.

• An extensive Grey Pages listing section, with over 13,000 addresses and phone numbers of photographers, stock photo agencies, representatives and other essential support services in the advertising industry.

• Clever and provocative essays written by creative leaders in the advertising industry, offering new, often unconventional viewpoints on the complex world of communication.

• A comprehensive list of Graphic Arts Organizations with dozens of names and addresses of associations, clubs, and guilds in the graphics/advertising community.

American Photography Showcase 10 meets all your creative and promotional needs—you'll never reach for another resource!

Complete your advertising library! Back issues of the American Showcase annuals are still available. For more information, call or write:

American Showcase, Inc.
724 Fifth Avenue
New York, New York 10019-4182
(212) 245-0981
Telex: 880356 AMSHOW P

NEW YORK CITY

NEW YORK CITY

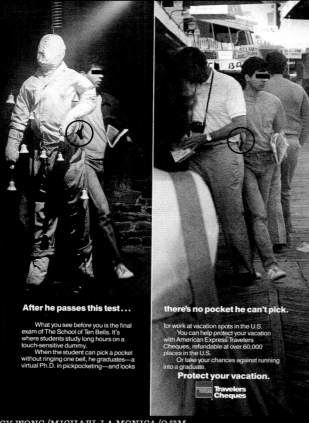

After he passes this test...

What you see before you is the final exam of The School of Ten Bells. It's where students study long hours on a touch-sensitive dummy.

When the student can pick a pocket without ringing one bell, he graduates—a virtual Ph.D. in pickpocketing—and looks

there's no pocket he can't pick.

for work at vacation spots in the U.S.

You can help protect your vacation with American Express Travelers Cheques, refundable at over 60,000 places in the U.S.

Or take your chances against running into a graduate.

Protect your vacation.

AMERICAN EXPRESS **Travelers Cheques**

TRACY WONG/MICHAEL LA MONICA/O&M

TIMBERLAND INTRODUCES THE ULTIMATE WATERPROOF, LIGHTWEIGHT BOOTS IN THE WORLD TODAY.

Timberland

CATHI MOONEY/ALLY & GARGANO

BOB TUCKER/DOYLE DANE & BERNBACH

There was something funny on News 4 New York last night.

Did you see it?

NEWS 4 NEW YORK
Is there any reason to watch anyone else?

STEVE SCHOLEM/LORD GELLER FEDERICO&EINSTEIN

We've been in this business since it started getting ugly.

Some 40 years ago in the car business, something happened.

It started getting fiercely competitive. With imports. And comparative advertising.

Something else happened, too. A new financial source from Marine Midland Bank started helping dealers play the new game.

Today, the competition is uglier than ever. Which makes Automotive Financial look better than ever.

We're now a national company. With the experience to understand the kinds of problems car dealers face.

Unlike many financial sources, the automotive business is our only business. So you get quick response. Plus some of the industry's most innovative financing options.

And we can finance virtually any need a dealership has. Covering everything from sales, to leasing, to construction.

Call 800-448-3400, ext. 329, for the

name and number of your local representative. We'll be glad to discuss any need you might have.

We know your business. Because it's your business. And we can help you get the bugs out.

AUTOMOTIVE FINANCIAL

MIKE FAZENDE/FALLON McELLIGOTT RICE

The most innovative option on this car is the loan.

Today's cars do just about everything but drive themselves.

Unfortunately, high technology leads to high prices. Which makes it harder for cars to sell themselves.

At Marine Midland Automotive Financial, we believe you have to be just as creative in selling today's cars as the factories were in designing them.

So while engineers work to develop the latest in technology, we work to develop the latest in financing.

You see, automotive financing is all we do. So we can see needs and design programs other financial sources never dream of.

Like our Reduced Auto Payment Plan. A unique method for making monthly payments more affordable.

Plus other creative packages that let a dealer offer as many options when financing a car as when ordering one.

Call 800-448-3400, ext. 334, for the name and number of your local representative.

We'd be glad to show you how a little innovation can help cars move faster.

AUTOMOTIVE FINANCIAL
A MARINE MIDLAND COMPANY

MIKE FAZENDE/FALLON McELLIGOTT RICE

FINALLY, AN ADVERTISEMENT BY PEOPLE WHO REALLY KNOW WHAT THEY'RE TALKING ABOUT.

DEGREGORIO/LEVINE HUNTLEY SCHMIDT & BEAVER

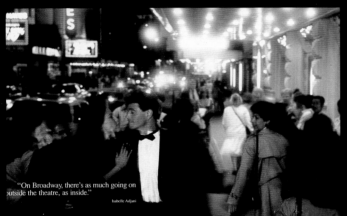

"On Broadway, there's as much going on outside the theatre, as inside."

Isabelle Adjani

DIANE FIUMARA/O&M

Maxell Corp. of America, 60 Oxford Drive, Moonachie, NJ 07074

David Langley Studio, Inc.,
536 W. 50 St., N.Y.C. 10019
(212) 581-3930

T.V. & Photomatic reel
upon request.

To see a portfolio, call
(212) 581-3930, and a
messenger will drop it off.

STARTING OCT. 26 THE NEW YORK SKYLINE WILL NEVER BE THE SAME.

CLARK FRANKEL/Y&R

maxell
FLOPPY DISKS
THE GOLD STANDARD

GEORGE POURIDAS/AC&R

David Langley

IT'S IN THERE!™

HOMEMADE TASTE
Prego Plus
GROUND BEEF
SIRLOIN
& FRESH
ONIONS
SPAGHETTI SAUCE

Homemade taste. It's in there!™

HENRY
WOLF

Some of us have more finely developed nesting instincts than others.

INVEST IN *Karastan*

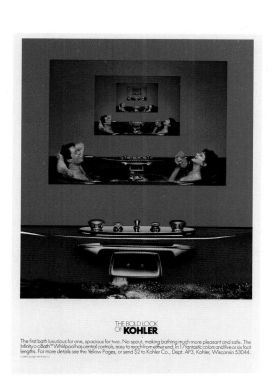

Represented by Jacqueline Dedell   **58 West 15 Street New York NY 10011 212.741.2539**

17

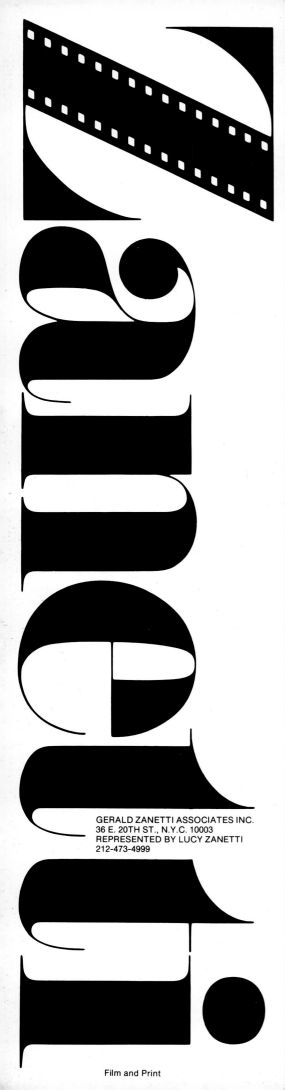

zanetti

GERALD ZANETTI ASSOCIATES INC.
36 E. 20TH ST., N.Y.C. 10003
REPRESENTED BY LUCY ZANETTI
212-473-4999

Film and Print

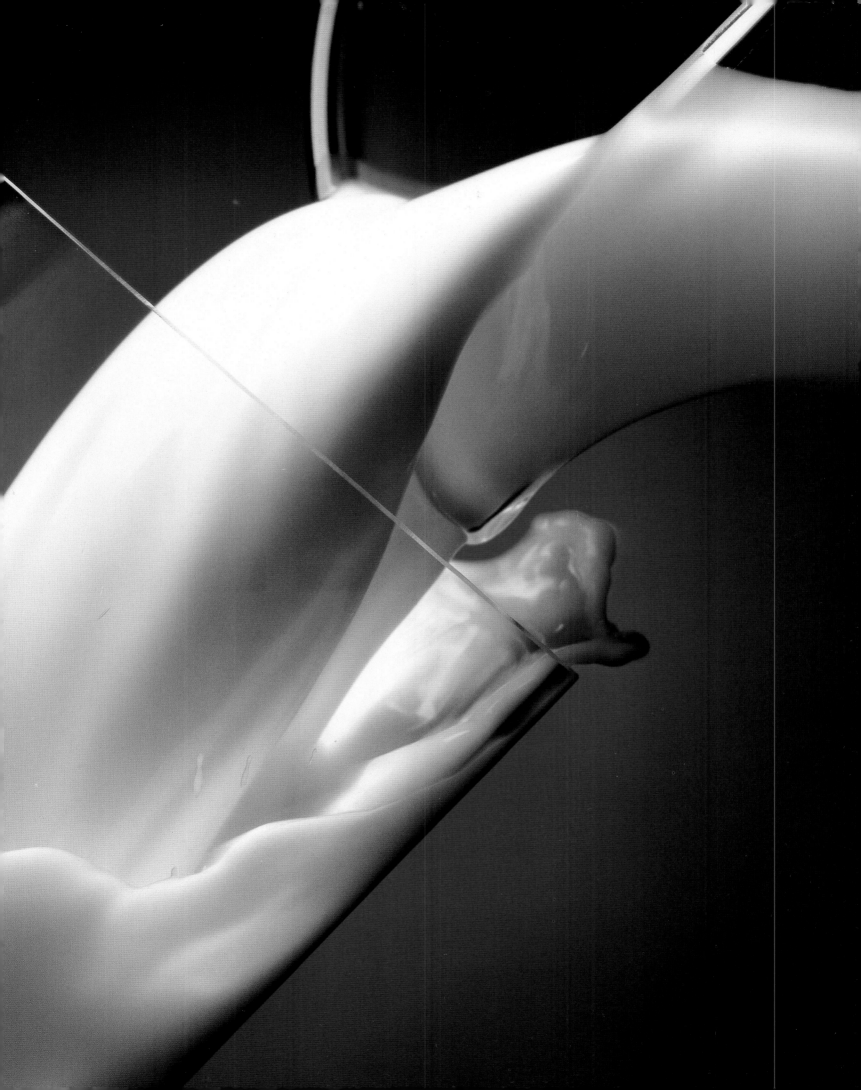

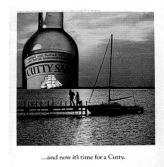

...and now it's time for a Cutty.

SCHLEMIEL CHILDREN

BY SEYMOUR AND RHODA LEE FISHER

Certain troubled children use the ridiculous to cope with life—much like the *schlemiel* of Yiddish folklore. Their development often parallels that of professional comics, according to elaborate testing of both groups.

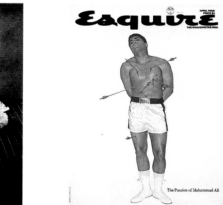

Esquire

The Passion of Muhammad Ali

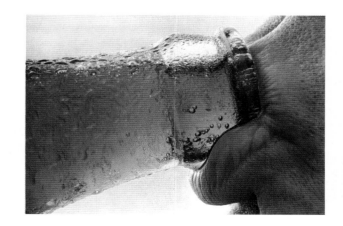

Fischer

121 East 83rd Street, New York, New York 10028 (212) 794-0400

Everybody deserves a chance to make it on their own.   Everybody.

The National Urban League is dedicated to achieving equal opportunity for all. And you can help. Contact your local Urban League or write:

National Urban League
500 East 62nd Street
New York, N.Y. 10021

WHEN YOU ASK US TO DO THE IMPOSSIBLE, WE'LL NEVER SAY IT'S IMPOSSIBLE.

We didn't get to be one of the most flexible, responsive knit fabric manufacturers in the industry by sitting on our hands. At Ti-Caro, we make superb 100% cotton knits and Fortrel® blends at price points for every market.

But what makes Ti-Caro is the way we turn ourselves inside out to meet your needs. Need a fabric that's fashion right? Chances are it's already in our sample room. If not, no problem. We'll create what you need on the spot. A computer network links all our mills, making execution quick and easy.

We're more responsive because as top managers we're more involved, and for the best of reasons: we own the company. Each of us has a personal stake in Ti-Caro's fortunes...in your fortune.

Ti-Caro let you down? Impossible.
Ti-Caro, 1071 Avenue of the Americas, NY, NY 10018.

TI-CARO
We have to come through for you.
Our assets are on the line.

Here, Mach II dominates the scene in a shirt that's sheer yet solid, with focus on the double-button pockets. Pants are striped to match the shirt, and feature a full-flare leg. Mach II. A slim and tapered look that's carried out in a whole new line of sport and dress shirts from Arrow.

A transparent state of mind. Mach II.

Inside Lindsay's Head, by Nicholas Pileggi
People I'm Not Speaking To, by Jimmy Breslin
Peter Blake's Cityscape Awards
Judith Crist's 10 Best/Worst Movies

New York

Dick Schaap on New York's Most Powerful People

JOHN PAUL ENDRESS

254 WEST 31 STREET (212) 736-7800
NEW YORK CITY, NEW YORK 10001
REPRESENTED BY BRUCE LEVIN (212) 410-0123

Some of you have been fans of my work for many years. Others have no idea of what I do. To repay the former and inform the latter, I'd like to send a selection of my favorite pieces to you…

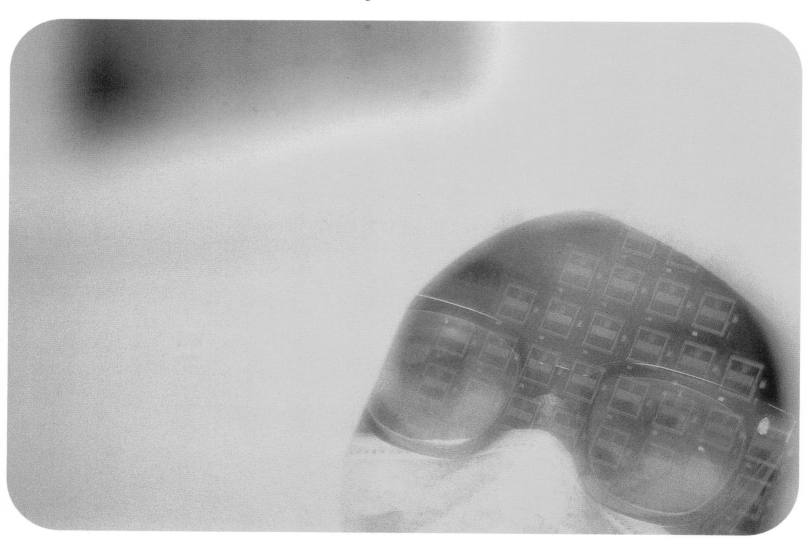

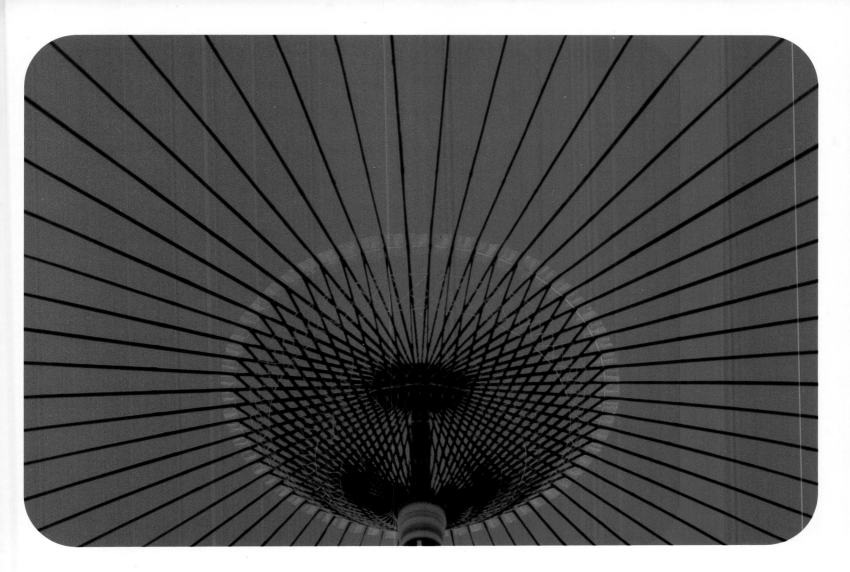

…If you would like a "maxifolio" of hundreds of images, please write me on your company letterhead. When you need to assign work or buy stock, and you want a different point of view, call and ask for Emily.

JAY MAISEL

190 The Bowery, NY, NY 10012 / 212-431-5013

WE GOT THE JUICE!

One of the few things on the Space Shuttle that didn't have a backup system.

Nikon
We take the world's greatest pictures.

THE FASTEST WAY TO GET OUT OF A MESS.

Swissair Business Class.

Comfort is the bottom line.

Europe. Africa. Middle East. Far East. North and South America. **swissair**

CAMPARI

SOONER OR LATER, AMERICA DISCOVERS YOU

CAMPARI THE SPIRIT OF ITALY

THE DESIRED EFFECT HASHI

TV AND PRINT

GORDON MUNRO
381 PARK AVENUE SOUTH
NEW YORK, N.Y. 10016

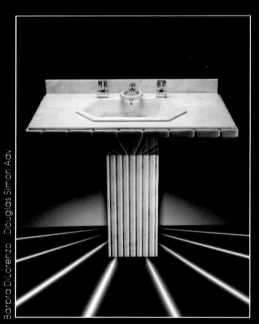
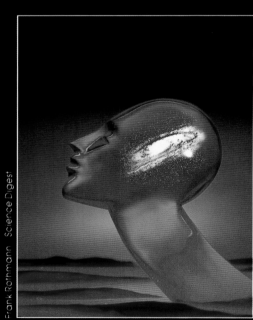

Barbra DiLorenzo Douglas Simon Adv

Frank Rothmann Science Digest

SHIG IKEDA

Photographer 636 Avenue of the Americas New York, New York 10011 212-924-4744
Representative: Joe Cahill 135 East 50th Street New York, New York 10022 212-751-0529

Now for the first time you can create custom eye shadow looks you choose...

...And collect them in a gorgeous new Revlon compact you fill. And refill!

You'll never buy another eye shadow you don't want again! Choose from Custom Eyes compacts that hold 2, or 3, interchangeable pans of color! Fill from a collection of 35 tempting new colors.

NEW
CUSTOM EYES

The First...
The Only...By REVLON

SHIG IKEDA

Larry Aarons/C
John Berg/Pat
Marshal Cetlin/
Epstein/George
Kurt Haiman/C
Manketo/Bill M
Peterson/Peter
Howard Smith/
Walters/Bill Wa
Ally & Gargano,
Company/Doyl
Haynes & Carr
Bates/William F
American Airlines/Amer
Columbia Records/Caesar's Board
Faberge/Fiat/Formica/Fuji/General Electric/Ge
Beach Hotel/N
Timex/Traveler

esh/Tony Angotti/Bill
ms/Peter Altman/John Andron.../Howard Brody/Le
Frank Bonagura/Stu Bresner/Vince Daddiego/Bob
Dennis D'Amico/Feldman/Len Fink/Ed Fla
rger/Pierre LeDuc/N
Andre Morkel/Roge
Tony Romeo/Ralph
Tesch/Joe Toto/Eli T
Wilmoth/Bill Yamada
wles/Compton Adver
pson/Ketchum Adve
W. Ayer/Nadler & La
e, Dane, Bernbach/C
Tourister/Atlantic Re
Charmin/Chase Mar
Gordons/Hanes/IB
Pfizer/Philip Morris/F
my Reserve/Vantage/

phone/Pan Am/Panasonic/M
ited States Post Office/U.S. Arm

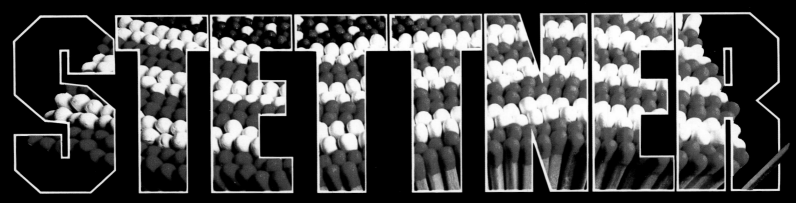

NICK SAMARDGE 212·226·6770

568 BROADWAY SUITE 706 NEW YORK NY 10012

YOU CAN TELL IT'S A NIVEA SUN TAN
EVEN WITH YOUR EYES CLOSED.

Now comes Miller time.

Summer Cruise.
Smirnoff Style

Hennessy
the civilized way
to lay down the law

The world's most civilized spirit

WITH US

WITH THE GOVERNMENT GIVING LESS
TO ART AND EDUCATION,
SOMEBODY'S GOT TO GIVE MORE.

CHASE

Raise your hand if you're Sure.

In '72, Corvette bonded a couple of
subassemblies with PLIOGRIP adhesive.
Now almost the whole car.

Ashland Chemical Company

NIVEA

**Hal Davis,
one of America's
leading
image makers**

PERWEILER

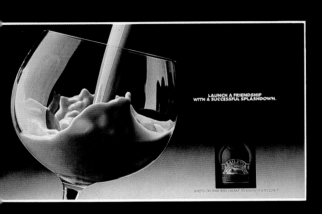

LAUNCH A FRIENDSHIP WITH A SUCCESSFUL SPLASHDOWN.

It says more about you than anything you can buy with it.

THE GOLD CARD

MINIMALISM

LO/OVRAL

If only Grammy choices were this simple.

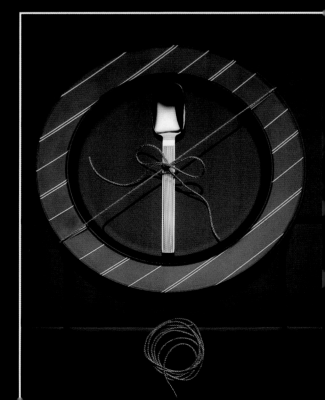

M I N I M A L I S M

GE OFFERS SOME THOUGHT FOR FOOD.

Within this classic bottle lies the promise of vibrant, radiant skin.

Every day, this bottle is opened with anticipation by millions of women around the world. For they know they are opening up the promise of radiant beauty. The promise of Oil of Olay.® Each drop, so sheer and light, penetrates beneath the skin's surface to replenish youthful fluids. Easing tiny dry lines, so that even in winter your skin stays soft and younger looking, just as you feel inside. After all, the bottle is just the beginning. Within it lies a promise that will be kept.

Beauty Hint: Share the secret of radiance this Christmas by giving Oil of Olay to someone you care about.

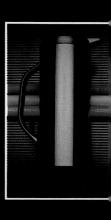

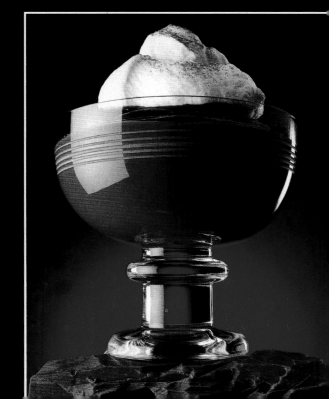

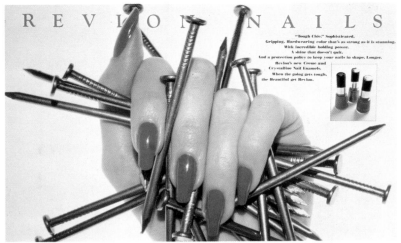

R · E · V · L · O · N   N · A · I · L · S

A.D. DICK LOPEZ

Great German bier. Brewed hier.

Löwenbräu. Classic American beer with a German heritage you can taste.

A.D. DICK LOPEZ

Don't you wish the whole world were as pure and natural as the wheat germ oil and honey in Fabergé Organics' Shampoo?

A.D. IRWIN GOLDBERG

"My dog's healthy and it shows, 'cause he's got the Hi-Pro Glow."

Purina Hi·Pro

A.D. HARVEY GABOR

DON'T BE CONFINED BY THEIR IDEAS.

WE'RE WIDE OPEN TO YOURS.

MOTOROLA Information Systems

A.D. HARRY WILSON

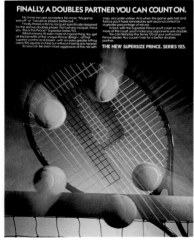

FINALLY, A DOUBLES PARTNER YOU CAN COUNT ON.

THE NEW SUPERSIZE PRINCE. SERIES 125.

A.D. VINCE SALMIERI

IT'S LIGHT YEARS AHEAD.

THE PRINCE MAGNESIUM PRO.

A.D. VINCE SALMIERI

DANSK

SUPER BOWL

A.D. LOU DORFSMAN

"It's worth $50,000 because there's nothing nearly so erotic at three times the price." Autoweek

"...turbo-monstered rocketry...with enough performance in all categories to send dilettantes screaming for cover." Car and Driver

Lotus

A.D. STAN KOVICS

R · E · V · L · O · N   N · A · I · L · S

THE FUTURE IS ON YOUR HANDS.

A.D. DICK LOPEZ

U.S. Postal Service

ENTER THE POLE VAULT EVENT.

A.D. JERRY ROACH

40

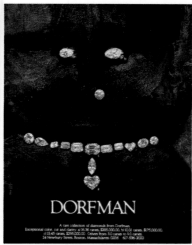

DORFMAN

A.D. STEVE COSMOPULOS

Great German bier. Brewed hier.

Löwenbräu. Classic American beer with a German heritage you can taste.

A.D. CHARLIE ABRAMS

At this minute, somewhere in the world, it's teatime on British Airways.

BRITISH AIRWAYS
The world's favourite airline

A.D. CHARLIE ABRAMS

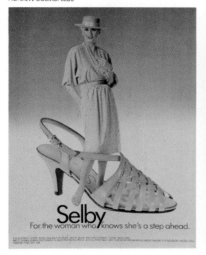

Selby
For the woman who knows she's a step ahead.

A.D. BETTE KLEGON

Scotch On The Rocks With A Twist
BRAEMAR

PACCIONE
REPRESENTED BY
DIANA DES VERGERS
(212) 691-8674
73 FIFTH AVENUE
N.Y. 10003 NY.

A.D. JOHN ANSADO

Lilith

A.D. LEN LEONE

PACCIONE

(212) 691-8674
73 FIFTH
AVENUE
NY 10003 NY

DRY SACK

A.D. CHARLIE ABRAMS

GLAMOUR
GUSTO

A.D. ROCCO CAMPANELLI

THE OCEAN.
AROMA DISC™ BRINGS IT HOME.

Aroma Disc
IT BRINGS IT HOME.

A.D. ANNMARIE LIGHT

IT'S A JUNGLE OUT THERE.

ROSSIGNOL

JIM DURFEE & MARTY SOLOW

THE AVERAGE MAN WILL PURCHASE 6.5 COATS
OVER THE NEXT 20 YEARS.
THE ABOVE AVERAGE MAN WILL PURCHASE JUST ONE.

LOEWE
Madrid 1846

CLASSIC NAPPA LEATHER CLOTHING. HANDMADE SINCE 1846.
FIFTH AVENUE AT 56 STREET, NEW YORK (212) 838-8260
MADRID BARCELONA LONDON BRUSSELS TOKYO JEDDAH HONG KONG SINGAPORE

A.D. TANA KLUGHERZ

Rumple
Minze
PEPPERMINT SCHNAPPS
LIQUEUR

White Magic from the Black Forest

A.D. CARL STEWART

TYPE & PRODUCTION: TSI COMMUNICATIONS PRINTING & SEPARATIONS: COLLIER COLORTYPE, INC. DUPS & CHROME ASSEMBLY: AUTHENTICOLOR

H. Mark Weidman

(215) 646-1745

ᓇᕿ ᐃᑯ

ᑲᑎ ᓕᐅᓂ ᖃᐊᒪᓐ ᑐᓗᒐ

ROGER SEVIGNY

ᑕᐸᔅᐱ ᑲ'ᓇᓕ
ᓇ

H. Mark Weidman

(215) 646-1745

On Friday, May 2, 1986, the Steger International Polar Expedition radioed base camp. After 56 grueling days, they had reached the North Pole! The team skied, walked, and dog sledded over 900 icy miles without any supply drops or outside navigational aid. This feat had never been accomplished.

Du Pont, the expedition's major corporate sponsor, assigned Mark Weidman to document the team's final on-ice training. The training camp was near the Arctic Circle in Canada's Northwest Territories. The photos promoted the expedition and the Du Pont materials used in the team's polar gear.

Most of the photography was done in −30° F. temperatures, some in blizzard conditions. Mark arranged to formally photograph the team in a makeshift studio in a school cafeteria. He also invited local Inuits (Eskimos) in for portraits. Over one hundred people came! Prints were sent to the Inuits, and the Canadian Government purchased a set for the regional museum.

H. Mark Weidman

(215) 646-1745

NEW YORK CITY

BOAT HOUSE ROW, PHILADELPHIA

CHICAGO

H. Mark Weidman

(215) 646-1745

For over a decade H. Mark Weidman has photographed for advertising and corporate clients. Assignments have taken him from the Arctic Circle to south of the Equator, through nearly every European country and to most of the States.

In addition to assignments, Mark has created thousands of personal photographs. The images shown here illustrate the individual style of photography in his extensive stock files. Subjects include computers and technology, people at work, industry, transportation, and science.

To receive printed samples, to review Mark's portfolio, or to request stock photographs, please call.

GUY POWERS

Represented by Carmel (212) 563-3177

Credit to Susan West food stylist

GUY POWERS

Represented by Carmel (212) 563-3177

Secunda

112 Fourth Avenue, New York, New York 10003 (212) 477-0241

Nationwide Insurance

Secunda

112 Fourth Avenue, New York, New York 10003 (212) 477-0241

F I N D E L

STEFAN FINDEL   NEW YORK 212-279-2838   ATLANTA 404-872-8103

Specialties: Concept, Lighting, Special Effects, Including Labwork

Clients include: Allegheny International, Amoco, Blue Cross/Blue Shield, CBS, Clairol, Coca-Cola, Concord Watch, DuPont, Georgia-Pacific, Hayes, Herculon, Hitachi, IBM, Kodak, Lufthansa, Martini, MSA, Philips, Procter & Gamble, Ryder Trucks, Scripto, Snapper, St. Pauli Girl, Sunbeam, Tenneco, Texize, Union Carbide, Valvoline

aiello

SPECIALIZING IN PHOTO ILLUSTRATION

35 S. Van Brunt St.
Englewood, NJ 07631
201-894-5120,21

NYC Studio Available:
212-686-6883

Represented by
John Henry
212-686-6883

© Frank J. Aiello 1986

"Only the Beginning"
Grant the Bearer One Free Cone of
Häagen-Dazs® ice cream.

Expires July 15, 1985.
See back for details.

A Black Forest Cake
worthy
of your talents.

CACAU BARRY

...the chocolate that can make great chefs even greater.

Jay Brenner
Studio (212) 741-2244

Jay Brenner Studio
18 East 17th Street
New York, NY 10003
(212) 741-2244

Long Island Studio
(516) 933-2055

Represented by: David Goldman Agency   (212) 807-6627

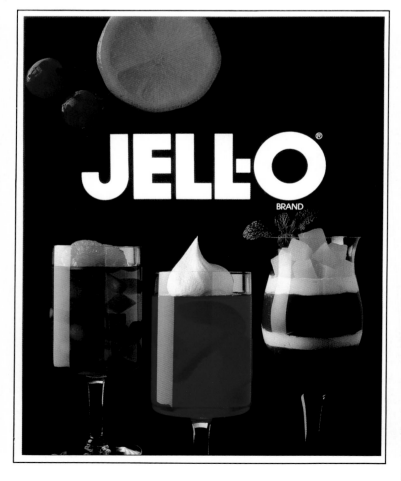

Peter Pioppo

50 West 17th Street • New York, N.Y. 10011 • Tel. 212-243 0661

DAVID HEDRICH

7 E. 17ᵗʰ St. New York (212) 924-3324 Phoenix (602) 220-0090

CAMILLE VICKERS
212/580-8649

AERIAL / INDUSTRIAL / CORPORATE / ADVERTISING / EDITORIAL / STOCK

JOSEPH MCLELLAN

Philadelphia, PA 19106

215 392-1339

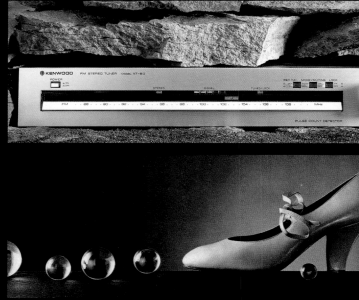

PETER NEUMANN
PHOTOGRAPHER
30 E. 20 ST. • N.Y.C. 10003 • (212) 420-9538

FELLERMAN

STAN FELLERMAN • 152 WEST 25TH STREET, NEW YORK, NY 10001 • **(212)-243-0027**

REPRESENTED BY • **JOSÉ IGLESIAS** • **(212)-929-7962**

Doug Abdelnour

Represented by:

Bedford Photo-Graphic

The Playhouse
Route 22
P.O. Box 64
Bedford, New York 10506
(914) 234-3123

Architectural and Industrial Photography:
Exteriors, interiors, models, and panoramas

Locations: Anywhere

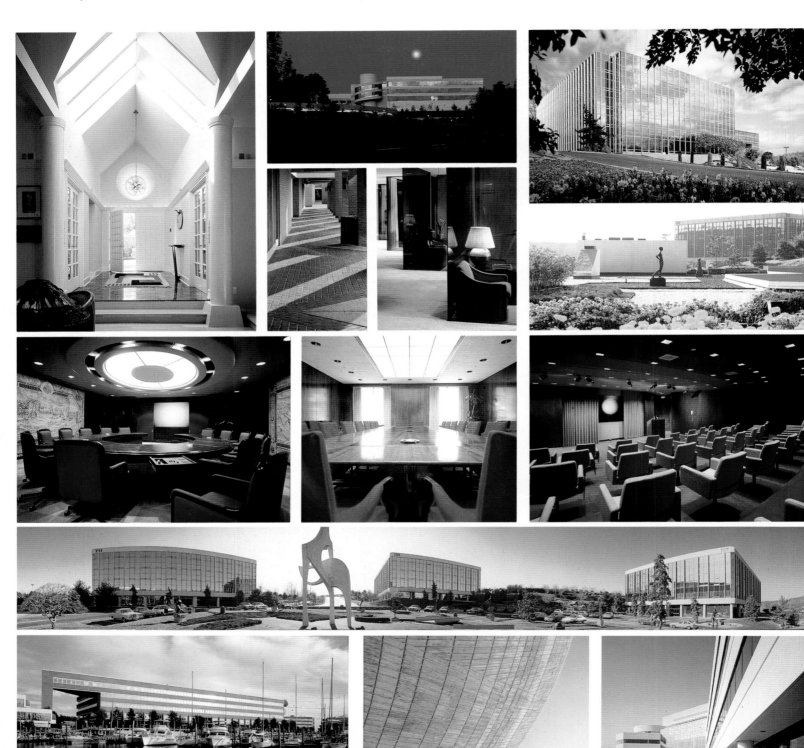

Andris · Hendrickson Photography

314 North 13th Street
Loft 404
Philadelphia, Pennsylvania 19107
(215) 925-2630

Portfolio available upon request.

Andris○Hendrickson Photography
Philadelphia, PA
215•925•2630

"THANKS TO LOU DORFSMAN FOR MAKING US AT CBS NEWS LOOK GOOD ON PAPER, ON THE TUBE, IN SO MANY WAYS, FOR SO MANY YEARS."
Mike Wallace
CBS News/60 Minutes

"Everything Lou Dorfsman has touched was made better for his efforts. Whether it was a television studio set, a matchbook cover, a book, a booklet, a paper cup, a cafeteria wall, an annual report, an annual meeting, Lou has done it with taste and style and integrity."
Dr. Frank Stanton
President Emeritus CBS

"QUITE SIMPLY THE BEST CORPORATE DESIGNER IN THE WORLD."
Milton Glaser
Designer

"CBS has a corporate commitment to excellence in design, but Lou Dorfsman is the one whose genius has translated that commitment into reality. Deservedly, he has become a legend in the annals of commercial design. He combines a lively creative flair with an innate, sure sense of style and superb taste. Lou is a man of great warmth, humor and kindness. He is also a total per-fectionist. The special 'CBS style' that he has created reflects to a large extent what I like to think of as the company personality. I am very proud of the way he has defined CBS visually. I doubt anyone else could have done it as well."
William S. Paley
Founder Chairman
CBS Inc.

"Lou is the ultimate in graphic design; his work is a reflection of his profound intellect, intuition and elegance."
David Levy
Executive Dean and Chief
Administrative Officer
Parsons School of Design

"I DID NOT GO TO ART SCHOOL. MUCH OF WHAT I LEARNED ABOUT THIS CRAFT I LEARNED BY STUDYING DORFSMAN. I WAS AMAZED TO DISCOVER HOW GREATLY I AM INDEBTED TO HIS EXAMPLE."
Dick Hess
Designer

"The CBS image has been helped more by Lou than anyone else."
Fred Friendly
Former President CBS News

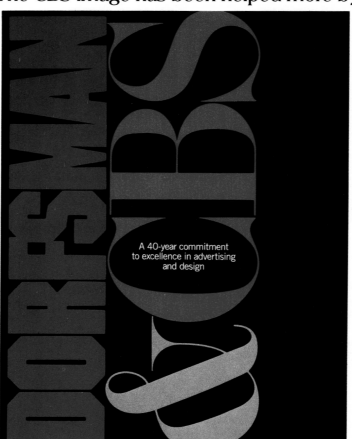

A 40-year commitment to excellence in advertising and design

"Anyone who's any good in the business keeps watching him to see what he's coming up with. He's done the most elegant design work in the world consistently over the years. And this isn't atelier stuff, but right on the firing lines at CBS."
George Lois Chairman
Lois Pitts Gershon PON/GGK

"I consider him one of the truly extraordinary talents in the field, one of the true luminaries in communications."
Saul Bass
Designer

"Lou Dorfsman is not just a designer, he is a thinker who solves problems and has wonderful ideas. He bears a good deal of the responsi-bility for the 'Tiffany image' of CBS."
Larry Grossman
President NBC News

Need we say more?

Yes, only that it is a 40-year retrospective of one of the greatest graphic designers of our time. Clothbound, 216 pages.

Take advantage of this special pre-publication offer! Send for your copy of DORFSMAN AND CBS and pay only $39.95 (retail price: $49.95). Postage and handling are FREE within the U.S. and Canada. To order, call 212-245-0981 and charge your AMEX, Visa or MasterCard. Or send your check or money order to:
American Showcase
724 Fifth Ave., NY, NY

Bill Ashe

534 West 35th Street
New York, New York 10001
(212) 695-6473

My specialties are still life, automobiles, advertising, corporate and editorial which I photograph on location and in my mid-town Studio. The studio facility is 6000 sq. feet, column free and accommodates trucks and cars through a 16'x22' door.

Twelve years of award winning photography for clients like Bulgari, Toshiba, Bristol Myers, Shell Oil, G.E., American Express, DeBeers, Oscar De La Renta, General Motors, Mitsui, American Cyanamid, Brown & Williamson, CBS, Newsweek, Hearst Corp., Dept. of Defense...

Scott Barrow, Incorporated

214 West 30th Street
Number Six
New York, New York 10001
Studio: (212) 736-4567

All photos © 1987 Scott Barrow

O&M asked me to shoot Christmas for Seagrams on the 3rd day of Spring. My staff scouted 3 states, cast models, organized an entire village, strung 7,000 white lights and fended off the advances of an amorous pet peacock named Elaine...all in 4 days. The rewards were great. I was presented with a gallon of maple syrup and a lifetime subscribtion to the local paper "Behind the Times."

CHRISTMAS IN SPRINGTIME FOR SEAGRAMS/OGILVY & MATHER

TRAVELMASTER

BARROW

Scott Barrow, Incorporated
214 West 30th Street
Number Six
New York, New York 10001
Studio:(212)736-4567

All photos © 1987 Scott Barrow

Clients: yes...
Air France, Air Portugal, American Express, Coca
Cola, Drake Hotel, Hilton Hotels, Lee Jeans, Mexican
Tourism, Procter & Gamble, St. Lucia Tourism, TWA,
Taylor Wines, Seagrams, Travelmaster, etc.

AAAH...   ...IXTAPA!

on Mexico's Pacific

Awaken your senses. Where rhythmic Pacific waves wash away your every care. While golden sundrenched beaches warm your heart, caress your soul. Aaah...Ixtapa. Sophisticated oceanfront hotels. World-class golf. And of course, nearby Zihuatanejo—a romantic village-on-the-sea, filled with old-world charm, warm smiles, and breezy cafés. Come and awaken your senses. Aaah...Ixtapa. Your travel agent will show you the way.

BARROW

Wendy Barrows

205 East 22 Street
New York, New York 10010
(212) 685-0799

Clients include:
AT&T
Burson-Marsteller
Chase NBW
Chemical Bank
Chermayeff & Geismar
Citicorp
Condé Nast Publications

Corporate Annual Reports
Foote Cone & Belding
Forbes Magazine
Hill & Knowlton
International Paper
Kidder, Peabody
Laurence Communications
Muir Cornelius Moore
Murdoch Magazines
Winkler McDermott Winkler

1. Malcolm Forbes
2. Louis Oliver Gropp, editor-in-chief, House & Garden
3. Donald McAllister, Jr., Geyer-McAllister Publications
4. Christopher L. Davis, president, Investment Partnership Assoc.
5. Lenore Benson, executive director, The Fashion Group

Ted Beaudin
Photographer

New York Studio:
450 West 31st Street
New York, New York 10001
Telephone (212) 563-6065

Connecticut Studio:
56 Arbor Street
Hartford, Connecticut 06106
Telephone (203) 232-4885

Photonet mailbox: PHO1334

Stock available through FPG
International, New York City

Member, ASMP

© 1987, Ted Beaudin

"Photography for advertising, brochures, and catalogs that has people looking natural at what they are doing, whether they are professional models or not."

"SEX AND ART—WHAT A COMBINATION! ONLY TWO 3—LETTER WORDS, BUT OH SO POWER-FUL AND LAST-ING."
*

BRAD BENEDICT'S

BLUEBOOK

An amazing all-color collection of funny, sexy, crazy, erotic fantasies by over 100 of the world's most successful artists.

*Brad Benedict

Barry Blackman
Special Effects Photography and techniques

115 East 23rd Street — 10th floor
New York, New York 10010
(212) 473-3100

Author of "Special Effects Photography For Print Art Directors, Designers and Photographers" published by Van Nostrand Reinhold

ALL PHOTOS UNRETOUCHED

Stock available

© Barry Blackman 1987

CLIENT LIST:

AT&T
IBM
Polaroid
AMF Voit
TWA
Federal Express
Colgate Palmolive
General Electric
Citibank
Sony
Reynolds Metals
Rubbermaid
Pepsi Cola

Marriott
Hilton Hotels
Holiday Inns
Hyatt Hotels
Quality Inns
Continental Telephone
N.U.S. Corporation
Fairchild Industries
London Fog
Union Camp
Sierra Corporation
Aeromaritime
Owens Corning
National Public Radio
Amtrack

Wool Institute of America
Xerox
Dynastar Skis
T-Bar Corporation
Bright Cigarettes
Hammermill Paper
Newsweek
USA Today
Life Magazine
U.S. News and World Report
Parents Magazine
National Geographic
Smithsonian Magazine
Business Week
America Illustrated

Science Digest
Discover Magazine
Nations Business Magazine
Avon Books
Ballentine Books
Fawcette Books
Gold Medal Books
Dell Publishing
Bantam Books

Line Drawing: Susan Hunt Yule
T.V. Illustration: David Schleinkofer

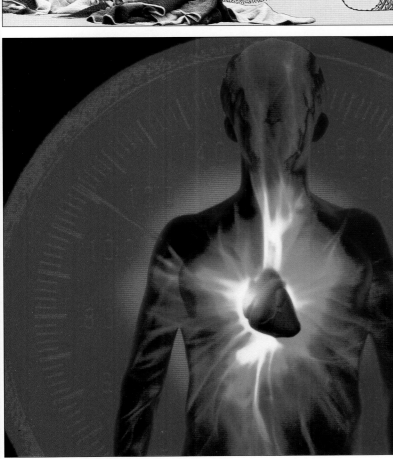

Leland Bobbé

51 West 28th Street
New York, New York 10001
(212) 685-5238

Represented by:
Dane Sonneville
(212) 603-9530

Clients include:

Avon, Bottecelli, Capital Records, Egon Von Furstenberg,
Fairchild Publications, Germaine Monteil, MCA
Records, Sebastian International, Spiegel, Redken

La Complexion
Clarité
Special Correctors
for Adult Oily Skin
GERMAINE
MONTEIL

A.D. BERETT FISHER

Leland Bobbé
51 West 28th Street
New York, New York 10001
(212) 685-5238

Represented by:
**Dane Sonneville
(212) 603-9530**

Clients include:

Avon
Bottecelli
Capital Records
Egon Von Furstenberg
Fairchild Publications
Germaine Monteil
MCA Records
Sebastian International
Spiegel
Redken

LELAND BOBBÉ

Barbara Bordnick

Photographer/Director
39 East 19th Street
New York, New York 10003
(212) 533-1180

Print and film.
Fashion/beauty advertising
editorial and illustration.
Celebrity and corporate
portraiture.
APA, ASMP member.

FABERGE

DONNA

REVLON

LIFE

CARIBBEAN CRUISE

74

Bruno Photography, Inc.

43 Crosby Street
New York, New York 10012
(212) 925-2929

Represented by Holly Kaplan

Bill Charles
265 West 37 Street PHD
New York, New York 10018
(212) 719-9156

Represented By Cassandra
(212) 751-1018

Portfolio Available Upon Request

Marc David Cohen/ Photography

5 West 19th Street
New York, New York 10011
(212) 741-0015

Represented by
Michael DeCunzo
(212) 741-0015

THE POWER BREAKFAST

I get a call from a headhunter.

She talks in a kind of telegraphic headhunter language. No conjunctions. No connectives. Only essence.

"Very *big* man. Very *busy* man..."

"Like to see you. Not just coffee danish Schrafft's chit chat.

"Inter-Conti. —7:45, make that 7:30 Gold Room AM breakfast. Four good places they hold them... Inter-Conti best..."

"Hold what?" I ask. Pause. Now the tone gets even terser.

"Power breakfast, Harv." Now slow, emphasizing each word. "Power...Breakfast. Madison Ave., Wall Street, Woman's Wear starting; Rag Trade just beginning to come. Talk Creative director, talk title, talk package...could be telephone numbers. Speak soon." She hangs up.

It's 7:30 in the morning and I stand in front of the headwaiter of the Inter-Continental Hotel. He's behind a podium looking into the pages of a two-foot-long ledger book. Above it, under a small light, is a diagram of all the breakfast tables. Red arrows sweep around tables going north. Green and yellow arrows surge against them to the south, like the allies pushing back Von Runstedt in the Battle of the Ruhr. Footsoldiers all around in white jackets with woven epaulets on the shoulders run with small trays of juice and coffee.

I mention the name of my party. "Ah yes, Monsieur, follow me." We stride quickly. He stops and pulls out a heavy Victorian flowered chair. My party rises to shake my hand. He's about 6 foot four, in his mid-fifties sporting a crew cut.

"Well Haar Yew...," he asks with that broad, possibly anywhere but New York accent. He shakes my hand. The Maitre d' stands smartly at attention. He folds, then snaps off two newspapers. "Pop!... Whap!..." First a *New York Times*, then a *Wall Street Journal*. He holds up both papers like a field marshal presenting arms. I point at the *Times*. He thrusts both the paper, then a menu at me. It's

a huge foot-long affair, four pages bound with a golden cord and tassels that looks like it was taken from an American Flag.

"Just a small orange juice, no ice." (I mean, who wants a stomach to rumble when you're talking "package.") "Just Raisin Bran and skim milk." The Maitre d' just stares at me. First, I think, with shock. And then with genuine pity.

"We do not serve the dry cereals here, perhaps some oatmeal?" A busboy darts to the table and pours coffee without even asking.

I'm learning. Among the power breakfasters, Raisin Bran is not one of the power orders.

I order eggs benedict and coffee. The recruiter orders his and we're off.

"Ah would take it that you are a native New Yorkah," he says warmly.

"Well, it's better than what one trade paper called me—A New York Native. Actually we've moved around quite a bit. New York, Westchester, back again, and when my son starting growing up, then back out again. And yourself?"

"Dallas now...originally from Elk City, Oklahoma. And I will tell you that we got ourselves a heckuva lifestyle down there." He smiles.

Now he gets serious. "I'm going to ask you two questions that we're going to ask all our candidates. The first one is: 'If Dallas Optical opens franchises in New York and New Jersey, do you think the name is going to help us or hurt us'?"

"And my second question is: 'Do you think you will be effective as a sales manager in Dallas; please remember we've got three hundred franchises in the one state alone'."

I feel my face flush with heat, and start trying to stand up.

"Excuse me. But you're not from Interpublic?" I ask him.

"Not this morning, I aint," he replies.

"Captain. CAPTAIN." As I summon him he rushes over followed by a busboy running behind him with reinforcements of two silver containers

continued on page 86

Peter Cunningham

Studio:
214 Sullivan Street
New York, New York 10012
(212) 475-4866

Advertising, Corporate,
and Entertainment photography.

Clients include:

CBS Records
Grey Advertising
The Shubert Organization
Rolling Stone Press
ABC Television

Manhattan Cable Television
Newsweek
Time
Texaco
Oldsmobile

Craig Cutler
536 West 50th Street
New York, New York 10019
(212) 315-3440

Craig Cutler
536 West 50th Street
New York, New York 10019
(212) 315-3440

Styling: Holly Hartman

Jorge Diaz

Photographer
142 West 24th Street 12th Floor
New York, New York 10011
(212) 675-4783

Advertising Still Life
Corporate
Editorial

Represented by: Meri Puccio

Warren Dittmar
217 Main Street
Ossining, New York 10562
(914) 762-6311

Representative: Geraldine Petty
(914) 762-6311

Advertising
Corporate
Editorial
Fashion
Photography

Studio and location.

Rich Dunoff

407 Bowman Avenue
Merion Station, Pennsylvania 19066
(215) 627-3690

People
Location
Advertising
Corporate

Stock available through:
The Stock Market (212) 684-7878

Rich Dunoff
215•627•3690

Rich Dunoff

407 Bowman Avenue
Merion Station, Pennsylvania 19066
(215) 627-3690

People
Location
Advertising
Corporate

Stock available through:
The Stock Market (212) 684-7878

Rich Dunoff
215•627•3690

continued from page 78

of coffee.

"I'm at the wrong table."

"I'm dreadfully sorry," I say to the Texan.

The Maitre d' pulls out a piece of paper. "You are Fortunato." He looks at me.

"No. I am Gabor."

"You are Fortunato." He repeats again with the accent.

"Close, I am Gabor."

He stares more intently. Looks at the paper once again.

"You are not Fortunato."

"Take my word for it," I tell him…

"Ah, Gabor, not Fortunato."

"Yes, take my word for it." I tell him as I start patting him on the shoulder. A long pause.

"Ah. Monsieur Gabor. Follow me, please." He apologizes then deposits me in front of another fellow. I quickly notice the Paul Stuart tie with the stickpin, and the red mallards on the gold background. He could be a stockbroker, but at least I'm getting warmer. My second glass of juice is placed in front of me, and again the Maitre d' stands at attention and snaps off both newspapers.

I apologize for being late. We go through the same stuff. Yes, married, lived in New York, out, in again, out again. Me, Cooper Union, he Tuck School of Business. Circle, jab, hold, clinch. I'm exhausted.

We discuss commercials we like. Marvin Hagler, Koch, Bernbach, Pro Choice, colored condoms.

My eggs benedict and his cheese omelette arrive. He proceeds to cut with knife and fork every bit of omelette acreage he can find before taking a single bite. Still nothing about the job.

I watch. Starving. I wonder what happens at a power breakfast if you strangle someone to death with your bare hands?

Finally I take a hearty forkful of egg white, liberally doused in Hollandaise sauce.

At that precise moment I learn that in the world of the power breakfast, nobody brings up money until the last ten minutes.

"May I ask you what salary area you are in now…?" he says.

After two orange juices, four newspapers, and five coffees someone asks.

"What salary area am I in now…" I think to myself. "How the hell should I know, I've got a mouthful of eggs benedict…"

I talk area. He flanks with perks and benefits. I round off numbers, he gives me a dental plan. We agree to agree to meet again and give it thought.

I've staggered through my first power breakfast. But at least I learned.

Want some advice? Never eat breakfast at a power breakfast. Eat at home, then hold a cup of coffee and sip.

Actually I've got a better idea: Tell them all you ever have for breakfast is a cigarette and a stinger. But you'll be happy to meet with them later in the day. I get a call from the headhunter that afternoon. I tell her nothing really happened. There is a pause. Again, the use of language without shock absorbers: "Likes you…next week, big one. Him…his boss…7 AM breakfast, St. Regis, …very very top of line…Varyshnikov…maybe an Ed Myer… Lois…Could see Kissingers…Billy fired there… are you tracking Harv…Harv?…HARV?…"

Harvey Gabor
Creative Director
MCA Advertising
New York City

Carlos Eguiguren

139 East 57th Street
3rd Floor
New York, New York 10022
(212) 888-6732

Represented by:
Eva Oye
(212) 286-9103

On this page:

Gregg Burge/Dial Magazine
Paul Jenkins/Artist
Judy Rodman/MTM Records
Eugene Friesen/Living Music
  Records
The Girls Next Door/MTM
  Records
Mitch Miller/Audio Magazine
Perry Ellis/United Airlines
  Magazines

Special thanks to Bob Cato
Art Director.

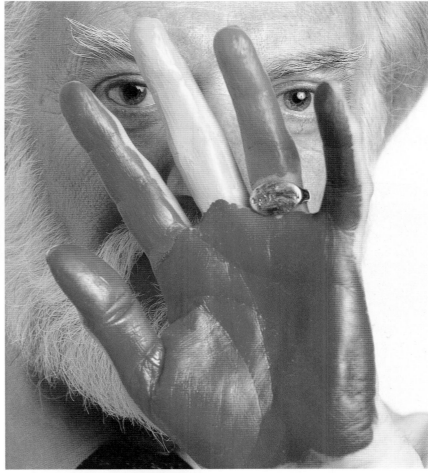

Chuck Fishbein
Photography

276 Fifth Avenue
New York, New York 10001
(212) 532-4452

"Still-Life"

Chuck Fishbein
Photography

276 Fifth Avenue
New York, New York 10001
(212) 532-4452

"Not-So-Still-Life"

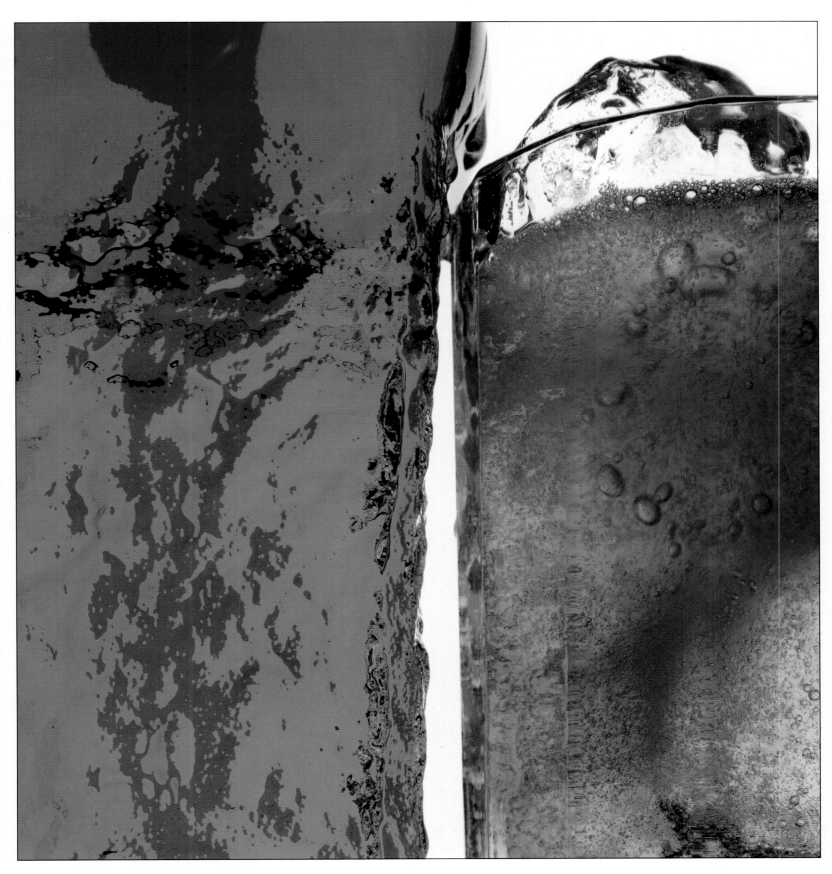

Robert Fishman

Robert Fishman Photography
153 West 27th Street, Studio 502
New York, New York 10001
(212) 620-7976

Additional work in ASMP Book 5

Bob Forrest

273 Fifth Avenue
New York, New York 10016
(212) 288-4458

Partial Client List:
American Motors, Buccelati, Charles of the Ritz,
Clairol, Pan Am, Polaroid, Sherle Wagner, Sony,
Warner Communications...

Additional work can be seen in:
ASMP Book 2, 3, 4, Showcase 9

Portfolio available upon request

Copyright 1986, Bob Forrest

Member:
ASMP
National Academy of Sciences
New York Academy of Sciences

Al Francekevich
73 Fifth Avenue
New York, New York 10003
(212) 691-7456

Al Francekevich
73 Fifth Avenue
New York, New York 10003
(212) 691-7456

Douglas Fraser
9 East 19th Street
New York, New York 10003
(212) 777-8404

Rob Fraser

211 Thompson Street
New York, New York 10012
(212) 677-4589

Corporate
Editorial
Travel
Advertising
Multi-Media

Also see:
American Showcase Vol. 9
Corporate Showcase Vol. 5

Stock available

A unique vision for the commercial world

WANTED

Sages. Wits. Philosophers.
Problem-solvers. Boat-rockers.

We hope you've enjoyed reading the **VIEWPOINTS** in this issue. This popular feature is designed to enlighten as well as entertain as it provides unique insights on the current state of advertising.

We'd like to take this opportunity to invite you to share your own thoughts, opinions and methods with thousands of your colleagues worldwide.

The average **VIEWPOINT** is 1000 words but we'll consider longer (or shorter) pieces. Have the article titled, typed double-space, and be sure to include your own name, title, company and address. Contributors to the next volume will receive a copy of the book, a small gift, and our eternal gratitude. (Of course, we can't guarantee that your article will be published but we do promise to acknowledge and read every submission.)

Go ahead, write down all those things you've always wanted to get off your chest. Speak out to those photographers, illustrators, and designers you hire...share confidences with your colleagues... tell off your boss. Do it while you're feeling outraged/satisfied/ frustrated about the work you create. Do it today and mail it to:

Wendl Kornfeld, V.P.
American Showcase, Inc.
724 Fifth Avenue—10th Floor
New York, New York 10019

Thanks a lot. We're looking forward to hearing from you and hope to see you in **AMERICAN SHOWCASE VOLUME 11!**

Brett Froomer

39 East 12th Street
New York, New York 10003
(212) 533-3113

Represented by:
Susan Boyer
(212) 533-3113

PEOPLE ON LOCATION for clients including: AT&T, Atlantic Financial Bank, Chemical Bank, Citibank, Digital Equipment, East/West Network, Family Circle, GQ, General Electric, Golf, IBM, J.C. Penney, McGraw-Hill Books, Metropolitan Life, Mitsubishi, Morgan Bank, Newsday, Newsweek, Olympus Camera, Quaker Oats, Reader's Digest, Signature, Times Mirror Corp., Toyota, Travel & Leisure.

Stock photography available through The Image Bank

All photographs © Brett Froomer 1986

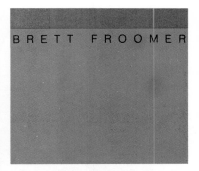

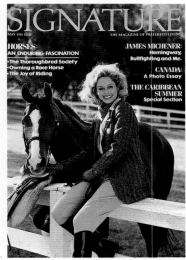

Mitchell Funk

500 East 77th Street
New York, New York 10162
(212) 988-2886

Large stock file available

Partial list of clients includes: IBM, AT&T, TWA, Nikon,
Newmont Mining, Inmont, Litton Industries, Life,
Fortune, Newsweek, New York Magazine, Polaroid,
Western Electric, Science Digest, J&B Scotch, Fuji,
Omni, Johnnie Walker Red, ABC, Modern
Photography.

Mitchell Funk

500 East 77th Street
New York, New York 10162
(212) 988-2886

Large stock file available

Partial list of clients includes: IBM, AT&T, TWA, Nikon,
Newmont Mining, Inmont, Litton Industries, Life,
Fortune, Newsweek, New York Magazine, Polaroid,
Western Electric, Science Digest, J&B Scotch, Fuji,
Omni, Johnnie Walker Red, ABC, Modern
Photography.

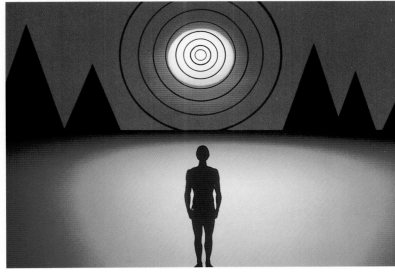

Michael Furman

115 Arch Street
Philadelphia, Pennsylvania 19106
(215) 925-4233

Represented by: Frank Reddan
and Victoria Satterthwaite

Michael Furman
115 Arch Street
Philadelphia, Pennsylvania 19106
(215) 925-4233

Represented by: Frank Reddan
and Victoria Satterthwaite

Joel Gordon Photography

112 Fourth Avenue
New York, New York 10003
(212) 254-1688

Whether your client's product is software or hardware… something to eat, drink or treasure… or a portrait of the Corporation President—I will HELP YOU CREATE THAT SPECIAL IMAGE on time, and within your budget.

Advertising, Corporate-image, Editorial. Location or Studio.

ASMP

Stock list (b/w and c/t) upon request. Stock also available through DPI.

Additional work can be seen in American Showcase volumes 3, 4, 5, & 7; Art Directors Index volumes 9 & 10; NY/NE Review '85.

© Joel Gordon 1986

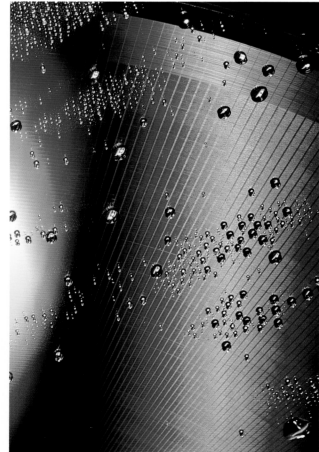

Geoffrey Gove

117 Waverly Place
New York, New York 10011
(212) 260-6051

Selected Stock:
The Image Bank

All work is done in camera utilizing basic optical principles. Whether the source is still life, location, or art work, the result is a uniquely photographic look that can't be duplicated in the computer.

Each of these images was self-assigned for SHOWCASE 10 from elements in my extensive resource files. Our other clients include:

American Bar Assoc.
Amtrak
Canon Cameras
Citibank
Diversion
Gips/Balkind
Games
HBO
Knopf
MD
Macmillan
McGraw-Hill
NY Times
Orion Films
Parke-Davis
Pfizer
Prentice Hall
Random House
Reader's Digest
Roche Labs
Runner
Sports Illustrated
TDK
Technology Illustrated
Time
Time-Life Books
WomenSports
World Tennis
Warner/Chilcott

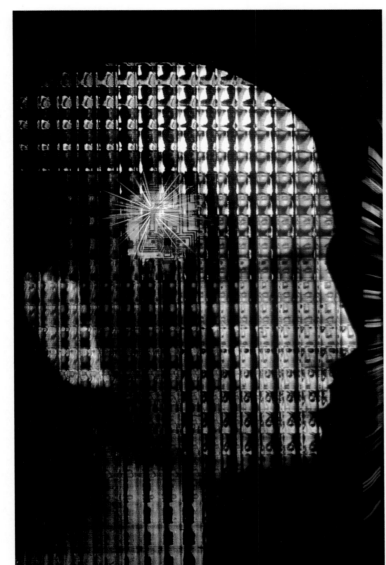

Stephen Green-Armytage

171 West 57th Street
New York, New York 10019
(212) 247-6314

Represented by: Ursula G. Kreis
(212) 562-8931

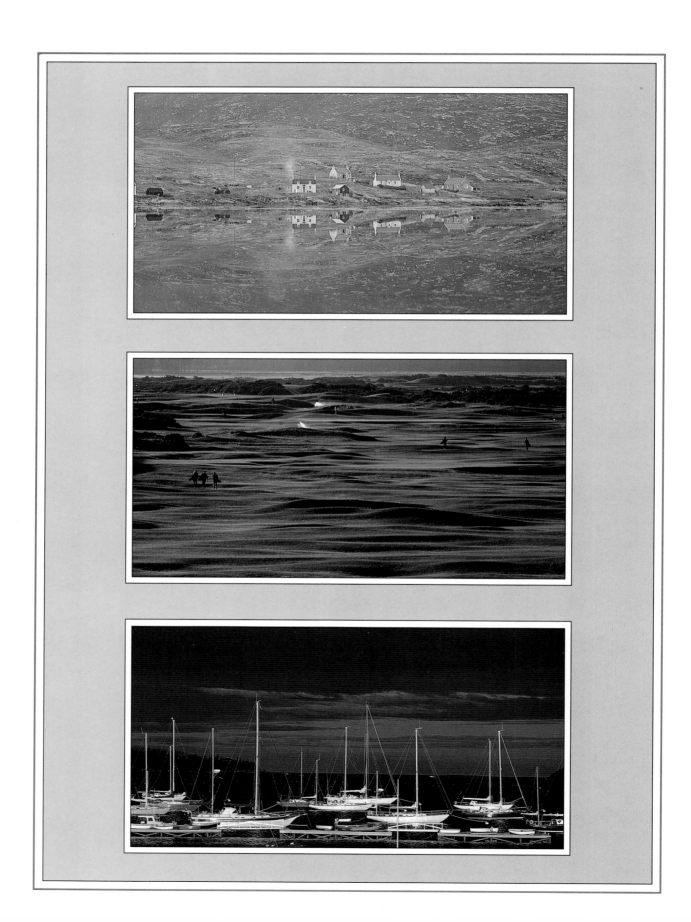

Stephen Green-Armytage

171 West 57th Street
New York, New York 10019
(212) 247-6314

Represented by: Ursula G. Kreis
(212) 562-8931

George Haling Productions: Industrial

NYC Photo District
(212) 736-6822

Energy
Esso-Rivista (Italy)
Exxon
Combustion Engineering
Conoco
Consolidated Natural Gas
PSE & G
Schlumberger Ltd.
Sun Company
Texaco

Transportation
American Airlines
Continental Airlines
Sabena
Seatrain

The Orient Express
TWA
United Airlines

Communications
ABC
CBS
IBM
ITT
Metromedia
NBC
New York Telephone
N.Y.C. Post Office
Perkin-Elmer
RCA
Sperry

Xerox
Blair Graphics
Inmont

**Forest Products/
Graphic Arts**
Champion International
Kimberly-Clark
Blair Graphics
Inmont
Sterling Roman Press

Editorial
Advertising Council
Camera Magazine
DU Magazine

Fortune Magazine
Ladies Home Journal
Lamp Magazine
LIFE Magazine
London Daily Telegraph
Money Magazine
Museum of Natural History
N.Y. Times Books
Réalités Magazine
Singer Corporation
Stern Magazine
Time-Life Books
United Fund

George Haling Productions: Corporate

NYC Photo District
(212) 736-6822

Photobases in New York and Europe.

Twenty-five years of excellence Here and There.

Great stock of Now and Then.

Corporate/Financial
ADT
Alexander & Alexander
American Express
Carteret
Citco
Citibank (N.Y.)
Emery Financial Services
Hartford Group
Manhattan Life
Merrill-Lynch
Mitchell-Hutchins
Mortgage Bankers Assn.
Morgan-Stanley
Salomon Brothers

The Travelers

Industrial
Alcoa
Amerace
American Can
Blount
Celanese
Chrysler Corp.
Fasco
GAF
General Cable
General Electric
Hunt Chemical
IBM

Indian Head
Inmont
ITT
3M
Otis
Perkin-Elmer
PepsiCo
Singer
Sperry Rand
Thomas & Betts
Xerox

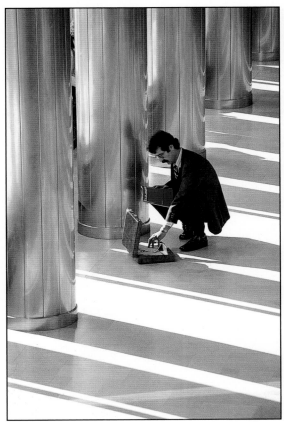

Blaine Harrington III

374 Old Hawleyville Road
Bethel, Connecticut 06801
(203) 798-2866

Specialist in world-wide location photography for advertising, corporate and editorial assignments.

Clients include:

Time
Discover
Fortune
Time-Life Books
National Geographic
New York Times
Travel & Leisure
TWA
Pan Am
Hertz

Stock Photography: The Stock Market (212) 684-7878

Haruo
Haruo Watabe
37 West 20th Street
New York, New York 10011
(212) 505-8800

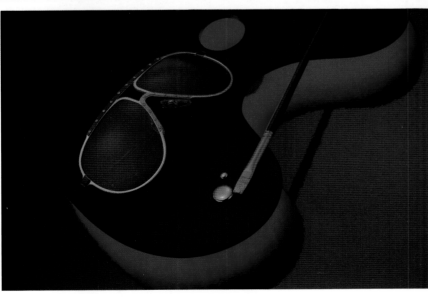

Ted Horowitz

465 West End Avenue
New York, New York 10024
(212) 595-0040

Specialist in world-wide location, corporate and people photography for an extensive range of advertising, annual report, and corporate assignments.

Blue Chip list of clients includes:
Bristol-Myers; Bank of America; General Electric; IBM; US Steel; AT&T; Paine Webber; Union Carbide; Allied Corporation; Hospital Corporation of America; American Express; Eastern Airlines; Time Inc.; Doyle Dane Bernbach; Compton, Marstellar; and Young and Rubicam Advertising.

Stock Photography: The Stock Market (212) 684-7878.

Ted Horowitz

465 West End Avenue
New York, New York 10024
(212) 595-0040

Specialist in world-wide location, corporate and people photography for an extensive range of advertising, annual report, and corporate assignments.

Blue Chip list of clients includes:
Bristol-Myers; Bank of America; General Electric; IBM; US Steel; AT&T; Paine Webber; Union Carbide; Allied Corporation; Hospital Corporation of America; American Express; Eastern Airlines; Time Inc.; Doyle Dane Bernbach; Compton, Marstellar; and Young and Rubicam Advertising.

Stock Photography: The Stock Market (212) 684-7878.

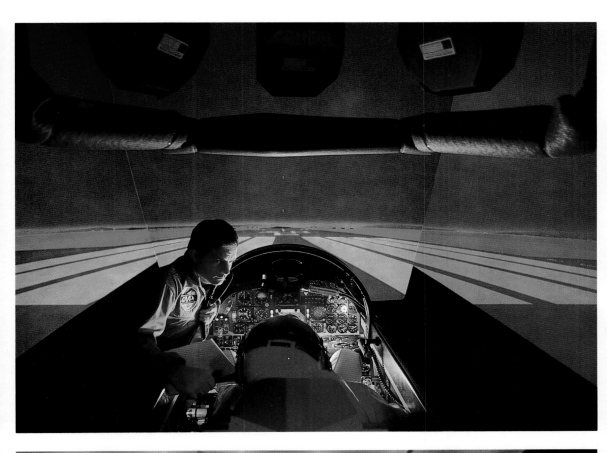

Peter Johansky

27 West 20th Street
New York, New York 10011
(212) 242-7013

Represented by:
Shelly Kopel & Associates
(212) 986-3282
See American Showcase: Volumes #7, 8, 9
ASMP Book #2

My special thanks to Rick Ellis and Elizabeth Woodson.

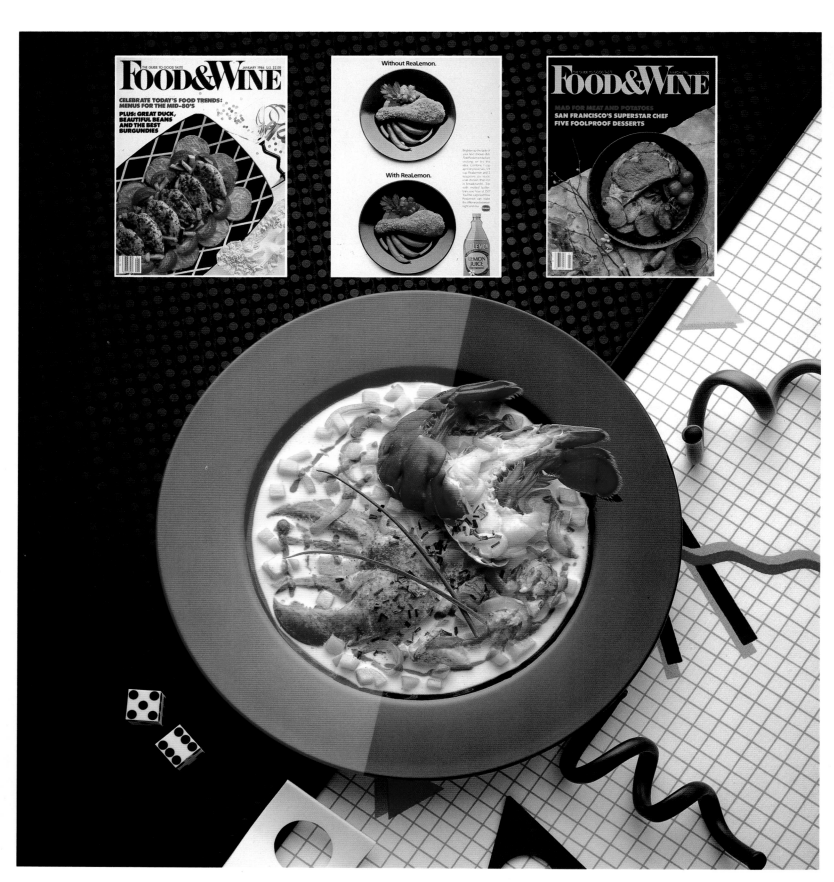

Peter Johansky

27 West 20th Street
New York, New York 10011
(212) 242-7013

Represented by:
Shelly Kopel & Associates
(212) 986-3282
See American Showcase: Volumes #7, 8, 9
ASMP Book #2

My special thanks to Rick Ellis and Elizabeth Woodson.

Lucille Khornak

425 East 58th Street
New York, New York 10022
(212) 593-0933

Fashion, Beauty & People
Advertising & Editorial
ASMP Member

Published Book: Fashion: 2001

Silver Award – Art Directors Club

Clients include:

Yves St. Laurent
Helena Rubinstein
Ungaro
Pernod Liquor
Coty Cosmetics
Maurice St. Michel
Johnson & Johnson
Lip Quencher
Concord Hotels
Alfa Romeo
Portfolio
Bon Jour
Pierre Cardin
Rive Gauche
Micar Communications
Omni Magazine
Givenchy Jewelry
Private Label
Richelieu
Maidenform.

Conceptual Photographer

Location & Studio

Write or call for your mini
portfolio.

Alfa Romeo

Alfa Romeo
feeling racy

LUCILLE
KHORNAK

Don Landwehrle
9 Hother Lane
Bay Shore, New York 11706
(516) 665-8221

Represented by:
Wendy Morgan
Network Studios
(516) 757-5609

Special effects, location and studio photography for
advertising, corporate and editorial.

Additional images can be seen in American Showcase
#8 and #9.

Portfolio Available Upon Request

Stock available through The Image Bank.

Styling by Jamie Nervo

Vive le style!

Thomas Leighton

321 East 43rd Street
New York, New York 10017
(212) 370-1835 (office)
(212) 714-2880 (service)

Architectural, interior, and structural photography

Clients include: IBM, Ford, Texaco, Honeywell, W. R. Grace, General Electric, Merrill Lynch, Salomon Brothers, Wurlitzer, European American Bank, Morgan Guaranty Trust, Equitable Life, New York Life, CIT, JMB Realty, Cushman & Wakefield, and Abitare.

Mark MacLaren

430 East 20th Street
New York, New York 10009
(212) 674-8615
(212) 674-0155

Portraits on location worldwide
for corporate and advertising clients.

Extensive stock photography covering a wide variety
of subjects in 50 states, 21 countries and 7 continents.

For additional work, please see American Showcase 9,
page 102.

REBA McENTIRE/McCALL'S

Mark MacLaren

430 East 20th Street
New York, New York 10009
(212) 674-8615
(212) 674-0155

People on location worldwide
for corporate and advertising clients.

Extensive stock photography covering a wide variety
of subjects in 50 states, 21 countries and 7 continents.

For additional work, please see American Showcase 9,
page 102.

CELEBRATE

As I write these words in mid-1986, the entire nation is celebrating the 100th anniversary of the Statue of Liberty—with far more grandiose spectacle than the original unveiling by President Grover Cleveland in 1886.

Texas is commemorating its Sesquicentennial, recalling the courage and tactical skill of Sam Houston and his motley band of Texans who defeated the magnificent army of Santa Anna in 1836. We also celebrate the founding of the city of Houston, shortly after the Texan victory at nearby San Jacinto.

In 1986 the Coca-Cola company celebrated its 100th birthday. Elsie the Borden Cow reached her 50th birthday. The Oreo cookie was 75 years old.

Film tributes and a TV special reminded one and all that 1986 was the 30th anniversary of the biggest film star of all—Godzilla.

Closer to our hearts, 1986 was observed as the "Linotype Centennial Year," to honor Ottmar Mergenthaler whose first Linotype machine set copy for the <u>New York Tribune</u> in 1886. Computer-set type has largely replaced the ubiquitous Linotype machines, but these machines produced the characters that formed the words that were the staple of the communications industry for almost a century.

It is right and fitting that we should honor and fete anniversaries and other observances of our history. These are landmarks that point out critical points in our heritage. If we don't know from whence we came, we'll never know where we are. Without that foundation, who knows where we are all going? Or why?

According to a poster produced by the American Association of Advertising Agencies, "1 out of 5 American adults can't read this word—AMERICA." Based on that, how many Americans do you think have read the Declaration of Independence? The Constitution? The writings of Thomas Paine?

(Hell, how many can read the words in the ads you're writing?) The celebration of anniversaries may be the only memorable exposure many Americans have to their heritage.

By now you are well aware that an outstanding event of 1987 will be the festivities associated with the 200th anniversary of the Constitution of these United States. This inspired document is a watershed of human progress in government.

Another 1986 anniversary marked the fiftieth year since *Gone With The Wind* was published in 1936. The theme of this enduring classic is a capacity for survival through times of cataclysmic change. Scarlett O'Hara called this drive to survive "gumption." Many of us, in these last decades of the 20th century, will see our "gumption" tested by increasingly frequent onsets of significant change in our society and our way of life. Computer graphics, mergers, desk-top publishing, mergers, satellite transmissions, and mergers will shake our trees. We will also be called upon to contend with the adverse effects of mergers, both of our clients and our competitors.

In these exciting times, Madison Avenue USA shakes and trembles as mega-mergers create giant mega-monster advertising agencies that span the entire free world. Creatives—copywriters, artists, designers, production people, and even account executives—cower in their caves as the financial moguls lead off in all directions. Alas. As agencies grow to giant size, ruled by financial wizards who are absorbed in stock-option deals, the creative may be ignored temporarily. But the day always comes when the clients wonder what they are receiving for their money.

The basic, essential product of an advertising agency is creative advertising. Which brings us straight to the anniversary of AMERICAN SHOWCASE. Through the magic windows of the pages of AMERICAN SHOWCASE, creative people all over

continued on page 136

Lee Marshall

201 West 89th Street
New York, New York 10024
(212) 799-9717

Additional work may be seen in
American Showcase Volumes 3
thru 9

Client list upon request

Member APA and ASMP
All photographs © Lee Marshall
1987

CHASE MANHATTAN BANK; ROBERT MEYER DESIGN; JULIA WYANT, DESIGNER.

EASTMAN KODAK; PIERCE BROWN ASSOC.;
CRAIG BROWN, DESIGNER

McDONALD'S; DAVID MURRAY, A.D.

AT&T BELL LABS; JOHN WATERS ASSOC.;
BETH STORY, DESIGNER

Bard Martin
142 West 26th Street
New York, New York 10001
(212) 929-6712

Just People...

Stock: The Image Bank

D.W. Mellor

1020 Mount Pleasant Road
Bryn Mawr, Pennsylvania 19010
Studio: (215) 527-9040

Specializing in executive portraiture.

Please refer to American Showcase Volumes
7, 8 and 9 for additional images.

Michael Merle
5 Union Square West
New York, New York 10003
(212) 741-3801

Studio and Location
Photography

Donald L. Miller

295 Central Park West
New York, New York 10024
(212) 496-2830

Specializing in C.E.O.s, Chairmen, Presidents,
Directors, and top management.

Donald L. Miller

295 Central Park West
New York, New York 10024
(212) 496-2830

Specializing in C.E.O.s, Chairmen, Presidents,
Directors, and top management.

Tina Mucci
129 West 22nd Street
New York, New York 10011
(212) 206-9402

PHOTOGRAPHY • 129 WEST 22ND STREET • NEW YORK, NEW YORK • 10011 • 212-206-9402

TINA MUCCI

Harold Naideau

233 West 26 Street
New York, New York 10001
(212) 691-2942

CLIENTS: Nikon; AT&T; Warner Communications; Standard Oil of California; The First National Bank of Chicago; Benton & Bowles; Phillip Morris; Avon; Clairol; J.C. Penney; Revlon; Holt, Rinehart Winston; McGraw-Hill; Harcourt Brace Jovanovich; EMI America Records.

Stock Photographs: The Stock Market

Member: ASMP

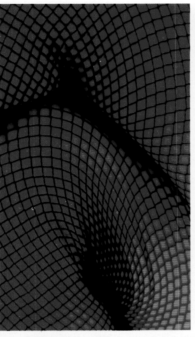
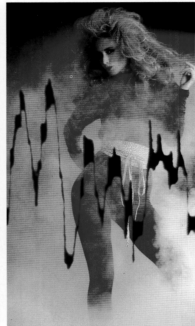

Dan Nelken Studio

43 West 27th Street
New York, New York 10001
(212) 532-7471

Corporate
Annual Reports
Advertising
Editorial

Major corporate clients in 1986: Canadian Imperial
Bank, CBS/Fox, Chase Manhattan Bank, Chemical
Bank, Dow Jones & Co., General Foods, Gulf &
Western Industries, IBM, NBC, Morgan Guaranty Trust,
Touche Ross.

Thom O'Connor
Photography

74 Fifth Avenue
New York, New York 10011
(212) 620-0723

Corporate and Editorial
Photography

For clients including:

Allstate
Sears
E. F. Hutton
Merrill, Lynch
Touche Ross
Business Week
PC Magazine
The New York Times

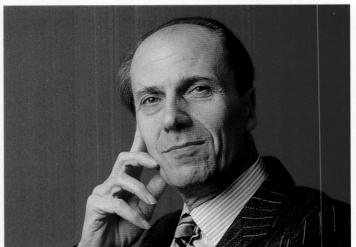

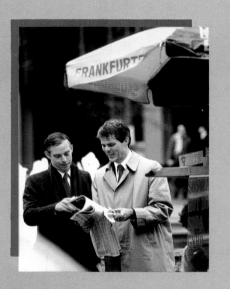

Gabe Palmer

**Gabe Palmer's
Mug Shots** ™
Fire Hill Farm
30 Rockledge Road
West Redding, Connecticut
06896
(203) 938-2514

Advertising and Corporate
photography on location and in
the studio.

Assignment:
Palmer/Kane
West Redding, Connecticut
06896
(203) 938-2514

Stock:
The Stock Market
New York
(212) 684-7878

After Image
Los Angeles
(213) 480-1105

Masterfile
Toronto
(416) 977-7267

Ace Photo
London
01 629 0303

Marka
Milan
02 439 1628

The Stock House
Hong Kong
5 220486

Stock Photos
Australia
699 7084

Stock...for people who need people.

Jerry Palubniak
144 West 27th Street
New York, New York 10001
(212) 645-2838

Portfolio On Request

Nancy Palubniak

144 West 27th Street
New York, New York 10001
(212) 645-2838

Portfolio On Request

continued from page 120

America can review the very best talent available. By intelligently utilizing the wealth of available talent for the jobs at hand, small local or regional agencies can compete with the largest agency anywhere. And advertising everywhere will be better.

The book you are holding is the 10th Anniversary Edition of AMERICAN SHOWCASE. This brilliant publishing achievement is an important service to advertising creatives from shore to shore, across America. Lives there a creative anywhere in the civilized world who doesn't salivate as he or she flips the pages of AMERICAN SHOWCASE?

In the spirit of this and all anniversaries, will you now put on your funny hat, tune up your kazoo, and sing along with me—

"Thanks, AMERICAN SHOWCASE;
Thanks, fabulously talented Artists and Photographers;
Thanks for putting your impressive works before us;
Thanks for the opportunity to work with you."

Now, let's get together and do some ads, brochures, catalogs, mailers, annual reports... and CELEBRATE!

(By the by, STAR Advertising Agency celebrated our 20th anniversary in 1986.)

Jim Saye
President
STAR Advertising Agency
Houston

Stuart Peltz

33 West 21st Street
New York, New York 10010
(212) 929-4600

Agent:
Anita Green
718 Broadway
New York, New York 10003
(212) 674-4788

Clients Include: Descente, Nikon, Perdue, Cunard,
Pioneer, Singer, Maxwell, Cooking Good, General
Foods, Sambucca, Procter & Gamble, Hebrew
National, U.P.S., *Geo*, Minolta, American Can,
Ponderosa, Arby's, Sharp, Western Union, Quaker,
Pepsi-Cola.

Clayton Price
Photographer
205 West 19th Street
New York, N.Y. 10011
212-929-7721

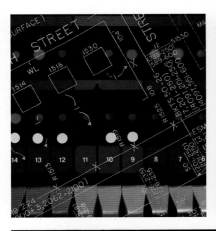

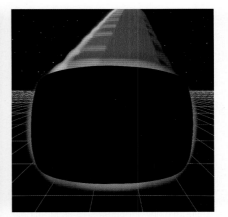

Clayton J. Price
Photographer
205 West 19th Street
New York, New York 10011
(212) 929-7721

Do you need another approach to the visuals for an established idea? Perhaps it's a whole new thought which requires a whole new translation.

Clayton Price understands the process of conceptual thinking. He has the experience and the knowledge to bridge the distance from mind to camera.

See more of Clayton's work in American Showcase, Vol. 9 and ASMP Books 2, 3, & 5.

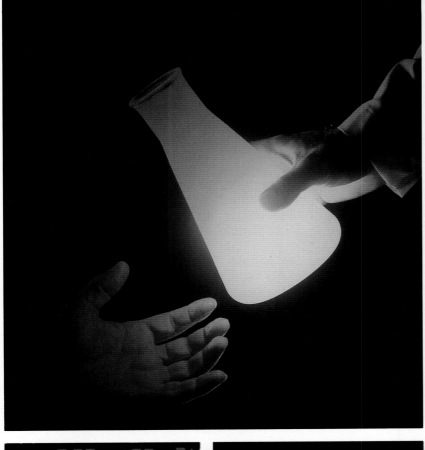

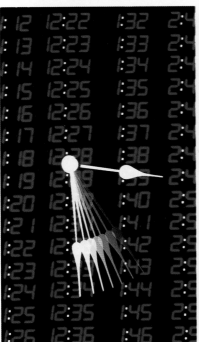

GROWTH. THE REAL CREATIVE KILLER.

With the final absorption of the legendary Doyle Dane Bernbach into the ominous sounding mega-structure of OMNICOM, there has been a rush of sentimental commentary and political public relations about the enduring creative legacy of DDB.

There's no argument that Bill Bernbach's vision of how to create brilliant advertising has forever changed the framework we use in practicing our creative skills, and the personal process we use in evolving our work.

But the legacy of the art and copy team or the constant search we go through to state a truth in a fresh way is <u>not</u> what all the talk is about.

The eulogizing is about DDB's clear and present impact on the creative quality of the advertising being produced today. The idea of a broad creative mantle upon the industry is appealing but is just wishful thinking.

The weight of visual evidence does not support it. It only shows up in intermittent doses. Just open the nearest magazine or turn on the tube for an hour to see what our industry mostly produces —bad, botched, and boring advertising. The isolated creative oasis we do enjoy only reminds us of the vast, bland desert we are working in.

So where is the enduring DDB legacy? And what did happen to Bill Bernbach's revolution?

The original DDB environment that spawned the exciting super-charged creative thrust was, indeed, revolutionary. It became the lightning rod for attracting unique creative talents and the measuring rod for the industry's creativity. The astounding ads coming out of this fountainhead opened our consciousness and dominated the award shows. Clients came knocking. Lots of them. In the early years, if a marketing v.p. put DDB on his agency review list, he was sticking his neck out. By the early 1970's, if he didn't put DDB on the agency review list, he wasn't doing his job.

In a relatively short time, the new kid on the block became part of the accepted establishment. Thus, success was assured. Followed quickly by growth and prosperity. And the inevitable happened. Over time, the DDB revolution succumbed to the assimilation process of evolution.

Any creative agency's success is a two-edged sword. The very growth it produces causes the gradual dilution of the singular creative force that helped the agency succeed in the first place.

It's a dilemma that no growth-minded creative agency has yet solved. With growth, new people are brought in to fill gaps at all levels. They bring different agency cultures with them and their subtle "alien" influences become part of the agency's process. In due time, more layers, more points of view, more egos and more consensus lead to less risk-taking and ultimately to mediocrity.

There is no other way to handle growth but to hire outsiders. Therefore, there is no way for a creative climate to remain untouched. The distinctive creative cultures that small agencies breed must be

continued on page 146

Bill Ray

350 Central Park West
New York, New York 10025

Represented by Marlys Ray
(212) 222-7680

© Bill Ray, 1987

For more of my work see pages
106-107 Corporate Showcase
3, Corporate Showcase 4,
American Showcase 9. Black
& white samples and portfolio
on request.

1. James C. Marlas, Chairman,
   CEO, Mickelberry Corp.

2. Walter J. O'Brien, Vice
   Chairman, J. Walter
   Thompson Group, Inc.

3. Don Johnston, Chairman,
   CEO, J. Walter Thompson
   Group, Inc.

4. Louis J. Forgione, Treasurer,
   General Re Corp.

5. James E. Burke, Chairman,
   CEO, Johnson & Johnson.

6. Frederick W. Smith,
   Chairman, CEO, Federal
   Express Corp.

7. Len Casillo, Designer,
   General Motors.

1.

2.

3.

4.

5.

6.

7.

Rep Rep
Gaylene Fraser (212) 475-5911
Valerie Kooyker (212) 673-4333

Photographer:

Marcus Tullis
400 Lafayette Street
New York, New York 10003
(212) 460-9096

OGILVY & MATHER ADV. A.D. LEE ERNST

Your baby's whole world should be as soft and safe as Q-tips.

Rep Rep
Valerie Kooyker (212) 673-4333
Gaylene Fraser (212) 475-5911

Photographer

Rosemary Howard
902 Broadway
New York, New York 10010
(212) 473-5552

CORPORATE ANNUAL REPORTS INC. A.D. LEN FURY

ANTHONY RUSSELL DESIGN A.D. JIM NOECKER

"I don't think of myself as too trendy. I just love the way Serendipity makes Hot Fudge Sundaes."

"He looked so tough... but he laughed when he ordered the Gun Powder Tea. Lord what a guy!"

"She ordered Hot Chocolate served frozen...she was spoiled rotten. I loved her."

serendipity 3

serendipity 3

serendipity 3

OWEN RYAN & ASSOCIATES A.D. BRIAN CORDELL

143

Jack Reznicki

568 Broadway
New York, New York 10012
(212) 925-0771

Represented by Elyse Weissberg
(212) 406-2566

People Photography:
Location and Studio

Clients include:

Crest
Panasonic
Sony
Personna
Cigna
Timex
Oragel
Wrangler
Stroh's Beer
Old Milwaukee Beer
Reader's Digest
Success
Money Magazine
American Baby
Video Magazine
Westvaco
Alka-Seltzer
Life of Virginia
Richmond County Bank
Pre-Sun
Watson-Guptill
NY Telephone
NYNEX
Chemical Bank
Xerox Computers
Foster-Wheeler
Cushman Wakefield

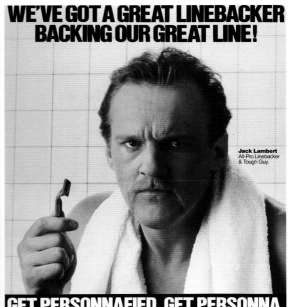

WE'VE GOT A GREAT LINEBACKER BACKING OUR GREAT LINE!

Jack Lambert
All-Pro Linebacker
& Tough Guy.

GET PERSONNAFIED. GET PERSONNA.

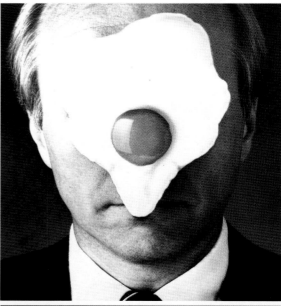

Rĕz-nick-i
(Just call me Jack).

Henry Ries

204 East 35th Street
New York, New York 10016
(212) 689-3794

HELIOPTIX © is a unique photographic concept. Controlled motion of light and lens creates designs of imaginative shapes and colors around words, logos, products and symbols.

Represented by
Sol Shamilzadeh
(212) 532-1977

Additional work may be seen in
American Showcase
Vol 1 Page   68
Vol 2 Page   74
Vol 3 Page 135
Vol 6 Page 120/121
Vol 8 Page 150

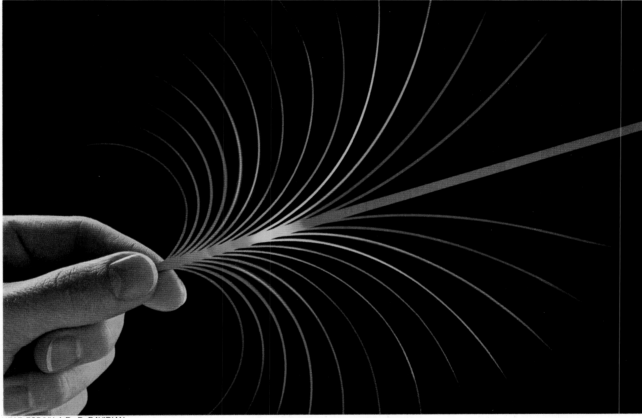

AT&T, FCB/NY, A.D.: D. DAVIDIAN

LEDERLE, CARRAFIELLO/DIEHL A.D. WALTER TREUER

continued from page 140

altered as they grow bigger. And that is the start of the blurring, the softening of the edges of the creative uniqueness that brought success.

When agency principals decide to expand, they are tacitly agreeing to a slow diminution of their original creative product. Of course, their hope is that the change will be for the better. History shows that it rarely is.

With growth, another important impact on the agency's creativity comes from the client side. Smaller and medium-sized agencies enjoy a more direct communication with like-sized clients. These clients have chosen the particular agency for their people and creative product. One-on-one contact is the norm allowing more mature partner relationships to develop. There are less layers of authority on both sides. The people who pay the bills talk directly with the people who create the advertising. But as companies grow, the original entrepreneurs, the decision makers move out of the hands-on process to be followed by second generation middle-level management people who are not initiators by nature. They tend to be the caretakers of the status quo. They equate new thinking with controversy and above all, they do not want to rock anybody's boat. They can easily question fresh thinking and are in positions to water it down or kill it off entirely. So once again, the muffling, the slow suffocation of the original breakthrough creative thinking happens, to be replaced with safe consensus advertising that won't cause too much conversation in the marketplace...or the halls.

It's no surprise that most of the new creative standard-bearers have shifted to places outside of New York. In the last decade the New York creative community has been traumatized by the abdication of upper management, a narrow bottom-line financial and marketing psychology and the insecurity that comes with mega-merger mania.

That part of Bernbach's vision, the insistence on searching for new ways to state old truths, seems to be kept alive mostly among small pockets of believers in cities like Minneapolis, Richmond, San Francisco, Seattle and Boston where the life-giving elements necessary for real creative reach seems to be flourishing.

The true DDB legacy is a very inward, personal one for most of us. It gives us a remarkable memory bank of the DDB experience. It lets us practice an uplifting inner creative process that is unassailable. And having been shown the difference between "good" and "bad," we cannot even willfully do the "bad" without betraying our creative selves.

Lee Epstein
Partner
Epstein & Walker Associates
New York City

Lee Epstein is a 20 year veteran of DDB taking part in that agency's tremendous growth period of the 60's and 70's. In 1981 he left to form his own agency and is presently a partner in Epstein & Walker Associates, a small New York City creative consulting firm providing a full range of creative and production services.

Susan Robins

124 North Third Street
Philadelphia, Pennsylvania 19106
(215) 238-9988

Advertising, Still Life.
Specializing in food and beverage.
© 1986 Susan Robins

James Robinson

1255 Fifth Avenue
New York, New York 10029
(212) 580-1793
(212) 996-5486

Location photography for
advertising and corporate
accounts.

Stock Available

See also Showcase Vol. 8 & 9.

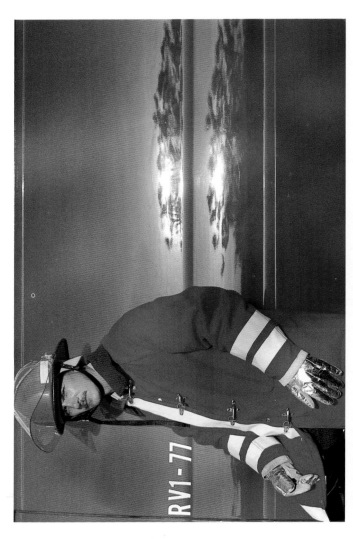

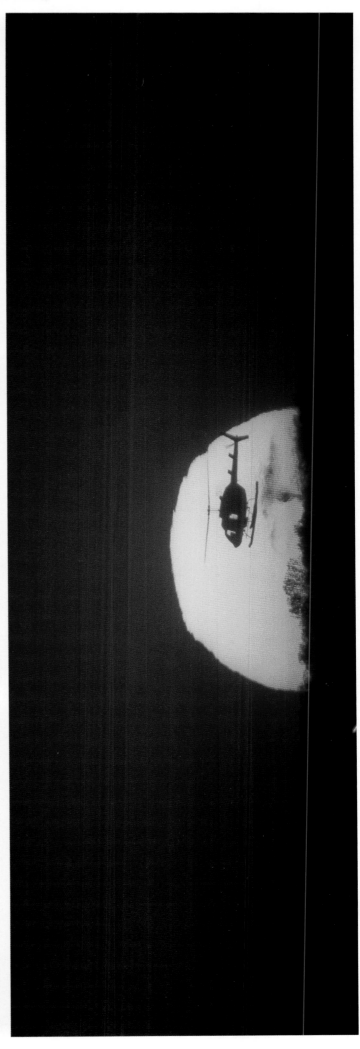

Steve Sharp
153 North Third Street
Philadelphia, Pennsylvania 19106
(215) 925-2890

Paul Sharratt

Multi-Media Photography

20 West 20th Street #703
New York, New York 10011
(212) 243-3281

Award winning optical special effect photography produced on 35mm and 4 × 5 transparency film for Print, Audio-Visual, and Broadcast purposes.

Strobes, zooms, stars, glows; drop shadows, posterizations, and airbrush look treatments are produced from elements including black and white line art, stock or original photography, computer generated images, and stills from video or film footage.

Component special effects are used as elements in photocomping, electronic separation processes, and video effects production.

1. BBDO/Hammermill Papers
   A.D. Tammy Sweet
2. CBS Records/
   A.D. Gene Seidman
3. Drury Design Dynamics
4. Kevin Biles Design
5. Rapideyemovement
   A.D. Bill Aylward

Shiki
119 West 23rd Street, 504
New York, New York 10011
(212) 929-8847

SHIKI

Ken Skalski

866 Broadway
New York, New York 10003
(212) 777-6207

APA

Client List:

Aramis
Buccellati
Corning Eye Wear
Dansk International Design
Estee Lauder
Grace Balducci's Marketplace
JC Penney
Lever Brothers
Maxim Company
Maximilian Furs
Merrill Lynch
Nestles
Polo
Sanyei America

KEN SKALSKI
PHOTOGRAPHY
866 BROADWAY
NY, NY 10003
212 777 6207

153

Howard Sochurek

680 Fifth Avenue
New York, New York 10019
Office (212) 582-1860
Home (914) 337-5014

Medical Scientific and Technical Photography

Electronic Graphics for both TV and print

Computer Imaging
Thermography
Tomography
Angiography

Color Xrays
Image Enhancement
Density Scanning

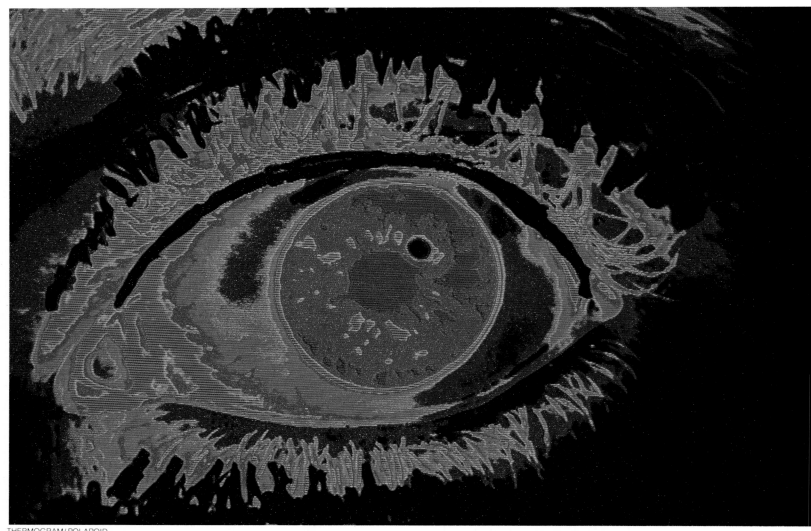

THERMOGRAM/ POLAROID

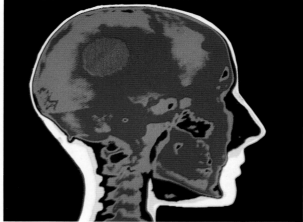

MAGNETIC RESONANCE/CIGNA

COMPUTER ENHANCED/OMNI

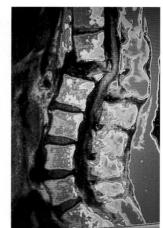

TOMOGRAPHY/ PFIZER

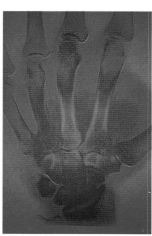

DIGITAL SUBTRACTION/N.G.S.

Olaf Sööt

419 Park Avenue South
New York, New York 10016
(212) 686-4565

9 Tomahawk Lane
Greenwich, Connecticut 06830
(203) 661-4522

Large stock available:

Land and mountains from Alaska to Patagonia:
Climbing, skiing, flying and boating. Mountain scenes,
moods, people and wildlife. Collection includes
Alaska, Canada, Western U.S., Mexico, Guatemala,
Peru, Bolivia, Argentina and Chile.

Northeast:
New York scenes and mountains, New England coast
and mountains. Aerial scenes. Abstract and realistic
details of nature.

Cities and places:
New York, California Coast, Vancouver, B.C., Houston,
Taxco and other Mexico, Tikal and other Guatemala,
Caracas and Maracaibo, Venezuela. Miscellaneous
South America, some Europe.

Activities:
Hiking, climbing, skiing, boating, camping, flying,
soaring, some hockey and other sports.

Additional portfolio available upon request.

Selective assignments accepted.

Don Spiro

(212) 484-9753

Represented by Alison Korman
Korman & Co.
381 Park Avenue South
New York, New York 10016
(212) 686-0525

We shoot for American Express, AT&T, McCann Erickson, Doyle Dane Bernbach, Leber Katz, Newsweek, General Electric, Colombian Coffee, Chase Manhattan, Hart Schaffner Marx, Corporate Graphics, Westvaco, Allegheny Beverage Corporation, Anthony Russell Design, World Magazine and lots of others.

For more of Don's work please see American Showcase Volumes 8 & 9.

Member ASMP

© 1987 Don Spiro

Don Spiro
212 484 9753

THE ANTENNAE OF YOUR IMAGINATION

There it was. Bigger than life. Well, actually it was about 8½″ by 11″ but it looked bigger because it jumped off the page and kicked me right between the eyes.

"It can't be!" I gulped as ice cubes filled my stomach. But there it was in black and white and cyan and magenta and yellow and ... and ... it was MY IDEA! I couldn't believe it. Somebody had already done MY IDEA!

There was MY headline. A different word here and there but it was the same concept. And the photo ... *of course,* it was weaker than MINE, but still ... it was *already there!*

Could I stop the ad? My mind raced. It was too late. The ad was finished and separated and on its way to every magazine in the country. Now I looked like the world's worst plagiarist. A dirt-bag, no-talent copycat. And in this business, that will make you a dead man. Maybe a small agency in Fort Worth, Texas would hire me as an errand boy, but my days in the Big Apple were numbered.

"How could this happen? It was MY idea!"

I had conceived it last November as I was sitting in traffic. I remember reaching over and fumbling for that chewing gum wrapper to write it on. Yes, it happened way before this ... *this other* ... ad was even running! I know it! I swear it's true!

But then the AE delayed it. And the account supervisor delayed it. Then the client sat on it for a few months. Then ... THEN, I got the OK. And now it was on its way to the eyes of the nation. I was sick ... no, it was worse than that. This had to have a much deeper meaning.

I may have had the idea first but someone else *DID IT* first. That's when I came up with THE THEORY ... *THE ANTENNAE THEORY.* And here it is:

Our imagination has these antennae that cover our heads in a twisted network of receivers. Some people call them hair, but they are really receivers ... *ANTENNAE.*

These antennae disguised as hair pick up all kinds of "signals" — TV signals, radio signals, microwave signals, telepathic signals ... even signals that we have no classification for.

These "unclassified signals" come from a *CENTRAL IMAGINATION CENTER* somewhere in Minneapolis. Nobody knows exactly where in Minneapolis, but we know that the signals originate from there because the agencies in Minneapolis get those signals first. This explains why they win all those awards.

Anyway, here's how it works: The "unclassified signals" (sometimes known as ideas) pulse out from their broadcast center and spread like circular waves across the country.

Most creative types keep their "antennae" (hair) long, so they can easily pick up these signals (One notable exception is Jerry Della Famina, whose bald pate serves more as a satellite dish than an antenna). When a person is bombarded by these transmissions, it is usually a good idea to either write them down or record them on a tape player for future use. And therein lies the catch ...

Everyone picks up these signals, just like your TV set receives *The Bill Cosby Show.* But not everyone watches Bill Cosby. Nor does everyone record the "signals." And even the ones that do don't always get the chance to use them. So there it is.

You've received the "signal." But so did the guy down the street ... and the guy across town ... and the guy in the next state. Are you catching on? Now if the other guy can get that "signal" reproduced before you do, then it's his IDEA. He is the original and you are the copy. Sure, you have no way of knowing if he is going to use it ... until he does.

In its simplest form, THE THEORY resembles the dilemma of man's struggle in the nuclear arms race. "Did they launch first? Or did we? Or did we both launch at the same time?"

Nevertheless, THE THEORY holds fundamental truths, whether we understand them or not. Our belief in them is not necessary for them to be true.

I have felt much better since I saw the light. But I do have to go run some errands for this little agency in Fort Worth, Texas. Oh, didn't I tell you about my new job?

Terry Taylor
Creative Director
Dally Advertising, Inc.
Fort Worth

Jeanne Strongin

61 Irving Place
New York, New York 10003
(212) 473-3718

Assignment Photography/
Portraits in the studio and on
location/Editorial/Annual
Report/Travel/Stock
Photography available

See American Showcase
Vol. Six page 135,
Vol. Seven page 176,
Vol. Nine page 147

Portfolio available on request

Photographs:
Artist Alex Katz, New York
   Times Magazine/
Musician Elliot Murphy,
   Interview/American Bar
   Assoc. Journal/
Kitty D'Alessio, Channel Inc./
Frank Wells, Walt Disney
   Productions/Promotion/
Senior Citizen Women,
   MS Magazine

Michel Tcherevkoff

873 Broadway
New York, New York 10003
(212) 228-0540

Represented in New York by Fran Black
(212) 580-4045

Stock available through studio

Michel Tcherevkoff

Represented in New York by Fran Black
(212) 580-4045

Call for Michel's mini-portfolio

UNCLEAR ABOUT INTEREST CHECKING?

Bank of America

The source of enchantment

Togashi
36 West 20th Street
New York, New York 10011
(212) 929-2290

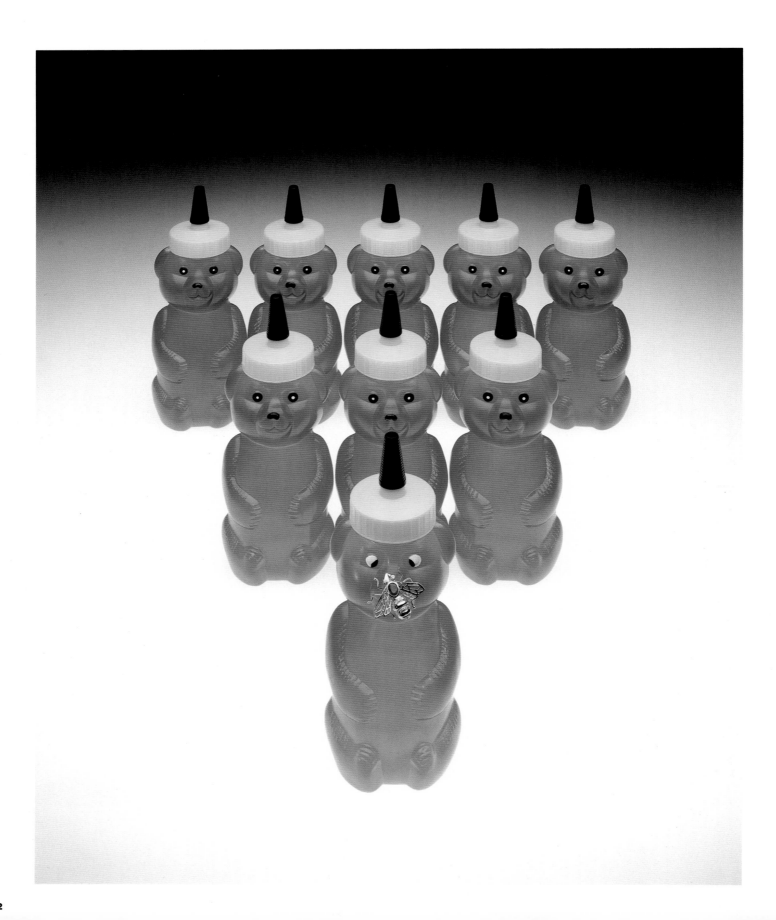

Bill Truran Studios

31 West 21st Street
New York, New York 10010
(212) 741-2285

Representative:

**Dane Sonneville
(212) 603-9530**

Portfolios available for:
• Consumer Advertising
• Food
• Medical
• Direct Market
• Trade Advertising
• Catalogue

31 West 21st Street   NYC 10010 (212) 741-2285
represented by Dane Sonneville (212) 603-9530

Julio Vega
417 3rd Avenue
New York, New York 10016
(212) 889-7568

Still Life neat and clean.

**Visual Impact
Productions**

Tony Cordoza/Chas. Pizzarello
15 West 18th Street
New York, New York 10011
(212) 243-8441

V.I.P.

Visual Impact Productions

SOURCEBOOKS AS TEXTBOOKS

Young people just getting a start in photography must relish opening a book like this.

It's not difficult to imagine them poring over it the very day it arrives in the mail, soaking up the information these pages offer on lighting, composition and conceptual thinking. And it's not hard to imagine them referring back to this book each time they need inspiration or answers to a problem they encounter on one of those first photo jobs they've managed to scrape up.

Industry books (specifically award books) have always been terribly important to young art directors, too.

Chances are that a typical art director started his career in a dead-end grunt job at a marginal agency. The ones that develop, and eventually progress to a better job, are the ones who subscribe to magazines like *Communication Arts* and *Archive,* the ones that wait in line to buy the new One Show annual, the ones that scrape up N.Y. Art Directors Club annuals from the 60's. They educate themselves. They mine advertising's past, memorizing the great ad campaigns and emulating the individuals who created them.

The beginners that have a real edge are the ones that were introduced to these publications by teachers early on in school. Unfortunately, their numbers are surprisingly small.

Colleges and art schools (with a few notable exceptions) are overrun with teachers whose qualifications are laughable—who reduce advertising to methodical textbook exercises, limited by rules, formulas and 30-year-old theories. They are teachers incapable of passing on the challenge and excitement of the field, because they lost or never had it themselves.

That's why these books are important. They can offer you a complete education, or fill in the gaps in the one you have. They let you know that there are people working out there who can be admired and emulated. And they serve as a teaching tool for those few enlightened souls out there who are sacrificing a part of their careers to teach the next generation.

I'll never stop reading them. And I'll never stop learning.

Dean Hanson
Art Director
Fallon McElligott
Minneapolis

Randall Wallace

43 West 13th Street, Studio 3F
New York, New York 10011
(212) 242-2930

(Fashion, Beauty, Editorial and Advertising
Photography)

Stock: Imperial Press, Tokyo
Contact: Dave Jampel
Telex: Imperial J25982

WAREHOUSE FASHIONS

Ed Wheeler
1050 King of Prussia Road
Radnor (Philadelphia)
Pennsylvania 19087
(215) 964-9294

Corporate/Industrial
Annual Reports
Advertising, Stock

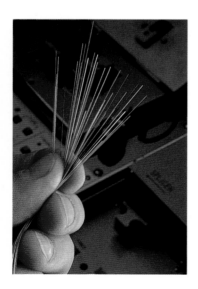

Ed Wheeler
(215) 964-9294
© Ed Wheeler 1986

Rick Young
Photography
Inc.

27 West 20th Street
New York, New York 10011
(212) 929-5701

Clients:

Pluzynski/Associates, Inc.
H. J. Delaney Company
Cooper Leder Advertising, Inc.
IMC Marketing Group
Mike Saltzman Design
    Group, Inc.
Ross, Culbert, Holland &
    Lavery, Inc.
P&D Group Marketing, Inc.
Ohrback & Benjamin
International Flavors &
    Fragrances
IDC Data Services, Inc.
Dorritie & Lyons, Inc.
Laurence, Charles & Free, Inc.
Kauftheil and Rothchild
    Advertising
American Safety Razors
Twentieth Century Fox
Dollar Dry Dock
Learning Corporation of
    America
Amtoy
American Greeting Company
Hasbro
Avon
Bonnie Boerer
John Wannamaker
Celebrity
Crystal Clear Industries
Imperial Crystal
Peter Pan Industries
National Gold Distributors
Dempster
Syed
De Francisco & Deluca, Inc.
Enquire Publishing
The Smart Group
Shaun Newton Design
Journey's End
Arthur Brown & Bros., Inc.
Simon & Schuster

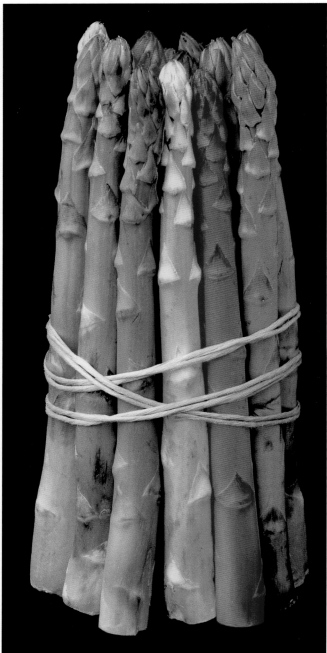

NORTHEAST

Connecticut
Massachusetts
New Hampshire
New York State
Pennsylvania

SIMMONS

Specializing in location photography for Advertising, Annual Reports, Corporations and Industry. Clients include: *Acushnet, Alpha Industries, Analog Devices, Avon, Bank of New England, Bose Corp., Bozell Jacobs Kenyon & Eckhardt, Citibank, Conde Naste Publications, Data Packaging, Digital Equipment Corp., Fairchild, Fidelity, Forbes Magazine, General Electric, Gillette Co., W.R. Grace, Grumman Aerospace, Heublein, Holt Rinehart & Winston, Houghton-Mifflin, IBM, Kimberly-Clark, McGraw-Hill, Microwave Associates, Nashua Corp., Polaroid, Prime Computer, Random House, Rockwell International, Scott Paper, Sola Basic Industries, State Street Bank & Trust, Syncor, Teradyne, 3M, Time Magazine, Touche-Ross, Vogue, S.D. Warren, Young & Rubicam.*

ERIK LEIGH SIMMONS
241 'A' Street
Boston, Massachusetts 02210
(617) 482-5325
Represented by Brigitte
(617) 542-6768

SIMMONS

Specializing in location photography for Advertising, Annual Reports, Corporations and Industry. Clients include: *Adage, Amtrak, Apollo Computer, Bank of Boston, Boise-Cascade, The Boston Company, CBS, Commercial Union Assurance, Data General, Deere & Company, EG&G, Ferrofluidics, Foote Cone & Belding, GCA, General Foods Corp., Goodyear, Graylock Industries, Harcourt Brace Jovanovich, HHCC, Horticulture, HBM-Creamer, John Hancock, LTX, Metagraphics, Moore Business Forms, New England Electric, Prentice Hall, Putnam Funds, Raymond Corp., St. Regis, Sheraton Corp., Sonat Inc., Sun Co., TWA, J. Walter Thompson, Time-Life Books, Touch of Class Catalog, Unionmutual, Warner Communications, Westinghouse.*

ERIK LEIGH SIMMONS
241 'A' Street
Boston, Massachusetts 02210
(617) 482-5325
Represented by Brigitte
(617) 542-6768

K U R T
S T I E R

represented by
Diane Worthington
(617) 247-2847

Studio:
Suite 402, 93 Massachusetts Avenue
Boston, Massachusetts 02115
(617) 247-3822

JO · HA · KYU

K U R T

S T I E R

represented by
Diane Worthington
(617) 247-2847

Studio:
Suite 402, 93 Massachusetts Avenue
Boston, Massachusetts 02115
(617) 247-3822

Jack Joyce/Merrill Lynch

Fred Luconi/Apex Corporation

Apollo Computer/Germany

GALE
HOWARD/JUDY

Model: Bonnie DeFinizio
Stylist: Daniel Citro

Model: Barbara Wheatley

t/a JOHN C. GALE & SON
712 CHESTNUT ST.
PHILADELPHIA, PA 19106
Phone 215/629-0506

THE *Smiths*

GORDON E. SMITH

Long established as a premier photographer creating distinctive images with food and still-life assignments.

& SONS
GARY AND RUSSELL SMITH

Russell and Gary Smith, producing quality people, product and still-life photography.

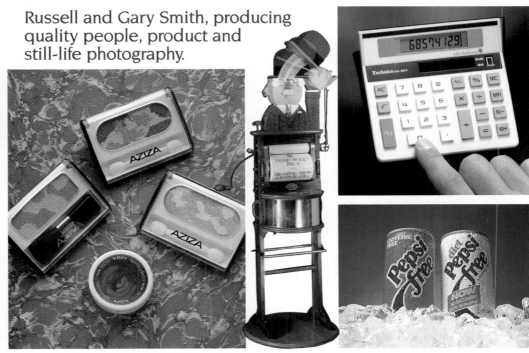

GORDON E. SMITH PHOTOGRAPHY • 65 WASHINGTON STREET, SOUTH NORWALK CT 06854 • PHONE 203-866-8871
STUDIOS IN NEW YORK AND CONNECTICUT

SAMARA INC.

PHOTOGRAPHY

SAMARA

TOM SAMARA

713 ERIE BLVD. WEST
SYRACUSE, NEW YORK 13204
315 476-4984

Carol Kaplan Studio, Inc.
20 Beacon Street
Boston, MA 02108
617 · 720 · 4400

Represented by Robin Fernsell

Kaplan

William Hubbell

General Foods Headquarters

Philip L. Smith, President, CEO, General Foods

Food—Editorial

Creative File—Stock

Bill Hubbell Corporate photographer specializes in Architectural,
Creative, and Food photographs—studio or location for Corporate,

William Hubbell
99 East Elm Street
Greenwich, Connecticut 06850

Ted Abell
51 Russell Road
Bethany, Connecticut 06525
(203) 777-1988

Kory Addis

144 Lincoln Street, Suite #4
Boston, Massachusetts 02111
(617) 451-5142

Advertising, editorial, people,
corporate and stock photography.

Clockwise from top:

Washington, D.C.
Palm Beach, Florida
Tiverton, Rhode Island
Spot-Bilt Athletic Shoes
Rolling Stones, Life Magazine

© Kory Addis Photography, 1987

Thomas W. Ames Jr.

Thetford Center, Vermont

People, places and things, specializing in New
England locations for commercial and editorial clients.

For assignment contact:
Hathorn Olson Photographers Inc.
1 Buck Road
Hanover, New Hampshire 03755
(603) 643-5523

Stock images available through
f/Stop Pictures Inc.
(See stock photography section)

ASMP

HOUGHTON MIFFLIN/EDUCATIONAL SOFTWARE

NEW ENGLAND EQUIPMENT COMPANY INC.

183

APPETIZING brt 'MAGES

BRT PHOTOGRAPHIC ILLUSTRATIONS

9 1 1   S T A T E   S T R E E T

L A N C A S T E R ,   P A   1 7 6 0 3

7 1 7 · 3 9 3 · 0 9 1 8

brt
Photographic
Illustrations

911 State Street
Lancaster, Pennsylvania 17603
(717) 393-0918

Brian R. Tolbert, ASMP
Kirk Zutell, ASMP
Fred C. Bogner, rep

A fine choice for mouth-watering photography.

ingredients:
Take three full-time photographers, add 12,000 sq feet of studio space, complete kitchen facilities, and top off with a comprehensive in-house lab.

We've combined all these ingredients to create one of the largest full-service studios in the northeast. And for best results, we'd like to suggest food photographer Brian Tolbert and stylist Bonnie Miller who are especially eager to please.

Try us once; you'll keep coming back for more.

Gerry Baskin

12 Union Park Street
Boston, Massachusetts 02118
(617) 428-3316

Other samples of my work can be seen in Corporate Showcase 4, American Showcase 9, and Boston's Designsource 83, 84, 85, & 87.

Thanks to the art directors who worked with me on these photographs: Glenn Cook, Norm Graf, Michael Haley, Joe Joslin, Chuck Lusignan, Judy Marlowe, and Susan Solomon.

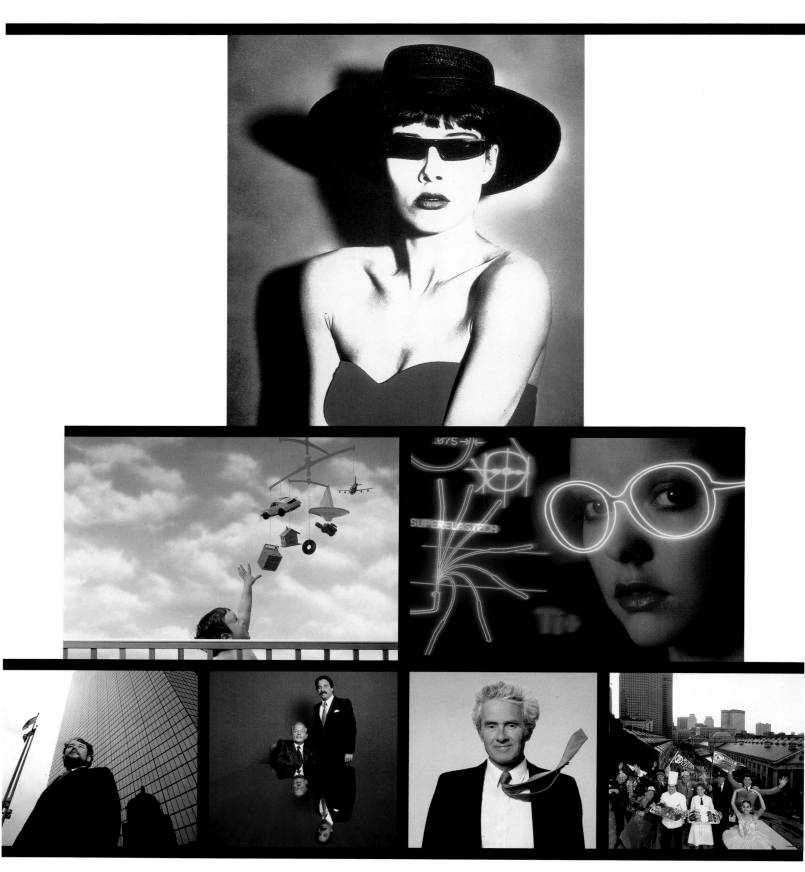

Ted Beaudin

Photographer

New York Studio:
450 West 31st Street
New York, New York 10001
(212) 563-6065

Connecticut Studio:
56 Arbor Street
Hartford, Connecticut 06106
(203) 232-4885

Photonet mailbox: PH01334

Stock available through FPG International,
New York City

Member, ASMP

© 1987, Ted Beaudin

"Photography for advertising, brochures, and catalogs
that has people looking natural at what they are doing,
whether they are professional models or not."

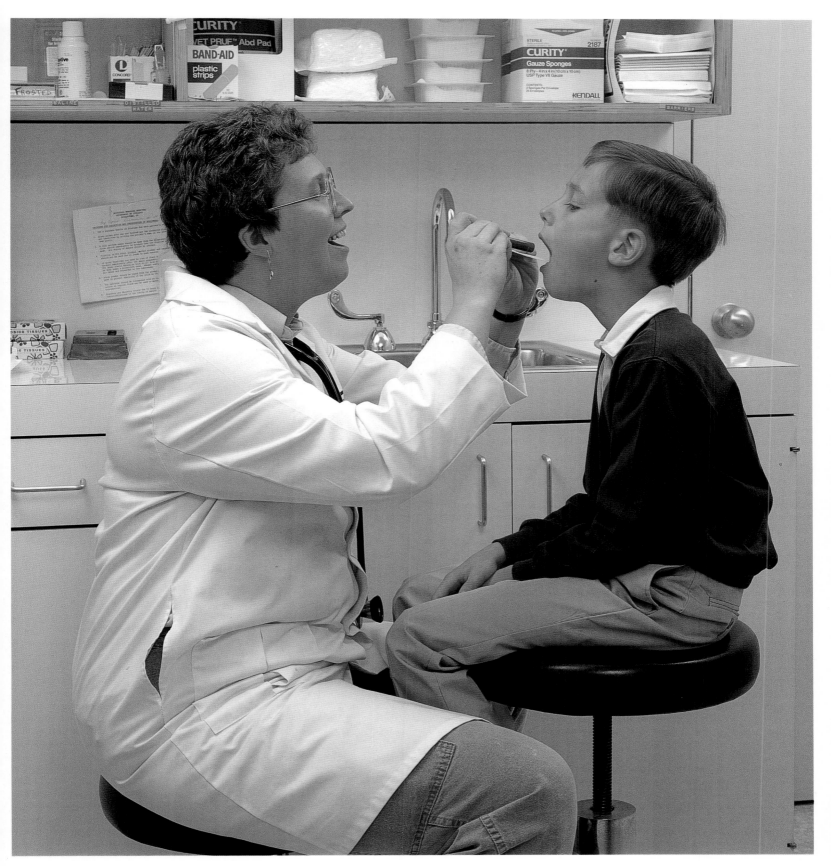

Rick Davis

Photographic Communications
No. 9, 210 Carter Drive
Matlack Industrial Center
West Chester, Pennsylvania 19382
(215) 436-6050

Represented by:
Nanette Hopkins
The a la Carte Solution
(215) 649-8589

PEOPLE WHO GAVE US A SHOT...

Mike Aloisi
Strategic Marketing

Mark Anderson
GOODLIFE Magazine

Mr. Arra
All-Fill Inc.

Kim Baker
Total Collateral Group

Susan Baltlake
Sommers/Rosen Inc.

Jay Barthmess
Total Collateral Group

Dan Bell
Users, Inc.

Joe Bewley
Bewley Irish Imports

Sandy Boucher
Rouse and Associates

David Bradford
Secrephone

Dan Braverman
Radio Systems

Dick Carlson
Madsen Interiors

Joe Carone
NUCORP Products

Kate Cherry
Peoples Light & Theater

Hobart Clark
Winchell Company

Mary Crowson
Knight-Ridder, Inc

Tracy Cunningham
Hawley Matthews Incorporated

Louise Cupelli
Rouse & Associates

Kevin Davies
Total Collateral Group

Donald Deyle
The Pflauder Company

Debra Diament
A.L. Diament & Co.

Pamela Dillett
William Jenkins Advertising

Brad Drexler
Binney & Smith

Marsha Drummond
CDQ Printers

Larry Eisman
Dopaco

Gene Ellick
Reese, Tomases, & Ellick

Donna Ellis
Charles Ganter Design

Joseph Fanelli
Rohm & Haas Company

Bruce Fisher
McNeil Consumer Product Co

Richard Florschultz
Graphic Design Associates

Bill Flynn
Montgomery & Associates

Kathy Fox
Iuppa McCartan, Inc

Joe Freeman
Total Collateral Group

Rolf Fricke
Eastman Kodak Company

Rodney Gentz
The Master Group

Jerry Giambatista
Newton Associates

Naomi Grass
Rittenhouse Market Associates

Lee Greenfield
Total Collateral Group

Vince Guiliano
Guiliano Design

Jay Gundel
Jay Gundel & Associates

Jack Harris
Charles Ganter Design

Jim Hashimoto
Denney-Reyburn

Linda Hawley
Hawley Matthews Incorporated

Frank Hesch
Bentley Harris Corporation

Russel Hirth
Kelley Michner, Inc.

Ray Hoffman
Boyd, Tamney & Cross

Jandon Hogan
Binney & Smith

David Hopkins
DATALOGIC

Nick Imperato
Tomark

Terry Johnson
Ebeling & Reuss

Barry Jones
Lloydes of Pennsylvania

Michael Jordan
Florida Trend, Inc.

Steve Kay
Quilt Classics

John Kilroy
Betz Labs Incorporated

Barney King
Fiber Metal Corporation

Marie King
Cyclop Strapping Corporation

Jack Lever
Compoa

Bruce Levey
O'Brian Machine Company

Merv Madsen
Madsen Interiors

Lindsey Marini
Rouse Chamberlain

George McCuetcheon
Homer & McCuetcheon, Inc.

Debbie McGann
Boyd, Tamney & Cross

Raymond McGlew
E. I. du Pont de Nemours

Glenda McIntyre
F. Daniel Cathers

Tim McKenna
McKenna Enterprises

Paul Meyers, Jr.
Valley Forge Tape & Label

Peg Miceli
Quad Systemc Corporation

Don Morris
Keystone Helicopter

Robert Morton
APEX Alkalai Products

Michael Mumma
Cell-Con, Inc

John Nearing
John Nearing Design

George Nolan
Spanco, Inc

Jerry Nook
Winchell Company

Gene Nopper
Hawley Matthews Incorporated

Ray Papale
Technitrol, Inc

Marvin Pekovsky
Eastrencraft

Steve Pinkston
Steve Pinkston & Others

Lou Rinko
Rinko Advertising

Russ Risko
Lindhult & Jones Advertising

Richard Rothwell
Reese, Tomases & Ellick

John Safrit
Lewis, Gilman & Kynett

Tom Schlenker
N.G.S. Design

Jerry Schneider
Schneider Studio

Jerry Schroder
McGrew Color Graphics

Al Schupp
Trend Industries

Nate Schwartz
Techniservice

Sue Shea
Outline Inc.

Marty Simon
The Simon Group

Joyce Skiffington
Boyd, Tamney & Cross

Lance Smith
Huntington Group

Nancy Smith
Nancy Smith Design

Beth Soldwich
Allester Manufacturing Co.

Gus Sortino
SKF Industries

Sara Stroud
Boyd, Tamney & Cross

Debra Thaler
McNeil Pharmaceutical

Marilyn Thompson
McNeil Consumer Products Co.

Jim Tobin
S.C.T. Corporation

Joan Toner
Valley Forge Country

Tony Trezza
Wright Associates, Inc.

Chris Truex
Direct Strategies, Inc.

Richard Uhlig
Spanco, Inc

Carola Vandenhouten
Modern Art Consultants

Jeff Vaughn
Elmark Packaging

Jim Verdun
Lindhult & Jones Advertising

Nancy Westlake
Crystal-X Corporation

Steve Whitman
Ted Thomas Associates

Phil Wickey
McNeil Consumer Products Co.

Richard Williams
General Ecology

Steve Winig
Isell Systems

Walt Winters
Triton Industries Ltd.

AND CONTINUE TO GET GREAT ONES IN RETURN

Rick Davis
Photographic Communications
No. 9, 210 Carter Drive
Matlack Industrial Center
West Chester, Pennsylvania 19382
(215) 436-6050

Represented by:
Nanette Hopkins
The a la Carte Solution
(215) 649-8589

Steven Edson
Photography
107 South Street
Boston, Massachusetts 02111
(617) 357-8032

Your reality.
My vision.

Steven Edson
Photography
107 South Street
Boston, Massachusetts 02111
(617) 357-8032

Your vision.
My reality.

C. Fatta Studio

Carol Fatta
25 Dry Dock Avenue
Boston, Massachusetts 02210
Boston Design Center
(617) 423-6638

Corporate, Advertising, Editorial
& Portrait Photography.
Location & Studio.
Portfolio & Client List Upon Request.

PAT MORITA

PARIS

RON

WCC, BB&K

RALPH WAITT

PHIL DONAHUE

WU, BOSTON

Bud Freund

Fotos by Freund
1425 Bedford Street – 9C
Stamford, Connecticut 06905
(203) 359-0147

Location Photography for:

AT&T Longlines, AMAX, American Can Company, Burson-Marsteller, Business Week, Cablevision of Connecticut, Chesebrough-Pond's, Combustion Engineering, Connecticut Magazine, Connecticut National Bank, Conrac, Continental Can Company, Cornell University, Dorr-Oliver, Exxon Chemical, Fisher-Camuto, GECC, GK Technologies, General Foods, General Reinsurance, Group W Satellite Communications, Hill & Knowlton, Howmet, IBM, Iroquois Brands, Ithaca College, Long Island Trust Company, Marquardt & Roche, Moore McCormack Resources, Nestle, New York Times, Newsweek, Olin, Padilla & Speer, Pitney Bowes, Pittston, Porter Novelli & Associates, Richardson-Vicks, Road & Track, SUNY Oswego, Xerox

Lou Jones

22 Randolph Street
Boston, Massachusetts 02118
(617) 426-6335
(212) 225-2259

Specializing in location and
illustration photography.

Clients include:

3M
MONY
Minolta
W R Grace
S D Warren
McDonald's
Stride Rite
Price Waterhouse
National Geographic
Blue Cross/Blue Shield

International representation by:
The Image Bank

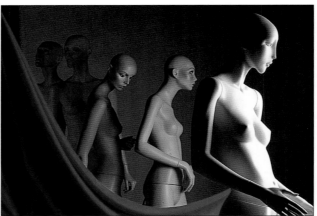

Lamar Photographics

P.O. Box 470
Framingham,
Massachusetts 01701
(617) 881-2512

© 1986 G. Lamar Rosier

Barney Leonard
Photography

518 Putnam Road
Merion, Pennsylvania 19066
(215) 664-2525

Corporate and Industrial
Location Photography for
annual reports, corporate
publications, and multi-image
presentations.

Barney Leonard
Photography

518 Putnam Road
Merion, Pennsylvania 19066
(215) 664-2525

Corporate and Industrial Location Photography for annual reports, corporate publications, and multi-image presentations.

Phil Matt

Box 10406
Rochester, New York 14610
(716) 461-5977

Phil's three specialties are location, location and location.

Locations courtesy:
Barron's
Bausch & Lomb
Bicycle Guide
Business Week
Cahners Publishing
Changing Times
Chase Manhattan Bank
Connoisseur
Eastman Kodak
Eastman School of Music
Entre' Computer
Essence
Farm Journal
Forbes
Fortune
Gannett
Goulds Pumps
GM/Delco
Grolier's
High Technology
Industry Week
I.B.M.
Inc.
Maclean's
National Law Journal
Newsweek
The New York Times
Nutri/System
Nynex
Ogilvy & Mather
Rochester Philharmonic
   Orchestra
Rumrill-Hoyt
Silver Burdett
Sybron
13-30 Corporation
Time
Travel & Holiday
United Press International
University of Rochester
USA Today
U.S. Information Agency
Venture
Xerox

Member: ASMP, NPPA

Extensive color and B/W stock—
fully computerized cross-
reference. See our ads in
American Showcase 8, 9, and
in Ad Index 11.

All photographs © Phil Matt.

Mozo

MOZO Photo/Design
282 Shelton Road (Route 110)
Monroe, Connecticut 06468
(203) 261-7400

For additional reference look up GRAPHIS/Packaging
4 Nos. 527/539/540, DesignSource '86 page 186,
Corporate Showcase Vol. 5 page 107, American
Showcase Vol. 8 page 206, Vol. 9 page 193.

Stock, mailers and portfolio available upon request.

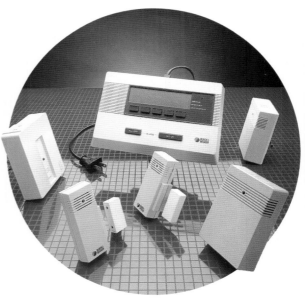

Oliver-McConnell
Photography, Inc.

8 Adler Drive
East Syracuse, New York 13057
(315) 433-1005

From micro-chips to cars, in the studio or on location,
from 35mm to 8 × 10;

Lou Oliver & Russ McConnell specialize in diversity.

Services Include:
Advertising/Illustration
Corporate/Industrial
Annual Reports
Architecture
Special Effects
Fashion
Large Sets
Food
Stock

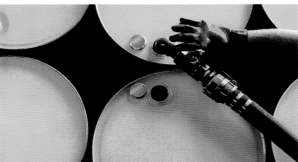

Ken Riemer

183 Saint Paul Street
Rochester, New York 14604
(716) 232-5450

Advertising & Corporate Photography

Available for Studio & East Coast Location
Assignments.

Clients include: A.C. Teleconnect, Analog Digital
Technology, Analytical Products Div. of Milton Roy,
Bausch & Lomb, Citibank, Crosman Airguns,
Detection Systems, DiPaolo Baking, Eastman Kodak,
Ernst & Whinney, Fahy-Williams Publishing, Ivaco,
Magnatag Products, Moscom, Newtex Industries,
Pro-Fac Cooperative, Rochester Community Savings
Bank, Rochester Telephone, Strasenburgh
Planetarium, United Way, Vari-Care, Xerox.

© Ken Riemer 1987

Eric Roth

337 Summer Street
Boston, Massachusetts 02210
(617) 338-5358

Portraiture on location or in the studio for advertising, editorial, corporate, or personal use.

DR. HERBERT V. SHUSTER   SCIENTIST, HERBERT V. SHUSTER, INC.

Eric Roth

337 Summer Street
Boston, Massachusetts 02210
(617) 338-5358

Portraiture on location and in the studio for advertising,
editorial, corporate, and personal use.

HUGH STUBBINS   ARCHITECT, THE STUBBINS ASSOCIATES

BOB KRANES   D.J., WBCN, BOSTON

DEAN JOHN C. MONKS   NORTHEASTERN UNIVERSITY LAW SCHOOL

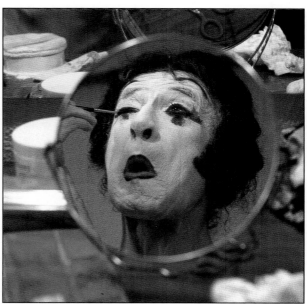

MARCEL MARCEAU   MIME ARTIST

Jeffrey L. Rotman

14 Cottage Avenue
Somerville, Massachusetts 02144
(617) 666-0874

On-location photography around the world, specializing in underwater. Available for assignments.

Extensive underwater stock including coral reefs, divers, marine life, and shipwrecks.

Exotic foreign stock including:
snake charming (India)
hippo hunting (Africa)
belly dancing (Egypt)

cocaine manufacture (Bolivia)
mud wrestling (Turkey)

Editorial clients include Audubon, Discover, Figaro, Geo, Life, Minolta Mirror, National Geographic, Natural History, New York Times, Omni, Penthouse, People, Science Digest, Sierra Club, Smithsonian, Time, Travel & Leisure, U.S. News & World Report, and Zoom.

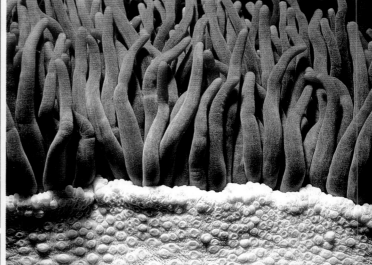

Ron Sauter

177 St. Paul Street
Rochester, New York 14604
(716) 232-1361

Studio and Locations
Stock available. Call the studio

Additional samples of my work
may be found in American
Showcase Vols 6, 7, 8 and
Corporate Showcase 3.

Clients include:

Alling & Cory
American Aeolian
Bausch & Lomb
Beacon Feeds
Black & Decker
Blair/BBDO
Burroughs
Canon
Carrier
Cloride
Computer Consoles
Corning
DuPont Chemicals
Eastman Kodak
Gould Pumps
Grumman Boats
Gunlocke Chair
Hardinge
Hutchins/Y&R
Interpace
Lincoln First Bank
Mutual of Omaha
National Audubon Magazine
Nestle's
Niagara Mohawk
Omega Watches
Penn Yan Boats
Perri, Debes, Looney & Crane
Raybestos Manhattan
Remington Arms
RJ Reynolds
Rochester Community
    Savings Bank
Rochester Gas & Electric
Rochester Philharmonic
    Orchestra
Rumrill Hoyt
Sarah Coventry
Sarroti Chocolates
Sentry Safes
Shimano Fishing Tackle
Smith, Kline & French
Swingline
J. Walter Thompson
Torin
Winross Models
Xerox

SAUTER

ALLING & CORY

SHIMANO FISHING TACKLE

EAGLE STOCK

EASTMAN KODAK

206

Russ Schleipman

Zero Nearen Row
Charlestown, Massachusetts 02129
(617) 242-9298

Advertising, Annual Report, Corporate, Editorial, Industrial, Travel.

AMCA International, Automatix, Bank of New England, Bausch & Lomb, Centocor, Chelsea, Digital, Dunkin' Donuts, Ernst & Whinney, First NH Banks, Forbes, Fortune, Integrated Genetics, Life, Macom, Money, Omni Flow, Outside, Polaroid, Raytheon, Repligen, Rockresorts, Sail, Shawmut.

Tim Schoon

P.O. Box 7446
Lancaster, Pennsylvania 17604
(717) 291-9483

Photography on location for advertising, corporate and industrial assignments.

Represented by Deborah Labonty
(717) 291-9483

© Tim Schoon, 1986

Amy I. Swertfager

Swertfager's Photography Studio
343 Manville Road
Pleasantville, New York 10570
(914) 747-1900

Advertising
Still life
Promotion
Product
Corporate

In studio and on location

Specializing in:
Reflective metals
Glassware
Problem solving

Carl Weese

140-50 Huyshope Avenue
Hartford, Connecticut 06106
(203) 246-6016

Editorial, advertising, and
corporate photography. Clients
this past year have included:

EDITORIAL
Home Mechanix
Popular Mechanics
Northeast

CORPORATE
Covenant Insurance Company
Barclay's American
TetraPak
Glastonbury Bank and Trust
New London Savings
Branson
Farmers and Mechanics Bank
Mechanics Bank
Leggo
Uniroyal
Corliss Data Systems
Eberhard

AGENCIES/DESIGNERS
Weiner and Mayer
Jonathan Wisconsin
Donahue
Adams, Rickard, Mason
Gamble & Bradshaw
Davidoff and Partners

CARL WEESE

WORKING PICTURES

ARCHIVE. IF YOU'RE WITHOUT IT,

YOU'RE NOT WITH IT.

Over 7,000 ad agency ADs, CDs and TV producers are with it.

Archive is the only magazine of its kind. No other publication shows you the newest, most innovative and successful print, television and poster advertising the way Archive does. Not just from the U.S, but around the world.

Advertising that's inspiring, stimulating, fresh and provocative. And you see it in a clear, visual format so you can quickly focus on your areas of interest.

You can get 6 idea-packed issues of Archive at an annual subscription price of $39.97. Call (212) 245-0981, or write:

ARCHIVE

c/o American Showcase,
724 Fifth Avenue,
New York, NY 10019.

MID-ATLANTIC

**Maryland
Pennsylvania
Virginia
Washington, D.C.**

A BETTER MOUSETRAP

ATV talk show host recently interviewed a California college professor who taught an intriguing course on making and marketing inventions. The bottom line of the interview was akin to the age-old advice of building a better mousetrap: find a public need—and devise a method to fill that need. It is much the same in the business world, with the world of advertising being no exception.

One of the most expensive, time-consuming, and traumatic tasks for an advertiser is searching for and selecting a new ad agency. The same could truly be said of ad agencies, in their own search of new clients—to assure their continued existence and even their growth—expensive, time-consuming, and traumatic. Anywhere from 1 million to 100 million dollars of business is often at stake. An agency switch can result in the loss of a dozen jobs in a small agency—to a hundred jobs in a larger shop. Yes, anyone would call that traumatic!

If one can picture the scenario of an agency hunt as it was for many decades, the inevitable muttering would be monitored..."there must be a better way." A better way than a slightly or greatly dissatisfied client stating—or leaking—to the press that he was either already decided on finding a new agency—or open to checking out the field and seeing what agencies other than their incumbent had to offer. The minute the message was out, the client was inundated with phone calls/telegrams/skywriting, etc. from agencies who wanted to pitch the account and land this new piece of business. The telephone time alone in trying to screen which agencies might be capable of handling the work was astronomical, repetitive, and even downright boring (after all, how many times can one repeat with enthusiasm a detailing of the corporate/product concept/history/goals?).

The next step of interviewing agency after agency, and seeing presentation upon presentation was time-consuming to the nth degree. Often good work blurred in memory after a dozen competitive offerings. And if it was time and agony on the client's side, just look at this scenario from an ad agency's side. Hours, perhaps weeks, of brainstorming meetings, creating sample ads/storyboards/campaigns, compiling an impressive and historical gathering of work for other clients that might sway the decision, rehearsals of the "pitch team" prior to the client presentation, and the equally painful job of then waiting...waiting... waiting for the agency selection.

Surely...there had to be a better way! And, as we all know, necessity is the mother of invention. Everyone concerned in this process was in search of a better way to mate clients in search of their ideal agency—with the "right" agency. In essence... a match-maker.

Enter—in 1974, that "match-maker"...in London ...and now in New York City, where I'm president of The Advertising Agency Register. Typically, so logical an answer, many quip "Why didn't I think of that?" The mark of a good "invention!!"

Actually, though I've been called "the match-maker of Madison Avenue," that isn't quite accurate. AAR doesn't match a client and their new agency; we bring the ideal candidates forward and the client makes the selection. But the process in achieving this is a painless method for a client in search of a new agency...an ingenious way of making maximum use of time and preserving anonymity. A process that can add up to a few days of the client's cumulative time, not a few weeks or even months. It is a unique way for a client to go literally unseen inside the offices of a number of preselected ad agencies and look them over, thereby deciding if he wants to meet them personally at a later date...and entertain a full-blown presentation of their work.

Here's the formula we developed in creating this "invention." As the name implies, we "register" —first agencies, and then clients. Agencies in our inventory provide us with a detailing of themselves (corporate biographies, bio's of principals in management and creative areas), a portfolio of what they consider to be their best past print work for clients, and a videotape that conveys the individual character of the agency, with samples of their TV work. In the videotape, usually one or more of the agency's top echelon discuss the shop's philosophy and qualifications and why they deserve consideration of a prospective client. It's rather like stocking a store—we have the "merchandise," now we need a customer.

Enter, a customer...that client about to search out a new agency...or who at least wants to look over the field to be further convinced that he already has the best agency the market has to offer.

AAR now registers the client's criteria. The size of an agency he's looking for...the size of his account...the nature of the account, which most often means eliminating prospective agencies who already carry a competitive account (unless they'd

continued on page 222

curt barlow/photography
washington, d.c. 202/543-5506

Cameron Davidson

Washington, DC
(202) 328-3344
(703) 845-0456

Represented in New York City by
Stuart L. Craig, Jr.
(212) 683-5475

Select stock available direct or from:

After-Image, Inc.
Los Angeles
(213) 480-1105

Bruce Coleman, Inc.
New York City
(212) 683-5227

Folio
Washington, DC
(202) 965-2410

Pacific Press Service
Tokyo
(03) 264-3821

Stock Photos
Melbourne
3-699-7084

Army National Guard
Bell Atlantic
C&P Telephone
C.A.T.S.
Cadillac Fairview
CITCOM
Danac
Fannie Mae
1st American Bankshares
Health & Human Services
Intercare
IWATSU
Life Technologies
Madison National Bank
Monsanto Chemical
National Geographic
Outside
Trans Financial Bancorp
Sibley Hospital
Success
The Washingtonian

Bob Emmott

Emmott Photography Inc.
700 South Tenth Street
Philadelphia,
Pennsylvania 19147
(215) 925-2773

Photography
Set creation
Models
Special effects

Represented by
Judy Yavorsky
(215) 557-0572

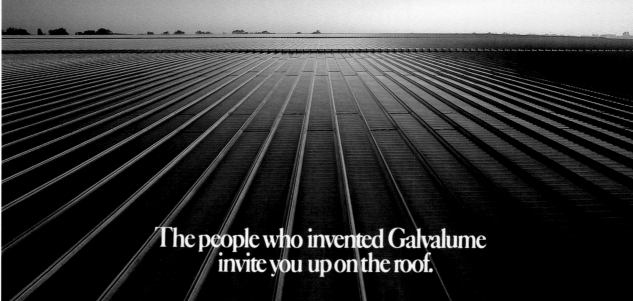

**Keith Lanpher
Photography**
Lanpher Productions
865 Monticello Avenue
Norfolk, Virginia 23510
(804) 627-3051

Greg Pease

23 East 22nd Street
Baltimore, Maryland 21218
(301) 332-0583

Stock photography available
Studio Manager: Kelly Baumgartner

Also see:

Greg Pease

23 East 22nd Street
Baltimore, Maryland 21218
(301) 332-0583

Stock photography available
Studio Manager: Kelly Baumgartner

Also see:
American Showcase 4, 5, 6, 7, 8, 9
Corporate Showcase 1, 4, 5

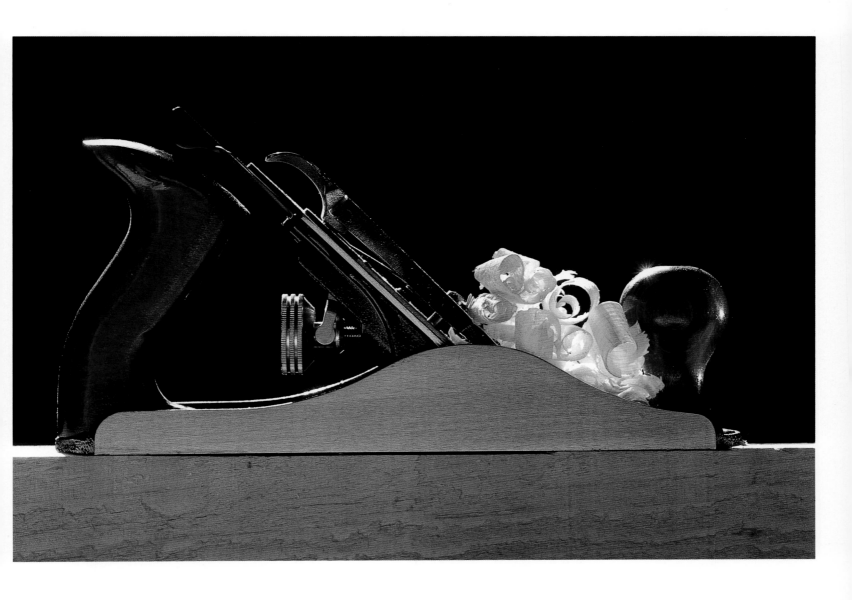

continued from page 214

drop it for a bigger piece of business), and numerous other goals. We then go to work, backing up the information already on file with dozens and dozens of phone calls to fill in additional areas of concern to the prospective client. And, NO agency we speak with or contact has the slightest idea of who the unseen prospective client might be. Once this phase has been completed, a specially-prepared brief is put into the client's hands—corresponding to his specific and earlier stated needs.

Step 2 is equally painless for the client. From all the information in the brief, he selects maybe 10 or 15 agencies he'd like to take a closer look at—still without meeting even one. A visit then to the AAR headquarters is scheduled. It's much like one-stop shopping. Or, as "we ladies" can relate to even better, it's like sitting in a private room in a chic dress salon, sipping tea, and having all the fashions brought in for viewing—contrasted with running around from department to department, sorting through dress racks, trying on, and being left exhausted and somewhat frustrated. The client review process is a joy by comparison to the old method. One by one, he is taken behind the scenes of an agency—via their portfolios and their video-tapes, with AAR giving guidance and answering all questions that come forth. At the end of just one day, or even less, the client has a list of perhaps from three to six agencies he'd like to consider.

Our final step is now a pleasant one—to inform those chosen of the client's name and that they will shortly receive a call for a personal meeting and a subsequent presentation date. We bow out, informing those who didn't make it through the final phase (who also know there'll be other clients, other reviews that result in their favor). We later hear who ultimately won the account. It is usually heralded on Madison Avenue as "a marriage made in heaven." We sit back and smile. We know the major part we played in this marriage. And how pleasant the period of courtship was, too. In one year alone, we were responsible for 20% of all client assignments to new agencies.

Leslie Winthrop
President
Advertising Agency Register
New York City

(Leslie Winthrop is also the elected President of the 80-year-old Advertising Club of New York.)

Robert Severi

Post Office Box 42378
Washington, DC 20015
(301) 585-1010

Portraits
Location or studio

Advertising
Annual Reports
Editorial

Additional work can be seen in
American Showcase Volume 8

Stock photography available.

Ira Wexler/
Photography

4893 MacArthur
Boulevard, N.W.
Washington, D.C. 20007
(202) 337-4886

Represented by
Marsha Brown Wexler

Advertising, industrial and
corporate photography.

Clients:
AAA
Amtrak
Bell Atlantic
Cargil
DuPont
EDS
Entre Computer
Fairchild Industries
Ford Aerospace
General Electric
General Motors
GTE
Holiday Inns
Honeywell

Howard Hughes Medical Inst.
IBM
James River
Magnavox
Manufacturers Hanover
Martin Marietta
McDonald's
MCI
Miles Laboratories
Miller Brewing
Mobil
NASD
NBC
National Guard
NIH

Philip Morris
RCA
Reynolds Metals
Rouse Company
Rubbermaid
Singer
Smith Kline
Smithsonian Books
Sperry
Time-Life Books
USAir
US Air Force
US Steel
Western Union
White Westinghouse

Ira Wexler/
Photography

Ira Wexler/
Photography

4893 MacArthur
Boulevard, N.W.
Washington, D.C. 20007
(202) 337-4886

Represented by
Marsha Brown Wexler

Advertising, industrial and
corporate photography.

Clients:
AAA
Amtrak
Bell Atlantic
Cargil
DuPont
EDS
Entre Computer
Fairchild Industries
Ford Aerospace
General Electric
General Motors
GTE
Holiday Inns
Honeywell

Howard Hughes Medical Inst.
IBM
James River
Magnavox
Manufacturers Hanover
Martin Marietta
McDonald's
MCI
Miles Laboratories
Miller Brewing
Mobil
NASD
NBC
National Guard
NIH

Philip Morris
RCA
Reynolds Metals
Rouse Company
Rubbermaid
Singer
Smith Kline
Smithsonian Books
Sperry
Time-Life Books
USAir
US Air Force
US Steel
Western Union
White Westinghouse

A DEFINITION OF CREATIVITY

"Be original." "Break new ground." "Find new ways of doing things." "Creativity." That's what advertising is all about. It's what people with big reputations preach. It's what people with small reputations torture. It's what people in stiff agencies avoid.

Yet it's ironic, I know of no other business that produces so much sameness, but embraces creativity so passionately as advertising.

The word bothers me.

Creative is a pretentious word. Not by itself, but how it applies to advertising generally.

I've been the Creative Director of the agency I helped co-found since we started. That was in 1962. Although that title serves the purpose of describing a long established agency function, it nevertheless makes me feel uncomfortable at times. Particularly when I meet people who know little or nothing of advertising. Can you imagine certain job titles if the situations were reversed? "Hello, I'm Stella, Creative Anthropologist." Or "Hi, my name's Ralph, Creative Proctology."

The advertising business is a business of communicating information. The wasteful part of advertising occurs when good solid information is taken and then so distorted no one understands what's being communicated. This is frequently referred to as the Creative Process.

Creativity is too heavy a burden to place on creative people. It's unfair. Think of all the undue anxiety it causes us. I'm not even sure how you describe it.

I'll settle for information. It's what I can understand. It's what people want. To be told something that's important to them about goods and services — specific, detailed, factual. For example: is the construction of your radial tire different from other radials? Does it hold the road better or last longer? What's its performance like on wet surfaces versus biased ply tires? Is the extra cost worth the investment in terms of value, safety, peace of mind? If the departure and return of your vacation is in mid-week, will the air fare be cheaper? Where is the gas tank positioned in your car in the event of rear-end collision? What's the nutritional value of your breakfast cereal?

Dig for information. Ask questions. Become as expert on the product and the category as you can. Absorb. Tell the truth. If a product has been around for any length of time, it must have some virtue. Find it. Explain it. Demonstrate it. If a product is new, why is it being introduced? To imitate other products previously launched with no particular advantage, or to produce its own special reason for being? Believe in what you do. If you don't believe it, how can you get other people to believe it?

I'd be foolish to deny the creativity of this business. It exists certainly. In small measure certainly.

But to my mind the real creative challenge of advertising begins before the ad is written. It's in the search, examination and discovery of new information. Confronting the reality of things. Dealing with the controversy of things. Dismissing the inappropriate. Answering the most pertinent questions. And finally, deciding on what is the most persuasive and substantive statement you can make about whatever it is you're about to sell somebody.

Amil Gargano
Chairman and CEO
Ally & Gargano/MCA Adv., Ltd.
New York City

(Originally published in American Showcase Volume 2, 1979.)

SOUTHEAST

Alabama
Florida
Georgia
Kentucky
Louisiana
North Carolina
South Carolina
Tennessee
Texas

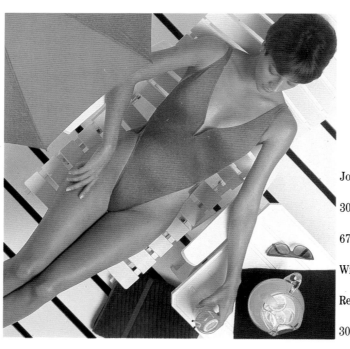

John Petrey

305-645-1718

670 Clay Street/P.O. Box 2401

Winter Park, (Orlando) Florida 32790

Represented by Karen Madoff

305-645-1935

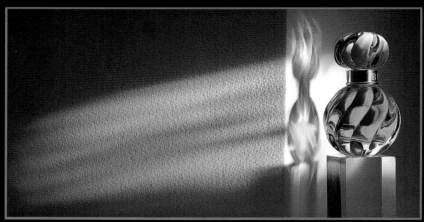

PARISH

Parish Kohanim

Parish Kohanim

P A R I S H

Atlanta (404) 892-0099
New York (212) 662-6611

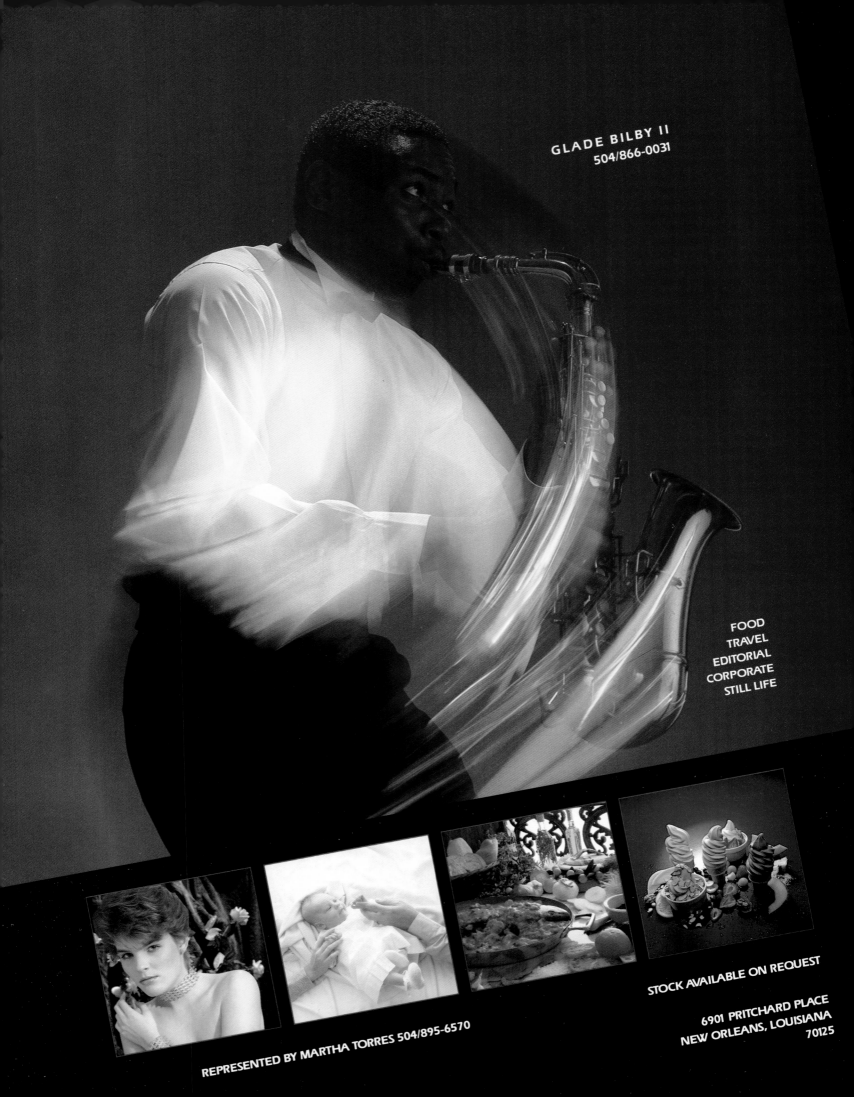

CHIPP JAMISON

ATLANTA (404) 873-3636

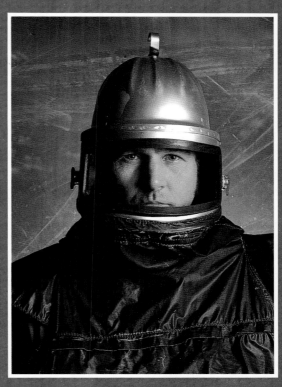

EXTENSIVE STOCK FILE ▪ PORTFOLIO ON REQUEST
MEMBER ASMP © CHIPP JAMISON 1987

Ball

**Roger Ball
Photography**

225-A West 4th St
Charlotte, NC
28202

704
335-0479

Also,
please see
Volumes 8 & 9.

CHARLES Beck STUDIOS

WHY ADVERTISING TRENDS
NEVER GET STARTED
'ROUND HEAH

Most advertising people working in the South will freely admit that we're behind the trends, if not the times. But I've never really heard a convincing explanation as to why this is true. So I offer herewith my own theory.

Folks who create advertising are notoriously susceptible to outside influences. This comes from always being open to anything and everything that could possibly be turned into an ad.

So, if you live in a place where you're constantly exposed to the avant-garde in art, theater and film, naturally you're gonna jump on the good stuff way before the boondocks catch wind of it. No doubt you read *CA* each month only to see how well your ads reproduced.

Influences down here tend to have a different effect on work. Take south Louisiana, for example, where I live. The flags of seven governments have flown over this part of the country: French, British, Spanish, West Florida Republic, Louisiana, Confederate States and the United States. So right away you know there's a real hodge-podge of influences to deal with. Here's what I mean:

Jean Lafitte—a pirate, sure. But he was also the most popular man in Louisiana in 1808. Lafitte plundered Spanish merchant ships and then sold the goods to the uppercrust of New Orleans society at bargain prices. People got spoiled. That explains why even today it's nearly impossible to get fair market value for good creativity around here.

Jim Garrison—the New Orleans wild man/district attorney who made national headlines in the 70's with his Kennedy assassination conspiracy theories. Seems like ever since then it's been hard to get the rest of the country to take anybody from Louisiana seriously. (I'm serious!)

OPEC—when they closed off the valves in Abu Dhabi, the ad business in Louisiana got well. Now they've opened them up all the way and shops are dropping like flies. Try making long-range plans based on those variables!

Heat & Humidity—go into the bathroom and turn the heater up full blast. Then wet a washcloth, put it over your face and breathe through it. At the same time, think up a clever headline. That's what summer can be like here. And now you know why we keep our sentences short and speak very slowly.

Hurricanes—several times a year nature boils up and blasts through, blowing away houses, pushing shrimp trawlers down the street, and driving pine needles through two by fours. Or, at the least, knocking out power for an afternoon. Either way, it's hardly conducive to sitting at the board or the typewriter. So we break for hurricane parties. (There's nothing like sipping on a cold one, watching a shrimp trawler blow by.)

Ice & Snow—because we get a lot more heat and humidity here than ice and snow, Louisianians don't behave well under these conditions. Ice turns every street into a demolition derby. And snow is so rare that any appearance of it has pretty much the same effect as a hurricane. (There's nothing like sipping on a cold one, watching snowflakes come down.)

Mardi Gras—the only thing that'll close down a shop in Louisiana quicker than snow or a hurricane is a parade. Especially if people on the floats are throwing cheap trinkets! Who can work when the world shows up at your place to party?

Food—it's been said that you either work to live or live to work. Here we live to eat. The food is fantastic. Crawfish, crabs, oysters, shrimp, Cajun, Creole—you can't believe how great the food is down here! But wait. I'm off the track.

I was discussing trends. Influences. Susceptibility…

I'll have to get back to you.

I hear an oyster calling my name.

Al McDuff
Creative Director
Diane Allen & Associates
Baton Rouge

LALLO

And Associates

573 Hill Street
Athens, Georgia 30606
(404) 353-8479
Message Service:
1-800-874-4143, Ext. W1
Toll free excludes Florida

Representing:

Dan McClure

320 North Milledge
Athens, Georgia 30606
(404) 354-1234

Dan McClure is at his best when he's shooting people on location. Whether it's a former U.S. Secretary of State, a college professor, or a young executive, Dan works easily with people; he's congenial, yet professional. He can make a busy executive ignore his schedule, a novice model forget her couture, a shy child "smile for the camera." When someone says, "I don't like to have my picture taken," Dan can change his mind.

Portfolio upon request.

And Associates

573 Hill Street
Athens, Georgia 30606
(404) 353-8479
Message Service:
1-800-874-4143, Ext. W1
Toll free excludes Florida

Representing:

Dennis O'Kain

219 Gilmer Street
Lexington, Georgia 30648
(404) 743-3140

Dennis O'Kain can be found on a bumpy back road or a super highway. He may be shooting a country store or a soaring high rise—historic landmarks or sleek interiors. But you can count on whatever he's shooting, it's strictly architecture. That's all he does, and he does it well.

Portfolio upon request.

Bill Barley

Bill Barley & Associates, Inc.
P.O. Box 2388
Columbia, S.C. 29202
(803) 755-1554

Location & studio photography:
Corporate, industrial, advertising
and aerial.

Tight deadline, distant or
multiple locations? Our personal
aircraft provides an easy solution.

Stock photography:
Shostal Associates, Inc.
New York City
(212) 686-8850

© Bill Barley, 1986
Member ASMP

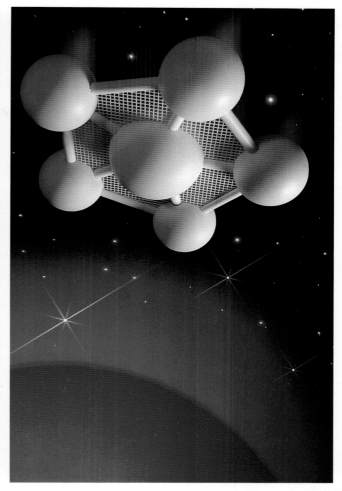

Ian Barr Photography Inc.

2640 S.W. 19th Street
Fort Lauderdale, Florida 33312
(305) 584-6247

Clients include:
Siemens; Bendix Avionics Division; Modular Computer
Systems, Inc.; Mitel; IBM.; Visual Graphics Corporation;
Lancetti Cosmetics; St. Mark V Cosmetics; STP.; Harris
Corporation, Computer Systems Division; Aloe;
Goldline Drugs

Jim Copeland Studio

2135-F Defoor Hills Road
Atlanta, Georgia 30318
(404) 352-2025

Representative Lisa Kellum
(404) 873-1805
(404) 352-2025

Lee Crum

P.O. Box 15229
New Orleans, Louisiana 70175
(504) 529-2156

See American Showcase Volume 9
See CA Photography Annual 84, 85

Bill Dawson

1853 Madison Avenue
Memphis, Tennessee 38104
(901) 726-6043

Photography by Bill and Jeanie
Dawson, Mark Istvanko. May we
send you a portfolio for your file?

Clients:

AT&T
Anheuser-Busch
Bendix
Coppertone
Federal Express
Grey Advertising
Holiday Corp.
IBM
Kraft
Lawn-Boy
Maybelline
Monsanto
Porter-Cable
Procter & Gamble
Richardson-Vicks, Inc.
Scholl

Jim DeVault

2400 Sunset Place
Nashville, Tennessee 37212
(615) 269-4538

Studio and location photography for advertising,
music and corporate accounts.

Jim DeVault

2400 Sunset Place
Nashville, Tennessee 37212
(615) 269-4538

Additional work in:
Black Book 1982, 1983
American Showcase 1984, 1985, 1986
Southwest Review 1986

GRAPHIC ARTS ORGANIZATIONS

Arizona:

Phoenix Society of Visual Arts
P.O. Box 469
Phoenix, AZ 85001

California:

Advertising Club of Los Angeles
514 Shatto Pl., Rm. 328
Los Angeles, CA 90020
(213) 749-3537

Art Directors and Artists Club
2791 24th St.
Sacramento, CA 95818
(916) 731-8802

Book Club of California
312 Sutter St., Ste. 510
San Francisco, CA 94108
(415) 781-7532

Graphic Artists Guild of Los Angeles
849 S. Broadway
Los Angeles, CA 90014
(213) 622-0126

Los Angeles Advertising Women
5300 Laurel Canyon Blvd. #103
North Hollywood, CA 91607
(818) 762-4669

Los Angeles Chapter of the Graphic Artists Guild
5971 W. 3rd St.
Los Angeles, CA 90036
(213) 938-0009

San Francisco Society of Communicating Arts
Fort Mason
Building A
San Francisco, CA 94123
(415) 474-3156

Society of Illustrators of Los Angeles
1258 N. Highland Ave.
Los Angeles, CA 90038
(213) 469-8465

Society of Motion Picture & TV Art Directors
14724 Ventura Blvd.
Sherman Oaks, CA
(818) 905-0599

Western Art Directors Club
P.O. Box 966
Palo Alto, CA 94302
(415) 321-4196

Women in Design
P.O. Box 2607
San Francisco, CA 94126
(415) 397-1748

Women's Graphic Center
The Woman's Building
1727 N. Spring St.
Los Angeles, CA 90012
(213) 222-5101

Colorado:

Art Directors Club of Denver
Suite 102
1550 S. Pearl Street
Denver, CO 80210

International Design Conference at Aspen
1000 N. 3rd
Aspen, CO 81612
(303) 925-2257

Connecticut:

Connecticut Art Directors Club
P.O. Box 1974
New Haven, CT 06521

District of Columbia:

American Advertising Federation
1400 K. St. N.W., Ste. 1000
Washington, DC 20005
(202) 898-0089

American Institute of Architects
1735 New York Avenue, N.W.
Washington, DC 20006
(202) 626-7300

Art Directors Club of Washington, DC
655 15th St., N.W.
Washington, DC 20005
(202) 347-5900

Federal Design Council
P.O. Box 7537
Washington, DC 20044

International Copyright Information Center, A.A.D.
1707 L Street, N.W.
Washington, DC 20036

NEA: Design Arts Program
1100 Pennsylvania Ave., N.W.
Washington, DC 20506
(202) 682-5437

Georgia:

Atlanta Art Papers, Inc.
P.O. Box 77348
Atlanta, GA 30357
(404) 885-1273

Graphics Artists Guild
3158 Maple Drive, N.E., Ste. 46
Atlanta, GA 30305
(404) 262-8077

Illinois:

Institute of Business Designers
National
1155 Merchandise Mart
Chicago, IL 60654
(312) 467-1950

Society of Environmental Graphics Designers
228 N. LaSalle St., Ste. 1205
Chicago, IL 60601

STA
233 East Ontario St.
Chicago, IL 60611
(312) 787-2018

Women in Design
2 N. Riverside Plaza
Chicago, IL 60606
(312) 648-1874

Kansas:

Wichita Art Directors Club
P.O. Box 562
Wichita, KS 67202

Maryland:

Council of Communications Societies
P.O. Box 1074
Silver Springs, MD 20910

Massachusetts:

Art Directors Club of Boston
50 Commonwealth Ave.
Boston, MA 02116
(617) 536-8999

continued on page 256

Gary Doty

P.O. Box 23697
Fort Lauderdale, Florida 33307-3697
(305) 928-0644

Location & studio photography for:
Advertising/Corporate
Interior/Architecture
Product

Additional work may be seen in the 1985 & 1986
Black Book and the 1986 Dynamic Publications
Mid Atlantic book.

Clients include:
IBM, Motorola, Johnson & Johnson, Hertz, Alamo,
Kiwi, Holiday Inn, Olympia & York, Iberia, Taco Viva,
Radice Corp., Sensormatic Corp, Keller Ind.

Portfolio available upon request.

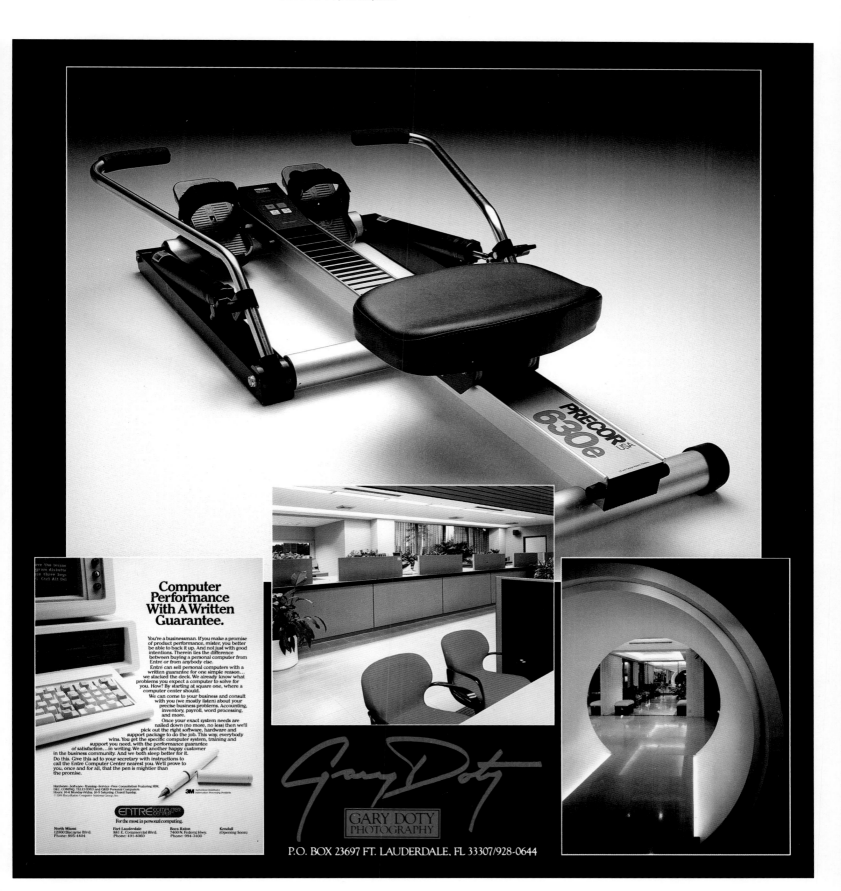

P.O. BOX 23697 FT. LAUDERDALE, FL 33307/928-0644

Jim Erickson

Erickson Photography, Inc.
302 Jefferson Street
Suite 300
Raleigh, North Carolina 27605
(919) 833-9955

Jim Erickson
Erickson Photography, Inc.
302 Jefferson Street
Suite 300
Raleigh, North Carolina 27605
(919) 833-9955

Jim Erickson
Erickson Photography, Inc.
302 Jefferson Street
Suite 300
Raleigh, North Carolina 27605
(919) 833-9955

GRAPHIC ARTS ORGANIZATIONS

continued from page 250

Center for Design of Industrial Schedules
221 Longwood Ave.
Boston, MA 02115
(617) 734-2163

Graphic Artists Guild
P.O. Box 1454–GMF
Boston, MA 02205
(617) 451-5362

Michigan:

Creative Advertising Club of Detroit
c/o Rhoda Parkin
30400 Van Dyke
Warren, MI 48093

Minnesota:

Minnesota Graphic Designers Association
P.O. Box 24272
Minneapolis, MN 55424

Missouri:

Advertising Center of Greater St. Louis
440 Mansion House Center
St. Louis, MO 63102
(314) 231-4185

Advertising Club of Kansas City
1 Ward Parkway Center, Ste. 102
Kansas City, MO 64112
(816) 753-4088

New Jersey:

Point-of-Purchase Advertising Institute
2 Executive Dr.
Fort Lee, NJ 07024
(201) 585-8400

New York:

The Advertising Club of New York
Roosevelt Hotel, Rm. 310
New York, NY 10017
(212) 697-0877

The Advertising Council, Inc.
825 Third Ave.
New York, NY 10022
(212) 758-0400

APA
Advertising Photographers of America, Inc.
45 E. 20th Street
New York, NY 10003
(212) 254-5500

Advertising Typographers Association of America, Inc.
5 Penn Plaza, 12th Fl.
New York, NY 10001
(212) 594-0685

Advertising Women of New York Foundation, Inc.
153 E. 57th St.
New York, NY 10022
(212) 593-1950

American Association of Advertising Agencies
666 Third Ave.
New York, NY 10017
(212) 682-2500

American Booksellers Association, Inc.
122 E. 42nd St.
New York, NY 10168
(212) 867-9060

The Public Relations Society of America, Inc.
845 Third Ave.
New York, NY 10022
(212) 826-1750

American Council for the Arts
570 Seventh Ave.
New York, NY 10018
(212) 354-6655

The American Institute of Graphic Arts
1059 Third Ave.
New York, NY 10021
(212) 752-0813

American Society of Interior Designers
National Headquarters
1430 Broadway
New York, NY 10018
(212) 944-9220

New York Chapter
950 Third Ave.
New York, NY 10022
(212) 421-8765

American Society of Magazine Photographers
205 Lexington Ave.
New York, NY 10016
(212) 889-9144

Art Directors Club of New York
488 Madison Ave.
New York, NY 10022
(212) 838-8140

Association of American Publishers, Inc.
1 Park Ave.
New York, NY 10016
(212) 689-8920

Center for Arts Information
625 Broadway
New York, NY 10012
(212) 677-7548

The Children's Book Council, Inc.
67 Irving Place
New York, NY 10003
(212) 254-2666

CLIO
336 E. 59th St.
New York, NY 10022
(212) 593-1900

Foundation for the Community of Artists
280 Broadway, Ste. 412
New York, NY 10007
(212) 227-3770

Graphic Artists Guild
30 E. 20th St., Rm. 405
New York, NY 10003
(212) 777-7353

Guild of Book Workers
663 Fifth Ave.
New York, NY 10022
(212) 757-6454

Institute of Outdoor Advertising
342 Madison Ave.
New York, NY 10017
(212) 986-5920

International Advertising Association, Inc.
475 Fifth Ave.
New York, NY 10017
(212) 684-1583

The One Club
251 E. 50th St.
New York, NY 10022
(212) 935-0121

Printing Industries of Metropolitan New York, Inc.
5 Penn Plaza
New York, NY 10001
(212) 279-2100

continued on page 262

Ken Glaser & Associates

5270 Annunciation Street
New Orleans, Louisiana 70115
(504) 895-7170

Advertising
Architectural
Corporate/Industrial

Represented by Dawn Wise
(504) 895-7170

Studio and Location
Photography

We Offer:
• Versatility
• Creativity
• Attention to detail
  and deadlines
• Studio with kitchen
  and dressing room
• Professional B&W
  processing/printing
• Audio visual production
  facilities
• The dedication and
  persistence to render ·
  exceptional images

Clients include:

U.S.F.&G.
Hyatt Hotels
AMI
Zotos International
Dean Witter Reynolds
Arby's
Dexitrim
Pepsi
Metal Sales Corporation
Tulane Medical Center
Louisiana Power & Light
New Orleans International
  Airport
New Orleans Convention Center

Eric Hansen

3005 7th Avenue South
Birmingham, Alabama 35233
(205) 251-5587

Outside of Alabama call toll free:
1-800-443-0601

24 × 30 Continuous Tone Poster Available

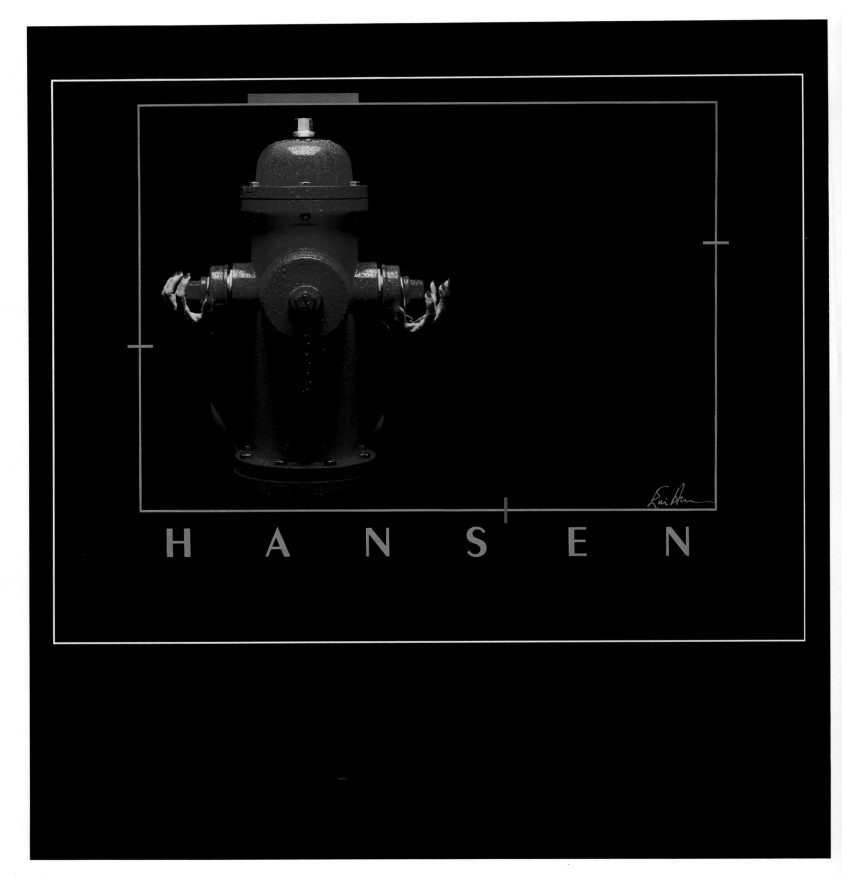

Henderson/Muir Photography

5700 New Chapel Hill Road
Raleigh, North Carolina 27606
(919) 851-0458

Stock Representation through:
Woodfin Camp & Associates
(212) 750-1020 New York
(202) 638-5705 Washington

Clients include:
Aerotron, Inc.; Ajinomoto, USA; Athol Vinyl Fabrics;
Bald Head Island; Blue Cross & Blue Shield; Branch
Banking & Trust; Colorcraft Corporation; Data General;
Entropy Environmentalists; Fails Management;
General Electric; Hardees Food Systems; Harlon
Properties Group; Highwoods Properties; Hilton
Hotels; IBM; Liggett and Myers; Mallinckrodt;
McDonalds; Mead CompuChem; NC Travel & Tourism;
North Carolina State Ports; Northern Telecom; Outward
Bound; Philip Morris, USA; Raychem; Research
Triangle Foundation; Sea Ox Boats; Southern Bell;
The New York Times Magazine; Thurston Trucking
Company; Time-Life Books; Union Carbide; U.S. Air;
Wachovia Bank & Trust.

Advertising, Business Publications, Annual Reports,
Corporate/Industrial, Travel/Personalities

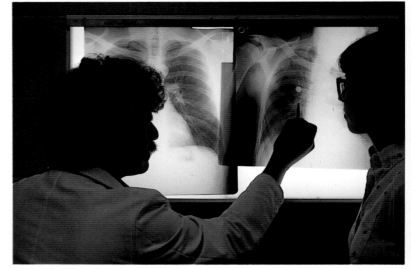

Jackson Hill

2032 Adams
New Orleans, Louisiana 70118
(504) 861-3000

Represented by:
Southern Lights Photography, Inc.
(504) 861-3000

Advertising, Annual Reports, Corporate/Industrial, Editorial, Fashion and Travel.

Location photography is Jackson's strong suit. The South is his special turf. Ask him to shoot wheeler dealers in a shiny Texas high-rise or pulpwood cutters in Red Dirt, Alabama. Jackson knows the people and he speaks the language.

Send him out to shoot heart surgery in Birmingham or high heel fashion on a Pensacola beach. Put him in a Montgomery mansion or a Mississippi micro-chip factory and he's right at home. Push Jackson hard. Dare him to make the humdrum hum. The years spent shooting in the real world pay off. Jackson can size it up, set it up and break it down right on schedule.

Next time you have a Southern project that you can't afford to have loused up, phone Jackson. Knock the concept around. Ask for names of art directors and editors who depended on Jackson to deliver. And if you make it down this way, drop by his New Orleans studio.

Call for a portfolio or see American Showcase Volumes #8 & #9.

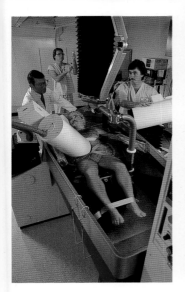

GRAPHIC ARTS ORGANIZATIONS

continued from page 256

Society of Illustrators
128 E. 63rd St.
New York, NY 10021
(212) 838-2560

Society of Photographers and Artists Representatives
1123 Broadway
New York, NY 10010
(212) 924-6023

Society of Publication Designers
25 W. 43rd St., Ste. 711
New York, NY
(212) 354-8585

Television Bureau of Advertising
485 Lexington Ave.
New York, NY 10017
(212) 661-8440

Type Directors Club of New York
545 W. 45th St.
New York, NY 10036
(212) 245-6300

U.S. Trademark Association
6 E. 45th St.
New York, NY 10017
(212) 986-5880

Volunteer Lawyers for the Arts
1560 Broadway, Ste. 711
New York, NY 10036
(212) 575-1150

Women in the Arts
325 Spring St.
New York, NY 10013
(212) 691-0988

Women in Design
P.O. Box 5315
FDR Station
New York, NY 10022

Ohio:

Advertising Club of Cincinnati
385 West Main St.
Batavia, OH 45103
(513) 732-9422

Cleveland Society of Communicating Arts
812 Huron Rd., S.E.
Cleveland, OH 44115
(216) 621-5139

Columbus Society of Communicating Arts
c/o Salvato & Coe
2015 West Fifth Ave.
Columbus, OH 43221
(614) 488-3131

Design Collective
D.F. Cooke
131 North High St.
Columbus, OH 43215
(614) 464-2883

Society of Communicating Arts
c/o Tailford Assoc.
1300 Indian Wood Circle
Maumee, OH 43537
(419) 891-0888

Pennsylvania:

Art Directors Club of Philadelphia
2017 Walnut St.
Philadelphia, PA 19103
(215) 569-3650

Tennessee:

Engraved Stationery Manufacturers Association
c/o Printing Industries Association of the South
1000 17th Ave. South
Nashville, TN 37212
(615) 327-4444

Texas:

Advertising Artists of Fort Worth
3424 Falcon Dr.
Fort Worth, TX 76119

Art Directors Club of Houston
2135 Bissonet
Housfon, TX 77005
(713) 523-1019

Dallas Society of Visual Communication
3530 High Mesa Dr.
Dallas, TX 75234
(214) 241-2017

Print Production Association of Dallas/Fort Worth
P.O. Box 160605
Irving, TX 75016
(214) 871-2151

Virginia:

Industrial Designers Society of America
6802 Poplar Pl., Ste. 303
McLean, VA 22101
(703) 556-0919

Tidewater Society of Communicating Arts
P.O. Box 153
Norfolk, VA 23501

Washington:

Puget Sound Ad Federation
c/o Sylvia Fruichantie
Kraft Smith Advertising
200 1st West St.
Seattle, WA 98119
(206) 285-2222

Seattle Design Association
P.O. Box 1097
Main Office Station
Seattle, WA 98111
(206) 285-6725
(Formerly Seattle Women in Design)

Seattle Women in Advertising
219 First Avenue N., Ste. 300
Seattle, WA 98109
(206) 285-0919

Society of Professional Graphic Artists
c/o Steve Chin, Pres.
85 S. Washington Street, Ste. 204
Seattle, WA 98104

Wisconsin:

The Advertising Club
407 E. Michigan St.
Milwaukee, WI 53202
(414) 271-7351

Illustrators & Designers of Milwaukee
c/o Don Berg
207 E. Michigan
Milwaukee, WI 53202
(414) 276-7828

Larry Keith Lackey

Park Avenue Ltd.
2400 Poplar Avenue, Suite 514
Memphis, Tennessee 38111
(901) 323-0811

Beauty, glamour, fashion, advertising.
Studio and location photography.

Peter Langone

Studio/Peter Langone, Inc.
516 Northeast 13th Street
Fort Lauderdale, Florida 33304
(305) 467-0654

For additional work see American Showcase
volumes 8 & 9.

"A slice of life"

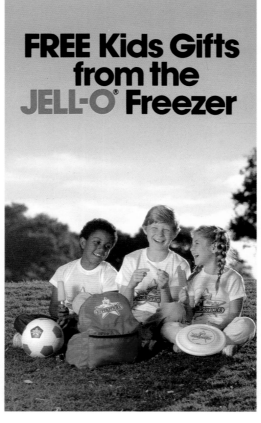

Peter Langone

Studio/Peter Langone, Inc.
516 Northeast 13th Street
Fort Lauderdale, Florida 33304
(305) 467-0654

For additional work see American Showcase
volumes 8 & 9.

"A slice of life"

NEWS FROM BEDLAM #4.
MERGER MANIA

Those of you who are loyal followers of the Diatribes of Leonard Roxbury have taken note, no doubt, that Leonard has been as silent as Stonehenge on the issue of the mergers of Certain Ad Agencies. Make it no wonder! (as Leonard would say). He has held his tongue—so to speak—for two good reasons. One: Roxbury spent the last two months in Venice entertaining, as it were, a number of clients and a select few members of the female sex. (Leonard is fond of elegant women and will indulge this proclivity without regard to time, money, or his status in the advertising business.)

Leonard Roxbury, who is best described as a cross between John Barrymore and P.T. Barnum (if one can imagine such a concoction of appearance and characteristics), is the owner and chairman of the board of one of the largest advertising agencies in the world, with offices in New York, Atlanta, London, Paris and Rome.

The second reason Leonard Roxbury has remained silent on the issue of mergers is that his mouth—which usually emits a resounding tirade on any issue you choose to introduce—was perpetually filled with food during his visit to Italy. (Leonard is partial to pasta—in its infinite varieties: i.e., pomodoro, putanesca, Bolognese, carbonara.) Thus his mouth was stuffed with such variety of food, and hence was in a constant state of relaxation, taking on board, along with his pasta, a considerable amount of regional Italian wines and a fair amount of Grappa!

But I learned the other day, when encountering Roxbury in the Peacock Alley of the Waldorf-Astoria (his favorite watering hole), that The Man was about to Speak His Mind. And if you mind the fact that I indicate the moment in capital letters— save your condemnation until you hear what the old gentleman had to say.

He sat across from me on a banquette, sipped his silver bullet—which is how he refers to a martini, and took a deep breath, suggestive of a skin diver about to descend into the depths. He said: "Yes! I suppose you're wondering what I make of all this merger mania. I've given it a thought, or two. And make no mistake! I think it's an arrant folly. Now if you'll settle back, and pay more attention to me than to the filly across the lobby with the perfect bouncers, you'll realize, once and for all, the baggage of atrocities that is part and parcel of a merger."

I took a deep breath, but I didn't regard myself a skin diver about to sweep toward the ocean floor. Rather, I knew—against my will—that I would be brought to new heights of Understanding. (And once again, if you take umbrage to the fact that I emphasize that prophecy with capital letters, listen as Roxbury hits His Stride.)

Roxbury took a pull at his silver bullet. Sniffed and arched an eyebrow. He announced: "You know I was born in New Orleans. My father was a Methodist preacher, and Ma was a Belle of the South—or so she pretended—for she was nothing more than a sharecropper's daughter. I had four brothers and a sister, and life was a hurly-burly, so I decided to run away from home. (The account of my life—as you know—has the makings of a movie). At any rate, I joined the circus. Indeed, life at home was insane enough, what with a father fond of quoting the Bible and Shakespeare, a mother who saw herself as Scarlett O'Hara, and a brood of brothers— and a sister—who were a touch doltish...and belligerent, to boot. Yes! After that insane set-up, a circus would afford me the perfect asylum to get my act together—as the suckers of the 70's used to say."

I knew Roxbury's story; he was a close friend. And I had listened to the details of his life with avid attention, over glasses of scotch, champagne and port. But I prompted my attentions to follow Leonard's line of reasoning; it always brought me to places I had never been before.

"At any rate," snorted Roxbury, fluttering his fingers across the rim of his glass, "at any rate, I wish to tell you a tale of merger mania, New Orleans style. By the age of fifteen, I was an accomplished trapeze artist. This background, no doubt, prepared me for a successful career in the advertising business. At any rate, I was working for the Fluster Brothers Circus. The year was 1938, and America was still rocking and reeling from the

continued on page 288

Lathem & Associates
Photography
Charles Lathem
559 Dutch Valley Road, Northeast
Atlanta, Georgia 30324
(404) 873-5858

Representative:
Linda Cain
(404) 873-5858

Albert Leggett

1415 Story Avenue
Louisville, Kentucky 40206
(502) 584-0255

To Albert, being a photographer is knowing how to see beyond the way things look. To anticipate. To interpret. To communicate with color. And to capture an emotion with such feeling that—sometime, somewhere—it will create itself all over again.

Yet, while he approaches each task with an insatiable appetite for creative expression, he knows how to keep an eye on the bottom line. He never loses sight of the cold, hard fact that his work must ultimately sell something to somebody. And, invariably the results are pleasing from a number of perspectives: his clients' and his clients' clients for starters.

If your assignment calls for location work, Albert Leggett can pack up his Piper and be where you need him in the time it takes some photographers to light a shot.

Assignments include still life, table top corporate annual reports and industrial. Both studio and location.

Clients include: BATUS, Blue Cross Blue Shield of Kentucky, Brown Forman Distillers, Eastern Airlines, Glenmore Distilleries, Humana.

For additional work see ASMP Book 4 & 5.

Member: APA, ASMP

All photos ©1987 Albert Leggett

Tom McCarthy
8960 Southwest 114 Street
Miami, Florida 33176
(305) 233-1703

Stock photography available.
See National Stock Network.

Clients:
IBM, Nikon, Kodak, Coca-Cola,
7-Up, Hilton, Holiday Inns,
Hertz, British Airways, Delta
Airlines, Eastern Airlines,
Bahamas, Mexico, Bacardi,
Johnny Walker, Seagrams,
Sears, Burger King, Lums,
Lipton, Sanka, Pillsbury,
DuPont, Hallmark, Salem,

Color separations by
Gold Coast Graphics, Inc.

Tom

McCarthy

Randy Miller

6666 Southwest 96th Street
Miami, Florida 33156
(305) 667-5765

Miami is one of those special places to shoot. I have shot in New York and L. A. and Miami still holds my eye. More and more art directors are finding their way here for innovative work. I work for such agencies as Ammirati & Puris, McKinney Silver Rocket, Cole Henderson Drake, Weiden & Kennedy, The Richards Group, and The Martin Agency. If quality and creativity are what you strive for in your work I hope to work with you some day.

COLE HENDERSON DRAKE/DICK HENDERSON/RITZ CARLTON HOTELS

SMITH GREENLAND ADV/JONAS GOLD   C.H.D./DAN SCARLOTTA   RICHARDS GROUP/GRANT RICHARDS

Randy Miller

6666 Southwest 96th Street
Miami, Florida 33156
(305) 667-5765

Miami is one of those special places to shoot. I have shot in New York and L. A. and Miami still holds my eye. More and more art directors are finding their way here for innovative work. I work for such agencies as Ammirati & Puris, McKinney Silver Rocket, Cole Henderson Drake, Weiden & Kennedy, The Richards Group, and The Martin Agency. If quality and creativity are what you strive for in your work I hope to work with you some day.

WEIDEN & KENNEDY/RICK McQUISTON/SPEEDO BATHING SUITS

STATE OF FLORIDA/JOEL FULLER

McKINNEY SILVER ROCKET/GINA MOREHEAD

C.H.D./DAN SCARLOTTA

Lloyd Noland Photography

P.O. Box 9456
Santa Fe, New Mexico 87504-9456

Represented by:
Jean Bissell
(505) 982-2488

Large Format Photography Areas include: Black and White, Hand Tint, and Color.

Location or studio work for clients in: Fine Art, Portrait, Corporate/Industrial, Editorial, Annual Reports and Advertising.

Lloyd Noland began his career in the Fine Arts field of Black and White photography using specially mixed formulas to get the effect he wanted. From this he evolved into hand tinting which gave his portrait work the richness that neither black and white nor color could exhibit. This brought commercial attention and has resulted in a movement into the field of color photography. His work portrays the corporate identity and still life images that excite the visual senses.

Ron Sherman

P.O. Box 28656
Atlanta, Georgia 30328
(404) 993-7197

Representative:
Bill Grubbs/WOODEN REPS
(404) 892-6303

Location photography for annual reports, advertising,
corporate, industrial, editorial, travel and sports
assignments.

Stock Photography available.
(404) 993-7197

Also see ads in American Showcase Volume 5, Volume
6, Volume 7, and Volume 8, and ASMP BOOK 1981,
BOOK 2, BOOK 3, and BOOK 4.

Member ASMP, APA

© 1986 Ron Sherman

Design: Critt Graham & Associates

Thompson & Thompson
Photography

5180 Northeast 12th Avenue
Fort Lauderdale, Florida 33334
(305) 772-4411

Keith Thompson
Jody Thompson

Advertising and Corporate Photography

Location or Studio

Stock Available

Rose Thompson

1802 Northwest 29th Street
Oakland Park, Florida 33311
(305) 485-0148

I specialize in photographic
illustration in the studio or
location. People, places,
product and food.

Partial client list:
IBM Corp.
Gould, Inc.
STP
Bendix Corp.
TRW Corp.
Macy's
Southeast Bank
Ford Motor Corp.
Jordan Marsh
J. Byrons
Mayor's Jewelry
Carteret Savings
First Bankers

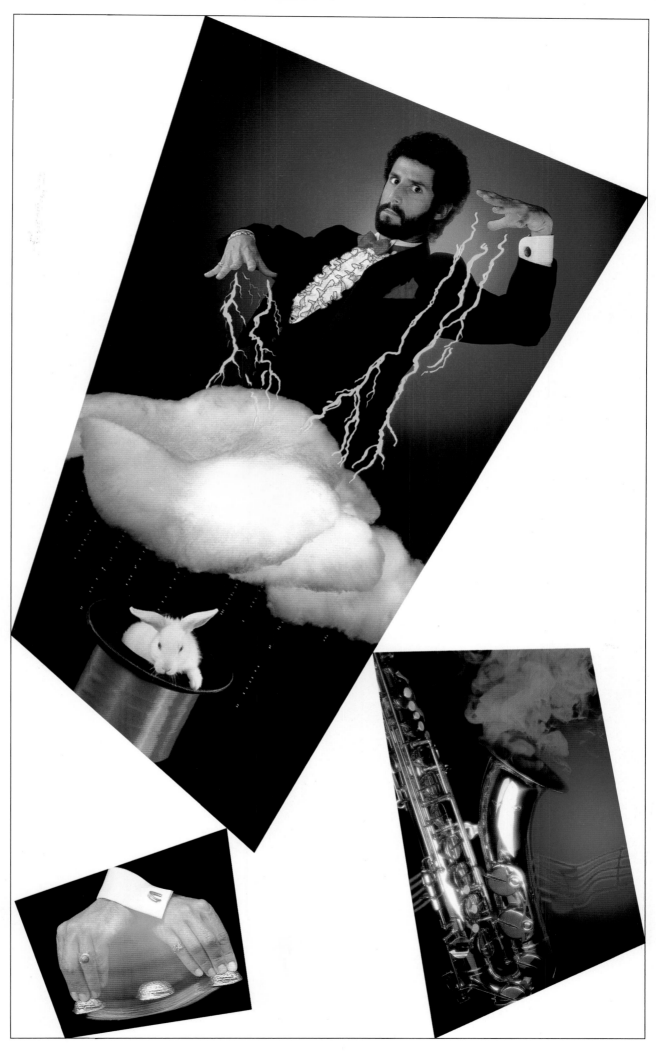

Charlie Westerman

Central American Building
Bowman Field
Louisville, Kentucky 40205
(502) 458-1532

Chicago Office:

59 East Cedar
Chicago, Illinois 60611
(312) 440-9422

A location photographer with offices in Louisville and Chicago, Westerman makes the set-up photograph believable and warm.

Charlie owns and pilots a Cessna 414, a pressurized twin-engine aircraft. This makes commuting between his offices and your location assignments both efficient and convenient.

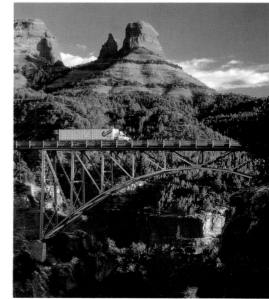

MIDWEST

Illinois
Indiana
Michigan
Minnesota
Missouri
Ohio
Wisconsin

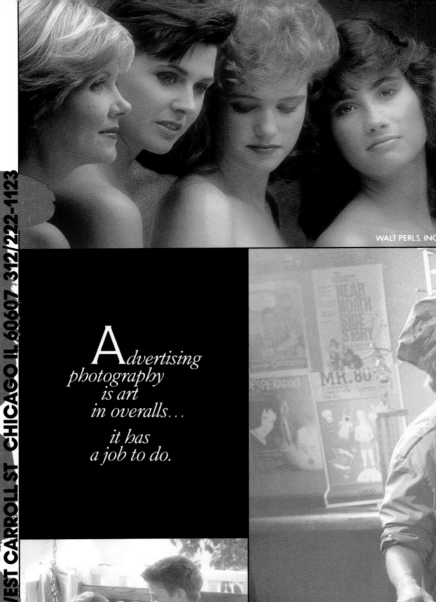

WALT PERLS, INC.

BEATRICE/HCM

Advertising photography is art in overalls...

it has a job to do.

BLUE CROSS/N.W. AYER   SEARS/NHW

BEATRICE/HCM

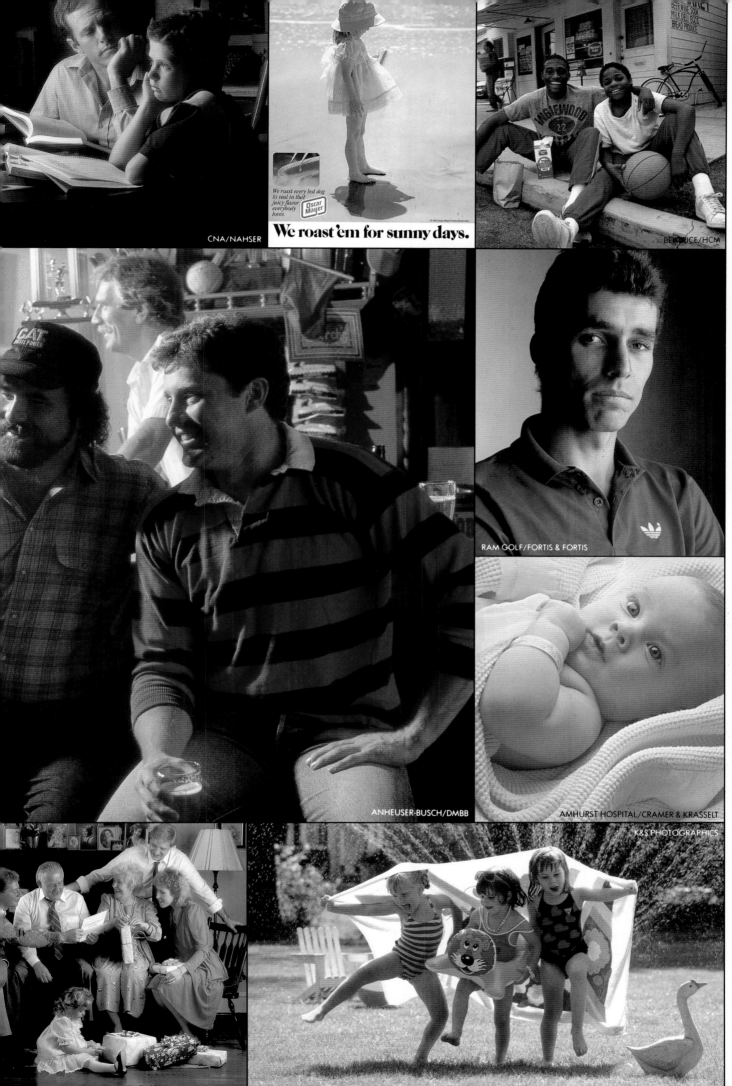

CNA/NAHSER

We roast every hot dog to seal in that juicy flavor everybody loves.

Oscar Mayer

We roast 'em for sunny days.

BEATRICE/HCM

RAM GOLF/FORTIS & FORTIS

ANHEUSER-BUSCH/DMBB

AMHURST HOSPITAL/CRAMER & KRASSELT

K&S PHOTOGRAPHICS

Richard Izui

Izui Photography

315 West Walton

Chicago, Illinois 60610

312 266.8029

CRAIG
VANDER LENDE

214 EAST FULTON
GRAND RAPIDS
MICHIGAN
49503

616 459 2880

TOM FRITZ
S T U D I O S
2320 N. 11th Street · Milwaukee, WI 53206 · (414) 263-6700

REPRESENTED BY DE WALT & ASSOCIATES · (414) 276-7990

285

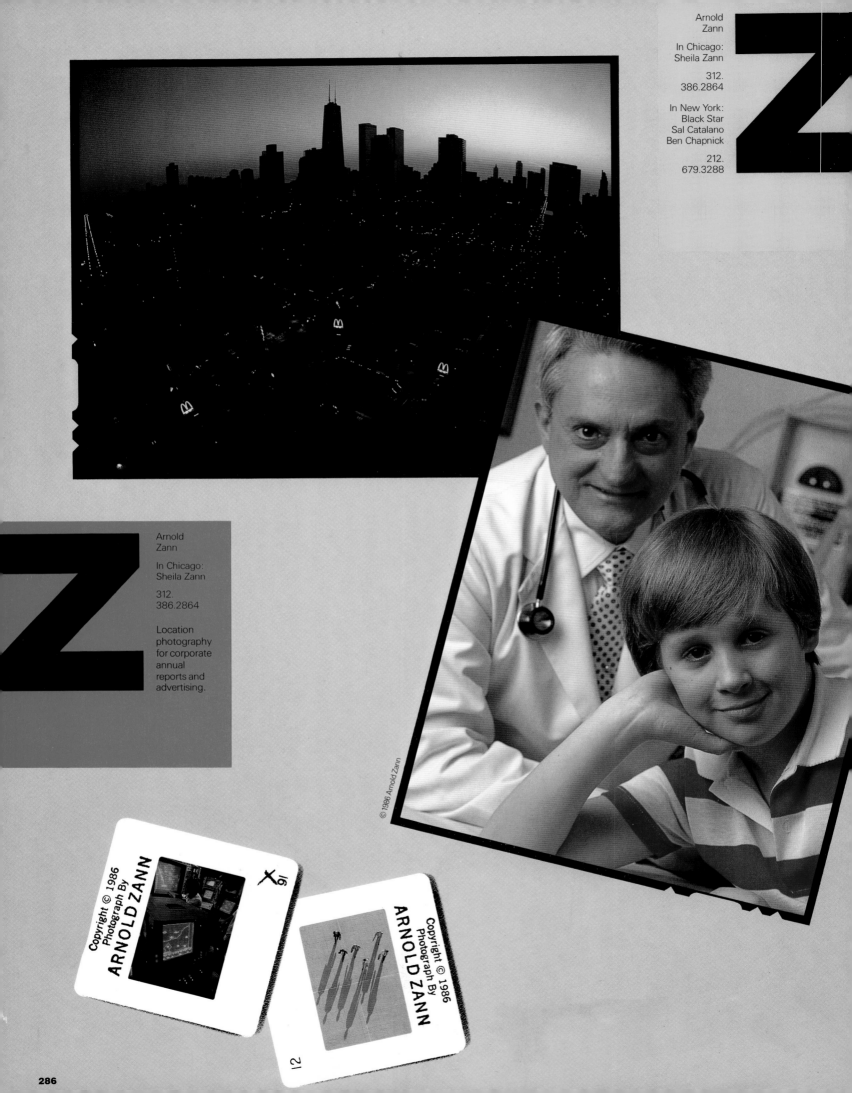

© 1986 Arnold Zann

Copyright © 1986
Photograph By
ARNOLD ZANN

X 9

Copyright © 1986
Photograph By
ARNOLD ZANN

12

WARKENTHIEN
PHOTOGRAPHY
117 S. MORGAN ST.　CHICAGO, IL 60607　312/666-6056

continued from page 266

Great Depression. The Fluster Brothers were not exactly businessmen of the first order—dedicated, as they were, to pleasures of the flesh, among them; drinking, carousing and galloping the female bare-back riders. I've committed a faux pas! (I'm nothing if not discreet.) So let me pass over their weaknesses of the flesh—some of which I've shared—and tell you that their ledgers looked like someone had run amok with a bottle of red ink.

"Make it no wonder; the Brothers Fluster had placed their attentions elsewhere, and with the economic situation being what it was, the bumpkinry surrounding the city of New Orleans didn't have the grease to spread across entertainments such as the circus. Therefore, the Fluster Brothers —in one of their more lucid moments—decided to merge with two other circuses who were hurting for cash in the same fashion as Byron and Bernard Fluster."

Roxbury bolted back the remainder of his drink. He took another furtive glance across the lobby, toward the filly with the perfect bouncers, and continued his tirade—wetting his lips with a last sip at his martini. "Needless to say, all of the circus personnel were purely delighted with the merger. The dwarfs appeared to be almost three feet tall. The lions cavorted and bristled their manes with pride. The clowns fell over each other in ecstacy. There was a general air of excitement about the whole thing. Until opening night.

"That was really a moment to remember, and make no mistake. I mean, you really had to be there to relish the imbecility of the moment. The local yokels had turned out in droves; seems they were throwing their last seedy dollar away on the ultimate entertainment, to wit, the spectacle of three circuses merging into one. Well, you can well imagine my attitude at the time. I was one of the star trapeze artists of the Fluster Brothers Circus, suddenly relegated to something like the second banana. (The Fluster Brothers had merged with the Clitwick Extravanganza, and the Grimley, Gamely Greatest Show.)

"It was at that moment, when I became keenly aware of the travesties committed in the name of merger. To wit, it was a pigstick, to be sure—and the following is gospel true. The evening unfolded,

and the bumpkins began shifting and stirring in their seats; they were witnessing a prime event, to be sure; a cast of thousands, spinning and spurting in every possible direction. Bareback riders, clashing into one another; clowns, falling over each other's false and floppy feet; lions growling—looking to find their proper trainers; tigers bawling and bleating for a recognizable figure with a whip. It was chaos all round, and no error. I make no bones about the fact that I took part in the whole catastrophic debacle; my innards were doing the polka. I felt my stomach heave, as I climbed to my perch, a hundred feet above the center circle. I observed the scene, from this rarified position and saw mayhem all round. Yes! I made a great show of pretending I knew what I was doing. But there were a dozen trapeze artists, whipping around the canvas heights of the big top. I was to catch one of the suckers by the wrists, while doing a triple (which I had learned only several weeks earlier).

"The band rendered their fanfare; the bumpkins clapped and snorted and stamped and cheered. My heart was pounding, and my hands were twitching like a landed fish. But make it no wonder; I was perched at the rafters of the canvas tent, with no less than twelve trapeze artists swinging, and swirling, and looking for somebody to catch.

"To say that my guts were quaking with fear would be the highest form of understatement. (It's not that I was suffering a suspicion of my own lack of talents as a high wire artist. Strictly speaking, I was simply confused with the mayhem and madness that was taking place above and below the confines of the big top. And then I felt ten thousand eyes turn in my direction, as if demanding me to display my tour de force (my triple somersault, while soaring in mid-air and finally catching… whoever happened to be around at the time).

"And then my heart took wing, and this is gospel true: I saw, across the arena, a familiar figure; a man who stopped my knees from knocking; a personage who stopped my stomach from churning. The man was Byron Fluster. Almost 200 pounds of puffy flesh, packed into the white and blue tights of a trapeze artist. He regarded me—across the expanse of the arena—with the look of a stricken seraph. He chomped on his cigar. Bellowed a loud

continued on page 294

Tom Berthiaume Studio

1008 Nicollet Mall
Minneapolis, Minnesota
(612) 338-1999

Represented in Chicago by
Vince Kamin & Associates
(312) 787-8834.

Tom leads and collaborates with
a small group of unusually
talented photographers. The
results have been winning
awards for over 10 years.

Clients include:

Apple Computers
Medtronics
Control Data
3M
AMF
Dayton-Hudson
Levi-Strauss
Nutra Sweet
Country Kitchen
Winnebago
Wall Street Journal
Marshall Field
Chicken-of-the-Sea
Nickelodeon
Carson, Pirie, Scott & Company
Jostens

CLICK/ Chicago Ltd.

213 West Institute Place
Suite 503
Chicago, Illinois 60610
(312) 787-7880

We are the most creative
and knowledgeable stock/
assignment agency in the
Midwest.

Our 40 assignment
photographers are spread
throughout the U.S.A. and Europe,
with the majority located in the
Midwest. All of our photographers
work both in color and b/w. We
have experts in the following
fields: Advertising, Aerial,
Annual Reports, Architecture,
Audiovisual, Illustration,
Location, Heavy and Light
Industry, Medical, Panoramic,
Photojournalism, Portraiture,
Products, Public Relations and
Still Life. We can show you
portfolios of photographers
whose work is relevant to
your needs.

We also have an extensive library
of current, top-quality stock
photographs and will be happy
to supply stock images where
available budget, season of the
year, or far-flung locations make
an assignment impractical.
Please see our other ad in the
Stock Section.

Ralph Cowan

452 North Halsted Street
Chicago, Illinois 60622
(312) 243-6696

Clients include: Abbott Laboratories, Advertising Age,
American Hospital Publishing, Armour Pharmaceutical,
Arthur Andersen, Blaupunkt, Boston Consulting
Group, Bristol-Myers, Citicorp, Continental Fibre Drum,
Eastman Kodak, Jim Beam, Kelloggs, Kemper
Financial Group, Montgomery Ward, Oster, Scott
Foresman Books, Standard Oil, Sunkist, Swift
Independent, Tampa Maid Seafoods, Weber Grills.

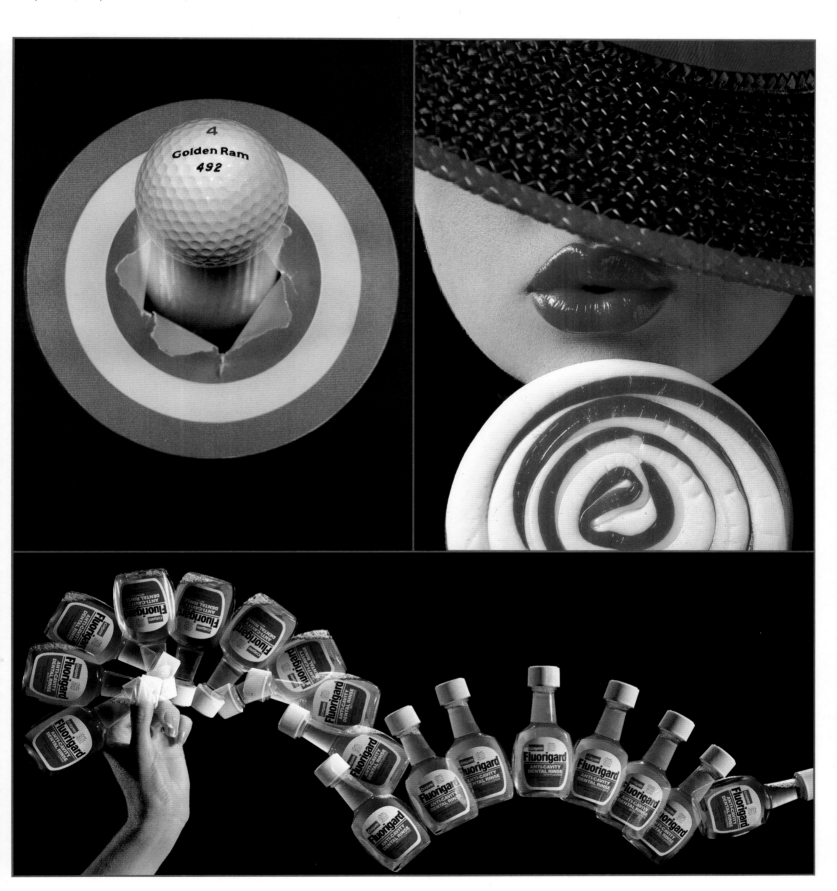

Lucky Curtis
1540 N. North Park Avenue
Chicago, Illinois 60610
(312) 787-4422

Represented by: Gigante Moore
(312) 558-1905

LUCKY CURTIS PHOTOGRAPHY INC./PHOTOMATICS/1540 N. NORTH PARK AVE./CHICAGO, IL 60610
REPRESENTED BY GIGANTE MOORE/312-787-4422

Paul Elledge
1808 West Grand Avenue
Chicago, Illinois 60622
(312) 733-8021

WILLIAM PERRY/EBONY MAGAZINE

DARYL HALL/RCA

TLK: AD/JAMES TROWELL

MARSHALL FIELDS

continued from page 288

and resounding cough, and made ready to swing toward me, while throwing caution to the wind.

"'Sweet Jeez!', I heard myself saying at the time, while I was fearing for my life. This sod hadn't been on a trapeze for twenty years—if I could trust the red of his eyes, and his billowing stomach. I execute the triple. The crowd goes wild. Yonder porko swings in my direction and misses me by a country mile. But the crowd was cheering (which was music to my ears), and through the fuzz and the haze and smoke, I went sailing, turning and twisting in mid-air. And suddenly, to my pleasure and longevity, I felt the grip of the fat and flabby stricken seraph, as he grunted and groaned, and prevented me from plunging to my death (for I worked without a net); another reason I'm so fit for the advertising business.

"Well, old Byron Fluster bellowed and belched. He bleated and squawked: 'Say there, young man, you're not half bad, at that! I commend you for not being confused. Damn distressing thing, this merger business. Wouldn't have done it, except that brother Bernard is a slave to the ledgers. Take a pull from this flask, and attend to me. Mergers are a damned confusing thing, don't you think. I've a mind to head back to the simple way of life. If the Fluster Brothers Circus is going to hit the skids, then let me do it alone. It's much less confusing, that way. On the other hand, maybe there's safety in numbers.'"

I recall myself shifting on the banquette. I recall myself summoning the waiter in order to order another round of drinks. I recollect Roxbury smil-ing, and fluttering his fingers across the knot of his gray tie. I recall the smile on his face, as he concluded his tirade (which was now settling into a mere benevolent observation).

He concluded: "I'm going to stay away from a merger; I gave up the swing and sway of the circus a long time ago. I like to know who the players are. And when I'm poised a hundred feet in the air, with a twenty million ad budget in my hands, I'd like to be reassured that there's some likely lad or gal ready to catch old Leonard by the wrists. It's nice to recognize a familiar face whilst dangling a hundred feet in mid air. It's rather preferable to see an old scout—the kind who has labored over numerous campaigns, deep into the night—turn a smiling face toward you, and say: 'Hey! We were in this thing from the beginning. I know you…and you know me. Now all we have to do is create the ads. And isn't that the bloody hell what we get paid for. The ledgers will take care of themselves, as long as we can command the attentions of the citizens of the world. And sell some of the client's product into the bargain.' Yes! The sound of those words sets my innards to relaxing. Yes! the sound of those words brings a slight smile to my lips. Yes! I'll sit this one out; this phenomenon known as merger mania, and attempt to stay lean and mean. My flabby friend, Byron Fluster, would have liked it that way."

And with that final remark, Leonard Roxbury rose from the banquette, and disappeared into the crowd which had gathered at the center of the Waldorf lobby. Leaving me to pay the check. A light price to pay for such a heavy lesson.

Vincent Daddiego
Senior Vice President
Associate Creative Director
Young & Rubicam
New York City

Jeff Grunewald
Photography

161 West Harrison Street
Chicago, Illinois 60605
(312) 663-5799

Special Effects, location and product photography for: TRW, U.S. Gypsum, Beatrice, Paterno Imports, Sears World Trade, Technical Publishing, Kerr-Sybron, Belden Wire, Revcor Fans, Alltest Diagnostic Equipment, Phillips Plastics, Graphic Technologies, ARA, Sears, Champion Parts Rebuilders, Diner's Club, American Hospital Supply, Abbott, Bruning, South Bend Sporting Goods, Ward's Auto Club, Degussa, Grayhill, Kemper Financial Services, Encyclopaedia Brittanica.

U.S. GYPSUM/A.D. ED WENTZ

CHICAGO HIGH TECH ASSN.

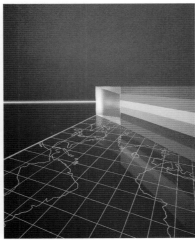

TRW/A.D. CLARKE KRUGER

SEARS WORLD TRADE/A.D. TOON LAIETMARK

Kazu Studio, Ltd.

1211 West Webster
Chicago, Illinois 60614
(312) 348-5393

Representative
Janice Tepke
(312) 348-5393

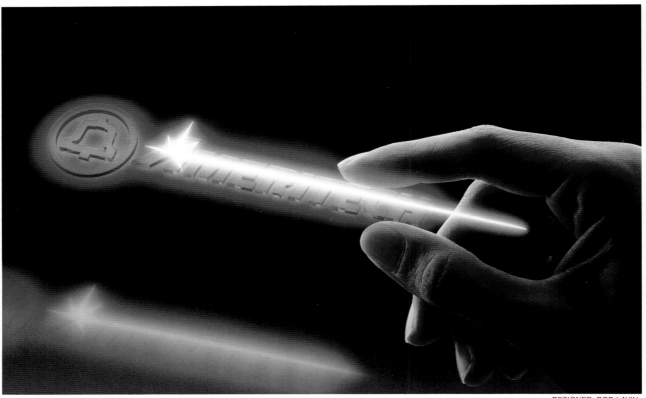

DESIGNER: BOB LAVIN

A.D. MICHAEL ROBERTS

Kondas
Associates, Inc.

1529 North Alabama Street
Indianapolis, Indiana
46202-2534
Post Office Box 1162,
46206-1162
(317) 637-1414

We see it this way.

Some people insist on 10,000
square feet of shooting space.
So, we have it.

Some want a fully-equipped
commercial kitchen. Okay, cook
your brains out. We've got that,
too.

Some insist on a full-time staff
of set designers, fabricators,
location scouts and model
coordinators, along with the
make-up artists and hair stylists.
Alright, alright. You've got it.

And some have the nerve to
want finished lab work the same
day of the shoot. So, what the
heck? We have complete
in-house lab facilities.

And on top of that, companies
like Sony, AT&T, Time-Life Corp.,
DOW, Eli Lilly, Mead-Johnson,
Bordens, McDonald's, FMC
Corp. and Frigidaire expect
us to consistently create and
capture the essence of their
fine products in compelling
photographic images.

Because we see it this way.

John Lehn & Associates

Advertising Photography, Inc.
2601 East Franklin
Minneapolis, Minnesota 55406
(612) 338-0257

You may notice something peculiar about this page.

No bathing beauties.

No muscle-bound motorcycles glistening in the moonlight or half-full mugs of foaming Bud.

No famous celebs or corporate moguls.

In fact, to the untrained eye, this page may be of very little interest at all.

Now that's not to say John Lehn and his partners don't shoot those things. But what they're very good at, indeed, best at, are the intricate, well thought-out shots that mere mortals simply take for granted. The kind of shot the almighty consumer simply looks at and says, "Oh, that's nice," while the all-knowing Art Director says, "Wow, how did they get that?"

If you have such a shot in mind, think of John Lehn. He knows how to get you there.

He also wouldn't mind a bathing beauty assignment now and then, either.

Eric Oxendorf

1442 North Franklin Place
P.O. Box 92337
Milwaukee, Wisconsin 53202
(414) 273-0654

East Coast Rep:
Jim Cuneo
(813) 848-8931

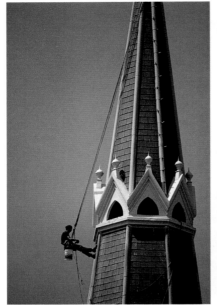

ARCHITECTURE AND RELATED INDUSTRIES

10,000 STOCK IMAGES AVAILABLE

R.D. Renken Photography

P.O. Box 11010
St. Louis, Missouri 63135
(314) 394-5055

Corporate Communications
Annual Reports
Product Advertising
Architecture

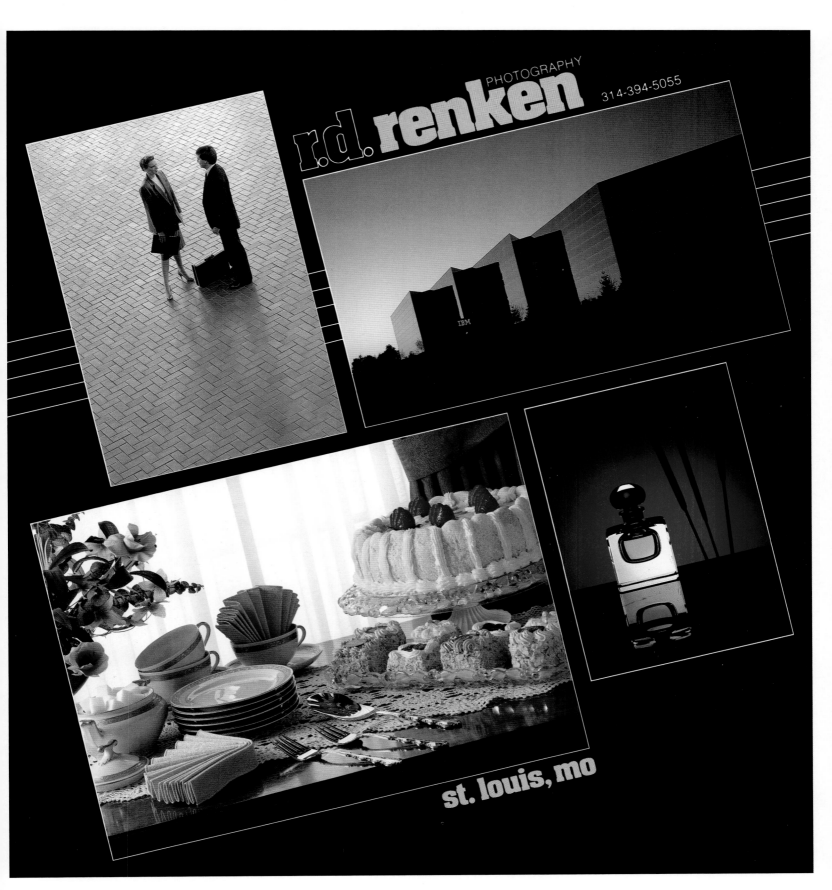

Charles Schridde
Photography, Inc.

600 Ajax Drive
Madison Heights (Detroit), Michigan 48071
(313) 589-0111

One Charlie Schridde is worth a thousand words. Unfortunately, we haven't got room for a thousand words. So we can only give highlights of the Charlie Schridde Legend. His childhood abduction by a crazed film salesman. His lifelong fear of sanity. His successful fight to have his name changed (to Schridde). And above all, his great eye (it's four inches across).

But his pictures say it all. See? They speak of light and mood and tight deadlines. They speak of everything from movie stars to sexy cars. And they whisper TRUTH. Listen. Closely. There!

JOHN LOUIS/AD

BRUCE ENGELSON/AD

TOM RICKEY/AD

JERRY EDMISON/AD

JERRY EDMISON/AD

FRANK BELT/AD

TOM RICKEY/AD

Greg Sereta

2108 Payne Avenue, Room 400
Cleveland, Ohio 44114
(216) 861-7227

Portfolio Available
Upon Request.

GREG SERETA

Alvis Upitis

620 Morgan Avenue South
Minneapolis, Minnesota 55405-2034
(612) 374-9375

SHOOTING THE PEOPLE AND PLACES OF
INDUSTRY FOR CORPORATE AND ADVERTISING
CLIENTS. ANYWHERE.

Clients Include: Avon, Ciba-Geigy, First Interstate
Corp, Fortune, General Foods, Hardee's, Honeywell,
IBM, Kodak, 3M, Money, Monsanto, Newsweek,
Pillsbury, Polaroid, St. Paul Companies, Time, US Air,
BBDO, Leo Burnett, Campbell-Mithun, Grey, Muller,
Jordan Weiss, Ogilvy & Mather, others. © 1987.

304

J. David Wilder

2300 Payne Avenue
Cleveland, Ohio 44114
(216) 771-7687

Represented in New York by:

Wendy Morgan

Network Studios
(516) 757-5609

See our pages in American
Showcase #8 and #9.

TRW

AMERITRUST

AMERITRUST

EDISON PROGRAM

EATON CORPORATION

Wolff Studios, Inc.

326 West Kalamazoo Avenue
Kalamazoo, Michigan 49007
(616) 342-0666

11357 South 2nd Street
Schoolcraft, Michigan 49087
(616) 679-4702

Advertising, Corporate/Industrial and Editorial
Photography, Studio or Location. Specializing in
food, Special Effects, Fashion and Product Still-Life.

Two shooting studios, complete lab services,
full kitchen facilities and large set design and
construction capability.

SOUTHWEST

Arizona
Texas

KENT KNUDSON IN FINE PRINT.

6 02·277·7701—ASSIGNMENT AND STOCK

Jim Caldwell

2422 Quenby
Houston, Texas 77005
(713) 527-9121

Industrial, advertising, corporate and editorial
photography. Stock available.

Major clients include: AT&T, Coca-Cola Foods,
Coldwell Banker, Exxon U.S.A., Exxon Americas,
Houghton-Mifflin Publishers, Kentucky Fried Chicken,
Kingdom of Saudi Arabia, *Newsweek,* Owens-Corning
Fiberglas, Prudential Insurance, *Shell Oil News,* Texas
Children's Hospital, Texas Heart Institute, *Texas
Monthly,* Warner Amex Communications.

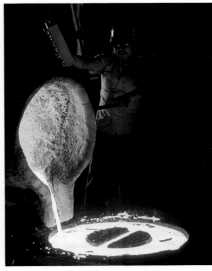

A CREATIVE DIRECTOR BY ANY OTHER NAME

The world of video and film production is the latest to be infiltrated by the agency creative director. To be sure, the transition from directing in a world of still, to a world that moves upon the command, "Ready on the set...annnnnd—action," is no minor undertaking.

But, the advertising world has seen the likes of Sam Scali, Bob Gage, and George Lois prove that art directors can make the transition to creative director. Not any easy accomplishment in a world that believed only writers qualified for that top creative post. (After all, art directors draw, writers write.) David Ogilvy proved that a cook could be a successful advertising professional.

Then along came the likes of Saul Bass and others providing that creative directors could make the transition to film and video.

Today, we have agencies that are no longer the creative boutiques they started out to be. Instead, they have become "full service agencies." Even that has changed to "marketing communications." They no longer merely create advertising, they are involved in all communications and planning functions that relate to marketing.

Of course, many of these agencies are now mega-merger goliaths with world-wide operations. It gets difficult to track. I recently overheard two ad executives discussing the sheer insanity of it all.

I realized they were wrong. It's not really so insane when one considers the world order which shows us that the only reliable constant is change. Think about it.

I know a man named Richard, and I call him Rich while others call him Dick. I also know a man named John and everybody calls him Jack. My friend Merton is called Gary. William is known by Willie, Billy, Bill, Will and sometimes "hey." Henry is

Hank. And of course my friend Samuel is called Bookie. (Don't ask.)

In addition, I've also known a few cabinet-makers who were really shoemakers. And even a shoemaker, who was a butcher.

Which brings me to the point of this article, essay, document or is it a composition? At any rate, the point or the purpose...

Many creative directors, art directors and writers have developed into very effective producers and directors in video, film and television. This exciting medium was introduced to me nearly ten years ago. It excited me then, and does so now. So I understand why creative types are drawn to it.

Regardless of where you stand, videos and film are hot. *Miami Vice,* cola wars and MTV have found their way into television spots, films and industrial videos. He was a courageous director who first mixed old movie footage with computer-generated visuals and music from MTV.

It is very exciting to see what is being produced to capture viewer attention due to heavy commercial-zapping.

However, all this visual appeal may not be selling products. Too often the main concentration is an image rather than an idea. It is very easy to wind up with puffery instead of substance. As Frank Gorman, a Chiat/Day graduate now behind the camera says, "There are a lot of non-concepts floating around that look great; the eyes like them but there's something missing for the mind."

It is in these areas that the transition may not be working as well as it could. The director, regardless of where he or she came from (art director, writer) must make a major effort to be a full-fledged director. Not an art director directing a film crew. Not a writer directing a film crew, but a direc-

continued on page 326

Cobb and Friend

2811 McKinney #224
Dallas, Texas 75204
(214) 855-0055

Representing:

Geof Kern

1337 Crampton
Dallas, Texas 75207
(214) 630-0856

Partial Client List

Fortune Magazine
Movie-goer Magazine

13-30 Corporation
American Airlines
M Bank
The Limited
Neiman-Marcus
Texas Monthly
Beverly Sassoon Cosmetics
Cigna
Haggar
Pearl Vision
Trammel Crow Development Corp.
Albritton Corporation
Texas Instruments

COBB AND FRIEND
ARTIST REPRESENTATIVES
2811 McKINNEY SUITE 224
DALLAS, TEXAS 75204
214-855-0055
ASK FOR
LISA COBB, SIMONE FRIEND,
OR BETH JOHNSON

311

Cobb and Friend

2811 McKinney #224
Dallas, Texas 75204
(214) 855-0055

Representing:

Tom Ryan

1821 Levee
Dallas, Texas 75207
(214) 651-7085

Partial client list:

Frito-Lay
Pepsi
Ben Hogan
Pier One
Neiman Marcus
Sanger-Harris
Anderson Clayton
Merico
Steak and Ale Corporation
Bennigans
El Chico
Southwest Airlines
Greyhound
Akai Stereo
Pizza Inn
Curtis Mathis
Del Taco
Pancho's Mexican Restaurants
KMW Computers
VMS Hotel Corporation

COBB AND FRIEND
ARTIST REPRESENTATIVES
2811 McKINNEY SUITE 224
DALLAS, TEXAS 75204
214-855-0055
ASK FOR
LISA COBB, SIMONE FRIEND,
OR BETH JOHNSON

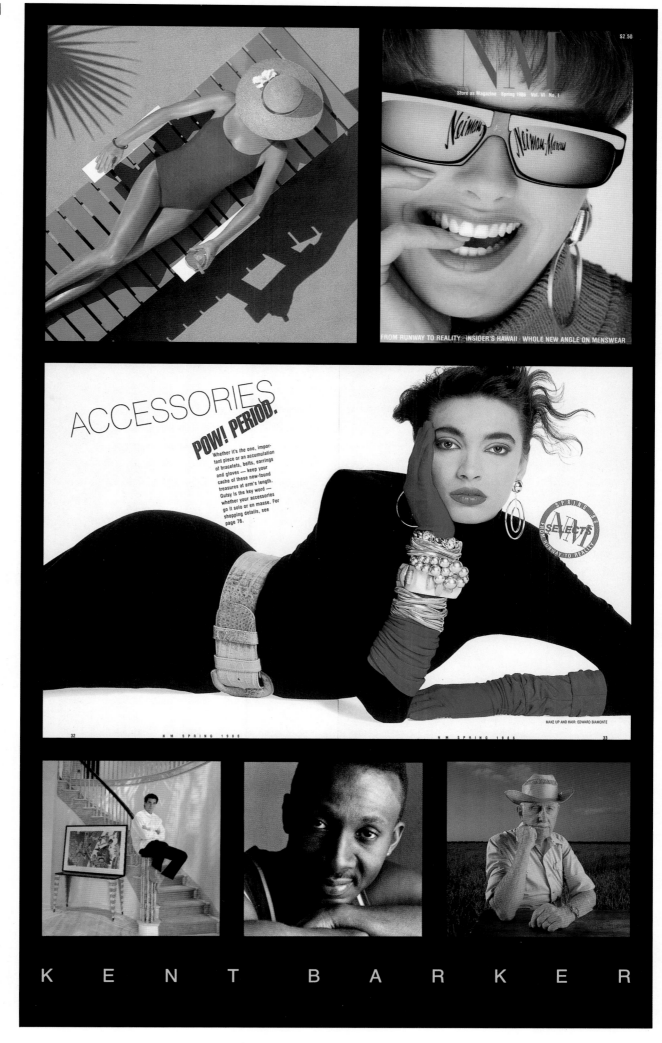

Cobb and Friend

2811 McKinney # 224
Dallas, Texas 75204
(214) 855-0055

Representing:

Dennis Murphy

101 Howell
Dallas, Texas 75207
(214) 651-7516

Partial client list:

Cigna Health
Jacuzzi
Poulan Chain Saws
American Airlines
Four Seasons Hotel Corporation
La Mansion Hotels
Haggar Corp.
Republic Bank
G.T.E.

Also see CA Art Annual 1981,
Photo Annual '84, '85, '86.

Cobb and Friend

2811 McKinney #224
Dallas, Texas 75204
(214) 855-0055

Representing:

Michael Johnson

830 Exposition #215
Dallas, Texas 75226
(214) 828-9550

Partial Client List

Neiman-Marcus
Almay Cosmetics
Allercreme Cosmetics
Diamond's Dept. Store
Wedding Magazine
Mary Kay Cosmetics
Marks and Spencer Dept.
  Store/England
Stanley Korshak
Dallas/Ft. Worth Ballet
Texas Monthly
Harrod's Department
  Store/London
House of Fraser Lingerie

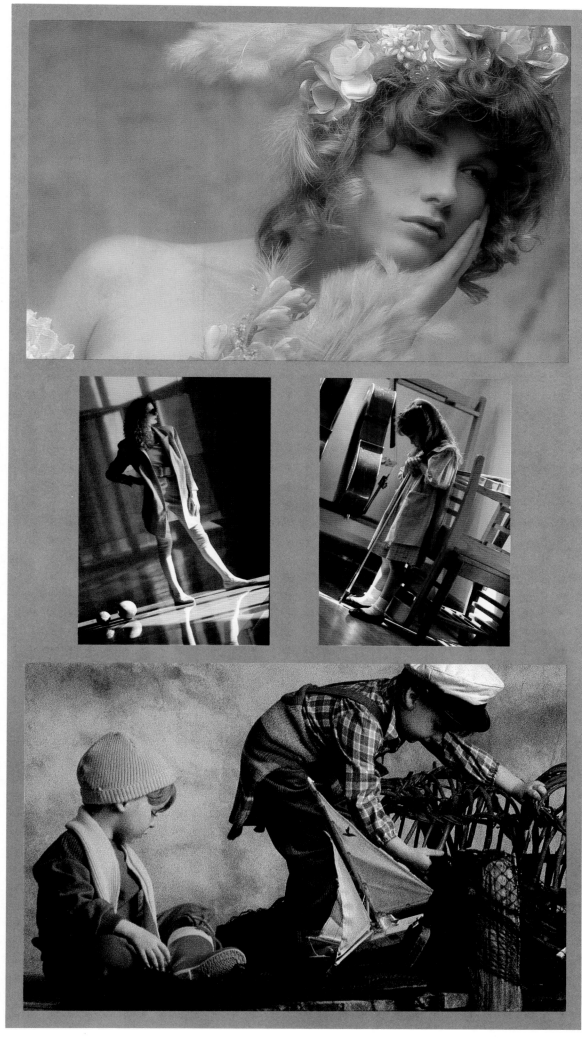

Arturo & Vallarie Enriquez

Vantage Point Visual Studios
1109 Arizona Avenue
El Paso, Texas 79902
(915) 533-9688

Distinctive location photography for fashion, advertising, editorial, and corporate assignments. We are photographers who passionately enjoy the challenge of getting those great angles and locations, and creating the right mood to complement your project...be it thru full color, black & white, or selective hand coloring.

Additional portfolio samples gladly sent upon request.

Stock photos available.

All photos © 1986 Arturo & Vallarie Enriquez

Tom Gerczynski

Gerczynski Photographs
2211 North 7th Avenue
Phoenix, Arizona 85007
(602) 252-9229

Citicorp, DuPont, Dow Chemical, Polaroid, USA Today, Honeywell, American Airlines, Chevron Oil, Aramis, Canadian Tire, Nissan, Ford Motor Company, IBM, AT&T, Mitsubishi Jets, Arizona Highways, Eldorado Motor Corporation, Carling O'Keefe Breweries, Rand McNally, Teledyne, Northwest Magazine, Mountain Bell, Thousand Trails Inc., Gates Learjet, Airborne Express, Circle K, American Hydrozone, Doubletree Inns, Cyma-McGraw Hill, Sheraton Hotels, Foxoboro Companies, Intel Corporation, Navistar, Phoenix Motion Picture Bureau, Ross Labs.

Represented by:
Joe Callahan
(602) 248-0777

Studio:
(602) 252-9229
Member ASMP, PPA

Additional work can be seen in American Showcase Volumes 6, 7, & 9, and Corporate Showcase Volume 4.

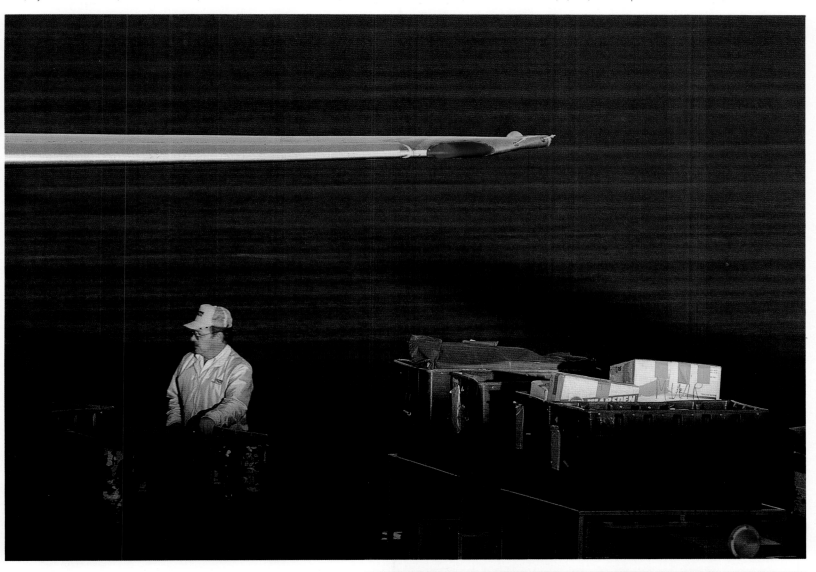

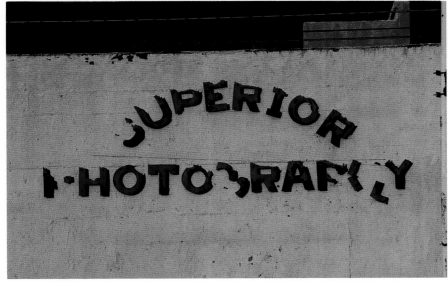

Boyce Graham

2707 Stemmons Freeway
Suite 160
Dallas, Texas 75207
(214) 631-4019

Boyce Graham photographs interiors,.architecture, and contract & residential furnishings for advertising and corporate marketing communications.

He is widely recognized in Texas and the Southwest as one of the top specialists in his field.

His work appears in national, regional and local publications.

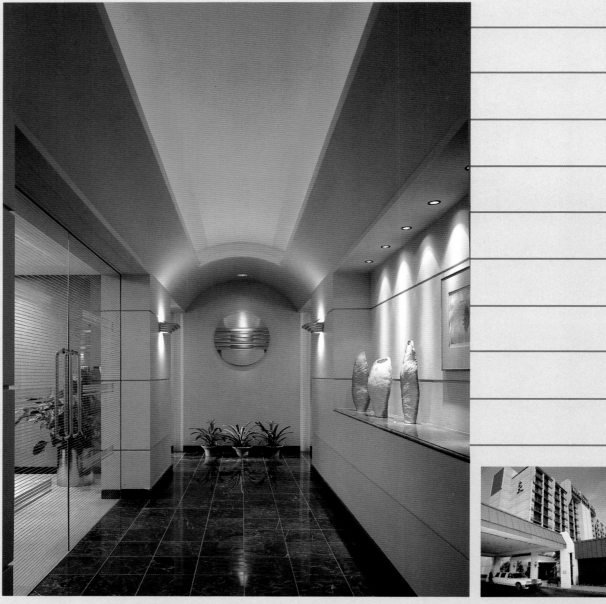

Boyce Graham
P H O T O G R A P H Y

Jeffrey Muir Hamilton

6719 Quartzite Canyon Place
Tucson, Arizona 85718
(602) 299-3624

Corporate, Editorial, Industrial

Zigy Kaluzny

4700 Strass Drive
Austin, Texas 78731
(512) 452-4463

© 1986 Zigy Kaluzny

Clients include:

Allied/Signal, Anthony Russell Inc., Business Week,
Deutsch Design, Exxon, Forbes, GEO, High
Technology, Life, Newsweek, New York Times, New
York Times Magazine, Smithsonian, Southwestern
Bell, Spiegel, Stern, Time, Westinghouse.

BOBBY RAY INMAN/MCC

DALLAS/SPIEGEL

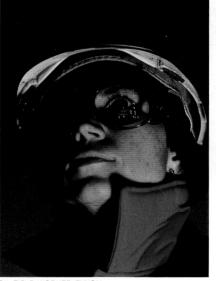

OIL FIELD WORKER/EXXON

TEXAS-MEXICO BORDER/NEWSWEEK

320

Lawrence J. Kuslich

5950 Westward Avenue
Houston, Texas 77081
(713) 988-0775
(713) 932-4525

FOOD • PRODUCT • PEOPLE

Studio or Location

Partial Client List:

3M
ITT
Amhoist
Honeywell
Texacraft
Sysco Foods
Delta Dental
General Mills
Boise Cascade
Riviana Foods
Coca Cola USA
Shell Chemical
Sheraton Hotels
Litton Microwave
Andersen Windows
Conwed Corporation
Hoffman Engineering
International Multifoods

For Additional Work, See
Vol. 5 of Corporate Showcase
and the S.W. Regional Review.

Food Stylist: Denise Leonhardt
(713) 729-1782

Member ASMP

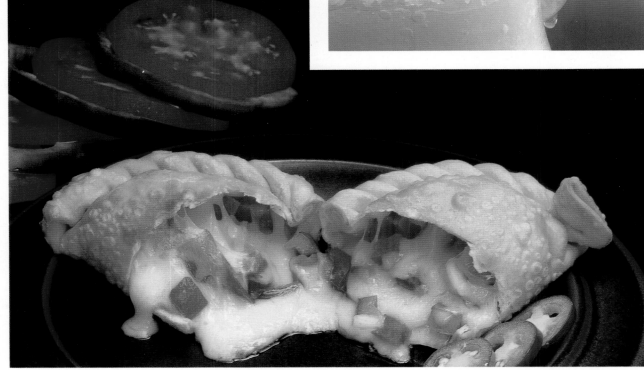

Paul E. Loven

2301 North 16th Street
Phoenix, Arizona 85006
(602) 253-0335

Represented by
Mary Holland
(602) 275-3563

Large stock file available through Visual Images West
(602) 820-5403
See Page 431 for more of my work.

Available for assignment location photography. Full
studio facilities with all formats available. Based in
Phoenix since 1979, previously worked out of N.Y.C.

Member A.S.M.P.

Dennis Meyler
7315 Ashcroft, Suite 110
Houston, Texas 77081
(713) 778-1700

Advertising/Editorial Illustration/Annual Reports/
Corporate

For additonal work see American Showcase, Volumes
7, 8 & 9.

Joseph Savant

4756 Algiers Street
Dallas, Texas 75207
(214) 951-0111

Specializing in still life, large product, special effect, problem solving, and conceptual images for advertising, corporate, and editorial needs.

All special effects done in-camera. Images have no stripping, retouching, or computer manipulation.

Portfolio available upon request.

Partial client list includes:

Aerospatiale
American Airlines
Arcoaire
Arthur Anderson Co.
Bell Helicopter
Crosby Group
Dr. Pepper
Emcom International
Foremost Insurance
Frito-Lay
G.E.
Halliburton
Hyatt Hotels
I.B.M.
Kaiser
Lomas & Nettleton
M-Corp
Mary Kay Cosmetics
Murata Business Systems
Neiman-Marcus
Northern Telecom
Olivetti
Otis Industries
PPG
St. Regis
Visa
Western Automotive, etc.

See our ad in Corporate Showcase 3 & 4 and American Showcase Volume 8 & 9.

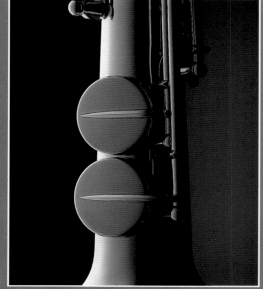

Joseph Savant

4756 Algiers Street
Dallas, Texas 75207
(214) 951-0111

Specializing in still life, large product, special effect, problem solving, and conceptual images for advertising, corporate, and editorial needs.

All special effects done in-camera. Images have no stripping, retouching, or computer manipulation.

Portfolio available upon request.

Partial client list includes:

Aerospatiale
American Airlines
Arcoaire
Arthur Anderson Co.
Bell Helicopter
Crosby Group
Dr. Pepper
Emcom International
Foremost Insurance
Frito-Lay
G.E.
Halliburton
Hyatt Hotels
I.B.M.
Kaiser
Lomas & Nettleton
M-Corp
Mary Kay Cosmetics
Murata Business Systems
Neiman-Marcus
Northern Telecom
Olivetti
Otis Industries
PPG
St. Regis
Visa
Western Automotive, etc.

See our ad in Corporate Showcase 3 & 4 and American Showcase Volume 8 & 9.

© JOSEPH SAVANT, 1986

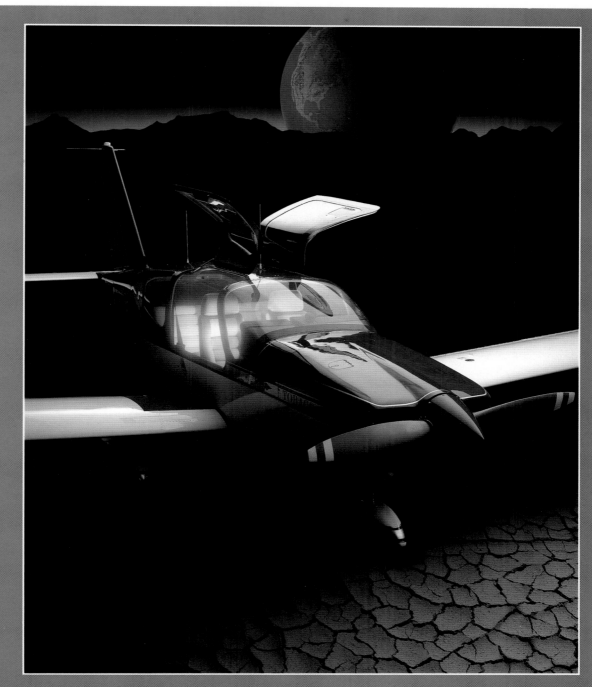

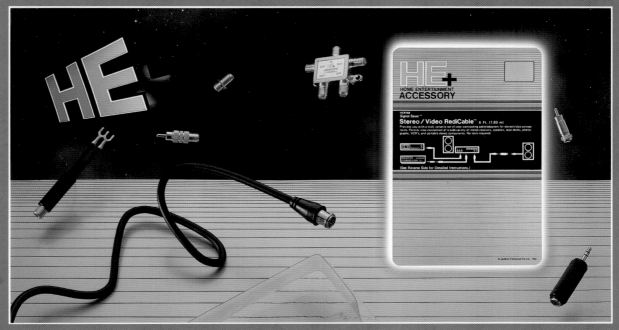

continued from page 310

tor directing a film crew. In this medium it just won't do to have Henry be a Hank. Either he's Henry or he's not. The director must direct. (A rose by any other name <u>MUST</u> still be a rose.)

He is responsible for non-exciting, non-glamorous items, also — such as budget. He may have to figure on a smaller crew shooting more days as opposed to a larger crew less days. It may keep production in budget.

Yes, transitions from one visual medium to another are great. I'm all for it. But the transition is not a game. It is serious business. One cannot succeed in looking at video, film and TV as just visual or just words and sounds.

All who have made the transition here should remember they are salespeople first. The work they create must sell a product, service, idea, position, whatever. It must sell something.

Yes, experiment with new ideas, sounds, images. Yes, don't let anyone tell you only writers can be directors. Don't let them convince you only art directors can be directors. Do it. But do it with passion. Look at the whole, not just a part. Actually, the titles are not so important, it's the end result.

I leave you with a request and an immortal thought. The request: Please create wonderful new films, videos, commercials but please, please, please, spare us any more break-dancing. The immortal thought: "You can call me Ray, you can call me Jay, you can call me Hey,......but you don't have to call me Johnson."

Alfred S. Pirozzoli
President/Creative Director
InComm, Inc.
Waterbury, CT

Michael Schneps
21 Pinedale #6
Houston, Texas 77006
(713) 520-8224

Michael Schneps creates graphic solutions for visual problems. He has worked both nationally and internationally for design, advertising, editorial and corporate clients. For additional work see *Showcase* Volumes 8 & 9, *A.R.*, *CA Photography Annual 1985*, and *The 65th Art Directors Annual*.

マイク・シネプスは日本に18年間滞在しました。彼は日本語を流暢に話し、仕事の関係もあり日本全国を旅行しました。日本そして日本人を良く理解した説得力のある彼のフォトグラフック・イメージは日本人の顧客の皆様に充分に御満足いただけるでしょう。

Scott/efx

1000 Jackson Boulevard
Houston, Texas 77006
(713) 529-5868

"People are amazed by the colors in my images, commenting on their saturation and purity. Although I have more than 16 million from which to choose, it isn't that I have found some magic combination that makes them look so good. I'd like to take all the credit but some of it must go to the science behind the images."

"Photography with a camera suffers the limitation that whatever colors are seen by the lens must be translated into colors that can be represented by the three colored dyes in the film itself. It is sort of like trying to copy an oil painting using water colors. You have to change mediums, for example, from the blue cloth of a designer dress to a color made up from a mixture of pinkish-red and greenish-blue dyes in the film. It is a compromise, albeit one that works quite well most often."

"My pictures never exist in any other medium until translated to film. The colors I use exist only as numbers. These numbers go directly to the film, exposing only the colored layer to which they correspond. Therefore if I select a pure color for my image it remains pure when it is placed on the film."

"Working with color this way is fun because not only are there so many to choose but once I find one that I like I just write down three numbers. When I want to use it again I just type in the numbers. And it is just as easy to try out new colors. I can make a picture with one set of colors and within just a few minutes see it with a completely new set of colors."

Contact Ron Scott if you would like to do something colorful.

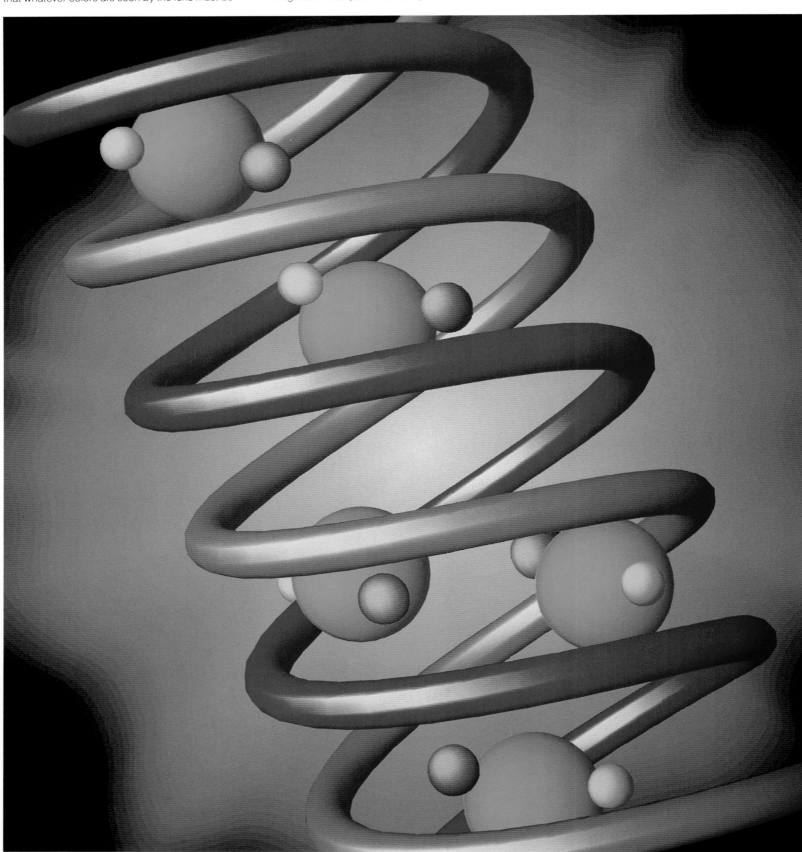

Scott/efx

1000 Jackson Boulevard
Houston, Texas 77006
(713) 529-5868

"It is common today for companies to use computers in designing and manufacturing products. I am using computers to illustrate and help market them. I build a model in the computer's memory of the product that mimics the original, often in great detail, and then the computer paints in the colors I select based on the lighting I choose. Since the model I build is three dimensional, just like the real item, I can view it from almost any angle."

"Once I have selected a position and viewing angle, the computer figures out how it should appear. This is the ultimate form of technical illustration, accurate to almost any level of detail, with unlimited views available. The 'look' is good too. The illustrative quality attracts attention and looks believable. Bright or subtle colors can be used for the best effect."

"When working with prototypes the computer can depict products as they should look in final production and not how they are at preliminary stages. This is great because no retouching is required since you don't have to model the blemishes! Cutaway views are no problem either. The computer can do the cutting and leave the prototype intact. Of course there are the other possibilities of exploded or transparent views as well as line drawings."

Contact Ron Scott for information and samples.

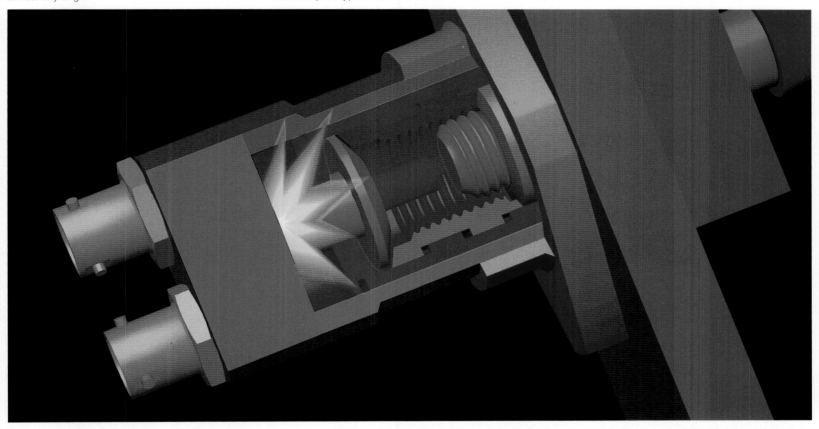

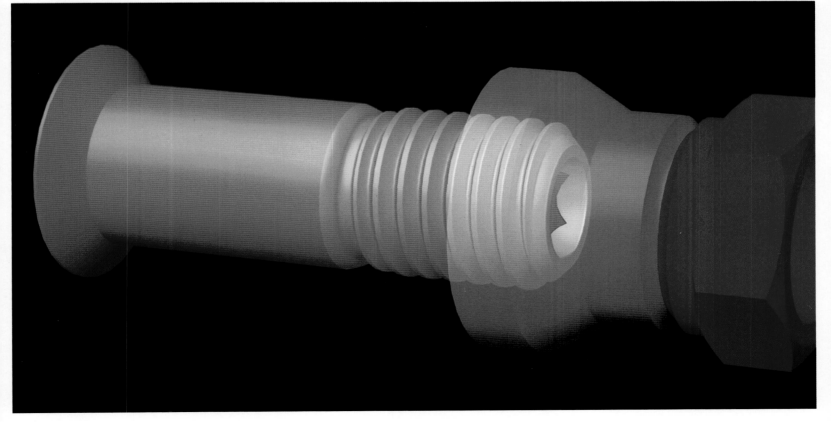

Hans Staartjes
20 Lana Lane
Houston, Texas 77027
(713) 621-8503

ROCKY MOUNTAIN

Colorado
Utah

Dirk Douglass

2755 South 300 West Suite D
Salt Lake City, Utah 84115
(801) 485-5691

The smiles, the people, the creative scenery of Utah.

Advertising, editorial, fashion, location and studio photography.

**Bob Fader
Studio**

14 Pearl Street
Denver, Colorado 80203
(303) 744-0711
(602) 941-3554 Phoenix

Represented by Patti Ryan
(303) 832-9214

Additional work can be
seen in American Showcase
Volume 7 page 363,
Volume 8 page 332,
Volume 9 page 297.

BOB FADER

DENVER   303/744-0711   •   PHOENIX   602/941-3554

Dirk Gallian
P.O. Box 4573
Aspen, Colorado 81612
(303) 925-8268

Stock agent:
Journalism Services
(312) 951-0269

GALLIAN

Gregory D. Gorfkle Photography, Inc.

6901 East Baker Place
Denver, Colorado 80224
(303) 759-2737

Represented in the southeast by:

Nancy Babcock
(404) 876-0117

Using a specially designed camera system, Greg creates unique and unusual images with people and products.

Done completely in the camera, motion, speed, panoramics and planned distortions can be applied to a wide variety of subjects.

See Showcase 5 and 8 for further examples.

Client list includes:

R. J. Reynolds
Hewlett Packard
Frontier Airlines
Adolph Coors Company
Mountain Bell
Consolidated Papers
Pentax
Voit Sports
No Nonsense Fashions
Kentucky Derby
Sheraton Hotels
Budget Rent-a-Car
Timex

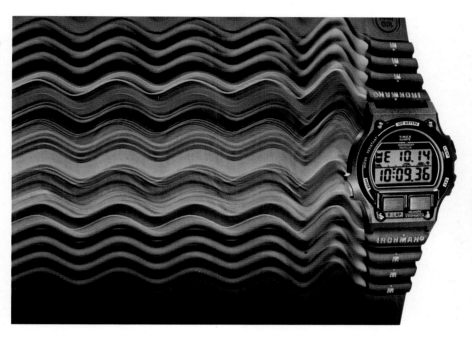

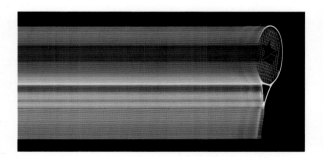

335

David Lissy

14472 Applewood Ridge Road
Golden, Colorado 80401
(303) 277-0232

Member ASMP
Portfolio available upon request
Stock images on varied subjects available
Photographs © David Lissy 1986

David brings with him to every job 15 years experience in photography. David's specialty is location photography for advertising, corporate communications/annual reports and editorial uses. He can handle all kinds of lighting conditions including the tough glare of snow & beaches, the soft backlighting of a sunrise or sunset and all kinds of indoor lighting. He is as comfortable photographing corporate executives as he is sports figures or families.

Clients include: Adolph Coors, American Airlines, Anheuser Busch, Arthur J. Gallegher & Co., Aspen Skiing Corp., Bank America, Carrera, Centrum, CHANGING TIMES, Comerica Bank, DENVER BUSINESS, Digital, Diners Club, DuPont, Eastman Kodak, Exploring Sports Books, GUTS, Hawaiian Tropic, Hoyle Calendars, Hydrafitness, IBM, Imperial Tobacco, Johnson & Johnson, K-2 skis, Marker, NEWSWEEK, NEW YORK MAGAZINE, Nikon, 1980 Winter Olympics, 1984 Summer Olympics, OUTSIDE MAGAZINE, Pfizer Pharmaceuticals, Porsche, POWDER MAGAZINE, Rossignol, Salomon North America, Sargent & Lundy, SKIING MAGAZINE, SKI MAGAZINE, SPORT MAGAZINE, SPORTS ILLUSTRATED, Sun Ger, Taylor California Cellar Wines, TIME, THE RUNNER, 13-30 Corp., VENTURE MAGAZINE, White Stag

The Quinney Group

David Quinney, Jr.
423 East Broadway
Salt Lake City, Utah 84111
(801) 363-0434

Clients include:
Amax Magnesium; Apple Computer; Axonix, Robert Bosch Corporation; CenTech; Cover Pools, Inc.; Hilton Hotel; Jetway Systems; Speech Plus O.C. Tanner; United States Film Festival; Utah Scientific.

Studio and location capabilities with emphasis toward advertising and corporate/industrial photographic illustration.

San Francisco representative
Kris Denton
(415) 383-6237

COVER POOLS INC. 1986 CORPORATE BROCHURE

Tom Travis

1219 South Pearl Street
Denver, Colorado 80210
(303) 377-7422

Advertising
Aerials
Annual Report
Architecture
Corporate Brochure
Industrial
Product.

Clients include: Adolph Coors Company; Aqua
Motion; Cobe Laboratories; Coke USA; Colorado
Lottery; Conant & Associates; Contact
Communications; The Creekside Company; C.W.
Fentress Architects; Hilton Hotel; Homart
Development; John Madden & Co.; Michael Barber
Architects; Osprey Development; Property Company
of America; Property Investors of Colorado; Pulte
Homes; Sanford Homes; Scott Rice Interiors; Silco Oil
Co.; Skidmore, Owings & Merrill; Sonnenblick-
Goldman; Sports Illustrated; Tele-Controls; The Witkin
Group; Venture Properties; Warsteiner Beer.

Brian Twede

430 South State Street
Salt Lake City, Utah 84111
(801) 534-1459

Illustrating on large format
Ektachrome. Specializing in
photographic manipulation. The
illustrations of the earth and the
logo were produced entirely
from line art.

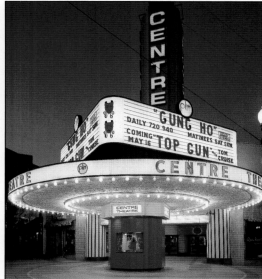

BEFORE MANIPULATION

AFTER MANIPULATION

GO BUY THE BOOK

Go buy Corporate Showcase. And you'll go by the book to find the right talent for the job. Over 18,000 buyers of corporate photography, illustration and design use it, so should you. Whether you're involved in everything from corporate advertising to sales brochures, calendars to catalogs, internal communications to annual reports. Corporate Showcase is unique. The only visual source book devoted exclusively to showing you the best talent on tap for corporate assign-

ments. Get Corporate Showcase and you get it all. Over 1,500 photography, illustration and design visuals featured on over 300 full-color art pages. All organized and cross-referenced for fast, easy use. That's not all. Order now and save 25% off the retail price of $32.50. Pay only $24.50 with free postage and handling. (N.Y. residents, please add sales tax.) Just call (212) 245-0981 or send check/money order to: American Showcase, 724 Fifth Avenue, NY, NY 10019

CORPORATE SHOWCASE 5

WEST

California
Hawaii
Oregon
Washington

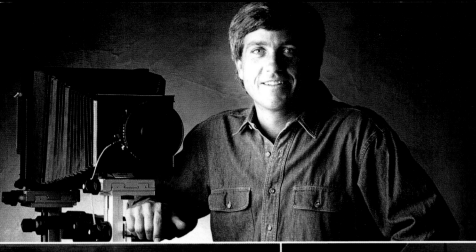

BILL WERTS
WERTS STUDIOS INC
732 N. HIGHLAND AVE
LOS ANGELES, CALIFORNIA 90038
REP: DIANNE BROWN & CO
(213) 464-2775
TELEX 650-296-9749
FAX 213-464-8373
REEL ALSO AVAILABLE ON REQUEST

DAVID LeBON
WERTS STUDIOS INC
732 N. HIGHLAND AVE
LOS ANGELES, CALIFORNIA 90038
REP: DIANNE BROWN & CO
(213) 464-2775
TELEX 650-296-9749
FAX 213-464-8373

SWARTHOUT

Swarthout & Associates, Inc., 370 Fourth Street, San Francisco, California 94107 (415) 543-2525

Represented by: Ron Sweet (415) 433-1222

I stand by my brandy. E&J.

Designed by Gary Keith Wong, AD.

JOHN ZIMMERMAN PERSONALITY

NEW YORK: O'ROURKE/PAGE ASSOC. (212) 772-0346 **LOS ANGELES:** DELORES ZIMMERMAN (213) 273-2642
CHICAGO: TIM HARWOOD & ASSOC. (312) 751-1552

SPORTS ILLUSTRATED

MINOLTA

KRAFT FOODS

CONTINENTAL CAN

CONTINENTAL CAN

PEBBLE BEACH APPAREL

JOHN ZIMMERMAN PERFORMANCE

NEW YORK: O'ROURKE/PAGE ASSOC. (212) 772-0346 **LOS ANGELES:** DELORES ZIMMERMAN (213) 273-2642
CHICAGO: TIM HARWOOD & ASSOC. (312) 751-1552

John Zimmerman specializes in automobile photography that captures motion and excitement. Call for samples of our latest high-performance work.

MARLBORO

FORD MOTORS/BRONCO

FORD MOTORS/BRONCO

FORD MOTORS/AEROSTAR

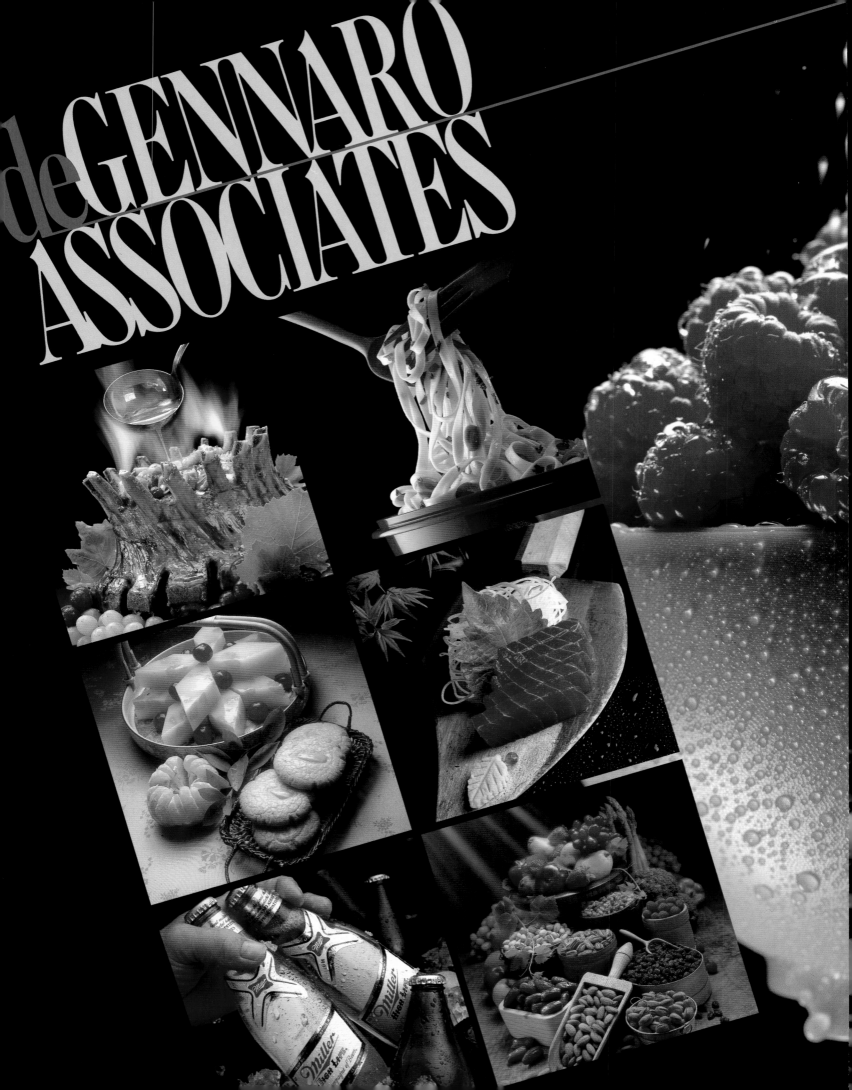

deGENNARO
ASSOCIATES

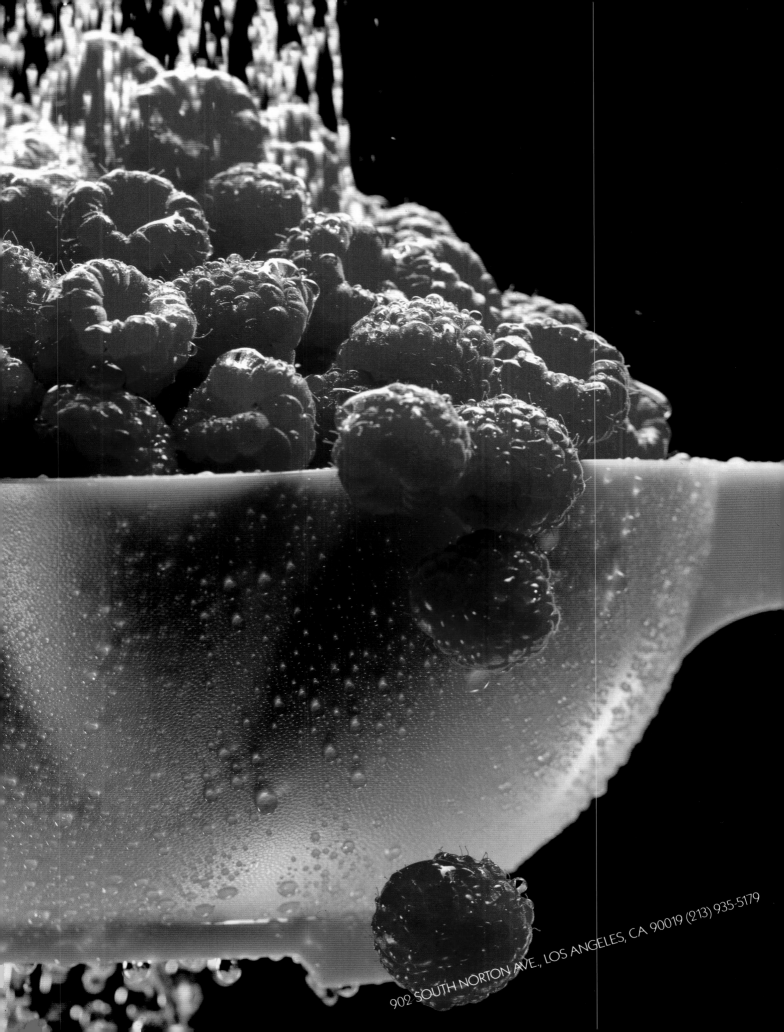

902 SOUTH NORTON AVE., LOS ANGELES, CA 90019 (213) 935-5179

HANK BENSON

653 Bryant Street
San Francisco, CA 94107
415 543 8153
Represented by
Ellen Phillips
415 928 6336
Food, Still Life, Sets
Reel On Request

653 Bryant Street
San Francisco, CA 94107
415 543 8153
Represented by
Ellen Phillips
415 928 6336
Food, Still Life, Sets
Reel On Request

HANK BENSON

In Northern California it's Fujioka for studio or location shoots. Studio has over 4,000 square feet with 30 foot hard cyclorama and a separate workshop for making props. And Fujioka's Iveco diesel grip truck with cellular phone helps make things go as smoothly on location as they do in the studio. All this plus great photography. Call Robert Fujioka at 415/960-3010.

Robert Fujioka Studios
715 Stierlin Road
Mountain View, CA 94043
415/960-3010

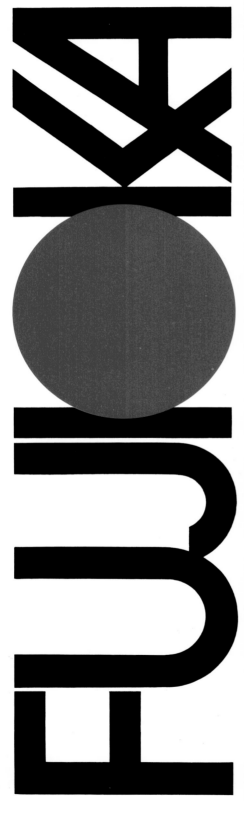

Born in the West

MASTERSON

11211 SORRENTO VALLEY RD., STE. S
SAN DIEGO, CALIFORNIA 92121
TELEPHONE: 619-457-3251

1986 ED MASTERSON

STEVE FRITZ

Partial Client List:
N.W. Ayer
McCann-Erickson
Grey Advertising
Applause/Division of Wallace Berrie Co.
Yamaha Keyboards
L.A. Museum of Contemporary Art
Brentwood Publishing
L.A. Olympics Organizing Committee
Santa Anita Racetrack
Soft Kat Inc.

Studio: 1023 So. Santa Fe Ave. Los Angeles CA 90021 (213) 629-8052

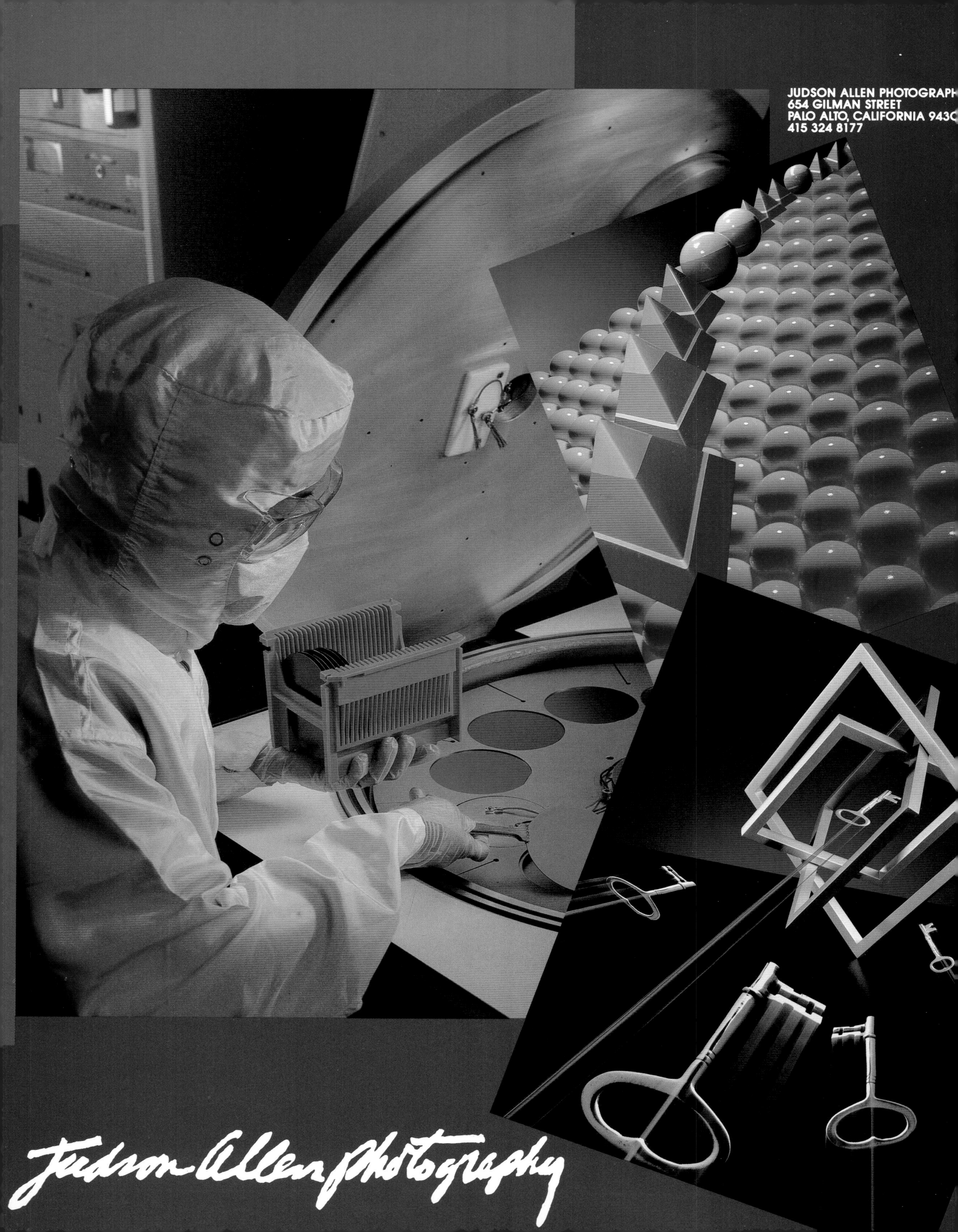

JUDSON ALLEN PHOTOGRAPH
654 GILMAN STREET
PALO ALTO, CALIFORNIA 9430
415 324 8177

Judson Allen photography

JOHN CLAYTON

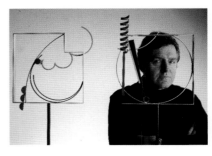

160 South Park San Francisco California 94107 415 495-4562

ALAN ABRAMOWITZ

P.O. BOX 45121
SEATTLE, WASHINGTON 98145
(206) 621-0710

ANNUAL REPORTS

ADVERTISING

CORPORATE/INDUSTRIAL

ARCHITECTURE

DOCUMENTARY

David Scharf

2100 Loma Vista Place
Los Angeles, California 90039
(213) 666-8657

New York representative:
Peter Arnold, Inc.
1181 Broadway
New York, New York 10001
(212) 481-1190
Stock Available

High tech imaging with electrons:
Photography with the scanning electron microscope for advertising, education, editorial, and research. Creative visions of places and things beyond the capability of the eye or regular microscopy, for almost any subject from the macro to the far-micro range. As illustrated below, we can now add natural looking color using our own recently developed techniques. An extensive stock is also available.

Clients include:
Time, Newsweek, National Geographic, U.S. News, National Wildlife, Natural History, Discover, Science, Scientific American, Omni, N.Y. Times, Time-Life Books, Prentice-Hall, McGraw Hill, Ziff-Davis, Scott Foresman, Houghton Mifflin, John Wiley, D.C. Heath, Norton, Harcourt Brace Jovanovich, Brittanica, Grolier, World Book, C.B.S., A.B.C., N.B.C., W.G.B.H., Nova, National Geographic Films—Cyanimide, Warner Lambert, Spectra Physics, American Burdick & Jackson, Cutter Biological Labs, Polaroid, Agfa, Kodak —Marsteller, J. Walter Thompson, Young & Rubicam, National Academy of Sciences...Etc.

MEDITERRANEAN FRUIT FLY

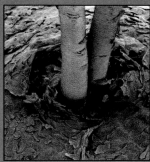

MEDITERRANEAN FRUIT FLY

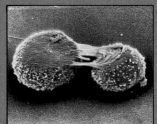

HUMAN HAIR AND SCALP

HYBRIDOMA CELLS

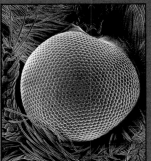

EYE OF A MOTH

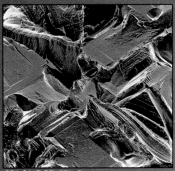

SEA SALT CRYSTALS

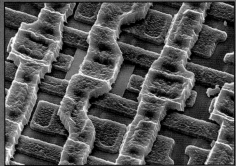

COMPUTER CHIP WITH CONTAMINATION

HUMAN DENTAL PLAQUE

BLACK FLY

ZIMMERMAN

Dick Zimmerman Studio 8743 W. Washington Blvd. LA, CA 90230 (213) 204-2911

"If you want romance to come on strong, you have to come on soft."
Jane Seymour

le Jardin
de MAX FACTOR
The incurably romantic fragrance.

JEANNIE FOR
Cole
JUNIORS

Rachel McLish
Ms. Olympia

Marie Osmond

Russell Abraham

17 Brosnan Place
San Francisco, California 94103
(415) 558-9100
In Los Angeles
(213) 381-3798

Russell Abraham photographs architecture, interiors, hotels, building products. His clients include a broad base of design firms, hotel chains, trade journals, and real estate interests.

Representative clients:

Architectural Record
Brown Matarazzi
Designers West Magazine
The Empire Group
Gensler & Associates
Hyatt Hotel Corp.
Interior Design Magazine
Johnson Burgee Architects
Alan Lucas & Associates
Robert Miller, A.S.I.D.
Marquis Associates
Ron Nunn & Associates
Michelle Pheasant Design
Progressive Architecture
Residence Inns
ROMA
Restaurant & Hotel Design Magazine
Sandy & Babcock
Skidmore, Owings & Merrill
Ruth Soforenko Associates
S&O Consultants
The Steinberg Group

The business of commercial art and photography.

The more than 300 SPAR members nationwide represent the best talent in the business.

For over 20 years, while we've been bringing talent and client together, SPAR members also have been working to promote high professional standards and to foster cooperation and understanding.

Our members today are not just salespeople but marketing specialists with a wide range of capabilities.

We are truly professionals doing business with professionals.

SOCIETY OF PHOTOGRAPHER AND ARTIST REPRESENTATIVES, INC.
1123 Broadway, Room 914 New York, New York 10010 212-924-6023

Bill Baker Photography, Inc.

265-29th Street
Oakland, California 94611
(415) 832-7685

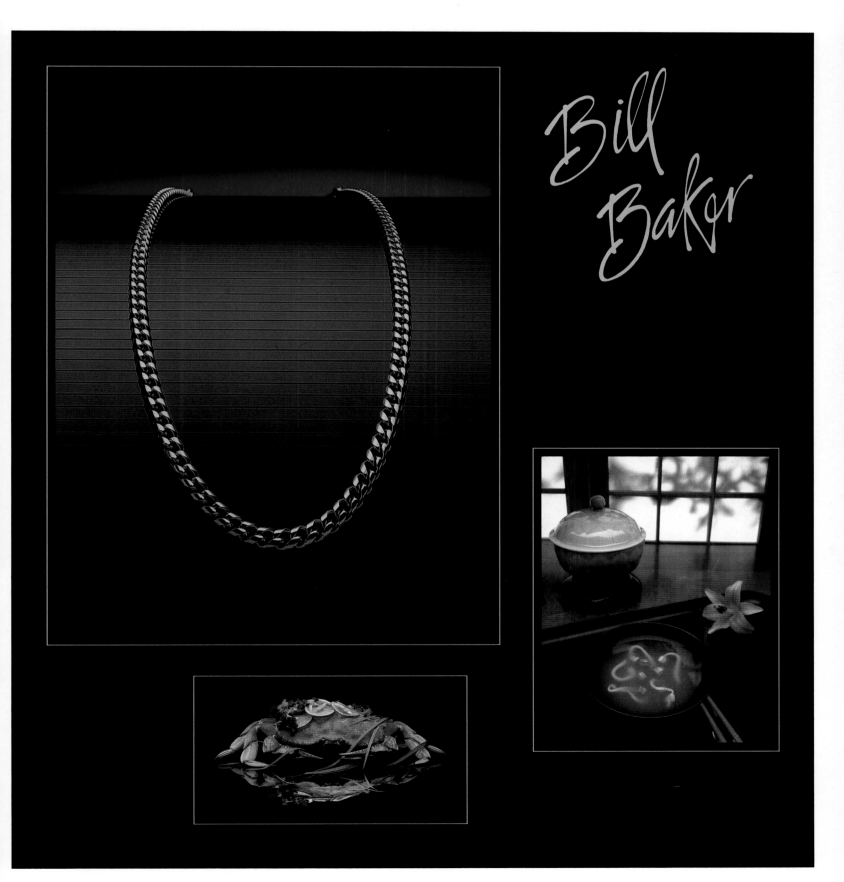

Louis Bencze

2442 N.W. Market Street
Suite 86
Seattle, Washington 98107
(206) 783-8033

Major clients include:
IBM, Xerox, Amoco Chemicals, Boeing, Hewlett-
Packard, Southwestern Bell, Pacific Northwest Bell,
AT&T, Microsoft, Exxon, Monsanto, Westinghouse,
Santa Fe Pacific, Airborne Express, USX.

"Wherever I go, whatever I shoot, I'm after the impact
beneath the obvious. I mine images."

LOUIS BENCZE

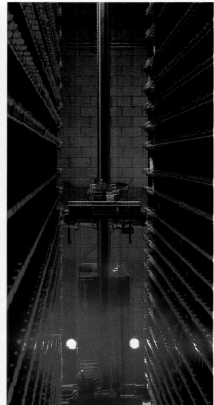

John Blaustein
San Francisco, California
(415) 525-8133

Also see: American Showcase Volume 5, 6, 7, 8 & 9;
Corporate Showcase Volume 1, 2, 3 & 4;
ASMP Book 1981; ASMP Book 2.

John Blaustein
(415) 525-8133

Jim Britt

140 North La Brea
Los Angeles, California 90036
(213) 936-3131

Editorial and advertising. Specializing in "people,"
location and studio.

Stock agency: Shooting Star.

Kathleen Norris Cook

P.O. Box 2159
Laguna Hills, California 92654
(714) 770-4619

Assignment and Stock
Landscapes
Aerials
Panoramics

REPRESENTED BY
Warren Cook
(714) 770-4619

RECENT CLIENTS
Audubon
California Tourism
Citicorp
Coldwell-Banker
Coors
Dupont
Eastman Kodak
Great American Bank
Great Western Savings
Mountain Bell
National Geographic
National Park Service
Prime Computer
PSA Airlines
Sierra Club
US West
The Paul Winter Consort

For additional examples,
please see Showcase
Volumes 4 thru 9 and
ASMP Book Vol. 5

Photographs © 1986
Kathleen Norris Cook

Dave Davidson

25003 South Beeson Road
Beavercreek, Oregon 97004
(503) 632-7650

Member ASMP
Stock available direct or through the Stock Market in
New York (212) 684-7878

**See feature article on my special effects in
Communication Arts Mag. March/April 85**

Also see American Showcase #8 and Corporate
Showcase #4

I've been shooting on location for over ten years, with
extensive experience in advertising, corporate and
editorial photography.

My expertise consists of capturing the drama and
dignity of hardworking people, as well as creating
distinctive and imaginative images through special
effects. My style includes a unique vision, with a bold
use of color and strong graphic composition.

Industrial
Exxon
AT&T
Western Aluminum Producers
Northwest Natural Gas
NEC Corp
PGE
Pacifico

Wacker Siltronics
Metra Steel
Gerber Knives
Precision Castparts

Forest Products
Weyerhaeuser
Louisiana Pacific
International Paper
Crown Zellerbach

Corporate/Financial
Warner Communications
U.S. Dept of Defense
Merrill-Lynch
U.S. Information Agency

TRW
U.S. Bancorp
Blue Cross
Sheraton Hotels
Safeco Insurance
The Koll Company
Olympia & York
U.S. Data Corp

Transportation
TWA
Pan Am
Alaska Airlines
Burlington Northern
Consolidated Air Freight

Digital Art

Computer Graphics
3699 Wilshire Boulevard, Suite 870
Los Angeles, California 90010
(213) 387-8384

Digital Art is a computer graphics studio. A computer graphic image can be created from any 35mm slide or any print up to 8½ by 11 inches. Finished work is provided on 35mm or 4x5 transparency film. The effects shown here include a color tone line (Tiger), posterization (Computer), block pixel (Handshake), and false color block pixel (Truck). The Handshake piece was assembled from several source transparencies, which were digitally combined before the special effect was created.

Clients include: Abert, Newhoff & Burr; Atlantic Records; Capitol Records; Carnation; Computer Sciences Corp.; Dancer Fitzgerald Sample; Dentsu Young & Rubicam; Embassy Home Video; Ernst & Whinney; Los Angeles Times; Mattel; MCA Records; Ogilvy & Mather; Petersen Publishing; RCA/Columbia Pictures Home Video.

Member of NCGA, SIGGRAPH, SILA.

For stock material call West Light, (213) 477-0421.

Additional images may be seen in The California Workbook.

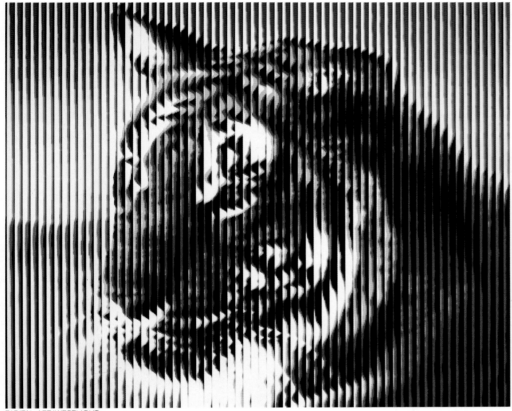

DIGITAL ART/WESTLIGHT

DELMATOFF, GEROW, MORRIS & LANGHAMS

MARTIN BRINKERHOFF & ASSOC.

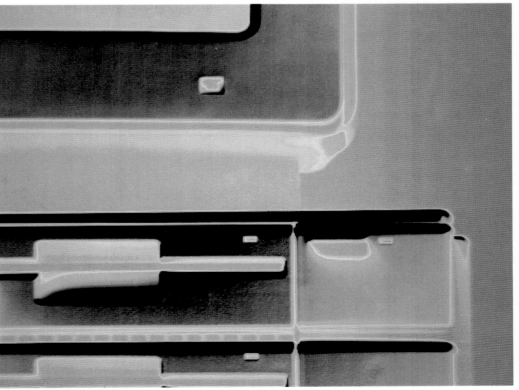

COCHRANE, CHASE/LIVINGSTONE

Charly Franklin

3352 20th Street
San Francisco, California 94110
(415) 543-5400

KBLX RADIO

SECURITY PACIFIC NATIONAL BANK

SIMPSON PAPER COMPANY

CALIFORNIA COLLEGE OF ARTS AND CRAFTS

PACIFIC TELESIS GROUP

TRANSAMERICA CORPORATION

George B. Fry III

PO Box 2465
Menlo Park, California 94026
(415) 323-7663

Member ASMP, PAPA

We shoot people and products
in the studio and on location. For
additional samples please call
the studio.

© George B. Fry III 1986

Gary Galván Studios

4626½ Hollywood Boulevard
Los Angeles, California 90027
(213) 667-1457

Clients include:

AT&T Communications
Disneyland
Mountain Bell
Petersens Photographic
Carnation
Stroh's Beer
Bueno Hand Bags
CBS
Pacific Bell
Invacare Corporation
South Pacific Lager
Integrated Circuit Development
   Corporation
Desert Horizons
Sears Savings Bank
Bugle Boy USA
La Blanca Sport
Jet Propulsion Laboratory
Los Angeles Times
Atrio Eyewear
Show Time the Movie Channel
Paramount Pictures
California Milk Advisory Board
etc.

Vast casting resources available
for the Hispanic market.

HEATEFLEX™
Strength in Technology
Flexibility in Design

HEATEFLEX™
Flexible Teflon® Heaters

Integrated Circuit Development Corp.
3724 Park Place, P.O. Box 728, Montrose, California 91020
818 957 2442   Telex: 887914

Life the way it was
meant to be lived.

WITH THE AT&T CARD...

You can always call from almost any telephone,
without coins!

AT&T
The right choice.

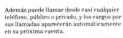

GALVAN

Gary Galván Photography   4626½ Hollywood Boulevard   Los Angeles, California 90027   213 667-1457

CAPTURE THE MOMENT

The fascinating thing about photography, beyond the wonderful design and the beautiful lighting, is that it captures moments in time. Moments in time that most of us spend little of our lives in. We live with one foot in the future and one foot in the past, and very seldom truly experience right now. Right Now. Right now.

Photography has a way of holding a moment for us to look at. A moment that would have slipped by barely noticed.

Everything is always moving, always changing, and for me, photography is a reminder that the way it is, is the way it is.

Ronald Travisano
Executive Vice President
Travisano–DiGiacomo Films, Inc.
New York City

(Originally published in American Showcase Volume 3, 1980.)

Robert Gardner Studios, Inc.

800 South Citrus Avenue
Los Angeles, California 90036
(213) 931-1108

Client Listing: American Express, Sports Illustrated, De Beers, Olga Lingerie, Cole of California, Tokina Optical, Neutrogena, Avon, Chanel, Clairol, Helena Rubenstein, Jean Naté, Revlon, Vidal Sassoon, Viviane Woodward, Rolex, Benson & Hedges, Continental Airlines, TWA, Volkswagen, Esquire, Tennis Magazine, Shape Magazine, Bazaar, Seagram, Canadian Lord Calvert, Pepsi, Coca-Cola, Shasta, Vassarette, Rogers,

Maidenform, Marantz, Clarion, 20th Century Fox, General Foods, Nestea, Carnation, Silverwoods, J.C. Penney, Bullock's, du Pont Qiana, Montgomery Ward, Broadway, Neiman-Marcus, IBM, Baskin-Robbins, Del Monte.

Celebrities Such As: Christy Brinkley, James Caan, Robert Wagner, Jack Lemmon, Jeff Bridges, Sally Field, Veronica Hammell, Ali MacGraw, Lou Ferigno, Arnold Schwarzenegger, Bob Newhart, George C. Scott, Cheryl Tiegs, Maude Adams, Dinah Shore.

Stock photography available through:
After-Image (213) 480-1105

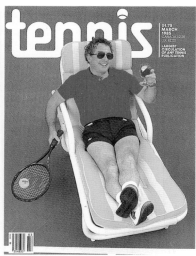

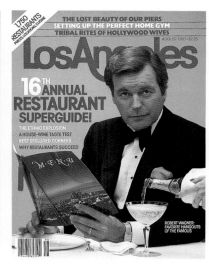

Paul Hoffman
Photo-Illustration
Studio
4500 19th Street
San Francisco, California 94114
(415) 863-3575

Representatives

Mary Busacca
San Francisco
(415) 381-9047

Alexis Dickinson
New York
(212) 473-8020

Michael D. Horikawa
MDH Studios

508 Kamakee Street
Honolulu, Hawaii 96814
(808) 538-7378

I shoot the best of Hawaii...luxury resorts, travel, location, studio, fashion, products and aerials.

Everything under the Hawaiian sun...
except weddings.

Thanks to AT&T, AMFAC, Aston Hotels, Catalina, General Foods, Hawaiian Airlines, Hilton Hotels, Hyatt Hotels, Lever Brothers, Mauna Lani Resort, Mercedes-Benz (Europe), Nissan (Japan), Pan Am, Panasonic, Playboy, Sheraton Hotels, Shiseido, Toshiba, United Airlines, and many others.

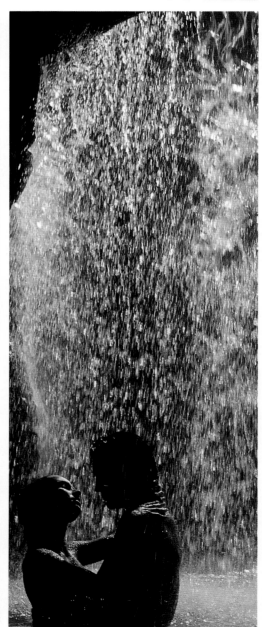

James F. Housel
84 University
Suite 409
Seattle, Washington 98101
(206) 682-6182

Corporate, industrial and architectural photography
for a wide variety of clients including:
Hewlett Packard, Exxon, Apple Computer Dealers,
Rainier Capital Management, Western Star Trucks,
and Safeco Properties.

H O U S E L

Come see the wide open spaces of Houston.

Jeff Hunter

4626½ Hollywood Boulevard
Los Angeles, California 90027
(213) 669-0468
(213) 937-2008

Corporate, Advertising, Industrial, Editorial and Travel
Photography

Clients include:
Pepsi-Co
Hilton Hotels
Best Western Hotels
Trust House Forte Hotels
Mexican Ministry of Tourism

Money Magazine
Woman's Day Magazine
Dynamic Years Magazine
Clairol
Great Western Financial Systems
Far East National Bank
Yamaha International
Ethan Allen Furniture
Sea World
The Image Bank
Urban Pacific Development Corp.
Tejon Ranch Corp.
Knoll International
Beneficial Standard Life Insurance

FINA
South Coast Medical Center
West Covina Medical Center
L.A. Herald Examiner
L.A. County Fair

Stock Photography: The Image Bank

For More Samples, see:
American Showcase, Vol. 8
Corporate Showcase, Vol. 4
New York Art Directors Club, 61st Annual

© Jeff Hunter, 1986

HUNTER

Jeff Hunter

4626½ Hollywood Boulevard
Los Angeles, California 90027
(213) 669-0468
(213) 937-2008

Corporate, Advertising, Industrial, Editorial and Travel Photography

Clients include:
Pepsi-Co
Hilton Hotels
Best Western Hotels
Trust House Forte Hotels
Mexican Ministry of Tourism
Money Magazine
Woman's Day Magazine
Dynamic Years Magazine
Clairol
Great Western Financial Systems
Far East National Bank
Yamaha International
Ethan Allen Furniture
Sea World
The Image Bank
Urban Pacific Development Corp.
Tejon Ranch Corp.
Knoll International
Beneficial Standard Life Insurance
FINA
South Coast Medical Center
West Covina Medical Center
L.A. Herald Examiner
L.A. County Fair

Stock Photography: The Image Bank

For More Samples, see:
American Showcase, Vol. 8
Corporate Showcase, Vol. 4
New York Art Directors Club, 61st Annual

© Jeff Hunter, 1986

HUNTER

Jim Karageorge
610 22nd Street #309
San Francisco, California 94107
(415) 648-3444

bringing the control of the studio
to location photography

all photos on both pages were
shot on location

stock is available
call the studio for a complete
portfolio
see previous pages in
Corporate Showcase Vols. 1, 2,
3, 4 & 5 and American
Showcase Vol. 9

member ASMP
© 1987 Jim Karageorge

MEMPHIS DISTRIBUTION CENTER/WILLIAMS-SONOMA ANNUAL REPORT

CALIFORNIA DRILL SITE/GEOTHERMAL RESOURCES ANNUAL REPORT

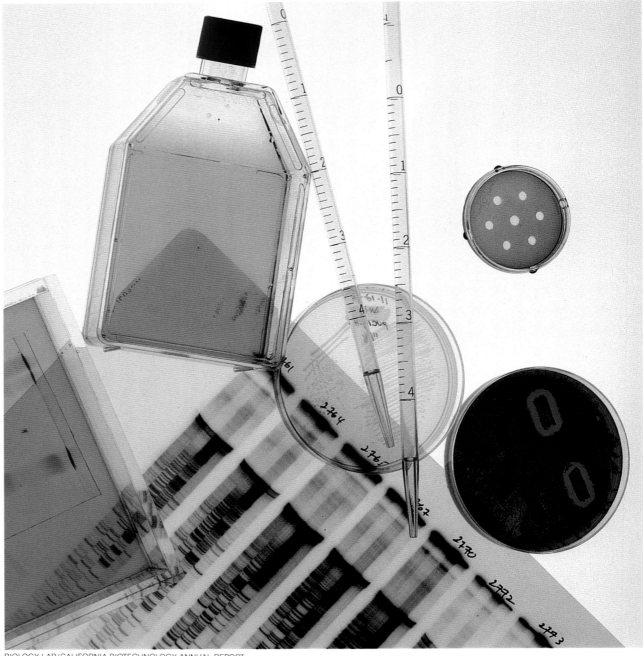

BIOLOGY LAB/CALIFORNIA BIOTECHNOLOGY ANNUAL REPORT

Jim Karageorge

610 22nd Street #309
San Francisco, California 94107
(415) 648-3444

bringing the control of the studio
to location photography

all photos on both pages were
shot on location

MERCEDES DEALERSHIP/BANK OF AMERICA AUTO LEASING BROCHURE.

RESEARCH LIBRARY/BANK OF AMERICA EXECUTIVE FINANCIAL COUNSELLING BROCHURE

Larry Keenan

421 Bryant Street
San Francisco, California 94107
(415) 495-6474

Advertising, annual reports,
corporate/industrial, travel,
conceptual and special effects
photography. International
experience, numerous awards.
Stock photography library.

Clients:

Activision
Ampex
Apple Computers
Blue Cross
Broderbund
CBS Records
Clorox
Coherent
Electronic Arts
Genentech
General Instrument
Hewlett-Packard
Levi-Strauss
Lorimar Productions
Microsoft
NorthStar Computers
Omni Magazine
PacBell
Syntex Labs
Tandem Computers
Triad Systems

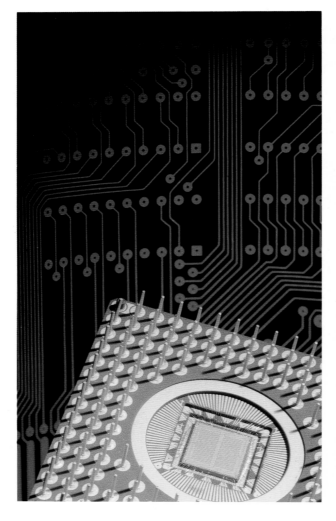

Ron Kimball

2582 Sun-Mor Avenue
Mountain View, California 94040
(415) 948-2939

Advertising, Calendars, Posters.
Animals, People, Fashion.
On location or in our studio.
Assignment or your choice of
over 100,000 quality stock shots.

Tom Landecker

1028 Folsom Street
San Francisco, California 94103
(415) 864-8888

**Larry Lee
Photography**

P.O. Box 4688
North Hollywood,
California 91607
(818) 766-2677
(24 hour Recorder)
(805) 259-1226
(Studio & Home)

Assignment and stock.

Specializing in industrial,
energy and travel locations
around the world.

Portfolio available by mail.

© 1986 Larry Lee

LARRY LEE

Mel Lindstrom
2510 Old Middlefield Way
Studio #H
Mountain View, California 94043
(415) 962-1313

Represented in Houston by:
Sandra Kline
(713) 522-1862

David Madison

2330 Old Middlefield
Mountain View, California 94043
(415) 961-6297

I specialize in ACTIVE PEOPLE and SPORTS. My San Francisco Bay Area location gives great access to wide-ranging outdoor locations, from beaches to mountains and deserts to vineyards. And beautiful West Coast light and weather.

Extensive stock available of all sports and fitness subjects, including recreational sports, many with model releases.

For additional work, see American Showcase Volumes 8 & 9 and Corporate Showcase Volume 2.

© David Madison 1987

David Muench

David Muench Photography, Inc.
P.O. Box 30500
Santa Barbara, California 93130
(805) 967-4488

A Collection of Stock Photography.
Focusing on the American Landscape...East...West
...North...and South. The wild beauty and presence
of mountain, desert, coast, prairie, water, texture and
sky...the elements.
Specializing in the mysterious moods, natural rhythms,
light and spacial forms. Over 20 large format books
exhibit his original photographs on the American
landscape. Photographs are made large format 4 x 5
and in 35mm size.
Available for advertising, annual reports, books,
editorial, calendar, poster and brochures.
Photography in bl/wt and color.

R. J. Muna
63 Encina
Palo Alto, California 94301
(415) 328-1131

When in San Francisco, please visit our
7000 square foot facility.

Portfolio samples on request.

David Perry

P.O. Box 4165
Pioneer Square Station
Seattle, Washington 98104
(206) 932-6614

Corporate/Annual Report/Advertising

Images found and produced on location.
Regionally. Nationally. Abroad.
Multiple assignment trips to Asia at least twice yearly.
Additional work may be seen in American Showcase,
Volumes 7 & 9.

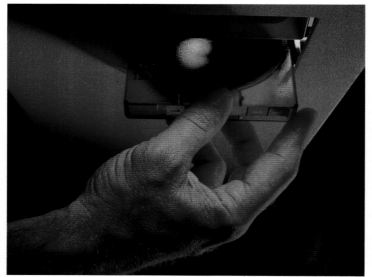

Marshal Safron

506 South San Vicente Boulevard
Los Angeles, California 90048
(213) 653-1234

Specializing in architecture, interiors, furniture, hotels
and building products on location and in the studio.
My work has appeared in all related national trade and
consumer publications.

Client list available upon request.

Additional work can be seen in American Showcase
Volume 9, page 373.

Paul Sanders

7378 Beverly Boulevard
Los Angeles, California 90036
(213) 933-5791

Joan Wood, Los Angeles
(213) 463-7717
(213) 933-5791

Warren Cook, Orange Co.
(714) 770-4619

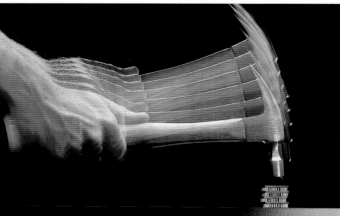

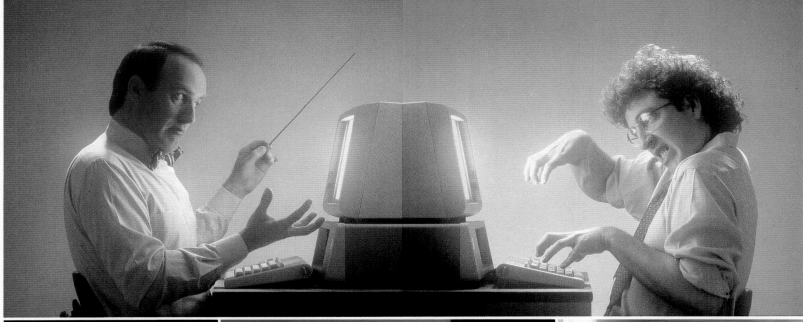

Teri Sandison
Lightra, Inc.

1545 North Wilcox Avenue, Suite 102
Hollywood, California 90028
(213) 461-3529

Clients include:

Van de Kamp's	California Avocado Commission	Hunt Wesson	
Nissin Foods	Meredith Publishing	The Benjamin Co.	
Las Palmas	California Date Commission	Security Pacific Bank	
Early California Foods	The Knapp Press	Leo's Meats	Heartland Bread
Sanyo, Inc.	Sears Roebuck and Co.	Kibun	Dow Ziploc
Sunset Magazine & Books	Chef Francisco	Contemporary Books	Naugle's
Martha White Co.	Bon Appètit	H.P. Books	California Table
Pizza Hut	Beverly Heritage Hotel	Emile Henry Cookware	Grape Commission
	Ralphs Grocery Co.	Entenmann's	Stouffer's

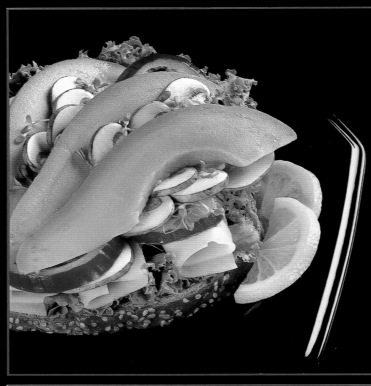

Larry Schenker

Larry Schenker Studio
5888 Smiley Drive
Los Angeles, California 90232
(213) 837-2020

Recent clients include:

American Commerce Exchange
Arrowhead, Inc.
C.B.S. Television
Cedars-Sinai Hospitals
Century Wilshire Hotels
Comdial
Computer Power Systems
Emerson Electronics
Fansteel
Flanigan Farms
Good Earth Restaurants
ITT Electronics
Juki Office Machines
Mobile Fidelity Sound Lab
Nissan Motor Corp.
Sunbank
Syntex Laboratories
Trus Joist Corp.
Warner/Elektra/Atlanta

See additional work in:

American Showcase Vol. 8
Western Review Vol. 1
California Workbook 1983,
   1984, 1985, 1986

A free minifolio of work
is available upon request.

WHO WAS HERB LUBALIN?

THE FACE BEHIND THE FACES.

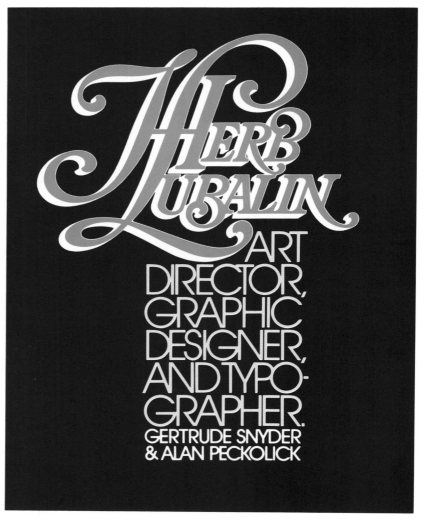

He was a skinny, colorblind, left-handed artist, known to friends and colleagues as a deafeningly silent man. But through his typography-based and editorial designs, he created bold new forms for communication and changed the dimensions of advertising and graphics.

Herb Lubalin is the definitive book about the typographic impresario and design master of our time. It is illustrated with more than 360 extraordinary examples of Lubalin's award-winning work, including: ■ Logos and Letterheads ■ Editorial and Book Design ■ Packaging ■ Advertising and Sales Promotion ■ Annual Reports ■ Best of *U&lc,* and more.

"The magnitude of Herb Lubalin's achievements will be felt for a long time to come....I think he was probably the greatest graphic designer ever."
—Lou Dorfsman, Vice President, Creative Director, Advertising and Design, CBS Inc.

184 pages, Color throughout, 9" x 11⅞"
Clothbound, Retail Value: $39.95

SPECIAL OFFER
Send for your copy of **Herb Lubalin** today and pay only $35.00.* Postage and handling are FREE within the U.S. and Canada. To order, **call 212-245-0981** and charge your AMEX, Visa or Mastercard. Or send your check or money order to:
AMERICAN SHOWCASE, INC.
724 Fifth Avenue, New York, NY 10019
*New York residents, please add appropriate sales tax.

Shaneff

Carl Shaneff
Photography
1100 Alakea Street
Honolulu, Hawaii 96813
(808) 533-3010

Hawaii. Sure, it's beautiful. But it isn't paradise unless you know your way around. And Carl Shaneff knows. He's been shooting his way around Hawaii for 15 years.

That's 15 years worth of advertising, corporate and editorial work. In that time, he's handled everything from nervous volcanoes to raging Art Directors.

He's worked for the likes of American Express, American Airlines and Avis. And that's just a few of the A's!

Between his studio and location work, he's put together a stock file that's become a major island attraction unto itself.

And he's an ASMP member. What more could you ask from a guy except, "What are you doing in Hawaii?" Carl would say, "Everything."

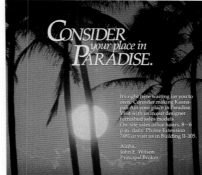

© CARL SHANEFF 1986

Marc Solomon

P.O. Box 480574
Los Angeles, California 90048
(213) 935-1771

Corporate
Industrial
Advertising
Editorial

A partial list of last year's clients:

AFG Industries
AT&T
Birtcher
Cardis Corp.
Dow
Dryden Press
Ethyl Corp.
Family Circle Magazine
Farmers Savings
First Business Bank
First Interstate Bank
Ford
Garrett
General Life Insurance
GTE
Guestinformant Books
ILFC
Institutional Investor
Integrated Resources
Maxicare
Personnel Journal
Pier One Imports
Southern Calif. Edison
Standard Pacific
Tishman
Titan Corp.
Warner Center Bank

Existing photography available
direct and select images
through: The Image Bank.

You can see more work in
American Showcase Volume
Six, Seven, Eight and Nine.
Corporate Showcase Volume
Three and Five.
Black Book 1985, 1986
and 1987.

Call for a portfolio.

© Marc Solomon 1987

INSTITUTIONAL INVESTOR

L.A. DEPT. OF CULTURAL AFFAIRS – "STREET SCENE"

GARRETT

SOUTHERN CALIF. EDISON

FIRST INTERSTATE BANK

Whittaker Photography

Steve Whittaker
111 Glenn Way, Suite #8
Belmont, California 94002
(415) 595-4242

Specializing in Architectural
Interiors and Exteriors, for
Hotels, Restaurants, Offices and
Residential, for brochures,
annual reports, corporate
publications and competitions.

Over 6000 stock images
available covering architectural,
construction, high tech, scenic,
agricultural, etc.

Partial List of Clients:

Amfac
Chevron USA
Skidmore
Owings & Merrill
Ehrlich-Rominger
The Koll Company
Lincoln Properties
Design Engineering Systems
Hewlett Packard
VISA
Eastman Kodak
Hutchins Young & Rubicam Inc.
Sheraton Sunnyvale
Perini Investments
Radison Suites Hotels
Rudolph & Slettin
McCann Ericson

Member of SIP, ASMP, APA, PPA

© 1986 Whittaker Photography

INTERIOR DESIGN: EHRLICH-ROMINGER
DEVELOPER: RAISER DEVELOPMENT CO.

ARCHITECT: DESIGN ENGINEERING SYSTEMS
DEVELOPER: SUTTER HILL LTD.

ARCHITECT: EHRLICH-ROMINGER
DEVELOPER: RAISER DEVELOPMENT CO.

410

Sandra Williams

P.O. Box 16130
San Diego
California 92116
(619) 283-3100

Specializing in
Photography of Architecture

Exteriors
Interiors
Models
Environments

Clients/Projects Include:

Formica Corporation
Chart House Enterprises
Del Mar Woven Woods
Marvin Windows
Irvine Company
Hirsch/Bedner Associates
San Diego Intercontinental
Hotel
Polo/Ralph Lauren
Vagabond Hotels
IBM
Harcourt/Brace/Jovanovich
Frazee Paints
John H. Harland Co.
Coastal Carpet Mills
U.S. Grant Hotel
Sheraton Hotels
Japan California Bank
Guardian Glass
American Institute of Architects
American Plywood Association
Bozell & Jacobs/Pacific
Hahn Corporation
Amfac
Ohbayashi America Corp.
Brehm Communities
Daniel/Mann/Johnson/
Mendenhall
Cannell & Chaffin
John Follis
Timothy Walker Associates
Langdon/Wilson/Mumper
William Pereira Associates
Maxwell Starkman Associates

Published Work Includes:

Architecture
Architectural Record
Better Homes & Gardens
Builder Magazine
Contract Interiors
Designers West
House & Garden
House Beautiful
Interior Design
Interiors
L.A. Times/Home Magazine
New West Magazine
Professional Builder
Progressive Architecture
Psychology Today
San Diego Home/Garden
San Diego Magazine
Sunset Magazine

Ken Wong
3522 West Temple Street
Los Angeles, California 90004
(213) 389-3081

STOCK & PHOTO SERVICES

Arizona
California
Colorado
Florida
Hawaii
Illinois
New York State
Oregon
Texas
Vermont
Washington

UNCOMMON STOCK

Peter Arnold, Inc.

THE INTERNATIONAL PHOTO AGENCY
1181 BROADWAY, NEW YORK, N.Y. 10001

212/481-1190   TELEX: ARNOLD 428281   PHOTONET: PHO 1448

**STOCK &
ASSIGNMENT**
Abstracts
Animals
Architecture
Birds
Cityscapes
Computers & Electronics
Ecology
Energy
Family & Children
Fish & Fishing
Industrial
Insects
Medical
National Parks &
  Monuments
Nature & Scenics
People
Photomicrography
Plants & Flowers
Pollution
Reptiles
Scanning Electron Micrography
Science & Technology

Sports
  (professional & recreational)
Travel & Foreign Cultures
Underwater

ASK FOR A COMPLETE
STOCK LIST.

© GÜNTER ZIESLER

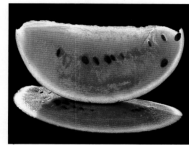
© MICHEL VIARD

© BRUNO J. ZEHNDER

© LIONEL ATWILL

© MARTHA COOPER

© HANSON CARROLL

© WERNER H. MÜLLER

© WERNER H. MÜLLER

© GALEN ROWELL

*See our ad in the "West" section
of this book featuring **David Scharf's**
Scanning Electron Micrography.

CLICK/ Chicago Ltd.

213 West Institute Place
Suite 503
Chicago, Illinois 60610
(312) 787-7880

We are the most creative and knowledgeable stock/ assignment agency in the Midwest.

Our 40 assignment photographers are spread throughout the U.S.A. and Europe, with the majority located in the Midwest. All of our photographers work both in color and b/w. We have experts in the following fields: Advertising, Aerial, Annual Reports, Architecture, Audiovisual, Illustration, Location, Heavy and Light Industry, Medical, Panoramic, Photojournalism, Portraiture, Products, Public Relations and Still Life. We can show you portfolios of photographers whose work is relevant to your needs.

We also have an extensive library of current, top-quality stock photographs and will be happy to supply stock images where available budget, season of the year, or far-flung locations make an assignment impractical. Please see our other ad in the Photography Section.

Leo de Wys, Inc.
Photo Agency
1170 Broadway
New York, New York 10001
(212) 689-1557

Stock and assignments/Color and black and white

Photo editor: Rana Youner

TRAVEL

LEISURE

SPORTS

When your image means the world...503/389-7662

f/Stop Pictures, Inc.

Post Office Box 359
Springfield, Vermont 05156

(802) 885-5261
Photonet PHO 1034
Telex: 4909963053 (PHO UI)

Member Picture Agency Council of America (PACA)

Specializing in stock and assignment photography of rural America and New England, we cover the country —call or write to find out how.

Photos clockwise from top left:
Seed head at sunset, © 1987 Budd Titlow;
Minnesota farmstead, © 1987 R. Hamilton Smith;
Bobcat, © 1987 Ron Sanford;
West Brookfield, Vermont,
© 1987 George A. Robinson;
Cub Scouts, Portsmouth, New Hampshire,
© 1987 Craig Blouin.

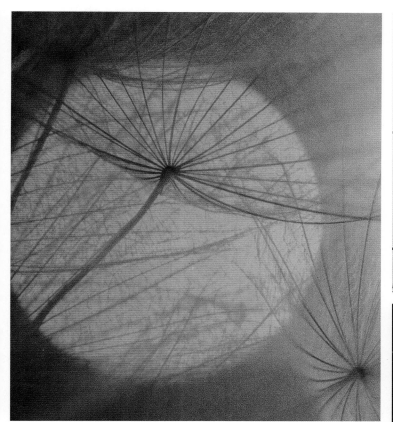

Journalism Services

A Stock and Assignment Agency
118 East Second Street
Lockport, Illinois 60441
(312) 951-0269

Specializing in High Quality Color Images

National Stock Network

8960 Southwest 114 Street
Miami, Florida 33176
(305) 233-1703

Unlimited categories to choose from. Specializing in Lifestyles, Florida, Latin America and The Caribbean.

© 1986 Tom McCarthy

© 1986 Chris Hetzer

© 1986 Red Morgan

© 1986 Stephen Frink

© 1986 Stephen Frink

© 1986 Network Productions

© 1986 Network Productions

© 1986 Tom McCarthy

© 1986 Suzanne Murphy

Color separations by Gold Coast Graphics, Inc.

© 1986 Bill Bachmann

© 1986 Bill Bachmann

© 1986 Network Productions

AMERICAN SHOWCASE

VOLUME 10

THIS BOOK WAS PRINTED BOUND AND SEPARATED BY

DAI NIPPON

SINCE VOLUME 3

DAI NIPPON PRINTING CO., LTD.

New York
Düsseldorf
Hong Kong
San Francisco
Chicago

International Sales Division
1-1, Ichigaya-Kagacho 1-chome, Shinjuku-ku,
Tokyo, 162 Japan. Telephone: 03-266-3307
Telex: J22737 DNPRINT TOKYO

London
Sydney
Jakarta
Singapore
Los Angeles

Ric Noyle
Visual Impact Hawaii

733 Auahi Street
Honolulu, Hawaii 96813
(808) 524-8269
FAX # (808) 533-2088

Paradise!!
The word conjures up many images...Describe one and we can find it for you.

The people, the places, the elements of paradise, the "wish you were here" looks, sundrenched beaches, breathtaking scenics, direct from heaven sunsets, volcanoes and snow covered mountains, as well as black sand beaches. We've got them on file waiting for you.

Taking stock of paradise is our specialty!

We can also create tailor made photographs to your exact specifications to produce images for advertising, corporate, and editorial assignments.

See more of our images in American Showcase '85, '86. Black Book '86, '87.

Member of PACA.

The Photo File

Show Place Square West
550 15th Street
San Francisco, California 94103
(415) 864-0505

This extraordinary collection includes over 800,000 original transparencies, not prints or duplicates.

Many are of such exceptional quality that they're hung as art in major corporations and institutions throughout the country.

Most importantly, The Photo File is a family business, and we provide the most personal service of any stock supplier anywhere. It's professional, courteous and instantaneous— in our office, by phone or by express mail. So you get precisely what you want, precisely when you want it.

So the next time you need fine photography fast, within hours, reach into The Photo File. And make your job a snap.

Our photographers are available for corporate/industrial, advertising and editorial assignments.

Members ASMP and PACA

THE WEST © 1986 GERALD L. FRENCH

LOCATION ©1986 CHRIS SPRINGMANN

TRAVEL ©1986 DAVE BARTRUFF

HIGH PERFORMANCE AIRCRAFT ©1986 GEORGE HALL

STUDIO ©1986 ED YOUNG

SPECIAL EFFECTS ©1986 TOM SKRIVAN

The Photo File

Show Place Square West
550 15th Street
San Francisco, California 94103
(415) 864-0505

Partial client list:

Apple Computer
American President Lines
Blue Shield
Bank of America
Bechtel
Brunswick Technetics
Leo Burnett
Burson Marsteller
Calma (GE)
Chevron
Cole & Webber
D'Arcy
Dancer, Fitzgerald, Sample
Doyle, Dane, Bernbach
Eastman Kodak
East/West Network
Foote, Cone Belding
General Electric
Grey Advertising
Hallmark Cards
Hewlett Packard
Holiday Inns
Hyatt Hotels
Imahara & Keep
Jonson, Pederson, Hinrichs and
    Shakery
Ketchum Communications
Leslie Salt
Landor and Associates
Levi Strauss
McCann Erickson
National Geographic
Pacific Bell
Pinne, Garvin, Herbers & Hock
PGE
PSA
Random House
Raymond, Kendall, Sherwood,
    Otto
Hal Riney & Partners
Shaklee
Sports Illustrated
Standard Oil
TWA
US News/World Report
Warner Bros Studio
Y&R

Our photographers are available
for corporate/industrial,
advertising and editorial
assignments.

Raphaële/Digital Transparencies, Inc.

616 Hawthorne
Houston, Texas 77006
(713) 524-2211

Raphaële/Digital Transparencies, Inc.
616 Hawthorne Houston, Texas 77006 713-524-2211

Showcase 1984 1985 1986   Black Book 1984 1985 1986 1987

Photographer: Jon Bruton   Designer: Joe Gray   Client: Anheuser Busch

Spectrum

A Photography Stockhouse with
over 2,000,000 Original Images

115 Sansome Street, Suite 812
San Francisco, California 94104
(415) 340-9811

A Division of Tom Tracy Photography

427

The Stock Broker

450 Lincoln Street, Suite 110
Denver, Colorado 80203
(303) 698-1734

Quality Images.

Quality Service.

Quality. It's that simple.

First page (clockwise): Allen Birnbach, Don Mattusch, Bruce Benedict, Perry Conway, David Tejada, Perry Conway.

Second page (clockwise): Jerry Downs, Jeff Cook, Kevin Saehlenou, James Cook, Bruce Benedict, James Cook.

Background: Dave Rosenberg.

© The Stock Broker 1987

THE STOCK BROKER

Visual Images West

600 East Baseline Road Suite B-6
Tempe, Arizona 85283
(602) 820-5403

Yep!* We've got your real West. Not a few token sunset/horse shots, but thousands and thousands of pure bred* Western images.

Don't think we're just cowboys and cactus, either. We've rounded up* the true Sun Belt lifestyle from luxury resorts and retirement communities to remote canyons and recreational sports.

You bet we're friendly and helpful, too. Call and we're out-of-the-gate* on a computerized search that puts our World Class* stock in your hands the next day. Put the Best of the West in your next project—Call Visual Images West.

*Call for the Western translation

Photographs ©1986 Paul E. Loven

(602) 820-5403

West Stock, Inc.

157 Yesler, Suite 600
Seattle, Washington 98104
(206) 621-1611
Call Toll Free 800-821-9600

"Existing Photography Of Practically Everything"

WEST STOCK

RICK MORLEY

DAVID STOECKLEIN

DAVID STOECKLEIN

CINDY MCINTYRE

KEITH GUNNAR

STEVE SOLUM

DICK GARVEY

West Stock, Inc.

157 Yesler, Suite 600
Seattle, Washington 98104
(206) 621-1611
Call Toll Free 800-821-9600

"Existing Photography Of Practically Everything"

WEST STOCK

JAY LURIE

DON MASON

PHIL SCHOFIELD

WALTER HODGES

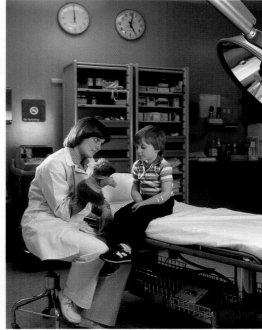

DAVID PERRY

MATT BROWN

DARRELL PETERSON

INDEX

INDEX

continued on next page

INDEX
Photographers

continued from previous page

PHONE LISTINGS & ADDRESSES OF REPRESENTATIVES, VISUAL ARTISTS & SUPPLIERS

Contents

Regions

New York City

Northeast
Connecticut
Delaware
Maine
Maryland
Massachusetts
New Hampshire
New Jersey
New York State
Pennsylvania
Rhode Island
Vermont
Washington, D.C.
West Virginia

Southeast
Alabama
Florida
Georgia
Kentucky
Louisiana
Mississippi
North Carolina
South Carolina
Tennessee
Virginia

Midwest
Illinois
Indiana
Iowa
Kansas
Michigan
Minnesota
Missouri
Nebraska
North Dakota
Ohio
South Dakota
Wisconsin

Southwest
Arizona
Arkansas
New Mexico
Oklahoma
Texas

Rocky Mountain
Colorado
Idaho
Montana
Utah
Wyoming

West Coast
Alaska
British Columbia
California
Hawaii
Nevada
Oregon
Washington

REPRESENTATIVES

NEW YORK CITY

A

Abbey, Ken & Assoc/421 Seventh Ave, New York, NY — 212-758-5259
David Greenberg, (P), Hal Oringer, (P), Ted Pobiner, (P), A J Sandone, (P)

Adams, Ray/22 W 38th St, New York, NY — 212-719-5514

Adler, Phil/35 W 38th St, New York, NY — 212-354-0456
Walter Auster, (P)

Altamore, Bob/237 W 54th St 4th Fl, New York, NY — 212-977-4300
Cailor/Resnick, (P)

American Artists/353 W 53rd St #1W, New York, NY — 212-682-2462
Don Almquist, (I), Joyce Ballantyne, (I), Keith Batcheller, (I), Frank Bolle, (I), Dan Bridy, (I), Rick Brown, (I), Bob Byrd, (I), Rob Cage, (I), Gary Ciccarelli, (I), Hank Connelly, (I), Jim Deigan, (I), Norm Doherty, (I), Alfred D'Ortenzio, (I), Lane DuPont, (I), Russell Farrell, (I), John Freas, (P), George Gaadt, (I), Jackie Geyer, (I), Michael Goodwin, (I), John Hamagami, (I), Karel Havileck, (I), Doug Henry, (I), John Holm, (I), Chris Hopkins, (I), Todd Kat, (I), Richard Kriegler, (I), Diane LaRoja, (I), Kaaren Lewis, (I), Ed Lindlof, (I), Jerry LoFaro, (I), Ron Mahoney, (I), Julia Manya, (I), Mick McGinty, (I), Steve Miller, (I), Richard Nelsen, (I), Jim Owens, (I), George Poladian, (I), Tony Randazzo, (I), Ed Renfro, (I), Paul Rogers, (I), Mike Ruland, (I), Jan Sawka, (I), Todd Schorr, (I), Victor Scocozza, (I), Joe Scrofani, (I), Mary Sherman, (I), Vince Streano, (I), Rudy Tesa, (I), Ron Wolin, (I), Jonathan Wright, (I), Andy Zito, (I), Craig Zuckerman, (I)

Anthony, Ed/133 W 19th St 3rd Fl, New York, NY — 212-924-7770

Anton, Jerry/107 E 38th St #5A, New York, NY — 212-679-4562
Bobbye Cochran, (I), Abe Echevarria, (I), Norman Green, (I), Aaron Rezny, (P), Bob Ziering, (I)

Arnold, Peter Inc/1181 Broadway 4th Fl, New York, NY — 212-840-6928
Fred Bavendam, (P), Bob Evans, (P), Jacques Jangoux, (P), Manfred Kage, (P), Stephen Krasemann, (P), Hans Pfletschinger, (P), David Scharf, (P), Erika Stone, (P), Bruno Zehnder, (P)

The Art Farm/420 Lexington Ave, New York, NY — 212-688-4555
Dick Carroll, (I), Sururi Gumen, (I), Bob Lubbers, (I), Dick Naugler, (I), Linda Pascual, (I), Scott Pike, (I), Bob Walker, (I), Kong Wu, (I), Bill Zdinak, (I)

Artco/24 W 57th St #605, New York, NY — 212-489-8777
Ed Acuna, (I), Peter Caras, (I), Jeff Cornell, (I), Bob Dacey, (I), Beau & Alan Daniels, (I), Ron DeFelice, (I), Christine Fromentine, (I), Enid Hatton, (I), Rick Mcullom, (I), Joseph Milioto, (I), Rick Tulka, (I), Sally Vitsky, (I)

Artists Associates/211 E 51st St #5F, New York, NY — 212-755-1365
Norman Adams, (I), Don Braupigam, (I), Michael Deas, (I), Mark English, (I), Alex Gnidziejko, (I), Robert Heindel, (I), Steve Karchin, (I), Dick Krepel, (I), Skip Liepky, (I), Fred Otnes, (I), Daniel Schwartz, (I)

Arton Associates/216 E 45th St, New York, NY — 212-661-0850
Paul Giovanopoulis, (I), Jacob Knight, (I), Carveth Kramer, (I), Michelle Laporte, (I), Karen Laurence, (I)

Asciutto Art Reps/19 E 48th St 3rd Fl, New York, NY — 212-838-0050
Anthony Accardo, (I), Alex Bloch, (I), Olivia Cole, (I), Kitty Diamantis, (I), Simon Galkin, (I), Donald Gates, (I), Meryl Henderson, (I), Taylor Jones, (I), Paul Lackner, (I), Sally Marshall Larrain, (I), Goran Lindgren, (I), Loreta Lustig, (I), Tod Mason, (I), Sal Murdocca, (I), Jan Pyk, (I), Donna Ward, (I), Fred Winkowski, (I)

Ash, Michael/5 W 19th St, New York, NY — 212-741-0015

Azzara, Louise/131 E 17th St, New York, NY — 212-674-8114

B

Backer, Vic/30 W 26th St, New York, NY — 212-620-0944

Badin, Andy/835 Third Ave 4th Fl, New York, NY — 212-986-8833
Jeff Feinen, (I), Vera, (I), Brad Guice, (P), Robert S Levy, (I), George Tsui, (I)

Bahm, Darwin/6 Jane St, New York, NY — 212-989-7074
Julian Allen, (I), Joan Landis, (I), Rick Meyerowitz, (I), Arno Sternglass, (I), Sketch Pad Studio, (I), John Thompson, (I), Robert Weaver, (I)

Baker, Valerie/152 W 25th St 12th Fl, New York, NY — 212-807-9754

Barboza, Ken Assoc/853 Broadway #1603, New York, NY — 212-505-8635

Barclay, R Francis/5 W 19th St, New York, NY — 212-255-3440

Bauchner, Susan/134 Beaumont St, Brooklyn, NY — 718-648-5345
Jacques Charlas, (P)

Becker, Erica/150 W 55th St, New York, NY — 212-757-7987
Richard Ely, (I), Esther Larson, (I)

Becker, Noel/150 W 55th St, New York, NY — 212-757-8987
Howard Tangye, (P), Sy Vinopoll, (P)

Beilin, Frank/405 E 56th St, New York, NY — 212-751-3074

Benedict, Brinker (Ms)/165 E 89th St, New York, NY — 212-534-1845

Bernstein & Andriulli/60 E 42nd St #505, New York, NY — 212-682-1490
Richard Anderson, (I), Tony Antonios, (I), Per Arnoldi, (I), Graphic Assoc, (I), Garin Baker, (I), Garie Blackwell, (I), Airstream, (I), Melinda Bordelon, (I), Rick Brown, (I), Everett Davidson, (I), Cathy Deeter, (I), Griesbach/Martucci, (I), Victor Gadino, (I), Joe Genova, (I), Marika Hahn, (I), Veronika Hart, (I), Catherine Huerta, (I), Cathy Johnson, (I), David McCall Johnston, (I), Kid Kane, (I), Mary Ann Lasher, (I), Bette Levine, (I), Todd Lockwood, (I), Michael Molkenthin, (I), Bill Morse, (I), Frank Moscati, (P), Simpson/Flint, (P), Craig Nelson, (I), Joe Salina, (I), Marla Shega, (I), Chuck Slack, (I), Peter Stallard, (I), Murray Tinkelman, (I), Clay Turner, (I), Chuck Wilkinson, (I), Paul Wollman, (I), James B. Wood, (P)

Bishop, Lynn/134 E 24th St, New York, NY — 212-254-5737
Irene Stern, (P)

Black Silver & Lord/415 Madison Ave, New York, NY — 212-580-4045
Gloria Baker, (P), Kip Brundage, (P), Norm Clasen, (P), Fred Mullane, (P), Michel Tcherevkoff, (P), Roger Tully, (P)

Black Star/450 Park Ave S, New York, NY — 212-679-3288
John W. Alexanders, (P), Nancy Rica Schiff, (P), Arnold Zann, (P)

Blum, Felice S/79 W 12th St, New York, NY — 212-929-2166

Boghosian, Marty/1123 Broadway #412, New York, NY — 212-242-1251
James Salzano, (P)

Booth, Tom Inc/425 W 23rd St #17A, New York, NY — 212-243-2750
Mike Datoli, (P), Joshua Green, (P), David Hartman, (P), Bob Hiemstra, (I), Patrick Russell, (P), John Stember, (P), Mike VanHorn, (I)

Brackman, Henrietta/415 E 52nd St, New York, NY — 212-753-6483

Brackman, Selma/251 Park Ave S, New York, NY — 212-777-4210

Brennan, Dan/32 E 38th St, New York, NY — 212-889-6555
Tom Biondo, (P), Knut Bry, (P), Francois Deconnick, (P), Renato Grignaschi, (P), Bob Krieger, (P), Michel Momy, (P)

Brindle, Carolyn/203 E 89th St #3D, New York, NY — 212-534-4177

Brody, Sam/230 E 44th St #2F, New York, NY — 212-758-0640
Robert Butler, (P), Linda Clenney, (I), Fred Hilliard, (I), Gary Kufner, (P), Stanford Smilow, (P), Steen Svenson, (P), Rudi Tesa, (P)

Brown Ink Assoc/267 Fifth Ave #1004, New York, NY — 212-686-5576
Deborah Albena, (I), Paulette Bogan, (I), Bob Brown, (I), Lisa Campbell, (I), Virginia Curtin, (I), Darrel Kanyok, (I), Richard Kushner, (I), Kurt Merkel, (I), John Reiner, (I), Christine Roose, (I), Jody Silver, (I), Conrad Weiss, (I)

Brown, Doug/17 E 45th St #1009, New York, NY — 212-980-4971
Abe Seltzer, (P), Andrew Unangst, (P)

Browne, Pema Ltd/185 E 85th St, New York, NY — 212-369-1925
George Angelini, (I), Robert Barrett, (I), Joe Burleson, (I), Peter Catalanotto, (I), Robert C Howe, (I), Ron Jones, (I), Kathy Krantz, (I), David Plourde, (I), Karen Pritchett, (I), John Rush, (I), John Sandford, (I), Alice deKok, (I)

Bruck, J S/157 W 57th St, New York, NY — 212-247-1130
Richard Anderson, (I), Eva Cellini, (I), Joseph Cellini, (I), Michael Dudash, (I), Tom Freeman, (I), Donald Hedlin, (I), Jim Mathewuse, (I), Richard Newton, (I), Victoria Vebell, (I), Gary Watson, (I)

Bruck, Nancy/315 E 69th St #2B, New York, NY — 212-288-6023
Gary Feinstein, (P), Pamela Patrick, (I)

Bruml, Kathy/262 West End Ave, New York, NY — 212-874-5659
Charles Folds, (P), Michael Skott, (P)

Byrnes, Charles/5 E 19th St #303, New York, NY — 212-473-3366
Steve Steigman, (P)

REPRESENTATIVES CONT'D.

Please send us your additions and updates.

C

Cafiano, Charles/140 Fifth Ave, New York, NY — 212-777-7654
  Kenro Izu, (P)
Cahill, Joe/135 E 50th St, New York, NY — 212-751-0529
  Shig Ikeda, (P), Brad Miller, (P), Howard Sochurek, (P)
Camera 5 Inc/6 W 20th St, New York, NY — 212-989-2004
  *Bob Bishop, (P), Peter Calvin, (P), Karin Epstein, (P), Curt
  Gunther, (P), Boyd Hagen, (P), Ralph Lewin, (P), Michael
  Marks, (P), Ralph Pabst, (P), Neal Preston, (P), Ken Regan, (P),
  Bob Sherman, (P), Ben Weaver, (P), Bob Wiley, (P)*
Camp, Woodfin & Assoc/415 Madison Ave, New York, NY — 212-750-1020
  Kip Brundage, (P)
Canter, Theresa/1483 First Ave #5G, New York, NY — 212-734-1352
  Denes Petoe, (P)
Caputo, Elise & Assoc/305 Madison #1805, New York, NY — 212-949-2440
  Ric Cohn, (P), Joe Toto, (P)
Carleo, Teresa/1328 Broadway PH, New York, NY — 212-244-5515
  Steve Chenn, (P)
Carmel/69 Mercer St, New York, NY — 212-925-6216
  Guy Powers, (P)
Carp, Stan/11 E 48th St, New York, NY — 212-759-8880
  Nick Samardge, (P), Allen Vogel, (P)
Casey, Judy/200 W 54th St #3C, New York, NY — 212-757-6144
  *Michael Doster, (I), Torkil Gudnason, (P), Michael O Brien, (P),
  Taolo Roversi, (P)*
Casey, Marge/245 E 63rd St, New York, NY — 212-486-9575
  *Peter Bosch, (P), Thomas Hooper, (P), John Manno, (P), Ken
  Nahoum, (I)*
Cedeno, Lucy/10 W 18th St, New York, NY — 212-255-9212
Celnick, Manny/36 E 12th St, New York, NY — 212-473-4455
  Edward Selnick, (P)
Chie/15 E 11th St #2M, New York, NY — 212-243-2353
Chislovsky, Carol/853 Broadway, New York, NY — 212-677-9100
  *Randal Birkey, (I), Alex Bostic, (I), Russell Cobane, (I), Bob
  Cooper, (I), Ignacio Gomez, (I), Ken Graning, (I), John Gray, (I),
  Michael Haynes, (I), Hubert, (I), Tim Herman, (I), William
  Hosner, (I), Jim Hunt, (I), Joe Lapinski, (I), Felix Marich, (I), Joe
  Ovies, (I), Vincent Petragnani, (I), Chuck Schmidt, (I), Sandra
  Shap, (I), Danny Smythe, (I), Randy South, (I), Nighthawk
  Studios, (I), Bob Thomas, (I)*
Cohen, Bruce/54 W 16th St, New York, NY — 212-620-7839
Collignon, Daniele/200 W 15th St, New York, NY — 212-243-4209
  *Bob Aiese, (I), Dan Cosgrove, (I), Bill Frampton, (I), David
  Gambale, (I), Mel Greifinger, (I), Richard Hughes, (P), Mike
  Lester, (I), Dennis Mukai, (I), Fran Oelbaum, (I), Cindy Pardy,
  (I), Alex Tiani, (I), Vicki Yiannias, (I), Varlet-Martinelli, (I)*
Conroy, Chris/124 E 24th St, New York, NY — 212-598-9766
  Howard Alt, (I), David Kennedy, (P)
Crawford, Janice/340 E 93rd St #9I, New York, NY — 212-722-4964
Creative Freelancers/62 W 45th St, New York, NY — 212-398-9540
  *Harold Brooks, (I), Howard Darden, (I), Claudia Fouse, (I),
  Rosanne Percivalle, (I)*
Creative Talent/62 LeRoy St, New York, NY — 212-243-7869
  Marshall Cetlin, (I), Alan Henderson, (I), Guy Smalley, (I)
Crecco, Michael/342 Madison Ave, New York, NY — 212-682-5663
Cullom, Ellen/55 E 9th St, New York, NY — 212-777-1749

D

Dagrosa, Terry/374 Eighth Ave 2nd Fl, New York, NY — 212-645-4082
  Rod Cook, (P)
Davies, Nora/370 E 76th St, New York, NY — 212-628-6657
DeBacker, Clo/29 E 19th St, New York, NY — 212-420-1276
  Bob Kiss, (P)
Dedell, Jacqueline/58 W 15th St, New York, NY — 212-741-2539
  *Teresa Fasolino, (I), Chermayeff and Geismar, (I), Ivan Powell,
  (I), Barry Root, (I), Richard Williams, (I), Henry Wolf, (P)*
Des Verges, Diana/73 Fifth Ave, New York, NY — 212-691-8674
Deverin, Daniele/226 E 53rd St, New York, NY — 212-755-4945
  *Paul Blakey, (I), Greg Couch, (I), Mort Drucker, (I), David
  Johnson, (I), Lazlo Kubinyi, (I), Charles Shields, (I), Jeff Smith,
  (I), Don Weller, (I)*
DeVito, Kitty/43 E 30th St 14th Fl, New York, NY — 212-889-9670
  Bart DeVito, (P)

DeVlieger, Mary/2109 Broadway, New York, NY — 212-903-4321
DeWan, Michael/250 Cabrini Blvd #2E, New York, NY — 212-927-9458
  Nancy Bundt, (P), Don Sparks, (P)
Dewey, Frank & Assoc/420 Lexington Ave, New York, NY — 212-986-1249
Dickinson, Alexis/175 Fifth Ave #1112, New York, NY — 212-473-8020
  *Jim Allen, (P), Robert Cohen, (P), Richard Dunkley, (P), Laura
  Ferguson, (S), Gregory King, (I), Jonathon Nix, (I), Eleanor
  Thompson, (P)*
DiMartino, Joseph/200 E 58th St, New York, NY — 212-935-9522
  *Mark Blanton, (I), Sid Evans, (I), Don Rogers, (I),
  Graphicsgroup, (I), Whistl'n-Dixie, (I)*
Dorman, Paul/419 E 57th St, New York, NY — 212-826-6737
  Studio DGM, (P)
Drexler, Sharon/451 Westminster Rd, Brooklyn, NY — 718-284-4779
  Les Katz, (I)
Droske, Diane/300 E 40th St #19R, New York, NY — 212-867-2383
  Tom Hollyman, (P), Nancy LeVine, (P), Tobey Sanford, (P)
DuBane, J J/130 W 17th St, New York, NY — 212-696-0274

E

Eagles, Betsy/130 W 57th St, New York, NY — 212-582-1501
  Ron Nicolaysen, (P), Lance Steadler, (P)
Edlitz, Ann/230 E 79th St #14F, New York, NY — 212-744-7945
Ellis, Mirjana/176 Westminster Rd, Brooklyn, NY — 718-282-6449
  Ray Ellis, (P)
Eng, Barbara/110 E 23rd St, New York, NY — 212-254-8334
Englert, Tim/305 W 84th St #313, New York, NY — 212-496-2074
Everly, Bart/156 Fifth Ave #327, New York, NY — 212-924-1510
Eyre, Susan/292 Marlboro Rd, Brooklyn, NY — 718-282-5034
  Robert Phillips, (P)

F

Feldman, Robert/358 W 18th St, New York, NY — 212-741-7254
  Alen MacWeeney, (P), Terry Niefield, (P)
Fischer, Bob/135 E 54th St, New York, NY — 212-755-2131
  James Moore, (P)
Fishback, Lee/350 W 21st St, New York, NY — 212-929-2951
Flesher, Lex/7 E 14th St #903, New York, NY — 212-255-4863
Folickman, Gail/399 E 72nd St, New York, NY — 212-879-1508
Foster, Peter/870 UN Plaza, New York, NY — 212-593-0793
  Charles Tracey, (P)
Friess, Susan/36 W 20th St, New York, NY — 212-675-3021
  Richard Goldman, (P)
Friscia, Salmon/20 W 10th St, New York, NY — 212-228-4134
Furst, Franz/420 E 55th St, New York, NY — 212-753-3148
  Greg Pease, (P)

G

Gargagliano, Tony/216 E 45th St, New York, NY — 212-661-0850
Gaynin, Gail/241 Central Park West, New York, NY — 212-255-3040
  Terry Clough, (P)
Gebbia, Doreen/156 Fifth Ave, New York, NY — 212-807-0588
Gelb, Elizabeth/856 West End Ave, New York, NY — 212-222-1215
Geng, Maud/, New York, NY — 212-513-1557
  Caroline Alterio, (I), Peter Barger, (I), Vicki Smith, (I)
Ginsberg, Michael/339 E 58th St, New York, NY — 212-628-2379
Giraldi, Tina/54 W 39th St, New York, NY — 212-840-8225
Godfrey, Dennis/95 Horatio St #203, New York, NY — 212-807-0840
  *Jeffrey Adams, (I), Daryl Cagle, (I), Joel Nakamura, (I), Karen
  Payne, (I), Morgan Pickard, (I), Wendy Popp, (I), Greg
  Ragland, (I), Lane Smith, (I)*
Goldman, David/18 E 17th St, New York, NY — 212-807-6627
  *Norm Bendell, (I), Jay Brenner, (P), Jim Kingston, (I), Joe
  Marvullo, (P)*
Goldmann, Howard/309 Fifth Ave #506, New York, NY — 212-481-0911
Goldstein, Michael L/107 W 69th St, New York, NY — 212-874-6933
  Carla Bauer, (I), Fred Schulze, (P)
Gomberg, Susan/145 E 22nd St, New York, NY — 212-473-8747
  *Julius Ciss, (I), Michael Conway, (I), Robert Dale, (I), Jeff Faria,
  (I), Richard Fried, (P), Allen Garns, (I), Ron Lieberman, (I),
  Janeart Limited, (P), Dan McGowan, (I), Enzo Messi & Urs
  Schmidt, (I), Kathy S Schorr, (I), James Tughan, (I)*
Goodman, Barbara L/50 W 34th St, New York, NY — 212-594-9209
Goodwin, Phyllis A/10 E 81st St, New York, NY — 212-570-6021
  Carl Furuta, (P), Cosimo, (P), Karen Leeds, (P)

REPRESENTATIVES CONT'D.

Please send us your additions and updates.

Ron Barry, (I), Linda Benson, (I), Judith Cheng, (I), Bob Clarke, (I), Keita Colton, (I), James Dietz, (I), Glenn Harrington, (I), Robert Hunt, (I), Nenad Jakesevic, (I), Jackie Jasper, (I), Sonja Lamut, (I), April Lawton, (I), Andrew Nitzberg, (I), Sharleen Pederson, (I), Jas Szygiel, (I), Jackie Vaux, (I)

Gordon, Fran/1654 E 13th St #5A, Brooklyn, NY	718-339-4277
Gotham Art Agency/25 Tudor Pl, New York, NY	212-286-9786
Green, Anita/160 E 26th St, New York, NY	212-674-4788

Alan Dolgins, (P), Stuart Peltz, (P)

Greenblatt, Eunice N/370 E 76th St, New York, NY	212-772-1776

Bob Brody, (P)

Grien, Anita/155 E 38th St, New York, NY	212-697-6170

Dolores Bego, (I), Fanny M Berry, (I), Hal Just, (I), Jerry McDaniel, (I), Don Morrison, (I), Marina Neyman-Levikova, (I), Alan Reingold, (I), Ellen Rixford, (I), Bill Wilkinson, (I), Mangal, (I)

Griffith, Valerie/10 Sheridan Square, New York, NY	212-675-2089
Gordon, Barbara Assoc/165 E 32nd St, New York, NY	212-686-3514
Groves, Michael/220 E 57th St #18D, New York, NY	212-532-2074

Ulf Skogsbergh, (P)

H

Hainy, Barry/82 Jane St, New York, NY	212-929-4313
Hajjar, Rene/220 Park Ave S, New York, NY	212-777-5361

Chris Jones, (P)

Hankins + Tegenborg Ltd/60 E 42nd St #428, New York, NY	212-867-8092

Peter Attard, (I), Ralph Brillhart, (I), George Bush, (I), Jamie Cavaliere, (I), John Cernak, (I), Jim Cherry, (I), Mac Conner, (I), David Cook, (I), John Dawson, (I), Guy Deel, (I), Ron DiScensa, (I), John Dismukes, (I), John Ennis, (I), George Fernandez, (I), David Gaadt, (I), Sergio Giovine, (I), James Griffin, (I), Tom Hall, (I), Ray Harvey, (I), Edwin Herder, (I), Michael Herring, (I), Kevin Hulsey, (I), Miro, (I), Aleta Jenks, (I), Rick Johnson, (I), Uldis Klavins, (I), Richard Lauter, (I), Cliff Miller, (I), Wendell Minor, (I), Greg Olanoff, (I), Walter Rane, (I), Robert Sabin, (I), Harry Schaare, (I), Bill Schmidt, (I), Dan Sneberger, (I), Frank Steiner, (I), Ludmilla Strugatsky, (I), Robert Travers, (I), Bob Trondsen, (I), Victor Valla, (I), Jeff Walker, (I)

Hansen, Wendy/126 Madison Ave, New York, NY	212-684-7139

Minh, (P)

Hare, Fran/126 W 23rd St, New York, NY	212-794-0043

Peter B Kaplan, (P)

Harmon, Rod/254 W 51st St, New York, NY	212-245-8935

Brian Hennessey, (P), Al Rubin, (P), Michael Sabanosh, (I), David Spagnolo, (P)

Henry, John/237 E 31st St, New York, NY	212-686-6883

Gregory Cannon, (P), Rosemary Howard, (P)

Herron, Pat/829 Park Ave, New York, NY	212-753-0462

Larry Dale Gordon, (P), Malcolm Kirk, (P)

Heyl, Fran/230 Park Ave #2525, New York, NY	212-581-6470

Phillip Harrington, (P)

Hoeye, Michael/120 W 70th St, New York, NY	212-362-9546

Leland Neff, (P), Lilo Raymond, (P), Richie Williamson, (P)

Holmberg, Irmeli/280 Madison Ave #1402, New York, NY	212-775-1810

Vincent Amicosante, (I), Rainbow Grinder, (I), Walter Gurbo, (I), Mitchell Hyatt, (I), Sharmen Liao, (I), John Martinez, (I), Barbara Maslen, (I), Lu Matthews, (I), Bill Nelson, (I), Debbie Pinkney, (I), Bob Radigan, (I), Bill Rieser, (I), Cameron Wasson, (I), Nicholas Wilton, (I)

Holt, Rita/280 Madison Ave, New York, NY	212-683-2002
Hovde, Nob/829 Park Ave, New York, NY	212-753-0462

Malcolm Kirk, (P), J Frederick Smith, (P)

Hurewitz, Gary/5 E 19th St #303, New York, NY	212-473-3366

Howard Berman, (P), Steve Bronstein, (P), Steve Steigman, (P)

Husak, John/568 Broadway #405, New York, NY	212-226-8110

Frank Marchese, (G), William Sloan, (I)

IJ

Iglesias, Jose/1123 Broadway #714, New York, NY	212-929-7962

Stan Fellerman, (P), Sven Lindman, (I), Akio Matsuyoshi, (I), George Ruentiz, (I)

Jacobsen, Vi/333 Park Ave S 2nd Fl, New York, NY	212-677-3770
Jedell, Joan/370 E 76th St, New York, NY	212-861-7861
Johnson, Bud & Evelyne/201 E 28th St, New York, NY	212-532-0928

Kathy Allert, (I), Betty de Araujo, (I), Irene Astrahan, (I), Rowan Barnes-Murphy, (I), Cathy Beylon, (I), Lisa Bonforte, (I), Carolyn Bracken, (I), Jane Chambliss-Rigie, (I), Roberta Collier, (I), Frank Daniel, (I), Larry Daste, (I), Ted Enik, (I), Carolyn Ewing, (I), Bill Finewood, (I), Robert Gunn, (I), Yukio Kondo, (I), Mei-ku-Huang, (I), Tom LaPadula, (I), Bruce Lemerise, (I), Turi MacCombie, (I), Dee Malan, (I), Brookie Maxwell, (I), Darcy May, (I), Eileen McKeating, (I), Steven Petruccio, (I), Mitch Rigie, (I), Christopher Santoro, (I), Stan Skardinski, (I), Barbara Steadman, (I), Pat Stewart, (I), Tom Tierney, (I), Tricia Zimic, (I)

Joseph Mindlin & Mulvey/1457 Broadway #1001, New York, NY	212-840-8223

Joseph Dawes, (I), John Dyess, (I), Paula Goodman, (I), Mark Hannon, (I), Tad Krumeich, (I), Mike McCreanor, (I), Justin Novak, (I), Frederick Porter, (I), Tom Powers, (I), Herb Reed, (I), John Rice, (I), Sally Scheadler, (I)

K

Kahn, Harvey Assoc Inc/50 E 50th St, New York, NY	212-752-8490

Alan Cober, (I), Bernard Fuchs, (I), Nicholas Gaetano, (I), Gerald Gersten, (I), Wilson McLean, (I), Bob Peak, (I), Isadore Seltzer, (I), Norman Walker, (I)

Kane, Barney & Friends/18 E 16th St 2nd Fl, New York, NY	212-206-0322

Margaret Brown, (P), Jack DeGraffenried, (I), Joe Denaro, (I), Michael Farina, (I), Nat Giorgio, (I), William Harrison, (I), Steve Hochman, (I), Steven Keyes, (I), Harvey Kurtzman, (I), Bob Lapsley, (I), Peter Lloyd, (I), Ted Lodigensky, (I), Rich Mahon, (I), Robert Melendez, (I), Sue Rother, (I), Gary Ruddell, (I), Doug Rosenthal, (I), Joseph Sellars, (I), Bill Thomson, (I), Glen Tunstull, (I), Larry Winborg, (I), Jenny Yip, (I)

Kane, Odette/119 W 23rd St, New York, NY	212-807-8730

Charles Seesselberg, (P)

Kaplan, Holly/35 W 36th St, New York, NY	212-563-2730

Bruno, (P)

Kaufman, Hillery/206 Lincoln Pl, Brooklyn, NY	718-230-3348
Kauss, Jean-Gabriel/122 E 42nd St #3103, New York, NY	212-370-4300

Guy Fery, (I), Jesse Gerstein, (P), Francois Halard, (P), Jacques Malignon, (P), Mike Noome, (I)

Keating, Peggy/30 Horatio St, New York, NY	212-691-4654

Bob Parker, (I), Frank Paulin, (I), Suzanne Peck, (I), Fritz Varady, (I), Carol Vennell, (I), Norma Welliver, (I)

Keiserman/Kandel/108 E 31st St, New York, NY	212-686-1042

Nicholas Baratta, (P), Vincent Ricucci, (P), Steve Young, (P)

Kenney, John Assoc/251 W 30th St 16th Fl, New York, NY	212-279-1515

Gary Hanlon, (P), Elizabeth Heyert, (P), David Stetson, (P)

Kestner, V G/427 E 77th St #4C, New York, NY	212-535-4144
Kim/209 E 25th St, New York, NY	212-679-5628
Kimche, Tania/470 W 23rd St, New York, NY	212-242-6367

Richard Goldberg, (I), Rafal Olbinski, (I), Miriam Schottland, (I), E T Steadman, (I)

Kirchoff-Wohlberg Inc/866 UN Plaza #4014, New York, NY	212-644-2020

Angela Adams, (I), Bob Barner, (I), Esther Baron, (I), Bradley Clark, (I), Brian Cody, (I), Gwen Connelly, (I), Floyd Cooper, (I), Betsy Day, (I), Lois Ehlert, (I), Al Fiorentino, (I), Frank Fretz, (I), Jon Friedman, (I), Jeremy Guitar, (I), Konrad Hack, (I), Ron Himler, (I), Rosekrans Hoffman, (I), Kathleen Howell, (I), Susan Jaekel, (I), Chris Kalle, (I), Mark Kelley, (I), Christa Kieffer, (I), Dora Leder, (I), Tom Leonard, (I), Susan Lexa, (I), Don Madden, (I), Jane McCreary, (I), Lyle Miller, (I), Carol Nicklaus, (I), Sharon O'Neil, (I), Ed Parker, (I), Jim Pearson, (I), Charles Robinson, (I), Bronwen Ross, (I), Arvis Stewart, (I), Pat Traub, (I), Lou Vaccaro, (I), Joe Veno, (I), John Wallner, (I), Alexandra Wallner, (I), Arieh Zeldich, (I)

Klein, Leslie D/104 E 40th St, New York, NY	212-490-1460

Eric Meola, (P), Digital Productions, (P)

Klimt, Bill & Maurine/15 W 72nd St, New York, NY	212-799-2231

Wil Cormier, (I), Jamie DeJesus, (I), Jacques Devaud, (I), Doug Gray, (I), Paul Henry, (I), Steven Huston, (I), Ken Joudrey, (I), Mike Kane, (I), Pinturov, (I), Frank Morris, (I), Alan Neider, (I), Gary Penca, (I), Bill Purdom, (I), Mark Skolsky, (I)

Kopel, Shelly & Assoc/51 E 42nd St #716, New York, NY	212-986-3282

Bliss Brothers, (I), Penny Carter, (I), Tom Christopher, (I), Marcus Hamilton, (I), Al Hering, (I), Jim Manos, (I), Meryl Rosner, (I)

REPRESENTATIVES CONT'D.

Please send us your additions and updates.

Korman, Alison/240 E 76th St, New York, NY	212-686-0525
David Bishop, (P), Susan Kravis, (I)	
Kramer, Joan & Assoc/720 Fifth Ave, New York, NY	212-567-5545
David Cornwell, (P), Clark Dunbar, (P), John Lawlor, (P),	
James McLoughlin, (P), Frank Moscati, (P), Jeff Perkell, (P),	
John Russell, (P), Glen Steiner, (P), Simpson/Flint, (P), Ken	
Whitmore, (P), Edward Young, (P)	
Kreis, Ursula G/63 Adrian Ave, Bronx, NY	212-562-8931
Stephen Green-Armytage, (P), John T. Hill, (P), Bruce	
Pendleton, (P), Jed Share, (P)	
Krongard, Paula/210 Fifth Ave #301, New York, NY	212-683-1020
Bill White, (P)	

L

LGI/241 W 36th St 7th Fl, New York, NY	212-736-4602
Lada, Joe/330 E 19th St, New York, NY	212-254-0253
George Hausman, (P)	
Lafayette-Nelson & Assoc/64 W 15th St, New York, NY	212-989-7059
Lamont, Mary/200 W 20th St, New York, NY	212-242-1087
Jim Marchese, (P)	
Lander/Osborn/333 E 30th St, New York, NY	212-679-1358
Francois Cloteaux, (I), Catherine Deeter, (I), Phil Franke, (I),	
Mel Furukawa, (I), Cathy Culp Heck, (I), Saul Lambert, (I),	
Frank Riley, (I), Barron Storey, (I)	
Lane Talent Inc/104 Fifth Ave, New York, NY	212-861-7225
Larkin, Mary/308 E 59th St, New York, NY	212-308-7744
Lynn St John, (P)	
Lavaty, Frank & Jeff/50 E 50th St #5, New York, NY	212-355-0910
John Berkey, (I), Jim Butcher, (I), Don Daily, (I), Bernard	
D'Andrea, (I), Roland DesCombes, (I), Christine Duke, (I),	
Bruce Emmett, (I), Gervasio Gallardo, (I), Tim Hildebrandt, (I),	
Martin Hoffman, (I), Stan Hunter, (I), Chet Jezierski, (I), Mort	
Kunstler, (I), Paul Lehr, (I), Lemuel Line, (I), Robert LoGrippo,	
(I), Darrel Millsap, (I), Carlos Ochagavia, (I)	
Lee, Alan/33 E 22nd St #5D, New York, NY	212-673-2484
Werner Kappes, (I), Peter Vaeth, (P)	
Leff, Jerry/420 Lexington Ave #2738, New York, NY	212-697-8525
Franco Accornero, (I), Ken Barr, (I), Tom Beecham, (I),	
Semyon Bilmes, (I), Mike Bryan, (I), Ron DiCianni, (I), Norm	
Eastman, (I), Bryant Eastman, (I), Charles Gehm, (I), Penelope	
Gottlieb, (I), Gary Lang, (I), Ron Lesser, (I), Dennis Magdich,	
(I), Frank Marciuliano, (I), Michael Nicastre, (I), Rosanne	
Nicotra, (I), Rick Ormond, (I), John Parsons, (I), Dazzeland	
Studios, (I), James Woodend, (I)	
Legrand, Jean Yves & Assoc/41 W 84th St #4, New York, NY	212-724-5981
Jim Cherry, (I), Holly Hollington, (I), Barry McKinley, (P), Peter	
Sato, (I), Jack Ward, (P)	
Leone, Mindy/381 Park Ave S #710, New York, NY	212-696-5674
Bill Kouirinis, (P)	
Leonian, Edith/220 E 23rd St, New York, NY	212-989-7670
Philip Leonian, (P)	
Lerman, Gary/113 E 31st St #4D, New York, NY	212-683-5777
Paul Barton, (P), John Bechtold, (P), Jan Cobb, (P)	
Levitt, Lee/43 W 16th St #16, New York, NY	212-206-7257
Levy, Leila/4523 Broadway #7G, New York, NY	212-942-8185
Yoav Levy, (P)	
Lewin, Betsy/152 Willoughby Ave, Brooklyn, NY	718-622-3882
Ted Lewin, (I)	
Lindgren, Pat/41 Union Sq W #1228, New York, NY	212-929-5590
Barbara Banthein, (I), Tom Bloom, (I), Regan Dunnick, (I),	
Charles White III, (I), Audrey Lavine, (I)	
Locke, John Studios Inc/15 E 76th St, New York, NY	212-288-8010
John Cayea, (I), John Clift, (I), Oscar DeMejo, (I), Jean-Pierre	
Desclozeaux, (I), Blair Drawson, (I), James Endicott, (I),	
Richard Erdoes, (I), Jean Michel Folon, (I), Michael Foreman,	
(I), Andre Francois, (I), George Giusti, (I), Edward Gorey, (I),	
Peter Lippman, (I), Sam Maitin, (I), Richard Oden, (I), William	
Bryan Park, (I), Colette Portal, (I), Fernando Puigrosado, (I),	
Hans-Georg Rauch, (I), Ronald Searle, (I), Tim, (I), Roland	
Topor, (I)	
Longobardi, Gerard/5 W 19th St, New York, NY	212-255-3440
Loshe, Diane/10 W 18th St, New York, NY	212-691-9920
Lott, Peter & George/60 E 42nd St #411, New York, NY	212-687-4185

Juan Barberis, (I), Ted Chambers, (I), Tony Cove, (I), Jim	
Dickerson, (I), David Halpern, (I), Ed Kurtzman, (I), Marie	
Peppard, (I), Steen Svenson, (P)	
Lynch, Alan/635 Madison Ave 6th Fl, New York, NY	212-688-1832

M

Madris, Stephen/445 E 77th St, New York, NY	212-744-6668
Gary Perweiler, (P)	
Manasse, Michele/1960 Broadway #2E, New York, NY	212-873-3797
Suzanne H Sullivan, (I)	
Mandell, Ilene/61 E 86th St, New York, NY	212-860-3148
Mann, Ken/20 W 46th St, New York, NY	212-944-2853
Rebecca Blake, (P), Hashi, (P), Dicran Studio, (P)	
Marchesano, Frank/35 W 36th St, New York, NY	212-563-2730
Marek & Assoc Inc/160 Fifth Ave, New York, NY	212-924-6760
Marie, Diana Rose/38 E 19th St, New York, NY	212-477-5107
Marino, Frank/35 W 36th St, New York, NY	212-563-2730
Bruno Benvenuti, (P)	
Mariucci, Marie A/32 W 39th St, New York, NY	212-944-9590
Mars/Barracca/156 Fifth Ave #1222, New York, NY	212-645-6772
Andrea Baruffi, (I), Robert Evans, (I), Rick Fischer, (I), Yan	
Nascimbene, (I), Larry Noble, (I), Donna Ruff, (I), JC Suares, (I)	
Marshall, Mel/40 W 77th St, New York, NY	212-877-3921
Mason, Kathy/101 W 18th St 4th Fl, New York, NY	212-675-3809
Don Mason, (P)	
Mathias, Cindy/7 E 14th St, New York, NY	212-741-3191
Vittorio Sartor, (I)	
Mattelson, Judy	212-684-2974
Karen Kluglein, (I), Marvin Mattelson, (I), Gary Viskupic, (I)	
Mautner, Jane/85 Fourth Ave, New York, NY	212-777-9024
Kozlowski, (P)	
Mayo, Vicki/225 E 31st St, New York, NY	212-686-1690
Harold Krieger, (P)	
McVey, Meg/54 W 84th St # 2F, New York, NY	212-362-3739
Meixler, Harriet/36 W 37th St, New York, NY	212-868-0078
Susanne Buckler, (P)	
Mendelsohn, Richard/353 W 53rd St #1W, New York, NY	212-682-2462
Mendola, Joseph/420 Lexington Ave #2911, New York, NY	212-986-5680
Paul Alexander, (I), Robert Berran, (I), Dan Brown, (I), Jim	
Campbell, (I), Carl Cassler, (I), Joe Csatari, (I), Kenneth Dewey,	
(I), Jim Dye, (I), John Eggert, (I), Jon Ellis, (I), Peter Fiore, (I),	
Antonio Gabriele, (I), Tom Gala, (I), Hector Garrido, (I), Mark	
Gerber, (I), Ted Giavis, (I), Dale Gustafson, (I), Chuck Hamrick,	
(I), Attila Hejja, (I), Dave Henderson, (I), Mitchell Hooks, (I),	
Joel Iskowitz, (I), Bob Jones, (I), Dave Kilmer, (I), Michael	
Koester, (I), Richard Leech, (I), Dennis Luzak, (I), Dennis Lyall,	
(I), Jeffrey Mangiat, (I), Goeffrey McCormack, (I), Ann Meisel,	
(I), Roger Metcalf, (I), Ted Michner, (I), Mike Mikos, (I),	
Jonathon Milne, (I), Barry Morgen, (I), Wally Neibart, (I), Chris	
Notarile, (I), Phil Roberts, (I), Rob Sauber, (I), David	
Schleinkofer, (I), Mark Schuler, (I), Mike Smollin, (I), Kip	
Soldwedel, (I), John Solie, (I), George Sottung, (I), Joel	
Spector, (I), Cliff Spohn, (I), Paul Tankersley, (I), Jeffrey	
Terreson, (I), Thierry Thompson, (I), Mark Watts, (I), Alan	
Welkis, (I), Ben Wohlberg, (I)	
Metz, Bernard/43 E 19th St, New York, NY	212-254-4996
Michalski, Ben/118 E 28th St, New York, NY	212-683-4025
Miller, Susan/1641 Third Ave #29A, New York, NY	212-905-8400
Mintz, Les/111 Wooster St #Ph C, New York, NY	212-925-0491
Bernard Bonhomme, (I), Robert Burger, (I), Hovik Dilakian, (I),	
Amy Hill, (I), George Masi, (I), Kirsten Soderlind, (I), Kurt Vargo,	
(I), Dennis Ziemienski, (I)	
Monomakhoff, Kathleen/304 E 20th St #7B, New York, NY	212-807-7703
Moretz, Eileen P/141 Wooster St, New York, NY	212-254-3766
Charles Moretz, (P), Jeff Morgan, (P)	
Morgan, Vicki Assoc/194 Third Ave, New York, NY	212-475-0440
John Alcorn, (I), Stephen Alcorn, (I), Willardson + Assoc, (I),	
Ray Cruz, (I), Sabina Fascione, (I), Vivienne Flesher, (I), Kathy	
& Joe Heiner, (I), Tim Lewis, (I), Emanuel Schongut, (I), Nancy	
Stahl, (I), Bruce Wolfe, (I), Wendy Wray, (I), Brian Zick, (I)	
Morse, Lauren/78 Fifth Ave, New York, NY	212-807-1551
Alan Zenreich, (P)	
Mosel, Sue/310 E 46th St, New York, NY	212-599-1806

REPRESENTATIVES CONT'D.

Please send us your additions and updates.

Gerard Gentil, (P), Stan Shaffer, (P)
Moskowitz, Marion/342 Madison Ave #469, New York, NY   212-719-9879
    Diane Teske Harris, (I), Arnie Levin, (I), Geoffrey Moss, (I)
Moss, Eileen/333 E 49th St #3J, New York, NY   212-980-8061
    Bill Cigliano, (I), Tom Curry, (I), Mike Davis, (I), Dennis Gottlieb,
    (I), Robert Pizzo, (I), Scott Pollack, (I)
Moss, Susan/29 W 38th St, New York, NY   212-354-8024
    Louis Mervar, (P)
Muth, John/37 W 26th St, New York, NY   212-532-3479
    Pat Hill, (P)

NO

Napaer, Michele/349 W Broadway, New York, NY   212-219-0325
    Michael Abramson, (P)
Neail, Pamela R Assoc/27 Bleecker St, New York, NY   212-673-1600
    Sean Daly, (I), Dennis DiVincenzo, (I), Barbara Goodrich, (I),
    Thea Kliros, (I), Tony Mascio, (I), Cary McKiver, (I), Ryuji Otani,
    (I), Brenda Pepper, (I), Janet Recchia, (I), Linda Richards, (I),
    Gail Severance, (I), Alex Vosk, (I), Pat Zadnik, (I)
Newborn, Milton/135 E 54th St, New York, NY   212-421-0050
    Braldt Bralds, (I), Carol Gillot, (I), Robert Giusti, (I), Dick Hess,
    (I), Mark Hess, (I), Victor Juhasz, (I), Simms Taback, (I), David
    Wilcox, (I)
O'Rourke-Page Assoc/219 E 69th St #11G, New York, NY   212-772-0346
    Jonathan Exley, (P), Honolulu Crtv Grp, (P), Sam Haskins, (P),
    Robert Kligge, (P), Rob Van Petten, (P), Lincoln Potter, (P), Jim
    Raycroft, (P), Smith/Garner, (P), Eric Schweikardt, (P), William
    Sumner, (P), John Thornton, (P), John Zimmerman, (P)
Oye, Eva/307 E 44th St, New York, NY   212-286-9103

P

Palmer-Smith, Glenn Assoc/160 Fifth Ave, New York, NY   212-807-1855
    James Moore, (P), Charles Nesbitt, (P)
Pelaez, Jose/568 Broadway #103, New York, NY   212-925-5149
Penny & Stermer Group/48 W 21st St 9th Fl, New York, NY   212-243-4412
    Bob Alcorn, (I), Manos Angelakis, (I), Ron Becker, (I), Jane
    Clark, (I), Julian Graddon, (I), Rich Grote, (I), Michael
    Hostovich, (I), Michael Kanarek, (I), Andy Lackow, (I), Julia
    Noonan, (I), Deborah Bazzel Pogue, (I), Steve Shub, (I), Gary
    Smith, (I), Page Wood, (I)
Peretti, Linda/420 Lexington Ave, New York, NY   212-687-7392
    Ken Tannenbaum, (P)
Peters, Barbara/One Fifth Ave, New York, NY   212-777-6384
    Jacques Dirand, (P), Lizzie Himmel, (P)
Petersen, Victoria/16 W 71st St, New York, NY   212-799-7021
Phyllis/38 E 19th St 8th Fl, New York, NY   212-475-3798
    John Weir, (P)
Powers, Elizabeth/1414 Ave of Americas, New York, NY   212-832-2343
    DiFranza Williamson, (P)
Pritchett, Tom/330 W 4th St, New York, NY   212-688-1080
    Steve Durke, (I), George Parrish Jr, (I), George Kanelous, (I),
    Mike Robins, (I), Terry Ryan, (I)
Puhalski, Ron & Assoc/156 Fifth Ave #417, New York, NY   212-242-2860
    Gregory Voth, (I)
Pushpin Assoc/215 Park Ave S, New York, NY   212-674-8080
    Istvan Banyai, (I), Lou Beach, (I), Christopher Blumrich, (I),
    Seymour Chwast, (I), Bob Crawford, (I), Jose Cruz, (I),
    Elizabeth Koda-Callan, (I), Richard McNeel, (I), Sarah Moon,
    (P), Roy Pendleton, (I), Stanislaw Zagorski, (I)

QR

Quercia, Mat/78 Irving Pl, New York, NY   212-477-4491
Rapp, Gerald & Cullen Inc/108 E 35th St #1C, New York, NY   212-889-3337
    Michael Brown, (I), Lon Busch, (I), Ken Dallison, (I), Jack
    Davis, (I), Bill Devlin, (I), Bob Deschamps, (I), Ray Domingo, (I),
    Ginnie Hoffman, (I), Lionel Kalish, (I), Sharon Knettell, (I), Lee
    Lorenz, (I), Allan Mardon, (I), Elwyn Mehlman, (I), Marie
    Michal, (I), Alex Murawski, (I), Lou Myers, (I), Gary Overacre,
    (I), Jerry Pinkney, (I), Charles Santori, (I), Bob Tanenbaum, (I),
    Michael Witte, (I), Barry Zaid, (I)
Ray, Marlys/350 Central Pk W, New York, NY   212-222-7680
    Bill Ray, (P)
Reese, Kay Assoc/175 Fifth Ave #1304, New York, NY   212-598-4848
    Jonathan Atkin, (P), Lee Balterman, (P), Gerry Cranham, (P),
    Ashvin Gatha, (P), Lowell Georgia, (P), Peter Gullers, (P), Arno

Hammacher, (P), Jay Leviton, (P), George Long, (P), George
Love, (P), Jon Love, (P), Lynn Pelham, (P), Richard Saunders,
(P), Milkie Studio, (P), T Tanuma, (P), Peter Treiber, (P)
Reid, Pamela/66 Crosby St, New York, NY   212-832-7589
    Thierry des Fontaines, (P), Sandy Hill, (P), Bert Stern, (P)
Renard, Madeline/501 Fifth Ave #1407, New York, NY   212-490-2450
    Guy Billout, (I), Steve Bjorkman, (I), Chas Wm Bush, (P), John
    Collier, (I), Etienne Delessert, (I), Bart Forbes, (I), Audra Geras,
    (I), Tim Girvin, (I), Lamb & Hall, (P), Miles Hardiman, (I),
    Personality Inc, (I), John Martin, (I), Richard Newton, (I), Al
    Pisano, (I), Robert Rodriguez, (I), Javier Romero, (I), Michael
    Schwab, (I), Jozef Sumichrast, (I), Kim Whitesides, (I)
REP REP/211 THOMPSON ST, NEW YORK, NY (P 142,143)   **212-475-5911**
    Rob Fraser, (P), Rosemary Howard, (P), Bernard Maisner, (L),
    Marcus Tullis, (P)
Ridgeway, Karen/1466 Broadway #1106, New York, NY   212-921-1919
    Scott Bricher, (I), Marilyn Jones, (I), Yemi Mardeigh, (I), David
    Rickerd, (I), Ron Ridgeway, (I), Gordon Swenarton, (I)
Riley, Edward T Inc/81 Greene St, New York, NY   212-925-3053
    Elliot Banfield, (I), Quentin Blake, (I), Zevi Blum, (I), CESC, (I),
    William Bramhall, (I), Chris DeMarest, (I), Paul Degen, (I), David
    Gothard, (I), David Gothard, (I), Carolyn Gowdy, (I), Paul
    Hogarth, (I), Edward Koren, (I), Pierre Le-Tan, (I), Joseph
    Mathieu, (I), Sara Midda, (I), Robert A Parker, (I), Jim
    Parkinson, (L), Cheryl Peterson, (I), J J Sempe, (I), Brenda
    Shahinian, (I), Philippe Weisbecker, (I)
Rindner, Barbara/216 E 45th St, New York, NY   212-661-0850
Rivelli, Cynthia/303 Park Ave S, New York, NY   212-254-0990
Roman, Helen Assoc/140 West End Ave #9H, New York, NY   212-874-7074
Rosenberg, Arlene/200 E 16th St, New York, NY   212-289-7701
Rudoff, Stan/271 Madison Ave, New York, NY   212-679-8780
    David Hamilton, (P), Gideon Lewin, (P)

S

S I International/43 East 19th St, New York, NY   212-254-4996
    Bob Bass, (I), Karen Baumann, (I), Stephen Berger, (I), Jack
    Brusca, (I), Ernie Colon, (I), Richard Corben, (I), Richard
    Courtney, (I), Allen Davis, (I), Robert DeMichiell, (I), Walt
    DeRijk, (I), Robert Fine, (I), Devis Grebu, (I), Sanjulian, (I),
    Enric, (I), Susi Kilgore, (I), Gaetano Liberatore, (I), Sergio
    Martinez, (I), Vince Perez, (I), Martin Rigo, (I), Doug Rosenthal,
    (I), Artie Ruiz, (I), Paul Tatore, (I), Bodhi Wind, (I), Kathy Wyatt, (I)
Sacramone & Valentine/302 W 12th St, New York, NY   212-929-0487
    Stephen Ladner, (P), Tohru Nakamura, (P), John Pilgreen, (P),
    Robin Saidman, (P), Gianni Spinazzola, (P)
Samuels, Rosemary/200 W 20th St, New York, NY   212-477-3567
Sander, Vicki/48 Gramercy Park North #3B, New York, NY   212-674-8161
    Ed Gallucci, (P), George Menda, (P)
Sandler, Cathy/470 W 24th St #5E, New York, NY   212-242-9087
    Aaron Rapoport, (P)
Scharak, Lisa/401 E 58th St #B-4, New York, NY   212-460-8067
Schecter Group, Ron Long/212 E 49th St, New York, NY   212-752-4400
Schickler, Paul/135 E 50th St, New York, NY   212-355-1044
Schochat, Kevin R/221 W 21st St #1D, New York, NY   212-243-6229
    Chuck Carlton, (P), Douglass Grimmett, (G), Bill Kramer, (P)
Schon, Herb/1240 Lexington Ave, New York, NY   212-737-2945
Schub, Peter & Robert Bear/37 Beekman Pl, New York, NY   212-246-0679
    Robert Freson, (P), Alexander Lieberman, (P), Irving Penn, (P),
    Rico Puhlmann, (P), Snowdon, (P), Albert Watson, (P)
Seigel, Fran/515 Madison Ave 22nd Fl, New York, NY   212-486-9644
    Leslie Cabarga, (I), Cheryl Cooper, (I), Kinuko Craft, (I), Peter
    Cross, (I), Joe English, (I), Earl Keleny, (I)
Shamilzadeh, Sol/1155 Broadway 3rd Fl, New York, NY   212-532-1977
    Ryszard Horowitz, (P), The Strobe Studio, (P)
Shapiro, Elaine/369 Lexington Ave, New York, NY   212-867-8220
Sharlowe Assoc/275 Madison Ave, New York, NY   212-683-2822
    Claus Eggers, (P), Nesti Mendoza, (P)
Sheer, Doug/29 John St, New York, NY   212-732-4216
    Karen Kent, (P)
Shepherd, Judith/186 E 64th St, New York, NY   212-838-3214
    Barry Seidman, (P)
Sigman, Joan/336 E 54th St, New York, NY   212-832-7980
    Robert Goldstrom, (I), John H Howard, (I), Jeff Seaver, (I),

REPRESENTATIVES CONT'D.

Please send us your additions and updates.

James Tennison, (I)
Simon, Debra/164 W 21st St, New York, NY — 212-505-5234
Uli Rose, (P)
Simoneau, Christine/PO Box 12541, New York, NY — 212-696-2085
Sims, Jennifer/1150 Fifth Ave, New York, NY — 212-860-3005
Clint Clemens, (P), Robert Latorre, (P)
Sjolin, Robert Nils/117 W 13th St, New York, NY — 212-242-7238
Richard Brummett, (P)
Slocum, Linda/15 W 24th St 11th Fl, New York, NY — 212-243-0649
Slome, Nancy/121 Madison Ave, New York, NY — 212-685-8185
Joe Berger, (P), Dennis Galante, (P)
Smith, Emily/30 E 21st St, New York, NY — 212-674-8383
Smith, Piper/484 W 43rd St #8R, New York, NY — 212-594-7756
Alexa Grace, (I), Michele Laporte, (I), Richard Mantel, (I)
Smith, Rita Assoc/1407 Broadway, New York, NY — 212-730-0065
Solomon, Richard/121 Madison Ave, New York, NY — 212-683-1362
Rick Brown, (I), Ray-Mel Cornelius, (I), Jack E. Davis, (I), Gary Kelley, (I), Elizabeth Koda-Callan, (I), David Palladini, (I), C F Payne, (I), Rodica Prato, (I), Ian Ross, (I), Douglas Smith, (I), John Svoboda, (I), Shelley Thornton, (I)
Sonneville, Dane/PO Box 20415 Greeley Sta, New York, NY — 212-603-9530
Leland Bobbe, (P), Jim Kinstrey, (I), John Pemberton, (P), Jamie Phillips, (P), Bob Shein, (I), Jane Sterrett, (I), Bill Truran, (P)
Stein, Jonathan & Assoc/353 E 77th St, New York, NY — 212-517-3648
Mitch Epstein, (P), Burt Glinn, (P), Ernst Haas, (P), Nathaniel Lieberman, (P), Alex McLean, (P), Gregory Murphey, (P), Kim Steele, (P), Joel Sternfeld, (P), Jeffrey Zaruba, (P)
Steiner, Susan/130 E 18th St, New York, NY — 212-673-4704
Stevens, Norma/1075 Park Ave, New York, NY — 212-427-7235
Richard Avedon, (P)
Stockland, Bill/17 E 45th St, New York, NY — 212-972-4747
Joel Baldwin, (P), Walter Iooss, (P), Eric Meola, (P), Michael Pruzan, (P)
Stogo, Donald/310 E 46th St, New York, NY — 212-490-1034
Tom Grill, (P), John Lawlor, (P), Tom McCarthy, (P), Peter Vaeth, (P)
Stringer, Raymond/123 W 44th St #8F, New York, NY — 212-840-2891
Ajin, (I)
Susse, Ed/56 W 22nd St 5th Fl, New York, NY — 212-243-1126
Karl Zapp, (P)

T
Taborda, Carlos/344 E 85th St #1E, New York, NY — 212-734-1903
Tanenbaum, Dennis/286 Fifth Ave 4th Fl, New York, NY — 212-279-2838
Taylor, Nancy/153 E 57th St, New York, NY — 212-223-0744
Therese, Jane/6 W 20th St, New York, NY — 212-675-8067
Nancy & David Brown, (P)
Thomas, Brenda & Assoc/127 W 79th St, New York, NY — 212-873-7236
Tise, Katherine/200 E 78th St, New York, NY — 212-570-9069
Raphael Boguslav, (I), John Burgoyne, (I), Bunny Carter, (I), Roberts & Van Heusen, (I), Judy Pelikan, (I), Cathleen Toelke, (I)
Townsend, Kris/18 E 18th St, New York, NY — 212-243-2484
David W Hamilton, (P)
Tralongo, Katrin/144 W 27th St, New York, NY — 212-255-1976
Mickey Kaufman, (P)

UV
Umlas, Barbara/131 E 93rd St, New York, NY — 212-534-4008
Hunter Freeman, (P)
Van Arnam, Lewis/154 W 57th St, New York, NY — 212-541-4787
Paul Amato, (P), Mike Reinhardt, (P)
Van Orden, Yvonne/119 W 57th St, New York, NY — 212-265-1223
Joe Schneider, (P)
Vance, Joy/515 Broadway #2B, New York, NY — 212-219-0808
Al Satterwhite, (P)
VisualWorks Inc/545 W 45th St, New York, NY — 212-489-1717
Vollbracht, Michelle/225 E 11th St, New York, NY — 212-475-8718
Walter Wick, (P)
Von Schreiber, Barbara/315 Central Pk West, New York, NY — 212-873-6594
Jean Pagliuso, (P), Hiro, (P), Neal Slavin, (P)

W
Ward, Wendy/200 Madison Ave #2402, New York, NY — 212-684-0590
Wasserman, Ted/310 Madison Ave, New York, NY — 212-867-5360

Watterson, Libby/350 E 30th St, New York, NY — 212-696-1461
Karen Leeds, (P)
Wayne, Philip/66 Madison Ave #9C, New York, NY — 212-696-5215
Roberto Brosan, (P)
Webb, Thomasina/350 W 24th St, New York, NY — 212-620-7832
Weissberg, Elyse/299 Pearl St #5E, New York, NY — 212-406-2566
Jack Reznicki, (P), Bill Smith, (P)
Wheeler, Paul/50 W 29th St #11W, New York, NY — 212-696-9832
John Dominis, (P), Greg Edwards, (P), Foto Shuttle Japan, (P), Seth Joel, (P), John McGrail, (P), Joe McNally, (P), Michael Melford, (P), Aaron Rapoport, (P), Steven Smith, (P), Peter Tenzer, (P), Leroy Woodson, (P)
Williamson, Jack/1414 Ave of the Americas, New York, NY — 212-832-2343
DiFranza Williamson, (P)

YZ
Yellen, Bert & Assoc/575 Madison Ave, New York, NY — 212-605-0555
Bill Connors, (P), Joe Francki, (P), Gordon Munro, (P)
Youngs, Maralee/318 E 39th St, New York, NY — 212-679-8124
Zanetti, Lucy/139 Fifth Ave, New York, NY — 212-473-4999
Zitsman, Cookie/30 Magaw Pl #3A, New York, NY — 212-928-6228
Zlotnick, Jenny/14 Prince St, New York, NY — 212-431-7680

NORTHEAST

A
Ackermann, Marjorie/2112 Goodwin Lane, North Wales, PA — 215-646-1745
H Mark Weidman, (P)
Andrews, Carolyn/109 Somerstown Rd, Ossining, NY — 914-762-5335
Whitney Lane, (P)
The Art Source/444 Bedford Rd, Pleasantville, NY — 914-747-2220
James Barkley, (I), Karen Baumann, (I), Paul Birling, (I), Vince Caputo, (I), Betsy Feeney, (I), Steve Haefele, (I) Robert Lee, (I), Harry Rosenbaum, (I), Jonathan Rosenbaum, (I)
Artco/227 Godfrey Rd, Weston, CT — 203-222-8777
Ed Acuna, (I), Peter Caras, (I), Jeff Cornell, (I), Bob Dacey, (I), Beau & Alan Daniels, (I), Ron DeFelice, (I), Christine Fromentine, (I), Enid Hatton, (I), Rick Mcullom, (I), Joseph Milioto, (I), Rick Tulka, (I), Sally Vitsky, (I)
Artifacts Agency/368 Grove St, Glenrock, NJ — 201-445-3635
Artists International/7 Dublin Hill Dr, Greenwich, CT — 203-869-8010

B
Bancroft, Carol & Friends/185 Goodhill Rd, Weston, CT — 203-226-7674
Bill & Judy Anderson, (I), Cal & Mary Bausman, (I), Wendy Biggins, (I), Jim Cummins, (I), Susan Dodge, (I), Andrea Eberbach, (I), Marla Frazee, (I), Bob Giuliani, (I), Fred Harsh, (I), Ann Iosa, (I), Laurie Jordan, (I), Bryan Jowers, (I), Barbara Lanza, (I), Mila Lazarevich, (I), Karen Loccisano, (I), Jimmy Longacre, (I), Al Lorenz, (I), Laura Lydecker, (I), Stephen Marchesi, (I), John Mardon, (I), Bob Masheris, (I), Elizabeth Miles, (I), Yoshi Miyake, (I), Nancy Munger, (I), Rodney Pate, (I), Cathy Pavia, (I), Ondre Pettingill, (I), Jackie Rogers, (I), Gail Roth, (I), Miriam Schottland, (I), Blanche Sims, (I), Charles Varner, (I), John Weecks, (I), Linda Boehm Weller, (I), Ann Wilson, (I), Chuck Wimmer, (I), Debby Young, (I)
Beckelman, Barbara/251 Greenwood Ave, Bethel, CT — 203-797-8188
Birenbaum, Molly/7 Williamsburg Dr, Cheshire, CT — 203-272-9253
Alice Coxe, (I), W E Duke, (I), Sean Kernan, (P), Joanne Schmaltz, (P), Paul Selwyn, (I), Bill Thomson, (I)
Black Silver & Lord/66 Union St, Belfast, ME — 207-338-1113
Gloria Baker, (P), Kip Brundage, (P), Norm Clasen, (P), Fred Mullane, (P), Michel Tcherevkoff, (P), Roger Tully, (P)
Brown, Jill/911 State St, Lancaster, PA — 717-393-0918
brt Photo Illustration, (P)

CDE
Camp, Woodfin Inc/925 1/2 F St NW, Washington, DC — 202-638-5705
Creative Advantage Inc/707 Union St, Schenectady, NY — 518-370-0312
Richard Siciliano, (P)
D'Angelo, Victoria/309 Madison Ave, Reading, PA — 215-921-8430
Andy D'Angelo, (P)
DeBren, Alan/355 Pearl St, Burlington, VT — 802-864-5916
John Goodman, (P)
Donaldson, Selina/37 Hemlock, Arlington, MA — 617-646-1687

443

Ella/229 Berkeley #52, Boston, MA   617-266-3858
Norman Adams, (P), Bente Adler, (I), Wilbur Bullock, (I), Rob Cline, (I), Jack Crompton, (I), Anna Davidian, (I), Sharon Drinkwine, (I), Anatoly Dverin, (I), Scott Gordley, (I), Eaton & Iwen, (I), Roger Leyonmark, (I), Janet Mager, (I), Bruce Sanders, (I), Ron Toelke, (I)

FG
Franco, Evelyn/1072 Greendale Ave, Needham, MA   617-444-4190
Geng, Maud/116 Commonwealth Ave, Boston, MA   617-236-1920
Caroline Alterio, (I), Peter Barger, (I), Vicki Smith, (I)
Giandomenico, Terry (Ms)/13 Fern Ave, Collingswood, NJ   609-854-2222
Bob Giandomenico, (P)
Gidley, Fenton/43 Tokeneke Rd, Darien, CT   212-772-0846
Goldstein, Gwen/91 Hundred Rd, Wellesley Hills, MA   617-235-8658
Michael Blaser, (I), Steve Fuller, (I), Lane Gregory, (I), Terry Presnall, (I), Susan Spellman, (I), Gary Torisi, (I), Joe Veno, (I)

HK
Haas, Ken/PO Box 86, Oley, PA   215-987-3711
Peter Leach, (P), Ken Ravel, (I), Michael Schroeder, (I), Emilie Snyder, (I)
Hone, Claire/2130 Arch Street, Philadelphia, PA   215-568-5434
Hopkins, Nanette/18 North New St, West Chester, PA   215-431-3240
Rick Davis, (P)
Hubbell, Marian/99 East Elm St, Greenwich, CT   203-629-9629
Kaltenbach, Faith/PO Box 317, Lititz, PA   717-626-0296
Grant Heilman, (P)
Kanefield, Andrew/14 North Gate, West Newton, MA   617-965-3557
Christopher Cunningham, (P), Peter Jones, (P), Bob O'Shaughnessy, (P), Lewis Portnoy, (P)
Kurlansky, Sharon/192 Southville Rd, Southborough, MA   617-872-4549
Steve Alexander, (I), Charles Freeman, (I), Judy Gailen, (I), John Gamache, (I), Susan Hanson, (I), Peter Harris, (I), Terry Van Heusen, (I), Geoffrey Hodgkinson, (I), Mark Kelly, (I), Dorthea Sierra, (I), Colleen, (I)

LM
Labonty, Deborah/PO Box 7446, Lancaster, PA   717-872-8198
Tim Schoon, (P)
Lipman, Deborah/506 Windsor Dr, Framingham, MA   617-451-6528
Mark Fisher, (I), Richard A. Goldberg, (I), James Hanlon, (I), Richard M. Joachim, (I), Armen Kojoyian, (I), Carol LaCourse, (I), Katherine Mahoney, (I)
Mattelson Assoc/37 Cary Rd, Great Neck, NY   212-684-2974
Karen Kluglein, (I), Marvin Mattelson, (I), Gary Viskupic, (I)
McNamara, Paula B/182 Broad St, Wethersfield, CT   203-563-6159
Jack McConnell, (P)
Metzger, Rick/186 South St, Boston, MA   617-426-2290
Steve Grohe, (P)
Montreal Crtv Consrtm/1155 Dorchester W #1520, Montreal H3B 2J6, QU   514-875-5426
Morgan, Wendy/5 Logan Hill Rd, Northport, NY   516-757-5609
Scott Gordley, (I), ParaShoot, (P), Fred Labitzke, (I), Don Landwehrle, (P), Preston Lyon, (P), Al Margolis, (I), David Rankin, (I), Fred Schrier, (I), Art Szabo, (P), David Wilder, (P)

OP
Oreman, Linda/15 Atkinson St, Rochester, NY   716-232-1585
Nick Angello, (I), Jim & Phil Bliss, (I), Roger DeMuth, (I), Jeff Feinen, (I), Bill Finewood, (I), Doug Gray, (I), Stephen Moscowitz, (I), Vicki Wehrman, (I)
Palulian, Joanne/18 Mckinley St, Rowayton, CT   203-866-3734
Scott Barrows, (I), M John English, (I), David Lesh, (I), Kirk Moldoff, (I), Dickran Palulian, (I), Walt Spitzmiller, (I)
Publishers Graphics/251 Greenwood Ave, Bethel, CT   203-797-8188
Paul Harvey, (I)
Putscher, Tony/2303 Green St, Philadelphia, PA   215-569-8890

R
Radxevich Standke/15 Intervale Terr, Reading, MA   617-944-3166
Christian Delbert, (P)
Reese-Gibson, Jean/4 Puritan Rd, N Beverly, MA   617-927-5006
Riley, Catherine/45 Circle Dr, Hastings On Hudson, NY   914-478-4377
Jon Riley, (P)
Robbins, David Group/256 Arch Rd, Avon, CT   203-673-6530
Mike Eagle, (I)

Rubenstein, Len/One Winthrop Sq, Boston, MA   617-482-0660
Jim Conaty, (P)

S
Satterthwaite, Victoria/115 Arch St, Philadelphia, PA   215-925-4233
Michael Furman, (P)
Sequis Ltd/PO Box 398, Sevenson, MD   301-583-9177
Jeremy Green, (P)
Shulman, Carol/6182 Chinquapin Pkwy, Baltimore, MD   301-323-8645
Smith, Russell/65 Washington St, S Norwalk, CT   203-866-8871
Gordon Smith, (P)
Smith, Wayne R/145 South St Penthouse, Boston, MA   617-426-7262
Robert Brooks, (I), John Holt, (I), Ben Luce, (I), Ed Porzio, (I)
Snyder, Diane/3 Underwood Rd, Wyncote, PA   215-572-1192
Craig Bakley, (I), Gordon Kibbee, (I), Michael McNelly, (I), Verlin Miller, (I), Shelly Roseman, (P), Lee Wojnar, (P)
Spencer, Sandy/700 S 10th St, Philadelphia, PA   215-238-1208
Anthony Ward, (P)
Spiak, Al/35 Monroe Ave, Dumont, NJ   201-387-9395
Stevens, Rick/925 Penn Ave #404, Pittsburgh, PA   412-765-3565
Stoller, Erica/222 Valley Pl, Mamaroneck, NY   914-698-4060
Peter Aaron, (P), Wolfgang Hoyt, (P)
Sweeny, Susan/425 Fairfield Ave, Stamford, CT

TUV
Ternay, Louise/119 Birch Ave, Bala Cynwyd, PA   215-667-8626
Vince Cuccinotta, (I), Don Everhart, (I), Geri Grienke, (I), Greg Purdon, (I), Peter Sasten, (G), Bill Ternay, (I), Victor Valla, (I), Kate Ziegler, (I)
Unicorn/1148 Parsippany Blvd, Parsippany, NJ   201-334-0353
Greg Hildebrandt, (I)
Valen Assocs/PO Box 8, Westport, CT   203-227-7806
Chas Adams, (I), George Booth, (C), Whitney Darrow, (C), Eldon Dedini, (C), Joe Farris, (C), William Hamilton, (C), Stan Hunt, (C), Anatol Kovarsky, (C), Henry Martin, (C), Warren Miller, (I), Frank Modell, (C), Mischa Richter, (C), Charles Saxon, (C), Jim Stevenson, (C), Henry Syverson, (C), Bob Weber, (C), Rowland Wilson, (I), Gahan Wilson, (I), Bill Woodman, (I), Bill Ziegler, (I)

WZ
Waterman, Laurie/130 South 17th St, Philadelphia, PA   215-988-0390
Wayne, Lynn/99 Wilson Ave, Windsor, CT   203-522-3143
Wigon, Leslie/191 Plymouth Dr, Scarsdale, NY   914-472-9459
Wolfe, Deborah Ltd/731 North 24th St, Philadelphia, PA   215-232-6666
Steve Cusano, (I), Harry Davis, (I), Jeff FitzMaurice, (I), Robin Hotchkiss, (I), Ron Lehew, (I), Bill Margerin, (I), Bob Schenker, (I), Jim Sharpe, (I), Jas Szygiel, (I), Charles Weckler, (P), Allan Weitz, (P), Frank Williams, (I)
Worrall, Dave/125 S 18th St, Philadelphia, PA   215-567-2881
Weaver Lilley, (P)
Worthington, Diane/372 Marlborough St, Boston, MA   617-247-2847
Kurt Stier, (P)
Zellner, Robin/54 Applecross Cir, Chalfont, PA   215-822-8258
Charles Callahan, (P)

SOUTHEAST

ABC
Ad Artist SE/1424 N Tryon, Charlotte, NC   704-372-6007
Aldridge, Donna/755 Virginia Ave, Atlanta, GA   404-872-7980
Chris Lewis, (I)
AND ASSOCIATES/573 HILL ST, ATHENS, GA (P 240-242)   **404-353-8479**
Dan McClure, (P), Dennis O'Kain, (P), Elaine H. Rabon, (I), Drake White, (P)
Babcock, Nancy/1496 N Morningside Dr NE, Atlanta, GA   404-876-0117
Beck, Susanne/2721 Cherokee Rd, Birmingham, AL   205-871-6632
Charles Beck, (P)
Burnett, Yolanda/559 Dutch Vall Rd, Atlanta, GA   404-873-5858
Jim Copland, (P), Charlie Lathem, (P)
Couch, Tom/1164 Briarcliff Rd NE #2, Atlanta, GA   404-872-5774
Granberry/Anderson Studio, (P)

FGH
Fink, Duncan/437 S Tryon St, Charlotte, NC   704-377-4217
Ron Chapple, (P), Mitchell Kearney, (P)

REPRESENTATIVES CONT'D.

Please send us your additions and updates.

Forbes, Pat/11459 Waterview Cluster, Reston, VA — 703-437-7042
  Kay Chenush, (P)
Grubbs/Bate & Assoc/1151 W Peachtree St NW, Atlanta, GA — 404-892-6303
  Image Electronic, (I), Stefan Findal, (P), Mike Hodges, (I),
  Johnna Hogenkamp, (I), Kevin Hulsey, (I), David Marks, (I),
  Theo Rudnak, (I), Joe Saffold, (I), Michael West, (P), Bruce
  Young, (I)
Hathcox, Julia/5730 Arlington Blvd, Arlington, VA — 703-845-5831
  David Hathcox, (P)

JLM

Jett & Agson/1340 S 6th St, Louisville, KY — 502-634-4911
Jourdan, Carolyn/520 Brickell Key Dr #1417, Miami, FL — 305-372-9425
Judge, Marie/9452 SW 77th Ave, Miami, Fl — 305-595-1700
Linden, Tamara/919 Lenox Hill Ct, Atlanta, GA — 404-262-1209
  Tom Fleck, (I), Joe Ovies, (I), Charles Passarelli, (I), Larry
  Tople, (I)
McGee, Linda/1816 Briarwood Ind Ct, Atlanta, GA — 404-633-1286
McLean Represents/401 W Peachtree St NW #1720, Atlanta,
  GA — 404-881-6627
  Joe Isom, (I), Jack Jones, (I), Martin Pate, (I), Steve Spetseris,
  (I), Warren Weber, (I)

PST

Phelps, Catherine/3210 Peachtree Rd NE, Atlanta, GA — 404-264-0264
  Tom McCarthy, (P), Tommy Thompson, (P), Bill Weems, (P)
Pollard, Kiki/848 Greenwood Ave NE, Atlanta, GA — 404-875-1363
  Betsy Alexander, (G), John Findley, (I), Dennis Guthrie, (I),
  James Soukup, (I), Mark Stanton, (I)
Prentice, Nancy/315-A Pharr Rd, Atlanta, GA — 404-266-9707
Propst, Sheryle/PO Box 1583, Norcross, GA — 404-263-9296
  Michael Davis, (I), Fred Gerlich, (P), Herring & Klem, (I), Reggie
  Stanton, (I)
Silva, Naomi/100 Colony Sq #200, Atlanta, GA — 404-892-8314
  Daryl Cagle, (C), Stefan Findel, (P), Kevin Hamilton, (I), Rob
  Horn, (L), Mike Moore, (I), Christy Sheets Mull, (I), Alan Patton,
  (I), Gary Penca, (I), Don Sparks, (P), John Yates, (G)
Sumpter, Will/1106 W Peachtree St #106, Atlanta, GA — 404-874-2014
Torres, Martha/927 Third St, New Orleans, LA — 504-895-6570

UW

Uter, Bonnie & Assoc/573 Hill St, Athens, GA — 404-353-8479
  Dan McClure, (P), Dennis O'Kain, (P), Elaine Rabon, (I), Drake
  White, (P)
Wells, Susan/5134 Timber Trail, Atlanta, GA — 404-255-1430
  Paul Blakey, (I), Jim Caraway, (I), Don Loehle, (I), Richard
  Loehle, (I), Randall McKissick, (I), Monte Varah, (I), Beth White, (I)
Wexler, Marsha Brown/6108 Franklin Pk Rd, McLean, VA — 703-241-1776
Williams, Phillip/1106 W Peachtree St #201, Atlanta, GA — 404-873-2287
  Jamie Cook, (P), Chipp Jamison, (P), Rick Lovell, (I), Kenvin
  Lyman, (G), Bill Mayer, (I), David McKelvey, (I), John Robinette, (I)

MIDWEST

AB

Andoniadis, Nina/900 Mark Ln #302, Wheeling, IL — 312-253-7488
Ball, John/203 N Wabash, Chicago, IL — 312-332-6041
Bartels, Ceci Assoc/111 Jefferson Rd, St Louis, MO — 314-961-1670
  Eric Dinyer, (I), Shannon Kriegshauser, (I), Don Kueker, (I),
  Greg MacNair, (I), Jean Probert, (I), Terry Sirrell, (I), Terry
  Speer, (I)
Berk, Ida/1350 N La Salle, Chicago, IL — 312-944-1339
Birdwell, Steven/208 W Kinzie St, Chicago, IL — 312-467-1430
Bonnen, Ed/913 Beach, Lansing, MI — 517-371-3086
Brenna, Allen/Southgate Plaza #515, Minneapolis, MN — 612-835-1831
Brenner, Harriet/660 W Grand Ave, Chicago, IL — 312-243-2730
Brooks, Douglas/1230 W Washington Blvd, Chicago, IL — 312-226-4060
  VanKirk Photo, (P)
Buermann, Jeri/321 N 22nd St, St Louis, MO — 314-231-8690
Bussler, Tom/19 E Pearson #410, Chicago, IL — 312-944-3837
  Sid Evans, (P)

CD

Carr, Ken/4715 N Ronald St, Harwood Heights, IL — 312-867-5445
Christell, Jim & Assoc/307 N Michigan Ave #1008, Chicago, IL — 312-236-2396
  Michel Ditlove, (P), Ron Harris, (P)

Coleman, Woody/490 Rockside Rd, Cleveland, OH — 216-621-1771
  Stuart Daniels, (I), Vladimir Kordic, (I), John Letostak, (I), Ernest
  Norcia, (I), Bob Novack, (I), Ezra Tucker, (I)
Commercial Images Group/15339 Center St, Harvey, IL — 312-333-1047
Daguanno, Donna/211 E Ohio #621, Chicago, IL — 312-644-0172
  Chris Hawker, (P)
Demunnik, Jack/2138 N Hudson #206, Chicago, IL — 312-883-7262
DeWalt & Assoc/210 E Michigan St #203, Milwaukee, WI — 414-276-7990
  Tom Fritz, (P), Don Glassford, (I), Mary Gordon, (G), Dennis
  Matz, (I), Tom Redman, (I)
Dodge, Tim/2412 E Stratford Ct, Milwaukee, WI — 414-964-9558
  Barbara Ericksen, (I), Jeff Hangartner, (I), Ken Hanson, (G),
  Paul Henning, (P), Tom Kwas, (P), Dave Vander Veen, (P)
Dolby, Karen/215 W Ohio, Chicago, IL — 312-321-1770

EF

Emerich Studios/300 W 19th Terrace, Kansas City, MO — 816-474-8888
Erdos, Kitty/210 W Chicago, Chicago, IL — 312-787-4976
Feldman, Kenneth/30 E Huron, Chicago, IL — 312-337-0447
Fiat, Randi/612 N Michigan, Chicago, IL — 312-784-2343
Fleming, Laird Tyler/1 Memorial Dr, St Louis, MO — 314-982-1700
  Willardson + Assoc, (P), John Bilecky, (P)
Fried, Monica/1546 N Orleans, Chicago, IL — 312-642-8715
Frost, Brent & Laumer, Dick/4037 Queen Ave S, Minneapolis,
  MN — 612-922-3440

GH

Green Gotfried & Assoc/29 E Ohio, Chicago, IL — 312-661-0024
Hanson, Jim/540 N Lake Shore Dr, Chicago, IL — 312-527-1114
  Bob Bender, (P), Richard Fegley, (P), Bob Gelberg, (P), Rob
  Johns, (P), Rick Mitchell, (P), Barry O'Rourke, (P), John Payne,
  (P), Al Satterwhite, (P)
Harlib, Joel/405 N Wabash #3203, Chicago, IL — 312-329-1370
  Bob August, (I), Nick Backes, (I), John Casado, (I), Lawrence
  Duke, (P), Peter Elliott, (P), Marty Evans, (P), Randy Glass, (I),
  Karel Havlicek, (I), Barbara Higgins-Bond, (I), DeWitt Jones,
  (P), Richard Leech, (I), Tim Lewis, (I), Peter Lloyd, (I), Bret
  Lopez, (I), David McMacken, (I), Joe Ovies, (I), Fred Prepera,
  (I), Matthew Rolston, (P), Todd Shorr, (I), Jay Silverman, (P),
  Robert Tyrrell, (I), Bill Vann, (I), Ron Villani, (I), Allan Weitz, (P),
  Kim Whitesides, (I), Bruce Wolfe, (I), Bob Ziering, (I)
Hartig, Michael/3620 Pacific, Omaha, NB — 402-345-2164
Heinen, Sandy/219 N 2nd St #409, Minneapolis, MN — 612-332-3671
Higgens Hegner Genovese Inc/510 N Dearborn St, Chicago, IL — 312-644-1882
Hogan, Myrna & Assoc/333 N Michigan, Chicago, IL — 312-372-1616
  Terry Heffernan, (P)
Hoke, Wayne & Assoc/17 N Elizabeth St, Chicago, IL — 312-666-0175
Horton, Nancy/939 Sanborn, Palatine, IL — 312-934-8966
Hull, Scott Assoc/20 Lynnray Circle, Dayton, OH — 513-433-8383
  Mark Braught, (I), Tracy Britt, (I), David Groff, (I), Julie Hodde,
  (I), Greg LaFever, (I), John Maggard, (I), Larry Martin, (I), Ted
  Pitts, (I), David Sheldon, (I), Don Vanderbeek, (I), Lee Woolery, (I)

JK

Jenkins, John/1147 W Ohio #403, Chicago, IL — 312-243-6580
Jeske, Kurt/612 S Clinton, Chicago, IL — 312-922-9200
Jordano, Charles/2623 Rhodes, Troy, MI — 313-528-0593
Kamin, Vince & Assoc/111 E Chestnut, Chicago, IL — 312-787-8834
  Dave Jordano, (P), Ron Lieberman, (I), Mary Anne Shea, (I),
  Roy Volkman, (P)
Kapes, Jack/233 E Wacker Dr #1412, Chicago, IL — 312-565-0566
  Stuart Block, (P), John Cahoon, (P), Jerry Friedman, (P), Carl
  Furuta, (P), Klaus Lucka, (P), Dan Romano, (I), Nicolas
  Sidjakov, (G)
Kezelis, Elena/215 W Illinois, Chicago, IL — 312-644-7108
Kleber, Gordon/125 W Hubbard, Chicago, IL — 312-661-1362
Koralik, Connie/26 E Huron, Chicago, IL — 312-944-5680
  Glenn Gustafson, (I), Robert Keeling, (P), Kazu, (I)

L

Lakehomer & Assoc/405 N Wabash #1402, Chicago, IL — 312-644-1766
  Tim Schultz, (P)
Lasko, Pat/452 N Halsted, Chicago, IL — 312-243-6696
  Ralph King, (P)
Levey, Rebecca/405 N Wabash, Chicago, IL — 312-329-9040
Linzer, Jeff/4001 Forest Rd, Minneapolis, MN — 612-926-4390

Please send us your additions and updates.

Lonier, Terry/215 W Ohio #5W, Chicago, IL — 312-527-1880
Lukmann, Geri/314 W Institute Pl, Chicago, IL — 312-787-1774
  Brent Carpenter, (P), Steve Nozicka, (P)

M

McMasters, Deborah/157 W Ontario, Chicago, IL — 312-943-9007
  Richard Foster, (P)
McNamara Associates/1250 Stephenson Hwy, Troy, MI — 313-583-9200
  Max Alterruse,(I), Gary Ciccarelli, (I), Garry Colby, (I), Hank
  Kolodziej, (I), Chuck Passarelli, (I), Tony Randazzo, (I), Gary
  Richardson, (I), Dick Scullin, (I), Don Wieland, (I)*
McNaughton, Toni/233 E Wacker #2904, Chicago, IL — 312-938-2148
  Pam Haller, (P), Rodica Prato, (I), James B. Wood, (P)
Miller Services/45 Charles St E, Toronto M4Y 1S6, ON — 416-925-4323
Miller, Richard/743 N Dearborn, Chicago, IL — 312-280-2288
  *Paul Barton, (P), Morton Beebe, (P), Rebecca Blake, (P), Chris
  Butler, (I), Geoffrey Clifford, (P), Marc Hauser, (P), Richard
  High, (C), Bob Krogle, (I), Jim Krogle, (I), Robert Sacco, (P)*
Mohlman, Jeanette/114 W Illinois, Chicago, IL — 312-321-1570
Mohlo, David/ Werremeyer Inc/12837 Flushing Meadow Dr, St
  Louis, MO — 314-966-3770
Moore, Amanda/1752 N Mohawk, Chicago, IL — 312-337-0880
  Peter Sagara, (P)
Moore, Connie/1540 N North Park, Chicago, IL — 312-787-4422
  Richard Shirley, (I)
Moshier & Maloney/535 N Michigan, Chicago, IL — 312-943-1668
  *Nicolette Anastas, (I), Dave Wilson & Assoc, (I), Steve Carr, (P),
  Dan Clyne, (I), Ron DiCianni, (I), David Gaadt, (I), John
  Hamagami, (I), Rick Johnson, (I), Bill Kastan, (I), Ed Lindlof, (I),
  Dennis Luzak, (I), Colleen Quinn, (I), Paul Ristau, (I), Stephen
  Rybka, (I), Skidmore-Sahratian, (I), Al Stine, (I), Jim Trusilo, (I),
  John Youssi, (I)*
Murphy, Sally/70 W Hubbard, Chicago, IL — 312-346-0720

NO

Nagan, Rita/1514 NE Jefferson St, Minneapolis, MN — 612-788-7923
Nelson, Sandy/315 W Walton, Chicago, IL — 312-266-8029
Newman, Richard/1866 N Burling, Chicago, IL — 312-266-2513
Nicholson, Richard B/2310 Denison Ave, Cleveland, OH — 216-398-1494
  *Martin Reuben, (P), Mike Steinberg, (P), Al Teufer, (P), J David
  Wilder, (P)*
Nicolini, Sandra/230 N Michigan #523, Chicago, IL — 312-346-1648
  Elizabeth Ernst, (P), Tom Petroff, (P)
O'Brien-Stieber/203 N wabash #1600, Chicago, IL — 312-726-9690
O'Farrel, Eileen/311 Good Ave, Des Plaines, IL — 312-297-5447
O'Grady Advertising Arts/333 North Michigan Ave #2200,
  Chicago, IL — 312-726-9833
O'Neill, Mary/17006 Woodbury Ave, Cleveland, OH — 216-252-6238
Osler, Spike/2616 Industrial Row, Troy, MI — 313-280-0640
  *Mark Coppos, (P), Madison Ford, (P), Rob Gage, (P), Rick
  Kasmier, (P), Jim Secreto, (P)*

PR

Parker, Tom/1750 N Clark, Chicago, IL — 312-266-2891
Peterson, Vicki/535 N Michigan Ave #2802, Chicago, IL — 312-467-0780
  *Charlie Gold, (P), Elyse Lewin, (P), Howard Menken, (P),
  Robert Stevens, (P), Charlie Westerman, (P)*
Phase II/155 N Michigan Ave, Chicago, IL — 312-565-0030
  *Bill Cigliano, (I), Michael Elins, (I), David Krainik, (I), Kathy
  Petrauskas, (I), Mark Sauck, (I), Richard Taylor, (I)*
Photo Services Owens-Corning/Fiberglass Towers, Toledo,
  OH — 419-248-8041
  Jay Langlois, (P), Joe Sharp, (P)
Platzer, Karen & Assoc/535 N Michigan Ave, Chicago, IL — 312-467-1981
  Larry Banner, (P), Michael Caporale, (P), Ray Cioni, (I)
Pool, Linda/6905 E 102nd St, Kansas City, MO — 816-761-7314
  Michael Radencich, (P)
Potts, Carolyn/3 E Ontario #25, Chicago, IL — 312-935-1707
  *Barbara Bersell, (P), John Craig, (I), Alan Dolgins, (P), Gregory
  Murphey, (P), Fred Nelson, (I), Joe Ovies, (I), Kulp
  Productions, (P), Leslie Wolf, (I)*
Potts, Vicki/139 N Wabash, Chicago, IL — 312-726-5678
  *Mitchell Einhorn, (P), Mercer Engelhard, (P), David Gerhardt,
  (P), Kathy Sanders, (P)*
Pride, Max/401 W Superior, Chicago, IL — 312-664-5392

Rabin, Bill & Assoc/666 N Lake Shore Dr, Chicago, IL — 312-944-6655
  *John Alcorn, (I), Joel Baldwin, (P), Joe Baraban, (P), Roger
  Beerworth, (I), Guy Billout, (I), Howard Bjornson, (P), Thomas
  Blackshear, (I), R O Blechman, (I), Charles William Bush, (P),
  JoAnn Carney, (P), John Collier, (I), Jackie Geyer, (I), Paul
  Giovanopoulos, (I), Tim Girvin, (G), Robert Giusti, (I), Kunio
  Hagio, (I), Lamb & Hall, (P), Mark Hess, (I), Richard Hess, (I),
  Walter Ioss, (P), Art Kane, (P), Rudi Legname, (P), Daniel
  Maffia, (I), Jay Maisel, (P), Dan Malinowski, (P), Jim Matusik,
  (P), Eric Meola, (P), Eugene Mihaesco, (I), Richard Noble, (P),
  Robert Rodriguez, (I), Reynold Ruffins, (I), Michael Shwab, (I),
  Ed Sorel, (I), George Stavrinos, (I), Simms Taback, (I), Ezra
  Tucker, (I), Pete Turner, (P), David Wilcox, (I)*
Ray, Rodney/405 N Wabash #3106, Chicago, IL — 312-472-6550

ST

Scarff, Signe/22 W Erie, Chicago, IL — 312-266-8352
  Larry Kolze, (P)
Sell, Dan/233 E Wacker, Chicago, IL — 312-565-2701
  *Alvin Blick, (I), Paul Bond, (I), Wayne Carey, (I), Justin Carroll,
  (I), Bobbye Cochran, (I), Wil Cormier, (I), Bill Ersland, (I), Rick
  Farrell, (I), Dick Flood, (I), Bill Harrison, (I), Dave LaFleur, (I),
  Gregory Manchess, (I), Bill Mayer, (I), Frank Morris, (I), Tim
  Raglin, (I), Ian Ross, (I), Mark Schuler, (I), R J Shay, (I), Jay
  Songero, (I), Dale Verzaal, (I), Jay, (I), Fran Vuksanovich, (I),
  Phil Wendy, (I), John Zielinski, (I)*
Shulman, Salo/215 W Ohio, Chicago, IL — 312-337-3245
  Stan Stansfield, (P)
Sims, Mel/233 E Wacker Dr #4304, Chicago, IL — 312-938-8937
  Britt Collins, (I)
Sinclair, Valerie/77 Florence St #301, Toronto M6K 1P4, ON — 416-588-1527
  John Martin, (P), James Toogan, (I)
Skillicorn, Roy/233 E Wacker #29031, Chicago, IL — 312-856-1626
  Wickart Brothers, (I), Tom Curry, (I), David Scanlon, (I)
Snowberger, Ann/3312 W Belle Plaine, Chicago, IL — 312-463-3590
  Tim Bieber, (P)
Timon, Clay & Assoc Inc/540 N Lake Shore Dr, Chicago, IL — 312-527-1114
  *Bob Bender, (P), Michael Fletcher, (P), Larry Dale Gordon, (P),
  Don Klumpp, (P), Chuck Kuhn, (P), Barry O'Rourke, (P), Al
  Satterwhite, (P), Michael Slaughter, (P)*
Trembeth, Rich/30 E Huron #4904, Chicago, IL — 312-727-1096
Trinko, Genny/126 W Kinzie St, Chicago, IL — 312-222-9242
  Cam Chapman, (P)
Trott, David/32588 Dequiendre, Warren, MI — 313-978-8932
Tuke, Joni/368 W Huron, Chicago, IL — 312-787-6826
  *Jay Ahrend, (P), David Beck, (I), Dan Blanchette, (I), Ken
  Goldammer, (I), Chris Hopkins, (I), Susan Kindst, (P), Brian
  Otto, (I), John Welzenbach, (P), Ken Westphal, (I)*

VYZ

Virnig, Janet/3308 Girard Ave S, Minneapolis, MN — 612-822-6444
Wainman, Rick & Assoc/166 E Superior #212, Chicago, IL — 312-337-3960
Warner, Rebecca/230 W Huron, Chicago, IL — 312-951-0880
Yunker, Kit/ Allchin, Scott/1335 N Wells St, Chicago, IL — 312-321-0655
Zann, Sheila/502 N Grove, Oak Park, IL — 312-386-2864
  Arnold Zann, (P)

SOUTHWEST

AB

Art Rep Inc/2801 W Lemmon #305, Dallas, TX — 214-521-5156
  *Tom Bailey, (I), Lee Lee Brazeal, (I), Ellis Chappell, (I), Dean St
  Clair, (I), Tom Curry, (I), M John English, (I), Tom Evans, (I),
  Tim Girvin, (I), Bill Harrison, (I), Jim Jacobs, (I), Kent Kirkley,
  (P), Gary McCoy, (P), Genevieve Meek, (I), Frank Morris, (I),
  Michael Schwab, (I), Andrew Vracin, (P), Kim Whitesides, (I),
  Terry Widener, (I)*
Assid, Carol/122 Parkhouse, Dallas, TX — 214-748-3765
Booster, Barbara/4001 Bryn Mawr, Dallas, TX — 214-373-4284
Boston, Belinda/PO Box 821095, Dallas, TX — 214-821-3042
  Kenneth Huey, (I)

CD

Callahan, Joe/330 E Mitchell, Phoenix, AZ — 602-248-0777
  Tom Gerczynski, (P), Mike Gushock, (I), Jon Kleber, (I),

REPRESENTATIVES CONT'D.

Please send us your additions and updates.

Howard Post, (I), Dan Ruiz, (I), Mark Sharpls, (I), Dan Vermillion, (P), Balfour Walker, (P)

Campbell, Patty/2610 Catherine, Dallas, TX	214-946-6597
Douglas Doering, (P)	
COBB & FRIEND/2811 MCKINNEY #224, DALLAS, TX	**214-855-0055**
(P 311-15)	

Kent Barker, (P), Greg Bates, (I), Cathie Bleck, (I), Margaret K Cheatham, (I), Michael Johnson, (P), David Kampa, (I), Geof Kern, (P), Rick Kroninger, (P), Mercedes McDonald, (I), Michael McGar, (I), Dennis Murphy, (P), R Kenton Nelson, (I), Steve Pietzsch, (I), Tom Ryan, (P), James N Smith, (I), James Tennison, (I), Michele Warner, (I), Ken Westphal, (I)

Crowder, Bob/4404 Main St, Dallas, TX	214-823-9000
Barry Kaplan, (P), Moses Olmoz, (P), Al Rubin, (P)	
Devereux, Julien/2707 Stemmons Frwy #160, Dallas, TX	214-634-0222
Faustino, (P)	
DiOrio, Diana/1819 Augusta Ct #148, Houston, TX	713-266-9390
John Collier, (I), Ray Mel Cornelius, (I), Regan Dunnick, (I), Larry Keith, (I), Bahid Marinfar, (I), Dennis Mukai, (I),	

EFH

Edwards, Nancy/2121 Regency Dr, Irving, TX	214-438-4114
Freeman, Sandra/3030 McKinney #1706, Dallas, TX	214-871-1956
Fuller, Alyson/5610 Maple Ave, Dallas, TX	214-688-1855
Hamilton, Chris/3900 Lemmon, Dallas, TX	214-526-2050
Holland, Nancy/1669 S Voss #590, Houston, TX	713-975-7279

LMN

Lynch, Larry/3527 Oak Lawn Ave #145, Dallas, TX	214-521-6169
Morton Beebe, (P), Robert Latorre, (P), Richard Wahlstrom, (P)	
McCann, Liz/3000 Carlisle #206, Dallas, TX	214-630-7756
Bill Crumpt, (P), Michael Doret, (I), Ben James, (I), Phil Kretchmar, (P), James B. Wood, (P)	
Noble, Peter/8344 East RL Thornton #300, Dallas, TX	214-328-6676

PSW

Photocom Inc/1707 S Ervay, Dallas, TX	214-428-8781
Louis Reens, (P)	
Production Services/1711 Hazard, Houston, TX	713-529-7916
George Craig, (P), C Bryan Jones, (P), Thaine Manske, (P)	
Spiegal, Melanie/2412 Converse, Dallas, TX	214-428-8781
Robb Debenport, (P), Jeff Haynie, (I), Louis Reens, (P), Michael Steirnagle, (I), Kelly Stribling, (I), Richard Wahlstrom, (P)	
Washington, Dick/914 Westmoreland, San Antonio, TX	512-342-2009
Willard, Paul Assoc/815 North First Ave #3, Phoenix, AZ	602-257-0097
Kevin Cruff, (P), Matthew Foster, (I), Rick Gayle, (P), Rick Kirkman, (I), Kevin MacPherson, (I), Curtis Parker, (I), Nancy Pendleton, (I), Bob Peters, (I), Roy & Peggy Roberts, (I), Norma Samuelson, (I), Wayne Watford, (I), Jean Wong, (I)	

ROCKY MOUNTAIN

FGK

Foremark Studios/PO Box 10346, Reno, NV	702-786-3150
Garrett, Ann/1100 Acoma, Denver, CO	303-893-1199
Goodman, Christine/1836 Blake St #201, Denver, CO	303-298-7085
Bill Koropp, (P), Geoffrey Wheeler, (P)	
Kelly, Rob/3113 E 3rd St #220, Denver, CO	303-399-3851
Pat Fujisaki, (I), Ron Sauter, (I)	

NRS

No Coast Graphics/2629 18th St, Denver, CO	303-458-7086
John Cuneo, (I), Cindy Enright, (I), Tom Nikosey, (I), Chris F Payne, (I), Mike Steirnagle, (I)	
Roberts, Hallie/16 W 13th Ave, Denver, CO	303-534-7267
Ryan, Patti/550 E 12th Ave #910, Denver, CO	303-832-9214
Bob Fader, (P)	
Sperling, Alice/1050 Corona #307, Denver, CO	303-832-4686
Synchrony/655 Broadway #800, Denver, CO	303-825-7513

WEST COAST

AB

Aline, France/1076 S Ogden Dr, Los Angeles, CA	213-933-2500
Guy Billout, (I), Thomas Blackshear, (I), Steve Hulen, (P), Michael Lamotte, (P), Bret Lopez, (P), Manuel Nunez, (I), Dave	

Scanlon, (I), Michael Schwab, (I), Veronica Sim, (P), Peggy Sirota, (P), Bob Stevens, (P), Ezra Tucker, (I), Kim Whitesides, (I), Bruce Wolfe, (I), Bob Zoell, (I)

Arnold, Wendy/4620 Coldwater Cnyn, Studio City, CA	818-762-8850
Ayerst, Deborah/828 Mission St, San Francisco, CA	415-974-1755
Azurite Productions/305 Boyd St, Los Angeles, CA	213-621-2700
Baker, Kolea/1822 N E Ravenna Rd, Seattle, WA	206-443-0326
George Abe, (I), Don Baker, (I)	
Becker, Roxanne/964 N Vermont Ave, Los Angeles, CA	213-684-7170
Braun, Kathy/75 Water St, San Francisco, CA	415-543-7377
Arnold & Assoc, (F), Sandra Belce, (L), Tandy Belew, (G), Michael Bull, (I), Anka, (I), Eldon Doty, (I), Boyington Film, (F), Jim Fulp, (I), Stephen Osborn, (I), Jim Parkinson, (L), Allan Rosenberg, (I), Diane Tyler, (MU)	
Brenneman, Cindy/1856 Elba Cir, Costa Mesa, CA	714-641-9700
Brooks/6632 Santa Monica Blvd, Los Angeles, CA	213-463-8844
Mike Chesser, (P)	
Brown, Dianne/732 N Highland, Los Angeles, CA	213-464-2775
David LeBon, (P), Bill Werts, (P)	
Burlingham, Tricia/10355 Ashton Ave, Los Angeles, CA	213-271-3982
Bob Stevens, (P)	
Busacca, Mary/130 Buena Vista, Mill Valley, CA	415-381-9047
Bob August, (I), Mark Busacca, (I), Ignacio Gomez, (I), Paul Hoffman, (P), Alton Kelley, (I), Rich Mahon, (I), Joe Murray, (C), Tom Nikosey, (I)	
Bybee, Gerald/1811 Folsom St, San Francisco, CA	415-863-6346

C

Caplan, Deborah/654 Cloverdale Ave #204, Los Angeles, CA	213-935-8248
Carroll, J J/PO Box 3881, Manhattan Beach, CA	213-318-1066
Fred Nelson, (I)	
Church, Spencer/425 Randolph Ave, Seattle, WA	206-324-1199
John Fretz, (I), Terry Heffernan, (P), Mits Katayama, (I), Ann Marra, (G), Scott McDougall, (I), Dale Nordell, (I), Marilyn Nordell, (I), Rusty Platz, (I), Ted Rand, (I), Diane Solvang-Angell, (I), Dugald Stermer, (I), West Stock, (S), Craig Walden, (I), Dale Windham, (P)	
Collier, Jan/166 South Park, San Francisco, CA	415-552-4252
Barbara Banthien, (I), Bunny Carter, (I), Chuck Eckart, (I), Cris Hammond, (I), Robert Hunt, (I), Kathy O'Brien, (I), Bernard Phillips, (P), Gretchen Schields, (I), Robert Steele, (I)	
Cook, Warren/PO Box 2159, Laguna Hills, CA	714-770-4619
Kathleen Norris Cook, (P)	
Copeland & Assoc/15726 Franciquito Ave, Valinda, CA	818-917-4940
Cormany, Paul/11607 Clover Ave, Los Angeles, CA	213-828-9653
Mark Busacca, (I), Bryant Eastman, (I), Dave Eichenberger, (I), Bob Gleason, (I), Lamb & Hall, (P), Jim Heimann, (I), Bob Krogle, (I), Gary Norman, (I), Ed Scarisbrick, (I), Stan Watts, (I), Dick Wilson, (I), Andy Zito, (I)	
Cornell, Kathleen/1046 N Orange Dr, Los Angeles, CA	213-462-5622
Nancy Duell, (I), Miles Hardiman, (I), Masami, (I), Daniel McGowan, (I), Jan Oswald, (P), Bonnie Timmons, (I)	
Courtney & Natale/8800 Venice, Los Angeles, CA	213-202-0344
Douglas Bevans, (I), Bart Doe, (I), Diane Teske Harris, (I), Matt Mahurin, (I), Paul Maxon, (I), Linda Medina, (I), Judy Reed, (I), Jeff Scales, (P), Chuck Schmidt, (I)	
Crosse, Annie/10642 Vanora Dr, Sunland, CA	818-352-5173
Wendy Lagerstrom, (I), Henri Parmentier, (I), Ted Sizemore, (I), Terry Smith, (I)	

DEF

Dicker, Debbie/765 Clementina St, San Francisco, CA	415-621-0687
Keith Ovregaard, (P)	
Diskin, Donnell/143 Edgemont, Los Angeles, CA	213-383-9157
Donnellan, Scott/112 Pine Pl #2, Santa Cruz, CA	408-425-1750
Drayton, Sheryl/5018 Dumont Pl, Woodland Hills, CA	818-347-2227
Dryden, Lorna/2104 Holly Dr, Los Angeles, CA	213-208-4920
DuCane, Alex/8350 Marmont Ln, Los Angeles, CA	213-654-3534
Dubow, Chuck/7461 Beverly Blvd #405, Los Angeles, CA	213-938-5177
Terry Anderson, (I), Rick Ellescas, (I), Marc Ericksen, (I), Roger Hubbard, (I), Richard Ikkanda, (I), Paul Kratter, (I), Mike Rogers, (I), Larry Salk, (I)	
Egbert, Lydia/190 Cervantes Blvd #7, San Francisco, CA	415-921-2415
Elliott, Christine/17806 Bailey Dr, Torrance, CA	213-542-7267

Please send us your additions and updates.

Epstein, Rhoni & Assoc/3814 Franklin Ave, Los Angeles, CA	213-663-2388
Ericson, William/1024 Mission St, South Pasadena, CA	213-461-4969
Faia, Michele/387 Brookmere Dr, San Jose, CA	408-281-2590
Feliciano, Terrianne/16782 Red Hill #B, Irvine, CA	714-250-4357
Fenton, Paul/1680 Vine St #819, Hollywood, CA	213-463-5596
Ferguson, Lynnda/6439 Cleon, N Hollywood, CA	818-761-3636
Finlayson & Assoc/1448 Portia St, Los Angeles, CA	213-481-0228
Fisher, Susan/22 Marinero Cir #37, Tiburon, CA	415-435-6198
Fleming, Laird Tyler/407 1/2 Shirley Pl, Beverly Hills, CA	213-552-4626

Willardson + Assoc, (P), John Bilecky, (P)

Fletcher, Lois/28956 West Lake Vista Dr, Agoura, CA	818-707-1010

Earl Miller, (P)

Fox & Clark/8350 Melrose Ave #201, Los Angeles, CA	213-653-6484

G

Gale, Gary/3539 Jennings St, San Diego, CA	619-222-6563
Gardner, Jean/4121 Wilshire Blvd #311, Los Angeles, CA	213-384-2615
Garvin, Bob/1100 Glendon Ave #732, Los Angeles, CA	213-279-1539
George, Nancy/360 1/2 N Mansfield Ave, Los Angeles, CA	213-935-4696

Brent Bear, (P), Sid Bingham, (I), Justin Carroll, (I), Randy Chewning, (I), Bruce Dean, (I), Steve Hendricks, (I), Hank Hinton, (I), Gary Hoover, (I), Richard Kriegler, (I), Larry Lake, (I), Gary Lund, (I), Rob Sprattler, (I), Bruce Wilson, (P), Jeannie Winston, (I)

Gilbert, Sam/410 Sheridan, Palo Alto, CA	415-325-2102
Glick, Ivy/350 Townsend St #421, San Francisco, CA	415-543-6056
Goldman, Caren/4521 Cleveland Ave, San Diego, CA	619-298-4043
Graham, Corey/2 Harbor Point #501, Mill Valley, CA	415-383-1134
Gray, Pam/1912 Hermosa Ave #F, Hermosa Beach, CA	213-374-3606
Group West Inc/5455 Wilshire Blvd #1212, Los Angeles, CA	213-937-4472

Neil Boyle, (I), Nixon Galloway, (I), Frank Germain, (I), Roger Hammond, (I), Fred Hatzer, (I), Ron McKee, (I), Norman Merritt, (I), Bill Robles, (I), Ren Wicks, (I)

H

Hackett, Pat/2030 First Ave #201, Seattle, WA	206-623-9459

Bill Cannon, (P), Steve Coppin, (I), Larry Duke, (I), Bill Evans, (I), Norman Hathaway, (I), Ed Hauser, (I), Gary Jacobsen, (I), Larry Lubeck, (P), Bill Mayer, (I), Mike Schumacher, (I), John C Smith, (I), John Terence Turner, (P)

Haigh, Nancy/90 Natoma St, San Francisco, CA	415-391-1646
Halcomb, Mark/1259-A Folsom, San Francisco, CA	415-861-8877
Hall, Marni & Assoc/620 N Citrus Ave, Los Angeles, CA	213-934-9420
Hart, Vikki/780 Bryant St, San Francisco, CA	415-495-4278

G K Hart, (P), Kevin Hulsey, (I), Aleta Jenks, (I), Tom Kamifuji, (I), Heather King, (I), Julie Tsuchiya, (I), Jonathan Wright, (I)

Hauser, Barbara/PO Box 1443, San Francisco, CA	415-339-1885
Hedge, Joanne/2433 28th St #O, Santa Monica, CA	213-874-1661

Delana Bettoli, (I), Chris Dellorco, (I), Ignacio Gomez, (I), Bette Levine, (I), Kenvin Lyman, (I), Rick McCollum, (I), David McMacken, (I), Dennis Mukai, (I), Vida Pavesich, (I), William Rieser, (I), Jim Salve..., (I), Joe Saputo, (I), Julie Tsuchiya, (I)

Heimberg, Nancy/351 1/2 N Sycamore Ave, Los Angeles, CA	213-933-8660
Hillman, Betsy/2230 Francisco #106, San Francisco, CA	415-563-2243

Chuck Bowden, (I), Tim Boxell, (I), Hiro Kimura, (I), John Marriott, (P), HKM Productions, (P), Greg Spalenka, (I), Joe Spencer, (I), Jeremy Thornton, (I), Jackson Vereen, (P)

Hjul, Diana/8696 Crescent Dr, Los Angeles, CA	213-654-9513

Neal Brisker, (P), John Reed Forsman, (P), Jim Greenberg, (P)

Hodges, Jeanette/12401 Bellwood, Los Alamitos, CA	213-431-4343

Ken Hodges, (I)

Hughes, April & Assoc/1350 California St #302, San Francisco, CA	415-441-4602

Romeo Bongrazio, (I), Steve Fukuda, (P), Kelly Hume, (L), David Jensen, (I), Paul Matsuda, (P), Bill Park, (I), Sue Rother, (I), Barton Stabler, (I), Diana Thewlis, (I), David Uhl, (I)

Hunt, Joann/3435 Army St #206, San Francisco, CA	415-821-9879
Hyatt, Nadine/PO Box 2455, San Francisco, CA	415-543-8944

Jeanette Adams, (I), Rebecca Archey, (I), Charles Bush, (P), Frank Cowan, (I), Marty Evans, (P), Gerry Gersten, (I), John Hyatt, (I), Bret Lopez, (P), Tom McClure, (I), Jan Schockner, (L), Victor Stabin, (I), Liz Wheaton, (I)

JK

Jorgensen, Donna/609 Summit Ave, Seattle, WA	206-284-5080

Alice Brickner, (I), Frank Denman, (P), Fred Hilliard, (I), Richard Kehl, (I), Doug Keith, (I), David Lund, (I), Robert Peckham, (I), Tim Stevenson, (I)

Kahn, Patrick/309 N Sycamore Ave, Los Angeles, CA	213-935-0071
Karpe, Michele/4328 Ben Ave, Studio City, CA	818-763-9686
Kersz, Valerie/183 N Martel Ave #220, Los Angeles, CA	818-763-9686
Kirsch, Melanie/825 1/2 Sweetzer Ave, Los Angeles, CA	213-651-3706

Bob August, (I), Kevin Hulsey, (I), Todd Smith, (P), Jeff Wack, (I)

Knable, Ellen/PO Box 67725, Los Angeles, CA	213-855-8855

Charles Bush, (P), Stan Caplan, (P), Mark Coppos, (P), David Erramouspe, (I), Joe Heiner, (I), Kathy Heiner, (I), John Hyatt, (I), Rudi Legname, (P), Vigon/Nahas/Vigon, (I), Robert Rodriguez, (I), Jonathan Wright, (I), Brian Zick, (I)

Koeffler, Ann/1555 Greenwich #9, San Francisco, CA	415-885-2714

Randy Berrett, (I), Karl Edwards, (I), Bob Hickson, (I), Paul Kratter, (I), Kevin O'Shea, (I), Michael Pearce, (I), Stephen Peringer, (I), Ken Rosenberg, (I), Chris Shorten, (P), Sarn Suvityasiri, (I)

Kovac, Elka/1609 Greenfield Ave, Los Angeles, CA	213-473-6316

Kate Lanier, (I)

LM

Laycock, Louise/8800 Venice Blvd, Los Angeles, CA	213-204-6401
Lee & Lou/1548 18th St #101, Santa Monica, CA	213-828-2259

Rob Gage, (P), Bob Grigg, (P), Richard Leech, (I)

Lilie, Jim/251 Kearny St #511, San Francisco, CA	415-441-4384

Lou Beach, (I), Alan Dolgins, (P), David Fischer, (P), Patricia Mahoney, (I), Masami Miyamoto, (I), Larry Noble, (I), Robert Rodriguez, (I), Dugald Stermer, (I), Ezra Tucker, (I), Stan Watts, (I), Dennis Ziemienski, (I)

Linville, Betty/6546 Hollywood Blvd #220, Los Angeles, CA	213-467-4455
Lippert, Tom/1100 Glendon #732, Los Angeles, CA	213-279-1539
London, Valerie/9756 Charleville Blvd, Beverly Hills, CA	213-277-8090
Luna, Tony/45 E Walnut St, Pasadena, CA	213-681-3130
MK Communications/2737 Polk St #2, San Francisco, CA	415-775-5110

Mike Godfrey, (I), Robert Holmes, (P), Jim Sadlon, (P), Max Seabuagh, (I)

MacKenzie, Stewart/515 Diamond St, San Francisco, CA	415-626-4542
Macias, Lori/16846 Armstead, Granada Hills, CA	818-368-2237
Magestic, Michael/23316 Burbank Blvd, Woodland Hills, CA	818-703-8348
Malone, Sara/26 Medway Rd #6, San Rafael, CA	415-459-6435
Marie, Rita & Friends/6376 W 5th St, Los Angeles, CA	213-934-3395

David Beck, (I), Chris Consani, (I), Mort Drucker, (I), Jim Endicott, (I), Marla Frazee, (I), Hiro Kimura, (I), Richard Milholland, (I), Gary Pierazzi, (I), Robert Pryor, (I), Paul Rogers, (I), Gary Ruddell, (I), Dick Sakahara, (I), Danny Smyhte, (I), Greg Wray, (I)

Martha Productions/1830 S Robertson Blvd #203, Los Angeles, CA	213-204-1771

Bob Brugger, (I), Jacques Devaud, (I), Stan Evenson, (I), Tracy Garner, (I), John Hamagami, (I), William Harrison, (I), Arthur Hill, (I), Catherine Leary, (I), Ed Lindlof, (I), Rudy Obrero, (I), Cathy Pavia, (I), Wayne Watford, (I)

Mastrogeorge, Robin/11020 Ventura Blvd Box 294, Studio City, CA	818-761-5677
May, William & Assoc/PO Box 781, Malibu, CA	213-457-1380
McBain, Morgan/650 San Juan Ave, Venice, CA	213-392-9341

Joann Daley, (I), Ron Derhacopian, (P), John Taylor Dismukes, (I), Scott Ernster, (I), Bob McMahon, (I), Greg Moraes, (I)

McBride, Elizabeth/70 Broadway, San Francisco, CA	415-863-0655

Keith Criss, (I), Robert Holmes, (P), Patricia Pearson, (I), Bill Sanchez, (I), Earl Thollander, (I), Tom Vano, (P)

McCargar, Lucy/652 Bair Isl Rd, Redwood City, CA	415-363-2130

Tim Mitoma, (I), Dennis Nolan, (I), Mary Ross, (I)

McKenzie, Dianne/125 King St, San Francisco, CA	415-541-9051

Victor Budnik, (P)

Melrose, Penny/1333 Lawrence Expwy #150, Santa Clara, CA	408-737-9494
Michaels, Martha/3279 Kifer Rd, Santa Clara, CA	408-735-8443
Mix, Eva/4985 S Santa Rosa Ave, Santa Ana, CA	707-584-1608
Mizejewski, Max/942 Shearwater St, Ontario, CA	714-947-8585
Moniz, Karletta/250 Newhall Ave, San Francisco, CA	415-821-6358
Morgan-Friedman/4411 Brookside, Irvine, CA	714-551-6445

REPRESENTATIVES CONT'D.

Please send us your additions and updates.

Morris, Leslie/1062 Rengstorff Ave, Mountain View, CA — 415-966-8301
 Paul Olsen, (I)

NOP

Newman & Franks/2956 Nicada Dr, Los Angeles, CA — 213-470-0140
Ogden, Robin/8126 Blackburn Ave, Los Angeles, CA — 213-858-0946
 Karen Bell, (I), Joe Crabtree, (I), Jan Evans, (I), Steve Gray, (I), Gerry Hampton, (I), Lou LaRose, (I), Jim Miller, (P), Julie Perron, (I), John Puchalski, (I), Ken Rosenberg, (I), Corey Wolfe, (I)
Ostan-Prentice/Ostan/13802 Northwest Passage #203, Marina Del Rey, CA — 213-823-4440
Padgett, Donna/13520 Terrace Pl, Whittier, CA — 213-945-7801
Parrish, Dave/Photopia/PO Box 2309, San Francisco, CA — 415-441-5611
Parsons, Ralph/1232 Folsom St, San Francisco, CA — 415-339-1885
Partners Reps/12813 Milbank St, Studio City, CA — 818-762-9007
Pate, Randy/The Source/3848 Ventura Canyon Ave, Sherman Oaks, CA — 818-985-8181
Patton, Robert/8228 Sunset Blvd #230, Los Angeles, CA — 213-650-8880
Peek, Pamela/1964 N Rodney Dr #201, Los Angeles, CA — 213-660-1596
Pepper, Don/638 S Van Ness Ave, Los Angeles, CA — 213-382-6281
Phillips, Ellen/1717 Mason St #2, San Francisco, CA — 415-928-6336
Pierceall, Kelly/25260 Piuma Rd, Malibu, CA — 213-559-4327
Piscopo, Maria/2038 Calvert Ave, Costa Mesa, CA — 714-556-8133
 Adrienne Warren, (P)
Pohl, Jacqueline/2947 Jackson St, San Francisco, CA — 415-563-8616
Pribble, Laurie/911 Victoria Dr, Arcadia, CA — 818-574-0288
Publication Arts Network/717 Market St, San Francisco, CA — 415-777-5988

RS

Reece, Sandra/2565 Canyon Dr, Los Angeles, CA — 213-465-7576
 Ken Chernus, (P), Ralph Pleasant, (P), David Zanzinger, (P)
Reese Causey & Assoc/2565 Canyon Dr, Los Angeles, CA — 213-465-7576
Rosen, Michael/870 N El Centro Ave #6, Los Angeles, CA — 213-462-5726
Rosenthal, Elise/3443 Wade St, Los Angeles, CA — 213-306-6878
 Saul Bernstein, (I), Chris Butler, (I), Alan Daniels, (I), Alan Hashimoto, (I), James Henry, (I), Tim Huhn, (I), Jim McKiernan, (I), Kenton Nelson, (I), Peter Palombi, (I), Tom Pansini, (I), Kim Passey, (I), Bill Robles, (I), Tom Tomita, (I), Larry Winborg, (I)
Salisbury, Sharon/116 W Blithedale, Mill Valley, CA — 415-495-4665
 Keith Batcheller, (I), Craig Calsbeck, (I), Jim Endicott, (I), Bob Graham, (I), Bo Hylen, (P), Larry Keenan, (P), Bette Levine, (I), Dave McMacken, (I), Robert Mizono, (P), Vida Pavesich, (I)
Salzman, Richard W/1352 Hornblend St, San Diego, CA — 619-272-8147
 Tony Baker, (I), Ruben DeAnda, (I), Manuel Garcia, (I), Jason Harlem, (P), Denise Hilton-Putnam, (I), Joyce Kitchell, (I), Bernie Lansky, (C), Gordon Menzie, (P), Dave Mollering, (I), Imagery That Moves, (G), Dianne O'Quinn-Burke, (I), Everett Peck, (I), Nono Remos, (R), Terry Smith, (I), Debra Stine, (I), Walter Stuart, (I), Jonathan Wright, (I), Daniels, (I)
Sandler, Neil/3443 Wade St, Los Angeles, CA — 213-306-6878
Scott, Alexis/940 N Highland Ave, Los Angeles, CA — 213-856-0008
Scott, Freda/244 Ninth St, San Francisco, CA — 415-621-2992
 Sherry Bringham, (I), David Campbell, (P), John Hersey, (I), Gayle Kabaker, (I), Jeff Leedy, (F), Francis Livingston, (I), Alan Mazzetti, (I), Diane Padys, (P), Susan Schelling, (P), Judy Unger, (I)
Scroggy, David/2124 Froude St, San Diego, CA — 619-222-2476
 Ed Abrams, (I), Jodell D Abrams, (I), Joe Chiado, (I), Rick Geary, (I), John Pound, (I), Hal Scroggy, (I), Debbie Tilley, (I)
Shaffer, Barry/PO Box 480888, Los Angeles, CA — 213-939-2527
Shigekuni, Cindy/PO Box 2336, Beverly Hills, CA — 213-858-3922
Slobodian, Barbara/745 N Alta Vista Blvd, Hollywood, CA — 213-935-6668
 Bob Greisen, (I), David Kaiser, (I), Tom O'Brien, (P), Forest Sigwart, (I), Scott Slobodian, (P)
Sobol, Lynne/4302 Melrose Ave, Los Angeles, CA — 213-665-5141
 Frank Marquez, (I), Arthur Montes de Oca, (P)
Stefanski, Janice/2022 Jones St, San Francisco, CA — 415-928-0457
 Adrian Day, (I), Michael Jay, (P), Barbara Kelley, (I), Steven Lyons, (I), George Olson, (P), Katherine Salentine, (I), Rolf Sieffe, (P), Cliff Spohn, (I)
Steinberg, John/11731 Crescenda, Los Angeles, CA — 213-471-0232
 Jay Ahrent, (P), John Alvin, (I), Bo Gehring & Associates, (I), Beau Daniels, (I), Alan Daniels, (I), Precision Illustration, (I),

David Kimble, (I), Reid Miles, (P), Richard Moore, (P), Larry Noble, (I), Frank Page, (I), Mark Stehrenberger, (I), Ed Wexler, (I)
Stern & Assoc/1083 Clay St #101, San Francisco, CA — 415-434-1010
Stivers, Robert/101 Scholz Plz PH 21, Newport Beach, CA — 714-645-9070
Stoffer, Barry/PO box 480888, Los Angeles, CA — 213-939-2527
Studio Artists Inc/638 S Van Ness Ave, Los Angeles, CA — 213-382-6281
 Chuck Coppock, (I), George Francuch, (I), Bill Franks, (I), Duane Gordon, (I), Larry Willett, (P)
Sullivan, Diane/3727 Buchanan St, San Francisco, CA — 415-563-8884
 Lawrence Duke, (P)
Sullivan, Martha/2395 Paradise Dr, Tiburon, CA — 415-435-4181
 Patricia Brabant, (P)
Sweet, Ron/716 Montgomery St, San Francisco, CA — 415-433-1222
 Charles East, (D), Randy Glass, (I), John Hamagami, (I), Bob Haydock, (I), Gregg Keeling, (I), Richard Leech, (I), Will Nelson, (I), Walter Swarthout, (P), Jack Unruh, (I), Don Weller, (I), Bruce Wolfe, (I), James B Wood, (P)

TV

Tabke, Tim/35-23 Ryder St, Santa Clara, CA — 408-733-5855
Taggard, Jim/PO 4064 Pioneer Square Station, Seattle, WA — 206-547-0807
 Sjef's-Photographie, (P)
Thomsen, Dale/40 Gold St, San Francisco, CA — 415-434-0380
Thornby, Kirk/1039 S Fairfax Ave, Los Angeles, CA — 213-933-9883
Todd, Deborah/259 Clara St, San Francisco, CA — 415-495-3556
Tomson, Jerry/1050 N Wilcox Ave, Hollywood, CA — 213-469-6316
 Robert Grigg, (P)
Tos, Debbie/7306 W 82nd St, Los Angeles, CA — 213-410-0402
 Carl Furuta, (P)
Tranter, Susan/23011 Moulton Pky #E-9, Lauguna Hills, CA — 714-770-1680
Trimpe, Susan/2717 Western Ave, Seattle, WA — 206-728-1300
 Don Baker, (I), Wendy Edelson, (I), Stephen Peringer, (I)
Turnbull, Gerry/9348 Santa Monica Blvd #101, Beverly Hills, CA — 213-659-1737
Vandamme, Mary/1242 Francisco #1, San Francisco, CA — 415-771-0494
 John Blaustein, (P), John Collier, (I), Robert Giusti, (I), Joe and Kathy Heiner, (I), Alan Krosnick, (P), Kenvin Lyman, (I), Dennis Mukai, (I), Bill Rieser, (I), Ed Scarisbrick, (I), Michael Schwab, (I), Charles Shields, (I), Rick Strauss, (P), Carol Wald, (I), Kim Whitesides, (I)

WYZ

Wagoner, Jae/200 Westminster Ave #A, Venice, CA — 213-392-4877
 Tim Alt, (I), Michael Backus, (I), Roger Beerworth, (I), Stephen Durke, (I), Steve Jones, (I), Lee MacLeod, (I), Craig Nelson, (I), Robert Tanenbaum, (I), Don Weller, (I)
Wiegand, Chris/7106 Waring Ave, Los Angeles, CA — 213-931-5942
Willey, David/1535 Green St #209, San Francisco, CA — 415-441-1623
Winston, Bonnie/228 S Beverly Dr #210, Beverly Hills, CA — 213-275-2858
 David Andrade, (P), Garry Brod, (P), Robert Ferrone, (P), Kiko Ricotti, (P), Rob White, (P)
Youmans, Jill/1021 1/2 N La Brea, Los Angeles, CA — 213-469-8624
 Dan Cooper, (I), Jeff George, (I), Brian Leng, (P), Jeff Leung, (I), Christine Nasser, (I), Joyce Patti, (I), Bill Salada, (I)
Young, Jill/Compendium Inc/945 Front St #206, San Francisco, CA — 415-392-0542
 Judy Clifford, (I), Armondo Diaz, (P), Celeste Ericsson, (I), Marilee Heyer, (I), Rae Huestis, (G), Mary Jew, (G), Bonnie Matza, (G), Barbara Muhlhauser, (G), Martin Schweitzer, (G), Donna Mae Shaver, (P), Cecily Starin, (I), Sarn Suvityasiri, (I), Ed Taber, (I), Carlotta Tormey, (I)
Zank, Elen/262 Donahue St, Sausalito, CA — 415-332-3739
 Chip Carroon, (P)
Zimmerman, Delores H/9135 Hazen Dr, Beverly Hills, CA — 213-273-2642

NOTES:

PHOTOGRAPHERS

NEW YORK CITY

A

Abatelli, Gary/80 Charles St #3W	212-254-2142
Abel, Jim/112 E 19th St	212-460-5374
Abramowitz, Ellen/166 E 35th St #4H	212-686-2409
Abramowitz, Jerry/680 Broadway	212-420-9500
Abramson, Michael/84 University Pl	212-691-2601
Adamo, Jeff/50 W 93rd St #8P	212-866-4886
Adams, Eddie/29 E 22nd St #68	212-477-5346
Adams, George G./15 W 38th St	212-391-1345
Adelman, Bob/151 W 28th St	212-736-0537
Adelman, Menachem Assoc/156 Fifth Ave #323	212-675-1202
Adler, Arnie/70 Park Terrace W	212-304-2443
Aerographics/514 W 24th St	212-362-9546
Agor, Alexander/108-28 Flatlands 7 St	212-777-1775
Aharoni, Oudi/704 Broadway	212-777-0847
Ahzzi, Robert/415 Madison Ave	212-750-1020
Aich, Clara/218 E 25th St	212-686-4220
Akis, Emanuel/6 W 18th St #803	212-620-0299
Albanese, Carlo/310 E 49th St	212-838-1507
Albert, Jade/59 W 19th St #3B	212-242-0940
Albert, Peter/59 W 71st St	212-787-1759
Alberts, Andrea/100 Fifth Ave	212-242-5794
Alcorn, Richard/160 W 95th St #7A	212-866-1161
Alexander, Robert/50 W 29th St	212-684-0496
Alexanders, John W/308 E 73rd St	212-734-9166
Allen, Jim/175 Fifth Ave #1112	212-473-8020
Allison, David/42 E 23rd St	212-460-9056
Alper, Barbara/202 W 96th St	212-316-6518
Alpern/Lukoski/250 W 88th St	212-724-5017
Alt, Howard/24 W 31st St	212-594-3300
Amato, Paul/154 W 57th St	212-541-4787
Ambrose, Ken/44 E 23rd St	212-260-4848
Amplo, Nick/271 1/2 W 10th St	212-741-2799
Amrine, Jamie/30 W 22nd St	212-243-2178
Andracke, Gregory/207 W 86th St	212-580-9964
Andrews, Bert/PO Box 20707	212-662-6732
Anik, Adam/111 Fourth Ave #1-I	212-228-4148
Antonio/Stephen Photo/45 E 20th St	212-674-2350
Apple, Richard/80 Varick St #4B	212-966-6782
Arakawa, Nobu/40 E 21st St	212-475-0206
Aranita, Jeffrey/60 Pineapple St	718-625-7672
Areman, Scott/50 Plaza St #5C	718-636-8217
Arky, David/57 W 19th St #2A	212-242-4760
Arlak, Victoria/40 East End Ave	212-879-0250
Arma, Tom/38 W 26th St	212-243-7904
Arndt, Dianne/400 Central Park West	212-866-1902
Arslanian, Ovak/344 W 14th St	212-255-1519
ASHE, BILL/534 W 35TH ST (P 65)	**212-695-6473**
Ashley, Pat/920 Broadway	212-473-6180
Atkin, Jonathan/23 E 17th St	212-242-5218
Aubry, Daniel/365 First Ave	212-598-4191
Augustine, Paula/50 Park Terr E	212-304-0234
Aurora Retouching/19 W 21st St	212-255-0620
Auster, Walter/35 W 38th St	212-354-0456
Avedis/381 Park Ave S	212-685-5888
Avedon, Richard/407 E 75th St	212-879-6325
Axon, Red/17 Park Ave	212-532-6317
Azzato, Hank/348 W 14th St 3rd Fl	212-929-9455
Azzi, Robert/415 Madison Ave	212-750-1020

B

Baasch, Diane/41 W 72nd St #11F	212-724-2123
Babushkin, Mark/110 W 31st St	212-239-6630
Back, John/15 Sheridan Sq	212-243-6347
Bagnato, Gene/230 Riverside Dr	212-222-8381
Bahrt, Irv/310 E 46th St	212-661-5260
Baillie, Allan & Gus Francisco/220 E 23rd St 11th Fl	212-683-0418
Bak, Sunny/876 Broadway 4th Fl	212-689-6045
Baker, Chuck/1630 York Ave	212-517-9060
Baker, Gloria/415 Central Park W	212-222-2866
Baker, Joe/156 Fifth Ave #925	212-924-3440

Bakerman, Nelson/342 W 56th St #1D	212-489-1647
Baldwin, Joel/29 E 19th St	212-533-7470
Bancroft, Monty/161 W 15th St	212-807-8650
Barash, Howard/349 W 11th St	212-242-6182
Baratta, Nicholas/511 W 33rd St	212-239-0999
Barba, Dan/201 E 16th St	212-420-8611
Barber, James/873 Broadway	212-598-4500
Barboza, Tony/108 E 16th St	212-674-5759
Barcellona, Marianne/36 E 20 St 5th Floor	212-460-8740
Barclay, Bob Studios/5 W 19th St 6th Fl	212-255-3440
Barkentin, George/15 W 18th St	212-243-2174
Barnell, Joe/164 Madison Ave	212-686-8850
Barnett, Peggy/26 E 22nd St	212-673-0500
Barns, Larry/21 W 16th St	212-242-8833
Barr, Neal/222 Central Park South	212-765-5760
Barrett, John/164 E 66th St	212-517-5210
Barrett, John E/40 E 20th St 7th Fl	212-777-7309
Barrick, Rick/12 E 18th St 4th Fl	212-741-2304
BARROW, SCOTT/214 W 30TH ST #6 (P 66,67)	**212-736-4567**
BARROWS, WENDY/205 E 22ND ST (P 68)	**212-685-0799**
Barton, Paul/101 W 18th St 4th Fl	212-533-1422
Bartone, Laurence/108 E 16th St	212-254-6430
Batlin, Lee/37 E 28th St 8th Fl	212-685-9492
Baumel, Ken/119 W 23rd St	212-929-7550
Bava, John/51 Station Ave	718-967-9175
Bealmear, Brad/54 Barrow St	212-675-8060
Bean, John/5 W l9th St	212-242-8106
BEAUDIN, TED/450 W 31ST ST (P 69,185)	**212-563-6065**
Bechtold, John/117 E 31st St	212-679-7630
Beck, Arthur/119 W 22nd St	212-691-8331
Becker, Jonathan/450 West 24th St	212-929-3180
Beckhard, Robert/130 E 24th St	212-777-1411
Beebe, Rod/790 Amsterdam #4D	212-678-7832
Beglieter, Steven/2025 Broadway #19K	212-580-7409
Belinsky, Jon/119 E 17th St	212-627-1246
Beller, Janet/48 W 21st St	212-741-2776
Benedict, William/5 Tudor City	212-697-4460
Bennett, Philip/1181 Broadway	212-683-3906
Benvenuti, Bruno/35 W 36th St	212-563-2730
Bercow, Larry/209 W 38th St	212-221-1598
Berenholtz, Richard/600 W 111th St #6A	212-222-1302
Berger, Joseph/121 Madison Ave	212-685-7191
Bergman, Beth/150 West End Ave	212-724-1867
Bergren, John/27 W 20th St #1003	212-989-4423
Berkun, Phil/119 Fifth Ave #801	212-254-7358
Berkwit, Lane/262 Fifth Ave	212-889-5911
Berman, Brad/295 Ecksford St	718-383-8950
Berman, Howard/5 E 19th St #303	212-473-3366
Berman, Malcolm/256 Fifth Ave	212-431-4446
Bernson, Carol/119 Fifth Ave #806	212-473-3884
Bernstein, Alan/365 First Ave 2nd Fl	212-254-1355
Bernstein, Bill/59 Thompson St #9	212-925-6853
Bester, Roger/55 Van Dam St 11th Fl	212-645-5810
Betz, Charles/50 W 17th St	212-807-0457
Bevan, David/536 W 50th St	212-582-5045
Bevilacqua, Joe/202 E 42nd St	212-490-0355
Bickford, Christopher/55 W 11th St	212-243-6638
Biddle, Geoffrey/5 E 3rd St	212-505-7713
Bies, William/221 W 21st St	212-924-6997
Big City Prodctns/5 E 19th St #303	212-473-3366
Bijur, Hilda/190 E 72nd St	212-737-4458
Bisbee, Terry/290 W 12th St	212-242-4762
Bishop, David/251 W 19th St	212-929-4355
Bishop, Randa/59 W 12th St	212-206-1122
Blackburn, Joseph M/116 W 29th St #2C	212-947-7674
BLACKMAN, BARRY/115 E 23RD ST 10TH FL (P 71)	**212-473-3100**
Blackman, Jeffrey/2323 E 12th St	718-769-0986
Blackstock, Ann/400 W 43rd St #4E	212-695-2525
Blake, Rebecca/35 W 36th St	212-695-6438
Blechman, Jeff/591 Broadway	212-966-1455
Blegen, Alana/	718-769-2619
Blinkoff, Richard/147 W 15th St 3rd Fl	212-620-7883

Please send us your additions and updates.

Block, Ira Photography/215 W 20th St	212-242-2728
Bloom, Teri/300 Mercer St #6C	212-475-2274
Blosser, Robert/741 West End Ave #3C	212-662-0107
BOBBE, LELAND/51 W 28TH ST (P 72,73)	**212-685-5238**
Bodi Studios/340 W 39th St	212-947-7883
Bodick, Gay/11 E 80th St	212-772-8584
Bogertman, Ralph Inc/34 W 28th St	212-889-8871
Bolesta, Alan/11 Riverside Dr #13SE	212-873-1932
Bonomo, Louis/118 W 27th St #2F	212-242-4630
BORDNICK, BARBARA/39 E 19TH ST (P 74)	**212-533-1180**
Bosch, Peter/477 Broome St	212-925-0707
Boszko, Ron/140 W 57th St	212-541-5504
Bottomley, Jim/125 Fifth Ave	212-677-9646
Bracco, Bob/43 E 19th St	212-228-0230
Brandt, Peter/73 Fifth Ave #6B	212-242-4289
Braun, Yenachem/666 West End Ave	212-873-1985
Braune, Peter/134 W 32nd St #602	212-244-4270
Braveman, Alan/485 Fifth Ave	212-674-1925
Brenner, George/15 W 24th St	212-691-7436
BRENNER, JAY/18 E 17TH ST (P 54,55)	**212-741-2244**
Breskin, Michael/324 Lafayette	212-925-2858
Brewster, Don/235 West End Ave	212-874-0548
Bridges, Kiki/147 W 26th St	212-807-6563
Brill Studio/270 City Island Ave	212-885-0802
Brill, James/237 E 79th St	212-744-4583
Britton, Peter/315 E 68th St	212-737-1664
Brizzi, Andrea/175 Washington Park	718-522-0836
Brody, Bob/5 W 19th 2nd Fl	212-741-0013
Bronstein, Steve/5 E 19th St #303	212-473-3366
Brooke, Randy/179 E 3rd St	212-677-2656
Brosan, Roberto/873 Broadway	212-473-1471
Brown, David/Nancy/6 W 20th St	212-675-8067
Brown, Owen Studio/134 W 29th St 2nd Fl	212-947-9470
Bruderer, Rolf/443 Park Ave S	212-684-4890
Bruno Burklin/873 Broadway	212-420-0208
BRUNO PHOTO/43 CROSBY ST 1ST FL (P 75)	**212-925-2929**
Brunswick, Cecile/127 W 96th St	212-222-2088
Bryce, Sherman E/269 W 90th St #3B	212-580-9639
Bryson, John/12 E 62nd St	212-755-1321
Buceta, Jaime/56 W 22nd St 6th Fl	212-807-8485
Buck, Bruce/39 W 14th St	212-645-1022
Buckler, Susanne/344 W 38th St	212-279-0043
Buckner, Bill/21 W 17th St	212-242-5129
Burns, Tom/534 W 35th St	212-927-4678
Burrell, Fred/16 W 22nd St	212-691-0808
Butler, Dennis/200 E 37th St 4th Fl	212-686-5084

C

Cadge, Bill & Jeff/15 W 28th St	212-685-2435
Cailor/Resnick/237 W 54th St 4th Fl	212-977-4300
Calicchio, Tom/30 E 21st St	212-473-8990
Callis, Chris/91 Fifth Ave	212-243-0231
Camera Communications/39 W 38th St	212-391-1373
Camp, E J/101 W 18th St	212-741-2872
Campbell, Barbara/147 W 22nd St	212-929-5620
Campos, John/132 W 21st St	212-675-0601
Canady, Philip/1411 Second Ave	212-737-3855
Cannon, Gregory/876 Broadway 2nd Fl	212-724-6196
Canton, Brian/205 E 42nd St	212-221-7318
Cantor, Phil/75 Ninth Ave 8th Fl	212-243-1143
Cardacino, Michael/20 Ridge Rd	212-947-9307
Cargasacchi, Gianni/175 Fifth Ave	212-473-8020
Carlton, Chuck/36 E 23rd St 7th Fl	212-777-1099
Carrino, John/160 Fifth Ave #914	212-243-3623
Carron, Les/15 W 24th St 2nd Fl	212-255-8250
Carson, Donald/115 W 23rd St	212-807-8987
Carter, Bill/39 E 12th	212-505-6088
Carter, Dwight/11 W 17th St	212-627-1266
Casey/10 Park Ave #3E	212-984-1397
Cashin, Art/5 W 19th St	212-255-3440
Casper, Mike/70 Wooster St	212-219-1257
Castellano, Peter/162 W 21st St	212-206-6320
Castillo, Luis A/60 Pineapple St	718-834-1380

Caulfield, Patricia/115 W 86th St #2E	212-362-1951
Caverly, Kat/414 W 49th St	212-757-8388
Cearley, Guy/25 W 31st St	212-714-0075
Celnick, Edward/36 E 12th St	212-420-9326
Cenicola, Tony Studio/503 W 43rd St	212-239-6634
Cerniglio, Tom/594 Broadway #8W	212-925-9583
Chakmakjian, Paul/35 W 36th St 8th Fl	212-563-3195
Chalk, David/265 37th St PH-A	212-302-6118
Chalkin, Dennis/5 E 16th St	212-929-1036
Chan, T S/174 Duane St	212-219-0574
Chaney, Scott/5 W 30th St	212-736-1720
Chanteau, Pierre/209 W 38th St	212-221-5860
Chao, John/51 W 81st St #6B	212-580-7912
Charlas, Jacques/134 Beaumont	718-648-5345
CHARLES, BILL/265 W 37TH ST #PH-D (P 76)	**212-719-9156**
Charles, Frederick/254 Park Ave S #7F	212-505-0686
Charles, Lisa/147 W 26th St	212-929-6958
Chauncy, Kim/123 W 13th St	212-242-2400
Checani, Richard/31 E 32nd St	212-889-2049
Chelsea Photo/Graphics/641 Ave of Americas	212-206-1780
Chen, Paul Inc/133 Fifth Ave	212-674-4100
Chernin, Bruce/330 W 86th St	212-496-0266
Chestnut, Richard/236 W 27th St	212-255-1790
Chiba/303 Park Ave S #506	212-674-7575
Chin, Ted/118 W 27th St #3R	212-691-7612
Chokel, Dan/135 W 29th St	212-947-5795
Choucroun, Irit/450 Broome St #3E	212-226-0191
Christensen, Paul H/286 Fifth Ave	212-279-2838
Chrynwski, Walter/154 W 18th St	212-675-1906
Chu, H L & Co Ltd/39 W 29th St	212-889-4818
Church, Diana/31 W 31st St	212-736-4116
Cipolla, Karen/103 Reade St 3rd Fl	212-619-6114
Cirone, Bettina/57 W 58th St	212-888-7649
Clarke, Kevin/900 Broadway 9th Fl	212-460-9360
Clayton, Tom/568 Broadway #601	212-431-3377
Clementi, Joseph Assoc/133 W 19th St 3rd Fl	212-924-7770
Clough, Terry/147 W 25th St	212-255-3040
Cobb, Jan/381 Park Ave S #922	212-889-2257
Cobin, Martin/145 E 49th St	212-758-5742
Cochran, George/381 Park Ave S	212-689-9054
Coggin, Roy/64 W 21st St	212-929-6262
Cohen, James/580 Eighth Ave	212-719-2790
Cohen, Joel/27 E 13th St #7E	212-691-5129
Cohen, Lawrence/277 E 10th St	212-777-3346
COHEN, MARC DAVID/5 W 19TH (P 77)	**212-741-0015**
Cohen, Robert/175 Fifth Ave #1112	212-473-8020
Cohn, Ric/137 W 25th St #1	212-924-6749
Colabella, Vincent/304 E 41st St	212-949-7456
Colby, Ron/140 E 28th St	212-684-3084
Cole, Bob/131-03 233rd St	718-525-7471
Coleman, Bruce/381 Fifth Ave 2nd Fl	212-683-5227
Coleman, Gene/250 W 27th St	212-691-4752
Colen, Corrine/519 Broadway	212-431-7425
Collins, Arlene/64 N Moore St #3E	212-431-9117
Collins, Chris/381 Park Ave S	212-725-0237
Collins, Joe J/208 Garfield Pl	718-965-4836
Collins, Sheldon/27 W 24th St	212-242-0076
Colliton, Paul/310 Greenwich St	212-619-6102
Colton, Robert/1700 York Ave	212-831-3953
Connelly, Hank/6 W 37th St	212-563-9109
Connors, William/310 E 46th St	212-490-3801
Contact Press Images/135 Central Park West	212-496-5300
Cook, Irvin/534 W 43rd St	212-925-6216
Cook, Rod/110 W 25th St	212-242-4463
Cooke, Colin/380 Lafayette St	212-254-5090
Cooper, Martha/310 Riverside Dr #805	212-222-5146
Cooper, Steve/5 W 31st St	212-279-4543
Cope, Gil/135 W 26th St	212-929-1777
Corbett, Jane/303 Park Ave S #512	212-505-1177
Cornicello, John/245 W 29th St	212-564-0874
Cornish, Dan/594 Broadway #1204	212-226-3183
Corporate Photographers Inc/45 John St	212-964-6515

PHOTOGRAPHERS CONT'D.

Please send us your additions and updates.

Cosimo/43 W 13th St	212-206-1818
Couzens, Larry/16 E 17th St	212-620-9790
Cowan, Frank/5 E 16th St	212-675-5960
Craig Jr, Stuart L/381 Fifth Ave 2nd Floor	212-683-5475
Crampton, Nancy/35 W 9th St	212-254-1135
Crocker, Ted/117 E 30th St	212-686-8684
Croner, Ted/15 W 28th St	212-685-3944
Cronin, Casey/115 Wooster St	212-334-9253
Crum, John R Photography/450 W 31st St	212-736-2693
Cserna, George/80 Second Ave #2	212-477-3472
Culberson, Earl/119 W 23rd St	212-473-3366
Culley, Brian/21-17 45th Ave	718-729-6311
CUNNINGHAM, PETER/214 SULLIVAN ST (P 79)	**212-475-4866**
Curatola, Tony/18 E 17th St	212-243-5478
CUTLER, CRAIG/536 W 50TH ST (P 80,81)	**212-315-3440**
Czaplinski, Czeslaw/90 Dupont St	718-389-9606

D

D'Addio, James/41 Union Sq W #1428	212-645-0267
D'Innocenzo, Paul/368 Broadway #604	212-925-9622
Daley, James D/568 Broadway	212-925-7192
Dantuono, Paul/433 Park Ave So	212-683-5778
Dantzic, Jerry/910 President St	718-789-7478
Dauman, Henri/4 E 88th St	212-737-1434
David, Gabrielle/109-35 Ditmars Blvd	718-429-0751
Davidson, Bruce/251 Park Ave S 11th Fl	212-475-7600
Davidson, Darwin K/32 Bank Street	212-242-0095
Davis, Dick/400 E 59th St	212-751-3276
Davis, Don/61 Horatio St	212-989-2820
DAVIS, HAL/131 SPRING ST (P 36,37)	**212-334-8113**
Davis, Harold/874 Broadway	212-228-0866
Davis, James/66 W 39th St	212-354-0339
Davis, Richard/17 E 16th St 9th Fl	212-675-2428
Day, Bob/29 E 19th St	212-475-7387
Day, Olita/239 Park Ave South	212-673-9354
De Zanger, Arie/80 W 40th St	212-354-7327
DeFrancis, Peter/424 Broome St	212-966-1357
DeGrado, Drew/250 W 40th St 5th Fl	212-860-0062
DeLessio, Len/7 E 17th St	212-206-8725
DeMarchelier, Patrick/162 W 21st St	212-924-3561
DeMelo, Antonio/126 W 22nd St	212-929-0507
DeMenil, Adelaide/222 Central Park South	212-541-8265
DeMilt, Ronald/873 Broadway 2nd Fl	212-228-5321
Denner, Manuel/249 W 29th St	212-947-6220
Dennis, Lisl/135 E 39th St	212-532-8226
Denson, Walt/70 W 83rd St Dplx B	212-496-7305
DePaul, Raymond/252 W 76th St #1A	212-769-2550
DePra, Nancy/15 W 24th St	212-242-0252
Derex, David/247 W 35th St	212-947-9302
Dermer, Ronald/Falmouth St	718-332-2464
DeRosa, Peter/117 W 95th St	212-864-3007
Derr, Stephen/418 W 46th St #4B	212-246-5920
DeSanto, Thomas/134 Fifth Ave 2nd Fl	212-989-5622
DeToy, Ted/205 W 19th St	212-675-6744
Deutsch, Jack/165 W 83rd St	212-799-7179
DeVito, Bart/43 E 30th St 14th Fl	212-889-9670
DeVito, Michael Jr/48 W 25th St	212-243-5267
DeVoe, Marcus E/34 E 81st St	212-737-9073
DEWYS, LEO/1170 BROADWAY (P 417)	**212-689-5580**
DeZitter, Harry/57 W 19th St	212-242-3124
Diamond, Joe/915 West End Ave	212-316-5295
DIAZ, JORGE/142 W 24TH ST 12TH FL (P 82)	**212-675-4783**
Dibue, Robert/40 W 20th St	212-490-0486
Dicran Studio/35 W 36th St 11th Fl	212-695-6438
DiFranza Williamson Photography/1414 Ave of Americas	212-832-2343
DiMartini, Sally/201 W 16th St	212-989-8369
Dodge, Jeff/133 Eighth Ave	212-620-9652
Doerzbacher, Cliff/12 Cottage Ave	718-984-7522
Doherty, Marie/43 E 22nd St	212-674-8767
Dominis, John/1271 6th Ave Rm 2850	212-841-2340
Dorf, Myron Jay/205 W 19th St 3rd Fl	212-255-2020
Dorin, Jay/220 Cabrini Blvd	212-781-7378
Dorot, Didier/48 W 21st St 9th Fl	212-206-1608

Doubilet, David/1040 Park Ave #6J	212-348-5011
Drabkin, Si Studios Inc/236 W 27th St	212-206-7040
Drew Studio/1200 Broadway	212-860-0062
Drew, Rue Faris/177 E 77th St	212-794-8994
Drivas, Joseph/15 Beacon Ave	718-667-0696
Duchaine, Randy/200 W 18th St #4F	212-243-4371
Duke, Dana/620 Broadway	212-260-3334
Dunand, Frank/18 W 27th St	212-686-3478
Duncan, Kenn/853 Seventh Ave	212-582-7080
Duncan, Nena/24 W 30th St 8th Fl	212-696-9652
Dunkley, Richard/175 Fifth Ave #1112	212-473-8020
Dunning, Hank/50 W 22nd St	212-675-6040
Dunning, Robert & Deane/57 W 58th St	212-688-0788
Duomo Photo Inc/133 W 19th St	212-243-1150

E

Eagan, Timothy/319 E 75th St	212-517-7665
Eastep, Wayne/443 Park Ave S #1006	212-686-8404
Eberstadt, Fred/791 Park Ave	212-794-9471
Eckstein, Ed/234 Fifth Ave 5th Fl	212-685-9342
Edahl, Edward/236 W 27th St	212-929-2002
Edgeworth, Anthony/333 Fifth Ave	212-679-6031
Edwards, Gregory/30 East End Ave	212-879-4339
EGUIGUREN, CARLOS/139 E 57TH ST 3RD FL (P 87)	**212-888-6732**
Ehrenpreis, Dave/156 Fifth Ave	212-242-1976
Eisenberg, Steve/448 W 37th St	212-563-2061
Elbers, Johan/18 E 18th St	212-929-5783
Elgort, Arthur/300 Central Park West	212-724-6557
Elios-Zunini Studio/142 W 4th St	212-228-6827
Elkins, Joel/5 E 16th St	212-989-4500
Ellis, Ray/176 Westminster Rd	718-282-6449
Elmer, Jo/200 E 87th St	212-369-7077
Elmore, Steve/1640 York Ave #3B	212-472-2463
Elness, Jack/236 W 26th St	212-242-5045
Elz, Barry/13 Worth St	212-431-7910
Emberling, David/38 W 26th St	212-242-7455
Emil, Pamela/327 Central Park West	212-749-4716
ENDRESS, JOHN PAUL/254 W 31ST ST (P 22,23)	**212-736-7800**
Englander, Maury/43 Fifth Ave	212-242-9777
Englehardt, Duk/80 Varick St #4E	212-226-6490
Epstein, Mitch/353 E 77th St	212-517-3648
Epstein, S Karin/233 E 70th St	212-472-0771
Essel, Robert/39 W 71st St	212-877-5228
Estrada, Sigrid/902 Broadway	212-673-4300
Everett, Michael/15 W 28th St	212-243-0627

F

Farber, Robert/232 E 58th St	212-486-9090
Faria, Rui/304 Eighth Ave #3	212-243-6343
Farrell, John/611 Broadway #905	212-460-9001
Favero, Jean P/208 Fifth Ave #3E	212-683-9188
Fay, Stephen Studios/154 W 57th St	212-757-3717
Feibel, Theodor/102-10 66th Rd #15C	718-897-2445
Feinstein, Gary/19 E 17th St	212-242-3373
Feldman, Andy/515 10th St	718-788-6585
FELLERMAN, STAN/152 W 25TH ST (P 61)	**212-243-0027**
Fellman, Sandi/548 Broadway	212-925-5187
Ferguson, Phoebe/289 Cumberland St	718-643-1675
Ferorelli, Enrico/50 W 29th St	212-685-8181
Ferri, Mark/463 Broome St	212-431-1356
Ferris, William/208 W 23rd St	212-691-7108
Fetter, Frank/400 E 78th St	212-249-3138
Fields, Bruce/71 Greene St	212-431-8852
FINDEL, STEFAN/ (P 50,51)	**212-279-2838**
Finkelman, Allan/118 E 28th St #608	212-684-3487
Finlay, Alastair/38 E 21st St 9th Fl	212-260-4297
Finley, Calvin/59 Franklin St	212-219-8759
Firman, John/434 E 75th St	212-794-2794
FISCHER, CARL/121 E 83RD ST (P 20,21)	**212-794-0400**
FISHBEIN, CHUCK/276 FIFTH AVE #1103 (P 88,89)	**212-532-4452**
Fisher, Jon/236 W 27th St	212-206-6311
Fishman, Chuck/69 1/2 Morton St	212-242-3987
FISHMAN, ROBERT/153 W 27TH ST #502 (P 90)	**212-620-7976**
Fiur, Lola Troy/360 E 65th St	212-861-1911

PHOTOGRAPHERS

453

Please send us your additions and updates.

Flatow, Carl/20 E 30th St	212-683-8688
Flores, Hilton/150 E 42nd St	212-883-2237
Floret, Evelyn/3 E 80th St	212-472-3179
Floyd, Bob/PO Box 216	212-684-0795
Flying Camera, Inc/114 Fulton St	212-619-0808
Flynn, Richard/306 W 4th St	212-243-0834
Forastieri, Marili/156 Fifth Ave #1301	212-431-1846
Forelli, Chip/316 Fifth Ave	212-564-1835
FORREST, BOB/273 FIFTH AVE 3RD FL (P 91)	**212-288-4458**
Forschmidt, Don S/160 St John's Pl	212-878-7454
Forte, John/162 W 21st St	212-620-0584
Foto Shuttle Japan/47 Greene St	212-966-9641
Foulke, Douglas/28 W 25th St	212-243-0822
Fox, Jeffrey/6 W 20th St	212-620-0147
Foxx, Stephanie/274 W 71st St	212-580-9158
FRANCEKEVICH, AL/73 FIFTH AVE (P 92,93)	**212-691-7456**
Frances, Scott/34 W 89th St	212-496-1440
Francisco, Gus/220 E 23rd St	212-683-0418
Francki, Joe/575 Madison Ave 10th Fl	212-605-0555
FRANK, DICK/11 W 25TH ST (P 14,15)	**212-242-4648**
Frank, Lawrence/784 Columbus Ave #17J	212-662-4037
FRASER, DOUGLAS/9 E 19TH ST (P 94)	**212-777-8404**
Fraser, Gaylene/211 Thompson St	212-677-4589
FRASER, ROB/211 THOMPSON ST #1E (P 95)	**212-677-4589**
Freed, Leonard/251 Park Ave S	212-475-7600
French, Larry/273 Fifth Ave 3rd Fl	212-685-2644
Freni, Al/381 Park Ave S #809	212-679-2533
Freson, Robert/881 Seventh Ave	212-246-0679
Fried, Richard/430 W 14th St	212-929-1052
Friedman, Benno/26 W 20th St	212-255-6038
Friedman, Jerry/873 Broadway	212-505-5600
Friedman, Steve/545 W 111th St	212-864-2662
Friedman, Walter/58 W 68th St	212-874-5287
FROOMER, BRETT/39 E 12TH ST (P 97)	**212-533-3113**
Fubini, Silvia/PO Box 2456	212-533-3042
FUNK, MITCHELL/500 E 77TH ST (P 98,99)	**212-988-2886**
Furones, Claude Emile/40 Waterside Plaza	212-683-0622
Fusco, Paul/251 Park Ave S	212-475-7600

G

Gairy, John/11 W 17th St 2nd Fl	212-242-5805
Galante, Dennis/9 W 31st St	212-239-0412
Gallucci, Ed/568 Broadway	212-226-2215
Galton, Beth/130 W 25th St	212-242-2266
Ganges, Halley/35 W 36th St	212-868-1810
Gans, Hank/40 Waterside Plaza	212-683-0622
Garetti, John/140 W 22nd St	212-242-1154
Garik, Alice/ Photo Comm/275 Clinton Ave	718-783-1065
Garn, Andrew/207 Eighth Ave #2R	212-532-7213
Gartel, Larry/152-18 Union Tnpk	718-969-8616
Gatehouse, Don/356 E 89th St	212-410-5961
Gee, Elizabeth/280 Madison #1109	212-683-6924
Geller, Bonnie/57 W 93rd St	212-864-5922
Gelsobello, Paul/245 W 29th St #1200	212-947-0317
Generico, Tony/124 E 27th St	212-685-3031
Gentieu, Penny/87 Barrow St	212-691-1994
Gentil, Gerard/310 E 46th St	212-599-1806
George Gibbions/292 City Island Ave	212-885-0769
George, Michael/525 Hudson St	212-924-5273
Geradi, Marcia/38 W 21st St	212-243-8400
Germana, Michael/64 Hett Ave	718-667-1275
Gesar, Aram/417 Lafayette St	212-228-1852
Gescheidt, Alfred/175 Lexington Ave	212-889-4023
Gibbons, George/292 City Islnd Ave	212-885-0769
Gidion Inc/119 Fifth Ave	212-677-8600
Gigli, Ormond/327 E 58th St	212-758-2860
Gillardin, Andre/6 W 20th St	212-675-2950
Gillette, Bruce/11 W 29th St	212-683-4626
Giordano, John A/60 E 9th St #538	212-477-3273
Giovanni, Raeanne/156 Fifth Ave #1230	212-206-7757
Giraldi, Frank/54 W 39th St	212-840-8225
Gladstone, Gary/237 E 20th St #2H	212-777-7772
Glancz, Jeff/38 W 21st St 12th Fl	212-741-2504

Glaser, Harold/143-30 Roosevelt Ave	718-939-1829
Glassman, Carl/80 N Moore St #37G	212-732-2458
Glassman, Keith/237 E 28th St #2A	212-213-5396
Glaviano, Marco/40 W 27th St 9th Fl	212-683-8680
Glinn, Burt/41 Central Park W	212-877-2210
Globus Brothers/44 W 24th St	212-243-1008
Goff, Lee/32 E 64th St	212-223-0716
Gold, Bernie/873 Broadway #301	212-677-0311
Gold, Charles/56 W 22nd St	212-242-2600
Goldberg, Ken/141 Fifth Ave	212-807-5559
Goldman, Richard/36 W 20th St	212-675-3021
Goldring, Barry/568 Broadway #608	212-334-9494
Goldsmith, Gary/201 E 66th St	212-288-4851
Goldstein, Arthur/149 Church St	212-233-6504
Goll, Charles R/404 E 83rd St	212-628-4881
Golob, Stanford/40 Waterside Plaza	212-532-7166
Gonzalez, Gilbert/322 W 53rd St #1	212-245-3762
Gonzalez, Luis/85 Livingston St	718-834-0426
Gonzalez, Manuel/127 W 26th St	212-254-2200
Goodman, Michael/115 Central Park W #32F	212-226-4541
Goodwin, Gary P/134 W 93rd St	212-866-7396
Gordon, Andrew/48 W 22nd St	212-807-9758
Gordon, Brad/259 W 12th St	212-206-7758
GORDON, JOEL/112 FOURTH AVE (P 102)	**212-254-1688**
Gore, Geoffrey/117 Waverly Pl	212-260-6051
Gorin, Bart/1160 Broadway	212-683-3743
Gorodnitzki, Diane/160 W 71st St	212-724-6259
Gotfryd, Bernard/46 Wendover Rd	718-261-8039
Gottheil, Philip/249 W 29th St	212-564-0971
Gottlieb, Dennis/5 Union Sq W	212-620-7050
Gould, Peter/ Images/7 E 17th St	212-675-3707
GOVE, GEOFFREY/117 WAVERLY PL (P 103)	**212-260-6051**
Gozo Studio/40 W 17th St	212-620-8115
Graff, Randolph/160 Bleecker St	212-254-0412
Graig, Eric/10 E 18th St	212-206-8695
Grand, Paul/1800 Ocean Pkwy	718-375-0138
Grant, Robert/62 Greene St	212-925-1121
Graves, Tom/136 E 36th St	212-683-0241
Gray, Mitchell/169 E 86th St	212-427-2287
Gray, Robert/160 West End Ave	212-496-0462
Green, Allen/1601 Third Ave	212-534-1718
Green, Anthony/335 W 35th St 11th Fl	212-239-4166
Green, Gary/200 W 95th St	212-678-0763
GREEN-ARMYTAGE, STEPHEN/171 W 57TH ST #7A (P 104,105)	**212-247-6314**
Greenberg, David/54 King St	212-243-7351
Greenberg, Joel/265 Water St	212-285-0979
Greene, Jim/20 W 20th St	212-674-1631
Greene, Joshua/448 W 37th St	212-243-2750
Greene, Richard/18 E 17th St	212-242-5282
Greenwald, Seth/195 Adams St	718-802-1531
Gregoire, Peter/329 W 87th St	212-496-0584
Gregory, John/105 Fifth Ave #9C	212-691-1797
Gregory, Kevin/237 W 26th St	212-807-9859
Grehan, Farrell/245 W 51st St #306	212-677-3999
Griffiths, Philip Jones/251 Park Ave S	212-475-7600
Grill, Tom/32 E 31st St	212-989-0500
Griner/Cuesta & Assoc/720 Fifth Ave	212-246-7600
Groff, Mark/357 W 11th St	212-807-1172
Gross, Cy/59 W 19th St	212-243-2556
Gross, David/922 Third Ave #3R	212-688-4729
Gross, Garry/907 Broadway	212-807-7141
Gross, Geoffrey/39 W 29th St	212-685-8850
Gross, Pat/315 E 86th St #1S East	212-427-9396
Grossman, Eugene/80 N Moore St Ste 14J	212-962-6795
Grossman, Henry/37 Riverside Dr	212-580-7751
Grotell, Al/170 Park Row	212-349-3165
Gruen, John/20 W 22nd St	212-242-8415
Gscheidle, Gerhard E/381 Park Ave S	212-532-1374
Gudnason, Torkil/58 W 15th St	212-929-6680
Guice, Brad Studio/132 W 21st St	212-206-0966
Gurovitz, Judy/207 E 74th St	212-988-8685

PHOTOGRAPHERS CONT'D.

Please send us your additions and updates.

Guyaux, Jean-Marie/29 E 19th St	212-529-5395

H

Haak, Ken/122 E 30th St	212-679-6284
Haar, Thomas/463 West St	212-929-9054
Haas, David/330 W 86th St	212-889-2878
Haas, Ernst/853 Seventh Ave	212-247-4543
Haas, Kenneth/15 Sheridan Square	212-255-0707
Hagen, Boyd/448 W 37th St #6A	212-244-2436
Haggerty, David/17 E 67th St	212-879-4141
Haidar/41 Union Sq	212-255-7225
Halaska, Jan/PO Box 6611 FDR Sta	718-389-8923
HALING, GEORGE/231 W 29TH ST #302 (P 106,107)	**212-736-6822**
Hall, Clayton/247 W 35th St	212-245-6366
Hamilton, Keith/749 FDR Dr	212-982-3375
Hammond, Maury/9 E 19th St	212-460-9990
Han, Anthony/143 Guernsey St	718-389-8973
Hanlon, Gary Inc/40 W 20th St	212-206-9144
Hansen, Constance/78 Fifth Ave	212-691-5162
Hanson, Kent/147 Bleecker St	212-777-2399
Hardin, Ted/119 W 23rd St #505	212-242-2958
Harrington, Grace/300 W 49th St	212-246-1749
Harris, Leslie/20 W 20th St #703	212-206-1934
Harris, Michael/18 W 21st St	212-255-3377
Harris, Ronald G/119 W 22nd St	212-255-2330
Harrison, Howard/20 W 20th St 8th Fl	212-989-9233
Hartman, Harry/61 W 23rd St 3rd Fl	212-675-5454
Hartmann, Erich/251 Park Ave S	212-475-7600
Harvey, Ned/129 W 22nd St	212-807-7043
HASHI STUDIO/49 W 23RD ST 3RD FL (P 26,27)	**212-675-6902**
Hathon, Elizabeth/8 Greene St	212-219-0685
Hausherr, Rosemary/145 W 17th St	212-691-3216
Hausman, George/1181 Broadway	212-686-4810
Haviland, Brian/34 E 23rd St 6th Fl	212-598-0070
Hayes, Kerry/35 Taft Ave	718-442-4804
Haynes, Richard/383 Madison Ave 2nd Fl	212-872-1927
Hayward, Bill/596 Broadway 8th Fl	212-966-6490
HEDRICH, DAVID/7 E 17TH ST (P 57)	**212-924-3324**
Heery, Gary/577 Broadway 2nd Fl	212-966-6364
Hege, Laszlo/13 E 30th St	718-706-0833
Heiberg, Milton/71 W 23rd St	212-741-6405
Hein, George/13 E 16th St 8th Fl	212-741-3211
Heir, Stuart/17 W 17th St	212-620-0754
Heisler, Gregory/568 Broadway #800	212-777-8100
Hellerstein, Stephen A/120 W 25th St #2E	212-741-2685
Helms, Bill/1175 York Ave	212-759-2079
Henze, Don Studio/126 Fifth Ave 7th Fl	212-989-3576
Heron, Michal (Ms)/28 W 71st St	212-787-1272
Herr, H Buff/56 W 82nd St	212-595-4783
Herrenbruck, David/119 Fifth Ave	212-477-5419
Hess, Brad/1201 Broadway	212-684-3131
Heuberger, William/28 W 25th St	312-242-1532
Heyert, Elizabeth/251 W 30th St	212-594-1008
Hill, Pat/37 W 26th St	212-532-3479
Hiller, Geoffrey/601 W 113th St	212-222-8823
Hine, Skip/34 W 17th St 9th Fl	212-691-5903
Hing/ Norton Photography/24 W 30th St 8th Fl	212-683-4258
Hiro/50 Central Park West	212-580-8000
Hirst, Michael/300 E 33rd St	212-982-4062
Hitz, Brad/377 W 11th St #2B	212-929-1432
Hochman, Allen Studio/9-11 E 19 St	212-777-8404
Hodges, Rose/158 W 15th St	212-929-5484
Hodgson, David/550 Riverside Dr	212-864-6941
Hogan, David/352 E 91st St	212-369-4575
Holbrooke, Andrew/50 W 29th St	212-679-2477
Holland, Robin/430 Greenwich St	212-431-5351
Hollyman, Tom/300 E 40th St #19R	212-867-2383
Holtzman Photography/41 Union Sq #425	212-242-7985
Hooper, Thomas/126 Fifth Ave	212-691-0122
Hopkins, Douglas/636 Sixth Ave	212-243-1774
Hopkins, Stephen/475 Carlton Ave #6F	718-783-6461
Hopson, Gareth/22 E 21st St	212-535-3800
Horn, Lawrence/599 Sixth Ave	212-242-3280
Horowitz, Ross M/206 W 15th St	212-206-9216
Horowitz, Ryszard/103 Fifth Ave	212-243-6440
HOROWITZ, TED/465 WEST END AVE (P 110,111)	**212-595-0040**
Horst/166 E 63rd St	212-751-4937
Horvath, Jim/95 Charles St	212-741-0300
Howard, Ken/130 W 17th St 9th Fl	212-777-1412
HOWARD, ROSEMARY/902 BROADWAY (P 143)	**212-473-5552**
Huang, Ming/3174 44th St	718-204-5912
Huibregtse, Jim/318 E 39th St	212-679-8125
Hume, Adam/12 E 89th St	212-758-8929
Huntzinger, Bob/514 W 37th St	212-947-4177
Huszar/156 Fifth Ave #836	212-929-2593
Hutchings, Richard/PO Box 45	212-885-0846
Hyatt, Morton/352 Park Ave S 2nd Fl	212-889-2955
Hyman, Barry/319 E 78th St #3C	212-879-3294
Hyman, Paul/236 W 26th St	212-255-1532

I

Ichi/303 Park Ave S #506	212-254-4168
Ihara/568 Broadway #507	212-219-9363
IKEDA, SHIG/636 SIXTH AVE (P 30,31)	**212-924-4744**
Illography/49 Crosby St	212-219-0244
Image Makers/310 E 23rd St #9F	212-533-4498
Ing, Francis/112 W 31st St 5th Fl	212-279-5022
Iooss, Walter/344 W 72nd St	212-769-1552
Irgens, O Christian/192-10 69th Ave #B	718-454-3157
Irish, Len/11 W 17th St	212-242-2237
Ishimuro, Eisuke/130 W 25th St 10th Fl	212-255-9198
Ivany, Sandra/6 W 90th St #6	212-580-1501

J

Jackson, Martin/181 E 78th St	212-288-3875
Jacobs, Marty/34 E 23rd St 5th Fl	212-475-1160
Jacobs, Robert/116 Lexington Ave	212-683-3629
Jacobsen, Paul/150 Fifth Ave	212-243-4732
Jacobson, Alan/250 W 49th St #800	212-265-0170
Janeart Ltd/161 W 15th St #1C	212-691-9701
Jann, Gail/352 E 85th St	212-861-4335
Janoff, Dean/514 W 24th St	212-362-9546
Jawitz, Louis H/13 E 17th St #PH	212-929-0008
Jeffery, Richard/119 W 22nd St	212-255-2330
Jeffrey, Lance/30 E 21st St #4A	212-674-0595
Jeffry, Alix/71 W 10th St	212-982-1835
Jenkinson, Mark/142 Bleecker St Box 6	212-529-0488
Jensen, Peter M/22 E 31st St	212-689-5026
Jenssen, Buddy/34 E 29th St	212-686-0865
Joel, Seth Photography/440 Park Ave S	212-685-3179
Joern, James/125 Fifth Ave	212-260-8025
JOHANSKY, PETER/27 W 20TH ST (P 112,113)	**212-242-7013**
Jones, Chris/220 Park Ave S #6B	212-777-5361
Jones, Liz/633 Third Ave 2nd Fl	212-953-0303
Jones, Spencer/400 E 71st St	212-734-2798
Jones, Steve Photo/120 W 25th St #3E	212-929-3641
Joseph, Meryl/158 E 82nd St	212-861-5057
Jurado, Louis/170 Fifth Ave	212-242-7480

K

Kachaturian, Armen/20 West 20th St 8th Fl	212-645-8865
Kahan, Eric/410 W 24th St	212-243-9727
Kahn, R T/156 E 79th St	212-988-1423
Kalan, Mark R/922 President St	718-857-3677
Kalinsky, George/4 Pennsylvania Plaza	212-563-8095
Kamp, Eric/98-120 Queens Blvd	718-896-7780
Kamsler, Leonard/140 Seventh Ave	212-242-4678
Kan Photography/122 W 26th St	212-989-1083
Kana, Titus/876 Broadway	212-473-5550
Kanakis, Michael/144 W 27th St 10th Fl	212-807-8232
Kane, Art/568 Broadway	212-925-7334
Kane, Peter T/236 W 26th St #502	212-924-4968
Kaplan, Alan/7 E 20th St	212-982-9500
Kaplan, Barry/323 Park Ave S	212-254-8461
Kaplan, Peter B/126 W 23rd St	212-989-5215
Kaplan, Peter J/924 West End Ave	212-222-1193
Karales, James H/147 W 79th St	212-799-2483
Karia, Bhupendra/9 E 96th St #15B	212-860-5479

PHOTOGRAPHERS CONT'D.

Please send us your additions and updates.

Kasoff, Brian/28 W 25th St	212-243-4880
Kassabian Photography/127 E 59th St	212-421-1950
Katvan, Moshe/40 W 17th St	212-242-4895
Katz, Paul/381 Park Ave S	212-684-4395
Katzenstein, David/99 Commercial St	718-383-8528
Kaufman, Micky/144 W 27th St	212-255-1976
Kaufman, Ted/121 Madison Ave #4E	212-685-0349
Kawachi, Yutaka/33 W 17th St 2nd Fl	212-929-4825
Kawalerski, Ted/	212-242-0198
Kaye, Nancy/77 Seventh Ave #7U	212-845-6463
Keaveny, Francis/260 Fifth Ave	212-683-1033
Keegan, Marcia/140 E 46th St	212-953-9023
Keller, Tom/440 E 78th St	212-472-3667
Kelley, Charles W Jr/649 Second Ave #6C	212-686-3879
Kelley, David/265 W 37th St	212-869-7896
Kellner, Jeff/16 Waverly Pl	212-475-3719
Kelly, Bill/140 Seventh Ave #1N	212-989-2794
Kennedy, David Michael/10 W 18th St	212-255-9212
Kennedy, Donald J/521 W 23rd St 10th Fl	212-206-7740
Kent, Karen/29 John St	212-962-6793
Kerr, Justin and Barbara/14 W 17th St	212-741-1731
KHORNAK, LUCILLE/425 E 58TH ST (P 114)	**212-593-0933**
Kiernan, Jim/34 W 17th St	212-243-3547
Kilkelly, James/30 W 73rd St #2B	212-496-2291
King, Bill/100 Fifth Ave	212-675-7575
Kingsford, Michael Studio/874 Broadway	212-475-0553
Kinmonth, Rob/85 E 10th St #5H	212-475-6370
Kirk, Barbara/447 E 65th St	212-734-3233
Kirk, Charles/333 Park Ave S	212-677-3770
Kirk, Malcolm/12 E 72nd St	212-744-3642
Kirk, Russell/31 W 21st St	212-206-1446
Kirkpatrick, Charla/348 E 92nd St	212-410-3496
Kiss, Bob/29 E 19th St	212-505-6650
Kitchen, Dennis/873 Broadway	212-674-7658
Kittle, Kit/511 E 20th St	212-673-0596
Klauss, Cheryl/463 Broome St	212-431-3569
Klein, Arthur/35-42 80th St	718-278-0457
Klein, Matthew/104 W 17th St	212-255-6400
Klein, Robert/215 W 90th St	212-580-0381
Klein, Rudi/873 Broadway	212-460-8245
Kligge, Robert/578 Broadway	212-226-7113
Klonsky, Arthur/161 W 15th St	212-691-9701
Knowles, Robert M/2 Fordham Hill Oval #9C	212-367-4430
Koenig, Phil/49 Market St	212-964-1590
Kolansky, Palma/291 Church St	212-431-5858
Komar, Greg/30 Waterside Sq #18A	212-685-0275
Kopelow, Paul/135 Madison Ave	212-689-0685
Koppelman, Jozef/1717 Ave N	718-645-3548
Korsh, Ken/118 E 28th St	212-685-8864
Kosoff, Brian/28 W 25th St 6th Fl	212-243-4880
Koudis, Nick/40 E 23rd St	212-475-2802
Kouirinis, Bill/381 Park Ave S #710	212-696-5674
Kozan, Dan/32 W 22nd St	212-691-2288
Kozlowski, Mark/39 W 28th St	212-684-7487
Kozyra, James/568 Broadway	212-431-1911
Kramer, Bill/33 W 17th St 4th Fl	212-242-7007
Kramer, Daniel/110 W 86th St	212-873-7777
Krein, Jeffrey/119 W 23rd St #800	212-741-5207
Krementz, Jill/228 E 48th St	212-688-0480
Kresch, Jerry/175 W 76th St	212-787-7396
Krieger, Harold/225 E 31st St	212-686-1690
Kristofik, Robert/334 E 90th St #2A	212-534-5541
Kroll, Eric/118 E 28th St #1005	212-684-2465
Kron, Dan/154 W 18th St	212-924-4432
Krongard, Steve/212-A E 26th St	212-689-5634
Krueger, Mike/300 E 95th St #6C	212-722-7638
Kuehn, Karen/49 Warren St	212-406-3005
Kufert, Lowell/160 W 96th St	212-663-2143
Kugler, Dennis/43 Bond St	212-677-3826
Kuhn, Ann Spanos/1155 Broadway	212-685-1774
Kupinski, Steven/50 W 17th St	212-206-0436

L

Labar, Elizabeth/327 W 18th St	212-929-7463
Lambray, Maureen/	212-879-3960
LaMonica, Chuck/121 E 24th St	212-673-4848
LANGLEY, DAVID/536 W 50TH ST (P 12,13)	**212-581-3930**
Larrain, Gilles/95 Grand St	212-925-8494
Laszlo Studio/28 W 39th St	212-736-6690
Lategan, Barry/502 LaGuardia Pl	212-228-6850
Laurance, Bruce Studio/253 W 28th St	212-947-3451
Laure, Jason/8 W 13th St 11th Fl	212-691-7466
Laurence, Mary/PO Box 1763	212-903-4025
Lavine, Arthur/1361 Madison Ave	212-348-2642
Lawrence, Christopher/12 E 18th St	212-807-8028
Lax, Ken/239 Park Ave S	212-228-6191
Layman/Newman/6 W 18th St 6th Fl	212-989-5845
Lazzarini, Bob/25 Park Place	212-513-7163
LeBaube, Guy/310 E 46th St	212-986-6981
Lederman, Ed/166 E 34th St #12H	212-685-8612
Leduc, Lyle/320 E 42nd St #1014	212-697-9216
Lee, Jung/132 W 21st St 3rd Fl	212-807-8107
Lee, Vincent/5 Union Sq West	212-354-7888
Leeds, Karen/43 W 13th St	212-206-1818
LEGRAND, MICHEL/152 W 25TH ST 12TH FL (P 116)	**212-807-9754**
Leicmon, John/353 W 39th St #204	212-563-5592
LEIGHTON, THOMAS/321 E 43RD ST (P 117)	**212-370-1835**
Leiter, Saul/111 E 10th St	212-475-6034
Lenore, Dan/249 W 29th St #2N	212-967-7115
Leo, Donato/170 Fifth Ave	212-989-4200
Leonian, Phillip/220 E 23rd St	212-989-7670
Lerner, Richard/34 E 23d St	212-598-0070
Lesinski, Martin/49 Willow St #3H	718-624-8475
Let There Be Neon/PO Box 337/Canal St	212-226-4883
Leung, Jook/110 E 23rd St	212-254-8334
Levin, James/1570 First Ave #3D	212-947-8127
Levine, Jonathan/11 W 9th St	212-673-4698
Levine, Nancy/60 E 9th St	212-473-0015
Levinson, Ken/35 East 10th St	212-254-6180
Levy, Peter/119 W 22nd St	212-691-6600
Levy, Richard/5 W 19th St	212-243-4220
Levy, Yoav/4523 Broadway	212-942-8185
Lewin, Gideon/271 Madison Ave	212-679-8780
Lewin, Ralph/156 W 74th St	212-580-0482
Lewis, Robert/333 Park Ave S 4th Fl	212-475-6564
Lewis, Ross/460 W 24th St	212-691-6878
Lieberman, Allen/5 Union Sq 4th Fl	212-243-2240
Liebman, Phil/315 Hudson	212-269-7777
Ligeti Inc/415 W 55th St	212-246-8949
Lindner, Steven/18 W 27th St	212-683-1317
Lipton, Trina/60 E 8th St	212-533-3148
Lisi-Hoeltzell Ltd/156 Fifth Ave	212-255-0303
Little, Christopher/4 W 22nd St	212-691-1024
Lloyd, Harvey/310 E 23rd St	212-533-4498
Lobell, Richard/25-12 Union St	718-445-6864
Loete, Mark/33 Gold St #405	212-571-2235
Loew, Anthony/32 E 22nd St	212-226-1499
Logan, Kevin/119 W 23rd St	212-206-0539
Lombardi, Frederick/180 Pinehurst Ave	212-568-0740
Lombroso, Dorit/67 Vestry St #B	212-219-8722
Lomeo, Angelo/336 Central Park W	212-663-2122
Londener, Hank/18 W 38th St	212-354-0293
Lonsdale, William J/35 Orange St	718-788-6652
Lorenz, Robert/873 Broadway	212-505-8483
Love, Robin/676 Broadway 4th Fl	212-777-3113
Lubianitsky, Leonid/1013 Ave of Americas	212-391-0197
Luce, Marcia Photography/132 W 21st St	212-807-6348
Lucka, Klaus/35 W 31st St	212-594-5910
Luftig, Allan/873 Broadway	212-533-4113
Luria, Dick/5 E 16th St 4th Fl	212-929-7575
Lusk, Frank/25 E 37th St	212-679-1441
Lustica, Tee/156 Fifth Ave #920	212-255-0303
Lypides, Chris/119 W 23rd St	212-741-1911

Please send us your additions and updates.

M

Macedonia, Carmine/866 Ave of Americas	212-889-8520
Mack, Donald/69 W 55th St	212-246-6086
Mackiewicz, Jim/208 E 28th St	212-689-0766
MACLAREN, MARK/430 E 20TH ST (P 118,119)	**212-674-8615**
MacWeeney, Alen Inc/171 First Ave	212-473-2500
Madere, John/306 W 80th St	212-724-3432
Maguire, William/111 W 24th St #7R	212-807-8138
MAISEL, JAY/190 BOWERY (P 24,25)	**212-431-5013**
Malignon, Jacques/34 W 28th St	212-532-7727
Mangia, Tony/11 E 32nd St #3B	212-889-6340
Mani, Monsor/40 E 23rd St	212-947-9116
Manna, Lou/20 E 30th St	212-683-8689
Manno, John/20 W 22nd St #802	212-243-7353
Mansour, Gozo/40 W 17th St	212-620-8115
Marchese, Jim/200 W 20th St	212-242-1087
Marco, Phil/104 Fifth Ave 4th Fl	212-929-8082
Marcus, Helen/120 E 75th St	212-879-6903
Marcusson, Eric E/85 Barrow St #2R	212-924-5437
Maresca, Frank/236 W 26th St	212-620-0955
Margerin, Bill/41 W 25th St	212-645-1532
Markowitz, Joel/PO Box 6242	212-744-6863
Marks, Michael/6 W 20th St 8th Fl	212-255-0740
Marshall, Alec/308 E 73rd St	212-772-8523
Marshall, Elizabeth/200 Central Pk S #31A	212-333-2012
MARSHALL, LEE/201 W 89TH ST (P 121)	**212-799-9717**
MARTIN, BARD/142 W 26TH ST (P 122,123)	**212-929-6712**
Martin, Butch/244 Madison Ave #2F	212-370-4959
Martin, Dennis/11 W 25th St	212-929-2221
Martinez, Oscar/303 Park Ave S #408	212-673-0932
Marvullo Photomontage/141 W 28th St #502	212-564-6501
Marx, Richard/8 W 19th St	212-929-8880
Masca/109 W 26th St	212-929-4818
Mason, Donald/101 W 18th St 4th Fl	212-675-3809
Masser, Randy/953 President	718-622-8274
Massey, Philip/475 W 186th St	212-928-8210
Masullo, Ralph/33 W 17th St	212-929-4825
Masunaga, Ryuzo/57 W 19th St #2D	212-807-7012
Mathews, Barbara Lynn/16 Jane St	212-691-0823
Matsumoto/PO Box 242 Cooper Station	212-228-7192
Matsuo, Toshi/135 Fifth Ave	212-532-1320
Matthews, Cynthia/200 E 78th St	212-288-7349
Maucher, Arnold/154 W 18th St	212-206-1535
May Tell, Susan/277 W 10th St	212-741-0189
Maynard, Chris/297 Church St	212-255-8204
Mayor, Randy/139 W 82nd St #7H	212-595-0896
Mazzurco, Phil/150 Fifth Ave #319	212-989-1220
McCabe, David/39 W 67th St #1403	212-874-7480
McCabe, Robert/117 E 24th St	212-677-1910
McCarthy, Margaret/31 E 31st St	212-696-5971
McCartney, Susan/902 Broadway #1608	212-533-0660
McCavera, Tom/450 W 31st St	212-745-9122
McConnell, Chester/31 W 21st St	212-255-8141
McCurdy, John Chang/156 Fifth Ave	212-243-6949
McFarland, Lowell/115 W 27th St	212-691-2600
McFarland, Nancy/115 W 27th St	212-691-2600
McGlynn, David/18-23 Astoria Blvd	718-626-9427
McGrath, Norman/164 W 79th St	212-799-6422
McKiernan, Scott/129 Front St	212-825-0073
McLaughlin-Gill, Frances/454 W 46th St #3D-S	212-664-7637
McLoughlin, James Inc/148 W 24th St 5th Fl	212-206-8207
McMullen, Mark/304 Eighth Ave #3	212-243-6343
McNally, Brian T/234 E 81st St #1A	212-744-1263
McNally, Joe/307-09 W Broadway	212-219-1014
McQueen, Hamilton/373 Park Ave S	212-689-7367
McSpirit, Jerry/413 E 82nd St	212-879-2332
Mead, Chris/108 Reade St	212-619-5616
Megna, Richard/210 Forsyth St	212-473-5770
Meiselas, Susan/251 Park Ave S	212-475-7600
Melford, Michael/32 E 22nd St	212-473-3095
Melillo, Nick/118 W 27th St #3R	212-691-7612
Mella, Michael/217 Thompson St	212-777-6012

Mellon/69 Perry St	212-691-4166
Meltzer, Irwin & Assoc/3 W 18th St	212-807-7464
Memo Studio/39 W 67th St #1402	212-787-1658
Menashe, Abraham/900 West End Ave #7C	212-254-2754
Menda, George/568 Broadway #403	212-431-7440
Menken, Howard Studios/119 W 22nd St	212-924-4240
Meola, Eric/535 Greenwich St	212-255-5150
MERLE, MICHAEL G/5 UNION SQUARE WEST (P 125)	**212-741-3801**
Merrell (Wood)/244 Fifth Ave #PH	212-686-4807
Mervar, Louis/29 W 38th St 16th Fl	212-354-8024
Messin, Larry/64 Carlyle Green	718-948-7209
Meyerowitz, Joel/151 W 19th St	212-242-0740
Michals, Duane/109 E 19th St	212-473-1563
Michelson, Eric T/101 Lexington Ave #4B	212-687-6190
Milbauer, Dennis/15 W 28th St	212-532-3702
Miles, Ian/313 E 61st St	212-688-1360
Miljakovich, Helen/114 Seventh Ave #3C	212-242-0646
Miller, Bert/30 Dongan Pl	212-567-7947
Miller, Bill Photo/36 E 20th St	212-674-8026
MILLER, DONALD L/295 CENTRAL PARK WEST (P 126,127)	**212-496-2830**
Miller, Eileen/28 W 38th St	212-944-1507
Miller, Myron/23 E 17th St	212-242-3780
Miller, Sue Ann/16 W 22nd St #406	212-645-5172
Miller, Wayne F/251 Park Ave S	212-475-7600
Ming Photo/1200 Broadway	212-213-1166
Ming Studio/110 E 23rd St	212-254-8570
Minh Studio/200 Park Ave S #1507	212-477-0649
Mitchell, Andrew/220 Berkeley Pl	718-783-6727
Mitchell, Benn/119 W 23rd St	212-255-8686
Mitchell, Diane/175 W 73rd St	212-877-7624
Mitchell, Jack/356 E 74th St	212-737-8940
Moer, Carla/485 Madison Ave	212-355-2323
Molkenthin, Michael/31 W 31st St #6E	212-594-0144
Molofsky, Rica/243 West End Ave	212-362-3592
Moon, Sarah/215 Park Ave S	212-674-8080
Moore, Chris/20 W 22nd St #810	212-242-0553
Moore, Jimmy/38 E 19th St	212-674-7150
Moore, Marvin/234 Fifth Ave 5th Fl	212-696-4001
Moore, Truman/873 Broadway 4th Fl	212-533-3655
Moran, Nancy/568 Broadway	212-925-7104
Morello, Joe/40 W 28th St	212-684-2340
Moretz, Charles/141 Wooster St	212-714-1357
Morgan, Jeff/27 W 20th St #604	212-924-4000
Morris, Bill/34 E 29th St 6th Fl	212-685-7354
Morris, Leonard/200 Park Ave S	212-473-8485
Morrison, Ted/286 Fifth Ave	212-279-2838
Morsch, Roy J/1200 Broadway #2B	212-679-5537
Morsillo, Les/20 St Marks Pl	212-674-3124
Morton/ Riggs Studio/39 W 29th St	212-889-6643
Moscati, Frank/5 E 16th St	212-255-3434
Moskowitz, Sonia/5 W 86th St #18B	212-877-6883
Mougin, Claude/227 W 17th St	212-691-7895
MUCCI, TINA/129 W 22ND ST (P 128)	**212-206-9402**
Mullane, Fred/415 Madison Ave	212-580-4045
Muller, Rudy/318 E 39th St	212-679-8124
MUNRO, GORDON/381 PARK AVE S (P 28,29)	**212-889-1610**
Munson, Russell/53 Crosby St	212-226-8875
Muresan, Jon/56 W 22nd St 5th Fl	212-242-1227
Murphey, Gregory/353 E 77th St	212-517-2648
Murray, Robert/149 Franklin St	212-226-6860
Myers, Robert J/407 E 69th St	212-249-8085
Myriad Communications Inc/208 W 30th St	212-564-4340

N

Naar, Jon/230 E 50th St	212-752-4625
Nadelson, Jay/116 Mercer St	212-226-4266
Nahoum, Ken/260 W Broadway #4G	212-219-0592
NAIDEAU, HAROLD/233 W 26TH ST (P 129)	**212-691-2942**
Nakamura, Tohru/112 Greene St	212-334-8011
Nakano, George/119 W 22nd St	212-228-9370
Namuth, Hans/20 W 22nd St	212-691-3220
Nardi, Bob/568 Broadway	212-219-8298
Nardiello, Carl/143 W 20th St	212-242-3106

PHOTOGRAPHERS CONT'D.

Please send us your additions and updates.

Nathan, Simon/275 W 96th St	212-873-5560
Nault, Corky/25 W 23rd St 3rd Fl	212-807-7310
Needham, Steven/6 W 18th St 10th Fl	212-206-1914
Neil, Joseph/247 W 20th St	212-961-1881
Neleman, Hans/205 E 14th St	212-973-1132
NELKEN, DAN/43 W 27TH ST (P 130)	**212-532-7471**
Nelson, Michael/7 E 17th St 5th Fl	212-924-2892
Nemeth Studio/220 E 23rd St #700	212-686-3272
NEUMANN, PETER/30 E 20TH ST (P 60)	**212-420-9538**
Newler, Michael/119 W 23rd St #409	212-242-2449
Newman, Allan/6 W 18th St 6th Fl	212-989-5845
Newman, Arnold/39 W 67th St	212-877-4510
Newman, Irving/900 Broadway	212-228-2760
Newman, Marvin E/227 Central Park West	212-362-2044
Ney, Nancy/108 E 16th St 6th Fl	212-260-4300
Ng, Norman Kaimen/36 E 20th St	212-982-3230
Niccolini, Dianora/356 E 78th St	212-564-4953
Nicholas, Peter/25 W 39th St	212-354-4681
Nicholson, Nick/121 W 72nd St #2E	212-362-8418
Nicolaysen, Ron/130 W 57th St	212-947-5167
Niederman, Mark/230 W 72nd St	212-362-3902
Niefield, Terry/12 W 27th St 13th Fl	212-686-8722
Nisnevich, Lev/133 Mulberry St	212-219-0535
Nivelle, Serge/36 Grammercy Pk E #3N	212-473-2802
Niwa-Ogrudek Ltd/30 E 23rd St	212-982-7120
Nobart NY Inc/33 E 18th St	212-475-5522
Nons, Leonard/5 Union Sq West	212-741-3990
Norstein, Marshall/248 6th Ave	718-768-0786

O O'Connor, Michael/216 E 29th St — 212-679-0396

O'CONNOR, THOM/74 FIFTH AVE (P 131)	**212-620-0723**
O'Neill, Michael/134 Tenth Ave	212-807-8777
O'Reilly, Robert/311 E 50th St	212-832-8992
O'Rourke, J Barry/578 Broadway #707	212-226-7113
Obremski, George/1200 Broadway	212-684-2933
Ochi, Toru/636 Sixth Ave	212-807-7711
Oelbaum, Zeva/600 W 115th St #84L	212-864-7926
Ogilvy, Stephen/876 Broadway	212-505-9005
Ohara, Ken/Pier 62/12th Ave @23rd St	212-255-0798
Ohringer, Frederick/514 Broadway	212-431-1064
Ohta Studio/15 E 11th St	212-243-2353
Okada, Tom/45 W 18th St	212-569-0726
Olds, H F/12 W 21st St	212-691-5614
Olivier, Paul/141 W 28th St	212-947-1077
Olivo, John/545 W 45th St	212-765-8812
Olman, Bradley/15 W 24th St	212-243-0649
Oppersdorff, Mathias/1220 Park Ave	212-860-4778
Orenstein, Ronn/55 W 26th St	212-685-0563
Oringer, Hal/568 Broadway #503	212-219-1588
Ort, Samuel/3323 Kings Hwy	718-377-1218
Ortner, Jon/64 W 87th St	212-873-1950
Osonitsch, Robert/112 Fourth Ave	212-533-1920
Otfinowski, Danuta/420 E 10th St	212-254-5799
Otsuki, Toshi/241 W 36th St	212-594-1939
Oudi/704 Broadway 2nd Fl	212-777-0847
Outerbridge, Graeme/PO Box 182	809-298-0888
Owens, Sigrid/221 E 31st St	212-686-5190
Ozgen, Nebil/37 E 18th St 3rd Fl	212-505-7770

P **PACCIONE/73 FIFTH AVE (P 40,41)** — **212-691-8674**

Page, Lee/310 E 46th St	212-286-9159
Paglailunga, Albert/450 Clarkson Ave Box 18	718-271-2760
Pagliuso, Jean/315 Central Pk West	212-873-6594
Pagnano, Patrick/217 Thompson St	212-475-2566
Palmisano, Georgio/309 Mott St	212-431-7719
PALUBNIAK, JERRY/144 W 27TH ST (P 134)	**212-645-2838**
PALUBNIAK, NANCY/144 W 27TH ST (P 135)	**212-645-2838**
Papadopolous, Peter/78 Fifth Ave	212-675-8830
Pappas, Tony/110 W 31st St 3rd Fl	212-868-2032
Paras, Michael N/28-40 34th St	718-278-6768
Parik, Jan/156 W 86th St	212-362-4087
Parks, Claudia/210 E 73rd St #1G	212-879-9841

Passmore, Nick/150 W 80th St	212-724-1401
Pastner, Robert L/166 E 63rd St	212-838-8335
Pateman, Michael/155 E 35th St	212-685-6584
Peacock, Christian/118 W 88th St	212-580-1422
Peden, John/155 W 19th St 6th Fl	212-255-2674
Pederson/Erwin/76 Ninth Ave	212-929-9001
PELTZ, STUART/33 W 21ST ST (P 137)	**212-929-4600**
Pemberton, John/37 E 28th St	212-532-9285
Pendleton, Bruce/5 Union Sq West 4th Fl	212-691-5544
Penn, Irving/443 W 50th St	212-695-0290
Penny, Donald Gordon/505 W 23rd St #PH	212-243-6453
Peress, Gilles/251 Park Ave S	212-475-7600
Perkell, Jeff/132 W 22nd St	212-645-1506
PERWEILER, GARY/873 BROADWAY (P 38,39)	**212-254-7247**
Peterson, Grant/876 Broadway	212-475-2767
Peticolas, Kip/210 Forsyth St	212-473-5770
Petoe, Denes/22 W 27th St	212-213-3311
Pettinato, Anthony/156 Fifth Ave #200	212-929-6016
Pfeffer, Barbara/40 W 86th St	212-877-9913
Pfizenmaier, Edward/42 E 23rd	212-475-0910
Phillips, James/82 Greene St	212-219-1799
Phillips, Robert/101 W 57th St	212-757-5190
Photoquest International/521 Madison Ave	212-986-1224
Photoscope Inc/12 W 27th St 12th Fl	212-696-0880
Pich, Tom/2870 Dudley Ave	212-863-1837
Piel, Denis/458 Broadway 9th Fl	212-925-8929
Pierce, Richard/241 W 36th St #8F	212-947-8241
Pilgreen, John/91 Fifth Ave #300	212-243-7516
Pilossof, Judd/142 W 26th St	212-989-8971
Pinney, Doris/555 Third Ave	212-683-0637
PIOPPO, PETER/50 W 17TH ST (P 56)	**212-243-0661**
Pipinou, Tom/35 Union Sq West	212-929-0098
Piscioneri, Joe/333 Park Ave S	212-533-7982
Pite, Jonathan/430 W 14th St #502	212-206-7377
Pittman, Dustin/45 W 18th St	212-243-2956
Plotkin, Bruce/3 W 18th St 7th Fl	212-691-6185
Plotkin, Burt/400 Lafayette St	212-260-5900
Pobereskin, Joseph/51 Warren St	212-619-3711
Pobiner, Ted/381 Park Ave S	212-679-5911
Pollack, David/132 W 15th St #4A	212-242-2115
Pollard, Kirsty/5 Union Sq West	212-243-2240
Polsky, Herb/1024 Sixth Ave	212-730-0508
Popper, Andrew J/330 First Ave	212-982-9713
Porta, Art/29 E 32nd St	212-685-1555
Porter, Alan/109 W 27th St	212-686-5493
Portnoy-Shung Studio/135 W 29th St	212-868-0521
Poster, James Studio/210 Fifth Ave #402	212-206-4065
Pottle, Jock/301 W 89th St #15	212-874-0216
Powell, Dean/32 Union Sq East	212-674-6280
POWERS, GUY/534 W 43RD ST (P 46,47)	**212-563-3177**
Pozarik, Jim/43-19 168th St	718-539-7836
Pressman, Herb/118 E 28th St #908	212-683-5055
Prezant, Steve Studios/1181 Broadway 9th Fl	212-684-0822
Pribula, Barry/59 First Ave	212-777-7612
PRICE, CLAYTON J/205 W 19TH ST (P 138,139)	**212-929-7721**
Price, David/4 E 78th St	212-794-9040
Priggen, Leslie/215 E 73rd St	212-772-2230
Probst, Kenneth/251 W 19 St	212-929-2031
Prochnow, Bob/9 E 32nd St	212-689-4133
Proctor, Keith/78 Fifth Ave	212-807-1044
Prozo, Marco/122 Duane St	212-766-4490
Pruitt, David/156 Fifth Ave	212-807-0767
Pruzan, Michael/1181 Broadway	212-686-5505
Puhlmann, Rico/156 Fifth Ave #1218	212-620-4211
Purvis, Charles/84 Thomas St #3	212-619-8028

QR Quat, Dan/57 Leonard St — 212-431-7780

R J Photo/711 Amsterdam Ave	212-865-8155
Raab, Michael/831 Broadway	212-533-0030
Rajs, Jake/36 W 20th St 11th Fl	212-675-3666
Rattner, Robert/106-15 Jamaica Ave	718-441-0826
Ratzkin, Lawrence/392 Fifth Ave	212-279-1314

458

PHOTOGRAPHERS CONT'D.

Please send us your additions and updates.

RAY, BILL/350 CENTRAL PARK WEST (P 141)	**212-222-7680**
Raymond, Lelo/212 E 14th St	212-362-9546
Rea, Jimmy/151 W 19th St 10th Fl	212-627-1473
Reed, Robert/25-09 27th St	718-278-2455
Regan, Ken/6 W 20th St	212-989-2004
Reichert, Robert/68-50 Burns St	718-263-7654
Reinhardt, Mike/881 Seventh Ave #405	212-541-4787
Reinmiller, Mary Ann/163 W 17th St	212-243-4302
Rentmeester, Co/4479 Douglas Ave	212-757-4796
REZNICKI, JACK/568 BROADWAY (P 144)	**212-925-0771**
Rezny, Aaron/119 W 23rd St	212-691-1894
Rezny, Abe/28 Cadman Plz W/Eagle Wrhse	212-226-7747
Rhodes, A Photography/325 E 64th St	212-249-3974
Ricucci, Vincent/59 W 19th St	212-691-5860
RIES, HENRY/204 E 35TH ST (P 145)	**212-689-3794**
Ries, Stan/48 Great Jones St	212-533-1852
Riggs, Robert/502 Laguardia Pl	212-254-7352
Riley, David-Carin/152 W 25th St	212-741-3662
Riley, Jon/12 E 37th St	212-532-8326
Rivelli, William/303 Park Ave S #204	212-254-0990
Rivera, Al/139 W 14th St	212-691-3930
Rizende, Sidney/64-48 Booth St	718-896-0660
Rizzo, Alberto/220 E 23rd St	212-736-1100
Roberts, Grant/11 W 20th St	212-620-7921
Roberts, Stefan K/155 E 47th St	212-688-9798
Robins, Lawrence/50 W 17th St	212-206-0436
Robinson, CeOtis/4-6 W 101st St #49A	212-663-1231
ROBINSON, JAMES/1255 FIFTH AVE (P 148,149)	**212-996-5486**
Robison, Chuck/21 Stuyvesant Oval	212-777-4894
Rockfield, Bert/31 E 32nd St	212-689-3900
Rodin, Christine/38 Morton St	212-242-3260
Rohr, Robert/325 E 10th St #5W	212-674-1519
Romanelli, Marc/244 Riverside Dr	212-865-5214
Romano, Robert/1155 Broadway	212-696-0264
Rose, Uli/234 W 21st St #33	212-505-5234
Rosen, David/238 E 24th St	212-684-5193
Rosenberg, Ken/514 West End Ave	212-362-3149
Rosenfeld, Stanley/175 Riverside Dr #8K	212-787-6653
Rosenthal, Barry/1155 Broadway 3rd Fl	212-889-5840
Rosenthal, Marshall M/231 W 18th St	212-807-1247
Ross, Ken/312 E 84th St #5C	212-734-2687
Ross, Mark/345 E 80th St	212-744-7258
Roth, Peter/8 W 19th St	212-242-4853
Rothaus, Ede/34 Morton St	212-989-8277
Rotkin, Charles E/1697 Broadway	212-757-9255
Roto Ad Print Studio/252 W 37th St	212-279-6590
Rozsa, Nick/325 E 64th St	212-734-5629
Rubenstein, Raeanne/8 Thomas St	212-964-8426
Rubin, Al/250 Mercer St #1501	212-674-4535
Rubin, Daniel/126 W 22nd St 6th Fl	212-989-2400
Rubin, Darleen/159 Christopher St	212-243-6973
Rubinstein, Eva/145 W 27th St	212-243-4115
Rudnick, James/799 Union St	718-783-4156
Rudolph, Nancy/35 W 11th St	212-989-0392
Rugen-Kory/150 E 18th St	212-777-3889
Ruggeri, Francesco/71 St Marks Pl #9	212-505-8477
Russell, Ted/67-25 Clyde St	718-263-3725
Russell, Tom/636 Ave of Americas	212-989-9755
Ryan, Will/16 E 17th St 2nd Fl	212-242-6270
Rysinski, Edward/636 Ave of Americas	212-807-7301
S Sabal, David/807 Ave of Americas	212-242-8464
Sacco, Vittorio/126 Fifth Ave #602	212-929-9225
Sacha, Bob/370 Central Park W	212-749-4128
Sahula, Peter/45 E 19th St	212-982-4340
Sailors, David/123 Prince St	212-505-9654
Sakas, Peter/400 Lafayette St	212-254-6096
Salaff, Fred/322 W 57th St	212-246-3699
Salvati, Jerry/206 E 26th St	212-696-0454
Salzano, Jim/29 W 15th St	212-242-4820
SAMARDGE, NICK/568 BROADWAY #706 (P 34,35)	**212-226-6770**
Sanchez, Alfredo/14-23 30th Dr	718-726-0182

Sanders, Chris/133 Eighth Ave 2nd Fl	212-724-6129
Sandone, A J/132 W 21st St 9th Fl	212-807-6472
Sanford, Tobey/888 Eighth Ave	212-245-2736
Sarapochiello, Jerry/47-A Beach St	212-219-8545
Sartor, Vittorio/32 Union Square E	212-674-2994
Sasson, Bob/352 W 15th St	212-675-0973
Sato Photo/152 W 26th St	212-741-0688
Satterwhite, Al/515 Broadway #2B	212-219-0808
Satterwhite, Steve/13 Avenue A	212-254-8844
Saunders, Michele/141 W 20th St	212-929-5705
Savas, James/37 W 20th St	212-620-0067
Savides, Harris/1425 Third Ave	212-772-8745
Saylor, H Durston/219 W 16th St #4B	212-620-7122
Scarlett, Nora/37 W 20th St	212-741-2620
Scavullo, Francesco/212 E 63rd St	212-838-2450
Schecter, Lee/440 Park Ave S	212-683-0370
Scheer, Stephen/9 Murray St #12NW	212-233-7195
Schein, Barry/118-60 Metropolitan Ave	718-849-7808
Schenk, Fred/112 Fourth Ave	212-677-1250
Schiavone, Carmen/271 Central Park West	212-496-6016
Schiff, Nancy Rica/24 W 30th St 7th Fl	212-679-9444
Schillaci, Michael/320 W 30th St #3A	212-564-2364
Schillaci/Jones Photo/400 E 71st St #14-O	212-734-2798
Schiller, Leif/244 Fifth Ave	212-532-7272
Schinz, Marina/222 Central Park S	212-246-0457
Schlachter, Trudy/160 Fifth Ave	212-741-3128
Schneider, Josef/119 W 57th St	212-265-1223
Schneider, Peter/902 Broadway	212-982-9040
Schneider, Roy/59 W 19th St	212-691-9588
Schreck, Bruno/873 Broadway #304	212-254-3078
Schuetz, Frank/117 W 17th St #5A	212-741-4661
Schulman, Richard/306 E 83rd St	212-737-9791
Schulze, Fred/38 W 21st St	212-242-0930
Schupf, John/568 Broadway #106	212-226-2250
Schurink, Yonah (Ms)/666 West End Ave	212-362-2860
Schuster, Sharon/320 W 90th St	212-877-1559
Schwartz, Marvin/223 W 10th St	212-929-8916
Schwartz, Sing-Si/15 Gramercy Park S	212-228-4466
Schweitzer, Andrew/333 Park Ave S	212-473-2395
Schwerin, Ron/889 Broadway	212-228-0340
Sclight, Greg/146 W 29th St	212-736-2957
Scocozza, Victor/117 E 30th St	212-686-9440
Seaton, Tom/91 Fifth Ave	212-989-3550
SECUNDA, SHELDON/112 FOURTH AVE (P 48,49)	**212-477-0241**
Seesselberg, Charles/119 W 23rd St	212-807-8730
Seghers, Carroll/441 Park Ave S	212-679-4582
Seidman, Barry/85 Fifth Ave	212-255-6666
Seitz, Sepp/530 W 25th St	212-255-5959
Selby, Richard/113 Greene St	212-431-1719
Seligman, Paul/163 W 17th St	212-242-5688
Selkirk, Neil/515 W 19th St	212-243-6778
Seltzer, Abe/524 W 23d St	212-807-0660
Seltzer, Kathleen/25 E 4th St	212-475-0314
Sewell, Jim/720 W 181st St	212-795-0537
Shaffer, Stan/2211 Broadway	212-807-7700
Shaman, Harvey/109 81st Ave	718-793-0434
Shapiro, Pam/11 W 30th St 2nd Fl	212-967-2363
Share, Jed/Tokyo/63 Adrian Ave	212-562-8931
Sharko, Greg/103-56 103rd St	718-738-9694
SHARRATT, PAUL/20 W 20TH ST #703 (P 151)	**212-243-3281**
Sherman, Guy/108 E 16th St 6th Fl	212-675-4983
Shiansky, Harry Studio/118 E 28th St	212-889-5489
SHIKI/119 W 23RD ST #504 (P 152)	**212-929-8847**
Shiraishi, Carl/137 E 25th St 11th Fl	212-679-5628
Silano, Bill/138 E 27th St	212-889-0505
Silbert, Layle/505 LaGuardia Pl	212-677-0947
Silver, Larry/236 W 26th St	212-807-9560
Silvia Jr, Peter/200 E 30th St	212-685-0407
Simko, Robert/437 Washington St	212-431-6974
Simon, Peter Angelo/568 Broadway #701	212-925-0890
Simpson, Coreen/599 West End Ave	212-877-6210
Simpson, Jerry/28 W 27th St	212-696-9738

PHOTOGRAPHERS

459

PHOTOGRAPHERS

Simpson/Flint/156 Fifth Ave #1214	212-741-3104
Singer, Michelle/251 W 19th St #5C	212-924-8485
Sirdofsky, Arthur/112 W 31st St	212-279-7557
SKALSKI, KEN/866 BROADWAY (P 153)	**212-777-6207**
Skelley, Ariel/249 W 29th St #3E	212-868-1179
The Sketch Pad Studio/6 Jane St	212-989-7074
Skogsbergh, Ulf/5 E 16th St	212-255-7536
Skolnik, Lewis/135 W 29th St	212-239-1455
Skott, Michael/244 Fifth Ave #PH	212-686-4807
Slade, Chuck/12 E 14th St #4B	212-807-1153
Slade, Mark/170 West End Ave	212-750-5112
Slavin, Fred/42 E 23rd St 7th Fl	212-505-1420
Slavin, Neal/62 Greene St	212-925-8167
Sleppin, Jeff/3 W 30th St	212-947-1433
Sloan-White, Barbara/372 Fifth Ave	212-760-0057
Small, John/156 Fifth Ave #834	212-645-4720
Smilow, Stanford/333 E 30th St/Box 248	212-685-9425
Smith, Jeff/30 E 21st St	212-674-8383
Smith, Kevin/446 W 55th St	212-757-4812
Smith, Michael/140 Claremont #5A	212-724-2800
Smith, Rita/666 West End Ave #10N	212-580-4842
Smith, Robert Photo/421 Seventh Ave	212-563-2535
Smith, William E/498 West End Ave	212-877-8456
Snedeker, Katherine/16 E 30th St	212-684-0788
Snider, Lee/221 W 82nd St #9D	212-873-6141
Snyder, Norman/514 Broadway #3H	212-219-0094
So Studio/34 E 23rd St	212-475-0090
Sobel, Jane/161 W 15th St	212-691-9701
SOCHUREK, HOWARD/680 FIFTH AVE (P 154)	**212-582-1860**
Solomon, Chuck/622 Greenwich St	212-243-4036
Solomon, Paul/440 W 34th St #13E	212-760-1203
Solowinski, Ray/154 W 57th St #826	212-757-7940
Soluri, Michael/95 Horatio St #633	212-645-7999
Somekh, Rick/13 Laight St	212-219-1613
SÖÖT, OLAF/419 PARK AVE S (P 155)	**212-686-4565**
Sorce, Wayne/20 Henry St #5G	718-237-0497
Sorensen, Chris/PO Box 1760	212-684-0551
Sotres, Craig/335 W 35th St 11thFl	212-239-4166
Spagnolo, David/144 Reade St	212-226-4392
Spahn, David/381 Park Ave S #915	212-689-6120
Spatz, Eugene/264 Sixth Ave	212-777-6793
Speier, Leonard/190 Riverside Dr	212-595-5480
Spindel, David M/18 E 17th St	212-989-4984
Spinelli, Frank/12 W 21st St 12th Fl	212-243-7718
Spinelli, Paul/1619 Third Ave #21K	212-410-3320
Spinelli, Phil/12 W 21st St	212-243-7718
Spiro, Edward/82-01 Britten	718-424-7162
Spreitzer, Andy/225 E 24th St	212-685-9669
St John, Lynn/308 E 59th St	212-308-7744
Stahman, Robert/1200 Broadway #2D	212-679-1484
Standard, Venus/115 Pendleton Pl	718-816-8702
Standart, Joe/5 W 19th St	212-924-4545
Stanton, Brian/175 Fifth Ave #3086	212-678-7574
Stanton, William/160 W 95th St #9D	212-662-3571
Stark, Philip/312 E 90th St	212-777-8070
Steadler, Lance/154 W 27th St	212-243-0935
Steedman, Richard C/214 E 26th St	212-684-7878
Steele, Kim/640 Broadway #7W	212-777-7753
Stegemeyer, Werner/377 Park Ave S	212-686-2247
Steigman, Steve/5 E 19th St #303	212-473-3306
Stein, Larry/568 Broadway #706	212-219-9077
Steinbrenner, Karl Photography/140 W 22nd St	212-807-8936
Steiner, Charles/61 Second Ave	212-777-0813
Steiner, Christian/300 Central Park West	212-724-1990
Steiner, Karel/349 W 46th St	212-460-8254
Stember, John/154 W 57th St	212-757-0067
Stern, Anna/261 Broadway #3C	212-349-1134
Stern, Bert/66 Crosby St	212-925-5909
Stern, Bob/12 W 27th St	212-889-0860
Stern, John/451 W Broadway	212-477-0656
Stern, Laszlo/57 W 19th St	212-691-7696
Sternfeld, Joel/353 E 77th St	212-517-3648

Stetson, David/251 W 30th St #16W	22-279-1515
STETTNER, BILL/118 E 25TH ST (P 32,33)	**212-460-8180**
Stevens, D David/175 Fifth Ave #3216	212-677-2200
Stiles, James/413 W 14th St	212-627-1766
Stock, Dennis/251 Park Ave S	212-475-7600
Stone, Erika/327 E 82nd St	212-737-6435
Stratigakis, John/2258 43rd St	718-274-1697
Stratos, Jim/176 Madison Ave	212-696-1133
The Strobe Studio/91 Fifth Ave	212-532-1977
Strode, Mark/2026 E 29th St	718-332-1241
Stroili, Elaine/416 E 85th St #3G	212-879-8587
STRONGIN, JEANNE/61 IRVING PL (P 159)	**212-473-3718**
Stuart, John/80 Varick St #4B	212-966-6783
Stucker, Hal/295 Washington Ave #5D	718-789-1180
Studio 17/149 W 14th St	212-929-8899
Studio Luna/335 W 35th St 11th Fl	212-239-4166
Stupakoff, Otto/80 Varick St	212-334-8032
Suanberg, Linda/20 E 49th St	212-319-6600
Sugarman, Lynn/40 W 22nd St	212-691-3245
Sun Photo/19 E 21st St	212-505-9585
Sussman, David/115 E 23rd St	212-254-9380
Sutton, Humphrey/18 E 18th St	212-989-9128
Svensson, Steen/52 Grove St	212-242-7272
Swedowsky, Ben/381 Park Ave S	212-684-1454
Swick, Danille/276 First Ave	212-777-0653
Symons, Abner/27 E 21st St 10th Fl	212-777-6660

T

Tamaccio, Larry/243 West End Ave	212-362-3592
Tanaka, Victor/30 W 26th St	212-675-3445
Tannenbaum, Ken/ 16 W 21st St	212-675-2345
Tanous, Dorothy/110 W 30th St #5R	212-563-2017
Taufic, William/166 W 22nd St	212-620-8143
Taylor, Curtise/29 E 22nd St #2S	212-473-6886
Taylor, Jonathan/5 W 20th St	212-741-2805
TCHEREVKOFF, MICHEL/873 BROADWAY (P 160,161)	**212-228-0540**
Tedesco, Frank/Union Sq West	212-777-3376
Tenzer, Peter/134 W 26th St	212-736-1252
Terk, Neil/400 E 59th St	212-838-1213
Tervenski, Steve/125 E 39th St	212-753-6990
Tessler, Stefan/115 W 23rd St	212-924-9168
Testa, Michelle/5 W 30th St	212-947-3364
Thomas, Mark/109 W 26th St #11B	212-741-7252
Thompson, Eleanor/147 W 25th St	212-675-6773
Thompson, Kenneth/220 E 95th St	212-348-3530
Tillman, Denny/39 E 20th St	212-674-7160
Today's Photos Inc/17 E 28th St	212-686-0071
TOGASHI/36 W 20TH ST (P 162)	**212-929-2290**
Tornberg-Coghlan Assoc/6 E 39th St	212-685-7333
Toto, Joe/148 W 24th St	212-620-0755
TRURAN, BILL/31 W 21ST ST 6TH FL (P 163)	**212-741-2285**
Trzeciak, Erwin/145 E 16th St	212-254-4140
TULLIS, MARCUS/40 LAFAYETTE ST, NEW YORK, NY (P 142)	**212-460-9096**
Tully, Roger/344 W 38th St	212-947-3961
Tung, Matthew/5 Union Sq West	212-741-0570
Turbeville, Deborah/160 Fifth Ave #907	212-924-6760
Turner, Pete Photography/154 W 57th St	212-765-1733
Turner, Sam/321 E 21st St #3E	212-777-8715
Tweedy-Holmes, Karen/180 Claremont Ave #51	212-866-2289
Tweel, Ron/241 W 36th St	212-563-3452
Tyler, Mark/233 Broadway #822	212-962-3690

UV

Umans, Marty/110 W 25th St	212-242-4463
Unangst, Andrew/381 Park Ave S	212-889-4888
Underhill, Les/10 W 18th St	212-691-9920
Ursillo, Catherine/1040 Park Ave	212-722-9297
Vaeth, Peter/295 Madison Ave	212-685-4700
Valente, Jerry/193 Meserole Ave	718-389-0469
Valentin, Augusto/202 E 29th St 6th Fl	212-888-1371
Vallini Productions/43 E 20th St 2nd Fl	212-674-6581
Vanglintenkamp, Rik/5 E 16th St 12th Fl	212-924-9210
Varnedoe, Sam/12 W 27th St #603	212-679-1230
Varon, Malcolm/125 Fifth Ave	212-473-5957

Vartoogian, Jack/262 W 107th St #6A	212-663-1341
Vava, John/51 Station Ave	718-967-9175
VEGA, JULIO/417 THIRD AVE #3B (P 164)	**212-889-7568**
Veldenzer, Alan/160 Bleecker St	212-420-8189
Vendikos, Tasso/59 W 19th St	212-206-6451
Vest, Michael/40 W 27th St 3rd Fl	212-532-8331
Vhandy Productions/225-A E 59th St	212-759-6150
Vicari, Jim/8 E 12th St	212-675-3745
VICKERS, CAMILLE/200 W 79TH ST PH #A (P 58)	**212-580-8649**
Victor, Thomas/131 Fifth Ave	212-777-6004
Vidal, Bernard/853 Seventh Ave	212-582-3284
Vidol, John/37 W 26th St	212-889-0065
Viesti, Joe/PO Box 20424 Cherokee Sta	212-734-4890
Vincenzo/327 W 30th St #1D	212-564-4100
Vine, David/873 Broadway 2nd Fl	212-505-8070
Vinopoll, Sy/39 W 38th St	212-840-6590
Vishniac, Roman/219 W 81st St	212-787-0997
VISUAL IMPACT PRODUCTIONS/15 W 18TH ST 10TH FL (P 165)	**212-243-8441**
Vitale, Peter/157 E 71st St	212-249-8412
Vogel, Allen/126 Fifth Ave	212-675-7550
Volpi, Rene/121 Madison Ave #11-I	212-532-7367
Von Hassell, Agostino/277 W 10th St PH-D	212-242-7290
Vos, Gene/440 Park Ave S	212-685-8384

W

Wadler, Lois/341 E 6th St	212-777-5638
Wagner Int'l Photos/216 E 45th St	212-661-6100
Wagner, Daniel/245 E 19th St	212-475-7397
Wagner, David/568 Broadway	212-925-5149
Wagoner, Robert/150 Fifth Ave	212-807-6050
Wahlund, Olof/7 E 17th St	212-929-9067
Waine, Michael/873 Broadway	212-533-4200
Waldo, Maje/873 Broadway	212-475-7886
Waldron, William/463 Broome St	212-226-0356
WALLACE, RANDALL/43 W 13TH ST #3F (P 167)	**212-242-2930**
Wallach, Louis/594 Broadway #8W	212-925-9553
Walsh, Bob/401 E 34th St	212-684-3015
Waltzer, Bill/110 Greene St #96	212-925-1242
Waltzer, Carl/873 Broadway #412	212-475-8748
Walz, Barbra/143 W 20th St	212-242-7175
Wang, John Studio Inc/30 E 20th St	212-982-2765
Warchol, Paul/133 Mulberry St	212-431-3461
Ward, Bob Studio/118 E 25th St 9th Fl	212-473-7584
Warsaw Photographic Assocs/36 E 31st St	212-725-1888
WATABE, HARUO/119 FIFTH AVE (P 109)	**212-505-8800**
Watanabe, Nana/130 W 25th St 10th Fl	212-741-3248
Watson, Albert M/80-82 Greene St	212-925-8552
Watson, Michael/133 W 19th St	212-620-3125
Watt, Elizabeth/141 W 26th St	212-929-8504
Watts, Cliff/536 W 50th St	212-581-3930
Weaks, Dan/175 Fifth Ave #3344	212-242-2105
Weatherly, Karl/235 E 11th St	212-736-1100
Webb, Alex/251 Park Ave S	212-475-7600
Weber, Bruce/37 W 26th St	212-685-5025
Weckler, Chad/256 Fifth Ave	212-632-8733
Weidlein, Peter/122 W 26th St	212-989-5498
Weinberg, Michael/5 E 16th St	212-691-1000
Weinberg, Steve/47 E 19th St	212-254-9571
Weinstein, Todd/47 Irving Pl	212-254-7526
Weir, John/38 E 19th St 8th Fl	212-475-3798
Weiss, Michael Photo/10 W 18th St 2nd Fl	212-929-4073
West, Bonnie/156 Fifth Ave #1232	212-929-3338
West, Charles/233 Court St	718-624-5920
Wettenstein, Raphael/165 Madison Ave	212-679-5555
Wexler, Mark/400 W 43rd St	212-564-7733
Wheatman, Truckin/251 W 30th St	212-239-1081
White, Bill/34 W 17th St	212-243-1780
White, Joel/36 W 20th St	212-620-3085
White, John/11 W 20th St 6th Fl	212-691-1133
White, Timothy/430 W 14th St #502	212-206-7377
Whitehurst, William/32 W 20th St	212-206-8825
Whitely Presentations/60 E 42nd St #419	212-490-3111

Wick, Walter/119 W 23rd St #210	212-243-3448
Wien, Jeffrey/160 Fifth Ave #912	212-243-7028
Wier, John Arthur/38 E 19th St 8th Fl	212-477-5107
Wier, Terry/38 E 19th St 8th Fl	212-477-5107
Wiesehahn, Charles/249 W 29th St #2E	212-563-6612
Wilcox, Shorty/DPI/521 Madison Ave	212-246-6367
Wilkes, Stephen/48 E 13th St	212-475-4010
Wilks, Harry/234 W 21st St	212-929-4772
Williams, Larry/43 W 29th St	212-684-1317
Williamson, Richie/514 W 24th St	212-362-9546
Wilson, Mike/441 Park Ave S	212-683-3557
Wilson, Vickie/37 E 29th St	212-685-9509
Wing, Peter/56-08 138th St	718-762-3617
Winkel, Peter/1413 York Ave	212-861-2563
Wolf, Bernard/214 E 87th St	212-427-0220
Wolf, Bruce/123 W 28th St	212-695-8042
WOLF, HENRY/58 W 15TH ST (P 16,17)	**212-741-2539**
Wolff, Brian R/503 Broadway	212-925-7772
Wolfson Photography/156 Fifth Ave #327	212-924-1510
Wolfson, Steve and Jeff/12 W 21st St 9th Fl	212-807-7866
Wong, Daniel Photography/652 Broadway #3	212-260-7058
Wong, Leslie/303 W 78th St	212-595-0434
Wood, Susan/641 Fifth Ave	212-371-0679
Woodward, Herbert/555 Third Ave	212-685-4385
Wormser, Richard L/800 Riverside Dr	212-928-0056
Wynn, Dan/170 E 73rd St	212-535-1551

YZ

Yalter, Memo/14-15 162nd St	718-767-3330
Yamashiro, Tad/224 E 12th St	212-473-7177
Yee, Tom/30 W 26th St	212-242-0301
Yoshitomo Photography/119 Fifth Ave #305	212-505-8800
Young, Donald/166 E 61st St #3C	212-593-0010
Young, James/56 W 22nd St	212-924-5444
YOUNG, RICK/27 W 20TH ST (P 170)	**212-929-5701**
Young, Steve/6 W 18th St	212-691-5860
Zager, Howard/450 W 31st St	212-239-8082
Zakarian, Aram/25 E 20th St	212-679-6203
Zander, George/30 W 26th St	212-620-0944
Zander, Peter/312 E 90th St #4A	212-348-2647
ZANETTI, GERRY/36 E 20TH ST (P 18,19)	**212-473-4999**
Zapp, Carl/873 Broadway	212-505-0510
Zappa, Tony/28 E 29th St	212-532-3476
Zegre, Francois/124 E 27th St	212-684-6517
Zehnder, Bruno/PO Box 5996	212-840-1234
Zenreich, Alan/78 Fifth Ave 3rd Fl	212-807-1551
Zens, Michael/15 W 29th St	212-683-7258
Zimmerman, David/119 W 23rd St #909	212-243-2718
Zingler, Joseph/18 Desbrosses St	212-226-3867
Zoiner, John/12 W 44th St	212-972-0357
Zwiebel, Michael/42 E 23rd St	212-477-5629

NORTHEAST

A

Aaron, Peter/222 Valley Pl, Mamaroneck, NY	914-698-4060
Abarno, Richard/11 Dean Ave, Newport, RI	401-846-5820
ABDELNOUR, DOUG/RT 22 PO BOX 64, BEDFORD VILLAGE, NY (P 62)	**914-234-3123**
ABELL, TED/51 RUSSELL RD, BETHANY, CT (P 181)	**203-777-1988**
Abend, Jay/511 East 5th St, Boston, MA	617-268-3334
Abrams, Larry/7 River St, Milford, CT	203-878-5090
Abramson, Dean/PO Box 610, Raymond, ME	207-655-7386
Adams Studio Inc/1523 22nd St NW Courtyard Washington, DC	202-785-2188
Adams, David/117 S Juliana St, Bedford, PA	814-623-2514
Adamstein, Jerome/3720 39th St NW #E167, Washington, DC	202-362-9315
ADDIS, KORY/144 LINCOLN ST #4, BOSTON, MA (P 182)	**617-451-5142**
Agelopas, Mike/2510 N Charles St, Baltimore, MD	301-235-2823
Ahrens, Gene/544 Mountain Ave, Berkeley Heights, NJ	201-464-4763
AIELLO, FRANK/35 S VAN BRUNT ST, ENGLEWOOD, NJ (P 52,53)	**201-894-5120**
Alexander, Jules/9 Belmont Ave, Rye, NY	914-686-7752

Please send us your additions and updates.

Allen, C J/89 Orchard St, Boston, MA	617-524-1925
Alonso, Manuel/425 Fairfield Ave, Stamford, CT	203-359-2838
Altman, Steve/79 Grand St, Jersey City, NJ	201-434-0022
AMES, THOMAS JR/MILLER POND RD BOX 66, THETFORD CENTER, VT (P 183)	**603-643-5523**
Ancona, George/Crickettown Rd, Stony Point, NY	914-786-3043
Anderson, Richard Photo/2523 N Calvert St, Baltimore, MD	301-889-0585
Anderson, Theodore/235 N Madison St, Allentown, PA	215-437-6468
ANDRIS-HENDRICKSON PHOTO/314 N 13TH #404, PHILADELPHIA, PA (P 63)	**215-925-2630**
Ankers Photo/316 F St NE, Washington, DC	202-543-2111
Ansell, Seth/6 Beach Dr, Littleton, MA	617-486-9116
Ansin, Mikki/2 Ellery Square, Cambridge, MA	617-661-1640
Anthony, Greg/15 East St, Boston, MA	617-423-4983
Anyon, Benjamin/206 Spring Run Ln, Downington, PA	215-363-0744
Anzalone, Joseph/PO Box 1802, South Hackensack, NJ	201-368-9275
Apoian, Jeffrey/202 Lincoln St, Kennett Square, PA	215-353-2210
Appleton, Hal/Kingston, Doug/44 Mechanic St PO Box 421, Newton, MA	617-969-5772
Arbor Studios/56 Arbor St, Hartford, CT	203-232-6543
Arce Studios/219 Henry St, Stanford, CT	203-661-4001
Armstrong, Christine/916 N Charles, Baltimore, MD	301-727-8800
Armstrong, James/127 Mill St, Springfield, MA	413-734-7337
Arruda, Robert/144 Lincoln St, Boston, MA	617-482-1425
Auerbach, Scott/32 Country Rd, Mamaroneck, NY	914-698-9073
Augenstein, Ron/509 Jenne Dr, Pittsburgh, PA	412-653-3583
Avanti Studios/46 Waltham St, Boston, MA	617-574-9424
Aviation Photo Service/65 Riverside Ave, Concord, MA	617-371-2079
Avis, Paul/310 Bedford, Manchester, NH	603-627-2659

B
B & H photographics/1210 Race St Box 1319, Philadelphia, PA	215-563-8611
Baehr, Sarah/708 South Ave, New Canaan, CT	203-966-6317
Baer, Rhoda/1648-A Beeckman Pl NW, Washington, DC	202-332-2879
Baese, Gary/2229 N Charles St, Baltimore, MD	301-235-2226
Bain, Christopher/11 Orchard Farm Rd, Port Washington, NY	516-883-2163
Baker, Bill Photo/1045 Pebble Hill Rd RD3, Doylestown, PA	215-348-9743
Baldwin, Steve/8 Eagle St, Rochester, NY	716-325-2907
Barbagallo, Ron/36 E 35th St, Bayonne, NJ	201-437-2394
Barber, Doug/1634 E Baltimore St, Baltimore, MD	301-276-1634
Bardes, Harold/1812 Kennedy Blvd, Union City, NJ	201-867-7808
BARLOW, CURTIS/PO BOX 8863, WASHINGTON, DC (P 215)	**202-543-5506**
Barlow, Len/392 Boylston, Boston, MA	617-266-4030
Barnes, Christopher/122 Winnisimmet St, Chelsea, MA	617-884-2745
Barocas, Melanie Eve/78 Hart Rd, Guilford, CT	203-457-0898
Barone, Christopher/381 Wright Ave, Kingston, PA	717-287-4680
Barrett, Bob/RD 1 Box 219 Creek Rd, High Falls, NY	914-687-0716
Barrow, Pat/3602 Spring St, Chevy Chase, MD	301-588-3131
Bartlett, Linda/3316 Runnymede Pl NW, Washington, DC	202-362-4777
Basch, Richard/2627 Connecticut Ave NW, Washington, DC	202-232-3100
BASKIN, GERRY/12 UNION PARK ST, BOSTON, MA (P 186)	**617-482-3316**
Bavendam, Fred/PO Box 276, Kittery, ME	207-439-0600
Bean, Jeremiah/96 North Ave, Garwood, NJ	201-789-2200
Beanchesne Photo/4 Bud Way/Vantage Pt III/#2, Nashua, NH	603-880-8686
Beards, James/409 Pine St, Providence, RI	401-273-9055
Beardsley, John/322 Summer St 5th Fl, Boston, MA	617-482-0130
BEAUDIN, TED/56 ARBOR ST, HARTFORD, CT (P 69,187)	**203-232-6198**
Becker, N Neesa/241 Monroe St, Philadelphia, PA	215-925-5363
Bedford Photo-Graphic Studio/PO Box 64 Rt 22, Bedford, NY	914-234-3123
Beigel, Daniel/2024 Chesapeake Road, Annapolis, MD	301-261-2494
Belmonte, William/43 Homestead Ave, Greenfield, MA	413-773-7744
Bender, Frank/2215 South St, Philadelphia, PA	215-985-4664
Benedetto, Angelo/1903 Chestnut St, Philadelphia, PA	215-627-1990
Benn, Nathan/925 1/2 F St NW, Washington, DC	202-638-5705
Bennett, George/1206 Tribbett Ave, Sharon Hill, PA	215-586-7095
Benson, Gary/50 Hillcrest Rd, Martinsville, NJ	201-356-6705
Benvenuti, Judi/12 N Oak Ct, Madison, NJ	201-377-5075
Berg, Hal/67 Hilary Circle, New Rochelle, NY	914-235-9356
Bergman, LV & Assoc/E Mountain Rd, S, Cold Spring, NY	914-265-3656
Berinstein, Martin/215 A St 6th Fl, Cambridge, MA	617-268-4117
Bernsau, W Marc/PO Box 1152, Sanford, ME	207-324-1741
Bernstein, Daniel/7 Fuller St, Waltham, MA	617-894-0473
Bethoney, Herb/1222 Washington St, Boston, MA	617-749-1124

Bezushko, Bob/1311 Irving St, Philadelphia, PA	215-735-7771
Bezushko, George/1311 Irving St, Philadelphia, PA	215-735-7771
Bibikow, Walter/76 Batterymarch St, Boston, MA	617-451-3464
Biegun, Richard/56 Cherry Ave, West Sayville, NY	516-567-2645
Bilyk, I George/314 E Mt Airy Ave, Philadelphia, PA	215-242-5431
Bindas Studio/205 A St, Boston, MA	617-268-3050
Bingham, Jack/8 Abbot St, E Rochester, NH	603-742-7718
Binzen, Bill/Indian Mountain Rd, Lakeville, CT	203-435-2485
Birn, Roger/150 Chestnut St, Providence, RI	401-421-4825
Bishop, Jennifer/2732 St Paul St, Baltimore, MD	301-366-6662
Blachut, Dennis/56 Leonard Dr, Massapequa, NY	516-795-0077
Blake, Mike/107 South Street, Boston, MA	617-451-0660
Blakeslee Lane Studios/916 N Charles St, Baltimore, MD	301-727-8800
Blank, Bruce/228 Clearfield Ave, Norristown, PA	215-539-6166
Blevins, Burgess/103 E Read St, Baltimore, MD	301-685-0740
Bliss, Brad/42 Audubon St, Rochester, NY	716-461-9794
Bloomberg, Robert/172 Kohanza St, Danbury, CT	203-794-1764
Blouin, Craig/14 Main St, Rollinsford, NH	603-742-0104
Boehm, J Kenneth/96 Portland Ave, Georgetown, CT	203-544-8524
Bognovitz, Murray/4980 Wyaconda Rd, Rockville, MD	301-984-7771
Bohm, Linda/7 Park St, Montclair, NJ	201-746-3434
Bolster, Mark/1235 Monterey St, Pittsburgh, PA	412-231-3757
Bolton, Bea/15 East St, Boston, MA	617-423-2050
Bookbinder, Sigmund/Box 833, Southbury, CT	203-264-5137
Borkoski, Matthew/1506 Noyes Dr, Silver Spring, MD	301-589-4858
Bossart, Bob/PO Box 734/Cathedral St, Boston, MA	617-423-2323
Bowman, Jo/1102 Manning St, Philadelphia, PA	215-625-0200
Bowman, Ron/PO Box 4071, Lancaster, PA	717-898-7716
Boxer, Jeff Photography/14 Newbury St, Boston, MA	617-266-7755
Boyer, Beverly/17 Llanfair Rd, Ardmore, PA	215-649-0657
Bradley, Dave/840 Summer St, Boston, MA	617-268-6644
Brady, Joseph/Rt 179 RD2 Box 198, Ringoes, NJ	201-788-5550
Braverman, Ed/337 Summer St, Boston, MA	617-423-3373
Bravo, David/383 Buena Vista Rd, Fairfield, CT	203-367-5919
Brignolo, Joseph B/Oxford Springs Rd, Chester, NY	914-496-4453
Brown, Jim/286 Summer St, Boston, MA	617-423-6484
Brown, Martin/Cathance Lake, Grove Post Office, ME	207-454-7708
Brown, Stephen R/1882 Columbia Rd NW, Washington, DC	202-667-1965
Brownell, David/Box 97, Hamilton, MA	617-468-4284
Brownell, William/1411 Saxon Ave, Bay Shore, NY	516-665-0081
brt PHOTOGRAPHIC ILLUSTRATIONS/911 STATE ST, LANCASTER, PA (P 184,185)	**717-393-0918**
Bruce, Bradley H/PO Box 1555, Beaver Falls, PA	412-843-7325
Bruemmer, Fred/5170 Cumberland Ave, Montreal H4V 2N8, QU	514-482-5098
Brundage, Kip/66 Union St, Belfast, ME	207-338-5210
Buchanan, Robert/12 Cleveland St, Valhalla, NY	914-997-1944
Buckman, Sheldon/15 Kiley Dr, Randolph, MA	617-986-4773
Bulkin, Susan/Photoghy Works/548 Fairway Terrace, Philadelphia, PA	215-483-8814
Bulvony, Matt/1003 E Carson St, Pittsburgh, PA	412-431-5344
Burak, Jonathan/50 Woodward, Quincy, MA	617-770-3380
Burdick, Gary Photography/9 Parker Hill, Brookfield, CT	203-775-2894
Burger, Oded/670 South St, Waltham, MA	617-527-1024
Burke, John/31 Stanhope St, Boston, MA	617-536-4912
Burke, John & Judy/116 E Van Buren Ave, New Castle, DE	302-322-8760
Burns, George/3909 State St, Schenectady, NY	518-393-3633
Burns, Terry/8409 Germantown Ave, Philadelphia, PA	215-843-1299
Burwell, John/3519 Bradley Ln, Chevy Chase, MD	301-986-1290
Buschner & Faust/450 W Menlo Park, Rochester, NY	716-475-1170
Butler, Herbert/200 Mamaroneck Ave, White Plains, NY	914-683-1767

C
C L M Photo/272 Nassau Rd, Huntington, NY	516-423-8890
Cali, Guy/Layton Rd, Clarics Summit, PA	717-587-1957
Callahan, Charles/54 Applecross Circle, Chalfont, PA	215-822-8258
Campione, David/2202 New Albany Rd, Cinnaminson, NJ	609-829-4937
Carbone, Fred/1018 Wood St, Philadelphia, PA	215-922-0220
Carrier, John/601 Newbury St, Boston, MA	617-262-4440
Carrino, Nick/710 S Marshall St, Philadelphia, PA	215-925-3190
Carroll, Hanson/11 New Boston Rd, Norwich, VT	802-649-1094
Carruthers, Alan/3605 Jeanne-Mamce, Montreal H2X 2K4, QU	514-288-4333
Carstens, Don/1021 Cathedral St, Baltimore, MD	301-385-3049
Carter, Philip/Seventeen Sunset Dr, Bedford Hills, NY	914-241-4901

PHOTOGRAPHERS CONT'D.

Please send us your additions and updates.

Cassaday, Bruce/RD 1 Box 345 Lockwood, Peekskill, NY	914-528-4343
Cataffo, Linda/30 W Harriet Ave, Palisades Park, NJ	201-945-5486
Catalano, John/48D Otis St, West Babylon, NY	516-491-5990
Certo, Rosemarie/2519 Parrish St, Philadelphia, PA	215-232-2814
Chadman, Bob/595-603 Newbury St, Boston, MA	617-426-4926
Chalifour, Benoit/1030 St Alexandre #812, Montreal, QU	514-879-1869
Chandoha, Walter/RD 1 PO Box 287, Annandale, NJ	201-782-3666
Chaput, Chuck/17 Stilling St, Boston, MA	617-542-8272
Chase Studio/5019 Wilson Ln, Bethesda, MD	301-986-1050
Chatwin, Jim/5459 Main St, Williamsville, NY	716-634-3436
Chauhan, Dilip/145 Ipswich St, Boston, MA	617-262-2359
Chawtsky, Ann/85 Andover Rd, Rockville Centre, NY	516-766-2417
Chen, Lillie/2 Columbine Rd, Whitehouse Station, NJ	201-534-9637
Chiusano, Michael/39 Glidden St, Beverly, MA	617-927-7067
Choroszewski, Walter J/10 Mohvale Path, Branchburg, NJ	201-526-2018
Chwatsky, Ann/85 Andover Road, Rockville Center, NY	212-870-0822
Ciaglia, Joseph/2036 Spruce St, Philadelphia, PA	215-985-1092
Clark, Conley/9814 Rosensteel Ave, Silver Spring, MD	301-585-4739
Clarke, Marna G/1571 Boulevard, West Hartford, CT	203-521-5127
Clayton-Hall, Gary/PO Box 38, Shelburne, VT	802-985-8380
Cleff, Bernie Studio/715 Pine St, Philadelphia, PA	215-922-4246
Clemens, Clint/346 Newbury St, Boston, MA	617-437-1309
Clemens, Peter/153 Sidney St, Oyster Bay, NY	516-922-1759
Clifford, Geoffrey C/Craggle Ridge, Reading, VT	802-484-5047
Clymer, Jonathan/208 Undercliff Ave, Edgewater, NJ	201-714-9041
Cohen, Daniel/744 Park Ave, Hoboken, NJ	201-659-0952
Cohen, Marc Assoc/23 Crestview Dr, Brookfield, CT	203-775-1102
Collette, Roger/7 N Main St Ste 300, Attleboro, MA	617-226-1856
Collins, Fred/186 South St, Boston, MA	617-426-5731
Colucci, Lou/128 Broadway #106, Patterson, NJ	201-881-7618
Conaty, Jim/1 Winthrop Sq, Boston, MA	617-482-0660
Conboy, John/1225 State St, Schenectady, NY	518-346-2346
Condax, John/1320 Nectarine St, Philadelphia, PA	215-923-7790
Confer, Holt/2016 Franklin Pl, Wyomissing, PA	215-678-0131
Congalton, David/206 Washington St, Pembroke, MA	617-826-2788
Conner, Marian/456 Rockaway Rd #15, Dover, NJ	201-328-1823
Connor, Donna/PO Box 272/Fourth Ave, Sweetwater, NJ	609-965-3396
Conouse, Scott/177 St Paul St, Rochester, NY	716-454-5618
Cooke, Doug/202 Beacon St, Boston, MA	617-267-1754
Coolidge, Jeffrey/322 Summer St, Boston, MA	617-338-6869
Corcoran, John/310 Eighth St, New Cumberland, PA	717-774-0652
Cordingley, Ted/Way Rd, Gloucster, MA	617-283-2591
Cortesi, Wendy/3034 'P' St NW, Washington, DC	202-965-1204
Cough, George/8 Bryant Dr, Huntington, NY	516-673-9376
Coughlin, Suki/Main St, New London, NH	603-526-4645
Crane, Tom/113 Cumberland Pl, Bryn Mawr, PA	215-525-2444
Crawford, Carol/14 Fortune Dr Box 221, Billerica, MA	617-663-8662
Creative Advantage/707 Union St, Schenectady, NY	518-370-0312
Creative Images/122 Elmcroft Rd, Rochester, NY	716-482-8720
Crossley, Dorothy/Mittersill Rd, Franconia, NH	603-823-8177
Cunningham, Chris/9 East St, Boston, MA	617-542-4640
Curtis, Bruce/70 Belmont Dr, Roslyn Heights, NY	516-484-2570
Curtis, Jackie/Alewives Rd, Norwalk, CT	203-866-9198
Curtis, John/50 Melcher St, Boston, MA	617-451-9117
Cushner, Susie/354 Congress St, Boston, MA	617-542-4070
Czamanske, Marty/2 Townline Circle, Rochester, NY	716-427-2333

D

D'Angelo, Andy/309 Madison Ave, Reading, PA	215-921-8430
Daigle, James/109 Broad St, Boston, MA	617-233-1284
Dannenberg, Mitchell/261 Averill Ave, Rochester, NY	716-473-6720
Dapkiewicz, Steve/121 Beach St, Boston, MA	617-357-6809
Davidson, Josiah Scenic Photography/PO Box 434, Jenkintown, PA	215-572-5757
Davis, Howard/19 E 21st St, Baltimore, MD	301-625-3838
Davis, Pat Photo/14620 Pinto Ln, Rockville, MD	301-279-8828
DAVIS, RICK/210 CARTER DR #9/MATLACK IND, WEST CHESTER, PA (P 188,189)	**215-436-6050**
De Lucia, Ralph/120 E Hartsdale Ave, Hartsdale, NY	914-472-2253
Dean, Floyd M/810 Tatnall St, Wilmington, DE	302-655-7193
Debren, Allen/355 Pearl St, Burlington, VT	802-864-5916
Degginger, Phil/PO Box 186, Convent Station, NJ	201-455-1733
Delbert, Christian/19 Linell Circle, Billerica, MA	617-273-3138

Dempsey-Hart/241 A St, Boston, MA	617-338-6661
Denuto, Ellen/3100 Stevens Rd #3133, Wallington, NJ	201-773-5345
Derenzis, Philip/PO Box 19, Wind Gap, PA	215-437-7832
DeWaele, John/14 Almy St, Lincoln, RI	401-726-0084
Di Maggio, Joe/512 Adams St, Centerport, NY	516-271-6133
Diamond, Joseph/534 Lotus Rd, Ridgewood, NJ	201-444-5957
Diane's Photo/1920 Washington Valley Rd, Martinsville, NJ	201-271-1215
DiBartolo, Joseph/5 Joni Dr, Hamilton Twnshp, NJ	609-585-0434
DiBenedetto, Emilo/32 Touro Ave, Medford, MA	617-396-0550
Dickens, James/1255 University Ave, Rochester, NY	716-244-6334
Dickstein, Bob/101 Hillturn Lane, Roslyn Heights, NY	516-621-2413
Diebold, George/416 Bloomfield Ave, Montclair, NJ	201-744-5789
Dietz, Donald/PO Box 177, Dorchester, MA	617-265-3436
DiGiacomo, Melchior/32 Norma Rd, Harrington Park, NJ	201-767-0870
Dillon, George/275 Tremont St, Boston, MA	617-482-6154
DiMarco, Salvatore C Jr/1002 Cobbs St, Drexel Hill, PA	215-789-3239
DiMarzo, Bob/109 Broad St, Boston, MA	617-482-0328
Dishman, Leon/3 Church Circle, Annapolis, MD	301-263-7330
DITTMAR, WARREN/217 MAIN ST, OSSINING, NY (P 83)	**914-762-6311**
Dixon, Mel/PO Box 468, Ossining, NY	914-941-9336
Dixon, Rodney/PO Box 113, Cedar Grove, NJ	201-239-6426
Dodson, George/PO Box 525, Bowie, MD	301-262-0702
Dolin, Penny Ann/190 Henry St, Stamford, CT	203-359-9932
Donovan, Bill/165 Grand Blvd, Scarsdale, NY	914-472-0938
Douglas Associates/3 Cove of Cork Ln, Annapolis, MD	301-266-5060
Douglass, James/5161 River Rd Bldg 2B, Bethesda, MD	301-652-1303
Dow, Norman/52 Concord Ave, Cambridge, MA	617-492-1236
Dreyer, Peter H/916 Pleasant St, Norwood, MA	617-762-8550
Ducote, Kimberly/18 Constitution Dr, Leonardo, NJ	201-872-1689
Dunham, Tom/20 Van Dyke Rd, Hopewell, NJ	609-259-6042
Dunn, Jeffery/32 Pearl St, Cambridge, MA	617-864-2124
Dunn, Paul/239 A Street, Boston, MA	617-542-9554
Dunn, Phoebe/20 Silvermine Rd, New Canaan, CT	203-966-9791
DUNOFF, RICH/407 BOWMAN AVE, MERION STATION, PA (P 84,85)	**215-627-3690**
Dunwell, Steve/20 Winchester St, Boston, MA	617-423-4916
Durrance, Dick/Dolphin Ledge, Rockport, ME	207-236-3990
Dvonch/ Seger/4025 Rt 8, Allison Park, PA	412-487-6474
Dwiggins, Gene/204 Westminster Mall, Providence, RI	401-421-6466
Dyekman, James E/14 Cherry Hill Circle, Ossining, NY	914-941-0821

E

Earle, John/PO Box 63, Cambridge, MA	617-628-1454
Edelman, Harry/1335 Brinton Rd, Pittsburgh, PA	412-371-6865
Edmunds, Skip/25 E Huron, Buffalo, NY	716-842-2272
Edson, Franz Inc/26 Watch Way, Huntington, NY	516-692-4345
EDSON, STEVEN/107 SOUTH ST, BOSTON, MA (P 190,191)	**617-357-8032**
Egan, Jim/Visualizations/220 W Exchange St, Providence, RI	401-521-7052
Ehrlich, George/PO Box 186, New Hampton, NY	914-355-1757
Eisenfeld, Robert/30 Lincoln Trail, Hopatcong, NJ	201-398-9366
Elder, Tommy/Chapelbrook & Ashfield Rds, Williamsburg, MA	413-628-3243
Ellis, Bob/15 Washington Ave, Emerson, NJ	212-874-5300
Elson, Paul/8200 Blvd East, North Bergen, NJ	201-662-2882
EMMOTT, BOB/700 S 10TH ST, PHILADELPHIA, PA (P 218)	**215-925-2773**
Epstein, Alan Photography/694 Center St, Chicopee, MA	413-736-8532
Ernest Creative Photo/47 Somerset St, N Plainfield, NJ	201-753-6342
Esposito, Anthony Jr/48 Old Amity Rd, Bethany, CT	203-393-2231
Evans, John C/808 Centennial Ave, Sewickley, PA	412-741-5580
Evans, Michael/5520 33rd St NW, Washington, DC	202-362-4901
Everett Studios/22 Barker Ave, White Plains, NY	914-997-2200
Eyle, Nicolas Edward/304 Oak St, Syracuse, NY	315-422-6231

F

F-90 Inc/60 Sindle Ave, Little Falls, NJ	201-785-9090
Falkenstein, Roland/Strawberry St #4, Philadelphia, PA	215-592-7138
Faragan, George/1621 Wood St, Philadelphia, PA	215-564-5711
Farris, Mark/3733 Benton St NW, Washington, DC	202-269-5963
FATTA, C/25 DRY DOCK AVE, BOSTON, MA (P 192)	**617-423-6638**
Faulkner, Robert I/52 Comstock St, New Brunswick, NJ	201-828-6984
Feehan, Stephen/86 Donaldson Ave, Rutherford, NJ	201-438-1514
Feil, Charles W III/PO Box 201, Washington Grove, MD	301-258-8328
Feiling, David/214 Scoville Ave, Syracuse, NY	315-474-0413
Felker, Richard/20 Melville St, Augusta, ME	207-623-2223
Fennell, Mary/57 Maple Ave, Hastings on Hudson, NY	914-478-3627

Feraulo, Richard/518 First Parish Rd, Scituate, MA	617-545-6654
Ferreira, Al/237 Naubuc Ave, East Hartford, CT	203-569-8812
Ferrino, Paul/PO Box 3641, Milford, CT	203-878-4785
Ficara Studios Ltd/880 Canal St, Stamford, CT	203-327-4535
Filipe, Tony/239 A St, Boston, MA	617-542-8330
Findlay, Christine/Hwy 36 Airport Plaza, Hazlet, NJ	201-264-2211
Fine, Jerome/4594 Brookhill Dr N, Manlius, NY	315-682-7272
Fine, Ron/8600 Longacre Ct, Bethesda, MD	301-469-7960
Finlayson, Jim/PO Box 337, Locust Valley, NY	516-676-5816
Finnegan, Michael/PO Box 901, Plandome, NY	516-365-7942
Fischer, John/9 Shore View Rd, Port Washington, NY	516-883-3225
Fish, Charles/240 Noroton Ave, Darien, CT	203-655-6798
Fish, Dick/40 Center St, Northampton, MA	413-584-6500
Fisher, Al/601 Newbury St, Boston, MA	617-536-7126
Fisher, Patricia/2234 Cathedral Ave NW, Washington, DC	202-232-3781
Fitzgerald, Mark/87 Daly Rd, E Northport, NY	516-462-5628
Fitzhugh, Susan/3809 Beech Ave, Baltimore, MD	301-243-6112
Five Thousand K/281 Summer St, Boston, MA	617-542-5995
Fland, Peter/20 Park St, Moravia, NY	315-497-3528
Flanigan, Jim/1325 N 5th St #F4, Philadelphia, PA	215-236-4448
Flowers, Morocco/520 Harrison Ave, Boston, MA	617-426-3692
Focus Photography/2300 Walnut St #421, Philadelphia, PA	215-567-0187
Fogliani, Tom/600 Thurnau Dr, River Vale, NJ	201-391-2245
Foley, Paul/791 Tremont, Boston, MA	617-266-9336
Folti, Arthur/8 W Mineola Ave, Valley Steam, NY	516-872-0941
Foote, James/22 Tomac Ave, Old Greenwich, CT	203-637-3228
Forbes, Fred/1 South King St, Gloucester City, NJ	609-456-1919
Fordham, Mark/2 Roselle Ave, Cranford, NJ	201-276-9515
Foster, Frank/323 Newbury St, Boston, MA	617-536-8267
Foster, Nicholas/143 Claremont Rd, Bernardsville, NJ	201-766-7526
Fournier, Walter/185 Forest St, S Hamilton, MA	617-468-2892
Fox, Peggy/701 Padonia Rd, Cockeysville, MD	301-252-0003
Fox, Seth/8 Roundtree Circle, Hockessin, DE	302-737-4300
Francois, Emmett W/208 Hillcrest Ave, Wycoff, NJ	201-652-5775
Frank, Richard/48 Woodside Ave, Westport, CT	203-227-0496
Frank-Adise, Gale/9012 Fairview Rd, Silver Spring, MD	301-585-7085
Fraser, Renee/1167 Massachusetts Ave, Arlington, MA	617-646-4296
Fredericks, Michael Jr/RD 2 Box 292, Ghent, NY	518-672-7616
Freer, Bonnie/265 S Mountain Rd, New City, NY	212-535-3666
Freeze Frame Studios/255 Leonia Ave, Bogota, NJ	201-343-1233
Freid, Joel Carl/812 Loxford Terr, Silver Spring, MD	301-681-7211
Frerking, Erich Photography Inc/1 Bridge St, Irvington, NY	914-591-6047
FREUND, BUD/1425 BEDFORD ST #9C, STAMFORD, CT	
(P 193)	**203-359-0147**
Fries, Janet/4439 Ellicott St NW, Washington, DC	202-362-4443
FURMAN, MICHAEL/115 ARCH ST, PHILADELPHIA, PA	
(P 100,101)	**215-925-4233**
Furore, Don/49 Sugar Hollow Rd, Danbury, CT	203-792-9395
G/Q Studios/1217 Spring Garden St, Philadelphia, PA	215-236-7770
GALE, JOHN & SON/712 CHESTNUT ST, PHILADELPHIA, PA	
(P 176)	**215-629-0506**
Galella, Ron/17 Glover Ave, Yonkers, NY	914-237-2988
Gallery, Bill/86 South St, Boston, MA	617-542-0499
Gallo, Peter/Philadelphia, PA	215-925-5230
Galvin, Kevin/PO Box 30, Hanover, MA	617-826-4795
Gans, Harriet/50 Church Lane, Scarsdale, NY	914-723-7017
Ganson, John/14 Lincoln Rd, Wayland, MA	617-358-2543
Garber, Ira/150 Chestnut St, Providence, RI	401-274-3723
Gardner, Charles/12 N 4th St, Reading, PA	215-376-8086
Garfield, Peter/3401 K St NW, Washington, DC	202-333-1379
Garrett-Stow, Liliane/18 Tuthill Point Rd, East Moriches, NY	516-878-8587
Gates, Ralph/364 Hartshorn Dr Box 233, Short Hills, NJ	201-379-4456
Geer, Garry/183 St Paul St, Rochester, NY	716-232-2393
George, Fred/737 Canal St, Stamford, CT	203-348-7454
George, Walter/863 Mountain Ave, Berkeley Heights, NJ	201-464-2180
Geraci, Steve/125 Wilbur Place, Bohemia, NY	516-567-8777
Giandomenico, Bob/13 Fern Ave, Collingswood, NJ	609-854-2222
Giese, Al/RR 1/Box 302, Poundridge, NY	914-764-5512
Giglio, Harry/925 Penn Ave #305, Pittsburgh, PA	412-261-3338
Gillette, Guy/133 Mountaindale Rd, Yonkers, NY	914-779-4684
Glasofer, David/PO Box 758, Woodbridge, NJ	201-750-2727
Glass, Mark/310 9th St, Hoboken, NJ	201-798-0219
Glass, Peter/63 Penn Dr, West Hartford, CT	203-233-2898
Gluck, Mike/2 Bronxville Rd, Bronxville, NY	914-961-1677
Goell, Jonathan J/109 Broad St, Boston, MA	617-423-2057
Goembl, Ponder/617 S 10th St, Philadelphia, PA	215-928-1797
Gold, Gary D/One Madison Pl, Albany, NY	518-434-4887
Goldblatt, Steven/32 S Strawberry St, Philadelphia, PA	215-925-3825
Goldenberg, Barry/1 Baltimore Ave Box 412, Cranford, NJ	201-276-1510
Golding, Robert D/1210 Race St/POB 1319, Philadelphia, PA	215-563-8611
Goldklang, Jay/778 New York Ave, Huntington, NY	516-421-3860
Goldman, Mel/329 Newbury St, Boston, MA	617-536-0539
Goldsmith, Alan/PO Box 260, Washington Depot, CT	203-263-3841
Goldstein, Robert/PO Box 1127, Dennis, MA	617-385-5030
Gooch-Mayer Studio/1728 Cherry St, Philadelphia, PA	215-567-3608
Good, Richard/5226 Osage Ave, Philadelphia, PA	215-472-7659
Goodman, Howard/Rt 100, Somers, NY	914-277-3591
Goodman, John/337 Summer St, Boston, MA	617-482-8061
Goodman, John D/One Mill Street, Burlington, VT	802-864-0200
Goodman, Lou/322 Summer St, Boston, MA	617-542-8254
Gorchev & Gorchev/11 Cabot Rd, Woburn, MA	617-933-8090
Gordon, David A/1413 Hertel Ave, Buffalo, NY	716-833-2661
Gordon, Lee/725 Boylston St, Boston, MA	617-423-1985
Goro, Fritz/324 N Bedford Rd, Chappaqua, NY	914-238-8788
Gorrill, Robert B/PO Box 206, North Quincy, MA	617-328-4012
Grace, Arthur/1928 35th Pl NW, Washington, DC	202-333-6568
Graham, Jim/720 Chestnut St, Philadelphia, PA	215-592-7272
Grant, Jarvis/1650 Harvard St NW #709, Washington, DC	202-387-8584
Graphic Accent/446 Main St PO Box 243, Wilmington, MA	617-658-7602
Graphic Horizons Ltd/3512 Mabank Ln, Bowie, MD	301-262-4512
Gray, Sam/886 Gay St, Westwood, MA	617-326-2624
Graybeal, Sharon/PO Box 896, Hockessin, DE	302-998-4037
Grayson, Jay/9 Cockenoe Dr, Westport, CT	203-222-0072
Green, Jeremy/15117 Wheeler Lane, Sparks, MD	301-366-0123
Green, Tom/511 Rutgers Ln, Parsippany, NJ	201-882-9826
Greenberg, Steven/28 Randolph St, Boston, MA	617-423-7646
Gregoire, Rogier/107 South St 2nd Fl, Boston, MA	617-574-9554
Greniers Commercial Photo/127 Mill St, Springfield, MA	413-532-9406
Griebsch, John/183 St Paul St, Rochester, NY	716-546-1303
Grohe, Stephen F/186 South St, Boston, MA	617-426-2290
Gross, Lance/PO Box 388, Manchester, CT	203-871-2641
Guarinello, Greg/252 Highwood St, Teaneck, NJ	201-836-2333
Hagerman, Ron/385 Westminster St, Providence, RI	401-272-1117
Hahn, Bob/2405 Exeter Ct, Bethlehem, PA	215-868-0339
Hakalski, Robert/731 N 24th St, Philadelphia, PA	215-925-4233
Halliwell, Harry/PO Box 1690 GMF, Boston, MA	617-623-7225
Halstead, Dirck/3332 P St NW, Washington, DC	202-338-2028
Hambourg, Serge/Box 753, Crugers, NY	212-866-0085
Hamlin, Elizabeth/Box 177, Dorchester, MA	617-265-3436
Hamor, Robert/2308 Columbia Cir, Merrimack, NH	603-882-6061
Handerhan, Jerome/ JJH Photo/113 Edgewood Ave, Pittsburgh, PA	412-242-6308
Hansen, Steve/1260 Boylston St, Boston, MA	617-236-2211
Hanstein, George/389 Belmont Ave, Haledon, NJ	201-790-0505
Haritan, Michael/1701 Eben St, Pittsburgh, PA	412-343-2112
Harkey, John/90 Larch Rd, Providence, RI	401-831-1023
Harrington, Phillip A/Wagner Ave/ PO Box 10 Fleischmann's, NY	914-254-5227
HARRINGTON, BLAINE/374 OLD HAWLEYVILLE RD, BETHEL, CT (P 108)	**203-798-2866**
Harrington, John/455 Old Sleepy Hollow Rd, Pleasantville, NY	914-939-0702
Harris, Bill/286 Summer St, Boston, MA	617-426-0989
Harris, Brownie/McGuire Lane	914-271-6426
Harris, Leonard/48 Sean's Circle, Centerville, MA	617-428-1118
Harrison, Jim/PO Box 266, Charleston, MA	617-242-4314
Harting, Christopher/327 Summer St, Boston, MA	617-451-6330
Harvey, Scott/273 Speedwell, Morristown, NJ	201-538-9410
Hausner, Clifford/10 Wayne Rd, Fairlawn, NJ	201-791-7409
Hayes, Eric/Rural Route #1, Jrdn Fls B0T1J0, NS	902-875-4260
Heayn, Mark/17 W 24th St, Baltimore, MD	301-235-1608
Hecker, David/285 Aycrigg Ave, Passaic, NJ	201-471-2496
Heilman, Grant/PO Box 317, Lititz, PA	717-626-0296

Heinz, F Michael Photography/17 Rose Hill, Southport, CT	203-259-7456
Heist, Scott/616 Walnut St, Emmaus, PA	215-965-5479
Helmar, Dennis/134 Beach St, Boston, MA	617-451-1496
Herwig/36 Gloucester St, Boston, MA	617-353-1262
Hewitt, Malcolm/179 Massachusetts Ave, Boston, MA	617-262-7227
Hill, Brian/PO Box 1823, Nantucket, MA	617-228-2210
Hill, John T/388 Amity Rd, New Haven, CT	203-393-0035
Hines, Harry/PO Box 10061, Newark, NJ	201-242-0214
Hirshfeld, Max/923 F Street NW, Washington, DC	202-638-3131
Hodges, Sue Anne/34 North St, Wilmington, MA	617-657-6417
Hoffman, Dave/PO Box 1299, Summit, NJ	201-277-6285
Hoffman, Steven/780 Eden Rd, Lancaster, PA	717-569-2631
Holland, James R/208 Commonwealth Ave, Boston, MA	617-321-3638
Hollander, David/11 S Springfield Ave/POB 443, Springfield, NJ	201-467-0870
Holmes, Greg/2007 Hickory Hill Ln, Silver Spring, MD	301-295-3338
Holniker, Barry/400 E 25th St, Baltimore, MD	301-889-1919
Holoquist, Marcy/424 N Craig St, Pittsburgh, PA	412-963-8021
Holt, Chuck/535 Albany St, Boston, MA	617-338-4009
Holt, John/145 South St, Boston, MA	617-426-7262
Holt, Walter/PO Box 936, Media, PA	215-565-1977
Holz, Thomas Jay/PO Box 4, Tribes Hill, NY	518-842-7730
Hone, Stephen/2130 Arch St, Philadelphia, PA	215-568-5434
Hopkins, Tom/15 Orchard Park, Box 7A, Madison, CT	203-245-0824
Hornick/ Rivlin/25 Dry Dock, Boston, MA	617-482-8614
Horowitz, Abby/922 Chestnut, Philadelphia, PA	215-925-3600
Hotshots/35 Congress St, Salem, MA	617-744-1557
Houck, Julie/535 Albany St, Boston, MA	617-338-4009
Houser, Robert/PO Box 299, Litchfield, CT	203-567-4241
Houser-Tartaglia Photoworks/23 Walnut Ave, Clark, NJ	201-388-8531
Howard, Alan B Assoc/27 Cleveland St, Valhalla, NY	914-946-0404
Howard, Carl/27 Huckleberry Ln, Ballston Lake, NY	518-877-7615
Howard, Jerry/12 Main St, Natick, MA	617-653-7610
Howard, Richard/144 Holworthy St, Cambridge, MA	617-576-6968
Hoyt, Russell/171 Westminister Ave, S Attleboro, MA	617-399-8611
Hoyt, Wolfgang/222 Valley Pl, Mamaroneck, NY	914-698-4060
HUBBELL, WILLIAM/99 EAST ELM ST, GREENWICH, CT (P 180)	**203-629-9629**
Hulbert, Steve/3642 N 3rd St, Harrisburg, PA	717-236-1906
Hulen, Steve/67 Catamount Rd, Fairfield, CT	203-255-2191
Hundertmark, Charles/6264 Oakland Mills Rd, Sykesville, MD	301-242-8150
Hungaski, Andrew/Merribrook Lane, Stamford, CT	203-327-6763
Hunsberger, Douglas/115 W Fern Rd, Wildwood Crest, NJ	609-522-6849
Hunter, Allan/56 Main St 3rd Fl, Milburn, NJ	201-467-4920
Hurwitz, Harrison/100 E Hartsdale Ave #6NW, Hartsdale, NY	914-725-4086
Hurwitz, Joel/PO Box 1009, Leominster, MA	617-537-6476
Hutchinson, Gardiner/280 Friend St, Boston, MA	617-523-5180
Hyde, Dana/PO Box 1302, South Hampton, NY	516-283-1001
IJ Iannazzi, Robert F/450 Smith Rd, Rochester, NY	716-624-1285
Ickow, Marvin/1824 35th St NW, Washington, DC	202-342-0250
Iglarsh, Gary/2229 N Charles St, Baltimore, MD	301-235-3385
Image Source Inc/PO Box 1929, Wilmington, DE	302-658-5897
Impact Multi Image Inc/53 Laurel Dr, Somers Point, NJ	609-927-8100
Industrial Photographic Service/10 Railroad St Box 6, North Abington, MA	617-878-3622
Jackson, Reggie/135 Sheldon Terr, New Haven, CT	203-787-5191
Jagger, Warren/150 Chestnut St Box 3330, Providence, RI	401-351-7366
Joachim, Bruno/326 A Street, Boston, MA	617-451-6156
Joel, Yale/Woodybrook Ln, Croton-On-Hudson, NY	914-271-8172
Johnson, Paul/38 Athens St, Boston, MA	617-269-4043
JONES, LOU/22 RANDOLPH ST, BOSTON, MA (P 194)	**617-426-6335**
Jones, Peter/43 Charles St, Boston, MA	617-227-6400
Joseph, George E/19 Barnum Rd, Larchmont, NY	914-834-5687
Joseph, Nabil/445 St Pierre St #402, Montreal H2Y 2M8, QU	514-842-2444
Julien, Martine/444 Bedford Rd	914-747-2220
K Kaetzel, Gary/PO Box 3514, Wayne, NJ	201-696-6174
Kalfus, Lonny/36 Myrtle Ave, Edgewater, NJ	201-886-0776
Kalish, Joanne/512 Adams St, Centerport, NY	516-271-6133
Kalisher, Simpson/, Roxbury, CT	203-354-8893
Kaminsky, Saul/36 Sherwood Ave, Greenwich, CT	203-531-4953
Kamper, George/62 North Union St, Rochester, NY	716-454-7006
Kan, Dennis/4200 Wisconsin Ave #106, Washington, DC	301-428-9417
Kane, Alice/3380 Emeric Ave, Wantagh, NY	516-781-7049
Kane, Martin/555 Chester Pike #2, Sharon Hills, PA	215-237-6897
Kannair, Jon/65 Water St, Worcester, MA	617-757-3417
KAPLAN, CAROL/20 BEACON ST, BOSTON, MA (P 179)	**617-720-4400**
Kasper, Ken/1232 Cobbs St, Drexel Hill, PA	215-446-0108
Katz, Dan/36 Aspen Rd, W Orange, NJ	201-731-8956
Katz, Geoffrey/156 Francestown Rd, New Boston, NH	603-487-3819
Kaufman, Robert/58 Roundwood Rd, Newton Upper Falls, MA	617-964-4080
Keene Studio/10510 Insley St, Silver Spring, MD	301-949-4722
Keller, Michael/15 S Grand Ave, Baldwin, NY	516-223-9604
Kelley, Edward/20 White St, Red Bank, NJ	201-747-0596
Kelly/Mooney Photography/87 Willow Ave, North Plainfield, NJ	201-757-5924
Kenik, David Photography/21 Countryside Dr, Nashua, NH	603-880-8108
Kernan, Sean/576 Leetes Island Rd, Stony Creek, CT	203-481-4478
Kim, Chang H/9425 Bethany Pl, Gaithersburg, MD	301-840-5741
King, Ralph/103 Broad St, Boston, MA	617-426-3565
Kinum, Drew/Glen Avenue, Scotia, NY	518-382-7566
Klapatch, David/350 Silas Deane Hwy, Wethersfield, CT	203-563-3834
Klein, Robert Photo/355 Boylston, Boston, MA	617-262-2278
Kligman, Fred/4733 Elm St, Bethesda, MD	301-652-6333
Klinefelter, Eric/10963 Hickory Ridge Rd, Columbia, MD	301-964-0273
Knapp, Stephen/74 Commodore Rd, Worcester, MA	617-757-2507
Kobrin, Harold/PO Box 115, Newton, MA	617-332-8152
Korona, Joseph/178 Superior Ave, Pittsburgh, PA	412-761-4349
Kovner, Mark/14 Cindy Lane, Highland Mills, NY	914-928-6543
Krist, Bob/228 Overlook Ave, Leonia, NJ	201-585-9464
Krubner, Ralph/4 Juniper Court, Jackson, NJ	201-364-3640
Kruper, Alexander Jr/70 Jackson Dr Box 152, Cranford, NJ	201-276-1510
Kugielsky, Joseph/Little Brook Ln, Newtown, CT	203-426-7123
L L M Associates/20 Arlington, Newton, MA	617-232-0254
Labranche, Rick/3 Crestview Rd, Terryville, CT	203-589-7543
LaBua, Frank/37 N Mountain Ave, Montclair, NJ	201-783-6318
Labuzetta, Steve/180 St Paul St, Rochester, NY	716-546-6825
LAMAR PHOTOGRAPHICS/PO BOX 470, FRAMINGHAM, MA (P 195)	**617-881-2512**
Landsman, Gary D/12115 Parklawn Dr, Rockville, MD	301-468-2588
LANDWEHRLE, DON/9 HOTHER LN, BAYSHORE, NY (P 115)	**516-665-8221**
Lane, Whitney/109 Somerstown Rd, Ossining, NY	914-762-5335
Lanman, Jonathan/41 Bristol St, Boston, MA	617-574-9420
Lapides, Susan Jane/451 Huron Ave, Cambridge, MA	617-864-7793
LaRiche, Michael/30 S Bank St, Philadelphia, PA	215-922-0447
Latham, Sid/3635 Johnson Ave, Riverdale, NY	212-543-0335
Laurino, Don Studio/220 Ferris Ave, White Plains, NY	914-949-5508
Lautman, Robert C/4906 41 St NW, Washington, DC	202-966-2800
Lavine, David S/4016 The Alameda, Baltimore, MD	301-467-0523
Lawfer, Larry/107 South St, Boston, MA	617-451-0628
Lawrence, Stephanie/2422 Chetwood Circle, Timonium, MD	301-252-3704
Leach, Peter/118 S Seventh St, Philadelphia, PA	215-574-0230
Leaman, Chris/105 Plant Ave, Wayne, PA	215-688-3290
LeBlond, Jerry/7 Court Sq, Rutland, VT	802-422-3115
Lee, Carol/214 Beacon St, Boston, MA	617-523-5930
Lee, Raymond/PO Box 9743, Baltimore, MD	301-323-5764
Leeming Studios Inc/222 Richmond St, Providence, RI	401-421-1916
Lefcourt, Victoria/1734 Linden Ave, Baltimore, MD	301-462-1331
Lehman, Amy/115 Old Short Hills Rd, W Orange, NJ	201-376-8734
Leney, Julia/PO Box 434, Wayland, MA	617-358-7229
Lent, Max/24 Wellington Ave, Rochester, NY	716-328-5126
Lent, Michael/PO Box 825, Hoboken, NJ	201-798-4866
LEONARD, BARNEY/518 PUTNAM RD, MERION, PA (P 196,197)	**215-664-2525**
Levart, Herb/566 Secor Rd, Hartsdale, NY	914-946-2060
Leveille, David/27-31 St Bridget's Dr, Rochester, NY	716-423-9474
Levin, Aaron M/200 N Pearl St, Baltimore, MD	301-528-1444
Lewitt, Peter/39 Billings Park, Newton, MA	617-244-6552
Ley, Russell/103 Ardale St, Boston, MA	617-325-2500
Lidington, John/2 "C" St, Hull, MA	617-246-0300
Lieberman, Fred/2426 Linden Ln, Silver Spring, MD	301-565-0644
Lightstruck Studio/519 W Pratt St #105, Baltimore, MD	301-727-2220
Lilley, Weaver/125 S 18th St, Philadelphia, PA	215-567-2881
Lillibridge, David/Rt 4 Box 1172, Burlington, CT	203-673-9786

Please send us your additions and updates.

Linck, Tony/2100 Linwood Ave, Fort Lee, NJ	201-944-5454
Lincon, James/30 St John Pl, Westport, CT	203-226-3724
Littlehale, David/301 N Harrison St #176, Princeton, NJ	609-924-5147
Littlehales, Breton/9520 Seminole St, Silver Spring, MD	202-737-6222
Littlewood, John/PO Box 141, Woodville, MA	617-435-4262
Lockwood, Lee/27 Howland Rd, West Newton, MA	617-965-6343
Loescher, Mark/29 Webb Rd, Westport, CT	203-227-5855
Lokmer, John/925 Penn Ave #404, Pittsburgh, PA	412-765-3565
Long Shots/4421 East West Hwy, Bethesda, MD	301-654-0279
Longley, Steven/2224 North Charles St, Baltimore, MD	301-467-4185
Lowe, T J II/1420 E Front St, Plainfield, NJ	201-757-6582
Lukowicz, Jerome/122 Arch St, Philadelphia, PA	215-922-7122
Lunan, David/535 Albany St, Boston, MA	617-542-7875

M
MacKay, Kenneth/127 Hillary Lane, Penfield, NY	716-385-1116
MacKenzie, Maxwell/2641 Garfield St NW, Washington, DC	202-232-6686
MacLeod, Richard/551 Boylston St, Boston, MA	617-267-6364
Maggio, Chris/180 St Paul St, Rochester, NY	716-454-3929
Maggio, Donald/Brook Hill Ln #5E, Rochester, NY	716-381-8053
Maglott, Larry/249 A St, Boston, MA	617-482-9347
Magnet, Jeff/628B 1620 Worchester Rd, Framingham, MA	617-547-8226
Magno, Thomas/19 Peters St, Cambridge, MA	617-492-5197
Makris, Dave/10 Newbold Dr, Hyde Park, NY	914-229-5012
Malitsky, Ed/337 Summer St, Boston, MA	617-451-0655
Malka, Daniel/1030 St Alexandre #203, Montreal H2Z 1P3, QU	514-397-9704
Maltz, Alan/182 Beach #136, Belle Harbour, NY	718-318-0110
Malyszko, Michael/90 South St, Boston, MA	617-426-9111
Mandelkorn, Richard/309 Waltham St, W Newton, MA	617-332-3246
Manheim, Michael Philip/PO Box 35, Marblehead, MA	617-631-3560
Mann, Richard J/PO Box 2712, Dix Hills, NY	516-673-3845
Marcelonis, George/291 Newbury St, Boston, MA	617-536-6777
Marchese, Frank/56 Arbor St, Hartford, CT	203-232-4417
Marcus, Joan/2311 Calvert St NW, Washington, DC	202-332-2828
Margolis, David/93 Audubon St, New Haven, CT	203-777-7288
Margolis, Paul/77 S Broadway, Nyack, NY	914-358-6749
Marinelli, Jack/673 Willow St, Waterbury, CT	203-756-3273
Marinelli, Mary Leigh/12 Curtis St, Salem, MA	617-745-7035
Mark Color Studios/286 Ridge Rd, Baltimore, MD	301-687-1222
Markel, Brad/1341 S Carolina Ave SE, Washington, DC	202-543-4806
Marshall, John/344 Boylston St, Boston, MA	617-536-2988
Martin Paul Ltd/247 Newbury St, Boston, MA	617-536-1644
Martin, Bruce/266-A Pearl St, Cambridge, MA	617-492-8009
Martin, Jeff/6 Industrial Way W, Eatontown, NJ	201-689-0888
Martin, Marilyn/130 Appleton St #2I, Boston, MA	617-262-5507
Massar, Ivan/296 Bedford St, Concord, MA	617-369-4090
Mastalia, Francesco/2 Midland Ave, Hawthorne, NJ	212-772-8449
MATT, PHILIP/PO BOX 10406, ROCHESTER, NY (P 198)	**716-461-5977**
Mattei, George Photography/179 Main St, Hackensack, NJ	201-342-0740
Mavodones, Bill/46 Waltham St #105, Boston, MA	617-423-7382
Mayer, Charles/108 Massachusetts Ave, Boston, MA	617-262-4448
Mayernik, George/41 Wolfpit Ave #2N, Norwalk, CT	203-846-1406
Mazzone, James/1201 82nd St, N Bergen, NJ	201-861-8992
McConnell, Jack/182 Broad St, Old Wethersfield, CT	203-563-6154
MCCONNELL, RUSS/8 ADLER DR, E SYRACUSE, NY (P 200)	**315-433-1005**
McCormick & Nelson, Inc/34 Piave St, Stamford, CT	203-348-5062
McCoy, Dan/Main St, Housatonic, MA	413-274-6211
McDermott, Brian/14 Sherwood Ave, Ossining, NY	914-941-6012
McDonald, Kevin R/319 Newtown Turnpike, Redding, CT	203-938-9276
McDonough Studio/3224 Kennedy Blvd, Jersey City, NJ	201-420-1056
McGrail, John/6576 Senator Ln, Bensalem, PA	215-750-6070
McKean, Thomas R/742 Cherry Circle, Wynnewood, PA	215-642-1412
McLaren, Lynn/42 W Cedar, Boston, MA	617-227-7448
McLean, Alex/65 E India Row #10D, Boston, MA	617-523-6446
McMullin, Forest/183 St Paul St, Rochester, NY	716-262-3944
McNeill, Brian/840 W Main St, Lansdale, PA	215-368-3326
McQueen, Ann/791 Tremont St #401, Boston, MA	617-267-6258
McWilliams, Jack/15 Progress Ave, Chelmsford, MA	617-256-9615
Meacham, Joseph/229 Brown St, Philadelphia, PA	215-925-8122
Mecca, Jack/1508 72nd St, North Bergen, NJ	201-869-7956
Mednick, Seymour/316 S Camac, Philadelphia, PA	215-735-6100
Medvec, Emily/151 Kentucky Ave SE, Washington, DC	202-546-1220
Meech, Christopher/20 Forest St, Stamford, CT	203-348-1158

Meek, Richard/8 Skyline Dr, Huntington, NY	516-271-0072
Mehne, Ralph/1501 Rose Terrace, Union, NJ	201-686-0668
Meiller, Henry Studios/1026 Wood St, Philadelphia, PA	215-922-1525
Melino, Gary/235 Simmonsville Ave, Johnston, RI	401-781-6320
MELLOR, D W/1020 MT PLEASANT RD, BRYN MAWR, PA (P 124)	**215-527-9040**
Melton, Janice Munnings/692 Walkhill St, Boston, MA	617-298-1443
Mendelsohn, David/Sky Farm Rd, Northwood, NH	603-942-7622
Mercer, Ralph/239 'A' St, Boston, MA	617-482-2942
Merchant, Martin/22 Barker Ave, White Plains, NY	914-997-2200
Merz, Laurence/215 Georgetown Rd, Weston, CT	203-222-1936
Meyers, Steve/Drawer 2, Almond, NY	607-276-6400
Michael's/481 Central Ave, Cedarhurst, NY	516-374-3456
Michael, Shawn/240 Prospect Ave, Hackensack, NJ	201-487-2865
Millard, Howard/220 Sixth Ave, Pelham, NY	914-738-3689
Miller, Bruce Photography/9 Tall Oaks Dr, East Brunswick, NJ	201-257-0211
Miller, Don/60 Sindle Ave, Little Falls, NJ	201-785-9090
Miller, Gary/PO Box 136, Bedford Hills, NY	914-666-4174
Miller, J T/12 Forest Edge Dr, Titusville, NJ	609-737-3116
Miller, Melabee/29 Beechwood Pl, Hillside, NJ	201-527-9121
Miller, Roger/1411 Hollins St Union Sq, Baltimore, MD	301-566-1222
Millman, Lester Jay/23 Court St #23, White Plains, NY	914-946-2093
Mincey, Dale/113 Brunswick St, Jersey City, NJ	201-420-9387
Mindell, Doug/811 Boylston St, Boston, MA	617-262-3968
Mink, Mike/180 St Paul St 5th Fl, Rochester, NY	716-325-4865
Miraglia, Elizabeth/29 Drummer Ln W Redding, CT	203-938-2261
Mirando, Gary/27 Cleveland St, Valhalla, NY	914-997-6588
Mitchell, Mike/930 'F' St #800, Washington, DC	202-347-3223
Moerder, Dan/2115 Wallace St, Philadelphia, PA	215-978-7414
Mogerley, Jean/1262 Pines Lake Dr W, Wayne, NJ	201-839-2355
Molinaro, Neil R/15 Walnut Ave, Clark, NJ	201-396-8980
Monroe, Robert/Kennel Rd, Cuddebackville, NY	914-754-8329
Monsees, Peter/150 River St, Hackensack, NJ	201-646-4130
Mopsik, Eugene/419 S Perth St, Philadelphia, PA	215-922-3489
Morgan, Bruce/55 S Grand Ave, Baldwin, NY	516-546-3554
Morley, Bob/129 South St, Boston, MA	617-482-7279
Morrow, Christopher W/163 Pleasant St, Arlington, MA	617-648-6770
Morse, Timothy/1133 Curve St, Carlisle, MA	617-369-8036
MOZO PHOTO DESIGN/282 SHELTON RD (RT 110), MONROE, CT (P 199)	**203-261-7400**
Mullen, Stephen/112 N 12th St, Philadelphia, PA	215-569-0930
Mulligan, Bob/109 Broad St, Boston, MA	617-542-7308
MULLIGAN, JOSEPH/239 CHESTNUT ST, PHILADELPHIA, PA (P 59)	**215-592-1359**
Munster, Joseph/Old Rt 28, Phoenicia, NY	914-688-5347
Murray, Ric/150 Chestnut St, Providence, RI	401-751-8806
Musto, Tom/225 S Main St, Wilkes-Barre, PA	717-822-5798
Mydans, Carl/212 Hommocks Rd, Larchmont, NY	212-841-2345
Myers Studios Inc/21 Princeton Place, Orchard Park, NY	716-662-6002
Myers, Steve/Drawer 2, Almond, NY	607-276-6400
Myron/127 Dorrance St, Providence, RI	401-421-1946

N
Nadel, Lee/10 Loveland Rd, Brookline, MA	617-277-8087
Nagler, Lanny/56 Arbor St, Hartford, CT	203-233-4040
National Imagemakers/30 Braod St, Denville, NJ	201-428-0212
Nelder, Oscar/Box 661 Main St, Presque Isle, ME	207-769-5911
Nelson, Janet/Finney Farm, Croton-On-Hudson, NY	914-271-5453
Nerney, Dan/137 Rowayton Ave, Rowayton, CT	203-853-2782
Nettis, Joseph/1717 Walnut St, Philadelphia, PA	215-563-5444
Neudorfer, Brien/46 Waltham St, Boston, MA	617-451-9211
Neumann, William/96 Carmita Ave, Rutherford, NJ	201-939-0370
Neumayer, Joseph/Chateau Rive #102, Peekskill, NY	914-739-3005
Nichols, Don/1241 University Ave, Rochester, NY	716-461-9666
Nighswander, Tim/315 Peck St, New Haven, CT	203-789-8529
Noble Inc/611 Cathedral St, Baltimore, MD	301-244-0292
Nochton, Jack/1238 W Broad St, Bethlehem, PA	215-691-2223
Noel, Peter/115 Cedar St, Malden, MA	617-321-1264
Norris, Robert/RFD 1 Box 4480, Pittsfield, ME	207-487-5981
Northlight Visual Comm Group Inc/21-23 Quine St Cranford, NJ	201-272-1155
Nurnberg, Paul/193 Florence St #3R, Roslindale, MA	617-327-3920

Please send us your additions and updates.

O

O'Donnell, John/179 Westmoreland St, White Plains, NY	914-948-1786
O'Donoghue, Ken/8 Union Park St, Boston, MA	617-542-4898
O'Neill, James/1543 Kater St, Philadelphia, PA	215-545-3223
O'Neill, Martin/1416 W Mt Royal Ave, Baltimore, MD	301-225-0522
O'Shaughnessy, Bob/50 Melcher, Boston, MA	617-542-7122
Obermeyer, Eva/PO Box 1722, Union, NJ	201-375-3322
Ogiba, Joseph/PO Box M, Somerville, NJ	201-874-8428
Olbrys, Anthony/41 Pepper Ridge Rd, Stamford, CT	203-322-9422
OLIVER, LOU/8 ADLER DR, E SYRACUSE, NY (P 200)	**315-433-1005**
Olivera, Bob/42 Weybossett St, Providence, RI	401-272-1170
Olmstead Studio/118 South St, Boston, MA	617-542-2024
Opfer, Robert M/20-35 Richmond St, Philadelphia, PA	215-563-0888
Orel, Mano/PO Box E, Dove Court, Croton-On-Hudson, NY	914-271-5542
Orkin, Pete/80 Washington St, S Norwalk, CT	203-866-9978
Orlando, Fran/329 Spruce St, Philadelphia, PA	215-629-9968
Orling, Alan S/Hawley Rd, North Salem, NY	914-669-5405
Orrico, Charles/72 Barry Ln, Syosset, NY	516-364-2257
Ouzer, Louis/120 East Ave, Rochester, NY	716-454-7582
Owens, John/93 Massachusetts Ave, Boston, MA	617-423-2452

P

PALMER, GABE/FIRE HILL FARM, WEST REDDING, CT (P 132,133)	**203-938-2514**
Panioto, Mark/95 Mohawk Ln, Weathersfield, CT	203-241-3202
Pantages, Tom/7 Linden Ave, Gloucester, MA	617-525-3678
Paradigm Productions/6437 Ridge Ave, Philadelphia, PA	215-482-8404
Paredes, Cesar/322 Clarksville Rd, Princeton Junction, NJ	609-799-4097
Parker, Bruce/Box 341 Eastwood Sta, Syracuse, NY	315-437-7804
Paskevich, John/1500 Locust St #3017, Philadelphia, PA	215-735-9868
Patrey, Dan/3 Cornell Pl, Great Neck, NY	516-466-4396
Patten, Michael/24-D Bartle Ct, Highland Park, NJ	201-846-8662
Paxenos, Dennis F/2125 Maryland Ave #103, Baltimore, MD	301-837-1029
PEASE, GREG/23 E 22ND ST, BALTIMORE, MD (P 220,221)	**301-332-0583**
Peckham, Lynda/65 S Broadway, Terrytown, NY	914-631-5050
Pellegrini, Lee/381 Newtonville Ave, Newtonville, MA	617-964-7925
Pelletier, Herve/329 A Street, Boston, MA	619-423-6724
Penneys, Robert/147 N 12th St, Philadelphia, PA	215-925-6699
The Peregrine Group/375 Sylvan Ave, Englewood Cliffs, NJ	201-567-8585
Perez, Paul R/143 Hoffman Ave, Lindenhurst, NY	516-226-0846
Perlmutter, Steven/246 Nicoll St, New Haven, CT	203-789-8493
Peterson, Brent/15 Davenport Ave #2G, New Rochelle, NY	212-573-7195
Petrecky, Sam/27 Reid St, Amsterdam, NY	518-842-7730
Petronio, Frank/74 Westchester Ave, Rochester, NY	716-288-4642
Pevarnik, Gervose/180 St Paul St, Rochester, NY	716-262-3579
Philiba, Allan A/3408 Bertha Dr, Baldwin, NY	516-623-7841
Photo Synthesis/524 Parkway View Dr, Pittsburgh, PA	412-787-7287
Photo-Colortura/PO Box 1749, Boston, MA	617-522-5132
Photographic Illustration Ltd/7th & Ranstead, Philadelphia, PA	215-925-7073
Photohandwerk/Michael D McGuire/51 W Walnut Lane, Philadelphia, PA	215-844-0754
Photown Studio/190 Vandervoort St, North Tonawanda, NY	716-693-2912
Pickerell, Jim H/110-E Frederick Ave, Rockville, MD	301-251-0720
Picture That Inc/880 Briarwood, Newtown Square, PA	215-353-8833
Picturehouse Assoc Inc/22 Elizabeth St, Norwalk, CT	203-852-1776
Pietersen, Alex/29 Raynor Rd, Morristown, NJ	201-267-7003
Piperno, Lauren/215 E Dean St, Freeport, NY	516-868-9107
Plank, David/981 River Rd, Reading, PA	215-376-3461
Platteter, George/82 Colonnade Dr, Rochester, NY	716-334-4488
Poggenpohl, Eric/1816 S Street NW, Washington, DC	202-387-0826
Pohuski, Michael/36 South Paca St, Baltimore, MD	301-962-5404
Polansky, Allen/1431 Park Ave, Baltimore, MD	301-383-9021
Polumbaum, Ted/326 Harvard St, Cambridge, MA	617-491-4947
Pope-Lance, Elton/117 Stacey Ave, Trenton, NJ	609-695-1040
Porcella, Phil/109 Broad St, Boston, MA	617-426-3222
Portsmouth Photography/259 Miller Ave, Portsmouth, NH	603-431-3351
Powell, Bolling/1 Worcester Sq, Boston, MA	617-536-1199
Pownall, Ron/7 Ellsworth Ave, Cambridge, MA	617-354-0846
Praus, Edgar G/176 Anderson Ave, Rochester, NY	716-442-4820
Pro Am Photo/4900 Merrick Rd, Massapequa Pk, NY	516-799-2580
Profit, Everett R/533 Massachusetts Ave, Boston, MA	617-267-5840
Prue, Sara/, Washington, DC	202-232-2330

Q R

Quin, Clark/241 A Street, Boston, MA	617-451-2686
Quindry, Richard/200 Loney St, Philadelphia, PA	215-742-6300
Raab, Timothy/163 Delaware Ave, Delmar, NY	518-439-2298
Ranck, Rosemary/323 W Mermaid Ln, Philadelphia, PA	215-242-3718
Rapp, Frank/327 A St, Boston, MA	617-542-4462
Rauch, Bonnie/Crane Rd, Somers, NY	914-277-3986
Rawle, Johnathan/PO Box 292, Lexington, MA	617-275-3030
Ray, Dean/13 W 25th St, Baltimore, MD	301-243-3441
Raycroft/McCormick/179 South St, Boston, MA	617-542-7229
Redding, Jim/105 Beach St, Boston, MA	617-482-2833
Reis, Jon Photography/141 The Commons, Ithaca, NY	607-272-1966
Renard, Jean/142 Berkeley St, Boston, MA	617-266-8673
Renckly, Joe/1200 Linden Pl, Pittsburgh, PA	412-323-2122
Retallack, John/207 Erie Station Rd, West Henrietta, NY	716-334-1530
Richard, George/PO Box 392, Walker Valley, NY	914-733-4300
Richards, Toby/244 Alexander St, Princeton, NJ	609-921-6830
Richman, Mel Inc/15 N Presidential Blvd, Bala-Cynwyd, PA	215-667-8900
Richmond, Jack/12 Farnsworth St, Boston, MA	617-482-7158
RIEMER, KEN/183 ST PAUL ST, ROCHESTER, NY (P 201)	**716-232-5450**
Riggs, Rollin/PO Box 9327, New Haven, CT	203-624-5485
Riley, George/Sisquisic Trail PO Box 840, Yarmouth, ME	207-846-5787
Riley, Laura/Hidden Spng Fm PO Box 186, Pittstown, NJ	201-735-7707
Ritter, Frank/2414 Evergreen St, Yorktown Hts, NY	914-962-5385
Rizzi, Leonard F/5161 River Rd Bldg 2B, Bethesda, MD	301-652-1303
Rizzo, John/36 St Paul St, Rochester, NY	716-232-5140
Robb, Steve/535 Albany St, Boston, MA	617-542-6565
Roberts, Mathieu/200 Henry St, Stamford, CT	203-324-3582
ROBINS, SUSAN/124 N THIRD ST, PHILADELPHIA, PA (P 147)	**215-238-9988**
Robinson, George A/4-A Stonehedge Dr, S Burlington, VT	802-862-6902
Robinson, Mike/2413 Sarah St, Pittsburgh, PA	412-431-4102
Rockhill, Morgan/204 Westminster Mall, Providence, RI	401-274-3472
Rode, Robert/2670 Arleigh Rd, East Meadow, NY	516-485-6687
Roseman, Shelly/723 Chestnut St, Philadelphia, PA	215-922-1430
Rosier, Gerald/PO Box 470, Framingham, MA	617-881-2512
Rosner, Eric/1133 Arch St 9th Fl, Philadelphia, PA	215-567-2758
Rosner, Stu/One Thompson Sq, Charlestown, MA	617-242-2112
Ross, Alex F/1622 Chestnut St, Philadelphia, PA	215-843-1274
Rossmeissl, Kirk/4810 Erpter Dr, Rockville, MD	301-465-6629
ROTH, ERIC/337 SUMMER ST, BOSTON, MA (P 202,203)	**617-338-5358**
Roth, Seth/264 9th St, Jersey City, NJ	201-792-9234
Rothstein, Jennifer/208 18th St, Union City, NJ	201-392-8958
ROTMAN, JEFFREY L/14 COTTAGE AVE, SOMERVILLE, MA (P 204,205)	**617-666-0874**
Rowan, Norm R/106 E 6th St, Clifton, NJ	201-772-5126
Roytos, Richard/PO Box 4000, Princeton, NJ	609-921-4983
Ruggeri, Lawrence/10 Old Post Office Rd, Silver Spring, MD	301-588-3131
Ruggieri, Ignazio/60 Sindle Ave, Little Falls, NJ	201-785-9090
Runyon, Paul/301 N 3rd St, Philadelphia, PA	215-238-0655
Russ, Clive/82 Barlett St, Charlestown, MA	617-242-5234
Russel, Rae/75 Byram Lake Rd, Mount Kisco, NY	914-241-0057
Russo, Rich/11 Clinton St, Morristown, NJ	201-538-6954
Ryder Photo/141 First St, Liverpool, NY	315-622-3499

S

Sa'Adah, Jonathan/PO Box 247, Hartford, VT	802-295-5327
Sagala, Steve/53-A Parsippany Rd, Whippany, NJ	201-377-1418
Sakmanoff, George/179 Massachusetts Ave, Boston, MA	617-262-7227
Salamone, Anthony/1277 Commonwealth Ave, Boston, MA	617-254-5427
Salant, Robin/216 Wadsworth Ave, South Plainfield, NJ	201-272-7195
Salomone, Frank/296 Brick Blvd, Bricktown, NJ	201-920-1525
Salsbery, Lee/14 Seventh St NE, Washington, DC	202-543-1222
Salstrand, Duane/503 Boylston #4, Brookline, MA	617-232-1795
SAMARA, THOMAS/713 ERIE BLVD WEST, SYRACUSE, NY (P 178)	**315-476-4984**
Samuels Studio/8 Waltham St, PO Box 201, Maynard, MA	617-897-7901
Sanford, Eric/219 Turnpike Rd, Manchester, NH	603-624-0122
Sansone, Nadine/7 River St, Milford, CT	203-878-5090
Sapienza, Louis A/96 West St, Colonia, NJ	201-382-5933
Saraceno, Paul/46 Waltham St, Boston, MA	617-542-2779
Sasso, Ken/116 Mattabaffa, Meriden, CT	203-235-1421

SAUTER, RON PHOTO/183 ST PAUL ST, ROCHESTER, NY (P 206)	**716-232-1361**
Savage, Sally/99 Orchard Terrace, Piermont, NY	914-359-5735
Saydah, Gerard/NJ	201-768-2582
Sayers, Jim/325 Valley Rd, West Orange, NJ	201-325-7826
Schadt, Bob/23 Ransom Rd, Brighton, MA	617-782-3734
Schaefer, Dave/48 Grove St, Belmont, MA	617-371-2850
Schaeffer, Bruce/510 Lancaster Ave, Frazer, PA	215-647-4446
Schembri, Joseph/PO Box 923, Metuchen, NJ	201-287-8561
Scherer, James/35 Kingston St, Boston, MA	617-338-5678
Scherzi, James/116 Town Line Rd, Syracuse, NY	315-455-7961
Schlanger, Irv/946 Cherokee Rd, Huntington Valley, PA	215-663-0663
SCHLEIPMAN, RUSS/ZERO NEAREN ROW, BOSTON, MA (P 207)	**617-242-9298**
Schlowsky Studios/145 South St, Boston, MA	617-338-4664
Schmitt, Steve/337 Summer St, Boston, MA	617-482-5482
Schoen, Robert/241 Crescent St, Waltham, MA	617-647-5546
SCHOON, TIM/PO BOX 7446, LANCASTER, PA (P 208)	**717-291-9483**
Schroeder, H Robert/PO Box 7361, W Trenton, NJ	609-883-8643
Schulmeyer, LT/2124 Maryland Ave, Baltimore, MD	301-332-0767
Schultz, Jurgen/Rt 100 N/Box 19, Londonderry, VT	802-824-3475
Schweikardt, Eric/PO Box 56, Southport, CT	203-375-8181
Sculnick, Herb/7 2nd St, Athens, NY	518-945-1598
Sedik, Joe/342 Perkiomen Ave, Lansdale, PA	215-368-6832
Segal Panorama Photo/2141 Newport Pl NW, Washington, DC	202-223-2618
Seger, Toby/5808 Holden St, Pittsburgh, PA	412-487-6474
Seng, Walt/810 Penn Ave #400, Pittsburgh, PA	412-391-6780
Serbin, Vincent/304 Church Rd, Bricktown, NJ	201-920-2249
Serio, Steve/10 Thatcher St #116, Boston, MA	617-227-3767
SEVERI, ROBERT/PO BOX 42378, WASHINGTON, DC (P 223)	**301-585-1010**
Shafer, Bob/3554 Quebec St N W, Washington, DC	202-362-0630
SHARP, STEVE/153 N 3RD ST, PHILADELPHIA, PA (P 150)	**215-925-2890**
Shelton, Sybil/416 Valley View Rd, Englewood, NJ	201-568-8684
Shepherd, Francis/PO Box 204, Chadds Ford, PA	215-347-6799
Sherer, Larry/5233 Eliots Oak Rd, Columbia, MD	301-730-3178
Sherman, Steve/49 Melcher St, Boston, MA	617-542-1496
Sherriff, Bob/963 Humphrey St, Swampscott, MA	617-599-6955
Shotwell, John/17 Stillings St, Boston, MA	617-357-7456
Shoucais, Bill/460 Harrison Ave 3rd Fl, Boston, MA	617-423-1774
Siciliano, Richard/707 Union St, Schenectady, NY	518-370-0312
Sickles Photo Reporting/PO Box 98, Maplewood, NJ	201-763-6355
Siegel, Hyam Photography/PO Box 356, Brattleboro, VT	802-257-0691
Siegler, William A/38 Orange Ave, Walden, NY	914-778-7300
Silk, Georgiana B/190 Godfrey Rd E, Weston, CT	203-226-0408
Silver, David/35 N Third St, Philadelphia, PA	215-925-7277
Silverman, Paul/49 Ronald Dr, Clifton, NJ	201-761-1497
Silverstein, Abby/3315 Woodvalley Dr, Baltimore, MD	301-486-5211
Simeone, J Paul/116 W Baltimore Pike, Media, PA	215-566-7197
Simian, George/9 Hawthorne Pl, Boston, MA	617-267-3558
SIMMONS, ERIK LEIGH/241 A ST, BOSTON, MA (P 172,173)	**617-482-5325**
Simon, David/263 110th St, Jersey City, NJ	201-795-9326
Simpson/Flint/2133 Maryland Ave, Baltimore, MD	301-837-9923
Singer, Arthur/Sedgewood RD 12, Carmel, NY	914-225-6801
Singer, Jay/20 Russell Park Rd, Syosset, NY	516-935-8991
Sint, Steven/6 Second Rd, Great Neck, NY	516-487-4918
Siteman, Frank/136 Pond St, Winchester, MA	617-729-3747
Sitkin, Marc B/23 Lincoln St, Hartford, CT	203-727-0605
Siuccoli, Stephen/152-A Prospect Ave, Shelton, CT	203-736-6100
Sklute, Kenneth/210 E Nassau St, Islip Terrace, NY	516-581-7276
Skoogford, Leif/415 Church Rd #B2, Elkins Park, PA	215-635-5186
Slide Graphics/262 Summer St, Boston, MA	617-542-0700
Sloan Photo/443 Albany St, Boston, MA	617-542-3215
Smith & Warren Photography/PO Box 205, Pittsburgh, PA	412-687-7500
Smith, Chris/19 E 22nd St, Baltimore, MD	301-659-0986
SMITH, GARY & RUSSELL/65 WASHINGTON ST, S NORWALK, CT (P 177)	**203-866-8871**
SMITH, GORDON E/65 WASHINGTON ST, S NORWALK, CT (P 177)	**203-866-8871**
Smith, Philip W/PO Box 400, Pennington, NJ	609-737-3370
Smith, Stuart/68 Raymond Lane, Wilton, CT	203-762-3158
Snyder, Clarence/717 Porter St, Easton, PA	215-252-2109

Solomon Assoc/PO Box 237, Glyndon, MD	301-833-5678
Soorenko, Barry/5161 River Rd Bldg 2B, Bethesda, MD	301-652-1303
Speedy, Richard/244 Alexander St, Princeton, NJ	609-921-6830
Spelman, Steve/15 A St Mary's Ct, Brookline, MA	617-566-6578
Spencer, Michael/735 Mt Hope Ave, Rochester, NY	716-475-6817
Sperduto, Stephen/18 Willett Ave, Port Chester, NY	914-939-0296
Spiegel, Ted/RD 2 Box 353 A, South Salem, NY	914-763-3668
SPIRO, DON/137 SUMMIT RD, SPARTA, NJ (P 156,157)	**212-484-9753**
St Niell Studio/209 Parker Ave, Clifton, NJ	201-340-1212
Staccioli, Marc/1480 Rt 46 #321B, Parsippany, NJ	201-334-7620
Stafford, Rick/26 Wadsworth, Allston, MA	617-495-2389
Stage, John Lewis/Iron Mountain Rd, New Milford, NY	914-986-1620
Stahl, Bill/87 Mulberry Ave, Garden City, NY	516-741-5709
Stapleton, John/6854 Radbourne Rd, Upper Darby, PA	215-626-0920
States, Randall Taylor/3016 Weaver Ave, Baltimore, MD	301-426-6910
Stearns, Stan/1814 Glade Ct, Annapolis, MD	301-268-5777
Stein, Geoffrey R/348 Newbury St, Boston, MA	617-536-8227
Steiner, Chuck/111 Newark Ave, Union Beach, NJ	201-739-0629
Steiner, Lisl/'El Retscho' Trinity Pass, Pound Ridge, NY	914-764-5538
Steiner, Peter/183 St Paul St 3rd Fl, Rochester, NY	716-454-1012
Stevens, Lee/2 Phillips Dr, Newburyport, MA	617-462-9385
STIER, KURT/93 MASSACHUSETTS AVE #402, BOSTON, MA (P 174,175)	**617-247-3822**
Stierer, Dennis/34 Plympton St, Boston, MA	617-357-9488
Still, John/17 Edinboro St, Boston, MA	617-451-8178
Stillings, Jamey/87 N Clinton Ave 5th Fl, Rochester, NY	716-232-5296
Stills/1 Winthrop Sq, Boston, MA	617-482-0660
Stock, Jack/Newberg, Art/155 Myrtle St, Shelton, CT	203-735-3388
Stoller, Bob/30 Old Mill Rd, Great Neck, NY	914-829-8906
Storch, Otto/Box 712, 22 Pondview Ln, East Hampton, NY	516-324-5031
Stromberg, Bruce/PO Box 2052, Philadelphia, PA	215-735-3520
Stuart, Stephen Photography/10 Midland Ave, Port Chester, NY	914-682-1418
Studio Assoc/30-6 Plymouth St, Fairfield, NJ	201-575-2640
The Studio Inc/818 Liberty Ave, Pittsburgh, PA	412-261-2022
Studio Tech/25 Congress St, Salem, MA	617-745-5070
Studio Three/1617 J F Kennedy Blvd, Philadelphia, PA	215-665-0141
Sullivan, Sharon/325 1/2 4th St, Jersey City, NJ	201-795-1930
Sunshine Photography/192 Newtown Rd, Plainview, NY	516-293-3376
Susoeff, Bill/3025 Wahangton Rd, McMurray, PA	412-941-8606
Sutphen, Chazz/22 Crescent Beach Dr, Burlington, VT	802-862-5912
Swann/ Niemann/1258 Wisconsin Ave NW 4th Fl, Washington, DC	201-342-6300
Sweeney, Dan/337 Summer St, Boston, MA	617-482-5482
Sweet, Ozzie/Mill Village Hill, Francestown, NH	603-547-6611
SWERTFAGER, AMY/343 MANVILLE RD, PLEASANTVILLE, NY (P 209)	**914-747-1900**
Swift, Dick/31 Harrison Ave, New Canaan, CT	203-966-8190
Swisher, Mark/5107 Herring Run Dr, Baltimore, MD	301-426-6665
Swoger, Arthur/18 Medway St #3, Providence, RI	401-331-0440
Szabo, Art/156-A Depot Rd, Huntington, NY	516-549-1699

T

Tadder, Morton/1010 Morton St, Baltimore, MD	301-837-7427
Tango, Rick/11 Pocconock Terrace, Ridgefield, CT	203-431-0514
Tardi, Joseph/125 Wolf Rd #108, Albany, NY	518-438-1211
Taylor, Alan/RD 1 Box 649, Saratoga Springs, NY	518-584-7937
Tchakirides, Bill/ Photography Assoc/140-50 Huyshope Ave, Hartford, CT	203-249-1105
TEC Photo/37 Huyler Ct, Setauket, NY	516-751-8300
Tenin, Barry/PO Box 2660 Saugatuck Sta, Westport, CT	203-226-9396
Tepper, Peter/195 Tunxis Hill Rd, Fairfield, CT	203-367-6172
Tesa, Rudi/194 Knickerbocker Rd, Demarest, NJ	212-620-4514
Tesi, Mike/12 Kulick Rd, Fairfield, NJ	201-575-7780
Thauer, Bill/542 Higgens Crowell Rd, W Yarmouth, MA	617-362-8222
Thayer, Mark/25 Dry Dock, Boston, MA	617-542-9532
Thellmann, Mark D/19 W Park Ave, Merchantville, NJ	609-488-9093
Thomas, Edward/140-50 Huyshope Ave, Hartford, CT	203-246-3293
Tkatch, James/2307 18th St NW, Washington, DC	202-462-2211
Tollen, Cynthia/50 Fairmont St, Arlington, MA	617-641-4052
Tong, Darren/28 Renee Terrace, Newton, MA	617-527-3304
Tornallyay, Martin/77 Taft Ave, Stamford, CT	203-357-1777
Total Concept Photo/95-D Knickerbocker Ave, Bohemia, NY	516-567-6010

PHOTOGRAPHERS

Please send us your additions and updates.

Touchton, Ken/PO Box 9435, Washington, DC	703-476-3628
Traub, Willard/PO Box 276, Lincoln, MA	617-259-9656
Traver, Joseph/187 Hodge Ave, Buffalo, NY	716-884-8844
Trefethen, Jim/14 Soley St Box 165, Charlestown, MA	617-242-0064
Treiber, Peter/917 Highland Ave, Bethlehem, PA	215-867-3303
Tretick, Stanley/4365 Embassy Park Dr NW, Washington, DC	202-537-1445
Tritsch, Joseph/507 Longstone Dr, Cherry Hill, NJ	609-424-0433
Troha, John/12258 St James Rd, Potomac, MD	301-340-7220
Trola, Bob/112 N 12th St, Philadelphia, PA	215-925-4322
Trzoniec, Stanley/58 W Main St, Northboro, MA	617-393-3800
Tur, Stefan/ NY	914-557-8857

UV

Uniphoto/1071 Wisconsin Ave, Washington, DC	202-333-0500
Urban, John/1424 Canton Ave, Milton, MA	617-333-0343
Urbina, Walt/7208 Thomas Blvd, Pittsburgh, PA	412-242-5070
Uzzle, Burk/537 Hilaire Rd, St Davids, PA	215-688-0507
Valerio, Gary/278 Jay St, Rochester, NY	716-352-0163
Van Petten, Rob/109 Broad St, Boston, MA	617-426-8641
Van Schalkwyk, John/50 Melcher St, Boston, MA	617-542-4825
Van Zandbergen Photo/187 Riverside Dr, Binghamton, NY	607-625-3408
Vandermark, Peter/523 Medford St, Charlestown, MA	617-242-2277
Vanderwarker, Peter/56 Boyd St, Newton, MA	617-964-2728
Vandevanter, Jan/2124 'I' St NW, Washington, DC	202-546-3520
Vaughan, Ted/423 Doe Run Rd, Manheim, PA	717-665-6942
Vecchio, Dan/129 E Water St, Syracuse, NY	315-471-1064
Vega, Eloise/1 Cobblestone Rd, Monsey, NY	212-512-1818
Vericker, Joe/111 Cedar St 4th Fl, New Rochelle, NY	914-632-2072
Verno, Jay/344 Third Ave, Pittsburgh, PA	412-562-9880
Vickery, Eric/4 Genetti Circle, Bedford, MA	617-275-0314
Vidor, Peter/70 Chestnut St, Morristown, NJ	201-267-1104
Viens, David/448 Smith St, Middletown, CT	203-632-2366
Visual Productions/2121 Wisconsin Ave NW #407, Washington, DC	202-337-7332
Vogt, Laurie/806 Garden St, Hoboken, NJ	201-792-0485
Von Hoffmann, Bernard/2 Green Village Rd, Madison, NJ	201-377-0317
Voscar The Maine Photographer/PO Box 661, Presque Isle, ME	207-769-5911

W

Waggaman, John/2746 N 46 St, Philadelphia, PA	215-473-2827
Wagner, William/208 North Ave, Cranford, NJ	201-276-2002
Walch, Robert/310 W Main St, Kutztown, PA	215-683-5701
Waldemar/386 Brook Ave, Passaic Park, NJ	201-471-3033
Waldman, Ed/109 Rochelle Ave, Philadelphia, PA	215-560-2088
Wallen, Jonathan/41 Lewis Pkwy, Yonkers, NY	914-476-8674
Walp's Photo Service/182 S 2nd St, Lehighton, PA	215-377-4370
Walsh, Dan/409 W Broadway, Boston, MA	617-268-7615
Walters, Day/PO Box 5655, Washington, DC	202-362-0022
Walther, Michael/2185 Brookside Ave, Wantagh, NY	516-783-7636
Wanamaker, Roger/PO Box 2800, Darien, CT	203-655-8383
Ward, Jack/221 Vine St, Philadelphia, PA	215-627-5311
Ward, Tony/704 South 6th St, Philadelphia, PA	215-238-1208
Warren Dittmar & Atelier/50 South Gate Dr, Spring Valley, NY	914-762-6311
Warren, Marion E/1935 Old Annapolis Blvd, Annapolis, MD	301-974-0444
Watson, H Ross/859 Lancaster Ave, Bryn Mawr, PA	215-527-1519
Watson, Linda M/38 Church St/Box 14, Hopkinton, MA	617-498-9638
Watson, Tom/2172 West Lake Rd, Skaneateles, NY	315-685-6033
Watson-Manning/972 E Broadway, Stratford, CT	203-375-3384
Wee, John/2100 Mary St, Pittsburh, PA	412-381-5555
Weems, Bill/2030 Pierce Mill Rd NW, Washington, DC	202-667-2444
Weems, Samuel/One Arcadia Pl, Boston, MA	617-288-8888
WEESE, CARL/140-50 HUYSHOPE AVE, HARTFORD, CT (P 210,211)	**203-246-6016**
WEIDMAN, H MARK/2112 GOODWIN LANE, NORTH WALES, PA (P 42-45)	**215-646-1745**
Weigand, Tom/717 North 5th St, Reading, PA	215-374-4431
Weinberg, Abe/1230 Summer St, Philadelphia, PA	215-567-5454
Weinrebe, Steve/354 Congress St, Boston, MA	617-423-9130
Weisenfeld, Stanley/135 Davis St, Painted Post, NY	607-962-7314
Weisgrau, Richard/1107 Walnut St 2nd Fl, Philadelphia, PA	215-923-0348
Weiss, Michael/212 Race St, Philadelphia, PA	215-629-1685
Weitz, Allan/209 Cuthbert St #301, Philadelphia, PA	215-923-1828
Wendler, Hans/RD 1 Box 191, Epsom, NH	603-736-9383
Werner, Perry/21 Sheridan Ave, Mt Vernon, NY	914-699-3637

Westwood Photo Productions/200 Gilbert St, Mansfield, MA	617-339-4141
WEXLER, IRA/4893 MACARTHUR BLVD NW, WASHINGTON, DC (P 224,225)	**202-337-4886**
WHEELER, EDWARD F/1050 KING OF PRUSSIA RD, RADNOR, PA (P 168,169)	**215-964-9294**
Wheeler, Nick/Turner Rd, Townsend Harbor, MA	617-597-2919
White, Frank/18 Milton Pl, Rowayton, CT	203-866-9500
White, Sharon/107 South St, Boston, MA	617-891-6011
Whitman, Edward/519 W Pratt St, Baltimore, MD	301-727-2220
Wickenheis, A/143 W Hoffman Ave, Lindenhurst, NY	516-226-0846
Wilcoxson, Steve/1820 Bolton St, Baltimore, MD	301-669-7447
Wiley, John Jay/147 Webster St, Boston, MA	617-567-0506
Williams, Lawrence S/9101 W Chester Pike, Upper Darby, PA	215-789-3030
Willinger, Dave/74 Pacific Blvd, Long Beach, NY	516-889-0678
Wilson, Paul S/6384 Overbrook Ave, Philadelphia, PA	215-473-4455
Wilson, Robert L/PO Box 1742, Clarksburg, WV	304-623-5368
Windman, Russell/348 Congress St, Boston, MA	617-357-5140
Wolff Freres/5811 Edson Ln #301, Rockville, MD	301-468-0833
Wolff, Randolph/5811 Edson Lane #301, Rockville, MD	301-468-0833
Wood, Jeffrey C/808 Monroe Ave, Ardsley, PA	215-572-6848
Wood, Richard/169 Monsgnr O'Brien Hwy, Cambridge, MA	617-661-6856
Wrenn, Bill/14 Rockland Pl, Old Greenwich, CT	203-637-1145
Wright, Jeri/PO box 7, Wilmington, NY	518-946-2658
Wu, Ron/179 St Paul St, Rochester, NY	716-454-5600
Wurster, George/22 Hallo St, Edison, NJ	201-352-2134
Wyman, Ira/14 Crane Ave, West Peabody, MA	617-535-2880

YZ

Yablon, Ron/PO Box 128, Exton, PA	215-363-2596
Yamashita, Michael/Roxticus Rd, Mendham, NJ	201-543-4473
Young, Don/PO Box 249, Exton, PA	215-363-2596
Yourman, Steve & Lisa/317 Plaza Rd N, Fairlawn, NJ	201-796-8091
Yuichi, Idaka/RR 2 Box 229D Wood Ave, Rindge, NH	603-899-6165
Zane, Steven/227 Grand St, Hoboken, NJ	201-420-8868
Zappala, John/Candlewood Echoes, Sherman, CT	203-354-6420
Zimbel, George/1538 Sherbrooke W #813, Montreal, QU	514-931-6387
Zimmerman, Larry/50 Grove St, Salem, MA	617-745-7117
Zmiejko, Tom/246 Center St #110, Freeland, PA	717-636-2304
Zuckerman, Robert/100 Washington St, South Norwalk, CT	203-853-2670
Zungoli, Nick/Box 5, Sugar Loaf, NY	914-469-9382
Zurich, Robert/105 Church St, Aberdeen, NJ	201-566-7076
Zutell, Kirk/911 State St, Lancaster, PA	717-393-0918

SOUTHEAST

A

Abel, Wilton/2609 Commonwealth Ave, Charlotte, NC	704-372-6354
Adcock, James/3108 1/2 W Leigh St #8, Richmond, VA	804-358-4399
The Alderman Co/325 Model Farm Rd, High Point, NC	919-889-6121
Alexander, Ric & Assoc Inc/212 S Graham St, Charlotte, NC	704-332-1254
Allard, William Albert/Marsh Run Farm Box 549, Somerset, VA	804-823-5951
Allen, Bob/710 W Lane St, Raleigh, NC	919-833-5991
Allen, Don/PO Box 56968, New Orleans, LA	504-737-6819
Alston, Cotten/Box 7927-Station C, Atlanta, GA	404-876-7859
Alterman, Jack/285 Meeting St, Charleston, SC	803-577-0647
Alvarez, Jorge/3105 W Granada, Tampa, FL	813-831-6765
Anderson, Susanne/PO Box 6, Waterford, VA	703-882-3244
Andrea, Michael/225 South Mint St, Charlotte, NC	704-334-3992
Arpino, Matthew/3731 Northcrest Rd #31, Atlanta, GA	404-266-8567
Arthur, Zinn/2661 S Course Dr, Pompano Beach, FL	305-973-3851
Ashcraft, Jeff/3611 Tanglewood Dr NW, Atlanta, GA	404-872-2551
Atlantic Photo/319 N Main St, High Point, NC	919-884-1474

B

Bachmann, Bill/PO Box 833, Lake Mary, FL	305-322-4444
Baker, I Wilson/PO Box 647, Mount Pleasant, SC	803-881-0811
Balbuza, Joseph/25 NE 210 St, Miami, FL	305-652-1728
BALL, ROGER/225 WEST 4TH ST #A, CHARLOTTE, NC (P 236)	**704-335-0479**
Ballenberg, Bill/200 Cortland Ln, Virginia Beach, VA	804-463-3505
Baptie, Frank/1426 9th St N, St Petersburg, FL	813-823-7319
BARLEY, BILL/PO BOX 2388, COLUMBIA, SC (P 243)	**803-755-1554**
Barnes, Billy E/313 Severin St, Chapel Hill, NC	919-942-6350

Please send us your additions and updates.

BARR, IAN/2640 SW 19TH ST, FORT LAUDERDALE, FL (P 244)	**305-584-6247**
Barrera, Louis/157-79 75 Ave North, Palm Beach Gardens, FL	305-744-6916
Barrs, Michael/6303 SW 69th St, Miami, FL	305-665-2047
Bartlett & Assoc/3007 Edgewater Dr, Orlando, FL	305-425-7308
Beardsley, Lawrence/PO Box 580657, Orlando, FL	305-297-8281
BECK, CHARLES/2721 CHEROKEE RD, BIRMINGHAM, AL (P 237)	**205-871-6632**
Beck, G & Assoc/176 Ottley Dr NE, Atlanta, GA	404-872-0728
Becker, Joel/5121 Virginia Beach Blvd, Norfolk, VA	804-461-7886
Bedgood, Bill/1292 Logan Cir, Atlanta, GA	404-351-4852
Behrens, Bruce/2920 N Orange Ave, Orlando, FL	305-898-2346
Belenson, Mark/8056 NW 41st Ct, Sunrise, FL	305-749-0675
Bennett, Ken/1001 Lockwood Ave, Columbus, GA	404-324-1182
Bentley, Gary/240 Great Circle Rd #330, Nashville, TN	615-242-4038
Berger, Erica/One Herald Plaza, Miami, FL	305-376-3750
Beswick, Paul/4479 Westfield Dr, Mableton, GA	404-944-8579
Bewley, Glen/428 Armour Circle, Atlanta, GA	404-872-7277
BILBY, GLADE/1715 BURGUNDY, NEW ORLEANS, LA (P 234)	**504-949-6700**
Blanton, Jeff/2086 Gatlin Ave, Orlando, FL	305-851-7279
Boatman, Mike/PO Box 11131, Memphis, TN	901-382-1656
Bollman, Brooks/1183 Virginia Ave NE, Atlanta, GA	404-876-2422
Bondarenko, Marc/212 S 41st St, Birmingham, AL	205-933-2790
Borchelt, Mark/4398-D Eisenhower Ave, Alexandria, VA	703-243-7850
Borum, Michael/625 Fogg St, Nashville, TN	615-259-9750
Bose, Patti/1245 W Fairbanks Ste 300, Winter Park, FL	305-629-5650
Bostick, Rick/6959-J Stapoint Ct, Winterpark, FL	305-677-5717
Boyd, Richard/PO Box 5097, Roanoke, VA	703-366-3140
Boyle, Jeffrey/7752 NW 54th St, Miami, FL	305-592-7032
Brack, Dennis/3609 Woodhill Pl, Fairfax, VA	703-280-2285
Brasher/Rucker Photography/3373 Park Ave, Memphis, TN	901-324-7447
Brill, David/Route 4, Box 121-C, Fairbourn, GA	404-461-5488
Brinson, Rob/486 14th St, Atlanta, GA	404-874-2497
Brooks, Charles/800 Luttrell St, Knoxville, TN	615-525-4501
Broomell, Peter/901 N Columbus St, Alexandria, VA	703-548-5767
Brown, Billy/2700 Seventh Ave S, Birmingham, AL	205-251-8327
Brown, Richard Photo/PO Box 1249, Asheville, NC	704-253-1634
Browne, Turner/1634 Washington Ave, New Orleans, LA	504-899-8883
Bruce, Thomas/79-25 4th St N, St Petersburg, FL	813-577-5626
Bryant, Donne/PO Box 80155, Baton Rouge, LA	504-769-1419
Bumpus, Ken/410 S Edgemon Dr, Winter Springs, FL	305-646-4387
Burgess, Ralph/PO Box 36, Chrstnsted/St Croix, VI	809-773-6541
Burns, Jerry/331-B Elizabeth St, Atlanta, GA	404-522-9377
Burris, Ned/2603 Treehouse Pkwy, Norcross, GA	404-938-8405
Byrd, Syndey/1205 Royal St, New Orleans, LA	504-588-9467
C	
Cabedo, Brent/108 E Franklin St, Richmond, VA	804-225-8324
Calamia, Ron & Assoc/8140 Forshey St, New Orleans, LA	504-482-8062
Camera Graphics/1230 Gateway Rd, Lake Park, FL	305-844-3399
Carnes, John/3307 Orleans Dr, Nashville, TN	615-383-1693
Carriker, Ronald/565 Alpine Rd, Winston Salem, NC	919-765-3852
Case, Sam/PO Box 1139, Purcellville, VA	703-338-2725
Caswell, Sylvia/807 9th Court S, Birmingham, AL	205-252-2252
Caudle, Rod Studio/1708 Defoor Pl, Atlanta, GA	404-351-6385
Cavedo, Brent/9 W Main St, Richmond, VA	804-344-5374
Centner, Ed Productions/12950 SW 122nd Ave, Miami, FL	305-238-3338
Cerri, Robert Noel/612-A NE Fourteenth Ave, Ft Lauderdale, FL	305-764-7259
Chalfant, Flip/283 Hope St, Marietta, GA	404-422-1796
Chambers, Terrell/6843 Tilton Lane, Doraville, GA	404-396-4648
Chamowitz, Mel/3931 N Glebe Rd, Arlington, VA	703-536-8356
Chapple, Ron/437 S Tryon St, Charlotte, NC	704-377-4217
Chernush, Kay/3855 N 30th St, Arlington, VA	703-528-1195
Chesler, Donna & Ken/6941 NW 12th St, Plantation, FL	305-581-6489
Choiniere, Gerin/900 Greenleaf Ave, Charlotte, NC	704-372-0220
Clark, Marty/1105 Peachtree St NE, Atlanta, GA	404-873-4618
Clayton, Al/141 The Prado NE, Atlanta, GA	404-577-4141
Cody, Dennie/5820 SW 51st Terrace, Miami, FL	305-666-0247
Colbroth, Ron/4421 Airlie Way, Annandale, VA	703-354-2729
Collins, Michael/229 Denise Ln, Auburndale, FL	813-965-1424
Compton, Grant/7004 Sand Nettles Dr, Savannah, GA	912-897-3771
Contorakes, George/PO Box 430901, South Miami, FL	305-661-0731

Cook, Jamie/653 Ethel St, Atlanta, GA	404-892-1393
Cooke, Bill/7761 SW 88th St, Miami, FL	305-596-2454
COPELAND, JIM/559 DUTCH VALLEY RD NE, ATLANTA, GA (P 245)	**404-873-5858**
Corn, Jack/27 Dahlia Dr, Brentwood, TN	615-373-3301
Cornelia, William/PO Box 5304, Hilton Head Island, SC	803-671-2576
Cosby-Bower Inc/209 N Foushee St, Richmond, VA	804-643-1100
Cox, Whitney/2042 W Grace St #3, Richmond, VA	804-358-3061
Creative Photographers Inc/2214 Hawkins St, Charlotte, NC	704-376-6475
Cromer, Peggo/1206 Andora Ave, Coral Gables, FL	305-667-3722
CRUM, LEE/PO BOX 15229, NEW ORLEANS, LA (P 246)	**504-529-2156**
D	
Dale, John/576 Armour Circle NE, Atlanta, GA	404-872-3203
Daniel, Ralph/915 Argonne Ave #2, Atlanta, GA	404-872-3946
David, Alan/1186-D N Highland Ave, Atlanta, GA	404-872-2142
DAVIDSON, CAMERON/1720 DOGWOOD DR, ALEXANDRIA, VA (P 216,217)	**202-328-3344**
DAWSON, BILL/1853 MADISON AVE, MEMPHIS, TN (P 247)	**901-726-6043**
Degast, Robert/Rt 1 Box 323, Onancock, VA	804-787-8060
DeKalb, Jed/PO Box 22884, Nashville, TN	615-331-8527
Demolina, Raul/3903 Ponce De Leon, Coral Gables, FL	305-448-8727
Design & Visual Effects/1228 Zonolite Rd, Atlanta, GA	404-872-3283
DEVAULT, JIM/2400 SUNSET PL, NASHVILLE, TN (P 248,249)	**615-269-4538**
Diaz, Rick/7395 SW 42nd St, Miami, FL	305-264-9761
Dickerson, John/1895 Annwicks Dr, Marietta, GA	404-977-4138
Dickinson, Dick/1854 University Pkwy, Sarasota, FL	813-351-2036
DiModica, Jim/6880 SW 80th St, Miami, FL	305-666-7710
Dix, Paul/106 W Bonito Dr, Ocean Springs, MS	601-875-7691
Dixon, Tom/3404-D W Windover Ave, Greensboro, NC	919-294-6076
Dobbs, David/1536 Monroe Dr NE #110, Atlanta, GA	404-885-1460
DOTY, GARY/PO BOX 23697, FT LAUDERDALE, FL (P 251)	**305-928-0644**
Draper, Fred/259 S Willow Ave, Cookeville, TN	615-526-1315
Dressler, Brian/3529 Yale Ave, Columbia, SC	803-254-7171
Drymon, Terry/6308 Benjamin Rd, Tampa, FL	813-888-7779
Dugas, Henri/PO Box 250, Amelia, LA	501-631-0687
Duvall, Thurman III/1021 Northside Dr NW, Atlanta, GA	404-875-0161
E	
Eastmond, Peter/PO Box 856 E, Barbados,W Indies,	809-429-7757
Edwards, Jack/209 N Rocheblave St, New Orleans, LA	504-822-2111
Edwards, Jim/416 Armour Circle NE, Atlanta, GA	404-875-1005
Eglof, Dan/PO Box 4301, Enterprise, FL	305-321-6623
Eighme, Bob/PO Box 7083, Ft Lauderdale, FL	305-527-8445
Elliot, Tom/19756 Bel Aire Dr, Miami, FL	305-251-4315
Ellis, Bill/406 Edwards Dr, Greensboro, NC	919-299-5074
Ellis, Gin/1203 Techwood Dr, Atlanta, GA	404-892-3204
Elmore, James/4807 5th St W, Bradenton, FL	813-755-0546
Engelman, Suzanne/1621 Woodbridge Lk Cir, W Palm Beach, FL	305-969-6666
English, Melissa Hayes/1195 Woods Circle NE, Atlanta, GA	404-261-7650
ERICKSON, JIM/302 JEFFERSON ST #300, RALEIGH, NC (P 252-255)	**919-833-9955**
F	
Felipe, Giovanni/3465 SW 73rd Ave, Miami, FL	305-266-5308
Fineman, Michael/7521 SW 57th Terrace, Miami, FL	305-666-1250
Fisher, Ray/10700 SW 72nd Ct, Miami, FL	305-665-7659
Fitzgerald, Barry/808 Charlotte St, Fredericksburg, VA	703-371-3253
Foley, Roger/519 N Monroe St, Arlington, VA	703-524-6274
Forer, Dan/1970 NE 149th St, North Miami, FL	305-949-3131
Fowley, Douglas/103 N Hite Ave, Louisville, KY	502-897-7222
Frazier, Steve/1425 US 19 S Bldg 26 #102, Clearwater, FL	813-531-3631
Freeman, Tina/2113 Decatur Sr, New Orleans, LA	504-949-1863
Frink, Stephen/PO Box 19-A, Key Largo, FL	305-451-3737
G	
Gandy, Skip/302 East Davis Blvd, Tampa, FL	813-253-0340
Gardella Photography & Design/781 Miami Cr NE, Atlanta, GA	404-231-1316
Garrett, Kenneth/PO Box 208, Broad Run, VA	703-347-5848
Garrison, Gary/4608 Tchoupitoulas, New Orleans, LA	504-899-8445
Gefter, Judith/1725 Clemson Rd, Jacksonville, FL	904-733-5498
Gelberg, Bob/7035-E SW 47th St, Miami, FL	305-665-3200
Gemignani, Joe/13833 NW 19th Ave, Miami, FL	305-685-7636
Genser, Howard/1859 Seventh Ave, Jacksonville, FL	904-734-9688

Please send us your additions and updates.

Gentile, Arthur Sr/7335 Connan Lane, Charlotte, NC	704-541-0227
Gerlich, Fred/1220 Spring St NW, Atlanta, GA	404-872-3487
Gibbs, Ernest/300 Regency Rd #C4, Spartanburg, SC	803-582-0471
GLASER, KEN & ASSOC/5270 ANNUNCIATION ST, NEW ORLEANS, LA (P 257)	**504-895-7170**
Gleasner, Bill/132 Holly Ct, Denver, NC	704-483-9301
Godfrey, Mark/3526 N Third St, Arlington, VA	703-527-8293
Graham, Curtis/648 First Ave S, St Petersburg, FL	813-821-0444
Graham, Urtim/648 First Ave S, St Petersburg, FL	813-821-0444
Granberry/Anderson Studios/1211 Spring St NW, Atlanta, GA	404-874-2426
Greer, Greg/2032 Adams, New Orleans, LA	504-861-3000
Grigg, Roger Allen/PO Box 52851, Atlanta, GA	404-876-4748
Grimes, Billy/PO Box 19739 N, Atlanta, GA	404-442-1414
Groendyke, Bill/6344 NW 201st Ln, Miami, FL	305-625-8293
Guider, John/517 Fairground Ct, Nashville, TN	615-255-4495
Gupton, Charles/Route 2 Box 206, Wake Forest, NC	919-556-6511
Guravich, Dan/PO Box 891, Greenville, MS	601-335-2444

H

Haggerty, Richard/656 Ward St, High Point, NC	919-889-7744
Hall, Don/29-22 Hyde Park St, Sarasota, FL	813-365-6161
Hall, Ed/7100 Citrus Point, Winter Park, FL	305-657-8182
Hamilton, Tom/1095 Greenleaf Rd, Atlanta, GA	404-622-0100
Hannau, Michael/3800 NW 32nd Ave, Miami, FL	305-633-1100
HANSEN, ERIC/3005 7TH AVE S/BOX 55492, BIRMINGHAM, AL (P 258,259)	**205-251-5587**
Harbison, Steve/2008 20th Ave S Box 120368, Nashville, TN	615-297-7611
Hardy, Frank/1003 N 12th Ave, Pensacola, FL	904-438-2712
Harkins, Lynn S/1900 Byrd Ave #101, Richmond, VA	804-285-2900
Harrelson, Keith/4505 131st Ave N, Clearwater, FL	813-577-9812
Harris, Christopher/PO Box 2926, Covington, LA	504-893-4898
Hathcox, David/PO Box 2477, Alexandria, VA	703-548-7217
Haviland, Patrick/3642 Tryclan Dr, Charlotte, NC	704-527-8795
HENDERSON/MUIR PHOTO/5700 NEW CHAPEL HILL RD, RALEIGH, NC (P 260)	**919-851-0458**
Hendley, Arington/454 Irwin St, Atlanta, GA	404-577-2300
Henley & Savage/113 S Jefferson St, Richmond, VA	804-780-1120
Higgins, Neal/1540 Monroe Dr, Atlanta, GA	404-876-3186
Hill, Dan/9132 O'Shea Ln, W Springfield, VA	703-451-4705
HILL, JACKSON/2032 ADAMS ST, NEW ORLEANS, LA (P 261)	**504-861-3000**
Hill, Tom/1538 Cortez Ln, Atlanta, GA	404-325-8806
Hillyer, Jonathan/450-A Bishop St, Atlanta, GA	404-351-0477
Hirsch, Alan/1259 Ponce de Leon #6C, San Juan, PR	809-723-2224
Hoflich, Richard/544 N Angier Ave NE, Atlanta, GA	404-584-9159
Hogben, Steve/468 Armour Dr, Atlanta, GA	404-266-2894
Holland, Ralph/3706 Alliance Dr, Greensboro, NC	919-855-6422
Holland, Robert/PO Box 162099, Miami, FL	305-255-6758
Holt Group/403 Westcliff Rd/Box 35488, Greensboro, NC	919-668-2770
Hood, Robin/1101 W Main St, Franklin, TN	615-794-2041
Hopkins, Allen W/627 King St, Alexandria, VA	703-549-2890
Horan, Eric/PO Box 6373, Hilton Head Island, SC	803-842-3233
Hosack, Loren/2301-F Sabal Ridge Ct, Palm Beach Gardens, FL	305-627-8313
Hunter, Bud/1917 1/2 Oxmoor Rd, Birmingham, AL	205-879-3153
Huntley, Robert/1210 Spring St NW, Atlanta, GA	404-892-6450

IJ

International Defense Images/2419 Mt Vernon Ave, Alexandria, VA	703-548-7217
Isaacs, Lee/807 9th Court South, Birmingham, AL	205-252-2698
JAMISON, CHIPP/2131 LIDDELL DR NE, ATLANTA, GA (P 235)	**404-873-3636**
Jeffcoat, Russell/620 Saluda Ave, Columbia, SC	803-799-8578
Jeffcoat, Wilber L/1864 Palomino Cir, Sumter, SC	803-773-3690
Jenkins, Dave Prdctns/1084 Duncan Ave, Chattanooga, TN	615-629-5380
Jimison, Tom/5929 Annunciation, New Orleans, LA	504-891-8587
Johns, Douglas/2535 25th Ave N, St Petersburg, FL	813-321-7235
Johnson, Silvia/6110 Brook Dr, Falls Church, VA	703-532-8653
Jones, Wesley/FL	305-483-8376
Jordan/Rudolph Studios/1446 Mayson St NE #5L, Atlanta, GA	404-874-1829
Jureit, Robert A/916 Aguero Ave, Coral Gables, FL	305-667-1346

K

Kaplan Studio/1491 Chain Bridge Rd #102, McLean, VA	703-893-1660
Kaplan, Al/PO Box 611373, North Miami, FL	305-891-7595
Kappiris, Stan/PO Box 14331, Tampa, FL	813-254-4866
Katz, Arni/PO Box 724507, Atlanta, GA	404-953-1168
Kaufman, Len/5119 Arthur St, Hollywood, FL	305-920-7822
Kearney, Mitchell/301 E 7th St, Charlotte, NC	704-377-7662
Kennedy, M Lewis/2700 7th Ave S, Birmingham, AL	205-252-2700
Kern Photography/1243 N 17th Ave, Lake Worth, FL	305-582-2487
Kersh, Viron/PO Box 51201, New Orleans, LA	504-524-4515
King, J Brian/1267 Coral Way, Miami, FL	305-856-6534
King, Tom/2806 Edgewater Dr, Orlando, FL	305-841-4421
Kinney, Greg/912 Burford Pl, Nashville, TN	615-297-8084
Kinsella, Barry/1010 Andrews Rd, West Palm Beach, FL	305-832-8736
Klass, Rubin & Erika/5200 N Federal Hwy #2, Fort Lauderdale, FL	305-565-1612
Klemens, Susan/7423 Foxleigh Way, Alexandria, VA	703-971-1226
Kling, David Photography/502 Armour Circle, Atlanta, GA	404-881-1215
Knibbs, Tom/5907 NE 27th Ave, Ft Lauderdale, FL	305-491-6263
Knight, Steve/1212 E 10th St, Charlotte, NC	704-334-5115
KOHANIM, PARISH/1130 W PEACHTREE NW, ATLANTA, GA (P 232,233)	**404-892-0099**
Kollar, Robert E/1431 Cherokee Trail #52, Knoxville, TN	615-573-8191
Koplitz, William/729 N Lime St, Sarasota, FL	813-366-5905
Kralik, Scott/210 N Fillmore, Arlington, VA	703-522-8261
Kufner, Gary/305 NW 10th Terr, Hallendale, FL	305-944-7740
Kunz, Grace/1104 W Newtown St, Dothan, AL	205-793-5723

L

LACKEY, LARRY/2400 POPLAR AVE #514, MEMPHIS, TN (P 263)	**901-323-0811**
Lair, John/1122 Roger St, Louisville, KY	802-589-7779
LALLO, ED/1183 HANCOCK DRIVE, ATLANTA, GA (P 239)	**404-876-8799**
LANGONE, PETER/516 NE 13TH ST, FT LAUDERDALE, FL (P 264,265)	**305-467-0654**
LANPHER, KEITH/865 MONTICELLO AVE, NORFOLK, VA (P 219)	**804-627-3051**
LATHEM, CHARLES/559 DUTCH VALLEY RD NE, ATLANTA, GA (P 267)	**404-873-5858**
Lavenstein, Lance/4605 Pembroke Lake Cir, Virginia Beach, VA	804-499-9959
Lawrence, David/PO Box 835, Largo, FL	813-586-2112
Lawrence, John R/Box 330570, Coconut Grove, FL	305-447-8621
Lawson, Slick/3801 Whitland Ave, Nashville, TN	615-383-0147
Lazzo, Dino/655 SW 20th Rd, Miami, FL	305-856-1148
Lee, Chung P/7820 Antiopi St, Annandale, VA	703-560-3394
Lee, George/PO Box 3923, Greenville, SC	803-232-4119
Lee, Joe/846 N President St, Jackson, MS	601-948-5255
LEGGETT, ALBERT/1415 STORY AVE, LOUISVILLE, KY (P 268,269)	**502-584-0255**
Leo, Victor/7100 Greenlawn Rd, Louisville, KY	502-423-8374
Little, Chris/PO Box 467221, Atlanta, GA	404-641-9688
Llewellyn, Robert/PO Drawer L, Charlottesville, VA	804-973-8000
Long, Lewis/3130 SW 26th St, Miami, FL	305-448-7667
Lubin, Jeff/8472 Rainbow Bridge Ln, Springfield, VA	703-569-5086
Lucas, Steve/7925 SW 104th St #E-202, Miami, FL	305-271-0778
Luttrell, David/1500 Highland Dr, Knoxville, TN	615-523-7121
Lynch, Warren/306 Production Ct, Louisville, KY	502-491-8233

M

Magruder, Mary and Richard/2156 Snap Finger Rd, Decatur, GA	404-289-8985
Mahen, Rich/4301 SW 10th St, Ft Lauderdale, FL	305-792-5429
Malles, Ed/355 Needle Blvd, Merritt Island, FL	305-452-0880
Mann, James/1007-B Norwalk, Greensboro, NC	919-292-1190
Mann, Rod/5082 Woodleigh Rd, Knotts Island, NC	919-429-3009
Maratea, Ronn/4338 Virginia Beach Blvd, Virginia Beach, VA	804-340-6464
Marden, Bruce F Productions/1379 Chattahoochee Ave, Atlanta, GA	404-351-8152
Markatos, Jerry/Rt 2 Box 419/Rock Rest Rd, Pittsboro, NC	919-542-2139
Marquez, Toby/1709 Wainwright Dr, Reston, VA	703-471-4666
Mason, Chuck/14115 NW 5th Court, North Miami, FL	305-769-0911
May, Clyde/1037 Monroe Dr NE, Atlanta, GA	404-873-4329
Mazey, Jon/2724 NW 30th Ave, Ft Lauderdale, FL	305-731-3300
McCannon, Tricia/1536 Monroe Dr, Atlanta, GA	404-873-3070
MCCARTHY, TOM/8960 SW 114TH ST, MIAMI, FL (P 270,271)	**305-233-1703**

PHOTOGRAPHERS

MCCLURE, DAN/320 N MILLEDGE, ATHENS, GA (P 240)	**404-354-1234**
McCord, Fred/2720 Piedmont Rd NE, Atlanta, GA	404-262-1538
McCoy, Frank T/131 Donmond Dr, Hendersonville, TN	615-822-4437
McGee, E Alan/1816-E Briarwd Ind Ct, Atlanta, GA	404-633-1286
McIntyre, William/3746 Yadkinville Rd, Winston-Salem, NC	919-922-3142
McKee, Lee/1004 Ruth Jordano Ct, Ocoee, FL	305-656-9289
McKee, Sandy/4264 Westroads Dr, W Palm Beach, FL	305-844-4667
McKelvey, Michael/682 Greenwood Ave, Atlanta, GA	404-892-8223
McKenzie & Dickerson/133 W Vermont Ave/Box 152, Southern Pines, NC	919-692-6131
McLaughlin, Ken/623 7th Ave S, Nashville, TN	615-256-8162
McNabb, Tommy/4015 Brownsboro Rd, Winston-Salem, NC	919-723-4640
McNeely, Burton/PO Box 338, Land O'Lakes, FL	813-996-3025
Medical Comm Group/816 Foucher St, New Orleans, LA	504-581-2167
Melyana Assoc/924 NE 78th St, Miami, FL	305-754-4400
Meredith, David/2900 NE 30th Ave #4E, Ft Lauderdale, FL	305-564-4579
Michot, Walter/1520 E Sunrise Blvd, Ft Lauderdale, FL	305-527-8445
Mikeo, Rich/5399 N E 14th Ave, Ft Lauderdale, FL	305-491-5399
Miller, Brad/3645 Stewart, Coconut Grove, FL	305-666-1617
Miller, Bruce/9401 61st Court SW, Miami, FL	305-666-4333
Miller, Frank Lotz/1115 Washington Ave, New Orleans, LA	504-899-5688
MILLER, RANDY/6666 SW 96TH ST, MIAMI, FL (P 272,273)	**305-667-5765**
Mills, Henry/5514 Starkwood Dr, Charlotte, NC	704-535-1861
Mims, Allen/107 Madison Ave, Memphis, TN	901-527-4040
Minardi, Mike/PO Box 14247, Tampa, FL	813-684-7138
Molony, Bernard/PO Box 15081, Atlanta, GA	404-457-6934
Moore, George Photography/1301 Admiral St, Richmond, VA	804-355-1862
Morgan, Frank/2414 Arctic Ave #5, Virginia Beach, VA	804-422-9328
Morgan, Red/970 Hickory Trail, W Palm Beach, FL	305-793-6085
Morrah, Linda/201 E Coffee St, Greenville, SC	803-242-9108
Morris, Paul/5420 NW 169th St, Miami, FL	305-625-0789
Mouton, Girard III/3535 Buchanan St, New Orleans, LA	504-255-2708
Mulvehill, Larry/60 Coral Dr, Key Largo, FL	305-931-2170
Murphy Jr, Lionel/2311 Waldemere, Sarasota, FL	813-365-0595
Murray, Kevin/1424 W 4th St, Winston-Salem, NC	919-722-5107
Murray, Steve/1330 Mordecai Dr, Raleigh, NC	919-828-0653
Myers, Fred/114 Regent Ln, Florence, AL	205-386-2207
Myhre, Gordon/PO Box 1226, Ind Rocks Beach, FL	813-584-3717
Mykietyn, Walt/10110 SW 133 St, Miami, FL	305-235-2342

NO Nelson, Jon/PO Box 8772, Richmond, VA	804-359-0642
Nemeth, Judy/PO Box 37108, Charlotte, NC	704-375-9292
Neubauer, John/1525 S Arlington Ridge Rd, Arlington, VA	703-920-5994
Nicholson, Nick/1503 Brooks Ave, Raleigh, NC	919-787-6076
Norling Studios Inc/221 Swathmore Ave/Box 7167, High Point, NC	919-434-3151
North Light Studio/1803 Hendricks Ave, Jacksonville, FL	904-398-2501
Norton, Mike/4917 W Nassau, Tampa, FL	813-876-3390
Novak, Jack/PO Box 971, Alexandria, VA	703-836-4439
Novicki, Norb/6800 North West 2nd St, Margate, FL	305-971-8954
O'Boyle, Erin/7001 N Atlantic Ave #122, Cape Canaveral, FL	305-783-1923
O'KAIN, DENNIS/219 GILMER ST, LEXINGTON, GA (P 241)	**404-743-3140**
O'Sullivan, Brian/1401 SE 8th St, Deerfield Beach, FL	305-429-0712
Olive, Tim/754 Piedmont Ave NE, Atlanta, GA	404-872-0500
Olson, Carl/3325 Laura Way, Winston, GA	404-949-1532
Osborne, Mitchel L/920 Frenchman St, New Orleans, LA	504-949-1366

P Parker, Phillip M/192 Williford, Memphis, TN	901-529-9200
Patterson, M N/1615 Brown Ave #2, Cookeville, TN	615-528-8025
Patterson, Pat/1635 Old Louisburg Rd, Raleigh, NC	919-834-2223
Payne, Steve/1524 Virginia St E, Charleston, WV	304-343-7254
Pelosi & Chambers/684 Greenwood Ave NE, Atlanta, GA	404-872-8117
Peters, J Dirk/PO Box 15492, Tampa, FL	813-884-6272
PETREY, JOHN/670 CLAY ST/BOX 2401, WINTER PARK, FL (P 230,231)	**305-645-1718**
Photo-Synthesis/1239 Kensington Rd, McLean, VA	703-734-8770
Photographic Group/7407 Chancery Ln, Orlando, FL	305-855-4306
Photographic Ideas/PO Box 285, Charleston, SC	803-577-7020
Photography Unlimited/3662 S West Shore Blvd, Tampa, FL	813-839-7710
Pierce, Nancy J/1715 Merry Oaks Rd, Charlotte, NC	704-535-7409
Pocklington, Mike/9 W Main St, Richmond, VA	804-783-2731
Posey, Mike/3524 Canal St, New Orleans, LA	504-488-8000

Prism Studios/1027 Elm Hill Pike, Nashville, TN	615-255-1919
Purin, Thomas/14190 Harbor Lane, Lake Park, FL	305-622-4131
R Ramirez, George/303 Canals St, Santurce, PR	809-724-5727
Ramos, Victor/8390 SW 132 St, Miami, FL	305-255-3111
Randolph, Bruce/132 Alan Dr, Newport News, VA	804-877-0992
Rank, Don/1980 Will Ross Ct, Atlanta, GA	404-452-1658
Rathe, Robert A/9018 Jersey Dr, Fairfax, VA	703-560-7222
Raymond, Tom/Rt 6 Box 424-C, Jonesborough, TN	615-753-9061
Reus-Breuer, Sandra/Cal Josefa Cabrera Final #3, Rio Piedras, PR	809-767-1568
Rickles, Tom/2655 Pinetree Dr, Miami Beach, FL	305-673-2401
Riggall, Michael/403 8th St NE, Atlanta, GA	404-872-8242
Riley, Richard/34 N Ft Harrison, Clearwater, FL	813-446-2626
Rippey, Ray/PO Box 50093, Nashville, TN	615-646-1291
Rodgers, Ted/544 Plasters Ave, Atlanta, GA	404-892-0967
Rogers, Brian/689 Antone St NW, Atlanta, GA	404-355-8069
Rogers, Chuck/508 Armour Cir NE, Atlanta, GA	404-872-0062
Rosen, Olive/3804 Moss Dr, Annandale, VA	703-256-6996
Rosenblum, Bruce/8618 Uranus Terrace, Lake Park, FL	305-627-9873
Rubio, Manny/1203 Techwood Dr, Atlanta, GA	404-892-0783
Runion, Britt/6414 Orange Bay Ave, Orlando, FL	305-351-3203
Russell, John/PO Box 2141, High Point, NC	919-887-1163
Rutherford, Michael W/623 Sixth Ave S, Nashville, TN	615-242-5953
Rutledge, Don/13000 Edgetree Ct, Midlothian, VA	804-353-0151
S Saenz, C M/PO Box 117, Alachua, FL	904-462-5670
Sahuc, Louis/530 Royal St, New Orleans, LA	504-523-2809
Salmon, George/10325 Del Mar Circle, Tampa, FL	813-961-8687
Sander, Neil/PO Box 819, Maggie Valley, NC	704-456-9912
Saylor, Ted/2312 Farwell Dr, Tampa, FL	813-879-5636
Schaedler, Tim/PO Box 1081, Safety Harbor, FL	813-796-0366
Schatz, Bob/112 Second Ave N, Nashville, TN	615-254-7197
Schenck, Gordon H/PO Box 35203, Charlotte, NC	704-332-4078
Schenker, Richard/6304 Benjamin Rd #504, Tampa, FL	813-885-5413
Schiavone, George/355 NE 59th Terr, Miami, FL	305-758-7334
Schiff, Ken/4406 SW 74th Ave, Miami, FL	305-262-2022
Schlinkert, Richard/5816 Sixth Ave, Birmingham, AL	205-595-7134
Schneider, John/3702-B Alliance Dr, Greensboro, NC	919-855-0261
Schulke, Flip/PO Box 570669, Miami, FL	305-251-7717
Schumacher, Karl/6254 Park Rd, McLean, VA	703-241-7424
Schwartz, Alan/PO Box 43-2775, Miami, FL	305-596-6720
Seifried, Charles/Rt 3 Box 162, Decatur, AL	205-535-0503
Seitelman, M D/PO Box 2477, Alexandria, VA	703-548-7217
Seitz, Arthur/615 NE 12th Ave #109, Ft Lauderdale, FL	305-764-5635
Sharpe, David/816 N St Asaph St, Alexandria, VA	703-683-3773
Shea, David/114 S Elgin Pkwy, Ft Walton Beach, FL	904-244-3602
Sheffield, Scott/2707 W Broad St, Richmond, VA	804-358-3266
Sheldon, Mike/Rt 2 Box 61A, Canton, NC	704-235-8345
Sherbow, Robert/1607 Colonial Terr, Arlington, VA	202-522-3644
Sherman, Pam/103 Bonnie Brae Way, Hollywood, FL	305-981-9485
SHERMAN, RON/PO BOX 28656, ATLANTA, GA (P 275)	**404-993-7197**
Shooters Photographic/PO Box 36464, Charlotte, NC	704-334-7267
Shrout, Bill/Route 1 Box 317, Theodore, AL	205-973-1379
Simmons, Roy/102 W Clinton Ave #404, Huntsville, AL	205-539-0407
Sink, Richard/1225 Cedar Dr, Winston Salem, NC	919-784-8759
Sisson, Barry/6813 Bland St, Springfield, VA	703-569-6051
Smeltzer, Robert/10-B Sevier St, Greenville, SC	803-235-2186
Smith, Clark/314 E Tyler, Dalken, GA	404-226-2508
Smith, Richard & Assoc/1007 Norwalk St #B, Greensboro, NC	919-292-1190
Smith, Richard Photo/5907 NE 27th Ave, Ft Lauderdale, FL	305-491-6263
Smith/Garner Studios/1114 W Peachtree St, Atlanta, GA	404-875-0086
Snow, Chuck/2700 7th Ave S, Birmingham, AL	205-251-7482
Sparkman, Clif/161 Mangum St SW #301, Atlanta, GA	404-588-9687
Sparks, Don/670 11th St NW, Atlanta, GA	404-876-7354
Speidell, Bill/PO Box 426, Madison Heights, VA	804-846-2133
St John, Chuck/2724 NW 30th Ave, Ft Lauderdale, FL	305-731-3300
St John, Michael/PO Box 1202, Oldsmar, FL	813-725-4817
Stansfield, Ross/4938 Eisenhower Ave #D, Alexandria, VA	703-370-5142
Stein Photo/20240 SW 92nd Ave, Miami, FL	305-251-2868
Stein, Art/1845 MacArthur Dr, McLean, VA	703-237-1482
Stein, Marc/402 Rustic Trail, Birmingham, AL	205-987-1359

Please send us your additions and updates.

Stewart, Harvey & Co Inc/836 Dorse Rd, Lewisville, NC	919-945-2101
Stoppee Photographics Group/13 W Main St, Richmond, VA	804-644-0266
Strode, William A/1008 Kent Rd, Prospect, KY	502-228-4446
Sweetman, Gary Photography/2904 Manatee Ave W, Bradenton, FL	813-748-4004
Symmes Jr, Edwin C/PO Box 8101, Atlanta, GA	404-876-7620

T
Tapp, Eddie/955 Smoketree Dr, Tucker, GA	404-493-7233
Tast, Jerry/7932 Southside Blvd #2303, Jacksonville, FL	904-642-8300
Tesh, John/904-A Norwalk St, Greenboro, NC	919-299-1400
Thomas, J Clark/2305 Elliston Place, Nashville, TN	615-327-1757
Thomas, Larry/1212 Spring St, Atlanta, GA	404-881-8850
THOMPSON & THOMPSON/5180 NE 12TH AVE, FT LAUDERDALE, FL (P 276)	**305-772-4411**
Thompson, Darrell/124 Rhodes Dr, Marietta, GA	404-641-2020
Thompson, Ed C/2381 Drew Valley Rd, Atlanta, GA	404-636-7258
Thompson, Michael Photography/710 Tenth St, Atlanta, GA	404-881-8435
THOMPSON, ROSE/1802 NW 29TH ST, OAKLAND PARK, FL (P 277)	**305-485-0148**
Thompson, Thomas L/3210 Peachtree Rd NW #14, Atlanta, GA	404-892-3499
Tilley, Arthur/1925 College Ave NE, Atlanta, GA	404-371-8086
Tilson, Mark/419 Sinclair Ave NE, Atlanta, GA	404-524-8569
Tobias, Jerry/2117 Opa-Locka Blvd, Miami, FL	305-685-3003
Trufant, David/1902 Highland Rd, Baton Rouge, LA	504-344-9690
Truman, Gary/PO Box 7144, Charleston, WV	304-755-3078
Tucker, Mark Studio/117 Second Ave N, Nashville, TN	615-254-5555
Turnau, Jeffrey/7210 Red Rd #216, Miami, FL	305-666-5454
Turner, Ken/PO Box 6792, Mobile, AL	205-476-6050
Tutino, Aldo/407 N Washington St, Alexandria, VA	703-549-8014

UV
Ustinick, Richard/12 North 18th St, Richmond, VA	804-649-1477
Uzzell, Steve/2505 N Custis Rd, Arlington, VA	703-522-2320
Valada, M C/8451 Hilltop Rd #A, Fairfax, VA	703-573-3006
Van Calsem, Bill/824 Royal St, New Orleans, LA	504-522-7346
Van Camp, Louis/713 San Juan Rd, New Bern, NC	919-633-6081
VANCE, DAVID/150 NW 164TH ST, MIAMI, FL (P 228,229)	**305-685-2433**
Vaughn, Marc/600 Curtis Pkwy/Box 660706, Miami Springs, FL	305-888-4926
Vern, Ike/10431 Larissa St, Orlando, FL	305-352-1620
Victor, Ira/2026 Prairie Ave, Miami Beach, FL	305-532-4444
Visual Zone/3804 Veterans Blvd, Metairie, LA	504-454-2409
Von Matthiessen, Maria/251 Royal Palm Way Ste 201, Palm Beach, FL	305-655-6889
Vullo, Phillip Photography/565 Dutch Valley Rd NE, Atlanta, GA	404-874-0822

W
Wagoner, Mark/12-H Wendy Ct Box 18974, Greensboro, NC	919-854-0406
Walker Jr, Reuel F/PO Box 5421, Greenville, SC	803-834-9836
Walters, Tom/804 Atando Ave, Charlotte, NC	704-333-6294
Webb, Jon/2023 Kenilworth Ave, Louisville, KY	502-459-7081
Webster & Co/2214 Hawkins St, Charlotte, NC	704-375-1709
Weinlaub, Ralph/81 SW 6th St, Pompano Beach, FL	305-941-1368
Weithorn, Mark/13740 NW 19th Ave #6, Miami, FL	305-688-7070
WESTERMAN, CHARLIE/CENTRAL AMER BLDG/BOWMAN FLD, LOUISVILLE, KY (P 278)	**502-458-1532**
Wheless, Rob/2239 Faulkner Rd NE, Atlanta, GA	404-321-3557
WHITE, DRAKE/PO BOX 40090, AUGUSTA, GA (P 242)	**404-733-4142**
White, Ellis/2286 Central Ave, Memphis, TN	901-725-4740
Whitman, Alan/PO Box 8446, Mobile, AL	205-478-5520
Whitman, John/604 N Jackson St, Arlington, VA	703-524-5569
Wiener, Ray/4300 NE 5th Terrace, Oakland Park, FL	305-565-4415
Wiley Jr, Robert/1145 Washington Ave, Winter Park, FL	305-629-5823
Williams, Jimmy/3801 Beryl Rd, Raleigh, NC	919-832-5971
Williams, Ron/105 Space Park Dr #A, Nashville, TN	615-331-2500
Williamson, Thomas A/9511 Colonial Dr, Miami, FL	305-255-6400
Willis, Joe/105 Lake Emerald Dr #314, Ft Lauderdale, FL	305-485-7185
Wilson, Andrew/1720 Cumberland Point Dr #20, Marietta, GA	404-980-1289
Wilt, Greg/PO Box 212, Clearwater, FL	813-442-4360
Winner, Alan/20151 NE 15th Court, Miami, FL	305-653-6778
Wray, Michael/3501 Royal Palm Ave, Coconut Grove, FL	305-446-1116
Wright, Chris (Ms)/4131 Walnut Grove, Memphis, TN	901-761-5215
Wright, Christopher/2001-A Dekle Ave, Tampa, FL	813-251-5206

Wrisley, Bard/55 Bennett St NW, Atlanta, GA	404-892-2928

YZ
Yankus, Dennis/223 S Howard Ave, Tampa, FL	813-254-4156
Yarbrough, Hal/12119 Muriel Ave #511, Baton Rouge, LA	504-275-6753
Young, Chuck/1199-R Howell Mill Rd, Atlanta, GA	404-351-1199
Zeck, Gerry/1939 S Orange Ave, Sarasota, FL	813-953-4888
Zimmerman, Mike/7821 Shalimar, Mira Mar, FL	305-987-8482

MIDWEST

A
Abel Photographics/7035 Ashland Dr, Cleveland, OH	216-526-5732
Abramson, Michael Photo/3312 W Belle Plaine, Chicago, IL	312-975-2454
Accola, Harlan J/210 W 29th St, Marshfield, WI	715-387-8682
Adamo, Sam/490 Parkview Dr, Seven Hills, OH	216-447-9249
Adams, Janet L/106 W Eighth Ave #B, Columbus, OH	614-294-8312
Adams, Steve Studio/3101 S Hanley, Brentwood, MO	314-781-6676
AGS & R Studios/425 N Michigan Ave, Chicago, IL	312-836-4500
Alan, Andrew/20727 Scio Church Rd, Chelsea, MI	313-475-2310
Albiez, Scott/4144 N Clarendon, Chicago, IL	312-327-8999
Albright, Dave/200 S Main, Northville, MI	313-348-2248
Aleksandrowicz, Frank/343 Canterbury Rd, Cleveland, OH	216-871-5081
Allan-Knox Studios/1014 N Van Buren St, Milwaukee, WI	414-272-4999
Altman, Ben/820 N Franklin, Chicago, IL	312-944-1434
Amenta/555 W Madison #3802, Chicago, IL	312-248-2488
Anderson Studios Inc/546 S Meridian #300, Indianapolis, IN	317-632-9405
Anderson, Curt/Box 3213, Minneapolis, MN	612-332-2008
Anderson, John/401 W Superior, Chicago, IL	312-944-3311
Anderson, Rob/900 W Jackson, Chicago, IL	312-666-0417
Anderson, Whit/219 W Chicago, Chicago, IL	312-973-5683
Andre, Bruce/436 N Clark, Chicago, IL	312-661-1060
Apolinski Photography/735 N Oriole Ave, Park Ridge, IL	312-696-3156
Ardisson Photography/436 N Clark, Chicago, IL	312-951-8393
Armour, Tony/ Bones Inc/1726 N Clybourn, Chicago, IL	312-664-2256
Arndt, David M/4620 N Winchester, Chicago, IL	312-334-2841
Arndt, Jim/400 First Ave N #510, Minneapolis, MN	612-332-5050
Arsenault, Bill/570 W Fulton, Chicago, IL	312-454-0544
Askenas, Ulf/409 W Huron, Chicago, IL	312-944-4630
Atevich, Alex/325 N Hoyne Ave, Chicago, IL	312-942-1453
Atkinson, David/3923 W Pine Blvd, St Louis, MO	314-535-6484
Audio Visual Impact Group/233 E Erie, Chicago, IL	312-664-6247
Ayala/431 E Illinois, Chicago, IL	312-329-0787
Azuma, Don/1335 N Wells, Chicago, IL	312-337-2101

B
Baer, Gordon/PO Box 2467, Cincinnati, OH	513-281-2339
Bagnoli, Susan/74-24 Washington Ave, Eden Prairie, MN	612-944-5750
Bahm, Dave/711 Commercial, Belton, MO	816-331-0257
Baker, Jim/1905 Main, Kansas City, MO	816-471-5565
Balterman, Lee/910 N Lake Shore Dr, Chicago, IL	312-642-9040
Bandle, Bruce/415 Delaware 3rd Fl, Kansas City, MO	816-471-1201
Banks, Mikes/1915 Parmenter #10, Royal Oak, MI	313-435-4031
Banner & Burns Inc/153 W Ohio, Chicago, IL	312-644-4770
Bannister, Will/2312 N Lincoln, Chicago, IL	312-327-2143
Barge, Mike/7618 W Myrtle, Chicago, IL	312-762-1749
Barkan Keeling Photo/905 Vine St, Cincinnati, OH	513-721-0700
Barlow Photography Inc/1125 S Brentwood Blvd, Richmond Hts, MO	314-721-2385
Barnett, Jim/1502 S Keystone Ave, Indianapolis, IN	317-783-6797
Barrett, Robert/3733 Pennsylvania, Kansas City, MO	816-753-3208
Bartholomew, Gary/263 Columbia Ave, Des Plaines, IL	312-824-8473
Bartz, Carl Studio Inc/321 N 22nd St, St Louis, MO	314-231-8690
Basdeka, Pete/1254 N Wells, Chicago, IL	312-944-3333
Bass, Alan/126 W Kinzie, Chicago, IL	312-280-9140
Battrell, Mark/1611 N Sheffield, Chicago, IL	312-642-6650
Baver, Perry L/2923 W Touhy, Chicago, IL	312-674-1695
Bayles, Dal/4431 N 64th St, Milwaukee, WI	414-464-8917
Beasley, Michael/1210 W Webster, Chicago, IL	312-248-5769
Beaulieu, Allen/127 N 7th St #208, Minneapolis, MN	612-338-2327
Beck, Peter/3409 W 44th St, Minneapolis, MN	612-920-4741
Beckett Photography/510 N Water St, Milwaukee, WI	414-271-2061
Beckett Studios/340 W Huron St, Chicago, IL	312-943-2648
Bellville, Cheryl Walsh/2823 8th St S, Minneapolis, MN	612-333-5788

Please send us your additions and updates.

Belter, Mark/640 N LaSalle St #555, Chicago, IL	312-337-7676
Benda, James/13282 Glendale Rd, Savage, MN	612-890-5914
Benda, Tom/20555 LaGrange, Frankfurt, IL	815-469-3600
Bender/Bender/281 Klingel Rd, Waldo, OH	614-726-2470
Benkert, Christine/27 N 4th St #501, Minneapolis, MN	612-340-9503
Benoit, Bill/1708 1/2 Washington, Wilmette, IL	312-251-7634
Bentley, David/208 West Kinzie, Chicago, IL	312-836-0242
Berglund, Peter/126 N 3rd St #402, Minneapolis, MN	612-371-9318
Bergos, Jim Studio/122 W Kinzie St, Chicago, IL	312-527-1769
Berkman, Elie/125 Hawthorn Ave, Glencoe, IL	312-835-4158
Berlin Chic Photo/1120 W Barry St, Chicago, IL	312-327-2266
Berliner, Sheri/2815 N Pine Grove #1A, Chicago, IL	312-477-6692
Berlow, Marc Photography/325 W Huron St #406, Chicago, IL	312-787-6528
Bernard, Jerry/2023 Beard St, Detroit, MI	313-841-9284
Berr, Keith/1220 W 6th St #608, Cleveland, OH	216-566-7950
BERTHIAUME, TOM/1008 NICOLLET MALL, MINNEAPOLIS, MN (P 289)	**612-338-1999**
Bidak, Lorne/570 W Fulton, Chicago, IL	312-263-0010
Bieber, Tim/3312 W Belle Plaine, Chicago, IL	312-463-3590
Biel Photographic Studios/2289-91 N Moraine Blvd Dayton, OH	513-298-6621
Bilsley, Bill/218 South Patton, Arlington Heights, IL	312-259-7633
Bishop, Robert/5622 Delmar #103, St Louis, MO	314-367-8787
Bjornson, Howard/671 N Sangamon, Chicago, IL	312-829-8516
Blasdel, John/3030 Roanoke, Kansas City, MO	816-561-8989
Block, Ernie/1138 Cambridge Cir Dr, Kansas City, KS	913-321-3080
Block, Stuart/1242 W Washington Blvd, Chicago, IL	312-733-3600
Bochsler, Tom/3514 Mainway, Burlington L7M 1A8, ON	416-529-9011
Bock, Edward/400 N First Ave #207, Minneapolis, MN	612-332-8504
Bodenhansen, Gary/306 W 8th St, Kansas City, MO	816-221-2456
Bolber Studio/6706 Northwest Hwy, Chicago, IL	312-763-5860
Bornefeld, William/586 Hollywood Pl, St Louis, MO	314-962-5596
Boschke, Les/4200 N Hermitage, Chicago, IL	312-929-1119
Bosek, George/118 W Kinzie, Chicago, IL	312-828-0988
Bosy, Peter/564 W Randolph, Chicago, IL	312-559-0042
Boucher, Joe/5765 S Melinda St, Milwaukee, WI	414-281-7653
Bowen, Paul/Box 3375, Wichita, KS	316-263-5537
Boyer, Dick/100 W Chicago, Chicago, IL	312-337-7211
Brackenbury, Vern/1516 N 12th St, Blue Springs, MO	816-229-6703
Braddy, Jim/PO Box 11420, Chicago, IL	312-337-5664
Brandt & Assoc/Route 5 Box 148, Barrington Hills, IL	312-428-6363
Brauer, Lloyd/3101 S Hanley, St Louis, MO	314-781-6667
Braun Photography/3966 W Bath Rd, Akron, OH	216-666-4540
Brettell, Jim/2122 Morrison Ave, Lakewood, OH	216-228-0890
Brewer, William/6252 S MLK Dr, Chicago, IL	312-493-1147
Brimacombe, Gerald/7212 Mark Terrace, Minneapolis, MN	612-941-5860
Broderson, Fred/215 W Huron, Chicago, IL	312-787-1241
Brody, David & Assoc/6001 N Clark, Chicago, IL	312-761-2735
Brody, Jerry/70 W Hubbard, Chicago, IL	312-329-0660
Brookins, Carl/PO Box 80096, St Paul, MN	612-636-1733
Brooks, John/5663 Carrollton Ave, Indianapolis, IN	317-253-5663
Brosilow, Michael/208 W Kinzie 4th Fl, Chicago, IL	312-645-0628
Brown, Alan J/145 W 4th St, Cincinnati, OH	513-421-5588
Brown, David/900 Jorie Blvd #70, Oak Brook, IL	312-355-4661
Brown, James F/1349 E McMillan St, Cincinnati, OH	513-221-1144
Brown, Ron/1324 N Street, Lincoln, NE	402-476-1760
Brown, Steve/107 W Hubbard, Chicago, IL	312-467-4666
Bruno, Sam/1630 N 23rd, Melrose Park, IL	312-345-0411
Bruton, Jon/3838 W Pine Blvd, St Louis, MO	314-533-6665
Brystrom, Roy/6127 N Ravenswood, Chicago, IL	312-973-2922
Bukva, Walt/118 Anchor Rd, Michigan City, IN	219-872-9469
Bundt, Nancy/4001 Forest Rd, Minneapolis, MN	612-927-7493
Burjoski, David/18 S Kings Hwy, St Louis, MO	314-367-4060
Burns Copeland Photography/6651 N Artesian, Chicago, IL	312-465-3240
Burress, Cliff/343 S Dearborn #608, Chicago, IL	312-427-3335
Burris, Zack/230 E Ohio, Chicago, IL	312-951-0131
Bush, Tim/1138 W 9th St, Cleveland, OH	216-621-2500

C

C-H Studios/600 W Jackson, Chicago, IL	312-726-7830
Cabanban, Orlando/410 S Michigan Ave, Chicago, IL	312-922-1836
Cable, Wayne/1302 W Waveland, Chicago, IL	312-248-2959
Cain, C C/420 N Clark, Chicago, IL	312-644-2371

Cairns, Robert/2035 W Charleston #4-SE, Chicago, IL	312-384-3114
Camacho, Mike/124 W Main St, West Dundee, IL	312-428-3135
Camera Works Inc/1260 Carnegie Ave, Cleveland, OH	216-687-1788
Camerawork, Ltd/1032 N LaSalle, Chicago, IL	312-321-0817
Camlen Studio/3695 #A N 126th St, Brookfield, WI	414-781-9477
Campbell, Bob/722 Prestige, Joliet, IL	815-725-1862
Candee & Assoc/1212 W Jackson, Chicago, IL	312-829-1212
Caporale, Michael/6710 Madison Rd, Cincinnati, OH	513-561-4011
Carell, Lynn/3 E Ontario #25, Chicago, IL	312-935-1707
Carney, Joann/368 W Huron, Chicago, IL	312-266-7620
Carosella, Tony/4138-A Wyoming, St Louis, MO	314-664-3462
Carr, Steve/311 N Desplaines #608, Chicago, IL	312-454-0984
Carter, Garry/179 Waverly, Ottawa K2P 0V5, ON	613-233-3306
Carter, Mary Ann/5954 Crestview, Indianapolis, IN	317-255-1351
Casalini, Tom/10 1/2 N Main St, Zionsville, IN	317-873-5229
Cascarano, John/657 W Ohio, Chicago, IL	312-733-1212
Caswell, George/700 Washington Ave N #308 Minneapolis, MN	612-332-2729
Cates, Gwendolen/1942 N Dayton, Chicago, IL	312-880-5571
Caulfield, James/430 W Erie, Chicago, IL	312-951-7260
Ceolla, George/5700 Ingersoll Ave, Des Moines, IA	515-279-3508
Cermak Photo/96 Pine Ave, Riverside, IL	312-447-6446
Chadwick Taber Inc/617 W Fulton, Chicago, IL	312-454-0855
Chambers, Tom/153 W Ohio, Chicago, IL	312-828-9488
Chapman, Cam/126 W Kinzie, Chicago, IL	312-222-9242
Chapman, John/125 W Hubbard, Chicago, IL	312-337-7347
Chare, Dave/1045 N Northwest Hwy, Park Ridge, IL	312-696-3188
Charlie Company/2000 Superior Ave #2, Cleveland, OH	216-566-7464
Chauncey, Paul C/1029 N Wichita #13, Wichita, KS	316-262-6733
Cherup, Thomas/PO Box 84, Dearborn Hts, MI	313-561-9376
Chicago Photographers/58 W Superior, Chicago, IL	312-944-4828
Chin, Ruth/108 E Jackson, Muncie, IN	317-284-4582
Chobot, Dennis/2857 E Grand Blvd, Detroit, MI	313-875-6617
Christian Studios Inc/5408 N Main St, Dayton, OH	513-275-3775
Christman, Gerald/985 Ridgewood Dr, Highland Park, IL	312-433-2279
Clark, Harold/9 Lloyd Manor, Islington M9B 5H5, ON	416-236-2958
Clark, Junebug/30419 W Twelve Mile Rd, Farmington Hills, MI	313-478-3666
Clarke, Jim/689 Craig Rd, St Louis, MO	314-872-7506
Clawson, David/6800 Normal Blvd, Lincoln, NE	402-483-4761
Clemens, Jim/1147 W Ohio, Chicago, IL	312-280-2289
CLICK* CHICAGO/213 W INSTITUTE PL #503, CHICAGO, IL (P 290,416)	**312-787-7880**
Cloudshooters/Aerial Photo/4620 N Winchester, Chicago, IL	312-334-2841
Clough, Jean/1059 W Columbia, Chicago, IL	312-262-1732
Coats & Greenfield Inc/2928 Fifth Ave S, Minneapolis, MN	612-827-4676
Cochrane, Jim/25 1/2 York St #1, Ottawa K1N 5S7, ON	613-234-3099
Coha, Dan/9 W Hubbard, Chicago, IL	312-664-2270
Coil, Ron Studio/15 W Hubbard St, Chicago, IL	312-321-0155
Compton, Ted/112 N Washington, Hinsdale, IL	312-654-8781
Condie, Thomas M/527 N 27th St, Milwaukee, WI	414-342-6363
Copeland, Burns/6651 N Artesian, Chicago, IL	312-465-3240
Corey, Carl/222 S Morgan, Chicago, IL	312-421-3232
Coster-Mullen, John E/2301 W Nordale Dr, Appleton, WI	414-766-4281
COWAN, RALPH/452 N HALSTED ST, CHICAGO, IL (P 291)	**312-243-6696**
Cox, D E/5856 Hartwell, Dearborn, MI	313-581-0116
CR Studio/1859 W 25th St, Cleveland, OH	216-861-5360
Cralle, Gary/83 Elm Ave #205, Toronto M4W 1P1, ON	416-923-2920
Crane, Arnold/666 N Lake Shore Dr, Chicago, IL	312-337-5544
Crane, Michael/1717 Wyandotte St, Kansas City, MO	816-221-9382
Creightney, Dorrell/116 W Illinois, Chicago, IL	312-528-0816
Crofoot, Ron/6140 Wayzata Blvd, Minneapolis, MN	612-546-0643
Crofton, Bill/205 Ridge Rd #102, Wilmette, IL	312-256-7862
Crosby, Paul/1701 E 79th St #17B, Minneapolis, MN	612-854-3060
Crowther Photography/2210 Superior Viaduct W, Cleveland, OH	216-566-8066
Culbert-Aguilar, Kathleen/1338 W Carmen, Chicago, IL	312-561-1266
Culver, Steve/115 N Washington Ave #200, Minneapolis, MN	612-332-2425
Cunningham, Elizabeth/1122 W Lunt Ave, Chicago, IL	312-998-1505
CURTIS, LUCKY/1540 N PARK AVE, CHICAGO, IL (P 292)	**312-787-4422**

D

D'Orio, Tony/1147 W Ohio, Chicago, IL	312-421-5532
Dacuisto, Todd/4455 W Bradley Rd #204, Milwaukee, WI	414-355-4947

Please send us your additions and updates.

Dale, LB/7015 Wing Lake Rd, Birmingham, MI	313-851-3296
Dali, Michael/1737 McGee, Kansas City, MO	816-931-0570
Dapkus, Jim/Westfield Photo/Rte 1 Box 247, Westfield, WI	608-296-2623
Davito, Dennis/638 Huntley Heights, Manchester, MO	314-394-0660
Day, Michael/264 Seaton St, Toronto M5A 2T4, ON	416-920-9135
Daytons/701 Industrial Blvd, Minneapolis, MN	612-623-7086
Deahl, David/70 W Hubbard, Chicago, IL	312-644-3187
Deart, Greg/4041 Beal Rd, Franklin, OH	513-746-5970
Debacker, Michael/231 Ohio, Wichita, KS	316-265-2776
Debold, Bill/1801 N Halsted, Chicago, IL	312-337-1177
DeLaittre, Bill/1307 5th St South, Minneapolis, MN	612-936-9840
Delich, Mark/304 W 10th St #200, Kansas City, MO	816-474-6699
DeMarco Photographers/7145 W Addison, Chicago, IL	312-282-1422
DeNatale, Joe/215 W Ohio, Chicago, IL	312-329-0234
Denning, Warren/27 Laurel, Wichita, KS	316-262-4163
Deutsch, Owen/1759 N Sedgewick, Chicago, IL	312-943-7155
Dieringer, Rick/19 West Court St, Cincinnati, OH	513-621-2544
Dinerstein, Matt/606 W 18th St, Chicago, IL	312-243-4766
Ditlove, Michel/18 W Hubbard, Chicago, IL	312-644-5233
Ditz, Michael/8138 W 9 Mile Rd, Oak Park, MI	313-546-1759
Dollahan, Sam/1043 W Grand, Chicago, IL	312-226-5620
Donner, Michael/5534 S Dorchester, Chicago, IL	312-241-7896
Donofrio, Randy/6459 S Albany, Chicago, IL	312-737-0990
Dorgay, Jeff/207 E Buffalo, Milwaukee, WI	414-271-8006
Dovey, Dean/531 S Plymouth Ct #303, Chicago, IL	312-427-0189
Doyle, Tim/259 E Frank, Birmingham, MI	313-642-5658
Drew, Terry-David/219 W Chicago, Chicago, IL	312-943-0301
Drickey, Pat/406 S 12th St, Omaha, NE	402-344-3786
Drier, David/804 Washington St #3, Evanston, IL	312-475-1992
Dublin, Rick/1019 Currie Ave N, Minneapolis, MN	612-332-8924
DuBroff, Don/2031 W Cortez, Chicago, IL	312-252-7390

E

Eagle, Joe/415 W Superior, Chicago, IL	312-280-1919
Eagle, Lin/415 W Superior, Chicago, IL	312-664-7650
EBEL, BOB PHOTOGRAPHY/415 N DEARBORN, CHICAGO, IL (P 280,281)	**312-222-1123**
Ebenoh, Tom/8439 Lake Dr, Cedar Hill, MO	314-285-2467
Ebert Photography/227 S Marion, Chicago, IL	312-386-6222
Eckhard, Kurt/1306 S 18th St, St Louis, MO	314-241-1116
Eggebenn, Mark/1217 Center Ave, Dostburg, WI	414-564-2344
Eiler, Lynthia & Terry/330 BArker Rd #B Rt 2, Athens, OH	614-592-1280
Einhorn, Mitchell/175 E Delaware Pl, Chicago, IL	312-944-7028
Eisner, Scott Photography/314 W Superior, Chicago, IL	312-670-2217
ELLEDGE, PAUL/511 N NOBLE, CHICAGO, IL (P 293)	**312-733-8021**
Ellingsen/1411 Peterson, Park Ridge, IL	312-823-0192
Elliott, Peter/405 N Wabash Ave, Chicago, IL	312-329-1370
Elmore, Bob and Assoc/315 S Green St, Chicago, IL	312-641-2731
Englehard, J Versar/522 W Eugene St, Chicago, IL	312-787-2024
Ennis, Janet/209 E 46th St #3, Kansas City, MO	816-561-2356
Erickson, Brett/15772 27th Ave N, Plymouth, MN	612-553-9274
Ernst, Elizabeth/1020 Elm St, Winnetka, IL	312-441-8993
ETM Studios/130 S Morgan, Chicago, IL	312-666-0660
Evans, Patricia/1153 E 56th St, Chicago, IL	312-288-2291
Ewert, Steve/17 N Elizabeth, Chicago, IL	312-733-5762

F

Faitage, Nick Photography/1910 W North Ave, Chicago, IL	312-276-9321
Farber, Gerald/10910 Whittier, Detroit, MI	313-371-4161
Faverty, Richard/340 W Huron, Chicago, IL	312-943-2648
Feferman, Steve/229 W Illinois #4E, Chicago, IL	312-644-5767
Fegley, Richard/6083 N Kirkwood, Chicago, IL	312-527-1114
Feher, Paul/3138 Flame Dr, Oregon, OH	419-698-4254
Feldman, Stephen L/2705 W Agatite, Chicago, IL	312-539-0300
Ferguson, Ken/920 N Franklin St, Chicago, IL	312-642-6255
Ferguson, Scott/7110 Oakland Ave, St Louis, MO	314-647-7466
Ficht, Bill/1207 Ford St, Geneva, IL	312-232-2874
Fichter, Russ/159 W Goethe, Chicago, IL	312-787-9768
Fine Art Photography/1619 Winchester, Schaumberg, IL	312-351-1702
Finlay & Finlay Photo/141 E Main St, Ashland, OH	419-289-3163
Firak Photography/11 E Hubbard, Chicago, IL	312-467-0208
First Light Assoc/78 Rusholme Rd, Toronto M6J 3H6, ON	416-532-6108
Fish Studios/125 W Hubbard, Chicago, IL	312-944-1570
Fitzsimmons, J Kevin/2380 Wimbledon Rd, Columbus, OH	614-457-2010

Fleming, Larry/1029 N Wichita #3, Wichita, KS	316-267-0780
Fletcher, Mike/7467 Kingsbury, St Louis, MO	314-721-2279
Flood, Kevin/1329 Macklind St, St Louis, MO	314-647-2485
Floyd, Bill/215 W Ohio, Chicago, IL	312-321-1770
Fong, John/13 N Huron St, Toledo, OH	419-243-7378
Fontayne Studios Ltd/4528 W Oakton, Skokie, IL	312-676-9872
Ford, Madison/2616 Industrial Row, Troy, MI	313-280-0640
Forrest, Michael/2150 Plainfield Ave NE, Grand Rapids, MI	616-361-2556
Forsyte, Alex/1180 Oak Ridge Dr, Glencoe, IL	312-835-0307
Forth, Ron/316 W 4th St, Cincinnati, OH	513-621-0841
Foss Studio/1711 N Honore, Chicago, IL	312-771-9347
Foss, Kurt/4147 Pleasant Ave S, Minneapolis, MN	612-822-4694
Foster, Richard/157 W Ontario St, Chicago, IL	312-943-9005
Foto-Graphics/2402 N Shadeland Ave, Indianapolis, IN	317-353-6259
Foto/Ed Sacks/Box 7237, Chicago, IL	312-871-4700
Fox Commercial Photo/119 W Hubbard, Chicago, IL	312-664-0162
Fox, Fred & Sons/2746 W Fullerton, Chicago, IL	312-342-3233
Frantz, Ken/706 N Dearborn, Chicago, IL	312-951-1077
Franz, Bill/820 E Wisconsin, Delavan, WI	414-728-3733
Freeman, George/1061 W Balmoral, Chicago, IL	312-275-1122
Frerck, Robert/4158 N Greenview 2nd Fl, Chicago, IL	312-883-1965
Frick, Ken/2255 Barry Dr, Colombus, OH	614-471-3090
Friedman, Susan J/215 W Ohio, Chicago, IL	312-527-1880
FRITZ, TOM/2320 N 11TH ST, MILWAUKEE, WI (P 285)	**414-263-6700**
Futran, Eric/6347 N Lakewood, Chicago, IL	312-338-3735

G

Gabriel Photo/160 E Illinois, Chicago, IL	312-787-2915
Gale, Bill/3041 Aldrich Ave S, Minneapolis, MN	612-827-5858
Gallagher, Colleen/300 W Grand St #440, Chicago, IL	312-467-0021
Galloway, Scott/177 Benson Rd, Akron, OH	216-864-7259
Gardner, Al/7120 Eugene, St Louis, MO	314-752-5278
Gates, Bruce/356 1/2 S Main St, Akron, OH	216-375-5282
Gaymont, Gregory/1812 N Hubbard St, Chicago, IL	312-421-3146
Gerding, Gary/8025 W Dodge Rd, Omaha, NE	402-390-2677
Getsug, Don/610 N Fairbanks Ct, Chicago, IL	312-440-1311
Giannetti, Joseph/127 N 7th St #402, Minneapolis, MN	612-339-3172
Gibbs, Stu/3244 N Cicero, Chicago, IL	312-725-8457
Gillette, Bill/2917 Eisenhower, Ames, IA	515-294-4340
Gilo, Dave/121 N Broadway, Milwaukee, WI	414-273-1022
Gilroy, John/2407 West Main St, Kalamazoo, MI	616-349-6805
Girard, Connie/316 Telford Ave, Dayton, OH	513-294-2095
Glenn, Eileen/123 W Chestnut, Chicago, IL	312-944-1756
Gluth, Bill/621 W Randolph, Chicago, IL	312-207-0055
Goddard, Will/1496 N Albert St, St Paul, MN	612-483-9068
Goez, Bill/9657 S Winchester, Chicago, IL	312-881-1964
Goff, P.R./66 W Wittier St, Columbus, OH	614-443-6530
Goldberg, Lenore/210 Park Ave, Glencoe, IL	312-835-4226
Goldstein, Steven/14982 Country Ridge, St Louis, MO	314-532-0660
Goodman, Anne Margaret/411 N LaSalle, Chicago, IL	312-670-3660
Gorecki Studio/5011 W Fullerton, Chicago, IL	312-622-8146
Goss, James M/1737 McGee St, Kansas City, MO	816-471-8069
Goss, Michael/1548 W Devon, Chicago, IL	312-262-6719
Gould, Christopher/224 W Huron, Chicago, IL	312-944-5545
Gould, Rick Studios/217 N 10th St, St Louis, MO	314-241-4862
Graenicher, Kurt/112 Seventh Ave, Monroe, WI	608-328-8400
Graham-Henry, Diane/2943 N Seminary, Chicago, IL	312-327-4493
Grajczyk, Chris/126 North 3rd St #405, Minneapolis, MN	612-333-6265
Graphic Arts Photo/100 E Ohio, Chicago, IL	312-944-1577
Gray, Walter/1035 W Lake, Chicago, IL	312-733-3800
Grayson, Dan/831 W Cornelia, Chicago, IL	312-477-8659
Greenblatt, William/20 Nantucket Ln, St Louis, MO	314-726-6151
Gregg, Rene/4965 McPherson, St Louis, MO	314-361-1963
Gregg, Robb T/4715 N Ronald St, Harwood Heights, IL	312-867-5445
Gremmler, Paul/221 W Walton, Chicago, IL	312-664-0464
Griffith, Sam/345 N Canal, Chicago, IL	312-648-1900
Griffith, Walter/719 S 75th St, Omaha, NE	402-391-8474
Grignon Studios/1300 W Altgeld Dr, Chicago, IL	312-975-7200
Grippentrag, Dennis/70 E Long Lake Rd, Bloomfield Hills, MI	313-645-2222
Groen, John/676 N LaSalle, Chicago, IL	312-266-2331
Grondin, Timothy/145 W 4th St, Cincinnati, OH	513-421-5588
Gross, Frank/125 W Hubbard, Chicago, IL	312-822-9374
Gross, Werner/465 S College, Valparaiso, IN	219-462-3453

Please send us your additions and updates.

Grubman, Steve/219 W Chicago, Chicago, IL	312-787-2272
GRUNEWALD, JEFF/161 W HARRISON ST, CHICAGO, IL	
(P 295)	**312-663-5799**
GSP/156 N Jefferson, Chicago, IL	312-944-3000
Gubin, Mark/2893 S Delaware Ave, Milwaukee, WI	414-482-0640
Guenther, Stephen/1939 Sherman Ave, Evanston, IL	312-864-5381
Guerry, Tim/411 S Sangamon #3B, Chicago, IL	312-666-0303

H Haberman, Mike/529 S 7th St #427, Minneapolis, MN — 612-338-4696

Haefner, Jim/1407 B Allen, Troy, MI	313-583-4747
Haines, W C (Bill)/3101 Mercier Ste 484, Kansas City, MO	816-531-0561
Halbe, Harrison/744 Office Pkwy #175, St Louis, MO	314-993-1145
Hall, Brian/1015 N LaSalle St, Chicago, IL	312-642-6764
Haller, Pam/215 W Huron, Chicago, IL	312-649-0920
Hammarlund, Vern/135 Park St, Troy, MI	313-588-5533
Hampton, Chris/120 W Kinzie St, Chicago, IL	312-467-0135
Handley, Robert E/1920 E Croxton, Bloomington, IL	309-828-4661
Hansen, Art/PO Box 8646, Detroit, MI	313-589-0066
Hansen, Lars/2817 33rd Ave S, Minneapolis, MN	612-332-5112
Harding Studio/727 Hudson, Chicago, IL	312-943-4010
Harlan, Bruce/52922 Camellia Dr, South Bend, IN	219-239-7350
Harquail, John/67 Mowat Ave #40, Toronto M6K 3E3,	416-535-1620
Harrig, Rick/3316 South 66th Ave, Omaha, NE	402-397-5529
Harris, Bart/70 W Hubbard St, Chicago, IL	312-751-2977
Hart, Bob/116 W Illinois, Chicago, IL	312-644-3636
Hatcher, Lois/32 W 58th St, Kansas City, MO	816-361-6230
Hauser, Marc/1810 W Cortland, Chicago, IL	312-486-4381
Hawker, Chris/119 N Peoria, Chicago, IL	312-829-4766
Hedrich-Blessing/11 W Illinois St, Chicago, IL	312-321-1151
Heil, Peter/213 W Institute Pl #707, Chicago, IL	312-544-9130
Heilbron, Kenneth/1357 N Wells, Chicago, IL	312-787-1238
Helmick, William/129 Geneva, Elmhurst, IL	312-834-4798
Henebry, Jeanine/1154 Locust Rd, Wilmette, IL	312-251-8747
Henning, Paul/PO Box 92218, Milwaukee, WI	414-765-9441
Hermann, Dell/676 N LaSalle, Chicago, IL	312-664-1461
Hertzberg, Richard/436 N Clark, Chicago, IL	312-836-0464
Hetisimer, Larry/1630 5th Ave, Moline, IL	309-797-1010
Hickson-Bender Photography/281 Klingel Rd Box 201	
Waldo, OH	614-726-2470
Hill, Roger/140 Jefferson SE, Grand Rapids, MI	616-451-2501
Hillery, John/PO Box 2916, Detroit, MI	313-345-9511
Hines, Tricia/PO Box 539, Creston, IA	515-782-9591
Hirschfeld, Corson/316 W Fourth St, Cincinnati, OH	513-241-0550
Hodes, Charles S/233 E Erie, Chicago, IL	312-951-1186
Hodges, Charles/539 W North Ave, Chicago, IL	312-664-8179
Hoffman-Wilber Inc/618 W Jackson, Chicago, IL	312-454-0303
Holcepl, Robert/2044 Euclid Ave, Cleveland, OH	216-621-3838
Holographics Design System/1134 W Washington, Chicago, IL	312-226-1007
Holzmer, Buck/3448 Chicago Ave, Minneapolis, MN	612-824-3874
Honor, David/415 W Superior, Chicago, IL	312-751-1644
Hooke Photography/1147 W Ohio, Chicago, IL	312-829-4568
Hoppe, Ed Photography/401 W Superior, Chicago, IL	312-787-2136
Houghton, Michael/Studiohio/55 E Spring St, Columbus, OH	614-224-4885
Howrani, Armeen/2820 E Grand Blvd, Detroit, MI	313-875-3123
Hrdlicka, Mitch/4201 Levinworth, Omaha, NE	402-551-0887
Hsi, Kai/160 E Illinois, Chicago, IL	312-642-9853
Hurling, Robert/225 W Huron, Chicago, IL	312-944-2022
Hutson, David/8120 Juniper, Prairie Village, KS	913-383-1123
Hyman, Randy/7709 Carnell Ave, St Louis, MO	314-721-7489

I Iann-Hutchins/2044 Euclid Ave, Cleveland, OH — 216-579-1570

Image Productions/115 W Church, Libertyville, IL	312-680-7100
Imagematrix/2 Garfield Pl, Cincinnati, OH	513-381-1380
Imagination Unlimited/PO Box 268709, Chicago, IL	312-764-1880
Imbrogno/411 N LaSalle St, Chicago, IL	312-644-7333
Inflight Photo/3114 St Mary's, Omaha, NE	402-345-2164
Ingram, Russell/1000-02 W Monroe St, Chicago, IL	312-829-4652
Ingve, Jan & Assoc/73 Elm St #14D, Chicago, IL	312-280-2289
International Photo Corp/1035 Wesley, Evanston, IL	312-475-6400
Irving, Gary/PO Box 38, Wheaton, IL	312-653-0641
Isenberg, Bill/27059 Arden Park Circle, Farmington Hills, MI	313-478-9709
Isenberger, Brent/1710-J Gutherie Ave, Des Moines, IA	515-262-5466

Issacs, Michael/2558 Madison Rd #7, Cincinnati, OH	513-241-4622
Itahara, Tets/676 N LaSalle, Chicago, IL	312-649-0606
Italo, Ed/1709 Washington #9000, St Louis, MO	314-231-4883
Iwata, John/336 W 15th Ave, Oshkosh, WI	414-424-0317
Izokaitis, Kastytis/441 N Clark, Chicago, IL	312-321-1388
Izquierdo, Abe/325 W Huron, Chicago, IL	312-787-9784
IZUI, RICHARD/315 W WALTON, CHICAGO, IL (P 282,283)	**312-266-8029**

J Jackson, David/1021 Hall St, Grand Rapids, MI — 616-243-3325

Jackson, Jack/207 E Buffalo #514, Milwaukee, WI	414-289-0890
Jacob, David/6412 N Glenwood, Chicago, IL	312-274-9191
Jacobs, Todd/3336 N Sheffield, Chicago, IL	312-472-4401
Jacquin Enterprise/1219 Holly Hills, St Louis, MO	314-832-4221
James Studio/730 Lee St, Des Plaines, IL	312-824-0007
James, E Michael/10757 S Peoria, Chicago, IL	312-928-5908
James, Phillip MacMillan/2300 Hazelwood Ave, St Paul, MN	612-777-2303
Jedd, Joseph/5931 N Keating, Chicago, IL	312-685-0641
Jenkins, David/1416 S Michigan Ave, Chicago, IL	312-922-2299
Jennings, Bill/1322 S Wabash, Chicago, IL	312-987-0124
Jensen, Michael/1101 Stinson Blvd NE, Minneapolis, MN	612-379-1944
Jilling, Helmut/1759 State Rd, Cuyahoga Falls, OH	216-928-1330
Jo, Isac/4344 N Wolcott, Chicago, IL	312-472-1607
Jochim, Gary/1324 1/2 N Milwaukee, Chicago, IL	312-252-5250
Joel, David/1342 W Hood Ave, Chicago, IL	312-262-0794
Johnson, Chaz T/225 N Park Ave Box 1813, Fond du Lac, WI	414-923-4494
Johnson, Dave/679 E Mandoline, Madison Hts, MI	313-589-0066
Johnson, Donald/2807 Brindle, Northbrook, IL	312-480-9336
Johnson, Jim/802 W Evergreen, Chicago, IL	312-943-8864
Jones, Arvell/8232 W McNichols, Detroit, MI	313-342-2000
Jones, Brent/9121 S Merrill Ave, Chicago, IL	312-933-1174
Jones, Dawson/46 E Franklin St, Dayton, OH	513-435-1121
Jones, Dick/325 W Huron, Chicago, IL	312-642-0242
Jones, Harrison/727 N Hudson #405, Chicago, IL	312-337-4997
Jons Studio/35 E Wacker, Chicago, IL	312-236-0243
Jordan, Jack/840 John St, Evansville, IN	812-423-7676
Jordano, Dave/1335 N Wells, Chicago, IL	312-280-8212
Joseph, Mark/1007 N La Salle, Chicago, IL	312-951-5333
Justice Patterson Horst/7613 Production Dr, Cincinnati, OH	513-761-4023

K Kahn, Dick/21750 Doral Rd, Waukesha, WI — 414-784-1994

Kalyniuk, Jerry/4243 N Winchester, Chicago, IL	312-975-8973
Kapal Photo Studio/233 Ridge Rd, Munster, IN	219-836-2176
Kaplan, Dick/1694 First St, Highland Park, IL	312-432-0632
Karant & Assoc/215 W Ohio St, Chicago, IL	312-527-1880
Kaspar, Tom/650 S Clark, Chicago, IL	312-987-0956
Kauck, Jeff/205 W Fourth, Cincinnati, OH	513-241-5435
Kauffman, Kim/913 Beech St, Lansing, MI	517-371-3036
Kavula, Ken/19 E Pearson, Chicago, IL	312-280-9060
KAZU STUDIO/1211 W WEBSTER, CHICAGO, IL (P 296,297)	**312-348-5393**
Kean, Christopher/624 West Adams St, Chicago, IL	312-559-0880
Keeling, Robert/26 E Huron St, Chicago, IL	312-944-5680
Keisman & Keisman/920 N Franklin St, Chicago, IL	312-337-5535
Kelly, Tony/828 Colfax, Evanston, IL	312-864-0488
Keltsch, Steve/7315 S Anthony Blvd/Box 6569, Ft Wayne, IN	219-447-0560
Kem, Patrick/1832 E 38th St, Minneapolis, MN	612-729-8989
Kemmetmueller Photo/973 East Lake St, Wayzata, MN	612-473-2142
Ketchum, Art/1 E Oak, Chicago, IL	312-544-1222
Kezar, Mitch/2207 Oakview Ln N, Minneapolis, MN	612-559-1733
Kinast, Susan/1035 Lake St, Chicago, IL	312-738-0068
King, Budde/1914 Gardner Rd, Westchester, IL	312-865-8316
King, Jay Studios/1024 W Armitage, Chicago, IL	312-327-0011
Kingsbury, Andrew/700 N Washington #306, Minneapolis, MN	612-340-1919
Kitahara, Joe/304 W 10th St, Kansas City, MO	816-474-6699
Klein Photography/952 W Lake, Chicago, IL	312-226-1878
Klein, Daniel/306 W 8th, Kansas City, MO	816-474-6491
Klutho, Dave/4617 Brookroyal Ct, St Louis, MO	314-487-3626
Knight, Bill/9906 Gilbrook Ave, St Louis, MO	314-968-9510
Knize, Karl/1024 W Armitage, Chicago, IL	312-327-0033
Kodama, Kiyoshi/424 N Benton, St Charles, MO	314-946-9247
Kogan, David/1313 W Randolph St #314, Chicago, IL	312-243-1929
Kolesar, Jerry Photographics/679 E Mandoline, Madison Hts, MI	313-589-0066

Kolze, Larry/22 W Erie, Chicago, IL	312-266-8352
KONDAS, THOM ASSOC/PO BOX 1162, INDIANAPOLIS, IN	
(P 298)	**317-637-1414**
Kondor, Linda/430 N Clark St, Chicago, IL	312-642-7365
Korab, Balthazar/PO Box 895, Troy, MI	313-641-8881
Kransberger, Jim/2247 Boston SE, Grand Rapids, MI	616-777-9404
Krantz, John/1791 W 31st Pl, Cleveland, OH	216-241-3411
Krantzen Studios/100 S Ashland, Chicago, IL	312-942-1900
Kraus, Gregor/213 W Institute Pl, Chicago, IL	312-266-6068
Krejci, Donald/1825 E 18th St, Cleveland, OH	216-831-4730
Krinsky, Jon A/85 Tahlequah Trail, Springboro, OH	513-746-5230
Krueger, Dick/660 W Grand, Chicago, IL	312-243-2730
Kufrin, George/500 N Dearborn, Chicago, IL	312-787-2854
Kulp, Curtis/222 W Ontario, Chicago, IL	312-266-0477
Kusel, Bob/1651 W Touhy, Chicago, IL	312-787-8220

L

Lacey, Ted/4733 S Woodlawn, Chicago, IL	312-624-2419
Lacroix, Pat/25 Brant St, Toronto, ON	416-864-1858
Laden, Murray/110 W Kinzie, Chicago, IL	312-222-0555
Landau, Allan/1147 West Ohio, Chicago, IL	312-942-1382
Lane, Jack Studio/5 W Grand Ave, Chicago, IL	312-337-2326
Lanza, Scott/, Milwaukee, WI	414-482-4114
LaRoche, Andrea/32588 Deguinder, Warren, MI	313-978-7373
Larsen, Kim/ Soren Studio/325 N Hoyne, Chicago, IL	312-666-5885
LaTona, Tony/1317 E 5th, Kansas City, MO	816-474-3119
Lauth, Lyal/833 N Orleans, Chicago, IL	312-787-5615
Leavenworth Photo Inc/929 West St, Lansing, MI	517-482-4658
Leavitt, Debbie/2756 N Pine Grove Ave #212, Chicago, IL	312-348-2833
Leavitt, Fred/916 Carmen, Chicago, IL	312-784-2344
Lecat, Paul/820 N Franklin, Chicago, IL	312-664-7122
Lee, Robert Photo/1512 Northlin Dr, St Louis, MO	314-965-5832
Lee, Terry/4420 N Paulina, Chicago, IL	312-561-1153
LeGrand, Peter/413 Sandburg, Park Forest, IL	312-747-4923
LEHN, JOHN/2601 E FRANKLIN AVE, MINNEAPOLIS, MN	
(P 299)	**612-338-0257**
Leick, Jim/1709 Washington Ave, St Louis, MO	314-241-2354
Leinwohl, Stef/439 W Oakdale #3, Chicago, IL	312-348-5862
Leonard, Steve/825 W Gunnison, Chicago, IL	312-275-8833
Leslie, William F/53 Tealwood Dr, Creve Coeur, MO	314-993-8349
Levey, Don/15 W Delaware Pl, Chicago, IL	312-329-9040
Levin, Jonathan/1035 W Lake St, Chicago, IL	312-226-3898
Levin, Marty/215 W Ohio, Chicago, IL	312-787-2586
Lewandowski, Leon/325 W Huron, Chicago, IL	312-467-9577
Lieberman, Archie/1135 Asbury, Evanston, IL	312-475-8508
Lightfoot, Robert/311 Good Ave, Des Plaines, IL	312-297-5447
Linc Studio/1163 Tower, Schaumberg, IL	312-882-1311
Lindblade, George R/PO Box 1342, Sioux City, IA	712-255-4346
Lindwall, Martin/1269 Briarwood Ln, Libertyville, IL	312-680-1578
Lipschis, Helmut Photography/903 W Armitage, Chicago, IL	312-871-2003
Liss, Leroy/6243 N Ridgeway Ave, Chicago, IL	312-539-4540
Little, Scott/1515 Linden, Des Moines, IA	515-243-4428
Lohbeck, Stephen/1226 Ambassador Blvd, St Louis, MO	314-991-4657
Lords Studio Ltd/162 N Clinton, Chicago, IL	312-332-0208
Lowenthal, Jeff/20 E Randolph #7948, Chicago, IL	312-938-0130
Lowry, Miles/222 S Morgan #3B, Chicago, IL	312-666-0882
Loynd, Mel/208 Queen St S, Streetsville L5M1L5, ON	416-821-0477
Lucas, John V/4100 W 40th St, Chicago, IL	312-927-4500
Lucas, Joseph/20 N Wacker Dr #1425, Chicago, IL	312-782-6905
Ludwigs, David/3600 Troost St, Kansas City, MO	816-531-1363
Lyles, David/401 W Superior 5th Fl, Chicago, IL	312-642-1223

M

Maas, Curt/7000 Pioneer Pkwy, Johnston, IA	515-270-3436
MacDonald, Al/32 Martin Lane, Elk Grove, IL	312-437-8850
Mack, Richard/2119 Lincoln, Evanston, IL	312-869-7794
MacTavish Arndt, David/4620 N Winchester, Chicago, IL	312-334-2841
Maguire, Jim/144 Lownsdale, Akron, OH	216-630-9050
Maki & Smith Photo/6156 Olson Mem Hwy, Golden Valley, MN	612-541-4722
Malinowski, Stan/1150 N State #312, Chicago, IL	312-951-6715
Mally Assoc/20 W Hubbard #3E, Chicago, IL	312-644-4367
Maloney, Michael/517 W Third St, Cincinnati, OH	513-721-2384
Manarchy, Dennis/229 W Illinois, Chicago, IL	312-828-9117
Mandel, Avis/40 E Cedar, Chicago, IL	312-642-4776

Mankus, Gary/1520 N LaSalle, Chicago, IL	312-787-5438
Mann, Milton & Joan/PO Box 413, Evanston, IL	312-777-5656
Manning, Russell/905 Park Ave, Minneapolis, MN	612-338-7761
Mar, Jan/111 Westgate, Oak Park, IL	312-524-1898
Marcus, Joel/23309 Commerce Park Rd, Cleveland, OH	216-831-0688
Marienthal, Michael/1832 S Halsted, Chicago, IL	312-226-5505
Marovitz, Bob/3450 N Lake Shore Dr, Chicago, IL	312-975-1265
Marsalle/PO Box 300063, Minneapolis, MN	612-872-8717
Marshall, Don Photography/361 W Superior, Chicago, IL	312-944-0720
Marshall, Paul/117 N Jefferson St #304, Chicago, IL	312-559-1270
Marshall, Simeon/1043 W Randolph, Chicago, IL	312-243-9500
Martin, Barbara E/46 Washington Terrace, St Louis, MO	314-361-0838
Marvy, Jim/41 Twelfth Ave N, Minneapolis, MN	612-935-0307
Masheris, R Assoc Inc/1338 Hazel Ave, Deerfield, IL	312-945-2055
Mathews, Bruce/16520 Ellison Way, Independence, MO	816-373-2920
Matlow, Linda/300 N State St #3926, Chicago, IL	312-321-9071
Matusik, Jim/3714 N Racine, Chicago, IL	312-327-5615
Mauney, Michael/1405 Judson Ave, Evanston, IL	312-869-7720
May, Ron/PO Box 8359, Ft Wayne, IN	219-483-7872
McCabe, Mark/1301 E 12th St, Kansas City, MO	816-474-6491
McCall Photo/900 N Franklin, Chicago, IL	312-951-5525
McCann, Larry/666 W Hubbard, Chicago, IL	312-942-1924
McCann, Michael/27 N 4th St, Minneapolis, MN	612-333-2115
McCay, Larry Inc/PO Box 927, Mishawaka, IN	219-259-1414
McClelan, Thompson/206 S First St, Champaign, IL	217-356-2767
McConnell & McConnell/1313 W Randolph #317, Chicago, IL	312-738-1444
McDonald, Neal/1515 W Cornelia, Chicago, IL	312-525-5401
McDonough, Ted/RR 3 PO Box W-30, Coon Rapids, IA	712-684-5449
McDunn, James/PO Box 8053, Rolling Meadows, IL	312-934-4268
McGinnis, Renee/907 E Fairchild, Iowa City, IA	319-395-9060
McGleam, Patrick/5422 N Paulina, Chicago, IL	312-989-0248
McHale Studios Inc/2349 Victory Pkwy, Cincinnati, OH	513-961-1454
McInturff, Steve/1795 E Kings Creek, Urbana, OH	513-789-3590
McKinley, William/847 W Jackson, Chicago, IL	312-666-5400
McLuckie Graphic Photo/121 S Wheeling, Wheeling, IL	312-639-8909
McMahon, Franklin/1319 Chestnut, Wilmette, IL	312-256-5528
McNichol, Greg/1638 W Greenleaf Ave, Chicago, IL	312-973-1032
Mead, Robert/711 Hillgrove Ave, La Grange, IL	312-354-8300
Meier, Lori/9100 Guthrie, St Louis, MO	314-428-0120
Meineke, David/703 E Golf Rd, Schaumburg, IL	312-884-6006
Melkus, Larry/679-E Mandoline, Madison Hts, MI	313-589-0066
Meoli, Rick/710 N Tucker #306, St Louis, MO	314-231-6038
Merrill, Frank/2939 West Touhy, Chicago, IL	312-764-1672
Merrithew, Jim/PO Box 1510, Almonte K0A 1A0, ON	613-729-3862
Meyer, Fred/415 N Dearborn, Chicago, IL	312-527-4873
Meyer, Gordon/216 W Ohio, Chicago, IL	312-642-9303
Meyer, Jim/7727 Frontier Trail, Chanhassen, MN	612-934-2908
Meyer, Robert/208 W Kinzie St, Chicago, IL	312-467-1430
Michael, William/225 W Hubbard, Chicago, IL	312-644-6137
Micus Photo/2777 S Finley, Downers Grove, IL	312-627-8181
Mignard Associates/1950-R South Glenstone, Springfield, MO	417-881-7422
Mihalevich, Mike/9235 Somerset Dr, Overland Park, KS	913-642-6466
Miller Photo/7237 W Devon, Chicago, IL	312-631-1255
Miller, Buck/PO Box 33, Milwaukee, WI	414-258-9473
Miller, Daniel D/1551 North Orleans, Chicago, IL	312-944-7192
Miller, Frank/6016 Blue Circle Dr, Minnetonka, MN	612-935-8888
Miller, Pat/1645 Ridgewood Ave, White Bear Lake, MN	612-426-9043
Miller, Spider/833 North Orleans, Chicago, IL	312-944-2880
Miller, William F/618 W Jackson, Chicago, IL	312-648-1818
Milne, Brian/78 Rusholme Rd, Toronto M6J 3H6, ON	416-532-6108
Mitchell, John Sr/2617 Greenleaf, Elk Grove, IL	312-956-8230
Mitchell, Rick/652 W Grand, Chicago, IL	312-829-1700
Mitzit, Bruce/331 S Peoria/Box 6638, Chicago, IL	312-733-5697
Mohlenkamp, Steve/632 West Pleasant, Freeport, IL	815-235-1918
Moore, Bob c/o Mofoto Graphics/1615 S 9th St, St Louis, MO	314-231-1430
Moore, Dan/1029 N Wichita #9, Wichita, KS	316-264-4168
Morrill, Dan/1811 N Sedgewick, Chicago, IL	312-787-5095
Morris, Merle Photography/614 Fifth Ave S, Minneapolis, MN	612-338-7829
Morrison, Guy/32049 Milton Ave, Madison Heights, MI	313-588-6544
Morton White & Cunningham/6665-H Huntley Rd	
Columbus, OH	614-885-8687
Moshman Photo/401 W Superior, Chicago, IL	312-377-3022

Moss, Jean/222 W Ontario, Chicago, IL	312-787-0260
Mottel, Ray/760 Burr Oak Rd, Westmont, IL	312-323-3616
Moustakas, Daniel/1255 Rankin, Troy, MI	313-589-0100
Moy, Clinton Photography/4728 N Spaulding, Chicago, IL	312-539-4297
Moy, Willie/364 W Erie, Chicago, IL	312-943-1863
Mueller, Linda/1709 Washington 7th Fl, St Louis, MO	314-231-3522
Musich, Jack/325 W Huron, Chicago, IL	312-644-5000
Mutrux, John L/5217 England, Shawnee Missn, KS	913-722-4343

N

Nagler, Monte/38881 Lancaster Dr, Farmington Hills, MI	313-661-0826
Nano, Ed/3413 Rocky River Rd, Cleveland, OH	216-941-3373
Nathanson, Neal/7531 Cromwell, St Louis, MO	314-727-7244
Nawrocki, William S/PO Box 43-007, Chicago, IL	312-445-8920
Neal, Les/319 N Albany, Chicago, IL	312-722-0116
Nelson, Tom/400 First Ave N, Minneapolis, MN	612-339-3579
Neumann, Robert/101 S Mason St, Saginaw, MI	517-790-9000
Nexus Productions/10-A Ashdale Ave, Toronto M4L 2Y7, ON	416-463-5078
Nible, R C/905 Broadway 4th Fl, Kansas City, MO	816-221-6110
Niedorf, Steve/700 N Washington, Minneapolis, MN	612-332-7124
Norris, James/2301 N Lowell, Chicago, IL	312-342-1050
Northlight Studio/1539 E 22nd St, Cleveland, OH	216-621-3111
Novak, Ken/2483 N Bartlett Ave, Milwaukee, WI	414-962-6953
Novak, Sam/230 W Huron, Chicago, IL	312-664-6733
Nozicka, Steve/314 W Institute Pl, Chicago, IL	312-787-8925
Nugent Wenckus Inc/110 Northwest Hwy, Des Plaines, IL	312-694-4151

O

O'Barski, Don/17239 Parkside, S Holland, IL	312-596-0606
O'Rourke, John/PO Box 52, Wilmington, OH	513-382-3782
Oakes, Kenneth Ltd/902 Yale Ln, Highland Park, IL	312-432-4809
Obata Design/1610 Menard, St Louis, MO	314-241-1710
Oberle, Frank/309 N Riverside Dr, St Charles, MO	314-946-0554
Officer, Hollis/819 Broadway 6th Fl, Kansas City, MO	816-474-5501
Okita, Clyde/865 N Sangamon 5th Fl, Chicago, IL	312-829-8283
Olausen, Judy/213 1/2 N Washington Ave, Minneapolis, MN	612-332-5009
Olsson, Russ/215 W Illinois, Chicago, IL	312-329-9358
Ontiveros, Don/5516 N Kenmore Ave, Chicago, IL	312-878-9009
Oscar & Assoc/63 E Adams, Chicago, IL	312-922-0056
OXENDORF, ERIC/1442 N FRANKLIN PL BOX 92337, MILWAUKEE, WI (P 300)	**414-273-0654**

P

Pacific Studio/632 Krenz Ave, Cary, IL	312-639-5654
Palmisano, Vito/1147 W Ohio St, Chicago, IL	312-565-0524
Panama, David/1100 N Dearborn, Chicago, IL	312-642-7095
Panich, Wil/20 W Hubbard, Chicago, IL	312-828-0742
Parker, Norman/710 N 2nd St #300N, St Louis, MO	314-621-8100
Parks, Jim/210 W Chicago, Chicago, IL	312-321-1193
Passman, Roger/719 W Willow, Chicago, IL	312-664-4085
Paszkowski, Rick/1637 W Estes, Chicago, IL	312-761-3018
Paternite, David/86 Elinor Ave, Akron, OH	216-784-9138
Paulson, Bill/5358 Golla Rd, Stevens Point, WI	715-341-6100
Payne, John/430 W Erie, Chicago, IL	312-280-8414
Payne, Scott/611 Lunt Unit B, Schaumburg, IL	312-980-3337
Pazovski, Kazik/2340 Laredo Ave, Cincinnati, OH	513-281-0030
Perkins, Ray/222 S Morgan St, Chicago, IL	312-421-3438
Perman, Craig/1645 Hennepin #311, Minneapolis, MN	612-338-7727
Perno, Jack/1147 W Ohio, Chicago, IL	312-829-5292
Perraud, Gene/535 N Michigan #2601, Chicago, IL	312-564-5278
Perspective Inc/2322 Pennsylvania St, Fort Wayne, IN	219-424-8136
Peterson, Garrick/216 W Ohio St, Chicago, IL	312-266-8986
Petroff, Tom/19 W Hubbard, Chicago, IL	312-836-0411
Phelps Photo/1057 W Dakin, Chicago, IL	312-248-2536
Phillips, David R/1230 W Washington Blvd, Chicago, IL	312-733-3277
Photo Concepts Inc/23042 Commerce Dr #2001, Farmington Hills, MI	313-477-4301
Photo Design/815 Main St, Cincinnati, OH	513-421-5588
Photo Group/1946-D Lehigh, Glenview, IL	312-998-4670
Photo Ideas Inc/804 W Washington Blvd, Chicago, IL	312-666-3100
Photo Images/430 W Erie St, Chicago, IL	312-664-5955
The Photo Place/4739 Butterfield, Hillside, IL	312-544-1222
Photographic Arts/624 W Adams, Chicago, IL	312-876-0818
Photographic Illustrators/405 1/2 E Main, Muncie, IN	317-288-1454
The Picture Place/689 Craig Rd, St Louis, MO	314-872-7506

Pierce, Rod/236 Portland Ave, Minneapolis, MN	612-332-2670
Pintozzi, Peter/42 E Chicago, Chicago, IL	312-266-7775
Pitt, Tom/1201 W Webster, Chicago, IL	312-281-5662
Pohlman Studios Inc/527 N 27th St, Milwaukee, WI	414-342-6363
Pokempner, Marc/1453 W Addison, Chicago, IL	312-525-4567
Polaski, James/9 W Hubbard, Chicago, IL	312-644-3686
Poli, Frank/158 W Huron, Chicago, IL	312-944-3924
Polin, Jack Photography/7306 Crawford, Lincolnwood, IL	312-676-4312
Pomerantz, Ron/325 W Huron #406, Chicago, IL	312-787-6407
Poon On Wong, Peter/516 First Ave #305, Minneapolis, MN	612-340-0798
Poplis, Paul/3599 Refugee Rd Bldg B, Columbus, OH	614-231-2942
Portnoy, Lewis/5 Carole Lane, St Louis, MO	314-567-5700
Powell, Jim/326 W Kalamazoo, Kalamazoo, MI	616-381-2302
Preszkop, Harry/332 S Cuyler, Oak Park, IL	312-524-9743
Price, Paul/8138 W Nine Mile Rd, Oak Park, MI	313-546-1759
Proctor & Proctor Photo/18126 Center Ave, Homewood, IL	312-789-6849
Progressive Visuals/2550 Northridge Ave, Arlington Hgts, IL	312-949-0886
Puffer, David/213 W Institute, Chicago, IL	312-266-7540
Puza, Greg/PO Box 1986, Milwaukee, WI	414-444-9882
Pyrzynski, Larry/691 N Sangamon, Chicago, IL	312-472-6550

QR

Quinn, James/518 S Euclid, Oak Park, IL	312-383-0654
Quist, Bruce/1370 N Milwaukee, Chicago, IL	312-252-3921
Rack, Ron/215 E Ninth St, Cincinnati, OH	513-421-6267
Raczynski, Walter/117 North Jefferson, Chicago, IL	312-454-0680
Radencich, Michael/1007 McGee, Kansas City, MO	816-421-5076
Radlund & Associates/4704 Pflaum Rd, Madison, WI	608-222-8177
Randall, Bob/325 W Huron, Chicago, IL	312-664-7008
Raynor, Dorka/1063 Ash St, Winnetka, IL	312-446-1187
Reames-Hanusin Studio/3306 Commercial Ave Northbrook, IL	312-564-2706
Reed, Dick/1330 Coolidge, Troy, MI	313-280-0090
Reeve, Catherine/822 Madison St, Evanston, IL	312-864-8298
Reffner, Wayne/4178 Dayton-Xenia Rd, Dayton, OH	513-429-2760
Reid, Ken/800 W Huron #3S, Chicago, IL	312-733-2121
Reiss, Ray/2144 N Leavitt, Chicago, IL	312-384-3245
Rekemeyer, Russ/Rt 3, Dewitt, IA	319-659-3789
Remington, George/1455 W 29th St, Cleveland, OH	216-241-1440
Renerts, Peter Studio/633 Huron Rd, Cleveland, OH	216-781-2440
RENKEN, ROGER/PO BOX 11010, ST. LOUIS, MO (P 301)	**314-394-5055**
Reuben, Martin/1231 Superior Ave, Cleveland, OH	216-781-8644
Ricco, Ron/207 E Buffalo #619, Milwaukee, WI	414-271-4360
Rich, Larry/29731 Everett, Southfield, MI	313-557-7676
Ritter, Gene/2440 W 14th St, Cleveland, OH	216-781-9461
Robert, Francois/740 N Wells, Chicago, IL	312-787-0777
Robinson, David/1147 W Ohio, Chicago, IL	312-942-1650
Roessler, Ryan/401 W Superior, Chicago, IL	312-951-8702
Rogers, Bill Arthur/846 Wesley, Oak Park, IL	312-848-3900
Rogowski, Tom/214 E 8th St, Cincinnati, OH	513-621-3826
Rohman, Jim/2254 Marengo, Toledo, OH	419-865-0234
Rosmis, Bruce/118 W Ohio, Chicago, IL	312-787-9046
Ross, Allan/3221 S Morgan, Chicago, IL	312-376-1011
Rostron, Philip/489 Wellington St W, Toronto, ON	416-596-6587
Rothrock, Douglas/215 W Ohio, Chicago, IL	312-951-9045
Rottinger, Ed/5409 N Avers, Chicago, IL	312-583-2917
Rowley, Joe/368 W Huron, Chicago, IL	312-266-7620
Rozzo, Richard/1707-B White Dr, Lee's Summit, MO	816-524-7296
Rubin, Laurie/719 W Willow St, Chicago, IL	312-266-1131
Rush, Michael/415 Delaware, Kansas City, MO	816-471-1200
Russetti, Andy/1260 Carnegie St, Cleveland, OH	216-687-1788
Rustin, Barry/934 Glenwood Rd, Glenview, IL	312-724-7600
Rutt, Don/324 Munson St, Traverse City, MI	616-946-2727
Ryan, Gary/23245 Woodward, Ferndale, MI	313-861-8199

S

S T Studio/325 W Huron St #711, Chicago, IL	312-943-2565
Sacco Photography Ltd/833 North Orleans St, Chicago, IL	312-943-5757
Sacks, Andrew/20727 Scio Church Rd, Chelsea, MI	313-475-2310
Sacks, Ed/Box 7237, Chicago, IL	312-871-4700
Sadin-Schnair Photo/820 N Franklin, Chicago, IL	312-944-1434
Sala, Don/950 W Willow, Chicago, IL	312-751-2858
Salter, Tom/685 Pallister, Detroit, MI	313-874-1155
Sanders, Kathy/368 W Huron, Chicago, IL	312-943-2627

PHOTOGRAPHERS CONT'D.

Please send us your additions and updates.

PHOTOGRAPHERS

Sanderson, Glenn/2936 Gross St, Green Bay, WI	414-336-6500
Sandoz Studios/415 Huron #3, Chicago, IL	312-440-0004
Sarnacki, Michael/18101 Oakwood Blvd, Dearborn, MI	313-548-1149
Sauer, Neil W/1554 S 7th St, St Louis, MO	314-241-9300
Schaefer, Ginzy/4336 Genesse, Kansas City, MO	816-753-4068
Schanuel, Anthony/10901 Oasis Dr, St Louis, MO	314-849-3495
Schaugnessy, Abe/32 Martin Ln, Elk Grove Village, IL	312-437-8850
Schewe, Jeff/624 West Willow, Chicago, IL	312-951-6334
Schnaible, Gerry/1888 Jamestown Cir, Hoffman Estates, IL	312-490-1191
Schrempp, Erich/932 W Washington Blvd, Chicago, IL	312-942-0045
SCHRIDDE, CHARLES/600 AJAX DR, MADISON HTS, MI	
(P 302)	**313-589-0111**
Schroeder, Loranelle/400 N First Ave 6th Fl, Minneapolis, MN	612-339-3191
Schube-Soucek/1735 Carmen Dr, Elk Grove Village, IL	312-439-0640
Schuemann, Bill/1591 S Belvoir Blvd, South Euclid, OH	216-382-4409
Schuessler, Dave/40 E Delaware, Chicago, IL	312-787-6868
Schuette, Bob/1221 Sixth Ave, Grafton, WI	414-377-2298
Schulman, Bruce/1102 W Columbia, Chicago, IL	312-338-0619
Schulman, Lee/669 College Ave Box 09506, Columbus, OH	614-235-5307
Schultz, Tim/2000 N Clifton, Chicago, IL	312-943-3318
Schwartz, Linda/72 E Oak #3E, Chicago, IL	312-266-7868
Scott, Denis/216 W Ohio St, Chicago, IL	312-467-5663
Secreto, Jim/2626 Industrial Row, Troy, MI	313-280-0640
Seed, Brian/213 W Institute Pl #503, Chicago, IL	312-787-7880
Seed, Suzanne/175 E Delaware, Chicago, IL	312-266-0621
Segal, Mark/230 N Michigan Ave, Chicago, IL	312-236-8545
Segielski, Tony/1886 Thunderbird, Troy, MI	313-362-3111
Semeniuk, Robert/78 Rusholme Rd, Toronto M6J 3H6, ON	416-532-6108
SERETA, GREG/2108 PAYNE AVE #400, CLEVELAND, OH	
(P 303)	**216-861-7227**
Severson, Kent/529 S 7th St #637, Minneapolis, MN	612-375-1870
Seymour, Ronald/314 W Superior, Chicago, IL	312-642-4030
Shafer, Ronald/4428 N Malden, Chicago, IL	312-878-1346
Shaffer, Mac/526 E Dunedin Rd, Columbus, OH	614-268-2249
Shambroom, Paul/529 S 7th St #537, Minneapolis, MN	612-340-9179
Shanoor Photo/116 W Illinois, Chicago, IL	312-266-1358
Shapiro, Terry/1147 W Ohio St, Chicago, IL	312-421-5631
Sharp, Joe/Owens Corning Fiberglass Tower, Toledo, OH	419-248-8041
Shaughnessy & MacDonald/32 Martin Ln, Elk Grove Village, IL	312-437-8850
Shay, Arthur/618 Indian Hill Rd, Deerfield, IL	312-945-4636
Shelli, Bob/PO Box 2062, St Louis, MO	314-772-8540
Sheppard, Richard/421 N Main St, Mt Prospect, IL	312-259-4375
Shigeta-Wright Assoc/1546 N Orleans St, Chicago, IL	312-642-8715
Shirmer, Bob/11 W Illinois St, Chicago, IL	312-321-1151
Shoots, Jim Weiner/230 E Ohio #402, Chicago, IL	312-337-0220
Shotwell, Chuck/2111 N Clifton, Chicago, IL	312-929-0168
Shoulders, Terry/676 N LaSalle, Chicago, IL	312-642-6622
Siede/Preis Photo/1526 N Halsted, Chicago, IL	312-787-2725
Sieracki, John/676 N LaSalle, Chicago, IL	312-664-7824
Sigman, Gary/2941 N Racine, Chicago, IL	312-871-8756
Silber, Gary Craig/300 Main St, Racine, WI	414-637-5097
Silker, Glenn/5249 W 73rd St #A, Edina, MN	612-835-1811
Sills, Anne Margaret/411 N LaSalle St, Chicago, IL	312-670-3660
Sills, Casey/411 N Lasalle, Chicago, IL	312-670-3660
Silver, Jared N/660 La Salle Pl, Chicago, IL	312-433-3866
Simmons Photography Inc/326 Chicago Ave, Chicago, IL	312-944-0326
Sindelar, Dan/2517 Grove Springs Ct, St Louis, MO	314-846-4775
Sinkler, Paul/510 N First Ave #307, Minneapolis, MN	612-343-0325
Skalak, Carl/47-46 Grayton Rd, Cleveland, OH	216-676-6508
Skrebneski, Victor/1350 N LaSalle St, Chicago, IL	312-944-1339
Skritski, Steve/2117 Gratiot, Detroit, MI	313-962-0877
Skutas, Joe/17 N Elizabeth, Chicago, IL	312-733-1266
Sladcik, William/215 W Illinois, Chicago, IL	312-644-7108
Slaughter, Michael/2051 Osage Ln, Hanover Park, IL	312-289-6662
Smetzer, Donald/2534 N Burling St, Chicago, IL	312-327-1716
Smith, Bill/600 N McClurgh Ct #802, Chicago, IL	312-787-4686
Smith, Doug Photo/2911 Sutton, St Louis, MO	314-645-1359
Smith, Mike/521 Cottonwood Circle, Bolingbrook, IL	312-759-0262
Smith, R Hamilton/1021 W Montana Ave, St Paul, MN	612-488-9068
Smith, Richard/PO Box 455, Round Lake, IL	312-546-0977
Smith, Robert/496 W Wrightwood Ave, Elmhurst, IL	312-941-7755
Snook, Allen/908 N Ernst Ct, Chicago, IL	312-943-7134
Snook, J J/118 W Ohio, Chicago, IL	312-664-0371
Snow, Andy/346 Shadywood Dr, Dayton, OH	513-836-8566
Snyder, John/368 W Huron, Chicago, IL	312-440-1053
Solis Studio/4161 S Archer, Chicago, IL	312-890-0555
Soluri, Tony/1147 W Ohio, Chicago, IL	312-243-6580
Sorokowski, Rick/1051 N Halsted, Chicago, IL	312-280-1256
Spahr, Dick/1133 E 61st St, Indianapolis, IN	317-255-2400
Spectra Studios/213 W Institute #512, Chicago, IL	312-787-0667
Spingola, Laurel/6225 N Forest Glen, Chicago, IL	312-883-0020
Spitz, Robert/317 Howard, Evanston, IL	312-869-4992
Sroka, Michael/5722 W Fillmore Dr, West Allis, WI	414-543-0512
Stansfield, Stan/215 W Ohio, Chicago, IL	312-337-3245
Starkey, John/2250 Rome Dr, Indianapolis, IN	317-299-5758
Starmark Photo/706 N Dearborn, Chicago, IL	312-922-3388
Stealey, Jonathan/PO Box 611, Findlay, OH	419-423-1149
Steele, Charles/531 S Plymouth Ct #22, Chicago, IL	312-922-0201
Stegbauer, Jim/421 Transit, Roseville, MN	612-333-1982
Stein, Frederic/409 W Huron St, Chicago, IL	312-642-7171
Steinberg, Mike/633 Huron Rd, Cleveland, OH	216-589-9953
Steinhart Photography/325 W Huron, Chicago, IL	312-944-0226
Stemo Photo/1880 Holste Rd, Northbrook, IL	312-498-4844
Stenberg, Pete Photography/225 W Hubbard, Chicago, IL	312-644-6137
Sterling, Joseph/2216 N Cleveland, Chicago, IL	312-348-4333
Stewart, Ron/314 E Downer Pl, Aurora, IL	312-897-4317
Stornello, Joe/4319 Campbell St, Kansas City, MO	816-756-0419
Straus, Jerry/247 E Ontario, Chicago, IL	312-787-2628
Strouss, Sarah/134 Upland Ave, Youngstown, OH	216-744-2774
Struse, Perry L Jr/232 Sixth St, West Des Moines, IA	515-279-9761
The Studio, Inc/730 N Franklin, Chicago, IL	312-337-1490
Stump Studio/3260 W Irving Park Rd, Chicago, IL	312-649-0084
Summers Studio/153 W Ohio, Chicago, IL	312-527-0908
Sundlof, John/401 W Superior, Chicago, IL	312-951-8701
Swan, Tom/2417 N Burling, Chicago, IL	312-871-8370
Swanson, Michael/215 W Ohio, Chicago, IL	312-337-3245
Sweeney, Kathi C/500 S Garth, Columbia, MO	314-442-3729

T

Taback, Sidney/415 Eastern Ave, Toronto M4M1B7, ON	416-463-5718
Taber, Gary/305 S Green St, Chicago, IL	312-726-0374
Taxel, Barney/4614 Prospect Ave, Cleveland, OH	216-431-2400
Taylor & Assoc/8601 Urbandale Rd, Des Moines, IA	515-276-0992
Taylor, Dale E/8505 Midcounty Ind Ctr, St Louis, MO	314-426-2655
Technigraph Studio/1212 Jarvis, Elk Grove Village, IL	312-437-3334
Teeter, Brian/6024 Blue Circle Dr, Minnetonka, MN	612-935-5666
Teschl, Josef/31 Brock Ave #203, Toronto, ON	416-532-3495
Teufen, Al/600 E Smith Rd, Medina, OH	216-723-3237
Thien, Alex/2754 N Prospect Ave, Milwaukee, WI	414-964-4349
Thoen, Greg/14940 Minnetonka Rd, Minnetonka, MN	612-938-2433
Thoman, Fred/6710 Madison Rd, Cincinnati, OH	513-561-4011
Thomas, Bill/Rt 4 Box 387, Nashville, IN	812-988-7865
Thomas, Tony/676 N Lasalle St 6th Fl, Chicago, IL	312-337-2274
Thompson, Dale/224 S Michigan Ave 14th Fl, Chicago, IL	312-347-2081
Thompson, Ken/225 W Huron, Chicago, IL	312-951-6356
Tillis, Harvey/501 N Wells, Chicago, IL	312-828-0731
Tolchin, Robert/2522 Fontana Dr, Glenview, IL	312-729-2522
Toro, Mark/778 S Wall St, Columbus, OH	614-460-4635
Tower Photo/4327 N Elston, Chicago, IL	312-478-8494
Townsend, Wesley/3825 Highland Ave, Downers Grove, IL	312-963-2403
TPS Studio/4016 S California, Chicago, IL	312-847-1221
Tracy, Janis/213 W Institute Pl, Chicago, IL	312-787-7166
Trantafil, Gary/3926 N Spaulding Ave, Chicago, IL	312-539-0150
Trujillo, Edward/345 N Canal St #1604, Chicago, IL	312-454-9798
Tucker, Bill/114 W Illinois, Chicago, IL	312-321-1570
Tunison, Richard/5511 E Lake Dr, Lisle, IL	312-944-1188
Tushas, Leo/111 N Fifth Ave #309, Minneapolis, MN	612-333-5774

U V

Uhlmann, Gina/1611 N Sheffield, Chicago, IL	312-642-6650
Umland, Steve/600 Washington Ave N, Minneapolis, MN	612-332-1590
UPITIS, ALVIS/620 MORGAN AVE S, MINNEAPOLIS, MN	
(P 304)	**612-374-9375**
Urba, Alexis/148 W Illinois, Chicago, IL	312-644-4466
Van Allen, John/U of Iowa Fndtn/Alumni Ctr, Iowa City, IA	319-453-6271
Van Marter, Robert/1209 Alstott Dr S, Howell, MI	517-546-1923

VANDER LENDE, CRAIG/214 EAST FULTON, GRAND RAPIDS, MI (P 284)	**616-458-4415**
Vander Veen, David/5151 N 35th St, Milwaukee, WI	414-527-0450
VanKirk Photography/1230 W Washington Blvd, Chicago, IL	312-226-4060
Vanmarter, Robert/1209 Alstott Dr S, Howell, MI	517-546-1923
Variakojis, Danguole/5743 S Campbell, Chicago, IL	312-776-4668
Vaughan, Jim/321 S Jefferson, Chicago, IL	312-663-0369
Vedros, Nick/215 W 19th St, Kansas City, MO	816-471-5488
Ventola, Giorgio/230 W Huron, Chicago, IL	312-951-0880
Vergos Studio/122 W Kinzie 3rd Fl, Chicago, IL	312-527-1769
Viernum, Bill/1629 Mandel Ave, Westchester, IL	312-562-4143
Villa, Armando/1872 N Clybourne, Chicago, IL	312-472-7003
Visual Data Systems Inc/5617 63rd Pl, Chicago, IL	312-585-3060
Vizanko Advertising Photo/11511 K-Tel Drive, Minnetonka, MN	612-933-1314
Vollan, Michael/222 W Huron, Chicago, IL	312-644-1792
Von Baich, Paul/78 Rusholme Rd, Toronto M6J 3H6, ON	416-532-6108
Von Photography/685 W Ohio, Chicago, IL	312-243-8578
Voyles, Dick & Assoc/2822 Breckenridge Ind Ctr, St Louis, MO	314-968-3851
Vuksanovich/401 W Superior St, Chicago, IL	312-664-7523

W

Wagenaar, David/1035 W Lake St, Chicago, IL	312-942-0943
Waite, Tim/717 S Sixth St, Milwaukee, WI	414-643-1500
Walker, Jessie Assoc/241 Fairview, Glencoe, IL	312-835-0522
Wans, Glen/325 W 40th, Kansas City, MO	816-931-8905
Ward, Les/17371 Beechwood, Birmingham, MI	313-548-4400
WARKENTHIEN, DAN/117 SOUTH MORGAN, CHICAGO, IL (P 287)	**312-666-6056**
Warren, Lennie/401 W Superior, Chicago, IL	312-664-5392
Watts, Dan/245 Plymouth, Grand Rapids, MI	616-451-4693
Watts, Ron/78 Rusholme Rd, Toronto M6J 3H6, ON	416-532-6108
Wedlake, James/750 Jossman Rd, Ortonville, MI	313-627-2711
Weidemann, Skot/1123 Sherman Ave, Madison, WI	608-251-7932
Weiner, Jim/540 N Lakeshore Dr, Chicago, IL	312-644-0054
Weinstein, John/3119 N Seminary Ave, Chicago, IL	312-327-8184
Weinstein, Michael/3 E Huron St, Chicago, IL	312-951-8683
Weinstein, Phillip/343 S Dearborn, Chicago, IL	312-922-1945
Weispfenning, Donna/815 W 53rd St, Minneapolis, MN	612-823-8405
Welzenbach, John/368 W Huron St, Chicago, IL	312-337-3611
Wengroff, Sam/2052 N Dayton, Chicago, IL	312-248-6623
West, Stu/430 First Ave #210, Minneapolis, MN	612-375-0404
WESTERMAN, CHARLIE/59 E CEDAR ST, CHICAGO, IL (P 278)	**312-440-9422**
Wheelock, Dan/1010 Currie Ave, Minneapolis, MN	612-333-5116
White, Christopher/169 MacKay St #3, Ottawa K1M 2B5, ON	613-741-3246
Whitehead, Jack/2117 Gratiot, Detroit, MI	313-962-0877
Whitford, T R/1709 Washington 7th Fl, St Louis, MO	314-231-3522
Whitman, Robert/529 S 7th St/Sexton Bldg, Minneapolis, MN	612-332-3200
Whitmer, Jim/125 Wakeman, Wheaton, IL	312-653-1344
Wicks, L Photography/1235 W Winnemac Ave, Chicago, IL	312-878-4925
Wigodsky, Steve/10326 Wright St, Omaha, NE	402-397-2697
WILDER, J DAVID/2300 PAYNE AVE, CLEVELAND, OH (P 305)	**216-771-7687**
Willett, Mike/221 W Walton, Chicago, IL	312-642-4282
Willette, Brady T/2720 W 43rd St, Minneapolis, MN	612-926-4261
Williams, Alfred G/5230 S Blackstone Ave #306, Chicago, IL	312-947-0991
Williams, Barry/2361 N High St, Columbus, OH	614-291-9774
Williams, Basil/4068 Tanglefoot Terrace, Bettendorf, IA	319-355-7142
Williamson, John/224 Palmerston Ave, Toronto M6J 2J4, ON	416-530-4511
Wilson, Dave & Assoc/1533 Seventh Ave, Moline, IL	309-762-1922
Wilson, Jack/2133 Bellvue, St Louis, MO	314-645-2211
Wilson, Tim/2330 N Sacramento, Chicago, IL	312-227-6914
Wimer, Scott K/555 W Adams #6E, Chicago, IL	312-372-7828
Wirthlin, Walter/6406 Morganford, St Louis, MO	314-351-7369
Witkin, L/11 E Hubbard, Chicago, IL	312-661-1099
Witte, Scott J/3025 W Highland Blvd, Milwaukee, WI	414-933-3223
Woburn/4715 N Ronald St, Harwood Heights, IL	312-867-5445
Woehrle, Mark/1709 Washington Ave, St Louis, MO	314-231-9949
Wojcik, Richard R/151 Victor Ave, Highland Park, MI	313-868-2200
Wolf, Bobbe/440 W Oakdale, Chicago, IL	312-472-9503
Wolf, Don/301 W 17th St, Kansas City, MO	816-421-0004
WOLFF, ED/11357 S SECOND ST, SCHOOLCRAFT, MI (P 306)	**616-679-4702**
Wooden, John/219 N 2nd St J#306, Minneapolis, MN	612-339-3032
Woodward, Greg/401 W Superior, Chicago, IL	312-337-5838
Worzala, Lyle/2954 W 57th St, Chicago, IL	312-434-7156
Wright, James/5740 S Kenwood #1, Chicago, IL	312-856-1838

YZ

Yamashiro, Paul Studio/125 W Hubbard St, Chicago, IL	312-321-1009
Yapp, Charles/932 W Washington, Chicago, IL	312-558-9338
Yates, Peter/515 Spring St, Ann Arbor, MI	313-995-0839
Yaworski, Don/10108 W 69th Terrace, Merriam, KS	913-384-2225
Yee, Henry/473 Cosburn Ave, Toronto M4J 2N6, ON	416-423-4883
Zamiar, Thomas/210 W Chicago, Chicago, IL	312-787-4976
ZANN, ARNOLD/502 N GROVE AVE, OAK PARK, IL (P 286)	**312-386-2864**
Zarlengo, Joseph/419 Melrose Ave, Boardman, OH	216-782-7797
Zena Photography/633 Huron Rd SE 5th Fl, Cleveland, OH	216-621-6366
Zimion/Marshall Studio/1043 W Randolph, Chicago, IL	312-243-9500
Zoom Photo/427 Queen St West, Toronto M5V 2A5, ON	416-593-0690
Zukas, R/311 N Desplaines #500, Chicago, IL	312-648-0100

SOUTHWEST

A

Abraham, Joe/11944 Hempstead Rd #C, Houston, TX	713-460-4948
Ad On/4404 Main St, Dallas, TX	214-823-9000
Aker, Joe/4710 Lillian, Houston, TX	713-862-6343
Alford, Jess/1800 Lear St #3, Dallas, TX	214-421-3107
Allen, Jim Photo/4410 Lovers Lane, Dallas, TX	214-368-0563
Anderson, Derek Studio/3959 Speedway Blvd E, Tucson, AZ	602-881-1205
Anderson, Randy/1606 Lewis Trail, Grand Prairie, TX	214-660-1071
Angle, Lee/1900 Montgomery, Fort Worth, TX	817-737-6469
Annerino, John/PO Box 1545, Prescott, AZ	602-445-4094
Ashe, Gil/Box 686, Bellaire, TX	713-668-8766
Ashley, Constance/2024 Farrington St, Dallas, TX	214-747-2501
Assid, Al/6311 N O'Connor #166, Irving, TX	214-869-7766
Associated Photo/2344 Irving Blvd, Dallas, TX	214-630-8730
Austin, David/2412 Fifth Ave, Fort Worth, TX	817-335-1881

B

Badger, Bobby/2707 Stemmons Frwy #160, Dallas, TX	214-634-0222
Bagshaw, Cradoc/603 High St NE, Albuquerque, NM	505-243-1096
Baird, Darryl/830 Exposition #215, Dallas, TX	214-826-3348
Baker, Bobbe C/1119 Ashburn, College Station, TX	409-696-7185
Baker, Jeff/2401 S Ervay #302, Dallas, TX	214-720-0178
Baker, Lane/7145 N 59th Ave, Glendale, AZ	602-937-4477
Baldwin/Watriss Assoc/1405 Branard St, Houston, TX	713-524-9199
Ballingham, Rodney/PO Box 35171, Dallas, TX	214-528-5434
Baraban, Joe/2426 Bartlett #2, Houston, TX	713-526-0317
BARKER, KENT/2039 FARRINGTON, DALLAS, TX (P 313)	**214-760-7470**
Bayanduryan, Rubik/PO Box 1791, Austin, TX	512-451-8960
Beebower Brothers/9995 Monroe #209, Dallas, TX	214-358-1219
Bender, Robert/1345 Chemical, Dallas, TX	214-631-4538
Benjamin, Barry/8008 Menaul Blvd NE, Albuquerque, NM	505-293-4040
Bennett, Sue/PO Box 1574, Flagstaff, AZ	602-774-2544
Bennett, Tony R/122 Parkhouse, Dallas, TX	214-747-0107
Benoist, John/PO Box 20825, Dallas, TX	214-692-8813
Berman, Bruce/140 N Stevens #301, El Paso, TX	915-544-0352
Bernhard, John/3700 Watonga #2210, Houston, TX	713-893-3555
Bernstein, Mal/ Bill Irwin/8001 E Second Ave, Mesa, AZ	602-986-5685
Berrett, Patrick L/2425-C NE Monroe, Albuquerque, NM	505-881-0935
Berry, George S Photography/Rt 2 Box 325B, San Marcos, TX	512-396-4805
Bictures/2410 Farrington, Dallas, TX	214-637-2747
Bishop, Gary/PO Box 12394, Dallas, TX	214-368-0889
Blackwell, J Michael/2032 Farrington, Dallas, TX	214-760-8742
Bland, Ron/201 NW 2nd St #108, Grand Prairie, TX	214-262-2650
Blockley, Gary/2121 Regency Dr, Irving, TX	214-438-4114
Blue, Janice/1708 Rosewood, Houston, TX	713-522-6899
Bondy, Roger/PO Box 3, Oklahoma City, OK	405-424-5224
Booth, Greg/1322 Round Table, Dallas, TX	214-688-1855
Bouche, Len/PO Box 5188, Sante Fe, NM	505-471-2044
Boulanger, Gary/2330 E Monterosa, Phoenix, AZ	602-264-1151
Bowman, Matt/3613 Parry, Dallas, TX	214-824-2142
Braden, Bruce E/4235 Rawlins #2, Dallas, TX	214-528-8249
Bradley, Jim/6411 Hillcrest, Dallas, TX	214-526-8559
Bradshaw, Reagan/PO Box 12457, Austin, TX	512-458-6101
Brady, Steve/5250 Gulfton #2G, Houston, TX	713-660-6663

Please send us your additions and updates.

Branner, Phillip/2700 Commerce St, Dallas, TX	214-939-0550
Brousseau, J/2408 Farrington, Dallas, TX	214-638-1248
Bryant, Ray/111-B Explorer, Duncanville, TX	214-691-9335
Buffington, David/2772 El Tivoli, Dallas, TX	214-943-4721
Bumpass, R O/2404 Farrington, Dallas, TX	214-630-0180
Bunch, Fred C/1809 Binz, Houston, TX	713-529-6211
Burger, Steven/544 E Dunlap Ave, Phoenix, AZ	602-997-4625
Burkes, Marsha/905 Iwo St, Alvin, TX	713-792-4266
Burkey, J W/2739 Irving Blvd, Dallas, TX	214-630-1369

C

Cabluck, Jerry/Box 9601, Fort Worth, TX	817-336-1431
CALDWELL, JIM/2422 QUENBY, HOUSTON, TX (P 309)	**713-527-9121**
Campbell, Doug/5617 Matalee, Dallas, TX	214-823-9151
Cannedy, Carl/2408 Farrington, Dallas, TX	214-638-1247
Captured Image Photography/5131 E Lancaster Fort Worth, TX	817-457-2302
Carr, Fred/8303 Westglen Dr, Houston, TX	713-266-2872
Case, Bob/126 E Texas St, Grapevine, TX	817-481-4854
Cathey Graphics Group/8585 Stemmons Frwy, Dallas, TX	214-638-0731
Chavanell, Joe/PO Box 32383, San Antonio, TX	512-377-1552
Chenn, Steve/6301 Ashcroft, Houston, TX	713-271-0631
Chisholm, Rich & Assoc/3233 Marquart, Houston, TX	713-623-8790
Clair, Andre/11415 Chatten Way, Houston, TX	713-465-5507
Clark, H Dean/18405 FM 149, Houston, TX	713-469-7021
Claussen, Peter/6901-C Mullins, Houston, TX	713-661-7498
Clintsman, Dick/3001 Quebec #102, Dallas, TX	214-630-1531
Cobb, Lynn/3505 Turtle Creek #109, Dallas, TX	214-528-6694
Cole, Alan Michael/Route A Box 197, Flippin, AR	501-425-9107
Colombo, Michel/2707 Stemmons Frwy #160, Dallas, TX	214-630-5317
Connolly, Danny F/PO Box 1290, Houston, TX	713-862-8146
Cook, Robert Ames/2608 Irving Blvd, Dallas, TX	214-634-7196
Cotter, Austin/1350 Manufacturing #211, Dallas, TX	214-742-3633
Countryman, Mike/1609 Grantland Circle, Fort Worth, TX	817-496-6348
Cowlin, James/PO Box 34205, Phoenix, AZ	602-264-9689
Craft, Bill/2008 Laws St #3A, Dallas, TX	214-748-1470
Craig, George/314 E 13th St, Houston, TX	713-862-6008
Crane, Christopher/5455 Dashwood #300, Bellaire, TX	713-661-1098
Creighton, Jim/5933 Bellaire #117, Houston, TX	713-669-1119
Crittendon, James/5914 Lake Crest, Garland, TX	214-226-2196
Cruff, Kevin/2318 E Roosevelt, Phoenix, AZ	602-267-8845
Crump, Bill/1357 Chemical, Dallas, TX	214-630-7745
Cunningham, Richard/6105 Belmont, Houston, TX	713-665-6833

D

David, Jerry/3314 Silver Maple Court, Garland, TX	214-495-9600
Davis, David/749 E Lola Dr, Phoenix, AZ	602-992-9770
Davis, Mark/8718 Boundbrook Ave, Dallas, TX	214-348-7679
Dawson, Greg/2211 Beall St, Houston, TX	713-862-8301
Dean, Don/5925 Maple #106/Box 36365, Dallas, TX	214-939-0005
Debenport, Robb/2412 Converse, Dallas, TX	214-631-7606
Denman, Merv/514 E Pipeline, Hurst, TX	817-268-2400
Dickman, Jay/11443 W Ricks Circle, Dallas, TX	214-696-9211
Doering, Douglas/2823 W Davis St, Dallas, TX	214-330-0304
Douglas, King Studio/1319 Conant St, Dallas, TX	214-630-4700
Drews, Buzzy/1555 W Mockingbird #202, Dallas, TX	214-351-9968
DuBose, Bill/5538 Dyer, Dallas, TX	214-630-0086
Duffield, Florine/4101 Commerce #4, Dallas, TX	214-823-7248
Duhon, Mike/4303 Jefferson, Houston, TX	713-921-1292
Duran, Mark/66 East Vernon, Phoenix, AZ	602-279-1141
Dyer, John/211 Richmond, San Antonio, TX	512-223-1891
Dykinga, Jack/3808 Calle Barcelona, Tucson, AZ	602-326-6094

E

Echo Image/1350 Manufacturing #206, Dallas, TX	214-742-1014
Edens, Swain/104 Heiman, San Antonio, TX	512-226-2210
Edwards, Bill/3820 Brown, Dallas, TX	214-521-8630
Eglin, Tom/3950 W Mais St, Tucson, AZ	602-748-1299
Eilers, Rick/4030 Swiss, Dallas, TX	214-823-2103
Endy, Mike/3800 Commerce, Dallas, TX	214-826-1361
ENRIQUEZ, ARTURO & VALLARIE/1109 ARIZONA AVE, EL PASO, TX (P 316)	**915-533-9688**
Evenson, Martin/5512 Dyer St, Dallas, TX	214-369-0798

F

Fantich, Barry/PO Box 70103, Houston, TX	713-862-6502
Faustino/PO Box 771234, Houston, TX	713-864-8454
Findysz, Mary/5740 E 22nd St, Tucson, AZ	602-745-8069
Fittipaldi, Mary Ann/3775 W Fourth St, Fort Worth, TX	817-735-9010
Fontenot, Dallas/6002 Burning Tree Dr, Houston, TX	713-988-2183
Forsyth, Mimi/PO Box 992, Santa Fe, NM	505-982-8891
Frady, Connie/2808 Fifth Ave, Fort Worth, TX	817-927-7589
Freeman, Charlie/3333-A Elm St, Dallas, TX	214-742-1446
Fry, Kristen Pearce/5416 Wateka, Dallas, TX	214-350-9565
Fuller, Timothy Woodbridge/135 1/2 S Sixth Ave, Tucson, AZ	602-622-3900

G

Gaber, Brad/4946 Glen Meadow, Houston, TX	713-723-0030
Galloway, Jim/2201 N Lamar, Dallas, TX	214-954-0355
Gary & Clark Photographic Studio/2702 Main, Dallas, TX	214-939-9070
Gatz, Larry/5250 Gulfton #3B, Houston, TX	713-666-5203
Gayle, Rick/2318 E Roosevelt, Phoenix, AZ	602-267-8845
Geffs, Dale/15715 Amapola, Houston, TX	713-933-3876
Gendreau, Raymond/2039 Farrington, Dallas, TX	214-760-1999
GERCZYNSKI, TOM/2211 N 7TH AVE, PHOENIX, AZ (P 317)	**602-252-9229**
Gilbert, Bruce/12335 Braesridge, Houston, TX	713-723-1486
Giles-Cardellino Inc/315 9th St #2, San Antonio, TX	512-224-9606
Gilmore, Dwight/2437 Hillview, Fort Worth, TX	817-536-4825
Gilstrap, L C/132 Booth Calloway, Hurst, TX	817-284-7701
Glentzer, Don Photography/3814 S Shepherd Dr, Houston, TX	713-529-9686
Gomel, Bob/5755 Bonhomme Rd #408, Houston, TX	713-977-6390
Gonzalez, Peter/PO Box 2775, Austin, TX	512-444-9737
Goodman, Robert/2025 Levee, Dallas, TX	214-653-1120
GRAHAM, BOYCE/2707 STEMMONS FRWY #160, DALLAS, TX (P 318)	**214-631-4019**
Grass, Jon/1345 Chemical St, Dallas, TX	214-634-1455
Green, Mark/2406 Taft St, Houston, TX	713-523-6146
Greene, Perry/170 Leslie, Dallas, TX	214-741-4383
Grider, James/732 Schilder, Fort Worth, TX	817-732-7472
Grossman, John/1752 Branard St #B, Houston, TX	713-523-2316
Guerrero, Charles/2207 Comal St, Austin, TX	512-477-6642

H

Hagler, Skeeter/PO Box 628, Red Oak, TX	214-576-5620
Hale, Butch Photography/1319 Conant, Dallas, TX	214-637-3987
Halpern, David/7420 E 70th St, Tulsa, OK	918-252-4973
Hamburger, Jay/1817 State St, Houston, TX	713-869-0869
HAMILTON, JEFFREY/6719 QUARTZITE CANYON PL, TUCSON, AZ (P 319)	**602-299-3624**
Handel, Doug/3016 Selma, Dallas, TX	214-241-1549
Harris, M D/2521 Pepperwood Pl #108, Dallas, TX	214-241-2800
Hart, Michael/7320 Ashcroft #105, Houston, TX	713-271-8250
Hartman, Gary/911 South St Marys St, San Antonio, TX	512-225-2404
Haskins, Ben/2712 Live Oak, Dallas, TX	214-827-8440
Hatcok, Tom/113 W 12th St, Deer Park, TX	713-479-2603
Hawks, Bob/1345 E 15th St, Tulsa, OK	918-584-3351
Hawn, Gray Photography/1608 W 35th St, Austin, TX	512-451-7561
Haynes, Mike/2700 Commerce St, Dallas, TX	214-939-0550
Heiner, Gary/2039 Farrington, Dallas, TX	214-760-7471
Heinsohn, Bill/5455 Dashwood #200, Bellaire, TX	713-666-6515
Heit, Don/8502 Eustis Ave, Dallas, TX	214-324-0305
Henry, Steve/7403 Pierrepont Dr, Houston, TX	713-937-4514
Hicks, Tracy/4228 Main, Dallas, TX	214-939-9085
Hight, George C/1404 Linda Dr Box 327, Gallup, NM	505-863-3222
Hix, Steve/209 E Ben White Blvd #109, Austin, TX	512-441-2600
Hollenbeck, Phil/9010 Windy Crest, Dallas, TX	214-340-1117
Hollingsworth, Jack/3141 Irving Blvd #209, Dallas, TX	214-634-2632
Hood, Bob/2312 Grand, Dallas, TX	214-428-6080
Hubbard, Tim/Box 44971/Los Olivos Sta, Phoenix, AZ	602-274-6985
Huber, Phil/13562 Braemar Dr, Dallas, TX	214-243-4011
Hulsey, Jim Photography/1135 E 9th St, Edmond, OK	405-348-5020
Hunt, John Photography/3322 White Oak, Houston, TX	713-862-7699

IJ

Ives, Michael/12225 Royal Coach Dr, Yukon, OK	405-373-3631
Ives, Tom/2250 El Moraga, Tucson, AZ	602-743-0750
Jacka, Jerry/PO Box 9043, Phoenix, AZ	602-944-2793
Jacoby, Doris/1317 Conant, Dallas, TX	214-631-5533
Jennings, Steve/PO Box 33203, Tulsa, OK	918-745-0836

PHOTOGRAPHERS

Jew, Kim/4013 Central NE, Albuquerque, NM	505-255-6424
JOHNSON, MICHAEL/830 EXPOSITION #215, DALLAS, TX	
(P 315)	**214-828-9550**
Jones, C Bryan/PO Box 7687, Houston, TX	713-861-5299
Jones, Jerry/6207 Edloe, Houston, TX	713-668-4328
K KALUZNY, ZIGY/4700 STRASS DR, AUSTIN, TX (P 320)	**512-452-4463**
Kasie Photos/2123 Avignon, Carrollton, TX	214-492-7837
Katz, John/5222 Red Field, Dallas, TX	214-637-0844
Kenny, Gill/3515 N Camino De Vista, Tucson, AZ	602-743-0963
KERN, GEOF/1337 CRAMPTON, DALLAS, TX (P 311)	**214-630-0856**
Kirkley, Kent/1345 Conant St, Dallas, TX	214-630-0051
Klumpp, Don/804 Colquitt, Houston, TX	713-521-2090
Knowles, Jim/6102 E Mockingbird Ln #499, Dallas, TX	214-699-5335
KNUDSON, KENT/PO BOX 10397, PHOENIX, AZ (P 308)	**602-277-7701**
Koelsch, David/PO Box 178, Jones, OK	405-399-5212
Kopacka, Greg/PO Box 680824, San Antonio, TX	512-688-9202
Koppes, Neil/1611 N 36th St, Phoenix, AZ	602-231-0918
Korab, Jeanette/2264 Vantage, Dallas, TX	214-337-0114
Kretchmar, Phil Photography/3333 Elm, Dallas, TX	214-744-2039
Kroninger, Rick/105 N Alamo #615, San Antonio, TX	512-222-8141
Kuper, Holly/5522 Anita St, Dallas, TX	214-750-6229
KUSLICH, LAWRENCE J/5950 WESTWARD AVE, HOUSTON,	
TX (P 321)	**713-988-0775**
L Langhammer, Gary/1350 Manufacturing #215, Dallas, TX	214-744-2255
Larson, Dennis/5353 Maple Suite 102, Dallas, TX	214-630-3418
Latorre, Robert/2336 Farrington St, Dallas, TX	214-630-8977
Lawrence, David/8612 Thackery, Dallas, TX	214-361-1013
Lawrie, Bill/313 Sundial Dr, Dallas, TX	214-243-4188
Lee & Lesser Photographics/3409 Oak Lawn, Dallas, TX	214-526-1522
Lettner, Hans/830 North 4th Ave, Phoenix, AZ	602-258-3506
Light Works/3303 Oak Lawn, Dallas, TX	214-939-9120
LJM Studios/216 W Main, Azle, TX	817-444-2712
LOVEN, PAUL/2301 N 16TH ST, PHOENIX, AZ (P 322)	**602-253-0335**
Luker, Tom/PO Box 6112, Coweta, OK	918-486-5264
M Mader, Bob/2570 Promenade Center N, Richardson, TX	214-690-5511
Mageors & Rice Photo Service Inc/240 Turnpike Ave,	
Dallas, TX	214-941-3777
Maloney, John W/170 Leslie, Dallas, TX	214-741-6320
Manley, Dan/1350 Manufacturing Suite 215, Dallas, TX	214-748-8377
Manske, Thaine/7313 Ashcroft #216, Houston, TX	713-771-2220
Manstein, Ralph/5353 Institute Ln, Houston, TX	713-523-2500
Markham, Jim/2739 S E Loop 410, San Antonio, TX	512-648-0403
Markow, Paul/2222 E McDowell Rd, Phoenix, AZ	602-273-7985
Marshall, Jim/7451 Long Rifle Rd/Box 2421, Carefree, AZ	602-488-3373
Matthews, Michael/2727 Cancun, Dallas, TX	214-492-5580
Maxham, Robert/319 E Huisache, San Antonio, TX	512-735-3537
Mayer, George H/933 Stonetrail, Plano (Dallas), TX	214-424-4409
McCormick, Mike/5950 Westward Ave, Houston, TX	713-988-0775
McCoy, Gary/2700 Commerce St, Dallas, TX	214-939-0550
McIntosh, W S/12201 Merit Dr #222, Dallas, TX	214-783-1711
McKee, Crane/9113 Sovereign Rd, Dallas, TX	214-638-1498
McMichael, Garry D/RT 1 Box 312, Paris, AR	501-963-6429
McNee, Jim/PO Box 741008, Houston, TX	713-796-2633
Meltzer, Andrea/11415 Chatten Way, Houston, TX	713-465-5507
Messina, John/4440 Lawnview, Dallas, TX	214-388-8525
Meyerson, Arthur/4215 Bellaire Blvd, Houston, TX	713-660-0405
MEYLER, DENNIS/7315 ASHCROFT #110, HOUSTON, TX	
(P 323)	**713-778-1700**
Mills, Jack R/PO Box 32583, Oklahoma City, OK	405-787-7271
Moberley, Connie/215 Asbury, Houston, TX	713-864-3638
Molen, Roy/3302 N 47 Pl, Phoenix, AZ	602-840-5439
Moore, Terrence/PO Box 41536, Tucson, AZ	602-623-9381
Moot, Kelly/6606 Demoss #508, Houston, TX	713-683-6400
Morgan, Roger/828 Birdsong, Bedford, TX	817-282-2170
Morris, Garry/9281 E 27th St, Tucson, AZ	602-795-2334
Morris, Mike/4003 Gilbert #6, Dallas, TX	214-528-3600
Morrison, Chet Photography/3102 Commerce St, Dallas, TX	214-939-0903
Muir, Robert/Box 42809 Dept 404, Houston, TX	713-784-7420
Murdoch, Lane/2707 Stemmons Frwy, Dallas, TX	214-634-2240

MURPHY, DENNIS/101 HOWELL ST, DALLAS, TX (P 314)	**214-651-7516**
Myers, Jim/165 Cole, Dallas, TX	214-698-0500
N Neely, David/2568 Southwell, Dallas, TX	214-241-1950
Netzer, Don/8585 Stemmons #M29, Dallas, TX	214-241-8530
Newby, Steve/4501 Swiss, Dallas, TX	214-821-0231
Newman, David/3319 Knight #1, Dallas, TX	214-522-8612
Noble, David/2543 Farrington, Dallas, TX	214-634-3939
NOLAND, LLOYD (WEAVER)/PO BOX 9456, SANTA FE, NM	
(P 274)	**505-982-2488**
Norrell, J B/7320 Ashcroft #106, Houston, TX	713-981-6409
O P Olvera, Jim/235 Yorktown St, Dallas, TX	214-760-0025
Palmetto, Chuck/2312 Grand Ave, Dallas, TX	214-321-7460
Pantin, Tomas/PO Box 1146, Austin, TX	512-474-9968
Parsons, Bill/518 W 9th St, Little Rock, AR	501-372-5892
Patrick, Richard/215 W 4th St #B, Austin, TX	512-472-9092
Payne, A F/830 North 4th Ave, Phoenix, AZ	602-258-3506
Payne, C Ray/2643 Manana, Dallas, TX	214-350-1055
Payne, Richard/2029 Haddon St, Houston, TX	713-524-7525
Payne, Tom/2425 Bartlett, Houston, TX	713-527-8670
Perlstein, Mark/1844 Place One Ln, Garland, TX	214-690-0168
Peterson, Bruce/1222 E Edgemont, Phoenix, AZ	602-265-6505
Pettit, Steve/206 Weeks, Arlington, TX	817-265-8776
Phelps, Greg/2360 Central Blvd, Brownsville, TX	512-541-4909
Photo Media, Inc/2805 Crockett, Fort Worth, TX	817-332-4172
Photographix of Dallas/2201 N Lamar St, Dallas, TX	214-954-0355
Poulides, Peter/PO Box 202505, Dallas, TX	214-350-5395
Prosen, Philip M/69-47 Coronado, Dallas, TX	214-321-2938
Q R The Quest Group/3007 Paseo, Oklahoma City, OK	405-525-6591
Quilia, Jim/3125 Ross, Dallas, TX	214-826-8327
Radcliff, Phillip/15 E Brady, Tulsa, OK	918-582-5850
RAPHAELE INC/616 HAWTHORNE, HOUSTON, TX (P 426)	**713-524-2211**
Raymond, Ray/1244 E Utopia, Phoenix, AZ	602-581-8160
Records, Bill/505 W 38, Austin, TX	512-458-1017
Redd, True/2328 Farrington, Dallas, TX	214-638-0602
Reens, Louis/4814 Sycamore, Dallas, TX	214-827-3388
Reese, Donovan/4801 Lemmon Ave, Dallas, TX	214-526-5851
Reisch, Jim/Studio 2025 Levee St, Dallas, TX	214-748-0456
Rich, Wilburn/3233 Marquart, Houston, TX	713-623-8790
Robbins Jr, Joe D/7320 Ashcroft Ste 213, Houston, TX	713-271-1111
Robbins, Mark/2520 Oakland Blvd, Ft Worth, TX	817-536-5061
Roe, Cliff/47 Woodelves Pl, The Woodlands, TX	713-363-5661
Rogers, John/PO Box 35753, Dallas, TX	214-351-1751
Running, John/PO Box 1237, Flagstaff, AZ	602-774-2923
Rusing, Rick/22 E 15th St, Tempe, AZ	602-967-1864
Russell, Gail/PO Box 241, Taos, NM	505-776-8474
Russell, Nicholas/849-F Harvard, Houston, TX	713-864-7664
RYAN, TOM/1821 LEVEE, DALLAS, TX (P 312)	**214-651-7085**
S Sall, Narinder/2024 Karbach #3, Houston, TX	713-680-3717
SAVANT, JOSEPH/4756 ALGIERS ST, DALLAS, TX	
(P 324,325)	**214-951-0111**
Sawada, Spencer/2810 S 24th St #109, Phoenix, AZ	602-275-5078
Saxon, John/1337 Crampton, Dallas, TX	214-630-5160
Scheer, Tim/1521 Centerville Rd, Dallas, TX	214-328-1016
Scheyer, Mark/3317 Montrose #A1003, Houston, TX	713-861-0847
Schlesinger, Terrence/PO Box 32877, Phoenix, AZ	602-957-7474
SCHNEPS, MICHAEL/21 PINEDALE #6, HOUSTON, TX	
(P 327)	**713-520-8224**
Schultz, David/4220 Main St, Dallas, TX	214-827-1453
Schuster, Ellen/3719 Gilbert, Dallas, TX	214-526-6712
SCOTT, RON/EFX/1000 JACKSON BLVD, HOUSTON, TX	
(P 328,329)	**713-529-5868**
Scruggs, Jim/2410 Taft, Houston, TX	713-523-6146
Segrest, Jerry Photography/1707 S Arvay, Dallas, TX	214-426-6360
Segroves, Jim/170 Leslie, Dallas, TX	214-827-5482
Sellers, Dan/2258 Vantage, Dallas, TX	214-631-4705
Shackelford, Robert/1515 Lomita Ave, Richardson, TX	214-234-4736
Shands, Nathan/1107 Bryan, Mesquite, TX	214-285-5382
Shaw, Robert/1723 Kelly SE, Dallas, TX	214-428-1757

Please send us your additions and updates.

Shultz, Dave/PO Box 59737, Dallas, TX	214-438-1549
Siegel, David Martin/224 N 5th Ave, Phoenix, AZ	602-257-9509
Sieve, Jerry/PO Box 1777, Cave Creek, AZ	602-488-9561
Simon, Frank/1012 N Seventh Ave, Phoenix, AZ	602-254-4018
Simpson, Micheal/415 N Bishop Ave, Dallas, TX	214-943-9347
Skelton, Rebecca/11443 W Ricks Cir, Dallas, TX	214-696-9211
Smith, Louis/9101 Jameel #190, Houston, TX	713-451-8094
Smith, Seth/1228 North 8th St, Abilene, TX	915-673-7505
Smith/Garza Photography/PO Box 10046, Dallas, TX	214-941-4611
Smothers, Brian/843 W 43rd St, Houston, TX	713-695-0873
Smusz, Ben/7313 Ashcroft #216, Houston, TX	713-772-5026
Snyder, Joe/1800 Lear #5, Dallas, TX	214-421-3993
Southan, Ron/2905 Sun Valley, Irving, TX	214-255-3741
Sperry, Bill/3300 E Stanford, Paradise Valley, AZ	602-955-5626
St Angelo, Ron/350 Turtle Creek #109, Dallas, TX	214-254-7703
St Gil & Associates/2230 Ashford Hollow Ln, Houston, TX	713-870-9458
STAARJES, HANS/20 LANA LANE, HOUSTON, TX (P 330)	**713-621-8503**
Starnes, Mac/2703 Fondren #136, Dallas, TX	214-692-1720
Stibbens, Steve/104 Cole St, Dallas, TX	214-651-8224
Stiller, Rick/1311 E 35th St, Tulsa, OK	918-749-0297
Stites, Bill/1600 Park St, Houston, TX	713-523-6439
Stroud, Dan/1350 Manufacturing #211, Dallas, TX	214-745-1933
Studio 3 Photography/2804 Lubbock, Fort Worth, TX	817-923-9931
Suddarth, Robert/3402 73rd St, Lubbock, TX	806-795-4553
Sumner, Bill/122 Parkhouse, Dallas, TX	214-748-3766
Svacina, Joe/2209 Summer, Dallas, TX	214-748-3260
Swindler, Mark/206 Santa Rita, Odessa, TX	915-332-3515

T

Tenney, Bob/PO Box 17236, Dallas, TX	214-288-9291
Terry, Phillip/1222 Manufacturing St, Dallas, TX	214-749-0515
Thatcher, Charles/4220 Main St, Dallas, TX	214-823-4356
Thompson, Dennis/4153 S 87th Ave, Tulsa, OK	918-252-4973
Thompson, Wesley/800 W Airport Frwy #301, Irving, TX	214-438-7762
Timmerman, Bill/2301 N 16th St, Phoenix, AZ	602-252-6501
Tomlinson, Doug/5651 East Side Ave, Dallas, TX	214-821-1192
Trent, Rusty/7205 Cecil, Houston, TX	713-797-1405
Turner, Rick/1117 Welch, Houston, TX	713-524-2576
Turtle Creek Studio/1405-B Turtle Creek Blvd, Dallas, TX	214-742-1045
Two Bob's Inc/3603 Parry Ave, Dallas, TX	214-823-9000

UV

Untersee, Chuck/2747 Seelcco, Dallas, TX	214-358-2306
Van Warner, Steven/1637 W Wilshire, Phoenix, AZ	602-254-2618
Vandivier, Kevin/1709 Iowa, Plano, TX	214-867-8512
Veeder, Bob/1922 N Haskell, Dallas, TX	214-826-2487
Vener, Ellis/3601 Allen Pkwy #123, Houston, TX	713-523-0456
Viewpoint Photographers/217 McKinley, Phoenix, AZ	602-245-0013
Vine, Terry/5455 Dashwood, Houston, TX	713-664-2920
Vinson, Phil/6216 Devonshire Terrace, Fort Worth, TX	817-451-4907
Von Helms, Michael/4212 San Felipe, Houston, TX	713-666-1212
Vracin, Andrew/4501 Swiss Ave, Dallas, TX	214-821-0231

WY

Walker, Balfour/1838 E 6th St, Tucson, AZ	602-624-1121
Wells, Craig/537 W Granada, Phoenix, AZ	602-252-8166
Welsch, Diana/PO Box 1791, Austin, TX	512-451-8960
Wheeler, Don/220 N Main, Tulsa, OK	918-592-5099
White, Frank Photo/2702 Sackett, Houston, TX	713-524-9250
Wilke, Darrell/2608 Irving Blvd, Dallas, TX	214-631-6459
Williams, Oscar/8535 Fairhaven, San Antonio, TX	512-690-8807
Wilson, Jennifer/8303 Westglen Dr, Houston, TX	713-266-2872
Wilson, Sandy/PO Box 49391, Austin, TX	512-452-1299
Wolenski, Stan/2410 Farrington, Dallas, TX	214-637-2747
Wolfhagen, Vilhelm/4916 Kelvin, Houston, TX	713-522-2787
Wollam, Les/5215 Goodwin Ave, Dallas, TX	214-760-7721
Wood, Keith/1308 Conant St, Dallas, TX	214-634-7344
Wristen, Don/2025 Levee St, Dallas, TX	214-748-5317
Yeung, Ka Chuen/4901 W Lovers Lane, Dallas, TX	214-350-8716

ROCKY MOUNTAIN

A

Aiuppy, Larry/PO Box 26, Livingston, MT	406-222-7308
Allen, Lincoln/1705 Woodbridge Dr, Salt Lake City, UT	801-277-1848
Alston, Bruce/PO Box 2480, Steamboat Springs, CO	303-879-1675
Anderson, Borge/234 South 200 East, Salt Lake City, UT	801-359-7703
Appleton, Roger/1420 N Weber, Colorado Springs, CO	303-635-0393
Appleton/ Kidder/1420 N Weber, Colorado Springs, CO	303-635-0393
Auben, Steven/590 Dover, Lakewood, CO	303-232-0243

B

Bako, Andrew/3047 4th St SW, Calgary T2S 1X9, AB	403-243-9789
Barber, Gene/21oo Blake St, Denver, CO	303-294-0004
Barry, Dave/6669 S Kit CArson St, Littleton, CO	303-798-9995
Bartek, Patrick/PO Box 26994, Las Vegas, NV	702-368-2901
Batchlor, Paul/655 Wolff St #42, Denver, CO	303-623-4465
Bator, Joe/2011 Washington Ave, Golden, CO	303-279-4163
Bauer, Erwin A/Box 543, Teton Village, WY	307-733-4023
Beery, Gale/1836 Blake, Denver, CO	303-296-2061
Bell, Phil/629 Grand Ave, Billings, MT	406-245-5168
Benedict, Bruce/PO Box 1096, Avon, CO	303-926-3210
Benschneider, Ben/1711 Alamo, Colorado Springs, CO	303-473-4294
Berchert, Jim/PO Box 903, Denver, CO	303-466-7414
Berge, Melinda/1280 Ute Ave, Aspen, CO	303-925-2317
Birnbach, Allen/3600 Tejon St, Denver, CO	303-455-7800
Black, Dave/PO Box 7522, Colorado Springs, CO	303-636-3510
Blake, John/4132 20th St, Greeley, CO	303-330-0980
Bluebaugh, David Studio/1594 S Acoma St, Denver, CO	303-778-7214
Bonmarito, Jim/PO Box 599, Durango, CO	303-247-1166
Bosworth/Graves Photo Inc/1055 S 700 W, Salt Lake City, UT	801-972-6128
Brantley, Robert/1414 S 7th West, Salt Lake City, UT	801-972-8293
Brofsky, Keith/2631 17th St, Denver, CO	303-458-5922
Burggraf, Chuck/2941 W 23rd Ave, Denver, CO	303-480-9053
Busath, Drake/701 East South Temple St, Salt Lake City, UT	801-364-6645

C

Cambon, Jim/216 Racquette Dr, Fort Collins, CO	303-221-4545
Carduino, Tony/1706 Palm Dr #3, Ft Collins, CO	303-493-4648
Chatman, Donna/3038 W 35th Ave, Denver, CO	303-480-1549
Chesley, Paul/Box 94, Aspen, CO	303-925-1148
Christensen, Barry/4505 South 2300 West, Roy, UT	801-731-3521
Christensen, Mark/2711 S Clarkson, Englewood, CO	303-458-0288
Clasen, Norm/PO Box 4230, Aspen, CO	303-925-4418
Coca, Joe/213 1/2 Jefferson St, Ft Collins, CO	303-482-0858
Collector, Stephen/1836 Mapleton Ave, Boulder, CO	303-442-1386
Colman, Mark/1505 E 13th Ave #9, Denver, CO	303-832-1243
Conrad, Bruce/PO Box 2606, Durango, CO	303-385-4265
Cook, James/PO Box 11608, Denver, CO	303-433-4874
Coppock, Ron/1443 Wazee St, Denver, CO	303-893-2299
Cravens, Karen/PO Box 26307, Lakewood, CO	303-423-1230
Cronin, Bill/2543 Xavier, Denver, CO	303-458-0883
Crowe, Steven/1150 S Cherry #1-202, Denver, CO	303-782-0346
Cruickshank/505 C Street, Lewiston, ID	208-743-9411
Cupp, David/2520 Albion St, Denver, CO	303-321-3581

D

Dahlquist, Ron/PO Box 1606, Steamboat Springs, CO	303-879-7075
Daly, Michael Kevin/PO Box 1987, Zephyr Cove, NV	916-577-7095
Dean, Bill/621 West 1000 North, West Bountiful, UT	801-295-9746
DeHoff, RD/632 N Sheridan, Colorado Springs, CO	303-635-0263
DeLespinasse, Hank/PO Box 14061, Las Vegas, NV	702-798-6693
Delmancznk, Phillip/1625 Wilber Pl, Reno, NV	702-329-0339
Dennis, Steven/350 Santa Fe Dr, Denver, CO	303-534-8400
DeSciose, Nick/2700 Arapahoe St #2, Denver, CO	303-296-6386
DeVore, Nicholas III/1280 Ute, Aspen, CO	303-925-2317
Dickey, Marc/2500 Curtis #115, Denver, CO	303-298-7691
Dimond, Craig/615 Simpson Ave, Salt Lake City, UT	801-484-7003
Dolan, J Ross/6094 S Ironton Ct, Englewood, CO	303-770-8454
Dondero, Donald/2755 Pioneer Dr, Reno, NV	702-825-7348
DOUGLASS, DIRK/2755 S 300 W #D, SALT LAKE CITY, UT (P 332)	**801-485-5691**
Downs, Jerry/1315 Oak Ct, Boulder, CO	303-444-8910

EF

Elder, Jim/PO Box 1600, Jackson Hole, WY	307-733-3555
Engel, Tom/1 Unicover Ctr, Cheyenne, WY	307-634-5911
FADER, BOB/14 PEARL ST, DENVER, CO (P 333)	**303-744-0711**
Farace, Joe Photo/11957 E Harvard Ave #8-301, Aurora, CO	303-830-2616
Farley, Malcolm/3870 Newland, Wheatridge, CO	303-420-9135
Feld, Stephen/1572 E 9350 S, Sandy, UT	801-571-1752

PHOTOGRAPHERS

Feller, Nora/1836 Blake St, Denver, CO	303-296-0236
Ford, David/954 S Emerson, Denver, CO	303-778-7044
Frazier, Van/2770 S Maryland Pkwy, Las Vegas, NV	702-735-1165
Freedman, Robert/739 Sherman St, Denver, CO	303-835-7458
Freeman, Hunter/852 Santa Fe Dr, Denver, CO	303-893-5730

G H
GALLIAN, DIRK/PO BOX 4573, ASPEN, CO (P 334)	**303-925-8268**
Gamba, Mark/705 19th St, Glenwood Springs, CO	303-945-5903
Goetze, David/3215 Zuni, Denver, CO	303-458-5026
GORFKLE, GREGORY D/6901 E BAKER PL, DENVER, CO	
(P 335)	**303-759-2737**
Gottlieb, Robert/PO Box 11235, Denver, CO	303-988-7097
Graf, Gary/1870 S Ogden St, Denver, CO	303-722-0547
H B R Studios/3310 South Knox Court, Denver, CO	303-789-4307
Harris, Richard/935 South High, Denver, CO	303-778-6433
Haun, Lora/8428 Fenton St, Arvada, CO	303-428-8834
Havey, James/1836 Blake St #203, Denver, CO	303-296-7448
Held, Patti/PO Box 44441, Denver, CO	303-341-7248
Henderson, Gordon/182 Gariepy Crescent, Edmonton T6M	
1A2, AB	403-483-8049
Herridge, Brent/736 South 3rd West, Salt Lake City, UT	801-363-0337
Hiser, David C/1280 Ute Ave, Aspen, CO	303-925-2317
Holdman, Floyd/1908 Main St, Orem, UT	801-224-9966
Hooper, Robert Scott/4330 W Desert Inn Rd, Las Vegas, NV	702-873-5823
Hunt, Steven/1139 W Shepard Ln, Farmington, UT	801-451-6552
Huntress, Diane/3337 W 23rd Ave, Denver, CO	303-480-0219

J
J T Photographics/10490-C West Fair Ave, Littleton, CO	303-972-8847
Janis, Brian/3110 Polaris #10, Las Vegas, NV	702-362-3605
Jensen, Curt/915 Walnut #A 305, Rock Spring, WY	307-382-7794
Johns, Rob/1075 Piedmont, Boulder, CO	303-449-9192
Johnson, Charles/PO Box 6580, Denver, CO	303-393-0990
Johnson, Jim Photo/12596 W Bayaud #290, Lakewood, CO	303-987-0760
Johnson, Ron/2460 Eliot St, Denver, CO	303-458-0288

K
Kay, James W/4463 Wander Ln, Salt Lake City, UT	801-277-4489
Kehrwald, Richard J/32 S Main, Sheridan, WY	307-674-4679
Kerr, Barnaby/900 Sherman #A-17, Denver, CO	303-839-1675
Kidder, Jeanne/1420 N Weber, Colorado Springs, CO	303-635-0393
Kitzman, J R/1285 Acropolis Dr, Lafayette, CO	303-440-7623
Koropp, Robert/901 E 17th Ave, Denver, CO	303-830-6000
Kramer, Andrew/PO Box 6023, Boulder, CO	303-449-2280
Krause, Ann/2450 8th St, Boulder, CO	303-447-9711

L
Lammers, Kathi/PO Box 8480, Breckenridge, CO	303-453-1860
Laszlo, Larry/1100 Acoma St, Denver, CO	303-893-1199
LeCoq, John Land/640 S University, Denver, CO	303-292-8433
Lee, Jess/6799 N Derek Ln, Idaho Falls, ID	208-529-4535
LeGoy, James M/PO Box 21004, Reno, NV	702-322-0116
Levy, Patricia Barry/4467 Utica, Denver, CO	303-458-6692
Lichter, Michael/3300 14th St, Boulder, CO	303-443-9198
LISSY, DAVID/14472 APPLEWOOD RIDGE RD, GOLDEN, CO	
(P 336)	**303-277-0232**
Lokey, David/PO Box 7, Vail, CO	303-949-5750
Lonczyna, Longin/257-R S Rio Grande St, Salt Lake City, UT	801-355-7513
Lotz, Fred/4220 W 82nd Ave, Westminster, CO	303-427-2875

M
MacDonald, Dan/PO Box 5133, Greeley, CO	303-352-5812
Mangelson, Tom/PO Box 205, Moose, WY	307-733-6179
Marlow, David/PO Box 4934, Aspen, CO	303-925-8882
Masamori, Ron/1261 Glenarm Pl, Denver, CO	303-892-6666
Mathews, T R/9206 W 100th St, Broomfield, CO	303-469-1436
Matthews, Don/PO Box 21169, Denver, CO	303-690-2125
McDonald, Kirk/350 Bannock, Denver, CO	303-733-2958
McDougal, Russ/PO Box 333, Boulder, CO	303-444-6984
McDowell, Pat/PO Box 283, Park City, UT	801-649-3403
McElhaney, Terry/Adolph Coors Co, Golden, CO	303-277-3819
McMahon, David/1553 Platte St #307, Denver, CO	303-480-0929
McManemin, Jack/662 S State St, Salt Lake City, UT	801-533-0435
Meleski, Mike/1420 Blake St, Denver, CO	303-297-0632
Melick, Jordan/1250 W Cedar St, Denver, CO	303-744-1414
Messineo, John/PO Box 1636, Fort Collins, CO	303-482-9349

Miles, Kent/25 South 300 East, Salt Lake City, UT	801-364-5755
Miller, Kenneth L/PO Box 57, Silver City, NV	702-847-9076
Milmoe, James O/14900 Cactus Cr, Golden, CO	303-279-4364
Milne, Lee/3615 W 49th Ave, Denver, CO	303-458-1520
Mitchell, Kurt/PO Box 3946, Jackson, WY	307-733-4376
Mitchell, Paul/1517 S Grant, Denver, CO	303-722-8852
Mock, Wanda/Po Box 85, Roberts, MT	406-445-2356
Moore, Janet/3250 S Elati St, Englewood, CO	303-781-0035
Mosbisch, Dick/1454 Dexter St, Denver, CO	303-333-9651
Munro, Harry/2355 W 27th Ave, Denver, CO	303-355-5612

O P
O'Hara, Timothy/PO Box 1802, Ft Collins, CO	303-224-2186
Oswald, Jan/921 Santa Fe, Denver, CO	303-893-8038
Patrick, Dick/650 Elkton Dr, Colorado Springs, CO	303-593-2120
Patryas, David/26 Birch Ct #4, Long Mont, CO	303-678-0959
Paul, Howard/2460 Eliot St, Denver, CO	303-458-0288
Paul, Ken/1523 E Montana Dr, Golden, CO	303-526-1162
Payne, Brian/2685 Forest, Denver, CO	303-355-5373
Peregrine Studio/1541 Platte St, Denver, CO	303-455-6944
Perkin, Jan/3194 Kaibob Way, Salt Lake City, UT	801-485-8100
Phillips, Ron/6500-K Stapleton S Dr, Denver, CO	303-321-6777

Q R
QUINNEY GROUP/423 E BROADWAY, SALT LAKE CITY, UT	
(P 337)	**801-363-0434**
Rafkind, Andrew/1702 Fairview Ave, Boise, ID	208-344-9918
Ramsey, Steve/4800 N Washington St, Denver, CO	303-295-2135
Ranson Photographers Ltd/26 Airport Rd, Edmonton T5G	
0W7, AB	403-454-9674
Rawls, Ray/4344 E 127th Pl, Denver, CO	303-452-5587
Redding, Ken/PO Box 717, Vail, CO	303-949-6123
Reed, Joe/9859 Orangewood Dr, Denver, CO	303-452-2894
Reynolds, Roger/3310 S Knox Ct, Englewood, CO	303-789-4307
Rosen, Barry/1 Middle Rd, Englewood, CO	303-758-0648
Rosenberg, David/1545 Julian SE, Denver, CO	303-893-0893
Rosenberger, Edward/2248 Emerson Ave, Salt Lake City, TX	801-355-9007
Russell, John/PO Box 4739, Aspen, CO	303-920-1431

S
Saehlenou, Kevin/3478 W 32nd Ave, Denver, CO	303-455-1611
Sammons, Steve/776 Santa Fe Dr, Denver, CO	303-623-1171
Satterly, David/5044 Gallatin Pl, Boulder, CO	303-443-2002
Saviers, Trent/2606 Rayma Ct, Reno, NV	702-747-2591
Scherer, William D/PO Box 274, Greeley, CO	303-353-6674
Schlack, Greg/1510 Lehigh St, Boulder, CO	303-499-3860
Schmiett, Skip/740 W 1700 S #10, Salt Lake City, UT	801-973-0642
Schneider, Beth/1666 Race St, Denver, CO	303-388-4909
Schoenfeld, Michael/925 SW Temple, Salt Lake City, UT	801-532-2006
Shupe, John R/4090 Edgehill Dr, Ogden, UT	801-392-2523
Simons, Randy/3320 S Knox Ct, Englewood, CO	303-761-1458
Smith, David Scott/1437 Ave E, Billings, MT	406-256-1612
Smith, Dorn/1201-A Santa Fe, Denver, CO	303-571-4331
Smith, Grafton Marshall/PO Box 3212, Aspen, CO	303-925-7120
Snyder, John P/PO Box 7429 University Sta, Provo, UT	801-373-5748
Sokol, Howard/3006 Zuni St, Denver, CO	303-433-3353
St John, Charles/PO Box 6580, Denver, CO	303-393-0990
Staver, Barry/5122 S Iris Way, Littleton, CO	303-973-4414
Stearns, Doug/1738 Wynkoop St #102, Denver, CO	303-296-1133
Stewert, Sandy/17618 W 14th Ave #1, Golden, CO	303-278-8039
The Stock Solution/6640 South, 2200 West, Salt Lake City, UT	801-569-1155
Stott, Barry/2427 Chamonix Rd, Vail, CO	303-476-5774
Stouder, Carol/5421 W Geddes Pl, Littleton, CO	303-979-5402
Studio Nine/283 N University, Provo, UT	301-374-6463
Swartz, Bill/5992 S Eudora Ct, Littleton, CO	303-773-2776
Sweitzer, David/4800 Washington, Denver, CO	303-295-0703

T V
Tanner, Scott/2755 South 300 West #D, Salt Lake City, UT	801-466-6884
Tatem, Mike/6256 S Albion Way, Littleton, CO	303-770-6080
Tejada, David X/901 E 17th Ave #205, Denver, CO	303-860-0104
Tharp, Brenda/901 E Seventeenth Ave, Denver, CO	303-830-0845
Till, Tom/796 Westwood, Moab, UT	801-259-5327
Tobias, Philip/3614 Morrison Rd, Denver, CO	303-936-1267
Tradelius, Bob/738 Santa Fe Dr, Denver, CO	303-825-4847
Trainor, Ted/1600 Broadway #540, Denver, CO	303-831-1113

TRAVIS, TOM/1219 S PEARL ST, DENVER, CO (P 338) 303-377-7422
Tregeagle, Steve/2994 S Richards St #C, Salt Lake City, UT 801-484-1673
Trice, Gordon/2046 Arapahoe St, Denver, CO 303-298-1986
TWEDE, BRIAN L/430 S STATE ST, SALT LAKE CITY, UT - (P 339) 801-534-1459
Van Hemert, Martin/5481 Cyclamen Ct, Salt Lake City, UT 801-969-3569
Vandenberg, Greg/1901 E 47th Ave, Denver, CO 303-295-2525
Varney, Frank/2600 King St, Denver, CO 303-458-8546
Viggio Studio/2400 Central Ave, Boulder, CO 303-444-3342

W
Walker, Rod/PO Box 2418, Vail, CO 303-926-3210
Wankelman, Peter/633 S College Ave, Ft Collins, CO 303-482-9424
Wapinski, David/10 Valdez Circle, Dugway, UT 801-522-4214
Warren, Cameron A/PO Box 10588, Reno, NV 702-825-5565
Wayda, Steve/5725 Immigration Canyon, Salt Lake City, UT 801-582-1787
Weeks, Michael/PO Box 6965, Colorado Springs, CO 303-632-2996
Wellisch, Bill/2325 Clay St, Denver, CO 303-455-8766
Wheeler, Geoffrey/721 Pearl St, Boulder, CO 303-449-2137
White, Stuart/4229 Clark Ave, Great Falls, MT 406-727-4664
Wiseman, Jay/6429 South 300 East, Murray, UT 801-261-2933
Wordal, Eric/3640 Keir Lane, Helena, MT 406-475-3304
Worden, Kirk/16 W 13th Ave, Denver, CO 303-629-5574

WEST COAST

A
Abecassis, Andree L/756 Neilson St, Berkeley, CA 415-526-5099
ABRAHAM, RUSSELL/17 BROSNAN ST, SAN FRANCISCO, CA (P 365) 415-558-9100
ABRAMOWITZ, ALAN/PO BOX 45121, SEATTLE, WA (P 362) 206-527-8111
Ackroyd, Hugh S/Box 10101, Portland, OR 503-227-5694
Addor, Jean-Michel/1311 63rd St, Emeryville, CA 415-653-1745
Adler, Allan S/PO Box 2251, Van Nuys, CA 818-901-6555
Adler, Gale/3740 Veteran Ave #1, Los Angeles, CA 213-837-9224
Agee, Bill & Assoc/715 Larkspur Box 612, Corona Del Mar, CA 714-760-6700
Ahlberg, Holly/1117 N Wilcox Pl, Los Angeles, CA 213-462-0731
Ahrend, Jay/1046 N Orange Dr, Hollywood, CA 213-462-5256
Albert, Betty/4900 Burrett Ave, Richmond, CA 415-235-2856
Alexander, David/1545 N Wilcox #202, Hollywood, CA 213-464-8690
Alexanian, Nubar/1821 Fifth Ave W, Seattle, WA 206-285-3787
All Sport Photo/23335 Lake Manor Dr, Chatsworth, CA 818-704-5118
Allan, Larry/3503 Argonne St, San Diego, CA 619-270-1850
Allen, Charles/537 S Raymond Ave, Pasadena, CA 818-795-1053
ALLEN, JUDSON PHOTO/654 GILMAN ST, PALO ALTO, CA (P 360) 415-324-8177
Allensworth, Jim/PO Box 2224, Newport Beach, CA 714-970-1395
Allison, Glen/PO Box 1833, Santa Monica, CA 213-392-1388
Alt, Tim/3699 Wilshire Blvd #870, Los Angeles, CA 213-387-8384
Ambrose, Paul Studios/1231 Alderwood Ave, Sunnyvale, CA 408-734-3211
Amer, Tommy/1858 Westerly Terrace, Los Angeles, CA 213-664-7624
Andersen, Kurt/250 Newhall, San Francisco, CA 415-641-4276
Andersen, Welden/2643 S Fairfax Ave, Culver City, CA 213-559-0059
Anderson, John D/6460 Byrnes Rd, Vacaville, CA 707-448-4926
Anderson, Karen/652 N Larchmont, Los Angeles, CA 213-461-9100
Anderson, Rick/8871-B Balboa Ave, San Diego, CA 619-268-1957
Andre Photography/5243 Tyler Ave #4, Temple City, CA 818-443-2468
Angelo, Michael/PO Box 2039, Mill Valley, CA 415-381-4224
Ansa, Brian/2605 N Lake Ave, Altadena, CA 818-797-2233
Aperture PhotoBank/1530 Westlake Ave N, Seattle, WA 206-282-8116
Apton, Bill/577 Howard St, San Francisco, CA 415-543-6313
Arend, Christopher/5401 Cordova St Ste 204, Anchorage, AK 907-562-3173
Armas, Richard/6913 Melrose Ave, Los Angeles, CA 213-931-7889
Arnesen, Erik/605 25th St, Manhattan Beach, CA 213-546-2363
Arnold, Robert Photo/1379 Natoma, San Francisco, CA 415-621-6161
Arnone, Ken/3830 Ray St, San Diego, CA 619-298-3141
Aron, Jeffrey/17801 Sky Park Cir #H, Irvine, CA 714-250-1555
Aronovsky, James/3356-B Hancock St, San Diego, CA 619-296-4858
Arsenault, Dan/, Los Angeles, CA 213-467-8495
Ashley, Chuck/329 San Francisco Blvd, San Anselmo, CA 415-453-2967
Askew, Don/8148 Ronson Rd #L, San Diego, CA 619-569-6274
The Association/151 Kalmuf #H 10, Costa Mesa, CA 714-631-4634
Atkinson Photo/505 S Flower B Level, Los Angeles, CA 213-624-5970

Atlas Photo-Video/11416 Harrisburg Rd, Los Alamitos, CA 213-430-8379
Attebery, Barton L/8406 Linden Ave, North Seattle, WA 206-783-0321
Aurness, Craig/1526 Pontius Ave #A, Los Angeles, CA 213-477-0421
Avery, Franklin/800 Duboce #101, San Francisco, CA 415 986-3701
Avery, Ron/820 N La Brea, Los Angeles, CA 213-465-7193
Avery, Sid/820 N La Brea, Los Angeles, CA 213-465-7193
Ayres, Robert Bruce/5635 Melrose Ave, Los Angeles, CA 213-461-3816

B
Bacon, Garth/18576 Bucknall Rd, Saratoga, CA 408-866-5858
Baer, Morley/PO Box 222537, Carmel, CA 408-624-3530
Bagley, John/730 Clemintina, San Francisco, CA 415-861-1062
Bailey, Brent P/759 W 19th St, Costa Mesa, CA 714-548-9683
BAKER, BILL/265 29TH ST, OAKLAND, CA (P 367) 415-832-7685
Baker, Frank/15031-B Parkway Loop, Tustin, CA 714-259-1462
Balderas, Michael/5837-B Mission Gorge Rd, San Diego, CA 619-563-7077
Baldwin, Doug/10518-2 Sunland Blvd, Sunland, CA 818-353-7270
Banko, Phil/1249 First Ave S, Seattle, WA 206-621-7008
Banks, Ken/135 N Harper Ave, Los Angeles, CA 213-930-2831
Bardin, James/111 Villa View Dr, Pacific Palisades, CA 213-459-4775
Bare, John/3001 Red Hill Ave #4-102, Costa Mesa, CA 714-979-8712
Barkentin, Pamela/1218 N LaCienega, Los Angeles, CA 213-854-1941
Barnes, David/PO Box 31498, Seattle, WA 206-282-8116
Barnes, John/637 Natoma St, San Francisco, CA 415-431-5264
Barnhurst, Noel/1417 15th St, San Francisco, CA 415-431-0401
Barros, Robert/E1813 Sprague, Spokane, WA 509-535-6455
Bartholick, Robin/89 Yesler Way 4th Fl, Seattle, WA 206-467-1001
Barton, Hugh G/230 Polk St, Eugene, OR 503-342-7072
Bartone, Tom/7403 W Sunset Blvd, Los Angeles, CA 213-469-4585
Bartruff, Dave/PO Box 800, San Anselmo, CA 415-457-1482
Bates, Frank/5158 Highland View Ave, Los Angeles, CA 213-258-5272
Batista-Moon Studio/444 Pearl #B-1, Monterey, CA 408-373-1947
Bauer, Karel M/141 10th St, San Francisco, CA 415-863-5155
Bayalis, John/583 Kamolku #2703, Honolulu, HI 808-943-0333
Bayer, Dennis/1261 Howard St, San Francisco, CA 415-552-6575
Bear, Brent/8566 W Pico Blvd, Los Angeles, CA 213-652-1156
Beatie, Chris/PO Box 1236, San Juan Capistrano, CA 714-240-3311
Becker Bishop Studios/1830 17th St, San Francisco, CA 415-552-4254
Bedilion, Michael/7272 Carlton Ave, Westminster, CA 714-894-3900
Beebe, Morton/150 Lombard St #207, San Francisco, CA 415-362-3530
Beer, Rafael/207 S Catalina Ste 4, Los Angeles, CA 213-384-9532
Behrman, C H/8036 Kentwood, Los Angeles, CA 213-216-6611
Belcher, Richard/2565 Third St #206, San Francisco, CA 415-641-8912
Benchmark Photo/1442 N Hundley, Anaheim, CA 714-630-7965
BENCZE, LOUIS/2442 NW MARKET ST #86, SEATTLE, WA (P 368,369) 206-783-8033
Benet, Ben/333 Fifth St #A, San Francisco, CA 415-974-5433
Bennett, James Photo/280 Cajon St, Laguna Beach, CA 714-497-4309
Bennion, Chris/5234 36th Ave NE, Seattle, WA 206-526-9981
BENSON, HANK/653 BRYANT ST, SAN FRANCISCO, CA (P 352,353) 415-543-8153
Benson, John/1261 Howard St 2nd Fl, San Francisco, CA 415-621-5247
Benton, Richard/4773 Brighton Ave, San Diego, CA 619-224-0278
Bergman, Alan/8241 W 4th St, Los Angeles, CA 213-852-1408
Berman, Ellen/5425 Senford Ave, Los Angeles, CA 213-641-2783
Berman, Steve/7955 W 3rd, Los Angeles, CA 213-933-9185
Bernstein, Andrew/1415 N Chester, Pasadena, CA 818-797-3430
Bernstein, Gary/8735 Washington Blvd, Culver City, CA 213-550-6891
Betz, Ted R/527 Howard 2nd Fl, San Francisco, CA 415-777-1260
Bez, Frank/1880 Santa Barbara Ave, San Luis Obispo, CA 805-541-2878
Bielenberg, Paul/2447 Lanterman Terr, Los Angeles, CA 213-669-1085
Biggs, Ken/1147 N Hudson Ave, Los Angeles, CA 213-462-7739
Bilecky, John/5047 W Pico Blvd, Los Angeles, CA 213-931-1610
Bilyell, Martin/600 NE Couch St, Portland, OR 503-238-0349
Bischoff & Assoc/1201 First Ave S #310, Seattle, WA 206-292-9931
Bishop, David/Photopia/PO Box 2309, San Francisco, CA 415-441-5611
Bjoin, Henry/146 N La Brea Ave, Los Angeles, CA 213-937-4097
Blakeley, Jim/1061 Folsom St, San Francisco, CA 415-558-9300
Blakeman, Bob/710 S Santa Fe, Los Angeles, CA 213-624-6662
Blattel, David/740 S Mariposa St, Burbank, CA 213-937-0366
BLAUSTEIN, JOHN/911 EUCLID AVE, BERKELEY, CA (P 370,371) 415-525-8133
Bleyer, Pete/807 N Sierra Bonita Ave, Los Angeles, CA 546-653-6567

Please send us your additions and updates.

PHOTOGRAPHERS

Blumensaadt, Mike/306 Edna, San Francisco, CA	415-333-6178
Bodnar, Joe/2817 Selby, Los Angeles, CA	213-838-6587
Boonisar, Peter/PO Box 2274, Atascadero, CA	805-466-5577
Bortvent, Jim/9100 SW Washington, Portland, OR	503-297-2976
Boudreau, Bernard/1015 N Cahuenga, Hollywood, CA	213-467-2602
Boulevard Photographic/5701 Buckingham Pky #F, Culver City, CA	213-649-0202
Boulger & Kanuit/503 S Catalina, Redondo Beach, CA	213-540-6300
Bourret, Tom/930 Alabama, San Francisco, CA	415-626-8425
Bowen, John E/PO Box 1115, Hilo, HI	808-959-9460
Boyd, Bill/614 Santa Barbara St, Santa Barbara, CA	805-962-9193
Boyd, Jack/2038 Calvert Ave, Costa Mesa, CA	714-556-8133
Boyer, Dale/PO Box 391535, Mountainview, CA	415-968-9656
Boyer, Neil/1416 Aviation Blvd, Redondo Beach, CA	213-374-0443
Brabant, Patricia/245 S Van Ness 3rd Fl, San Francisco, CA	415-864-0591
Bracke, Vic/560 S Main St #4N, Los Angeles, CA	213-623-6522
Bradley, Leverett/Box 1793, Santa Monica, CA	213-394-0908
Bragstad, Jeremiah O/1041 Folsom St, San Francisco, CA	415-776-2740
Brandon, Randy/PO Box 1010, Girdwood, AK	907-783-2773
Braun, Ernest/PO Box 627, San Anselmo, CA	415-454-2791
Brenneis, Jon/2576 Shattuck, Berkeley, CA	415-845-3377
Brewer, Art/27324 Camino Capistrano #161, Laguna Nigel, CA	714-831-9885
Brian, Rick/555 S Alexandria Ave, Los Angeles, CA	213-387-3017
BRITT, JIM/140 N LABREA, LOS ANGELES, CA (P 372)	**213-936-3131**
Broberg, Ed/PO Box 1892, Walla Walla, WA	509-529-5189
Brod, Garry/6502 Santa Monica Blvd, Hollywood, CA	213-463-7887
Brown, George/1417 15th St, San Francisco, CA	415-621-3543
Brown, Matt/420 Commercial Ave, Anacortes, WA	206-293-3540
Brown, Michael/PO Box 45969, Los Angeles, CA	213-379-7254
Browne, Rick/145 Shake Tree Ln, Scotts Valley, CA	408-438-3919
Brum, Kim/5555-L Santa Fe St, San Diego, CA	619-483-2124
Brummett, Richard/515 N 50th St, Seattle, WA	206-633-5995
Bryan, J Y/3594 Ramona Dr, Riverside, CA	714-684-8266
Bubar, Julie/12559 Palero Rd, San Diego, CA	619-234-4020
Buchanan, Craig/1026 Folsom St #207, San Francisco, CA	415-861-5566
Budnik, Victor/125 King St, San Francisco, CA	415-541-9050
Burke, Kevin/1015 N Cahuenga Blvd, Los Angeles, CA	213-467-0266
Burke, Leslie/947 La Cienega, Los Angeles, CA	213-652-7011
Burke/Triolo Photo/940 E 2nd St #2, Los Angeles, CA	213-687-4730
Burkhart, Howard Photography/231 Olive #10, Inglewood, CA	213-671-2283
Burr, Bruce/2867 1/2 W 7th St, Los Angeles, CA	213-388-3361
Burr, Lawrence/76 Manzanita Rd, Fairfax, CA	415-456-9158
Burroughs, Robert/6713 Bardonia St, San Diego, CA	619-469-6922
Burry, D L/PO Box 1611, Los Gatos, CA	408-354-1922
Burt, Pat/1412 SE Stark, Portland, OR	503-284-9989
Bush, Chan/PO Box 819, Montrose, CA	818-957-6558
Bush, Charles/940-N Highland, Los Angeles, CA	213-937-8246
Bush, Dave/2 St George St, San Francisco, CA	415-981-2874
Busher, Dick/7042 20th Place NE, Seattle, WA	206-523-1426
Bussey, Bill/7915 Via Stefano, Burbank, CA	818-767-5078
Butchofsky, Jan/7219 Hampton Ave, Los Angeles, CA	213-874-5313
Butler, Erik/161 King St, San Francisco, CA	415-777-1656

C

C & I Photography/3523 Ryder St, Santa Clara, CA	408-733-5855
Cable, Ron/17835 Skypark Cir #N, Irvine, CA	714-261-8910
Caccavo, James/10002 Crescent Hts Blvd, Los Angeles, CA	213-939-9594
Cacitti, Stanley R/589 Howard, San Francisco, CA	415-974-5668
Caddow, Thomas/1944 University #10, Palo Alto, CA	415-329-0334
Cahoon, John/613 S LaBrea Ave, Los Angeles, CA	213-930-1144
Camera Hawaii/875 Waimanu St #110, Honolulu, HI	808-536-2302
Cameron, Robert/543 Howard, San Francisco, CA	415-777-5582
Camp, James Lee/1248 Jedburgh St, Glendora, CA	818-966-9240
Campbell Comm Photo/8586 Miramar Pl, San Diego, CA	619-587-0336
Campbell, David/244 Ninth St, San Francisco, CA	415-864-2556
Campbell, Kathleen Taylor/4751 Wilshire Blvd, Los Angeles, CA	213-931-6202
Campos Photography/705 13th St, San Diego, CA	619-233-9914
Candid Photo/9602 Orange Ave, Anaheim, CA	800-336-3838
Cannon, Bill/516 Yale Ave North, Seattle, WA	206-682-7031
Caplan, Stan/7014 Santa Monica Blvd, Los Angeles, CA	213-462-1271
Capps, Alan/137 S La Peer Dr, Los Angeles, CA	213-276-3724
Caputo, Tony/6636 Santa Monica Blvd, Hollywood, CA	213-464-6636
Carey, Ed/60 Federal St, San Francisco, CA	415-543-4883

Carlson, Craig/266 J Street, Chula Vista, CA	619-422-4937
Carofano, Ray/1011 1/4 W 190th St, Gardena, CA	213-515-0310
Carpenter, Mert/2020 Granada Wy, Los Gatos, CA	408-370-1663
Carr, Melanie/2120 J Durante Blvd #U, Del Mar, CA	619-755-1200
Carroll, Bruce/517 Dexter Ave N, Seattle, WA	206-623-2119
Carroll, Tom/26712 Calle Los Alamos, Capistrano Beach, CA	714-493-2665
Carroon, Chip/PO Box 5545, Mill Valley, CA	415-864-1082
Carruth, Kerry/7153 Helmsdale Circle, Canoga Park, CA	818-704-6570
Carry, Mark/2224 Old Middlefield Way, Mountain View, CA	415-967-8470
Casemore, Rick/111 N Tamarind Ave, Los Angeles, CA	213-461-9384
Casilli, Mario/2366 N Lake Ave, Altadena, CA	213-681-4476
Casler, Christopher/1600 Viewmont Dr, Los Angeles, CA	213-854-7733
Cato, Eric/3456 1/2 Floyd Terr, Los Angeles, CA	213-851-5606
Caulfield, Andy/PO Box 41131, Los Angeles, CA	213-258-3070
Chamberlain, Paul/319 1/2 S Robertson Blvd, Beverly Hills, CA	213-652-5885
Chaney, Brad/370 4th St, San Francisco, CA	415-543-2525
Chang, Richard/17911 Skypark Cir #M, Irvine, CA	714-261-5119
Charles, Cindy/1040 Noe St, San Francisco, CA	415-821-4457
Chen, James/1917 Anacapa St, Santa Barbara, CA	805-569-1849
Cherin, Alan/220 S Rose St, Los Angeles, CA	213-680-9893
Chernus, Ken/9531 Washington Blvd, Culver City, CA	213-838-3116
Chesser, Mike/6632 Santa Monica Blvd, Los Angeles, CA	213-463-5678
Chester, Mark/PO Box 99501, San Francisco, CA	415-922-7512
Chiarot, Roy/846 S Robertson Blvd, Los Angeles, CA	213-659-9173
Chin, K P/PO Box 421737, San Francisco, CA	415-282-3041
Chmielewski, David/458 Crescent Ave, Sunnyvale, CA	408-773-9507
Chun, Mike/35 Russia St #H, San Francisco, CA	415-469-7220
Chung, Ken-Lei/5200 Venice Blvd, Los Angeles, CA	213-938-9117
Church, Jim & Cathy/PO Box 80, Gilroy, CA	408-842-9682
Ciskowski, Jim/2444 Wilshire Blvd #B100, Santa Monica, CA	213-829-7375
Clark, Richard/334 S LaBrea, Los Angeles, CA	213-933-7407
Claxton, William/1368 Angelo Dr, Beverly Hills, CA	213-854-2222
CLAYTON, JOHN/160 SOUTH PARK, SAN FRANCISCO, CA (P 361)	**415-495-4562**
Cobb, Bruce/1537-A 4th St #102, San Rafael, CA	415-454-0619
Coccia, Jim/PO Box 81313, Fairbanks, AK	907-479-4707
Cogen, Melinda/1112 N Beachwood Dr, Hollywood, CA	213-467-9414
Cohn, Steven/2036 Eunice St, Berkeley, CA	415-525-0982
Coit, Jim/5555-L Santa Fe St, San Diego, CA	619-272-2255
Coleberd, Frances/1273 Mills St Apt 3, Menlo Park, CA	415-325-4731
Coleman, Arthur Photography/303 N Indian Ave, Palm Springs, CA	619-325-7015
Colladay, Charles/711 12th Ave, San Diego, CA	619-231-2920
Collison, James/6950 Havenurst, Van Nuys, CA	818-902-0770
Coluzzi, Tony Photography/897 Independence Ave #2B, Mountain View, CA	415-969-2955
COOK, KATHLEEN NORRIS/PO BOX 2159, LAGUNA HILLS, CA (P 373)	**714-770-4619**
Cormier, Glenn/ PO Box 351, Santa Barbara, CA	805-963-4853
Cornfield, Jim/454 S La Brea Ave, Los Angeles, CA	213-938-3553
Correll, Volker/6614 Aldama St, Los Angeles, CA	213-255-3336
Corwin, Jeff/CPC Assoc/1910 Weepah Way, Los Angeles, CA	213-656-7449
Courbet, Yves/6516 W 6th St, Los Angeles, CA	213-655-2181
Courtney, William/4524 Rutgers Way, Sacramento, CA	916-487-8501
Cowin, Morgin/325 Bocana St, San Francisco, CA	415-648-2600
Crane, Wally/PO Box 81, Los Altos, CA	415-960-1990
Crawford, Dick/PO Box 747, Sanger, CA	209-875-3800
Crowley, Eliot/706 W Pico Blvd, Los Angeles, CA	213-742-0367
Cruver, Dick/517 Aloha St, Seattle, WA	206-283-7900
Cummings, Ian/2400 Kettner Blvd, San Diego, CA	619-231-1270
Cummins, Jim/1527 13th Ave, Seattle, WA	206-322-4944

D

Dahlstrom Photography Inc/2312 NW Savier St, Portland, OR	503-222-4910
Dang, Tai/426 Jefferson St, Oakland, CA	415-832-8642
Daniel, Hank/PO Box 15779, Sacramento, CA	916-321-1278
Daniel, Jay/517 Jacoby St #11, San Raphael, CA	415-459-1495
Davey, Robert/PO Box 69291, Los Angeles, CA	213-659-3542
David/Gayle Photo/911 Western Ave #510, Seattle, WA	206-624-5207
DAVIDSON, DAVE/25003 S BEESON RD, BEAVERCREEK, OR (P 374)	**503-632-7650**
Davidson, Jerry/3923 W Jefferson Blvd, Los Angeles, CA	213-735-1552
Davis, Tim/PO Box 1278, Palo Alto, CA	415-327-4192

Please send us your additions and updates.

Dayton, Ted/4415 Ventura Canyon #103, Sherman Oaks, CA	818-906-2565
DeCastro, Mike/2415 De La Cruz, Santa Clara, CA	408-988-8696
DeCruyenaere, Howard/1825 E Albion Ave, Santa Ana, CA	714-997-4446
DEGENNARO, GEORGE ASSOC/902 SOUTH NORTON AVE, LOS ANGELES, CA (P 350,351)	**213-935-5179**
Degler, Curtis/1050 Carolan Ave #311, Burlingame, CA	415-342-7381
Delancie, Steve/1129 Folsom St, San Francisco, CA	415-864-2640
Demerdjian, Jacob/3331 W Beverly Blvd, Montebello, CA	213-724-9630
DeMont, Debbi/3736 E 7th St, Long Beach, CA	213-433-1087
Denman, Frank B/1201 First Ave S, Seattle, WA	206-325-9260
Denny, Michael/2631 Ariane Dr, San Diego, CA	619-272-9104
DePaola, Mark/1560 Benedict Cnyn Dr, Beverly Hills, CA	213-550-5910
Der, Rick Photography/50 Mandell St #10, San Francisco, CA	415-824-8580
Derhacopian, Ronald/3109 Beverly Blvd, Los Angeles, CA	213-388-6724
Devine, W L Studios/PO Box 67, Maple Falls, WA	206-599-2927
DeWilde, Roc/139 Noriega, San Francisco, CA	415-681-4612
DeYoung, Skip/1112 N Beachwood, Los Angeles, CA	213-462-0712
Diaz, Armando/19 S Park, San Francisco, CA	415-495-3552
DIGITAL ART/3699 WILSHIRE BLVD #870, LOS ANGELES, CA (P 375)	**213-387-8384**
Dinn, Peter/2776 Humboldt Ave, Oakland, CA	415-532-7792
Divine, Jeff/PO Box 3778, San Clemente, CA	714-432-1333
Dolgins, Alan/1640 S La Cienega Blvd, Los Angeles, CA	213-273-5794
Dominick/833 N LaBrea Ave, Los Angeles, CA	213-934-3033
Donaldson, Peter/118 King St, San Francisco, CA	415-957-1102
Dow, Larry/1537 W 8th St, Los Angeles, CA	213-483-7970
Dowbanko, Uri/PO Box 1201, Aguroa Hills, CA	818-706-8838
Drake, Brian/407 Southwest 11th Ave, Portland, OR	503-241-4532
Dreiwitz, Herb/145 N Edgemont St, Los Angeles, CA	213-383-1746
Dressler, Rick/1322 Bell Ave #M, Tustin, CA	714-730-9113
Driver, Wallace/2510 Clairemont Dr #113, San Diego, CA	619-275-3159
Drumbor, David C/1125 Stewart Ct #E, Sunnyvale, CA	408-554-6420
Dudley, Hardin & Yang/3839 Stone Way North, Seattle, WA	206-632-3001
Duff, Rodney/4901 Morena Blvd #323, San Diego, CA	619-270-4082
Duffey, Robert/9691 Campus Dr, Anaheim, CA	714-956-4731
Duka, Lonnie/919 Oriole Dr, Laguna Beach, CA	714-494-7057
Dull, Ed/1745 NW Marshall, Portland, OR	503-224-3754
Dumentz, Barbara/1615 N Cahuenga, Los Angeles, CA	213-467-6397
Dunbar, Clark/1260-B Pear Ave, Mountain View, CA	415-964-4225
Dunmire, Larry/PO Box 338, Balboa Island, CA	714-673-4058
Dyna Pac/7926 Convoy St, San Diego, CA	619-560-0280

E

Ealy, Dwayne/2 McLaren #B, Irvine, Ca	714-951-5089
Eastabrook, William R/3281 Oakshire Dr, Los Angeles, CA	213-851-3281
Eclipse Anonymous/PO Box 689, Haines, AK	907-766-2670
Edmunds, Dana/188 N King St, Honolulu, HI	808-521-7711
Edwards, Grant P/6837 Nancy Ridge Dr #G, San Diego, CA	619-458-1999
Ekdahl, Dean/2025 W Balboa Blvd #D, Newport Beach, CA	714-675-3902
Elias, Robert Studio/959 N Cole, Los Angeles, CA	213-460-2988
Elk, John III/583 Weldon, Oakland, CA	415-834-3024
Emanuel, Manny/2257 Hollyridge Dr, Hollywood, CA	213-465-0259
Emberly, Gordon/1479 Folsom, San Francisco, CA	415-621-9714
Enkelis, Liane/764 Sutter Ave, Palo Alto, CA	415-326-3253
Epstein, Mike/PO Box 6753, Bend, OR	503-382-7370
Esgro, Dan/PO Box 38536, Los Angeles, CA	213-932-1919
Estel, Suzanne/2325 3rd St, San Francisco, CA	415-864-3661
Evans, Marty/11112 Ventura Blvd, Studio City, CA	818-762-5400

F

Falk, Randolph/123 16th Ave, San Francisco, CA	415-751-8800
Fallon, Bernard/524 N Juanita Ave #3, Redondo Beach, CA	213-318-6006
Faries, Tom/16431 Sandalwood, Fountain Valley, CA	714-775-5767
Farruggio, Matthew J/855 Folsom St #203, San Francisco, CA	415-543-6161
Faubel, Warren/1317 Scott Ave, Pomona, CA	714-623-7342
Fauguet, Emile/PO Box 2662, Everett, WA	206-353-9595
Feldman, Marc/6442 Santa Monica Blvd, Hollywood, CA	213-463-4829
Felt, Jim/1316 SE 12th Ave, Portland, OR	503-238-1748
Felzman, Joe/421 NW Fourth Ave, Portland, OR	503-224-7983
Finn, Dennis/1520 Tower Grove Dr, Beverly Hills, CA	213-274-4014
Finnegan, Kristin/3045 NW Thurman St, Portland, OR	503-241-2701
Firebaugh, Steve/3107 S Dearborn, Seattle, WA	206-721-5151
Fischer, Curt/51 Stillman, San Francisco, CA	415-974-5568
Fischer, David/340 Harriet, San Francisco, CA	415-495-4585

Fisher, Arthur Vining/271 Missouri St, San Francisco, CA	415-626-5483
Fitch, Wanelle/17845-D Sky Pk Cir, Irvine, CA	714-261-1566
Flavin, Frank/PO Box 141172, Anchorage, AK	907-561-1606
Flinn, Jim/8617 Sandpoint Way NE, Seattle, WA	206-524-1409
Flood, Alan/206 14th Ave, San Mateo, CA	415-572-0439
Fogg, Don/259 Clara St, San Francisco, CA	415-974-5244
Foothorap, Robert/426 Bryant St, San Francisco, CA	415-957-1447
Ford Photography/906 1/2 S Robertson Blvd, Los Angeles, CA	213-655-7655
Forsman, John/8696 Crescent Dr, Los Angeles, CA	213-933-9339
Forster, Bruce/431 NW Flanders, Portland, OR	503-222-5222
Forsyth, Dan/2311 Fifteenth Ave, San Francisco, CA	415-753-8451
Fort, Daniel/691 Center St, Costa Mesa, CA	714-546-5709
Fortson, Ed/Shoshana/400 S June St, Los Angeles, CA	213-934-6368
Fowler, Bradford/1946 N Serrano Ave, Los Angeles, CA	213-464-5708
Fox, Arthur/2194 Cable St, San Diego, CA	619-223-4784
Frankel, Tracy/7250 Hillside Ave #308, Los Angeles, CA	213-851-9668
FRANKLIN, CHARLY/3352 20TH ST, SAN FRANCISCO, CA (P 376)	**415-543-5400**
Franzen, David/746 Ilaniwai St #200, Honolulu, HI	808-537-9921
Frazier, Kim Andrew/PO Box 6132, Hayward, CA	415-889-7050
Freed, Jack/749 N La Brea, Los Angeles, CA	213-931-1015
Freis, Jay/416 Richardson St, Sausalito, CA	415-332-6709
French, Gerald/550 15th St #31/Showpl Sq, San Francisco, CA	415-397-3040
French, Peter/PO Box 100, Kamuela, HI	808-889-6488
Friedlander, Ernie/82 Ringold Alley, San Francisco, CA	415-626-6111
Friedman, Todd/PO Box 3737, Beverly Hills, CA	213-550-0831
Friend, David/3886 Ampudia St, San Diego, CA	619-260-1603
Frisch, Stephen/ICB - Gate 5 Rd, Sausalito, CA	415-332-4545
Frisella, Josef/340 S Clark Dr, Beverly Hills, CA	213-462-2593
FRITZ, STEVE/1023 S SANTA FE AVE, LOS ANGELES, CA (P 359)	**213-629-8052**
Fritze, Jack/2106 S Grand, Santa Ana, CA	714-545-6466
Fronk, Peter/203 Indian Way, Novato, CA	415-883-5253
Fruchtman, Jerry/8735 Washington Blvd, Culver City, CA	213-839-7891
FRY, GEORGE B III/PO BOX 2465, MENLO PARK, CA (P 377)	**415-323-7663**
FUJIOKA, ROBERT/715 STIERLIN RD, MT VIEW, CA (P 354,355)	**415-960-3010**
Fukuda, Curtis/2239-F Old Middlefield Way, Mountain View, CA	415-962-9131
Fukuda, Steve/454 Natoma, San Francisco, CA	415-543-9339
Fukuhara, Richard Yutaka/3267 Grant St, Signal Hill, CA	213-597-4497
Furuta, Carl/7360 Melrose Ave, Los Angeles, CA	213-655-1911
Fusco, Paul/7 Melody Ln, Mill Valley, CA	415-388-8940

G

Gage, Rob/789 Pearl St, Laguna Beach, CA	714-494-7265
Gallagher, John/PO Box 4070, Seattle, WA	206-937-2422
GALVAN, GARY/4626 1/2 HOLLYWOOD BLVD, LOS ANGELES, CA (P 378,379)	**213-667-1457**
GARDNER, ROBERT/800 S CITRUS AVE, LOS ANGELES, CA (P 381)	**213-931-1108**
Garrabrandts, Doug/431 Winchester Ave, Glendale, CA	818-502-0271
Garretson, Jim/333 Fifth St, San Francisco, CA	415-974-6464
Gascon, Enrique Jr/143 S Edgemont St, Los Angeles, CA	213-383-9157
Gatley, David/14341 Aedan Ct, Poway, CA	619-748-0405
Geissler, Rick/1729 Vista Del Valle, El Cajon, CA	619-440-5594
Gelineau, Val/1041 N McCadden Pl, Los Angeles, CA	213-465-6149
Gerba, Peter/50 Ringold St, San Francisco, CA	415-864-5474
Gerretsen, Charles/1714 N Wilton Pl, Los Angeles, CA	213-462-6342
Gersten, Paul/1021 1/2 N La Brea, Los Angeles, CA	213-850-6045
Gervase, Mark/732 N Highland Ave, Los Angeles, CA	213-464-2775
Giannetti Photography/730 Clementina St, San Francisco, CA	415-864-0270
Gibbs, Christopher/4640 Business Pk Blvd, Anchorage, AK	907-563-6112
Gibson, Mark/PO Box 14542, San Francisco, CA	415-524-8118
Giefer, Sebastian/3132 Hollyridge Dr, Hollywood, CA	213-461-1122
Gilbert, Elliot/311 N Curson Ave, Los Angeles, CA	213-939-1846
Gillman, Mitchell/610 22nd St #307, San Francisco, CA	415-621-5334
Gilmore, Ed/9000 Broadway Terrace, Oakland, CA	415-547-2194
Giraud, Steve/2960 Airway Ave #B-103, Costa Mesa, CA	714-751-8191
Gleis, Nick/10421 Venice Blvd, Los Angeles, CA	213-204-4229
Glenn, Joel/439 Bryant St, San Francisco, CA	415-957-1273
Gnass, Jeff/PO Box 2196, Oroville, CA	916-533-6788
Goavec, Pierre/1464 La Plaza #303, SAn Francisco, CA	415-564-2252

Please send us your additions and updates.

Goble, James/620 Moulton Ave #205, Los Angeles, CA	213-222-7661
Godwin, Bob/1427 E 41st St #1, Los Angeles, CA	213-269-8001
Going, Michael/1117 N Wilcox Pl, Los Angeles, CA	213-465-6853
Goldman, Larry/5310 Circle Dr #206, Van Nuys, CA	818-995-4121
Goldner, David/833 Traction Ave, Los Angeles, CA	212-617-0761
Goodman, Jamison/1001 E 1st St, Los Angeles, CA	213-617-1900
Goodman, Todd/1417 26th #E, Santa Monica, CA	213-453-3621
Gordon, Charles M/19226 35th Pl NE, Seattle, WA	206-365-2132
Gordon, David/905 Cole Ave, Los Angeles, CA	213-464-1846
Gordon, Jon/2052 Los Feliz Dr, Thousand Oaks, CA	805-496-1485
Gordon, Larry Dale/2047 Castilian Dr, Los Angeles, CA	213-874-6318
Gorman, Greg/1351 Miller Dr, Los Angeles, CA	213-650-5540
Gottlieb, Mark/1915 University Ave, Palo Alto, CA	415-321-8761
Gowans, Edward/10316 NW Thompson Rd, Portland, OR	503-297-5110
Grady, Noel/277 Rodney Ave, Encinitas, CA	619-753-8630
Graham, Don/1545 Marlay Dr, Los Angeles, CA	213-656-7117
Graham, Ellen/614 N Hillcrest Rd, Beverly Hills, CA	213-275-6195
Gray, Dennis/250 Newhall St, San Francisco, CA	415-641-4009
Gray, Keehn/625 Locust St, San Francisco, CA	415-332-8831
Gray, Marion/42 Orben Pl, San Francisco, CA	415-931-5689
Gray, Todd/1962 N Wilcox, Los Angeles, CA	213-466-6088
Greenberg, Jim/17518 Castellammare, Pacific Palisades, CA	213-454-9911
Greenleigh, John/756 Natoma, San Francisco, CA	415-864-4147
Grigg, Robert/1050 N Wilcox Ave, Hollywood, CA	213-469-6316
Grimm, Tom & Michelle/PO Box 83, Laguna Beach, CA	714-494-1336
Groenekamp, Greg/2922 Oakhurst Ave, Los Angeles, CA	213-838-2466
Gross, Richard/1810 Harrison St, San Francisco, CA	415-558-8075
Groutoge, Monty/2214 S Fairview Rd, Santa Ana, CA	714-751-8734
Gullette, William/3410 Villa Terr, San Diego, CA	619-692-3801
Gurente, Paul/1005 W Olive Ave, Burbank, CA	818-841-4050
H Hagopian, Jim/915 N Mansfield Ave, Hollywood, CA	213-856-0018
Hagyard, Dave/1205 E Pike, Seattle, WA	206-322-8419
Haislip, Kevin/PO Box 1862, Portland, OR	503-254-8859
Hale, Don/460 NE 70th St, Seattle, WA	206-524-5220
Hall, Alice/1033 N Myra Ave, Los Angeles, CA	213-666-0535
Hall, George/82 Macondray Ln, San Francisco, CA	415-775-7373
Hall, Steven/645 N Eckhoff St #P, Orange, CA	714-634-1132
Hall, William/19881 Bushard St, Huntington Bch, CA	714-968-2473
Hamilton, David W/511 The Alameda, San Anselmo, CA	415-459-0625
Hammid, Tino/PO Box 69-A109, Los Angeles, CA	213-652-6626
Hampton, Ralph/PO Box 480057, Los Angeles, CA	213-934-5781
Hanauer, Mark/1717 N Vine St #12, Los Angeles, CA	213-462-2421
Handleman, Doris/10108 Lovelane, Los Angeles, CA	213-838-0088
Hands, Bruce/PO Box 16186, Seattle, WA	206-938-8620
Hansen, Jim/2800 S Main St #1, Santa Ana, CA	714-545-1343
Hara/265 Prado Rd #4, San Luis Obispo, CA	805-543-6907
Harder, Paul/731 Kala Point, Port Townsend, WA	206-385-4878
Harding, C B/660 N Thompson St, Portland, OR	503-281-9907
Harlem, Jason/2534 W 7th St, Los Angeles, CA	213-383-2774
Harmel, Mark/714 N Westbourne, West Hollywood, CA	213-659-1633
Harrington, Lewis/746 Ilaniwai #200, Honolulu, HI	808-533-3696
Harrington, Marshall/2775 Kurtz St #2, San Diego, CA	619-291-2775
Harris, Paul/4601 Larkwood Ave, Woodland Hills, CA	818-347-8294
Hart, G K/780 Bryant St, San Francisco, CA	415-495-4278
Hartman, Raiko/6916 Melrose, Los Angeles, CA	213-278-4700
Harvey, Stephen/7801 W Beverly Blvd, Los Angeles, CA	213-934-5817
Hathaway, Steve/173 Bluxome 4th Fl, San Francisco, CA	415-495-3473
Hawkes, William/5757 Venice Blvd, Los Angeles, CA	213-931-7777
Hawley, Larry/6502 Santa Monica Blvd, Hollywood, CA	213-466-5864
Heffernan, Terry/352 6th St, San Francisco, CA	415-626-1999
Henderson, Tom/11722 Sorrento Vly Rd #A, San Diego, CA	619-481-7743
Henneg, Robert/3435 Army St #336, San Francisco, CA	415-282-7302
Herrmann, Karl/3165 S Barrington Ave #F, Los Angeles, CA	213-397-5917
Herron, Matt/PO Box 1860, Sausalito, CA	415-479-6994
Hewett, Richard/5725 Buena Vista Terr, Los Angeles, CA	213-254-4577
Hicks, Alan/333 N W Park, Portland, OR	503-226-6741
Hicks, Jeff & Assoc/41 E Main, Los Gatos, CA	408-395-2277
Higgins, Donald/201 San Vincente Blvd #14, Santa Monica, CA	213-393-8858
Higgins, Errol/2 McLaren #B, Irvine, CA	714-951-5089
Hildreth, James/40 Lundys Lane, San Francisco, CA	415-821-7398
Hill, Dennis/994 North Altadena, Pasadena, CA	818-795-2589

Hines, Richard/734 E 3rd St, Los Angeles, CA	213-625-2333
Hirshew, Lloyd/750 Natoma, San Francisco, CA	415-861-3902
Hishi, James/612 S Victory Blvd, Burbank, CA	213-849-4871
Hixson, Richard/1468 Huston Rd, Lafayette, CA	415-621-0246
Hodge, Nettie/9687 Adams Ave, Huntington Beach, CA	714-964-3166
Hodges, Walter/1605 Twelfth Ave #25, Seattle, WA	206-325-9550
Hoffman, Davy/1923 Colorado Ave, Santa Monica, CA	213-453-4661
HOFFMAN, PAUL/4500 19TH ST, SAN FRANCISCO, CA (P 382,383)	**415-863-3575**
Hofmann, Mark/827 N Fairfax Ave, Los Angeles, CA	213-658-7376
Hogg, Peter/1221 S La Brea, Los Angeles, CA	213-937-0642
Hollenbeck, Cliff/Box 4247 Pioneer Sq, Seattle, WA	206-682-6300
Hollingsworth, Mike/164 N La Brea Ave, Los Angeles, CA	213-936-0310
Holmes, Mark/347 S Wilton Pl, Los Angeles, CA	213-933-5242
Holmes, Robert/PO Box 556, Mill Valley, CA	415-383-6783
Holt, David/1624 Cotner Ave #B, Los Angeles, CA	213-478-1188
Holz, William/7630 W Norton Ave, Los Angeles, CA	213-656-4061
Honolulu Creative Group/424 Nahua St, Honolulu, HI	808-926-6188
Honowitz, Ed/512 N Hobart Blvd, Los Angeles, CA	213-669-1785
Hooper, H Lee/30708 Monte Lado Dr, Malibu, CA	213-457-2897
Hopkins, Stew/345 5th Ave, Venice, CA	213-396-8649
HORIKAWA, MICHAEL/508 KAMAKEE ST, HONOLULU, HI (P 384)	**808-538-7378**
HOUSEL, JAMES F/84 UNIVERSITY PL #409, SEATTLE, WA (P 385)	**206-682-6181**
Houser, Dave/249 S Hwy 101 #336, Solana Beach, CA	619-755-2828
Hudetz, Larry/11135 SE Yamhill, Portland, OR	503-245-6001
Hunt, Phillip/3435 Army St #206, San Francisco, CA	415-821-9879
HUNTER, JEFF/4626 1/2 HOLLYWOOD BLVD, LOS ANGELES, CA (P 386,387)	**213-937-2008**
Hussey, Ron/1499 Bluebird Canyon, Laguna Beach, CA	714-494-6988
Hylen, Bo/1640 S LaCienega, Los Angeles, CA	213-271-6543
I I P C Photo/4320 Viewridge Ave #C, San Diego, CA	619-565-0672
Illusion Factory/4657 Abargo St, Woodland Hills, CA	818-883-4501
Illustration West/4020 N Palm #207, Fullerton, CA	714-773-9131
Imstepf, Charles/620 Moulton Ave #216, Los Angeles, CA	213-222-8773
In Vision/2004 Martin Ave, Santa Clara, CA	408-496-6030
Inahara, Sharon/178 N Mansfield, Los Angeles, CA	213-463-8318
Iri, Carl/929 S Hampshire Ave, Los Angeles, CA	213-388-5737
Isaacs, Robert/1646 Mary Ave, Sunnyvale, CA	408-245-1690
Iverson, Bruce/2511 W Sunflower #D9, Santa Ana, CA	714-546-0485
Iverson, Michele/1527 Princeton #2, Santa Monica, CA	213-829-5717
J Jacobs, Lou/296 Avenida Andorra, Cathedral City, CA	619-324-5505
Jacobs, Michael/646 N Cahuenga Blvd, Los Angeles, CA	213-461-0240
James, Patrick/2231 Mesa, San Pedro, CA	213-519-1357
Jarrett, Michael/16782 Red Hill #B, Irvine, CA	714-250-4357
Jasmine Photography/1746 N Ivar, Hollywood, CA	213-851-2775
Jay, Michael/1 Zeno Pl #345 Folsom Cmplx, San Francisco, CA	415-543-7101
Jenkin, Bruce/11577-A Slater Ave, Fountain Valley, CA	714-546-2949
Jensen, John/449 Bryant St, San Francisco, CA	415-957-9449
Johnson, Dave Photo/2081 Bering Dr #F, San Jose, CA	408-436-8778
Johnson, Diane Photo/3018 Columbia St, San Diego, CA	619-295-2369
Johnson, Payne B/4650 Harvey Rd, San Diego, CA	619-299-4567
Jones, Aaron/608 Folsom St, San Francisco, CA	415-495-6333
Jones, DeWitt/Box 116, Bolinas, CA	415-868-0674
Jones, Douglas/918 Lombard St, Costa Mesa, CA	714-557-2300
Jones, William B/2171 India St #B, San Diego, CA	619-235-8892
K Kaestner, Reed/2120 J Durante Blvd #4, Del Mar, CA	619-755-1200
Kahn, Steve/622 Rose Ave, Venice, CA	213-450-5576
Kakuk, Ted/PO Box 1030, Glendora, CA	818-335-8729
Kaldor, Kurt/1011 Grandview Dr, S San Francisco, CA	415-583-8704
KARAGEORGE, JIM/610 22ND ST #309, SAN FRANCISCO, CA (P 388,389)	**415-648-3444**
Karjalas' Photo Vision/231 E Imperial Hwy #260, Fullerton, CA	714-992-1210
Kasmier, Richard/441 E Columbine #I, Santa Ana, CA	714-545-4022
Kasparowitz, Josef/PO Box 4308, San Luis Obispo, CA	805-544-8209
Katano, Nicole/2969 Jackson #104, San Francisco, CA	415-563-2646
Katzenberger, George/211-D E Columbine St, Santa Ana, CA	714-545-3055
Kauffman, Helen/9017 Rangeley Ave, Los Angeles, CA	213-275-3569

Kaufman, Robert/819 Stonegate Dr, S San Francisco, CA	415-588-6385
Kauschke, Hans-Gerhard/16 Una Way #D, Mill Valley, CA	415-383-4230
Keenan, Elaine Faris/90 Natoma St, San Francisco, CA	415-546-9246
KEENAN, LARRY/421 BRYANT ST, SAN FRANCISCO, CA	
(P 390)	**415-495-6474**
Kehl, Robert/769 22nd St, Oakland, CA	415-452-0501
Keller, Greg/769 22nd St, Oakland, CA	415-452-0501
Kelley, Tom/8525 Santa Monica Blvd, Los Angeles, CA	213-657-1780
Kent, Betty McAlinden/2317 Cliff Dr, Newport Beach, CA	714-631-1141
Kermani, Shahn/109 Minna St #210, San Francisco, CA	415-567-6073
Kessler/McKinnon Photo/2101 Las Palmas, Carlsbad, CA	619-931-9299
Kiesow, Paul/459 1/2 N Fairfax Ave, Los Angeles, CA	213-655-1897
Kilberg, James/3371 Cahuenga Blvd W, Los Angeles, CA	213-874-9514
Killian, Glen/245 N Lake Ave, Pasadena, CA	213-681-2114
KIMBALL, RON/2582 SUN-MOR AVE, MT VIEW, CA (P 391)	**415-948-2939**
Kimball-Nanessence/3421 Tripp Ct #4, San Diego, CA	619-453-1922
King, Nicholas/3356 Hancock St #B, San Diego, CA	619-296-8200
Kinon, Ed/PO Box 590805, San Francisco, CA	415-752-0807
Kious, Gary/9800 Sepulvada Blvd #304, Los Angeles, CA	213-536-4880
Kirkendall/ Spring/18819 Olympic View Dr, Edmonds, WA	206-776-4685
Kirkland, Douglas/9060 Wonderland Park Ave, Los Angeles, CA	213-656-8511
Kirkpatrick, Mike/1115 Forest Way, Brookdale, CA	408-395-1447
Kleinman, Kathryn/542 Natoma St, San Francisco, CA	415-864-2406
Klimek & Weislein/, Los Angeles, CA	213-253-1049
Koch, Jim/1360 Logan Ave #106, Costa Mesa, CA	714-957-5719
Kodamama & Moriarty Photo/4081 Glencoe Ave, Marina Del Rey, CA	213-306-7574
Koehler, Rick/1622 Moulton Pkwy #A, Tustin, CA	714-259-8787
Koga, Dean/20219 SW Birch St, Santa Ana Hts, CA	714-756-9185
Kohler, Heinz/163 W Colorado Blvd, Pasadena, CA	213-681-9195
Kopp, Pierre/PO Box 8337, Long Beach, CA	213-430-8534
Kosta, Jeffrey/2565 Third St #306, San Francisco, CA	415-285-7001
Kramer, David/5121 Santa Fe St #A, San Diego, CA	619-270-5501
Krasner, Carin/5923 W Pico Blvd, Los Angeles, CA	213-937-4686
Kredenser, Peter/2551 Angelo Dr, Los Angeles, CA	213-278-6356
Kremers, Henry/1105 N Pcfic Cst Hwy #I, Laguna Beach, CA	714-494-3767
Krisel, Ron/1925 Pontius Ave, Los Angeles, CA	213-477-5519
Krosnick, Alan/2800 20th St, San Francisco, CA	415-285-1819
Krueger, Gary/PO Box 543, Montrose, CA	818-249-1051
Krupp, Carl/PO Box 910, Merlin, OR	503-479-6699
Kubly, Jon/1816 S Flower St, Los Angeles, CA	213-747-7259
Kuhn, Chuck/206 Third Ave S, Seattle, WA	206-624-4706
Kuhn, Robert/3022 Valevista Tr, Los Angeles, CA	213-461-3656
Kupersmith, Dan/823 N LaBrea, Los Angeles, CA	213-935-6232
Kurihara, Ted/680 Beach St #484, San Francisco, CA	415-771-5100
Kurisu/819 1/2 N Fairfax, Los Angeles, CA	213-655-7287
L Lachata, Carol/77 S Michigan Ave, Pasadena, CA	818-795-3797
Lamb & Hall/7318 Melrose, Los Angeles, CA	213-931-1775
Lammers, Bud/211-A East Columbine, Santa Ana, CA	714-546-4441
Lamont, Dan/117 W Denny Way #213, Seattle, WA	206-285-8252
Lamotte, Michael/828 Mission St, San Francisco, CA	415-777-1443
Landau, Robert/7275 Sunset Blvd #4, Los Angeles, CA	213-851-2995
LANDECKER, TOM/1028 FOLSOM ST, SAN FRANCISCO, CA	
(P 392,393)	**415-864-8888**
Lane, Bobbi/7213 Santa Monica Blvd, Los Angeles, CA	213-874-0557
Langdon, Harry/8275 Beverly Blvd, Los Angeles, CA	213-651-3212
LaRocca, Jerry/3734 SE 21st Ave, Portland, OR	503-232-5005
Larson, Dean/7668 Hollywood Blvd, Los Angeles, CA	213-876-1033
Latana Photo/6938 Wildlife Rd, Malibu, CA	213-457-1705
LaTona, Kevin/159 Western Ave W #454, Seattle, WA	206-285-5779
Laughmiller, Allen/1140 Irving, Glendale, CA	213-735-1551
Lawder, John/2672 S Grand, Santa Ana, CA	714-557-3657
Lawlor, John/6101 Melrose, Hollywood, CA	213-468-9050
Lea, Thomas/181 Alpine, San Francisco, CA	415-864-5941
Leach, David/7408 Beverly Blvd, Los Angeles, CA	213-932-1234
Leatart, Brian/520 N Western, Los Angeles, CA	213-856-0121
LEBON, DAVID/732 N HIGHLAND AVE, LOS ANGELES, CA	
(P 344,345)	**213-464-2775**
LEE, LARRY/PO BOX 4688, NORTH HOLLYWOOD, CA	
(P 394)	**818-766-2677**
Lee, Roger Allyn/1628 Folsom St, San Francisco, CA	415-861-1147
Lee, Sherwood/909 Micheltorena St, Los Angeles, CA	213-660-4230
Legname, Rudi/389 Clementina St, San Francisco, CA	415-777-9569
Lehman, Danny/6643 W 6th St, Los Angeles, CA	213-652-1930
Leighton, Ron/1360 Logan #105, Costa Mesa, CA	714-641-5122
Leng, Brian/1021 1/2 N La Brea, Los Angeles, CA	213-469-8624
Lennon Photographer/1015 N Cahuenga Blvd, Hollywood, CA	213-469-2212
Levasheff, Michael/1112 N Beachwood, Los Angeles, CA	213-462-0712
Levy, Paul/2830 S Robertson Blvd, Los Angeles, CA	213-838-2252
Lewin, Elyse/820 N Fairfax, Los Angeles, CA	213-655-4214
Lewine, Rob/8929 Holly Pl, Los Angeles, CA	213-654-0830
Lewis, Cindy/3960 Laurel Canyon Blvd #310, Studio City, CA	818-761-2911
Lewis, Don/2350 Stanley Hills Dr, Los Angeles, CA	213-656-2138
Li, Jeff/234 N Juanita Ave, Los Angeles, CA	213-383-3077
Lidz, Jane/33 Nordhoff St, San Francisco, CA	415-587-3377
Lightra/1545 N Wilcox Ave #102, Hollywood, CA	213-461-3529
Liles, Harry/1060 N Lillian Way, Hollywood, CA	213-466-1612
Lind, Lenny/1559 Howard St, San Francisco, CA	415-563-2020
Lindsey, Gordon/2311 Kettner Blvd, San Diego, CA	619-234-4432
Lindstrom, Eric/414 Olive Way #B29, Seattle, WA	206-583-0601
LINDSTROM, MEL/2510-H OLD MIDDLEFLD WAY,	
MOUNTAIN VIEW, CA (P 395)	**415-962-1313**
Livzey, John/1510 N Las Palmas, Hollywood, CA	213-469-2992
Lockwood, Scott/1317 Willow St, Los Angeles, CA	213-617-2222
Loeser, Peter/1431 Ocean Ave #819, Santa Monica, CA	213-393-5576
London, Matthew/10141 Maya Linda Rd #109, San Diego, CA	619-457-3251
Long, John/815 High St, Palo Alto, CA	415-328-5664
Longsdorf Jr, Robert/636 Lynwood St, Thousand Oaks, CA	805-492-3008
Lopez, Bret/533 Moreno Ave, Los Angeles, CA	213-393-8841
Lorenzo/4654 El Cajon Blvd, San Diego, CA	619-280-6010
Loveless, Roger/1700 Yosemite #201D, Simi Valley, CA	805-522-0961
Lovell, Craig/Rt 1 Box 53A, Carmel, CA	408-624-5241
Lowry, Alexander/PO Box 1500, Santa Cruz, CA	408-425-8081
Luhn, Jeff/ Visioneering/2565 3rd St #339, San Francisco, CA	415-282-6630
Lund, John M/860 Second St, San Francisco, CA	415-957-1775
Lund, John William/741 Natoma St, San Francisco, CA	415-552-7764
Lyon, Fred/237 Clara St, San Francisco, CA	415-974-5645
Lyons, Marv/2865 W 7th St, Los Angeles, CA	213-384-0732
M Machat, Mike/4426 Deseret Dr, Woodland Hills, CA	818-702-9433
Madden, Daniel J/PO Box 965, Los Alamitos, CA	213-429-3621
MADISON, DAVID/2284 OLD MIDDLEFIELD #8, MOUNTAIN	
VIEW, CA (P 396)	**415-961-6297**
Maharat, Chester/74 Clearbrook, Irvine, CA	714-832-6203
Maher, John/10413 NW Laidlaw Rd, Portland, OR	503-297-7451
Mahieu, Ted/PO Box 42578, San Francisco, CA	415-641-4747
Maloney, Jeff/2646 Taffy Dr, San Jose, CA	408-274-6027
Malphettes, Benoit/816 S Grand St, Los Angeles, CA	213-629-9054
Mangold, Steve/PO Box 1001, Palo Alto, CA	415-969-9897
Manning, Lawrence/15507 Doty Ave, Lawndale, CA	213-679-4774
Mar, Tim/PO Box 3488, Seattle, WA	206-583-0093
Maraldo, Vshanna/23316 Burbank Blvd, Woodland Hills, CA	818-703-8348
Marcus, Ken/6916 Melrose Ave, Los Angeles, CA	213-937-7214
Mareschal, Tom/5816 182nd Pl SW, Lynnwood, WA	206-771-6932
Margolies, Paul/480 Potrero, San Francisco, CA	415-621-3306
Marley, Stephen/1062 N Rengstorff Ave Bldg D, Mountain View, CA	415-966-8301
Marriott, John/1830 McAllister, San Francisco, CA	415-922-2920
Marsden, Dominic/3783 W Cahuenga Blvd, Studio City, CA	818-508-5222
Marshall, Jim/3622 16th St, San Francisco, CA	415-864-3622
Marshutz, Roger/1649 S La Cienega Blvd, Los Angeles, CA	213-273-1610
Martin Photography/1053 Blossom Dr, Santa Clara, CA	408-985-9378
Martin, Glenn/335 Oak Meadow Dr, Los Gatos, CA	408-354-0986
Martin, John F/118 King St, San Francisco, CA	415-957-1355
Martinelli, Bill/608 S Railroad Ave, San Mateo, CA	415-347-3589
Martinez, David/2325 Third St #433, San Francisco, CA	415-558-8088
Mason, Pablo/3026 North Park Way, San Diego, CA	619-298-2200
MASTERSON, ED/11211-S SORRENTO VAL RD, SAN DIEGO,	
CA (P 356,357)	**619-457-3251**
Matoso, Gary/161 King St, San Francisco, CA	415-777-1656
Mauskopf, Norman/615 W California Blvd, Pasadena, CA	818-578-1878
McAfee, Lynn/11159 1/4 Acama St, North Hollywood, CA	818-761-1317

McAfee, Tom/930 Alabama, San Francisco, CA	415-777-1736
McClain, Stan/39 E Walnut St, Pasadena, CA	818-795-8828
McCracken, Sabra K/200 W 34th St #190, Anchorage, AK	907-345-5941
McCrary, Jim/211 S LaBrea Ave, Los Angeles, CA	213-936-5115
McCumsey, Robert/2600 E Coast Hwy, Corona Del Mar, CA	714-720-1624
McDermott, John/31 Genoa Place, San Francisco, CA	415-982-2010
McGraw, Chelsea/838 Eolus Ave, Leucadia, CA	619-436-0602
McHugh, Jim/3009 Linda Ln, Santa Monica, CA	213-392-3010
McIntyre, Don/515 S Harbor Blvd, Anaheim, CA	714-635-9491
McIntyre, Gerry/3385 Lanatt Way #B, Sacramento, CA	916-736-2108
McIntyre, Mark/380 Del Mar Blvd, Pasadena, CA	818-796-1841
McKinney, Andrew/1628 Folsom St, San Francisco, CA	415-552-6974
McMahon, Steve/1164 S LaBrea, Los Angeles, CA	213-937-3345
McNeil, Larry/3605 Arctic #1617, Anchorage, AK	907-561-4308
McVay, Matt/PO Box 1103, Mercer Island, WA	206-236-1343
Meisels, Penina/917 20th St, Sacramento, CA	916-443-3330
Melgar Photographers Inc/2971 Corvin Dr, Santa Clara, CA	408-733-4500
Mendenhall, Jim/PO Box 10547, Santa Ana, CA	714-834-9240
Menzel, Peter J/136 N Deer Run Lane, Napa, CA	707-255-3528
Menzie, W Gordon/2311 Kettner Blvd, San Diego, CA	619-234-4431
Merfeld, Ken/3951 Higuera St, Culver City, CA	213-837-5300
Merkel, Dan/PO Box 1025, Haleiwa, HI	808-373-2710
Merken, Stefan/900 N Citrus Ave, Los Angeles, CA	213-466-4533
Meyers, Deborah/405 1/2 S Fairfax Ave, Los Angeles, CA	213-655-4444
MIAD Photography/3220 S Susan St, Santa Ana, CA	714-549-4101
Micoine, Christian/, Los Angeles, CA	213-856-0008
Mihulka, Chris/PO Box 1515, Springfield, OR	503-741-2289
Miles, Reid/1136 N Las Palmas, Hollywood, CA	213-462-6106
Milholland, Richard/8271 W Norton, Los Angeles, CA	213-650-5458
Milkie Studio Inc/127 Boylston Ave E, Seattle, WA	206-324-3000
Miller, Bill/7611 Melrose Ave, Los Angeles, CA	213-651-5630
Miller, Donald/415 Molino, Los Angeles, CA	213-680-1896
Miller, Earl/3212 Bonnie Hill Dr, Los Angeles, CA	213-851-4947
Miller, Ed/705 32nd Ave, San Francisco, CA	415-221-5687
Miller, Jim/1122 N Citrus Ave, Los Angeles, CA	213-466-9515
Miller, Jordan/506 S San Vicente Blvd, Los Angeles, CA	213-655-0408
Miller, Peter Read/3413 Pine Ave, Manhattan Beach, CA	213-545-7511
Miller, Ray/PO Box 450, Balboa, CA	714-646-5748
Miller, Wynn/4083 Glencoe Ave, Marina Del Rey, CA	213-821-4948
Milliken, Brad/583 Vista Ave, Palo Alto, CA	415-424-8211
Milne, Robbie/2717 Western, Seattle, WA	206-682-6828
Milroy/ McAleer/3857 Birch St #170, Newport Beach, CA	714-957-0219
Mineau, Joe/8921 National Blvd, Los Angeles, CA	213-558-3878
Mishler, Clark/1238 G St, Anchorage, AK	907-279-8847
Mitchell, David Paul/564 Deodar Ln, Bradbury, CA	818-358-3328
Mitchell, Josh/706 W Pico Blvd 4th Fl, Los Angeles, CA	213-742-0368
Mitchell, Margaretta K/280 Hillcrest Rd, Berkeley, CA	415-655-4920
Mizono, Robert/14 Otis St 3rd Fl, San Francisco, CA	415-558-8663
Montague Studio/18005 Skypark Cir #E, Irvine, CA	714-250-0254
Monteaux, Michele/8741 Washington Blvd, Culver City, CA	213-839-6439
Montes de Oca, Arthur/4302 Melrose Ave, Los Angeles, CA	213-665-5141
Moore, Charles/PO Box 1876, Columbia, CA	415-451-1088
Moore, Gary/1125 E Orange Ave, Monrovia, CA	818-359-9414
Moran, Edward/5264 Mount Alifan Dr, San Diego, CA	619-693-1041
Moratti, Brian/27411 Lindvog Rd NE, Kingston, WA	206-297-3158
Morduchowicz, Daniel/2020 N Main St #223, Los Angeles, CA	213-223-1867
Morfit, Mason/897 Independence Ave #D, Mountain View, CA	415-969-2209
Morgan, Scott/2210 Wilshire #433, Santa Monica, CA	213-829-5318
Mosgrove, Will/250 Newhall, San Francisco, CA	415-282-7080
Motil, Guy/253 W Canada, San Clemente, CA	714-492-1350
Moulin, Tom/465 Green St, San Francisco, CA	415-986-4224
Muckley, Mike Photography/8057 Raytheon Rd #3, San Diego, CA	619-565-6033
Mudford, Grant/5619 W 4th St #2, Los Angeles, CA	213-936-9145
MUENCH, DAVID/PO BOX 30500, SANTA BARBARA, CA (P 397)	**805-967-4488**
Mullenski, Steven/7718 1/2 Herschel Ave, La Jolla, CA	619-454-4331
Mulligan, Frank/392 Coogan Way, El Cajon, CA	619-444-5555
MUNA, R J/63 ENCINA AVE, PALO ALTO, CA (P 398,399)	**415-328-1131**
Murphy, Suzanne/2442 Third St, Santa Monica, CA	213-399-6652
Murphy, William/7771 Melrose Ave, Los Angeles, CA	213-651-4800
Murray, Derik/1128 Homer St, Vancouver V6B 2X6, BC	604-669-7468

Murray, Michael/15431 Redhill Ave #E, Tustin, CA	714-259-9222
Murray, Tom/592 N Rossmore Ave, Los Angeles, CA	213-937-3821
Murray, William III/1507 Belmont Ave, Seattle, WA	206-322-3377
Musilek, Stan/610 22nd St #307, San Francisco, CA	415-621-5334
Myers, Jeffry W Photography/Joseph Vance Bldg #414, Seattle, WA	206-621-7609
Myers, Tom/1737 Markham Way, Sacramento, CA	916-443-8886

N

Nadler, Jeff/520 N Western Ave, Los Angeles, CA	213-467-2135
Nahoum, Ken/6609 Orange St, Los Angeles, CA	213-559-3244
Nakamura, Michael/5429 Russell NW, Seattle, WA	206-784-4323
Nance, Ancil/9217 N Hudson, Portland, OR	503-286-0941
Narciso, Mike/31 Union St, San Jose, CA	408-298-7688
Nation, Bill/1514 S Stanley, Los Angeles, CA	213-937-4888
Nease, Robert/441 E Columbine #E, Santa Ana, CA	714-545-6557
Nebeux, Michael/1633 W 144th St, Gardena, CA	213-532-0949
Nels/811 Traction Ave, Los Angeles, CA	213-680-2414
Newman, Greg/1356 Brampton Rd, Pasadena, CA	213-257-6247
Niedopytalski, Dave/1415 E Union, Seattle, WA	206-329-7612
Noble, Richard/7618 Melrose Ave, Los Angeles, CA	213-655-4711
Nolan, Terry/431 Termino Ave, Long Beach, CA	213-439-1158
Nolton, Gary/107 NW Fifth Ave, Portland, OR	503-228-0844
Normark, Don/1622 Taylor Ave N, Seattle, WA	206-284-9393
Norwood, David/21 Laguna Ct, Manhattan Beach, CA	213-827-2020
NOYLE, RIC/733 AUAHI ST, HONOLULU, HI (P 423)	**808-524-8269**
NTA Photo/600 Moulton Ave #101-A, Los Angeles, CA	213-226-0506
Nuding, Peter/3181 Melendy Dr, San Carlos, CA	415-967-4854
Nyerges, Suzanne/413 S Fairfax, Los Angeles, CA	213-938-0151

O

O'Brien, George/1515 Merced St, Fresno, CA	209-226-4000
O'Brien, Tom/450 S La Brea, Los Angeles, CA	213-938-2008
O'Hara, Yoshi/6341 Yucca St, Hollywood, CA	213-466-8031
O'Rear, Chuck/PO Box 361, St Helena, CA	707-963-2663
Odgers, Jayme/703 S Union, Los Angeles, CA	213-484-9965
Ogilvie, Peter/90 Natoma, San Francisco, CA	415-391-1646
Oldenkamp, John/3331 Adams Ave, San Diego, CA	619-283-0711
Olson, George/451 Vermont, San Francisco, CA	415-864-8686
Olson, Jon/4045 32nd Ave SW, Seattle, WA	206-932-7074
Oppenheimer, Kent/1344 Devlin Dr, Los Angeles, CA	213-652-3923
Orazem, Scott/1150 1/2 Elm Dr, Los Angeles, CA	213-277-7447
Osbourne, Jan/460 NE 70th St, Seattle, WA	206-524-5220
Otto, Glenn/10625 Magnolia Blvd, North Hollywood, CA	818-762-5724
Ounjian, Michael/612 N Myers St, Burbank, CA	818-842-0880
Outland, Joe/Box 6202 Pt Loma Station, San Diego, CA	619-222-4558
Ovregaard, Keith/765 Clementina St, San Francisco, CA	415-621-0687
Owen & Owen Photo/4114 Kilauea Ave, Honolulu, HI	808-737-9123
Owyang, William/211 Bradford St, San Francisco, CA	415-558-4167

P

Pacheco, Robert/11152 3/4 Morrison, N Hollywood, CA	818-761-1320
Padys, Diane/PO Box 77307, San Francisco, CA	415-285-6443
Pagos, Terry/3622 Albion Pl N, Seattle, WA	206-633-4616
Painter, Charles/2513 Devri Ct, Mountain View, CA	415-968-7467
Pan, Richard/6227 Alcove Ave, N Hollywood, CA	818-508-0800
Parks, Ayako/PO Box 6552, Laguna Nigel, CA	714-240-8347
Parks, Jeff/12936 133rd Pl NE, Kirkland, WA	206-821-5450
Parrish, Al/3501 Buena Vista Ave, Glendale, CA	818-957-3726
Parry, Karl/8800 Venice Blvd, Los Angeles, CA	213-558-4446
Pasley, Raymond/1240 Merkley Ave #108, W Sacramento, CA	916-372-6952
Pasquali, Art/1061 Sunset Blvd, Los Angeles, CA	213-250-0134
Patterson, Marion/1745 Croner Ave, Menlo Park, CA	209-379-2838
Patterson, Robert/915 N Mansfield Ave, Hollywood, CA	213-462-4401
Paulus, Bill/612 Lighthouse Ave, Pacific Grove, CA	408-375-0446
Pavloff, Nick/PO Box 2339, San Francisco, CA	415-452-2468
Peais, Larry/95 Minna, San Francisco, CA	415-957-1366
Pearson, Charles R/PO Box 350, Leavenworth, WA	509-763-3333
Pearson, John/1343 Sacramento, Berkeley, CA	415-525-7553
Pearson, Victoria/560 S Main St #4-N, Los Angeles, CA	213-627-9256
Pedrick, Frank/2690 Union st, Oakland, CA	415-465-5080
Peebles, Douglas Photography/1100 Alekea St #221, Honolulu, HI	808-533-6686
Pelton & Assoc/36 14th St, Hermosa Beach, CA	213-376-8061
Percey, Roland/626 N Hoover, Los Angeles, CA	213-660-7305

Please send us your additions and updates.

PERRY, DAVID/BOX 4165 PIONEER SQ STA, SEATTLE, WA (P 400,401) | **206-932-6614**
Peterman, Joan & Herbert/1118 Fifth St #7, Santa Monica, CA | 213-395-7668
Petersen, Ragnar M/1467 Laurelwood Rd, Santa Clara, CA | 408-748-9049
Peterson, Bryan/PO Box 892, Hillsboro, OR | 503-985-3276
Peterson, Darrell/1004 Turner Way E, Seattle, WA | 206-324-0307
Peterson, Richard/733 Auahi St, Honolulu, HI | 808-536-8222
Peterson, Richard Studio/711 8th Ave #A, San Diego, CA | 619-236-0284
Peterson, Robert/1220 42nd Ave E, Seattle, WA | 206-329-2299
Pett, Laurence J/5907 Cahill Ave, Tarzana, CA | 818-344-9453
Pfleger, Mickey/PO Box 280727, San Francisco, CA | 415-355-1772
Phillips, Bernard/166 South Park, San Francisco, CA | 415-552-4252
Photo Graphics West/15811 Debesor St, Valinda, CA | 818-918-5491
Photography Northwest/1415 Elliot Ave W, Seattle, WA | 206-285-5249
Pierazzi, Gary/1928 Cooley Ave #49, Palo Alto, CA | 415-325-2677
Pildas, Ave/1568 Murray Circle, Los Angeles, CA | 213-664-1313
Pinckney, Jim/PO Box 1149, Carmel Valley, CA | 408-375-3534
Piper, Jim/922 SE Ankeny, Portland, OR | 503-231-9622
Piscitello, Chuck/6502 Santa Monica Blvd, Los Angeles, CA | 213-460-6397
Place, Chuck/2940 Lomita Rd, Santa Barbara, CA | 805-682-6089
Pleasant, Ralph B/8755 W Washington Blvd, Culver City, CA | 213-202-8997
Poppleton, Eric/1341 Ocean Ave #259, Santa Monica, CA | 213-209-3765
Porter, James/3955 Birch St #F, Newport Beach, CA | 714-852-8756
Poulsen, Chriss/104-A Industrial Center, Sausalito, CA | 415-331-3495
Powers, David/17 Brosnan St, San Francisco, CA | 415-864-7974
Powers, Lisa/2073 Outpost Dr, Los Angeles, CA | 213-874-5877
Prater, Yvonne/Box 940 Rt 1, Ellensburg, WA | 509-925-1774
Preuss, Karen/369 Eleventh Ave, San Francisco, CA | 415-752-7545
Pribble, Paul/120 S Vignes St, Los Angeles, CA | 213-617-7182
Price, Mark/2337 El Camino Real, San Mateo, CA | 415-345-8377
Price, Tony/PO Box 5216, Portland, OR | 503-239-4228
Prince, Norman/3245 25th St, San Francisco, CA | 415-821-6595
Pritchett, Bill/1771 Yale St, Chula Vista, CA | 619-421-6005
Proehl, Steve/916 Rodney Dr, San Leandro, CA | 415-483-3683
Professional Photo Services/1011 Buenos Ave #A-B, San Diego, CA | 619-276-4780
Pruitt, Brett/2343-B Rose St, Honolulu, HI | 808-845-3811

R
Raabe, Dan/5923 W Pico Blvd, Los Angeles, CA | 213-934-8447
Rahn, Stephen/259 Clara St, San Francisco, CA | 415-495-3556
Ramey, Michael/612 Broadway, Seattle, WA | 206-329-6936
Ramsey, Gary/1412 Ritchey #A, Santa Ana, CA | 714-547-0782
Rand, Marvin/13432 Beach, Marina Del Rey, CA | 213-306-9779
Randklev, James/1471 S Bradford St, Los Angeles, CA | 213-825-5893
Randlett, Mary/Box 10536, Bainbridge Island, WA | 206-842-3935
Ransier, Richard/3923 W Jefferson Blvd, Los Angeles, CA | 213-735-1553
Ranson, James/PO Box 501, Laguna Beach, CA | 714-634-6688
Rapoport, Aaron/3119 Beverly Blvd, Los Angeles, CA | 213-738-7277
Rausin, Chuck/1020 Woodcrest Ave, La Habra, CA | 213-697-0408
Rawcliffe, David/7609 Beverly Blvd, Los Angeles, CA | 213-938-6287
Ream-Stuart Visual Productions/3405 Industrial Dr, Santa Rosa, CA | 707-523-0125
Reed, Bob/1816 N Vermont Ave, Los Angeles, CA | 213-662-9703
Reiff, Robert/1920 Main St #2, Santa Monica, CA | 213-470-1146
Reitzel, Bill/49 Keats Dr, Mill Valley, CA | 415-383-3031
Ressmeyer, Roger/1230 Grant Ave #574, San Francisco, CA | 415-921-1675
Rhoney, Ann/2264 Green St, San Francisco, CA | 415-922-4775
Ricketts, Mark/2809 NE 55th St, Seattle, WA | 206-526-1911
Riggs, Robin/3785 Cahuenga W, N Hollywood, CA | 818-506-7753
Ripley, Michael & Assoc/13985 E 6th St, Corona, CA | 714-737-5118
Ritts, Herb/7927 Hillside Ave, Los Angeles, CA | 213-876-6366
Roark, James/18913 Napa St, Northridge, CA | 818-886-7654
Robbins, Bill/7016 Santa Monica Blvd, Los Angeles, CA | 213-930-1382
Roberge, Earl/764 Bryant, Walla Walla, WA | 509-525-7385
Rodal, Arney A/395 Winslow Way E, Bainbridge Island, WA | 206-842-4989
Rogers, George/2111 Moreland Dr, Chico, CA | 916-345-2347
Rogers, Kenneth/6221 W 6th St, Los Angeles, CA | 213-553-5532
Rojas, Art/1588 N Batavia, Orange, CA | 714-921-1710
Rokeach, Barrie/32 Windsor, Kensington, CA | 415-527-5376
Rolston, Matthew/8259 Melrose Ave, Los Angeles, CA | 213-658-1151
Rorke, Lorraine/146 Shrader St, San Francisco, CA | 415-386-2121
Ros-Lynn Photo/405 E Olive, Fresno, CA | 209-266-0305

Rose, Peter/651 N Russell, Portland, OR | 503-249-5864
Rosenberg, Allan/963 North Point St, San Francisco, CA | 415-673-4550
Ross, Alan C/202 Culper Ct, Hermosa Beach, CA | 213-379-2015
Ross, Bill/1526 Pontius Ave #A, Los Angeles, CA | 818-703-7605
Ross, Dave/130 McCormick #106, Costa Mesa, CA | 714-432-1355
Ross, James Studio/2565 3rd St #220, San Francisco, CA | 415-821-5710
Rothman, Michael/1816 N Vermont Ave, Los Angeles, CA | 213-662-9703
Rouse, Victoria/4411 Geary Blvd #244, San Francisco, CA | 415-621-5660
Rowan, Bob/209 Los Banos Ave, Walnut Creek, CA | 415-930-8687
Rowell, Galen/PO Box 6312, Albany, CA | 415-524-9343
Rubins, Richard/3757 Wilshire Blvd #204A, Los Angeles, CA | 213-387-9989
Ruggles, Joan/4132 Holly Knoll Dr, Los Angeles, CA | 213-667-2488
Ruppert, Michael/5086 W Pico, Los Angeles, CA | 213-938-3779
Ruscha, Paul/940 N Highland Ave, Los Angeles, CA | 213-465-3516
Ruthsatz, Richard/8735 Washington Blvd, Culver City, CA | 213-838-6312

S
Sabransky, Cynthia/3331 Adams Ave, San Diego, CA | 619-283-0711
Sadlon, Jim/2 Clinton Park, San Francisco, CA | 415-626-1900
SAFRON, MARSHAL/506 S SAN VINCENTE BLVD, LOS ANGELES, CA (P 402) | **213-653-1234**
Sagara, Peter/736 N LaBrea, Los Angeles, CA | 213-933-7531
Saitta, Joseph/2000 Old Page Mill Rd, Palo Alto, CA | 415-494-1684
Salas, Michael/5307 1/2 Seashore Dr, Newport Beach, CA | 213-930-2935
Salazar, Tim/4057 Brant St #6, San Diego, CA | 619-574-1176
Saloutos, Pete/11225 Huntley Pl, Culver City, CA | 213-397-5509
Samerjan, Peter/743 N Fairfax, Los Angeles, CA | 213-653-2940
SANDERS, PAUL/7378 BEVERLY BLVD, LOS ANGELES, CA (P 403) | **213-933-5791**
Sandford, Eric/Mazama Meadows, Mazama, WA | 509-996-2250
SANDISON, TERI/1545 N WILCOX #102, HOLLYWOOD, CA (P 404) | **213-461-3529**
Santullo, Nancy/7213 Santa Monica Blvd, Los Angeles, CA | 213-874-1940
Sarpa, Jeff/555 Rose Ave #G, Venice, CA | 213-392-7400
Sassy, Gene/PO Box 3114, Pomona, CA | 714-623-7424
Sato, Garry/645 N Martel Ave, Los Angeles, CA | 213-658-8645
SCHARF, DAVID/2100 LOMA VISTA PL, LOS ANGELES, CA (P 363) | **213-666-8657**
Schelling, Susan/1440 Bush St, San Francisco, CA | 415-441-3662
SCHENKER, LARRY/5888 SMILEY DR, LOS ANGELES, CA (P 405) | **213-837-2020**
Scherl, Ron/1717 Mason St #4, San Francisco, CA | 415-421-1160
Schermeiserper, Phil/472 22nd Ave, San Francisco, CA | 415-386-0218
Schiff, Darryll/8153 W Blackburn Ave, Los Angeles, CA | 213-658-6179
Schmidt, Brad/1417 26th St, Santa Monica, CA | 213-828-0754
Schubert, John/5959 W Third, Los Angeles, CA | 213-935-6044
Schwartz, George J/PO Box 413, Bend, OR | 503-389-4062
Schwartz, Monserrate/PO Box 413, Bend, OR | 503-389-4062
Schwob, Bill/1033 Heinz St, Berkeley, CA | 415-848-3579
Scoffone, Craig/1169 Husted Ave, San Jose, CA | 408-723-7011
Scott, Mark/7207 Melrose Ave, Hollywood, CA | 213-931-9319
Sebastian Studios/5161-A Santa Fe St, San Diego, CA | 619-581-9111
Segal, Susan/11738 Moor Pk #B, Studio City, CA | 818-763-7612
Seidemann, Bob/703 S Union Ave, Los Angeles, CA | 213-483-6046
Seiffe, Rolf/2022 Jones St, San Francisco, CA | 415-928-0457
Selig, Jonathan/29206 Heathercliff Rd, Malibu, CA | 213-457-5856
Selland Photography/461 Bryant St, San Francisco, CA | 415-495-3633
Serbin, Glen/905 Chelham Way, Montecito, CA | 805-969-9186
Sessions, David/2210 Wilshire Blvd #205, Santa Monica, CA | 213-394-8379
Sexton, Richard/128 Laidley St, San Francisco, CA | 415-550-8345
Shaffer, Bob/1250 Folsom, San Francisco, CA | 415-552-4884
Shahood, Chuck/10725 Ellis Ave #A, Fountain Valley, CA | 714-963-2142
SHANEFF, CARL/1100 ALAKEA ST #224, HONOLULU, HI (P 407) | **808-533-3010**
Sharpe, Dick/2475 Park Oak Dr, Los Angeles, CA | 213-462-4597
Sheret, Rene/2532 W 7th St, Los Angeles, CA | 213-385-8587
Shipps, Raymond/1325 Morena Blvd #A, San Diego, CA | 619-276-1690
Shirley, Ron/706 W Pico Blvd, Los Angeles, CA | 213-747-6608
Sholik, Stan/15455 Red Hill Ave #E, Tustin, CA | 714-259-7826
Short, Glenn/14641 La Maida, Sherman Oaks, CA | 818-990-5599
Shorten, Chris/60 Federal St, San Francisco, CA | 415-543-4883
Shrum, Steve/PO Box 6360, Ketchikan, AK | 907-225-5453
Shuman, Ronald/1 Menlo Pl, Berkeley, CA | 415-527-7241

PHOTOGRAPHERS

Shvartzman, Eddie/224 Barbara Dr, Los Gatos, CA	408-559-6490
Sibley, Scott/764 Bay, San Francisco, CA	415-673-7468
Sievert, John/2421 Cabrillo St, San Francisco, CA	415-751-2369
Silk, Gary Photography/6546 Hollywood Blvd #215, Hollywood, CA	213-466-1785
Silva, Keith/771 Clementina Alley, San Francisco, CA	415-863-5655
Silverek, Don/914 Ripley St, Santa Rosa, CA	707-525-1155
Silverman, Jay Inc/920 N Citrus Ave, Hollywood, CA	213-466-6030
Sim, Veronica/4961 W Sunset Blvd, Los Angeles, CA	213-661-7356
Simmerman, Nancy L/PO Box 548, Girdwood, AK	907-783-2501
Simon, Marc/1031 Sanchez, San Francisco, CA	415-647-9547
Simon, Wolfgang/PO Box 807, La Canada, CA	818-790-1605
Simpson, Ed/2038 Milan Ave, S Pasadena, CA	213-682-3131
Simpson, Stephen/701 Kettner Blvd #124, San Diego, CA	619-239-6638
Sinick, Gary/3246 Ettie St, Oakland, CA	415-655-4538
Sirota, Peggy/451 N Harper Ave, Los Angeles, CA	213-653-1903
Sjef's Fotographie/2311 NW Johnson St, Portland, OR	503-223-1089
Skarsten & Dunn Studios/1062 N Rengstorff #E, Mountain View, CA	415-969-5759
Skelton, Keith/3032 Vista St, Long Beach, CA	213-439-8584
Slabeck, Bernard/2565 Third St #316, San Francisco, CA	415-282-8202
Slatery, Chad/11627 Ayres Ave, Los Angeles, CA	213-477-0734
Slaughter, Paul D/771 El Medio Ave, Pacific Palisades, CA	213-454-3694
Slenzak, Ron/7106 Waring Ave, Los Angeles, CA	213-934-9088
Slobin, Marvin/1065 15th St, San Diego, CA	619-239-2828
Slobodian, Scott/6519 Fountain Ave, Los Angeles, CA	213-464-2341
Smith, Charles J/7163 Construction Crt, San Diego, CA	619-271-6525
Smith, Derek/1811 Folsom, San Francisco, CA	415-558-9803
Smith, Diane/428 Kurdson Way, Spring Valley, CA	619-470-0861
Smith, Don/1527 Belmont #1, Seattle, WA	206-324-5748
Smith, Elliott Varner/PO Box 5268, Berkeley, CA	415-654-9235
Smith, Gil/2865 W 7th St, Los Angeles, CA	213-384-1016
Smith, Steve/228 Main St #E, Venice, CA	213-392-4982
Smith, Todd/2643 S Fairfax, Culver City, CA	213-559-0059
SNYDER, MARK/2415 THIRD ST #265, SAN FRANCISCO, CA (P 358)	**415-861-7514**
Sokol, Mark/6518 Wilkinson Ave, North Hollywood, CA	818-506-4910
Sollecito, Tony/1120-B W Evelyn Ave, Sunnyvale, CA	408-773-8118
SOLOMON, MARC/PO BOX 480574, LOS ANGELES, CA (P 408,409)	**213-935-1771**
Speier, Brooks/6022 Haviland Ave, Whittier, CA	213-695-3552
Spitz, Harry Photography/6153 Carpenter Ave, North Hollywood, CA	818-761-9828
Sporkin, Lee/135 S Detroit, Los Angeles, CA	213-934-6737
Spradling, David/2515 Patricia Ave, Los Angeles, CA	213-477-0467
Spring, Bob & Ira/18819 Olympic View Dr, Edmonds, WA	206-776-4685
Springmann, Christopher/PO Box 745, Point Reyes, CA	415-663-8428
St Jivago Desanges/PO Box 24AA2, Los Angeles, CA	213-931-1984
Staley, Bill/1401 Crown St, Vancouver V7J 1G4, BC	604-986-1174
Starkman, Rick/544 N Rios Ave, Solana Beach, CA	619-481-8259
Steele, Melissa/PO Box 280727, San Francisco, CA	415-355-1772
Stees, M S/PO Box 2775, Costa Mesa, CA	714-545-7993
Stein, Robert/319 1/2 S Robertson Blvd, Beverly Hills, CA	213-652-2030
Steinberg, Bruce/2128 18th St, San Francisco, CA	415-864-0739
Steinberg, Mike Photo/715 S Coast Hwy, Laguna Beach, CA	714-240-2997
Steiner, Glenn Rakowsky/3356 Hancock St #D, San Diego, CA	619-299-0197
Steinheimer, Richard/2648 Fifth Ave, Sacramento, CA	916-457-1908
Stevens, Bob/9048 Santa Monica Blvd, Los Angeles, CA	213-271-8123
Stewart, Stephen/939 N Alfred #7, West Hollywood, CA	213-656-2270
Stewart, Tom/Studio 3/PO Box 5063, Portland, OR	503-238-1748
Stinson, John/376 W 14th St, San Pedro, CA	213-831-8495
Stoaks, Charles/PO Box 6417, Portland, OR	503-243-2635
Stock, Richard Photography/1767 N Orchid Ave #312, Los Angeles, CA	213-876-7436
Stockton, Michael/567 Prescott St, Pasadena, CA	818-794-6087
Stone, Pete/1410 NW Johnson, Portland, OR	503-224-7125
Stoy, Werner/287 Chestnut St, San Carlos, CA	415-591-4155
Strauss, Andrew/6442 Santa Monica Blvd, Los Angeles, CA	213-464-5394
Streano, Vince/PO Box 662, Laguna Beach, CA	714-497-1908
Street-Porter, Tim/6938 Camrose Dr, Los Angeles, CA	213-874-4278
Streshinsky, Ted/PO Box 674, Berkeley, CA	415-526-1976
Strick, David/3865 Beethoven St, Los Angeles, CA	213-397-0147
Strickland, Steve/Box 3486, San Bernardino, CA	714-883-4792
Stryker, Ray/12029 76th Ave S, Seattle, WA	206-772-5680
Stuart, James Peter/PO Box 84744, Seattle, WA	206-587-0588
Studio AV/1227 First Ave S, Seattle, WA	206-223-1007
Studio B/5121-B Santa Fe St, San Diego, CA	619-483-2122
Studio IV/29141 Kensington, Laguna Niguel, CA	714-495-5898
Su, Andrew/5733 Benner St, Los Angeles, CA	213-256-0598
Sugar, James/45 Midway Ave, Mill Valley, CA	415-388-3344
Sugiyama, Ron/PO Box 665, San Francisco, CA	415-563-8052
Sullivan, Jeremiah S/PO Box 7870, San Diego, CA	619-224-0070
Sullivan, Michael/2247 Boundary St, San Diego, CA	619-282-5001
Sund, Harald/PO Box 16466, Seattle, WA	206-938-1080
Super, Rob/PO Box 210, Volcano, CA	209-296-4077
Surber, Bruce/13600 NE 20th St #E, Bellevue, WA	206-641-6003
Sutton, David/11502 Dona Teresa Dr, Studio City, CA	213-654-7979
Sutton, John/333 Fifth St, San Francisco, CA	415-974-5452
Swanson, Van/41195 Academy Dr, Hemet, CA	714-658-8125
SWARTHOUT, WALTER & ASSOC/370 FOURTH ST, SAN FRANCISCO, CA (P 346,347)	**415-543-2525**
Swartz, Fred/135 S LaBrea, Los Angeles, CA	213-939-2789
Swenson, John/4353 W 5th St #D, Los Angeles, CA	213-384-1782

T

Tachibana, Kenji/1067 26th Ave East, Seattle, WA	206-325-2121
Taggart, Fritz/1117 N Wilcox Pl, Los Angeles, CA	213-469-8227
Tang, Dai/426 Jefferson St, Oakland, CA	415-832-8642
Tapp, Carlan/114 Alaskan Way S, Seattle, WA	206-621-8344
Taub, Doug/8712 Duncamp Pl, Los Angeles, CA	213-650-1221
Tauber, Richard/4221 24th St, San Francisco, CA	415-824-6837
Teeter, Jeff/2205 Dixon St, Chico, CA	916-895-3255
Teke/4338 Shady Glade Ave, Studio City, CA	818-985-9066
Theis, Rocky/2955 4th Ave, San Diego, CA	619-295-1923
Thimmes, Timothy/2805 S La Cienega Blvd, Los Angeles, CA	213-204-6851
Thomas, Neil/4686 Woodside Dr, Los Angeles, CA	213-202-0051
Thompson, Michael/7811 Alabama Ave #14, Canoga Park, CA	818-883-7870
Thompson, William/PO Box 4460, Seattle, WA	206-621-9069
Thomson, Sydney (Ms)/PO Box 1032, Keaau, HI	808-966-8587
Thornton, Tyler/4706 Oakwood Ave, Los Angeles, CA	213-465-0425
Tichenor, K C/2395 El Camino Ave, Sacramento, CA	916-971-1771
Tilger, Stewart/71 Columbia #206, Seattle, WA	206-682-7818
Tise, David/975 Folsom St, San Francisco, CA	415-777-0669
Tokar, John/1360 Logan Ave #105, Costa Mesa, CA	714-733-8572
Tracy, Tom/37 Crystal Springs, San Mateo, CA	415-340-9811
Trafficanda, Gerald/1111 N Beachwood Dr, Los Angeles, CA	213-466-1111
Trailer, Martin/11125-D Flintkote Ave, San Diego, CA	619-452-7759
Trank, Steven/706 W Pico Blvd, Los Angeles, CA	213-749-1220
Trexler, Pete/5888 Smiley Dr Std B, Culver City, CA	213-558-8226
Trindl, Gene/3950 Vantage Ave, Studio City, CA	213-877-4848
Tucker, Kim/2428 Canyon Dr, Los Angeles, CA	213-465-9233
Turner & DeVries/1200 College Walk #212, Honolulu, HI	808-537-3115
Turner, John Terence/173 37th Ave E, Seattle, WA	206-325-9073
Turner, Richard P/Box 64205 Rancho Pk Sta, Los Angeles, CA	213-279-2127
Tuschman, Mark/300 Santa Monica, Menlo Park, CA	415-322-4157

UV

Ueda, Richard/1816 South Flower St, Los Angeles, CA	213-747-7259
Underwood, Ron/918 Hilldroft Rd, Glendale, CA	818-246-3628
Undheim, Timothy/8535 Arjohns Dr #L, San Diego, CA	619-549-3322
Uniack/8933 National Blvd, Los Angeles, CA	213-938-0287
Upfront Communication/227 5th St #A, Encinitas, CA	619-273-8544
Upton, Tom/1879 Woodland Ave, Palo Alto, CA	415-325-8120
Urie, Walter Photography/1810 E Carnegie, Santa Ana, CA	714-261-6302
Vanderpoel, Fred/1118 Harrison, San Francisco, CA	415-621-4405
Varie, Bill/2210 Wilshire Blvd, Santa Monica, CA	213-395-9337
Vega, Raul/3511 W 6th Tower Suite, Los Angeles, CA	213-387-2058
Veitch, Julie/5757 Venice Blvd, Los Angeles, CA	213-936-4231
Venezia, Jay/1373 Edgecliffe Dr, Los Angeles, CA	213-665-7382
Vereen, Jackson/570 Bryant St, San Francisco, CA	415-777-5272
Viarnes, Alex/Studio 33/Clementina, San Francisco, CA	415-543-1195
Vignes, Michelle/654 28th St, San Francisco, CA	415-550-8039
Villaflor, F/PO Box 883274, San Francisco, CA	415-921-4248
Visually Speaking/3609 E Olympic Blvd, Los Angeles, CA	213-269-9141
Vogt, Jurgen/936 E 28th Ave, Vancouver V5V 2P2, BC	604-876-5817
Vollenweider, Thom/3430 El Cajon Blvd, San Diego, CA	619-280-3070

Please send us your additions and updates.

Vollick, Tom/415 28th St, Hermosa Beach, CA	213-316-3196

W

Wade, Bill/5608 E 2nd St, Long Beach, CA	213-439-6826
Wahlstrom, Richard/650 Alabama St 3rd Fl, San Francsico, CA	415-550-1400
Wallace, Marlene/7801 Beverly Blvd, Los Angeles, CA	213-478-8488
Wallick, Philip/PO Box 3096, Chico, CA	916-893-8464
Warden, John/9201 Shorecrest Dr, Anchorage, AK	907-243-1667
Warren Aerial Photography/PO Box 60155, Pasadena, CA	213-681-1006
Warren, Adrienne/3001 Crown Valley Pkwy, Laguna Niguel, CA	714-643-0333
Warren, William James/509 S Gramercy Pl, Los Angeles, CA	213-383-0500
Watamura, Ed Photography/17962 Sky Park Cir #J, Irvine, CA	714-261-0575
Watanabe, David/14355 132nd Ave NE, Kirkland, WA	206-823-0692
Waterfall, William/826 15th Ave, Honolulu, HI	808-735-6035
Watson, Alan/3157 Maple St, San Diego, CA	619-239-5555
Watson, Stuart/560 S Main St #4N, Los Angeles, CA	213-627-9256
Waz, Tony/1115 S Trotwood Ave, San Pedro, CA	213-548-3758
Webber, Phil/2466 Westlake Ave N, Seattle, WA	206-282-2423
Weissman, Jeff/3025 Jordan Rd, Oakland, CA	415-482-3891
Werner, Jeffery R/14002 Palawan Way, Marina Del Rey, CA	213-821-2384
Werner, Joel/930 W 16th St #E1, Costa Mesa, CA	714-650-0999
WERTS STUDIO INC/732 N HIGHLAND, LOS ANGELES, CA (P 342-345)	**213-464-2775**
WERTS, BILL/732 N HIGHLAND, LOS ANGELES, CA (P 342-343)	**213-464-2775**
West, Andrew/342 Sycamore Rd, Santa Monica, CA	213-459-7774
Wexler, Glen/736 N Highland, Los Angeles, CA	213-465-0268
Wheeler, Nik/7444 Woodrow Wilson Dr, Los Angeles, CA	213-850-0234
Wheeler, Richard/PO Box 3739, San Rafael, CA	415-457-6914
Whetstone, Wayne/149 W Seventh Ave, Vancouver BC	604-873-8471
Whitmore, Ken/PO Box 49373, Los Angeles, CA	213-472-4337
WHITTAKER, STEVE/111 GLEN WAY #8, BELMONT, CA (P 410)	**415-595-4242**
Wiener, Leigh/2600 Carman Crest Dr, Los Angeles, CA	213-876-0990
Wietstock, Wilfried/877 Valencia St, San Francisco, CA	415-285-4221
Wilcox, Jed/PO Box 4091, Palm Springs, CA	714-659-3945
Wildschut, Sjef/2311 NW Johnson, Portland, OR	503-223-1089
Wilhelm, Dave/2565 Third St #303, San Francisco, CA	415-826-9399
Wilkings, Steve/Box 22810, Honolulu, HI	808-732-6288
Willett, Larry/450 S LaBrea, Los Angeles, CA	213-935-6047
Williams, David Jordan/6122 W Colgate, Los Angeles, CA	213-936-3170
Williams, Harold/705 Bayswater Ave, Burlingame, CA	415-648-6644
WILLIAMS, SANDRA/PO BOX 16130, SAN DIEGO, CA (P 411)	**619-234-0447**
Williams, Steven Burr/5315 Clinton, Los Angeles, CA	213-469-5749
Williams, Wayne/7623 Beverly Blvd, Los Angeles, CA	213-937-2882
Williamson, Scott/1901 E Carnegie #1G, Santa Ana, CA	714-261-2550
Wilson, Bruce/1022 1st Ave South, Seattle, WA	206-621-9182
Wilson, Don/10754 2nd Ave NW, Seattle, WA	206-367-4075
Wilson, Douglas M/10133 NE 113th Pl, Kirkland, WA	206-822-8604
Wimpey, Christopher/627 Eighth Ave, San Diego, CA	619-232-3222
Wincott, Gary Photography/1087 Robbia Dr, Sunnyvale, CA	408-245-9559
Windus, Scott/916 N Formosa, Beverly Hills, CA	213-276-0968
Winholt, Bryan/PO Box 331, Sacramento, CA	916-725-0592
Winter-Green Photo/7936 Miramar Rd, San Diego, CA	619-693-1652
Wittner, Dale/507 Third Ave #209, Seattle, WA	206-623-4545
Wolfe, Dan E/45 E Walnut, Pasadena, CA	213-681-3130
Wolman, Baron/PO Box 1000, Mill Valley, CA	415-388-0181
WONG, KEN/3522 W TEMPLE ST, LOS ANGELES, CA (P 412)	**213-389-3081**
Wood, Darrell/517 Aloha St, Seattle, WA	206-283-7900
Wood, Harold/314 NW Glisan, Portland, OR	503-248-0534
Wood, James/1746 N Ivar, Los Angeles, CA	213-461-3861
Woolslair, James/17229 Newhope St #H, Fountain Valley, CA	714-957-0349
Wortham, Robert/521 State St, Glendale, CA	818-243-6400
Wright, Armand/4026 Blairmore Ct, San Jose, CA	408-629-0559
Wyatt, Tom Photography/215 Second St, San Francisco, CA	415-543-2813

YZ

Young, Bill/PO Box 27344, Honolulu, HI	808-595-7324
Young, Edward/860 2nd St, San Francisco, CA	415-543-6633
Youngblood, Lee/501 Forest Ave #608, Palo Alto, CA	415-329-1085
Yudelson, Jim/33 Clementina, San Francisco, CA	415-543-3325
Zajack, Greg/1517 W Alton Ave, Santa Ana, CA	714-432-8400
Zak, Ed/80 Tehama St, San Francisco, CA	415-781-1611

Zanzinger, David/2411 Main St, Santa Monica, CA	213-399-8802
Zaruba, Jeff/833 N Fairfax Ave, Los Angeles, CA	213-653-3341
Zenuk, Alan/POB 3531, Vancouver BC, Canada V6B 3Y6,	604-733-8271
Zimberoff, Tom/PO Box 5212, Beverly Hills, CA	213-271-5900
ZIMMERMAN, DICK/8743 W WASHINGTON BLVD, LOS ANGELES, CA (P 364)	**213-204-2911**
ZIMMERMAN, JOHN/9135 HAZEN DR, BEVERLY HILLS, CA (P 348,349)	**213-273-2642**
Zippel, Arthur/2110 E McFadden #D, Santa Ana, CA	714-835-8400
Zlozower, Neil/6341 Yucca, Los Angeles, CA	213-935-0606
Zurek, Nikolay/276 Shipley St, San Francisco, CA	415-777-9210
Zwart, Jeffrey R/1900-E East Warner, Santa Ana, CA	714-261-5844
Zyber, Tom/11577-A Slater Ave, Fountain Valley, CA	714-546-2949

PHOTOGRAPHERS

STOCK

NEW YORK CITY

American Heritage Picture Library/10 Rockefeller Plaza	212-399-8930
American Library Color Slide Co/222 W 23rd St	212-255-5356
Archive Pictures/111 Wooster St	212-431-1610
Argent and Aurum/470 W 24th St	212-807-1186
ARNOLD, PETER/1181 BROADWAY 4TH FL (P 415)	**212-481-1190**
Art Resource Inc/65 Bleecker St 9th Fl	212-505-8700
Beck's Studio/37-44 82nd St	718-424-8751
The Bethel Agency/513 W 54th St #1	212-664-0455
Bettmann Archive/136 E 57th St	212-758-0362
Five Inc/6 W 20th St	212-989-2004
Camp, Woodfin Assoc/415 Madison Ave	212-750-1020
Coleman, Bruce Inc/381 Fifth Ave 2nd Fl	212-683-5227
Colour Library Int'l/99 Park Ave	212-557-2929
COMSTOCK/32 E 31ST ST (INSIDE FRONT COVER)	**212-889-9700**
Consolidated Poster Service/341 W 44th St	212-581-3105
Contact Stock Images/415 Madison Ave	212-750-1020
Cooke, Jerry/161 E 82nd St	212-288-2045
Culver Pictures Inc/150 W 22nd St 3rd Fl	212-684-5054
Design Conceptions/Elaine Abrams/112 Fourth Ave	212-254-1688
DEWYS, LEO INC/1170 BROADWAY (P 417)	**212-986-3190**
DMI Inc/341 First Ave	212-777-8135
Dot Picture Agency/50 W 29th St	212-684-3441
DPI Inc/521 Madison Ave 5th Fl	212-752-3930
Galloway/1466 Broadway	212-719-4720
Flex Inc/342 Madison Ave	212-722-5816
Flying Camera Inc/114 Fulton St	212-619-0808
Focus on Sports/222 E 46th St	212-661-6860
by Five Inc/485 Madison Ave	212-355-2323
FPG International/251 Park Ave S	212-777-4214
Fundamental Photographs/210 Forsythe St	212-473-5770
Gabriel Graphic News Service/38 Madison Sq Sta	212-254-8863
Gamma-Liaison Photo Agency/150 E 58th St	212-888-7272
Globe Photos Inc/275 Seventh Ave 21st Fl	212-689-1340
Gottscho-Schleisner Inc/150-35 86th Ave	718-526-2795
The Granger Collection/1841 Broadway	212-586-0971
Gross, Lee Assoc/366 Madison Ave	212-682-5240
Heyman, Ken/3 E 76th St	212-226-3725
THE IMAGE BANK/633 THIRD AVE (BACK COVER)	**212-953-0303**
Image Resources/134 W 29th St	212-736-2523
Index Stock International Inc/126 Fifth Ave	212-929-4644
Stock Photos/113 E 31st St #1A	212-696-4666
Keystone Press Agency Inc/202 E 42nd St	212-924-8123
Kramer, Joan & Assoc Inc/720 Fifth Ave	212-567-5545
Frederick Inc/134 W 29th St #1003	212-594-8816
Life Picture Service/Rm 28-58 Time-Life Bldg	212-841-4800
Magnum Photos Inc/251 Park Ave S	212-475-7600
MAISEL, JAY/190 BOWERY (P 24,25)	**212-431-5013**
Manhattan Views/41 Union Sq W #1027	212-255-1477
MediChrome/271 Madison Ave	212-679-8480
Memory Shop Inc/109 E 12th St	212-473-2404
Press Photo Agency/118 E 28th St #615	212-689-2242
Omni Photo Communication/521 Madison Ave	212-751-6530
Photo Assoc News Service/PO Box 306 Station A	718-961-0909
Photo Files/1235 E 40th St	718-338-2245
Photo Library Inc/325 W 45th St	212-246-1349
Photo Researchers Inc/60 E 56th St	212-758-3420
Photo Unique/1328 Broadway PH	212-244-5511
Photo World/251 Park Ave S	212-777-4214
Photofile International Ltd/32 E 31st St	212-989-0500
Photography for Industry/230 W 54th St	212-757-9255
PhotoNet/250 W 57th St	212-307-6999
Photoreporters/875 Ave of Americas #1003	212-736-7602
Phototake/4523 Broadway #76	212-942-8185
Phototeque/156 Fifth Ave #415	212-242-6406
Pictorial Parade/130 W 42nd St	212-840-2026
RDR Productions/351 W 54th St	212-586-4432
Reese, Kay/175 Fifth Ave #1304	212-598-4848
Pictures/119 Fifth Ave	212-254-0008
Retna Ltd/36 W 56th St	212-489-1230
Roberts, H Armstrong/1181 Broadway	212-685-3870
Science Photo Library Int'l/118 E 28th St	212-683-4025
Photo/501 Fifth Ave #2102	212-490-2180
Shostal Assoc/164 Madison Ave	212-686-8850
SO Studio Inc/34 E 23rd St	212-475-0090
Sochurek, Howard Inc/680 Fifth Ave	212-582-1860
Sovfoto-Eastphoto Agency/25 W 43rd St	212-921-1922
Spano/Roccanova/16 W 46th St	212-840-7450
Sports Illustrated Pictures/Time-Life Bldg 19th Fl	212-841-3663
Stock Market/1181 Broadway	212-684-7878
The Stock Shop/271 Madison Ave	212-679-8480
Stockphotos Inc/373 Park Ave S 6th Fl	212-686-1196
The Strobe Studio Inc/91 Fifth Ave	212-691-5270
Sygma Photo News/225 W 57th St 7th Fl	212-765-1820

NORTHEAST

Authenticated News Int'l/29 Katonah Ave, Katonah, NY	914-232-7726
Bergman, LV & Assoc/East Mountain Rd S, Cold Spring, NY	914-265-3656
Blizzard, William C/PO Box 1696, Beckley, WV	304-755-0094
Camerique Stock Photography/1701 Skippack Pike, Blue Bell, PA	215-272-7649
Camerique Stock Photography NE/45 Newbury St, Boston, MA	617-267-6450
Cape Scapes/542 Higgins Crowell Rd, West Yarmouth, MA	617-362-8222
Chandoha, Walter/RD 1 PO Box 287, Annandale, NJ	201-782-3666
Consolidated News Pictures/209 Pennsylvania Ave SE, Washington, DC	202-543-3203
Cyr Color Photo/PO Box 2148, Norwalk, CT	203-838-8230
DCS Enterprises/12806 Gaffney Rd, Silver Spring, MD	301-622-2323
Devaney Stock Photos/7 High St #308, Huntington, NY	516-673-4477
Earth Scenes/Animals Animals/17 Railroad Ave, Chatham, NY	518-392-5500
Educational Dimension Stock/PO Box 126, Stamford, CT	203-327-4612
Esto Photographics/222 Valley Pl, Mamaroneck, NY	914-698-4060
F/STOP PICTURES INC/PO BOX 359, SPRINGFIELD, VT (P 419)	**802-885-5261**
First Foto Bank/2637 Connecticut Ave NW, Washington, DC	301-670-0299
Folio/2651 Conn Ave NW 3rd Fl, Washington, DC	202-965-2410
Heilman, Grant/506 W Lincoln Ave, Lititz, PA	717-626-0296
Illustrators Stock Photos/PO Box 1470, Rockville, MD	301-279-0045
Image Photos/Main St, Stockbridge, MA	413-298-5500
The Image Works Inc/PO Box 443, Woodstock, NY	914-679-7172
In Slide Out/1701 Eben St, Pittsburgh, PA	412-343-2112
Jones, G P - Stock/45 Newbury St, Boston, MA	617-267-6450
Lambert, Harold M Studio/2801 W Cheltenham Ave, Philadelphia, PA	215-224-1400
Light, Paul/1430 Massachusetts Ave, Cambridge, MA	617-628-1052
Lumiere/512 Adams St, Centerport, NY	516-271-6133
Mercier, Louis/15 Long Lots Rd, Westport, CT	203-227-1620
Newsphoto Worldwide/902 National Press Bldg, Washington, DC	202-737-0450
Photo Media Ltd/3 Forest Glen Rd, New Paltz, NY	914-255-8661
The Picture Cube/89 State St, Boston, MA	617-367-1532
Picture Group/5 Steeple St, Providence, RI	401-273-5473
Picture Research/6107 Roseland Dr, Rockville, MD	301-230-0043
Positive Images/12 Main St, Natick, MA	617-653-7610
Rainbow/PO Box 573, Housatonic, MA	413-274-6211
Roberts, H Armstrong/4203 Locust St, Philadelphia, PA	215-386-6300
Sandak Inc/180 Harvard Ave, Stamford, CT	203-348-4721
Siquis Stock Photography/PO Box 215, Stevenson, MD	301-583-9177
Sportschrome/270 Sylvan Ave, Englewood Cliffs, NJ	201-568-1412
Starwood/PO Box 40503, Washington, DC	202-362-7404
Stock Boston Inc/36 Gloucester St, Boston, MA	617-266-2300
Undersea Systems/PO Box 29M, Bay Shore, NY	516-666-3127
Unicorn/Photographic Images Div/1148 Parsippany Blvd, Parsippany, NJ	201-334-0353
Uniphoto Picture Agency/1071 Wisconsin Ave NW, Washington, DC	202-333-0500
View Finder Stock Photo/818 Liberty Ave, Pittsburg, PA	412-391-8720
WEIDMAN, H MARK/2112 GOODWIN LANE, NORTH WALES, PA (P 42-45)	**215-646-1745**

STOCK

494

STOCK CONT'D.

Please send us your additions and updates.

SOUTHEAST

Cactus Clyde/3623 Perkins Rd Box 14876, Baton Rouge, LA	504-887-3704
Camera MD Studios/8290 NW 26 Pl, Ft Lauderdale, FL	305-741-5560
Florida Image File/222 2nd St N, St Petersburg, FL	813-894-8433
THE IMAGE BANK/255 PEACHTREE ST NE #800, ATLANTA, GA (BACK COVER)	**404-223-0133**
McCarthy's National Stock/8960 SW 114th St, Miami, FL	305-233-1703
NATIONAL STOCK NETWORK/8960 SOUTHWEST 114TH ST, MIAMI, FL (P 421)	**305-233-1703**
Phelps Agency/3210 Peachtree St NW, Atlanta, GA	404-264-0264
Photo Options/1432 Linda Vista Dr, Birmingham, AL	205-979-8412
Photri(Photo Research Int'l)/505 W Windsor/PO Box 971, Alexandria, VA	703-836-4439
Sharp Shooters/7210 Red Rd #216, Miami, FL	305-666-1266
Sherman, Ron/PO Box 28656, Atlanta, GA	404-993-7197
SOUTHERN STOCK PHOTO/3601 W COMMERCIAL BLVD #33, FT LAUDERDALE, FL (P 414)	**305-486-7117**
Stills Inc/3210 Peachtree Rd NE, Atlanta, GA	404-233-0022
The Waterhouse/PO Box 2487, Key Largo, FL	305-451-3737

MIDWEST

A-Stock Photo Finder & Photographers/1030 N State St, Chicago, IL	312-645-0611
Artstreet/111 E Chestnut St, Chicago, IL	312-664-3049
Bundt, Nancy/4001 Forest Rd, Minneapolis, MN	612-927-7493
Cameramann International/PO Box 413, Evanston, IL	312-777-5657
Camerique Stock Photography/233 E Wacker Dr #4305, Chicago, IL	312-938-4466
Camerique Stock Photography/45 E Charles St, Toronto M4Y 1S6	416-925-4323
Campbell Stock Photo/28000 Middlebelt Rd #260, Farmington Hills, MI	313-626-5233
Charlton Photos/11518 N Pt Washington Rd, Mequon, WI	414-241-8634
CLICK* CHICAGO INC/213 W INSTITUTE PL #503, CHICAGO, IL (P 290,416)	**312-787-7880**
Collectors Series/161 W Harrison, Chicago, IL	312-427-5311
Gartman, Marilyn/5549 N Clark St, Chicago, IL	312-561-5504
Hedrich-Blessing/11 W Illinois St, Chicago, IL	312-321-1151
Historical Picture Service/601 W Randolph St, Chicago, IL	312-346-0599
Ibid Inc/727 N Hudson, Chicago, IL	312-944-0020
THE IMAGE BANK/510 DEARBORN, CHICAGO, IL (BACK COVER)	**312-329-1817**
JOURNALISM SERVICES STOCK/118 E 2ND ST, LOCKPORT, IL (P 420)	**312-951-0269**
Krinsky, Jon A/85 Tahlequah Trail, Springboro, OH	513-746-5230
Masterfile/2 Carlton St #617, Toronto M5B 1J3, ON	
Miller Services/45 East Charles St, Toronto M4Y 1S6, ON	416-925-4323
Photo Reserve/842 W Lill St, Chicago, IL	312-871-7371
The Photoletter/Pine Lake Farm, Osceola, WI	715-248-3800
Pix International/300 N State #3926, Chicago, IL	312-321-9071
Third Coast Stock/PO Box 92397, Milwaukee, WI	414-765-9442
Weathers, Ginny/708 Gage, Topeka, KS	913-272-1190
Zehrt, Jack/PO Box 122A Rt5, Pacific, MO	314-458-3600

SOUTHWEST

Cochise Photographics/1500 Martingale Rd, Sierra Vista, AZ	602-458-2400
Far West Photo/1104 Hermosa Dr SE, Albuquerque, NM	505-255-0646
THE IMAGE BANK/1336 CONANT ST, DALLAS, TX (BACK COVER)	**214-869-0474**
Image Venders/2404 Farrington, Dallas, TX	214-630-0183
Images Unlimited/13510 Floyd #100, Dallas, TX	214-644-6595
McLaughlin, Herb & Dorothy/2344 W Holly, Phoenix, AZ	602-258-6551
Photobank/PO Box 1086, Scottsdale, AZ	602-948-8805
Photoworks/Uniphoto International/215 Asbury, Houston, TX	713-864-3638
RAPHAELE/DIGITAL TRANSPARENCIES INC/616 HAWTHORNE, HOUSTON, TX (P 426)	**713-524-2211**
Running Productions/PO Box 1237, Flagstaff, AZ	602-774-2923
Southern Images/Rt 1 Box 312, Paris, AR	501-963-6429
The Stock House Inc/1622 W Alabama, Houston, TX	713-526-3007

VISUAL IMAGES WEST/600 E BASELINE RD #B-6, TEMPE, AZ (P 431)	**602-820-5403**
Westlake, Jude/PO Box 791, Tempe, AZ	602-968-9078

ROCKY MOUNTAIN

Amwest Picture Agency/1595 S University, Denver, CO	303-777-2770
Aspen Stock Photo/PO Box 4063, Aspen, CO	303-925-8280
Bair, Royce & Assoc/6640 South 2200 West, Salt Lake City, UT	801-569-1155
Dannen, Kent & Donna/Moraine Route, Estes Park, CO	303-586-5794
International Photo File/PO Box 343, Magna, UT	801-250-3447
The Photo Bank/271 Second Ave N Box 3069, Ketchum, ID	208-726-5731
Stack, Tom & Assoc/1322 N Academy Blvd #209, Colorado Springs, CO	303-570-1000
THE STOCK BROKER/450 LINCOLN ST #110, DENVER, CO (P 428,429)	**303-698-1734**
STOCK IMAGERY/711 KALAMATH ST, DENVER, CO (P 430)	**303-592-1091**
Visual Media Inc/2661 Vassar St, Reno, NV	702-322-8868

WEST COAST

After Image Inc/3807 Wilshire Blvd #250, Los Angeles, CA	213-480-1105
Alaska Pictorial Service/Drawer 6144, Anchorage, AK	907-344-1370
AlaskaPhoto/1530 Westlake Ave N, Seattle, WA	206-282-8116
American Stock Photos/6842 Sunset Blvd, Los Angeles, CA	213-469-3908
Aperture PhotoBank/1530 Westlake Ave N, Seattle, WA	206-282-8116
Beebe, Morton & Assoc/150 Lombard St #207, San Francisco, CA	415-362-3530
Burr, Lawrence/76 Manzanita Rd, Fairfax, CA	415-456-9158
Camera Hawaii/875 Waimanu, Honolulu, HI	808-536-2302
Cornwell, David/1311 Kalakaua Ave, Honolulu, HI	808-949-7000
Dae Flights/PO Box 1086, Newport Beach, CA	714-675-3902
Dandelet Interlinks/126 Redwood Rd, San Anselmo, CA	415-456-1260
Eclipse & Suns/PO Box 689, Haines, AK	907-766-2670
Elich, George/PO Box 255016, Sacramento, CA	916-481-5021
Environmental Communications/62 Windward Ave, Venice, CA	213-392-4964
ERGENBRIGHT, RIC/PO BOX 1067, BEND, OR (P 418)	**503-389-7662**
Focus West/4112 Adams Ave, San Diego, CA	619-280-3595
Fort, Daniel/691 Center St, Costa Mesa, CA	714-549-5709
French, Peter/PO Box 100, Kamuela, HI	808-889-6488
Gemini Smith/5858 Desert View Dr, La Jolla, CA	619-454-4321
Globe Photos/8400 W Sunset Blvd #2B, Los Angeles, CA	213-654-3350
Gornick Film Production/4200 Camino Real, Los Angeles, CA	213-223-8914
Great American Stock/3955 Pacific Hwy, San Diego, CA	619-297-2205
Grimm, Tom & Michelle/PO Box 83, Laguna Beach, CA	714-494-1336
Grubb, T D/11102 Blix St, N Hollywood, CA	818-760-1236
THE IMAGE BANK/8228 SUNSET BLVD #310, LOS ANGELES, CA (BACK COVER)	**213-656-9003**
Jerobam Inc/1041 Folsom St, San Francisco, CA	415-863-7975
Jeton/483 Index Pl NE, Kenton, WA	206-226-1408
Long Photo Inc/1265 S Cochran, Los Angeles, CA	213-933-7219
Lundberg Photo/1370 Logan Ave #6, Costa Mesa, CA	714-631-4177
Lundberg, Bret/PO Box 7542, Newport Beach, CA	714-631-4177
Peebles, Douglas Photography/1100 Alakea St #221, Honolulu, HI	808-533-6686
PHOTO FILE/550 15TH ST #31/1 SHWPLCE SQ, SAN FRANCISCO, CA (P 424,425)	**415-397-3040**
Photo Network/1541 Parkway Loop #J, Tustin, CA	714-259-1244
Photo Vault/1045 17th St, San Francisco, CA	415-552-9682
Photographsanstuff/730 Clementina, San Francisco, CA	415-861-1062
Photophile/2311 Kettner Blvd, San Diego, CA	619-234-4431
Pitcairn, Alan/555 Santa Fe St #L, San Diego, CA	619-270-8851
Shooting Star Inc/PO Box 93368, Hollywood, CA	213-874-9000
SPECTRUM/115 SANSOME ST #812, SAN FRANCISCO, CA (P 427)	**415-340-9811**
Stock Orange/2511 W Sunflower #D9, Santa Ana, CA	714-546-0485
Take Stock/2831 7th Street, Berkeley, CA	415-644-2988
Terraphotographics/BPS/PO Box 490, Moss Beach, CA	415-726-6244
TRW/9841 Airport Blvd #1414, Los Angeles, CA	213-536-4880
VISUAL IMPACT/733 AUAHI ST, HONOLULU, HI (P 423)	**808-524-8269**
West Light/1526 Pontius Ave #A, Los Angeles, CA	213-477-0421
WEST STOCK/157 YESLER WAY #600, SEATTLE, WA	

Please send us your additions and updates.

(P 432,433)	**206-621-1611**
Zephyr Pictures/2120 Jimmy Durante Blvd #4, Del Mar, CA	619-755-1200
Zephyr Pictures/2725 Van Ness #5, San Francisco, CA	415-775-7757
Zoological Society of San Diego/PO Box 551/Photo Lab, San Diego, CA	619-231-1515

STOCK

GRAPHIC DESIGNERS

NEW YORK CITY

A
Abramson, Michael R Studio	212-683-1271
Adams, Gaylord Design	212-684-4625
Adlemann, Morton	212-564-8258
Adzema, Diane	212-982-5657
AKM Associates	212-687-7636
Album Graphics Inc	212-489-0793
Alexander, Martha	212-772-7382
Aliman, Elie	212-925-9621
Allied Graphic Arts	212-730-1414
American Express Publishing Co	212-382-5600
Amorello, Frank Assoc	212-972-1775
Anagraphics Inc	212-279-2370
Ancona Design Atelier	212-947-8287
And Co	212-213-8888
Anspach Grossman Portugal	212-692-9000
Antler & Baldwin Graphics	212-751-2031
Antupit and Others Inc	212-686-2552
Appelbaum Company	212-593-0003
Art Department	212-391-1826
Athey, Diane	212-787-7415

B
Balasas, Cora	718-633-7753
Bantam Books Inc	212-765-6500
Barmache, Leon Design Assoc Inc	212-752-6780
Barnett Design Group	212-677-8830
Barry, Jim	212-873-6787
Basilion, Nick	212-645-6568
Becker Hockfield Design Assoc	212-505-7050
Beckerman, Ann Design	212-684-0496
Bell, James Graphic Design Inc	212-929-8855
Bellows, Amelia	212-777-7012
Benvenutti, Chris	212-696-0880
Bernhardt/Fudyma	212-889-9337
Besalel, Ely	212-759-7820
Bessen & Tully, Inc	212-838-6406
Binns, Betty Graphic Design	212-679-9200
Biondo, Charles Design Assoc	212-645-5300
Birch, Colin Assoc Inc	212-223-0499
Bloch, Graulich & Whelan, Inc	212-473-7033
BN Associates	914-964-8102
Boker Group	212-686-1132
Bonnell Design Associates Inc	212-921-5390
Bordnick, Jack & Assoc	212-563-1544
Botero, Samuel Assoc	212-935-5155
Bradford, Peter	212-982-2090
Brainchild Designs	212-420-1222
Branin, Max	212-254-9608
Braswell, Lynn	212-222-8761
Bree/Taub Design	212-254-8383
Breth, Jill Marie	212-781-8370
Brochure People	212-696-9185
Brodsky Graphics	212-684-2600
Brown, Alastair Assoc	212-221-3166
Brown, Kim	212-567-5671
Buckley Designs Inc	212-861-0626
Burns, Tom Assoc Inc	212-594-9883
By Design	212-684-0388
The Byrne Group	212-889-0502

C
Cain, David	212-691-5783
Cannan, Bill & Co Inc	212-563-1004
Caravello Studios	212-620-0620
Carnase, Inc	212-679-9880
Cetta, Al	212-989-9696
Chajet Design Group Inc	212-684-3669
Chang, Ivan	212-777-6102
Chapman, Sandra S	718-855-7396
Charles, Irene Assoc	212-765-8000
Chermayeff & Geismar	212-532-4499

Chu, H L & Co Ltd	212-889-4818
Church, Wallace Assoc	212-755-2903
Cliffer, Jill	212-691-7013
Cohen, Norman Design	212-679-3906
Comart Assoc	212-714-2550
Condon, J & M	212-242-7811
Corchia Woliner Assoc	212-977-9778
Corey & Co	212-924-4311
Corpographics, Inc.	212-483-9065
Corporate Annual Reports Inc.	212-889-2450
Corporate Graphics Inc	212-599-1820
Cosgrove Assoc Inc	212-889-7202
Cotler, Sheldon Inc	212-719-9590
Cousins, Morison S & Assoc	212-751-3390
Crane, Eileen	212-644-3850
Crane, Susan Inc	212-260-0580
Cranner, Brian Inc	212-582-2030
Creamer Dickson Basford	212-887-8670
Csoka/Benato/Fleurant Inc	212-242-6777
Cuevas, Robert	212-661-7149
Curtis Design Inc.	212-685-0670

D
Daniels Design	212-889-0071
Danne & Blackburn Inc.	212-371-3250
Davis-Delaney-Arrow Inc	212-686-2500
DeHarak, Rudolph	212-929-5445
Deibler, Gordon	212-565-8022
Delgado, Lisa	212-645-0097
Delphan Company	212-371-6700
DeMartin-Marona-Cranstoun-Downes	212-682-9044
DeMartino/Schultz	212-513-0300
Design Derivatives Inc	212-751-7650
Design Influence Inc	212-840-2155
Designed to Print	212-924-2090
Designframe	212-924-2426
Deutsch Design	212-684-4478
Diamond Art Studio	212-685-6622
Dickens, Holly	212-682-1490
DiComo, Charles & Assoc	212-689-8670
DiFranza Williamson Inc	212-832-2343
Dinand, Pierre Design	212-751-3086
Displaycraft	718-784-8186
Donovan & Green Inc	212-725-2233
Doret, Michael	212-929-1688
Douglas, Barry Design	212-734-4137
Downey Weeks + Toomey	212-564-8260
Drate, Spencer	212-620-4672
Dreyfuss, Henry Assoc	212-957-8600
Dubins, Milt Designer Inc	212-691-0232
Dubourcq, Hilaire	212-924-1564
Dubrow, Oscar Assoc	212-688-0698
Duffy, William R	212-682-6755
Dwyer, Tom	212-986-7108

E
Edge, Dennis Design	212-679-0927
Eichinger, Inc	212-421-0544
Eisenman and Enock	212-431-1000
Emerson, Matt	212-807-8144
Environetics Inc	212-759-3830
Environment Planning Inc	212-661-3744
Erikson Assoc.	212-688-0048
ETC Communications Grp	212-645-6800
Etheridge, Palombo, Sedewitz	212-944-2530
Eucalyptus Tree Studio	212-226-0331

F
Failing, Kendrick G Design	212-677-5764
Falkins, Richard Design	212-840-3045
Farmlett Barsanti Inc	212-691-9398
Farrell, Bill	212-562-8931
FDC Planning & Design Corp	212-355-7200
Feucht, Fred Design Group Inc	212-682-0040
Fineberg Associates	212-734-1220

Please send us your additions and updates.

Florville. Patrick Design Research	718-475-2278
Flying Eye Graphics	212-725-0658
Forman, Yale Designs Inc	212-799-1665
Foster, Stephen Design	212-532-0771
Freeman, Irving	212-674-6705
Freyss, Christina	212-571-1130
Friday Saturday Sunday Inc	212-260-8479
Friedlander, Ira	212-580-9800
Fulgoni, Louis	212-243-2959
Fulton & Partners	212-695-1625

G Gale, Cynthia 212-860-5429

Gale, Robert A Inc	212-535-4791
Gamarello, Paul	212-485-4774
Gardner, Beau Assoc Inc	212-832-2426
Gaster, Joanne	212-686-0860
Gentile Studio	212-986-7743
George, Hershell	212-929-4321
Gerstman & Meyers Inc.	212-586-2535
Gianninoto Assoc, Inc.	212-759-5757
Giber, Lauren	212-473-2062
Giovanni Design Assoc.	212-725-8536
Gips & Balkind & Assoc	212-421-5940
Gladstein, Renee	212-877-2966
Gladych, Marianne	212-925-9712
Glaser, Milton	212-889-3161
Glazer & Kalayjian	212-687-3099
Glusker Group	212-757-4438
Goetz Graphics	212-679-4250
Goldman, Neal Assoc	212-687-5058
Gorbaty, Norman Design	212-684-1665
Gorman, Chris Assoc	212-696-9377
Grant, Bill	718-996-3555
The Graphic Expression Inc.	212-759-7788
Graphic Art Resource Assoc	212-929-0017
Graphics 60 Inc.	212-687-1292
Graphics by Nostradamus	212-581-1362
Graphics for Industry	212-889-6202
Graphics Institute	212-887-8670
Graphics to Go	212-889-9337
Gray, George	212-873-3607
Green, Douglas	212-752-6284
Griffler Designs	212-794-2625
Grossberg, Manuel	212-620-0444
Grunfeld Graphics Ltd	212-431-8700
Gucciardo & Shapokas	212-683-9378

H Halle, Doris 212-321-2671

Halversen, Everett	718-438-4200
Handler Group Inc	212-391-0951
Haydee Design Studio	212-242-3110
HBO Studio Productions Inc	212-477-8600
Hecker, Mark Studio	212-620-9050
Heimall, Bob Inc	212-245-4525
Herbick, David	718-852-6450
Holden, Cynthia	212-222-4214
Holland, DK	718-789-3112
Holzsager, Mel Assoc Inc	212-741-7373
Hooper, Ray Design	212-924-5480
Hopkins, Will	212-580-9800
Horvath & Assoc Studios Ltd	212-741-0300
Hub Graphics	212-675-8500
Human Factors/Industrial Design Inc	212-730-8010

IJ Image Communications Inc 212-807-9677

Infield & D'Astolfo	212-924-9206
Inkwell Inc	212-279-2066
Inner Thoughts	212-674-1277
Intersight Design Inc	212-696-0700
Jaffe Communications, Inc	212-697-4310
Johnson, Dwight	718-834-8529
Johnston, Shaun & Susan	212-663-4686

Jonson Pedersen Hinrichs & Shakery	212-889-9611

K Kacik Design 212-753-0031

Kaeser & Wilson Design	212-563-2455
Kahn, Al Group	212-580-3517
Kahn, Donald	212-889-8898
Kallir Phillips Ross Inc.	212-878-3700
Kass Communications	212-868-3133
Kass, Milton Assoc Inc	212-874-0418
Kaye Graphics	212-924-7800
Keithley & Assoc	212-807-8388
Kleb Associates	212-246-2847
KLN Publishing Services Inc	212-686-8200
Kneapler, John	212-696-1150
Ko Noda and Assoc International	212-759-4044
Kollberg-Johnson Assoc Inc	212-686-3648
Koons, Irv Assoc	212-752-4130
Koppel & Scher Inc	212-683-0870

L Lacy, N Lee 212-532-6200

Lake, John	212-644-3850
Lamlee, Stuart	212-844-8991
The Lamplight Group	212-682-6270
LCL Design Assoc Inc	212-758-2604
Leach, Richard	212-869-0972
Lebbad, James A	212-645-5260
Lee & Young Communications	212-689-4000
Lefkowith Inc.	212-758-8550
Leo Art Studio	212-736-8785
Lesley-Hille Inc	212-677-7570
Lester & Butler	212-889-0578
Levine, Gerald	212-986-1068
Levine, William V & Assoc	212-683-7177
Levirne, Joel	212-869-8370
Lichtenberg, Al Graphic Art	212-865-4312
Lieberman, Ron	212-947-0653
Liebert Studios Inc	212-686-4520
Lika Association	212-490-3660
Lind Brothers Inc	212-924-9280
Lippincott & Margulies Inc	212-832-3000
Little Apple Art	718-499-7045
Loiacono Adv	212-683-5811
Loukin, Serge Inc	212-255-5651
Lubliner/Saltz	212-679-9810
Luckett Slover & Partners	212-620-9770
Lukasiewicz Design Inc	212-581-3344
Lundgren, Ray Graphics	212-370-1686
Luth & Katz Inc	212-644-5777

M M & Co Design Group 212-243-0082

Maddalone, John	212-807-6087
Maggio, Ben Assoc Inc	212-697-8600
Maggio, J P Design Assoc Inc	212-725-9660
Maleter, Mari	718-726-7124
Marchese, Frank	212-988-6267
Marckrey Design Group Inc	212-620-7077
Marcus, Eric	718-789-1799
Marino, Guy Graphic Design	212-935-1141
Mauro, C L & Assoc Inc	212-868-3940
Mauro, Frank Assoc Inc	212-719-5570
Mayo-Infurna Design	212-888-7883
McDonald, B & Assoc	212-869-9717
McGovern & Pivoda	212-840-2912
McNicholas, Florence	718-965-0203
Meier Adv	212-355-6460
Mendola Design	212-986-5680
Mentkin, Robert	212-534-5101
Merrill, Abby Studio Inc	212-753-7565
The Midnight Oil	212-582-9071
Millenium Design	212-683-3400
Miller, Irving D Inc	212-755-4040
Mirenburg, Barry	718-885-0835

Please send us your additions and updates.

Mitchell, E M Inc	212-986-5595
Mizerek Design	212-986-5702
Modular Marketing Inc	212-581-4690
Mont, Howard Assoc Inc	212-683-4360
Morris, Dean	212-420-0673
Moshier, Harry & Assoc	212-873-6130
Moskof & Assoc	212-333-2015
Mossberg, Stuart Design Assoc	212-873-6130
Muir, Cornelius, Moore	212-687-4055
Murtha Desola Finsilver Fiore	212-832-4770

N

N B Assoc Inc	212-684-8074
Nelson, George & Assoc Inc	212-777-4300
Nemeser, Robert Assoc	212-832-9595
New American Graphics	212-532-3551
Newman, Harvey Assoc	212-391-8060
Nicholson Design	212-206-1530
Nightingale, Gordon	212-685-9263
Nitzburg, Andrew	212-686-3514
Nobart NY Inc	212-475-5522
Noneman & Noneman Design	212-473-4090
North, Charles W Studio	212-242-6300
Notovitz & Perrault Design Inc	212-677-9700
Novus Visual Communications Inc	212-689-2424

O

Oak Tree Graphics Inc	212-398-9355
Offenhartz, Harvey Inc	212-751-3241
Ohlsson, Eskil Assoc Inc	212-758-4412
Ong & Assoc	212-355-4343
Orlov, Christian	212-873-2381
Ortiz, Jose Luis	212-831-6138
Oz Communications Inc	212-686-8200

P

Page Arbitrio Resen Ltd	212-421-8190
Pahmer, Hal	212-889-6202
Palladino, Tony	212-751-0068
Parsons School of Design	212-741-8900
Patel, Harish Design Assoc	212-686-7425
Pellegrini & Assoc	212-686-4481
Pencils Portfolio Inc	212-355-2468
Penpoint Studio Inc	212-243-5435
Penraat Jaap Assoc	212-873-4541
Performing Dogs	212-260-1880
Perlman, Richard Design	212-935-2552
Perlow, Paul	212-758-4358
Peters, Stan Assoc Inc	212-684-0315
Peterson Blythe & Cato	212-557-5566
Pettis, Valerie	212-683-7382
Plumb Design Group Inc	212-673-3490
Podob, Al	212-697-6643
Pop Shots Corporate Design	212-489-1717
Pouget, Evelyn	212-228-7935
Prendergast, J W & Assoc Inc	212-687-8805
Primary Design Group	212-219-1000
Projection Systems International	212-682-0995
Puiying	212-689-5148
PushPin	212-674-8080

QR

Quon, Mike Design Office	212-226-6024
Rafkin Rubin Inc	212-869-2540
Ratzkin, Lawrence	212-279-1314
RC Graphics	212-755-1383
RD Graphics	212-889-5612
Regn-Califano Inc	212-239-0380
Robinson, Mark	718-638-9067
Rogers, Ana	212-741-4687
Rogers, Richard Inc	212-685-3666
Romero, Javier	212-206-9175
Rosenthal, Herb & Assoc Inc	212-685-1814
Ross Culbert Holland & Lavery	212-206-0044
Ross/Pento Inc	212-757-5604
Royce Graphics	212-239-1990

Russell, Anthony Inc	212-255-0650

S

Sabanosh, Michael	212-947-8161
Saiki & Assoc	212-255-0466
Sakin, Sy	212-688-3141
Saks, Arnold	212-861-4300
Saksa Art & Design	212-255-5539
Salisbury & Salisbury Inc	212-575-0770
Salpeter, Paganucci, Inc	212-683-3310
Saltzman, Mike Group	212-929-4655
Sandgren Associates Inc	212-679-4650
Sawyer, Arnie Studio	212-685-4927
Saxton Communications Group	212-953-1300
Say It In Neon	212-691-7977
Schaefer-Cassety Inc	212-840-0175
Schaeffer/Boehm Ltd	212-947-4345
Schechter Group Inc	212-752-4400
Schecterson, Jack Assoc Inc	212-889-3950
Schumach, Michael P	718-539-5328
Scott, Louis Assoc	212-674-0215
SCR Design Organization	212-752-8496
Serge Loukin Inc	212-255-5651
Shapiro, Ellen Graphic Design	212-221-2625
Shareholder Graphics	212-661-1070
Shareholders Reports	212-686-9099
Sherin & Matejka Inc	212-686-8410
Sherowitz, Phyllis	212-532-8933
Shreeve, Draper Design	212-675-7534
Siegel & Gale Inc	212-730-0101
Silberlicht, Ira	212-595-6252
Silverman, Bob Design	212-371-6472
Singer, Paul Design	718-449-8172
Sloan, William	212-226-8110
Smith, Edward Design	212-255-1717
Smith, Laura	212-206-9162
Sochynsky, Ilona	212-686-1275
Solay/Hunt	212-840-3313
Sorvino, Skip	212-580-9638
St Vincent Milone & McConnells	212-921-1414
Stillman, Linda	212-410-3225
Stuart, Gunn & Furuta	212-689-0077
Studio 42	212-354-7298
The Sukon Group, Inc	212-986-2290
Swatek and Romanoff Design Inc	212-807-0236
Systems Collaborative Inc	212-608-0584

T

Tapa Graphics	212-243-0176
Taurins Design Assoc	212-679-5955
Tauss, Jack George	212-279-1658
Taylor & Ives	212-244-0750
Taylor, Stan Inc	212-685-4741
Teague, Walter Dorwin Assoc	212-557-0920
Tercovich, Douglas Assoc Inc	212-838-4800
Theoharides Inc	212-838-7760
Thompson Communications	212-685-4400
Three	212-988-6267
Tobias, William	212-741-1712
Todd, Ann	212-799-1016
Tower Graphics Arts Corp	212-421-0850
Tribich/Glasman Design	212-679-6016
Tscherny, George Design	212-734-3277
Tunstull Studio	718-875-9356
Turner/Miller	212-371-3035

UV

Ultra Arts Inc	212-679-7493
Un, David	212-924-2090
Vecchio, Carmine	212-683-2679
Viewpoint Graphics	212-685-0560
Visible Studio Inc	212-683-8530
Visual Accents Corp	212-777-7766

W

Wajdowicz, Jurek	212-807-8144

Please send us your additions and updates.

Waldman, Veronica	212-260-3552
Waters, John Assoc Inc	212-807-0717
Waters, Pamela Studio Inc	212-620-8100
Webster, Robert Inc	212-677-2966
Weed, Eunice Assoc Inc	212-725-4933
Whelan Design Office	212-691-4404
The Whole Works	212-575-0765
Wijtvliet, Ine	212-684-4575
Wilke, Jerry	212-689-2424
Wilson, Rex Co	212-594-3646
Withers, Bruce Graphic Design	212-599-2388
Wizard Graphics Inc	212-686-8200
Wolf, Henry Production Inc	212-472-2500
Wolff, Rudi Inc	212-873-5800
Wood, Alan	212-889-5195
Word-Wise	212-246-0430
Works	212-696-1666

YZ

Yoshimura-Fisher Graphic Design	212-431-4776
Young Goldman Young Inc	212-697-7820
Zahor & Bender	212-686-1121
Zazula, Hy Inc	212-531-2747
Zeitsoff, Elaine	212-580-1282
Zimmerman & Foyster	212-674-0259

NORTHEAST

A

Action Incentive/Rochester, NY	716-427-2410
Adam Filippo & Moran/Pittsburgh, PA	412-261-3720
Adler-Schwartz Graphics/Hunt Valley, MD	301-628-0600
Advertising Design Assoc Inc/Baltimore, MD	301-752-2181
Another Color Inc/Washington, DC	202-328-1414
Aries Graphics/Manchester, NH	603-668-0811
Art Service Assoc Inc/Pittsburgh, PA	412-391-0902
The Artery/Baltimore, MD	301-752-2979
Arts and Words/Washington, DC	202-463-4880
Artwork Unlimited Inc/Washington, DC	202-638-6996
Autograph/Annapolis, MD	301-268-3300
The Avit Corp/Fort Lee, NJ	201-886-1100

B

Bain, S Milo/Hartsdale, NY	914-946-0144
Baker, Arthur/Germantown, NY	518-537-4438
Baldwin, Jim/Salem, MA	617-745-6462
Bally Design Inc/Carnegie, PA	412-276-5454
Banks & Co/Boston, MA	617-262-0020
Barancik, Bob/Philadelphia, PA	215-893-9149
Barton-Gillet/Baltimore, MD	301-685-6800
Bedford Photo-Graphic Studio/Bedford, NY	914-234-3123
Belser, Burkey/Washington, DC	202-462-1482
Bennardo, Churik Design Inc/Pittsburgh, PA	412-963-0133
Berns & Kay Ltd/Washington, DC	202-387-7032
Beveridge and Associates, Inc/Washington, DC	202-337-0400
Blum, William Assoc/Boston, MA	617-232-1166
Bogus, Sidney A & Assoc/Melrose, MA	617-662-6660
Bomzer Design Inc/Boston, MA	617-227-5151
Bookmakers/Westport, CT	203-226-4293
Booth, Margot/Washington, DC	202-244-0412
Boscobel Advertising/Laurel, MD	301-953-2600
Bradbury, Robert & Assoc/Closter, NJ	201-768-6395
Brady, John Design Consultants/Pittsburgh, PA	412-288-9300
Breckenridge Designs/Washington, DC	202-833-5700
Bressler, Peter Design Assoc/Philadelphia, PA	215-925-7100
Bridy, Dan/Pittsburgh, PA	412-288-9362
Brier, David/E Rutherford, NJ	201-896-8476
Brown and Craig Inc/Baltimore, MD	301-837-2727
Buckett, Bill Assoc/Rochester, NY	716-546-6580
Burke & Michael Inc/Pittsburgh, PA	412-321-2301
Byrne, Ford/Philadelphia, PA	215-564-0500

C

Cable, Jerry Design/Madison, NJ	201-966-0124
Calingo, Diane/Kensington, MD	301-949-3557
Cameron Inc/Boston, MA	617-338-4408
Carlson, Tim/Brookline, MA	617-566-7330
Carmel, Abraham/Peekskill, NY	914-737-1439
Case/Washington, DC	202-328-5900
Casey Mease Inc/Wilmington, DE	302-655-2100
Chaparos Productions Limited/Washington, DC	202-289-4838
Charysyn & Charysyn/Westkill, NY	518-989-6720
Chase, David O Design Inc/Skaneateles, NY	315-685-5715
Chronicle Type & Design/Washington, DC	202-828-3519
Clark, Dave/Riva, MD	301-956-4160
Colangelo, Ted Assoc/Greenwich, CT	203-531-3600
Colopy Dale Inc/Pittsburgh, PA	412-332-6706
Communications Graphics Group/Arlington, VA	703-979-8500
Concept Packaging Inc/Ft Lee, NJ	201-224-5762
Consolidated Visual Center Inc/Tuxedo, MD	301-772-7300
Cook & Shanosky Assoc/Princeton, NJ	609-452-1666
Creative Communications Center/Pennsauken, NJ	201-894-2566
Creative Presentations Inc/Washington, DC	202-737-7152
The Creative Dept/Philadelphia, PA	215-988-0390
Crozier, Bob & Assoc/Washington, DC	202-638-7134
Curran & Connors Inc/Jericho, NY	516-433-6600

D

D'Art Studio Inc/Boston, MA	617-482-4442
Dakota Design/King of Prussia, PA	215-265-1255
Dale, Terry/Washington, DC	202-244-3866
Daroff Design Inc/Philadelphia, PA	215-636-9900
Dawson Designers Associates/Assonet, MA	617-644-2940
DeCesare, John/Darien, CT	203-655-6057
DeMartin-Marona-Cranstoun-Downes/Wilmington, DE	302-654-5277
Design Associates/Arlington, VA	703-243-7717
Design Center Inc/Boston, MA	617-542-1254
Design Communication Collaboration/Washington, DC	202-833-9087
Design for Medicine Inc/Philadelphia, PA	215-925-7100
Design Group of Boston/Boston, MA	617-437-1084
Design Technology Corp/Billerica, MA	617-272-8890
Design Trends/Valhalla, NY	914-948-0902
Designworks Inc/Watertown, MA	617-926-6286
DiFiore Associates/Pittsburgh, PA	412-471-0608
Dimmick, Gary/Pittsburgh, PA	412-321-7223
Dohanos, Steven/Westport, CT	203-227-3541
Downing, Allan/Needham, MA	617-449-4784
Duffy, Bill & Assoc/Washington, DC	202-965-2216

E

Edigraph Inc/Katonah, NY	914-232-3725
Educational Media/Graphics Division/Washington, DC	202-625-2211
Egress Concepts/Katonah, NY	914-232-8433
Erickson, Peter/Maynard, MA	617-369-8060
Eucalyptus Tree Studio/Baltimore, MD	301-243-0211
Evans Garber & Paige/Utica, NY	315-733-2313

F

Fader Jones & Zarkades/Boston, MA	617-267-7779
Falcone & Assoc/Chatham, NJ	201-635-2900
Fannell Studio/Boston, MA	617-267-0895
Flat Tulip Studio/Marietta, PA	717-426-1344
Forum Inc/Fairfield, CT	203-259-5686
Fossella, Gregory Assoc/Boston, MA	617-267-4940
Fowler, Cynthia/Silver Spring, MD	301-445-1217
Fraser, Robert & Assoc Inc/Baltimore, MD	301-685-3700
Fresh Produce/Lutherville, MD	301-821-1815
Froelich Advertising Service/Mahwah, NJ	201-529-1737

G

Galasso, Gene Assoc Inc/Silver Spring, MD	202-439-1282
Gasser, Gene/Chatham, NJ	201-635-6020
Gateway Studios/Pittsburgh, PA	412-471-7224
Gatter Inc/Rye, NY	914-967-5600
Genesis Design/Ashland, MA	617-881-2471
GK+D Communications/Washington, DC	202-328-0414
Glass, Al/Washington, DC	202-333-3993
Glickman, Frank Inc/Boston, MA	617-524-2200
Good, Peter Graphic Design/Chester, CT	203-526-9597
Gorelick, Alan & Assoc/Clark, NJ	201-382-4141
Graham Associates Inc/Washington, DC	202-833-9657

Please send us your additions and updates.

Grant Marketing Assoc./Conshohocken, PA	215-834-0550
The Graphic Suite/Pittsburgh, PA	412-661-6699
Graphic Workshop/Emerson, NJ	201-967-8500
Graphicenter/Washington, DC	202-544-0333
Graphics By Gallo/Washington, DC	202-234-7700
Graphics Plus Corp/St Malden, MA	617-321-7500
Graphicus Corp/Baltimore, MD	301-727-5553
Grear, Malcolm Designers Inc/Providence, RI	401-331-5656
Green, Mel/Needham Hts, MA	617-449-6777
Greenebaum Design/Natick, MA	617-655-8146
Greenfield, Peggy/Foxboro, MA	617-543-6644
Gregory & Clyburne/New Canaan, CT	203-966-8343
Groff, Jay Michael/Silver Spring, MD	301-565-0431
Groff-Long Associates/Bethesda, MD	301-654-0279
Group Four Inc/Avon, CT	203-678-1570
Gunn Associates/Boston, MA	617-267-0618

H

Hain, Robert Assoc/Scotch Plains, NJ	201-322-1717
Hammond Design Assoc/Milford, NH	603-673-5253
Harrington-Jackson/Boston, MA	617-536-6164
Harvey, Ed/Washington, DC	703-671-0880
Hegemann Associates/Nyack, NY	914-358-7348
Herbick & Held/Pittsburgh, PA	412-321-7400
Herbst Lazar Rogers & Bell Inc/Lancaster, PA	717-291-9042
Herman & Lees/Cambridge, MA	617-876-6463
Hill, Michael/Towson, MD	301-821-0729
Hillmuth, James/Washington, DC	202-244-0465
Holl, RJ/ Art Directions/Wales, MA	413-267-5024
Holloway, Martin/Springfield, NJ	201-563-0169
Hough, Jack Inc/Norwalk, CT	203-846-2666
Hrivnak, James/Silver Spring, MD	301-681-9090
Huerta, Gerard/Darien, CT	203-656-0505
Huyysen, Roger/Darien, CT	203-656-0200

IJ

Image Consultants/Amherst, NH	603-673-5512
Innovations & Development Inc/Ft Lee, NJ	201-944-9317
Irish, Gary Graphics/Boston, MA	617-247-4168
Itin, Marcel/Visual Concepts/Greenwich, CT	203-869-1928
Jaeger Design Studio/Washington, DC	202-785-8434
Jarrin Design Inc/Pound Ridge, NY	914-764-4625
Jensen, R S/Baltimore, MD	301-727-3411
Jezierny, John Michael/Westville, CT	203-689-8170
Johnson & Simpson Graphic Design/Newark, NJ	201-624-7788
Johnson Design Assoc/Acton, MA	617-263-5345
Johnson, Charlotte/Washington, DC	202-544-7936
Jones, Tom & Jane Kearns/Washington, DC	202-232-1921

K

Kahana Associates/Jenkintown, PA	215-887-0422
Karp, Rudi/Landsowne, PA	215-284-5949
Katz-Wheeler Design/Philadelphia, PA	215-567-5668
Kaufman, Henry J & Assoc Inc/Washington, DC	202-333-0700
KBH Graphics/Baltimore, MD	301-539-7916
Kell & Co/Silver Spring, MD	202-585-4000
Ketchum International/Pittsburgh, PA	412-456-3693
King-Casey Inc/New Canaan, CT	203-966-3581
Klim, Matt & Assoc/Avon, CT	203-678-1222
Klotz, Don/Wilton, CT	203-762-9111
Knox, Harry & Assoc/Washington, DC	202-833-2305
Kostanecki, Andrew Inc/New Canaan, CT	203-966-1681
Kovanen, Erik/Wilton, CT	203-762-8961
Kramer/Miller/Lomden/Glossman/Philadelphia, PA	215-545-7077
Krohne, David/Washington, DC	202-265-2371
Krone Graphic Design/Lemoyne, PA	717-774-7431
Krueger Wright Design/Somerville, MA	617-666-4880

L

LAM Design Inc/White Plains, NY	914-948-4777
Landersman, Myra/Malaga, NJ	609-694-1011
Langdon, John/Wenonah, NJ	609-468-7868
Lapham/Miller Assoc/Andora, MA	617-367-0110
Latham Brefka Associates/Boston, MA	617-536-8787
Lausch, David Graphics/Baltimore, MD	301-235-7453
Lebowitz, Mo/N Bellemore, NY	516-826-3397

Leeds, Judith K Studio/N Caldwell, NJ	201-226-3552
Lenney, Ann/Washington, DC	202-667-1786
Leotta Designers Inc/Conshohocken, PA	215-828-8820
Lester Associates Inc/West Nyack, NY	914-358-6100
Levinson Zaprauskis Assoc/Philadelphia, PA	215-248-5242
Lewis, Hal Design/Philadelphia, PA	215-563-4461
Lion Hill Studio/Baltimore, MD	301-837-6218
Livingston Studio/Elmsford, NY	914-592-4220
Lizak, Matt/N Smithfield, RI	401-766-8885
Lose, Hal/Philadelphia, PA	215-849-7635
Luma/Baltimore, MD	301-523-5903
Lussier, Mark/E Norwalk, CT	203-852-0363

M

M&M Graphics/Baltimore, MD	301-747-4555
MacIntosh, Rob Communication/Boston, MA	617-267-4912
Maglio, Mark/Plainville, CT	203-793-0771
Mahoney, Ron/Pittsburgh, PA	412-261-3824
Major Assoc/Baltimore, MD	301-752-6174
Mandala/Philadelphia, PA	215-923-6020
Marcus, Sarna/Bethesda, MD	301-951-7044
Mariuzza, Pete/Briarcliff Manor, NY	914-769-3310
Martucci Studio/Boston, MA	617-266-6960
Mason, Kim/Washington, DC	202-646-0118
MDB Communications Inc/Rockville, MD	301-279-9093
Media Concepts/Boston, MA	617-437-1382
Media Loft/Minneapolis, MN	612-831-0226
Melanson, Donya Assoc/Charlestown, MA	617-241-7300
Micolucci, Nicholas Assoc/King of Prussia, PA	215-265-3320
Miho, J Inc/Redding, CT	203-938-3214
Mitchell & Company/Washington, DC	202-342-6025
Monti, Ron/Baltimore, MD	301-366-8952
Morlock Graphics/Towson, MD	301-825-5080
Moss, John C/Chevy Chase, MD	301-320-3912
Mossman Art Studio/Baltimore, MD	301-243-1963
Mueller & Wister/Philadelphia, PA	215-568-7260
Muller-Munk, Peter Assoc/Pittsburgh, PA	412-261-5161
Myers, Gene Assoc/Pittsburgh, PA	412-661-6314

NO

Nason Design Assoc/Boston, MA	617-266-7286
Navratil Art Studio/Pittsburgh, PA	412-471-4322
Nimeck, Fran/South Brunswick, NJ	201-821-8741
Nolan & Assoc/Washington, DC	202-363-6553
North Charles St Design/Baltimore, MD	301-539-4040
Odyssey Design Group/Washington, DC	202-783-6240
Ollio Studio/Pittsburgh, PA	412-281-4483
Omnigraphics/Cambridge, MA	617-354-7444
On Target/Riverside, CT	203-637-8300

P

Paganucci, Bob/Montvale, NJ	201-391-1752
Paine/ Bluett/ Paine Inc/Bethesda, MD	301-493-8445
Papazian Design/Boston, MA	617-262-7848
Paragraphics Inc./White Plains, NY	914-948-4777
Parks, Franz & Cox, Inc/Washington, DC	202-797-7568
Parry, Ivor A/Eastchester, NY	914-961-7338
Parshall, C A Inc/Stamford, CT	212-947-5971
Pasinski, Irene Assoc/Pittsburgh, PA	412-683-0585
Patazian Design Inc/Boston, MA	617-262-7848
Peck, Gail M/Washington, DC	202-667-7448
Pentick, Joseph/Kingston, NY	914-331-8197
Perspectives In Communications/Washington, DC	202-667-7448
Pesanelli, David Assoc/Washington, DC	202-363-4760
Petty, Daphne/Washington, DC	202-667-8222
Phillips Design Assoc/Boston, MA	617-423-7676
Picture That Inc/Newtown Square, PA	215-353-8833
Planert, Paul Design Assoc/Pittsburgh, PA	412-621-1275
Plataz, George/Pittsburgh, PA	412-322-3177
Plumridge Artworks/Bethesda, MD	301-231-5110
Porter, Al/Graphics Inc/Washington, DC	202-244-0403
Prelude to Print/Rockville, MD	301-984-1488
Presentation Associates/Washington, DC	202-333-0080
Production Studio/Port Washington, NY	516-944-6688
Profile Press Inc/E Islip, NY	516-277-6319

Please send us your additions and updates.

Publication Services Inc/Stamford, CT	203-348-7351

R

Ralcon Inc/West Chester, PA	215-692-2840
Rand, Paul Inc/Weston, CT	203-227-5375
Redtree Associates/Washington, DC	202-628-2900
Renaissance Communications/Silver Spring, MD	301-587-1505
Research Planning Assoc/Philadelphia, PA	215-561-9700
Rieb, Robert/Westport, CT	203-227-0061
Ringel, Leonard Lee Graphic Design/Kendall Park, NJ	201-297-9084
Ritter, Richard Design Inc/Berwyn, PA	215-296-0400
RKM Inc/Washington, DC	202-364-0148
Rogalski Assoc/Boston, MA	617-451-2111
Romax Studio/Stamford, CT	203-324-4260
Rosborg Inc/Newton, CT	203-426-3171
Roth, J H Inc/Peekskill, NY	914-737-6784
RSV/Boston, MA	617-262-9450
Rubin, Marc Design Assoc/Breesport, NY	607-739-0871
RZA Inc/Park Ridge, NJ	201-391-8500

S

Sanchez/Philadelphia, PA	215-564-2223
Schneider Design/Baltimore, MD	301-467-2611
Schoenfeld, Cal/Parsippany, NJ	201-263-1635
Selame Design Associates/Newton Lower Falls, MA	617-969-6690
Shapiro, Deborah/Jersey City, NJ	201-432-5198
Silvia, Ken/Cambridge, MA	617-451-1995
Simpson Booth Designers/Cambridge, MA	617-661-2630
Smarilli Graphics Inc/Mechanicsburg, PA	717-697-8094
Smith, Agnew Moyer/Pittsburgh, PA	412-322-6333
Smith, Doug/Larchmont, NY	914-834-3997
Smith, Gail Hunter/Barnegat Light, NJ	609-494-9136
Smith, Tyler Art Direction/Providence, RI	401-751-1220
Smizer Design/Boston, MA	617-423-3350
Snowden Associates Inc/Washington, DC	202-362-8944
Sparkman & Bartholomew/Washington, DC	202-785-2414
Spectrum Boston/Boston, MA	617-367-1008
Stansbury Ronsaville Wood Inc/Annapolis, MD	301-261-8662
Star Design Inc/Moorestown, NJ	609-235-8150
Steel Art Co Inc/Allston, MA	617-566-4079
Stettler, Wayne Design/Philadelphia, PA	215-235-1230
Stockman & Andrews Inc/E Providence, RI	401-438-0694
Stolt, Jill Design/Rochester, NY	716-461-2594
Stuart, Neil/Mahopac, NY	914-618-1662
The Studio Group/Washington, DC	202-332-3003
Studio Six Design/Springfield, NJ	201-379-5820

T

Takajian, Asdur/N Tarrytown, NY	914-631-5553
Taylor, Pat/Washington, DC	202-338-0962
Telesis/Baltimore, MD	301-235-2000
Tetrad Inc/Annapolis, MD	301-268-8680
Thompson, Bradbury/Riverside, CT	203-637-3614
Thompson, George L/Reading, MA	617-944-6256
Toelke, Cathleen/Boston, MA	617-242-7414
Torode, Barbara/Philadelphia, PA	215-732-6792
Town Studios Inc/Pittsburgh, PA	412-471-5353
Troller, Fred Assoc Inc/Rye, NY	914-698-1405

V

Van Der Sluys Graphics Inc/Washington, DC	202-265-3443
Vance Wright Adams & Assoc/Pittsburgh, PA	412-322-1800
VanDine, Horton, McNamara, Manges Inc/Pittsburgh, PA	412-261-4280
Vinick, Bernard Assoc Inc/Hartford, CT	203-525-4293
Viscom Inc/Baltimore, MD	301-764-0005
Visual Research & Design Corp/Boston, MA	617-536-2111
The Visualizers/Pittsburgh, PA	412-488-0944

W

Warkulwiz Design/Philadelphia, PA	215-546-0880
Wasserman's, Myron Graphic Design Group/Philadelphia, PA	215-922-4545
Weadock, Rutka/Baltimore, MD	301-563-2100
Webb & Co/Boston, MA	617-262-6980
Weitzman & Assoc/Bethesda, MD	301-652-7035
Weymouth Design/Boston, MA	617-542-2647
White, E James Co/Alexandria, VA	703-750-3680
Wickham & Assoc Inc/Washington, DC	202-296-4860

Willard, Janet Design Assoc/Allison Park, PA	412-486-8100
Williams Associates/Lynnfield, MA	617-599-1818
Wilsonwork Graphic Design/Washington, DC	202-332-9016
Wright, Kent M Assoc Inc/Sudbury, MA	617-443-9909

YZ

Yeo, Robert/Hoboken, NJ	201-659-3277
Yurdin, Carl Industrial Design Inc/Port Washington, NY	516-944-7811
Zeb Graphics/Washington, DC	202-293-1687
Zmiejko & Assoc Design Agcy/Freeland, PA	717-636-2304

SOUTHEAST

A

Ace Art/New Orleans, LA	504-861-2222
Alphabet Group/Atlanta, GA	404-892-6500
Alphacom Inc/N Miami, FL	305-949-5588
Art Services/Atlanta, GA	404-892-2105
Arts & Graphics/Annandale, VA	703-941-2560
Arunski, Joe & Assoc/Miami, FL	305-271-8300
The Associates Inc/Arlington, VA	703-534-3940
Aurelio & Friends Inc/Miami, FL	305-385-0723

B

Baskin & Assoc/Alexandria, VA	703-836-3316
Bender, Diane/Arlington, VA	703-521-1006
Blair Incorporated/Bailey's Crossroads, VA	703-820-9011
Bodenhamer, William S Inc/Miami, FL	305-253-9284
Bonner Advertising Art/New Orleans, LA	504-895-7938
Bono Mitchell Graphics/Arlington, VA	703-276-0612
Bowles, Aaron/Reston, VA	703-471-4019
Brimm, Edward & Assoc/Palm Beach, FL	305-655-1059
Brothers Bogusky/Miami, FL	305-891-3642
Bugdal Group/Miami, FL	305-264-1860
Burch, Dan Associates/Louisville, KY	502-895-4881

C

Carlson Design/Gainesville, FL	904-373-3153
Chartmasters Inc/Atlanta, GA	404-262-7610
Cooper-Copeland Inc/Atlanta, GA	404-892-3472
Corporate Design/Atlanta, GA	404-876-6062
Creative Design Assoc/Lake Park, FL	305-627-2467
Creative Services Inc/New Orleans, LA	504-943-0842
Creative Services Unlimited/Naples, FL	813-262-0201
Creative Technologies Inc/Annandale, VA	703-256-7444
Critt Graham & Assoc/Atlanta, GA	404-320-1737

DEF

Design Consultants Inc/Falls Church, VA	703-241-2323
Design Inc/Fairfax, VA	703-273-5053
Design Workshop Inc/Miami, FL	305-884-6300
Designcomp/Vienna, VA	703-938-1822
Dodane, Eric/Knoxville, TN	615-693-6857
Emig, Paul E/Arlington, VA	703-522-5926
First Impressions/Tampa, FL	813-875-0555
Foster, Kim A/Miami, FL	305-642-1801
From Us Advertising & Design/Atlanta, GA	404-373-0373

G

Gerbino Advertising Inc/Ft Lauderdale, FL	305-776-5050
Gestalt Associates, Inc/Alexandria, VA	703-683-1126
Get Graphic Inc/Vienna, VA	202-938-1822
Graphic Arts Inc/Alexandria, VA	703-683-4303
Graphic Consultants Inc/Arlington, VA	703-536-8377
Graphics Group/Atlanta, GA	404-391-9929
Graphicstudio/N Miami, FL	305-893-1015
Great Incorporated/Alexandria, VA	703-836-6020
Gregg, Bill Advertising Design/Miami, FL	305-854-7657
Group 2 Atlanta/Atlanta, GA	404-262-3239

H

Haikalis, Stephanie/Alexandria, VA	703-998-8695
Hall Graphics/Coral Gables, FL	305-443-8346
Hall, Stephen Design Office/Louisville, KY	502-584-5030
Hannau, Michael Ent. Inc/Hialeah, FL	305-887-1536
Hauser, Sydney/Sarasota, FL	813-388-3021
Helms, John Graphic Design/Memphis, TN	901-363-6589

Please send us your additions and updates.

I J K

Identitia Incorporated/Tampa, Fl	813-221-3326
Jensen, Rupert & Assoc Inc/Atlanta, GA	404-352-1010
Johnson Design Group Inc/Arlington, VA	703-525-0808
Jordan Barrett & Assoc/Miami, FL	305-667-7051
Kelly & Co Graphic Design Inc/St Petersburg, FL	813-526-1009
Ketchum, Barbara/Raleigh, NC	919-782-4599
Kjeldsen, Howard Assoc Inc/Atlanta, GA	404-266-1897
Klickovich Graphics/Louisville, KY	502-459-0295

L M

Lowell, Shelley Design/Atlanta, GA	404-636-9149
Marks, David/Atlanta, GA	404-872-1824
Maxine, J & Martin Advertising/McLean, VA	703-356-5222
McGurren Weber Ink/Alexandria, VA	703-548-0003
MediaFour Inc/Falls Church, VA	703-573-6117
Michael, Richard S/Knoxville, TN	615-584-3319
Miller, Hugh K/Orlando, FL	305-293-8220
Moore, William "Casey"/Duluth, GA	404-449-9553
Morgan-Burchette Assoc/Alexandria, VA	703-549-2393
Morris, Robert Assoc Inc/Ft Lauderdale, FL	305-973-4380
Muhlhausen, John Design Inc/Roswell, GA	404-642-1146

P

Parallel Group Inc/Atlanta, GA	404-261-0988
Pertuit, Jim & Assoc Inc/New Orleans, LA	504-568-0808
PL&P Advertising Studio/Ft Lauderdale, FL	305-776-6505
Platt, Don Advertising Art/Hialeah, FL	305-888-3296
Point 6/Ft Lauderdale, FL	305-563-6939
Polizos, Arthur Assoc/Norfolk, VA	804-622-7033
Positively Main St Graphics/Sarasota, FL	813-366-4959
PRB Design Studio/Winter Park, FL	305-671-7992
Pre-Press Studio Design/Alexandria, VA	703-548-9194
Prep Inc/Arlington, VA	703-979-6575
Price Weber Market Comm Inc/Louisville, KY	502-499-9220
Promotion Graphics Inc/N Miami, FL	305-891-3941

Q R

Quantum Communications/Arlington, VA	703-841-1400
Rasor & Rasor/Cary, NC	919-467-3353
Rebeiz, Kathryn Dereki/Vienna, VA	703-938-9779
Reinsch, Michael/Hilton Head Island, SC	803-842-3298
Revelations Studios/Orlando, Fl	305-896-4240
Rodriguez, Emilio Jr/Miami, FL	305-235-4700

S

Sager Assoc Inc/Sarasota, FL	813-366-4192
Salmon, Paul/Burke, VA	703-250-4943
Santa & Assoc/Ft Lauderdale, FL	305-561-0551
Schulwolf, Frank/Coral Gables, FL	305-665-2129
Showcraft Designworks/Clearwater, FL	813-586-0061
Sirrine, J E/Greenville, SC	803-298-6000

T U V

Tash, Ken/Falls Church, VA	703-237-1712
Thayer Dana Industrial Design/Monroe, VA	804-929-6359
Thomas, Steve Design/Charlotte, NC	704-332-4624
Turpin Design Assoc/Atlanta, GA	404-320-6963
Unique Communications/Herndon, VA	703-471-1406
Varisco, Tom Graphic Design Inc/New Orleans, LA	504-949-2888
Visualgraphics Design/Tampa, FL	813-877-3804

W

Walton & Hoke/Falls Church, VA	703-538-5727
Whitford, Kim/Decatur, GA	404-371-0860
Whitver, Harry K Graphic Design/Nashville, TN	615-320-1795
Winner, Stewart Inc/Louisville, KY	502-583-5502
Wood, Tom/Atlanta, GA	404-262-7424

MIDWEST

A

Aarons, Allan Design/Northbrook, IL	312-291-9800
Ades, Leonards Graphic Design/Northbrook, IL	312-564-8863
Album Graphics/Melrose Park, IL	312-344-9100
Allied Design Group/Chicago, IL	312-743-3330
Anderson Studios/Chicago, IL	312-922-3039
Anderson, I K Studios/Chicago, IL	312-664-4536

Art Forms Inc/Cleveland, OH	216-361-3855
Arvind Khatkate Design/Chicago, IL	312-337-1478

B

Babcock & Schmid Assoc/Bath, OH	216-666-8826
Bagby Design/Chicago, IL	312-861-1288
Bal Graphics Inc/Chicago, IL	312-337-0325
Banka Mango Design Inc/Chicago, IL	312-467-0059
Barnes, Jeff/Chicago, IL	312-951-0996
Bartels & Cartsens/St Louis, MO	314-781-4350
Beda Ross Design/Chicago, IL	312-944-2332
Benjamin, Burton E Assoc/Highland Park, IL	312-432-8089
Berg, Don/Milwaukee, WI	414-276-7828
Bieger, Walter Assoc/Arden Hills, MN	612-636-8500
Blake, Hayward & Co/Evanston, IL	312-864-9800
Blau-Bishop & Assoc/Chicago, IL	312-321-1420
Boelter Industries Inc/Minneapolis, MN	612-831-5338
Boller-Coates-Spadero/Chicago, IL	312-787-2798
Bowlby, Joseph A/Chicago, IL	312-922-0890
Bradford-Cout Graphic Design/Skokie, IL	312-539-5557
Brooks Stevens Assoc Inc/Mequon, WI	414-241-3800
Busch, Lonnie/Fenton, MO	314-343-1330

C

Campbell Art Studio/Cincinnati, OH	513-221-3600
Campbell Creative Group Inc/Milwaukee, WI	414-351-4150
Carter, Don W/ Industrial Design/Kansas City, MO	816-356-1874
Centaur Studios Inc/St Louis, MO	314-421-6485
Chartmasters Inc/Chicago, IL	312-787-9040
Chestnut House/Chicago, IL	312-822-9090
Claudia Janah Designs Inc/Chicago, IL	312-726-4560
Clifford, Keesler/Kalamazoo, MI	616-375-0688
CMO Graphics/Chicago, IL	312-527-0900
Combined Services Inc/Minneapolis, MN	612-339-7770
Container Corp of America/Chicago, IL	312-580-5500
Contours Consulting Design Group/Bartlett, IL	312-837-4100
Coons/Beirise Design Assoc/Cincinnati, OH	513-751-7459

D

Day, David Design & Assoc/Cincinnati, OH	513-621-4060
DeBrey Design/Minneapolis, MN	612-935-2292
DeGoede & Others/Chicago, IL	312-951-6066
Dektas Eger Inc/Cincinnati, OH	513-621-7070
Design Alliance Inc/Cincinnati, OH	513-621-9373
Design Consultants/Chicago, IL	312-642-4670
Design Factory/Overland Park, KS	913-383-3085
The Design Group/Madison, WI	608-274-5393
Design Group Three/Chicago, IL	312-337-1775
Design Innovations Inc/Toronto M5A 2W5, ON	416-362-8470
Design Mark Inc/Indianapolis, IN	317-872-3000
Design Marks Corp/Chicago, IL	312-327-3669
Design North Inc/Racine, WI	414-639-2080
Design One/Highland Park, IL	312-433-4140
The Design Partnership/Minneapolis, MN	612-338-8889
Design Planning Group/Chicago, IL	312-943-8400
Design Train/Cincinnati, OH	513-761-7099
Design Two Ltd/Chicago, IL	312-642-9888
Dezign House III/Cleveland, OH	216-621-7777
Di Cristo & Slagle Design/Milwaukee, WI	414-273-0980
Dickens Design Group/Chicago, IL	312-222-1850
Dimensional Designs Inc/Indianapolis, IN	317-637-1353
Doty, David Design/Chicago, IL	312-348-1200
Douglas Design/Cleveland, OH	216-621-2558
Dresser, John Design/Libertyville, IL	312-362-4222
Dynamic Graphics Inc/Peoria, IL	309-688-9800

E

Eaton and Associates/Minneapolis, MN	612-871-1028
Egger/Assoc Inc/Park Ridge, IL	312-296-9100
Ellies, Dave Indstrl Design/Columbus, OH	614-488-7995
Elyria Graphics/Elyria, OH	216-365-9384
Emphasis 7 Communications/Chicago, IL	312-951-8887
Engelhardt Design/Minneapolis, MN	612-377-3389
Environmental Graphics Inc/Indianapolis, IN	317-634-1458
Epstein & Assoc/Cleveland, OH	216-421-1600
Eurographics/Chicago, IL	312-951-5110

Please send us your additions and updates.

F

Falk, Robert Design Group/St Louis, MO	314-531-1410
Feldkamp-Malloy/Chicago, IL	312-263-0633
Ficho & Corley Inc/Chicago, IL	312-787-1011
Fleishman-Hillard, Inc/St Louis, MO	314-982-1700
Fleming Design Office/Minneapolis, MN	612-830-0099
Flexo Design/Chicago, IL	312-321-1368
Ford & Earl Assoc Inc/Warren, MI	313-536-1999
Forsythe-French Inc/Kansas City, MO	816-561-6678
Frederiksen Design/Villa Park, IL	312-343-5882
Frink, Chin, Casey Inc/Minneapolis, MN	612-333-6539

G

Garmon, Van/W Des Moines, IA	515-225-0001
Gellman, Stan Graphic Design Studio/St Louis, MO	314-361-7676
Gerhardt and Clements/Chicago, IL	312-337-3443
Glenbard Graphics Inc/Carol Stream, IL	312-653-4550
Goldsholl Assoc/Northfield, IL	312-446-8300
Goldsmith Yamasaki Specht Inc/Chicago, IL	312-266-8404
Goodwin, Arnold/Chicago, IL	312-787-0466
Goose Graphics/Minneapolis, MN	612-333-3502
Gournoe, M Inc/Chicago, IL	312-787-5157
Graphic Corp/Des Moines, IA	515-247-8500
Graphic House Inc/Detroit, MI	313-259-7790
Graphic Productions/Chicago, IL	312-236-2833
Graphic Specialties Inc/Minneapolis, MN	612-722-6601
Graphica Corp/Troy, MI	313-649-5050
Graphics Group/Chicago, IL	312-782-7421
Graphics-Cor Associates/Chicago, IL	312-332-3379
Greenberg, Jon Assoc Inc/Berkley, MI	313-548-8080
Greenlee-Hess Ind Design/Mayfield Village, OH	216-461-2112
Greiner, John & Assoc/Chicago, IL	312-644-2973
Grusin, Gerald Design/Chicago, IL	312-944-4945

H

Handelan-Pedersen/Chicago, IL	312-782-6833
Hans Design/Northbrook, IL	312-272-7980
Harley, Don E Associates/West St Paul, MN	612-455-1631
Herbst Lazar Rogers & Bell Inc/Chicago, IL	312-454-1116
Higgins Hegner Genovese Inc/Chicago, IL	312-644-1882
Hirsch, David Design Group Inc/Chicago, IL	312-329-1500
Hirsh Co/Skokie, IL	312-267-6777
Hoekstra, Grant Graphics/Chicago, IL	312-641-6940
Hoffar, Barron & Co/Chicago, IL	312-922-0890
Hoffman York & Compton/Milwaukee, WI	414-259-2000
Horvath, Steve Design/Milwaukee, WI	414-271-3992

IJ

Identity Center/Schaumburg, IL	312-843-2378
IGS Design Div of Smith Hinchman & Grylls/Detroit, MI	313-964-3000
Indiana Design Consortium/Lafayette, IN	317-423-5469
Industrial Technological Assoc/Cleveland, OH	216-349-2900
Ing, Victor Design/Morton Grove, IL	312-965-3459
Intelplex/Maryland Hts, MO	314-739-9996
J M H Corp/Indianapolis, IN	317-639-2535
James, Frank Direct Marketing/Clayton, MO	314-726-4600
Jansen, Ute/Chicago, IL	312-922-5048
Johnson, Stan Design Inc/Brookfield, WI	414-783-6510
Johnson, Stewart Design Studio/Milwaukee, WI	414-265-3377
Jones, Richmond Designer/Chicago, IL	312-935-6500
Joss Design Group/Chicago, IL	312-828-0055

K

Kaulfuss Design/Chicago, IL	312-943-2161
KDA Industrial Design Consultants Inc/Addison, IL	312-495-9466
Kearns, Marilyn/Chicago, IL	312-645-1888
Keller Lane & Waln/Chicago, IL	312-782-7421
Kovach, Ronald Design/Chicago, IL	312-461-9888
Krupp, Merlin Studios/Minneapolis, MN	612-871-6611

L

Lange, Jim Design/Chicago, IL	312-943-2589
Larson Design/Minneapolis, MN	612-835-2271
Lehrfeld, Gerald/Chicago, IL	312-944-0651
Lenard, Catherine/Chicago, IL	312-248-6937
Lerdon, Wes Assoc/Columbus, OH	614-486-8188
Lesniewicz/Navarre/Toledo, OH	419-243-7131

Lipson Associates Inc/Cincinnati, OH	513-961-6225
Lipson Associates Inc/Northbrook, IL	312-291-0500
Liska & Assoc/Chicago, IL	312-943-5910
Loew, Dick & Assoc/Chicago, IL	312-787-9032
Lubell, Robert/Toledo, OH	419-531-2267
LVK Associates Inc/St Louis, MO	314-534-2104

M

Maddox, Eva Assoc Inc/Chicago, IL	312-670-0092
Madsan/Kuester/Minneapolis, MN	612-378-1895
Manning Studios Inc/Cincinnati, OH	513-621-6959
Market Design/Cleveland, OH	216-771-0300
Marsh, Richard Assoc Inc/Chicago, IL	312-236-1331
McCoy, Steven/Omaha, NE	402-554-1416
McDermott, Bill Graphic Design/St Louis, MO	314-962-6286
McGuire, Robert L Design/Kansas City, MO	816-523-9164
McMurray Design Inc/Chicago, IL	312-527-1555
Media Corporation/Columbus, OH	614-488-7767
Minnick, James Design/Chicago, IL	312-527-1864
Moonink Inc/Chicago, IL	312-565-0040
Murrie White Drummond Leinhart/Chicago, IL	312-943-5995

NO

Naughton, Carol & Assoc/Chicago, IL	312-454-1888
Nobart Inc/Chicago, IL	312-427-9800
Nottingham-Spirk Design Inc/Cleveland, OH	216-231-7830
Oak Brook Graphics, Inc/Elmhurst, IL	312-832-3200
Obata Design/St Louis, MO	314-241-1710
Osborne-Tuttle/Chicago, IL	312-565-1910
Oskar Designs/Evanston, IL	312-328-1734
Our Gang Studios/Omaha, NE	402-341-4965
Overlock Howe Consulting Group/St Louis, MO	314-533-4484

P

Pace Studios/Lincolnwood, IL	312-676-9770
Painter/Cesaroni Design, Inc/Glenview, IL	312-724-8840
Palmer Design Assoc/Wilmette, IL	312-256-7448
Paramount Technical Service Inc/Cleveland, OH	216-585-2550
Perman, Norman/Chicago, IL	312-642-1348
Phares Associates Inc/Farmington Hills, MI	313-553-2232
Pitlock Design/South Bend, IN	219-233-8606
Pitt Studios/Cleveland, OH	216-241-6720
Polivka-Logan Design/Minnetonka, MN	612-474-1124
Porter-Matjasich/Chicago, IL	312-670-4355
Powell/Kleinschmidt Inc/Chicago, IL	312-726-2208
Pride and Perfomance/St Paul, MN	612-646-4800
Prodesign Inc/Plymouth, MI	612-476-1200
Purviance, George Marketing Comm/Clayton, MO	314-721-2765
Pycha and Associates/Chicago, IL	312-944-3679

QR

Qually & Co Inc/Chicago, IL	312-944-0237
Ramba Graphics/Cleveland, OH	216-621-1776
Red Wing Enterprises/Chicago, IL	312-951-0441
Redmond, Patrick Design/St Paul, MN	612-926-3951
Reed, Stan/Madison, WI	608-238-1900
RHI Inc/Chicago, IL	312-943-2585
Richardson/Smith Inc/Worthington, OH	614-885-3453
Roberts Webb & Co/Chicago, IL	312-861-0060
Robinson, Thompson & Wise/Overland Park, KS	913-451-9473
Ross & Harvey/Chicago, IL	312-467-1290
Roth, Randall/Chicago, IL	312-467-0140
Rotheiser, Jordan I/Highland Park, IL	312-433-4288

S

Samata Assoc/West Dundee, IL	312-428-8600
Sargent, Ann Design/Minneapolis, MN	612-870-9995
Savlin/Williams Assoc/Evanston, IL	312-328-3366
Schlatter Group Inc/Battle Creek, MI	616-964-0898
Schmidt, Wm M Assoc/Harper Woods, MI	313-881-8075
Schultz, Ron Design/Chicago, IL	312-528-1853
Scott, Jack/Chicago, IL	312-922-1467
Seltzer, Meyer Design & Illustration/Chicago, IL	312-348-2885
Sherman, Roger Assoc Inc/Dearborn, MI	313-582-8844
Simanis, Vito/St Charles, IL	312-584-1683
Simons, I W Industrial Design/Columbus, OH	614-451-3796
Skolnick, Jerome/Chicago, IL	312-944-4568

Slavin Assoc Inc/Chicago, IL	312-822-0559
Smith, Glen Co/Minneapolis, MN	612-871-1616
Sosin, Bill/Chicago, IL	312-751-0974
Source Inc/Chicago, IL	312-236-7620
Space Design International Inc/Cincinnati, OH	513-241-3000
Spatial Graphics Inc/Milwaukee, WI	414-545-4444
Stepan Design/Mt Prospect, IL	312-364-4121
Strandell Design Inc/Chicago, IL	312-861-1654
Strizek, Jan/Chicago, IL	312-664-4772
Stromberg, Gordon H Visual Design/Chicago, IL	312-275-9449
Studio One Graphics/Livonia, MI	313-522-7505
Studio One Inc/Minneapolis, MN	612-831-6313
Swoger Grafik/Chicago, IL	312-943-2491
Synthesis Concepts/Chicago, IL	312-787-1201

T

T & Company/Chicago, IL	312-463-1336
Tassian, George Org/Cincinnati, OH	513-721-5566
Taylor & Assoc/Des Moines, IA	515-276-0992
Tepe Hensler & Westerkamp/Cincinnati, OH	513-241-0100
Thorbeck & Lambert Inc/Minneapolis, MN	612-871-7979
Toth, Joe/Rocky River, OH	216-356-0745
Turgeon, James/Chicago, IL	312-861-1039

UV

Underwood, Muriel/Chicago, IL	312-236-8472
Unicom/Milwaukee, WI	414-354-5440
UVG & N/Hillside, IL	312-449-1500
Vallarta, Frederick Assoc Inc/Chicago, IL	312-944-7300
Vanides-Mlodock/Chicago, IL	312-663-0595
Vann, Bill Studio/St Louis, MO	314-231-2322
Vista Three Design/Minneapolis, MN	612-920-5311
Visual Image Studio/St Paul, MN	612-644-7314

WXZ

Wallner Harbauer Bruce & Assoc/Chicago, IL	312-787-6787
Weber Conn & Riley/Chicago, IL	312-527-4260
Weiss, Jack Assoc/Evanston, IL	312-866-7480
Widmer, Stanley Assoc Inc/Staples, MN	218-894-3466
Winbush Design/Chicago, IL	312-527-4478
Wooster + Assoc/Winnetka, IL	312-726-7944
Worrel, W Robert Design/Minneapolis, MN	612-340-1300
Xeno/Chicago, IL	312-327-1989
Zender and Associates/Cincinnati, OH	513-561-8496

SOUTHWEST

A

A&M Associates Inc/Phoenix, AZ	602-263-6504
Ackerman & McQueen/Oklahoma City, OK	405-843-9451
The Ad Department/Ft Worth, TX	817-335-4012
Ad-Art Studios/Ft Worth, TX	817-335-9603
Advertising Inc/Tulsa, OK	918-747-8871
Anderson Pearlstone & Assoc/San Antonio, TX	512-826-1897
Apple Graphics/Dallas, TX	214-522-6261
Ark, Chuck/Dallas, TX	214-522-5356
Arnold Harwell McClain & Assoc/Dallas, TX	214-521-6400
Art Associates/Irving, TX	214-258-6001
The Art Works/Dallas, TX	214-521-2121

B

Baugh, Larry/Irving, TX	214-438-5696
Beals Advertising Agency/Oklahoma City, OK	405-848-8513
The Belcher Group Inc/Houston, TX	713-271-2727
Bentterman & Assoc/Fort Worth, TX	817-731-9941
Bleu Design Assoc/Phoenix, AZ	602-279-1131
Boughton, Cindy/Houston, TX	713-951-9113
Brooks & Pollard Co/Little Rock, AR	501-375-5561

C

Central Advertising Agency/Fort Worth, TX	817-390-3011
Chandler, Jeff/Dallas, TX	214-946-1348
Chesterfield Interiors Inc/Dallas, TX	214-747-2211
Clark, Betty & Assoc/Dallas, TX	214-696-6611
Coffee Design Inc/Houston, TX	713-780-0571
Connaster & Co/Dallas, TX	214-744-3555

Cranford/ Johnson & Assoc/Little Rock, AR	501-376-6251
Creative Directions/Dallas, TX	214-358-3433

D

Davis, George/Dallas, TX	214-631-1356
Dennard, Bob/Dallas, TX	214-233-0430
Design Bank/Austin, TX	512-445-7584
Design Enterprises, Inc/El Paso, TX	915-594-7100
Design Group/Dallas/Dallas, TX	212-241-4085
Designmark/Houston, TX	713-626-0953
Drebelbis, Marsha/Dallas, TX	214-951-0266

EF

Eisenberg Inc/Dallas, TX	214-528-5990
Ellies, Dave Industrial Design Inc/Dallas, TX	214-742-8654
Executive Image/Dallas, TX	214-733-0496
Fedele Creative Consulting/Dallas, TX	214-528-3501
Fischer, Don/Dallas, TX	214-522-2995
Friesenhahn, Michelle/San Antonio, TX	512-822-3325
Funk, Barbara/Dallas, TX	214-357-7961

G

Galen, D/Dallas, TX	214-385-7855
GKD/Oklahoma City, OK	405-943-2333
Gluth & Weaver/Houston, TX	713-784-4141
The Goodwin Co/El Paso, TX	915-584-1176
Graphic Designers Group Inc/Houston, TX	713-622-8680
Graphics Hardware Co/Phoenix, AZ	602-242-4687
Gregory Dsgn Group/Dallas, TX	214-522-9360
Grimes, Don/Dallas, TX	214-526-0040

H

Hanagriff-King/Houston, TX	714-622-4260
Harman, Gary/Ft Worth, TX	817-332-7687
Harrison Allen Design/Houston, TX	713-771-9274
Hermsen Design Assoc/Dallas, TX	214-233-5090
Herring, Jerry/Houston, TX	713-526-1250
High, Richard/Houston, TX	713-521-2772
Hill, Chris/Houston, TX	713-523-7363
Hixo/Austin, TX	512-477-0050
Hood Hope & Assoc/Tulsa, OK	918-250-9511
Hubler-Rosenburg Assoc/Dallas, TX	214-742-2491

IJK

Image Excellence/Dallas, TX	214-352-9958
Image Group Studio/Dallas, TX	214-745-1411
Jacob, Jim/Dallas, TX	214-939-0033
Jettun, Carol/Ft Worth, TX	817-737-4708
Johnson, Carla/Dallas, TX	214-341-2158
Jones, Don/Dallas, TX	214-327-0819
Kilmer/Geer/Houston, TX	713-668-1708
Konig Design Group/San Antonio, TX	512-824-7387

L

Lawrence Design/Dallas, TX	214-522-0620
Ledbetter, James/Dallas, TX	214-341-4858
Lindgren Design/Dallas, TX	214-742-3573
Loucks Atelier/Houston, TX	713-877-8551
Lowe Runkle Co/Oklahoma City, OK	405-848-6800
Lyons, Dan/Dallas, TX	214-368-4890

M

Mantz & Associates/Dallas, TX	214-521-7432
Martin, Hardy/Dallas, TX	214-630-2977
Martin, Randy/Dallas, TX	214-826-3630
McBride, Tom/Dallas, TX	214-521-5320
McCulley, Mike/Euless, TX	214-528-4889
McEuen, Roby/Ft Worth, TX	817-335-5153
McFarlin, Steven/Dallas, TX	214-340-3459
McGrath, Michael Design/Richardson, TX	214-644-4358
Moore Co/Dallas, TX	214-631-9443
Morales, Frank Design/Dallas, TX	214-233-0667
Morris, Carroll/Dallas, TX	214-233-6616
Morrison & Assoc/Dallas, TX	214-528-7410

NOP

Nelson, Mary/Dallas, TX	214-742-6259
Neumann, Steve & Friends/Houston, TX	713-629-7501
Overton, Janet/Dallas, TX	214-357-1272
Owen-Garritson Inc/Dallas, TX	214-991-3577

Please send us your additions and updates.

Owens & Assoc Advertising Inc/Phoenix, AZ	602-264-5691
Parnell, Cap/Dallas, TX	214-826-5441
Pencil Point/Dallas, TX	214-233-0776
Pirtle Design/Dallas, TX	214-522-7520

QRS

Quad Type & Graphics/Dallas, TX	214-238-0733
Richards Brock Miller Mitchell & Assoc/Dallas, TX	214-386-9077
Riechers, Ann/Dallas, TX	214-369-7219
Sawyer, Sandra/Ft Worth, TX	817-332-1611
Serigraphics Etc/Dallas, TX	214-352-6440
Shiels, Henry/Dallas, TX	214-521-7461
Slaton, Richard/Dallas, TX	214-522-6241
Squires, James/Dallas, TX	214-739-1114
Stoler, Scott/Dallas, TX	214-521-4024
Stotts, Billie/Dallas, TX	214-744-0997
Strickland, Michael & Co/Houston, TX	713-961-1323
Struthers, Yvonne/Arlington, TX	214-469-1377
Studio Renaissance/Dallas, TX	214-939-0401
Studiographix/Dallas, TX	214-258-8446
Sullivan, Jack Design Group/Phoenix, AZ	602-271-0117
Suntar Designs/Prescott, AZ	602-778-2714
Sweeney, Jim/Irving, TX	214-258-1705

TUVW

Tarasoff, Neal/Mesquite, TX	214-681-0480
Tellagraphics/Richardson, TX	214-238-9297
Texas Art & Media/Ft Worth, TX	817-334-0443
3D/International/Houston, TX	713-871-7000
Total Designers/Houston, TX	713-688-7766
Turnipseed, Allan/Dallas, TX	214-651-7832
Unigraphics/Dallas, TX	214-526-0930
Vanmar Assoc/Dallas, TX	214-630-7603
Varner, Charles/Dallas, TX	214-744-0148
Walker Fuld & Assoc/Dallas, TX	214-692-7775
Warden, Bill/Dallas, TX	214-634-8434
A Worthwhile Place Comm/Dallas, TX	214-946-1348
WW3 Papagalos/Phoenix, AZ	602-279-2933

ROCKY MOUNTAIN

ABC

Allison & Schiedt/Denver, CO	303-830-1110
Ampersand Studios/Denver, CO	303-388-1211
Arnold Design Inc/Denver, CO	303-832-7156
Barnstorm Studios/Colorado Springs, CO	303-630-7200
Blanchard, D W & Assoc/Salt Lake City, UT	801-484-6344
Chen, Shih-chien/Edmonton T6L5K2, AB	403-462-8617
CommuniCreations/Denver, CO	303-759-1155
Consortium West/Concept Design/Salt Lake City, UT	801-278-4441
Cuerden Advertising Design/Denver, CO	303-321-4163

DEFG

Danford, Chuck/Denver, CO	303-320-1116
Design Center/Salt Lake City, UT	801-532-6122
Duo Graphics/Ft Collins, CO	303-463-2788
Entercom/Denver, CO	303-393-0405
Fleming, Ron/Great Falls, MT	406-761-7887
General Graphics/Denver, CO	303-832-5258
Gibby, John Design/Layton, UT	801-544-0736
Graphic Concepts Inc/Salt Lake City, UT	801-359-2191
Graphien Design/Englewood, CO	303-779-5858

MOR

Malmberg & Assoc/Aurora, CO	303-699-9364
Markowitz & Long/Boulder, CO	303-449-7394
Martin, Janet/Boulder, CO	303-442-8202
Matrix International Inc/Denver, CO	303-388-9353
Monigle, Glenn/Denver, CO	303-388-9358
Multimedia/Denver, CO	303-777-5480
Okland Design Assoc/Salt Lake City, UT	801-484-7861
Radetsky Design Associates/Denver, CO	303-629-7375

TVW

Tamburello, Michael Communications/Littleton, CO	303-733-0128
Tandem Design Group Inc/Denver, CO	303-831-9251
Taylor, Robert W Design Inc/Boulder, CO	303-443-1975

Three B Studio & Assoc/Denver, CO	303-777-6359
Visual Communications/Littleton, CO	303-773-0128
Visual Images Inc/Denver, CO	303-388-5366
Walker Design Associates/Denver, CO	303-773-0426
Weller Institute for Design/Park City, UT	801-649-9859
Wilson, Cheryl/Boulder, CO	303-444-0979
Woodard Racing Graphics Ltd/Boulder, CO	303-443-1986
Worthington, Carl A Partnership/Boulder, CO	303-443-7271

WEST COAST

A

A & H Graphic Design/Rancho Bernardo, CA	619-486-0777
Ace Design/Sausalito, CA	415-332-9390
Adfiliation Design/Eugene, OR	503-687-8262
ADI/Los Angeles, CA	213-254-7131
Advertising Design & Production Service/San Diego, CA	619-483-1393
Advertising/Design Assoc/Walnut Creek, CA	415-421-7000
AGI/Los Angeles, CA	213-462-0821
Alatorre, Sean/Santa Monica, CA	213-209-3765
Alvarez Group/Los Angeles, CA	213-876-3491
Andrysiak, Michele/Hawthorne, CA	213-973-8480
Antisdel Image Group/Santa Clara, CA	408-988-1010
Art Zone/Honolulu, HI	808-537-6647
Artists In Print/San Francisco, CA	415-673-6941
Artmaster Studios/San Fernando, CA	818-365-7188
Artworks/Los Angeles, CA	213-380-2187
Asbury & Assoc/Long Beach, CA	213-595-6481

B

Bailey, Robert Design Group/Portland, OR	503-228-1381
Ballard, Laurie/Santa Monica, CA	213-392-9749
Banuelos Design/Orange, CA	714-771-4335
Barile, Michael & Assoc/Oakland, CA	415-339-8360
Barnes, Herb Graphics/S Pasadena, CA	213-682-2420
Basic Designs Inc/Sausalito, CA	415-388-5141
Bass, Yager and Assoc/Hollywood, CA	213-466-9701
Beggs Langley Design/Palo Alto, CA	415-323-6160
Bennett, Douglas Design/Seattle, WA	206-324-9966
Bennett, Ralph Assoc/Van Nuys, CA	818-782-3224
Beuret, Janis/Honolulu, HI	808-537-6647
Bhang, Samuel Design Assoc/Los Angeles, CA	213-382-1126
The Blank Co/San Jose, CA	408-289-9095
Blazej, Rosalie Graphics/San Francisco, CA	415-586-3325
Blik, Ty/San Diego, CA	619-232-5707
Bloch & Associates/Santa Monica, CA	213-450-8863
Boelter, Herbert A/Burbank, CA	818-845-5055
Bohn, Richard/Costa Mesa, CA	714-548-6669
Boyd, Douglas Design/Los Angeles, CA	213-655-9642
Bright & Associates, Inc/Los Angeles, CA	213-658-8844
Briteday Inc/Mountain View, CA	415-968-5668
Brookins, Ed/Studio City, CA	213-766-7336
Brosio Design/San Diego, CA	619-226-4322
Brown, Bill/Los Angeles, CA	213-386-2455
Burns & Associates Inc/San Francisco, CA	415-567-4404
Burridge, Robert/Santa Barbara, CA	805-964-2087
Business Graphics/Los Angeles, CA	213-467-0292

C

Camozzi, Teresa/San Francisco, CA	415-392-1202
Campbell, Tom + Assoc/Los Angeles, CA	213-931-9990
Carlson, Keith Advertising Art/San Francisco, CA	415-397-5130
Carre Design/Santa Monica, CA	213-395-1033
Catalog Design & Production Inc/San Francisco, CA	415-468-5500
Chan Design/Santa Monica, CA	213-393-3735
Chartmasters Inc/San Francisco, CA	415-421-6591
Chase, Margo/Los Angeles, CA	213-937-4421
Churchill, Steven/San Diego, CA	619-560-1225
Clark, Tim/Los Angeles, CA	213-202-1044
Coak, Steve/Altadena, CA	818-797-5477
The Coakley Heagerty Co/Santa Clara, CA	408-249-6242
Coates Advertising/Portland, OR	503-241-1124
Cognata Associates Inc/San Francisco, CA	415-931-3800
Conber Creations/Portland, OR	503-288-2938

GRAPHIC DESIGNERS

Please send us your additions and updates.

Corporate Comms Group/Marina Del Rey, CA	213-821-9086
Corporate Graphics/San Francisco, CA	415-474-2888
Cowart, Jerry/Los Angeles, CA	213-278-5600
Crawshaw, Todd Design/San Francisco, CA	415-956-3169
Creative Source/Los Angeles, CA	213-462-5731
Cross Assoc/San Francisco, CA	415-777-2731
Cross, James/Los Angeles, CA	213-474-1484
Crouch + Fuller Inc/Del Mar, CA	619-450-9200
Curtis, Todd/Los Angeles, CA	213-452-0738

D

Dahm & Assoc Inc/Torrance, CA	213-320-0460
Dancer Fitzgerald & Sample/San Francisco, CA	415-981-6250
Danziger, Louis/Los Angeles, CA	213-935-1251
Davis, Pat/Sacramento, CA	916-442-9025
Dawson, Chris/Los Angeles, CA	213-937-5867
Dayne, Jeff The Studio/Portland, OR	503-232-8777
Daystar Design/La Mesa, CA	619-463-5014
Dellaporta Adv & Graphic/Santa Monica, CA	213-452-3832
DeMaio Graphics & Advertising/Reseda, CA	818-342-1800
Denny, Dianne/San Diego, CA	619-272-9104
Design & Direction/Torrance, CA	213-320-0822
Design Corps/Los Angeles, CA	213-651-1422
Design Direction Group/Pasadena, CA	818-792-4765
Design Element/Los Angeles, CA	213-656-3293
Design Graphics/Los Angeles, CA	213-749-7347
Design Graphics/Portland, OR	503-223-0678
Design Group West/Del Mar, CA	619-450-9200
Design Office/San Francisco, CA	415-543-4760
Design Projects Inc/Encino, CA	818-995-0303
Design Vectors/San Francisco, CA	415-391-0399
The Design Works/Los Angeles, CA	213-477-3577
Designage/Newport Beach, CA	714-852-1585
The Designory Inc/Long Beach, CA	213-432-5707
Detanna & Assoc/Beverly Hills, CA	213-852-0808
Diniz, Carlos/Los Angeles, CA	213-387-1171
Doane, Dave Studio/Orange, CA	714-548-7285
Doerfler Design/La Jolla, CA	619-455-0506
Dowlen, James/Santa Rosa, CA	707-576-7286
Dupre Design/Coronado, CA	619-435-8369
Dyer-Cahn/Los Angeles, CA	213-937-4100
Dyna Pac/San Diego, CA	619-560-0280

EF

Earnett McFall & Assoc/Seattle, WA	206-364-4956
Ehrig & Assoc/Seattle, WA	206-623-6666
Engle, Ray & Assoc/Los Angeles, CA	213-381-5001
English, Rick/Palo Alto, CA	415-326-1273
Exhibit Design Inc/San Mateo, CA	415-342-3060
Farber, Melvyn Design Group/Santa Monica, CA	213-829-2668
Finger, Julie Design Inc/Los Angeles, CA	213-653-0541
Five Penguins Design/Burbank, CA	213-841-5576
Floyd Design & Assoc/Lafayette, CA	415-283-1735
Flying Colors/San Francisco, CA	415-563-0500
Follis, Dean/Los Angeles, CA	213-735-1283
Fox, BD & Friends Advertising Inc/Los Angeles, CA	213-464-0131
Frazier, Craig/San Francisco, CA	415-863-9613
Furniss, Stephanie Design/San Rafael, CA	415-459-4730

G

Garner, Glenn Graphic Design/Seattle, WA	206-323-7788
Garnett, Joe Design/Illus/Los Angeles, CA	213-279-1539
Georgopoulos/Imada Design/Los Angeles, CA	213-933-6425
Gerber Advertising Agency/Portland, OR	503-221-0100
Gillian/Craig Assoc/San Francisco, CA	415-558-8988
Girvin, Tim Design/Seattle, WA	206-623-7918
Glickman, Abe Design/Van Nuys, CA	818-989-3223
Global West Studio/Los Angeles, CA	213-384-3331
The Gnu Group/Sausalito, CA	415-332-8010
Gohata, Mark/Gardena, CA	213-327-6595
Gold, Judi/West Hollywoood, CA	213-659-4690
Gotschalk's Graphics/San Diego, CA	619-298-0085
Gould & Assoc/W Los Angeles, CA	213-208-5577
Graformation/N Hollywood, CA	818-985-1224
Graphic Data/San Diego, CA	619-274-4511

Graphic Designers Inc/Los Angeles, CA	213-381-3977
Graphic Ideas/San Diego, CA	619-299-3433
Graphic Studio/Los Angeles, CA	213-466-2666

H

Hale, Dan Ad Design Co/Woodland Hills, CA	818-347-4021
Harper and Assoc/Bellevue, WA	206-462-0405
Harrington and Associates/Los Angeles, CA	213-876-5272
Harte-Yamashita & Forest/Los Angeles, CA	213-462-6486
Hauser, S G Assoc Inc/Calabasas, CA	818-884-1727
Helgesson, Ulf Ind Dsgn/Woodland Hills, CA	213-883-3772
Hernandez, Daniel/Whittier, CA	213-696-0607
Hornall Anderson Design Works/Seattle, WA	206-467-5800
Hosick, Frank Design/Vashon Island, WA	206-463-5454
Hubert, Laurent/Menlo Park, CA	415-321-5182
Humangraphic/San Diego, CA	619-299-0431
Hyde, Bill/Foster City, CA	415-345-6955

IJ

Imag'Inez/San Francisco, CA	415-254-2444
Image Stream/Los Angeles, CA	213-933-9196
ImageMakers/Santa Barbara, CA	805-965-8546
Imagination Creative Services/Santa Clara, CA	408-988-8696
Imagination Graphics/Santa Ana, CA	714-662-3114
J J & A/Burbank, CA	213-849-1444
Jaciow Design Inc/Mountain View, CA	415-962-8860
Jerde Partnership/Los Angeles, CA	213-413-0130
Johnson Rodger Design/Rolling Hills, CA	213-377-8860
Johnson, Paige Graphic Design/Palo Alto, CA	415-327-0488
Joly Major Product Design Group/San Francisco, CA	415-641-1933
Jones, Steve/Venice, CA	213-396-9111
Jonson Pedersen Hinrichs & Shakery/San Francisco, CA	415-981-6612
Juett, Dennis & Assoc/Los Angeles, CA	213-385-4373

K

K S Wilshire Inc/Los Angeles, CA	213-879-9595
Kageyama, David Designer/Seattle, WA	206-622-7281
Kamins, Deborah/Encino, CA	818-905-8536
Keating, Kate Assoc/San Francisco, CA	415-398-6611
Keser, Dennis/San Francisco, CA	415-387-6448
Kessler, David & Assoc/Hollywood, CA	213-462-6043
Klein/Los Angeles, CA	213-278-5600
Kleiner, John A Graphic Design/Santa Monica, CA	216-472-7442
Kuey, Patty/Yorba Linda, CA	714-970-5286
Kuwahara, Sachi/Los Angeles, CA	213-277-0872

L

Lacy, N Lee Assoc Ltd/Los Angeles, CA	213-852-1414
Lancaster Design/Santa Monica, CA	213-450-2999
Landes & Assoc/Torrance, CA	213-540-0907
Landor Associates/San Francisco, CA	415-955-1200
Larson, Ron/Los Angeles, CA	213-465-8451
Laurence-Deutsch Design/Los Angeles, CA	213-937-3521
Leong, Russell Design/Palo Alto, CA	415-321-2443
Leonhardt Group/Seattle, WA	206-624-0551
Lesser, Joan/Etcetera/Los Angeles, CA	213-450-3977
Levine, Steve & Co/Venice, CA	213-399-9336
Logan Carey & Rehag/San Francisco, CA	415-543-7080
Loveless, J R Design/Santa Ana, CA	714-754-0886
Lumel-Whiteman Assoc/North Hollywood, CA	818-769-5332

M

Mabry, Michael/San Francisco, CA	415-982-7336
Maddu, Patrick & Co/San Diego, CA	619-238-1340
Manwaring, Michael Office/San Francisco, CA	415-421-3595
Marketing Comm Grp/San Bernadino, CA	714-885-4976
Marketing Tools/Encinitas, CA	619-942-6042
Markofski, Don/Monrovia, CA	818-446-1222
Marra & Assoc/Portland, OR	503-227-5207
Matrix Design Consultants/Los Angeles, CA	213-487-6300
Matthews, Robert/Campbell, CA	408-378-0878
McCargar Design/Redwood City, CA	415-363-2130
McKee, Dennis/San Francisco, CA	415-543-7107
Media Services Corp/San Francisco, CA	415-928-3033
Meek, Kenneth/Pasadena, CA	818-449-9722
Mikkelson, Linda S/Hollywood, CA	213-463-3116
Miller, Marcia/Ingelwood, CA	213-677-4171

GRAPHIC DESIGNERS CONT'D.

Please send us your additions and updates.

Miura Design/Torrance, CA	213-320-1957
Mize, Charles Advertising Art/San Francisco, CA	415-421-1548
Mizrahi, Robert/Buena Park, CA	714-527-6182
Mobius Design Assoc/Los Angeles, CA	213-937-0331
Molly Designs Inc/Irvine, CA	714-768-7155
Monahan, Leo/Los Angeles, CA	213-463-3116
Mortensen, Gordon/Santa Barbara, CA	805-962-5315
Murphy, Harry & Friends/Mill Valley, CA	415-383-8586
Murray/Bradley Inc/Seattle, WA	206-622-7082

N

N Graphic/San Francisco, CA	415-896-5806
Naganuma, Tony K Design/San Francisco, CA	415-433-4484
Nagel, William Design Group/Palo Alto, CA	415-328-0251
New Concepts Industrial Design Corp/Seattle, WA	206-633-3111
Nicholson Design/San Diego, CA	619-235-9000
Nicolini Associates/Oakland, CA	415-531-5569
Niehaus, Don/Los Angeles, CA	213-279-1559
Nine West/Pasadena, CA	818-799-2727
Nordenhook Design/Newport Beach, CA	714-752-8631

OP

Olson Design Inc/Del Mar, CA	619-450-9200
Orr, R & Associates Inc/El Toro, CA	714-770-1277
Osborn, Michael Design/San Francisco, CA	415-495-4292
Oshima, Carol/Covina, CA	818-966-0796
Pacific Rim Design/Vancouver V5V2K9, BC	604-879-6689
Package Deal/Tustin, CA	714-541-2440
Pease, Robert & Co/Alamo, CA	415-820-0404
Peddicord & Assoc/Santa Clara, CA	408-727-7800
Persechini & Co/Beverly Hills, CA	213-657-6175
Petzold & Assoc/Lake Oswego, OR	503-246-8320
Pihas Schmidt Westerdahl Co/Portland, OR	503-228-4000
Popovich, Mike/City of Industry, CA	818-336-6958
Powers Design International/Newport Beach, CA	714-645-2265
Primo Angeli Graphics/San Francisco, CA	415-974-6100

R

The Quorum/Seattle, WA	206-522-6872
Rand, Vicki/Marina Del Rey, CA	213-306-9779
Reid, Scott/Santa Barbara, CA	805-963-8926
Reineck & Reineck/San Francisco, CA	415-566-3614
Reineman, Richard Industrial Design/Newport Beach, CA	714-673-2485
Reis, Gerald & Co/San Francisco, CA	415-543-1344
Rickabaugh Design/Portland, OR	503-223-2191
Ritola, Roy Inc/San Francisco, CA	415-788-7010
RJL Design Graphics/Fremont, CA	415-657-2038
Roberts, Eileen/Carlsbad, CA	619-439-7800
Robinson, David/San Diego, CA	619-298-2021
Rogow & Bernstein Dsgn/Los Angeles, CA	213-936-9916
Rohde, Gretchen/Seattle, WA	206-623-9459
Rolandesign/Woodland Hills, CA	818-346-9752
Runyan, Richard Design/West Los Angeles, CA	213-477-8878
Runyan, Robert Miles & Assoc/Playa Del Rey, CA	213-823-0975
Rupert, Paul Designer/San Francisco, CA	415-391-2966

S

Sackheim, Morton Enterprises/Beverly Hills, CA	213-652-0220
San Diego Art Prdctns/San Diego, CA	619-239-6666
Sanchez/Kamps Assoc/Pasadena, CA	213-793-4017
Sant'Andrea, Jim West Inc/Compton, CA	213-979-5449
Schaefer, Robert Television Art/Hollywood, CA	213-462-7877
Schorer, R Thomas/Palos Verdes, CA	213-377-0207
Schwab, Michael Design/San Francisco, CA	415-546-7559
Schwartz, Bonnie/Clem/San Diego, CA	619-291-8878
Seiniger & Assoc/Los Angeles, CA	213-653-8665
Shaw, Michael Design/Manhattan Beach, CA	213-545-0516
Shenon, Mike/Palo Alto, CA	415-326-4608
Shimokochi/Reeves Design/Los Angeles, CA	213-460-4916
Shoji Graphics/Los Angeles, CA	213-384-3091
Shuman, Sharon Designer/Los Angeles, CA	213-837-6998
Sidjakov, Nicholas/San Francisco, CA	415-931-7500
Signworks/Seattle, WA	206-525-2718
Smidt, Sam/Palo Alto, CA	415-327-0707
The Smith Group/Portland, OR	503-224-1905
Sorensen, Hugh Industrial Design/Brea, CA	714-529-8493

Soyster & Ohrenschall Inc/San Francisco, CA	415-956-7575
Spear, Jeffrey A/Santa Monica, CA	213-395-3939
Specht/Watson Studio/Los Angeles, CA	213-652-2682
Sperling, Lauren/Los Angeles, CA	213-472-9957
Spivey, William Design Inc/Lake Forrest, CA	714-770-7931
The Stansbury Company/Beverly Hills, CA	213-273-1138
Starr Seigle McCombs Inc/Honolulu, HI	808-524-5080
Stephenz, The Group/Campbell, CA	408-379-4883
Strong, David Design Group/Seattle, WA	206-447-9160
The Studio/San Francisco, CA	415-928-4400
Studio A/Los Angeles, CA	213-721-1802
Sugi, Richard Design & Assoc/Los Angeles, CA	213-385-4169
Superior Graphic Systems/Long Beach, CA	213-433-7421
Sussman & Prejza/Santa Monica, CA	213-829-3337

T

Tackett/Barbaria/Sacramento, CA	916-442-3200
Tartak, Donald H Design/Los Angeles, CA	213-477-3571
Thomas & Assoc/Santa Monica, CA	213-451-8502
Thomas, Greg/Los Angeles, CA	213-479-8477
Thomas, Keith M Inc/Santa Ana, CA	714-979-3051
Torme, Dave/San Francisco, CA	415-391-2694
Trade Marx/Seattle, WA	206-623-7676
Tribotti Design/Sherman Oaks, CA	818-784-6101
Trygg Stefanic Advertising/Los Altos, CA	415-948-3493
Tycer Fultz Bellack/Palo Alto, CA	415-856-1600

V

Valentino Graphic Design/Thousand Oaks, CA	805-495-9933
Vanderbyl Design/San Francisco, CA	415-543-8447
VanNoy & Co Inc/Los Angeles, CA	213-329-0800
Vantage Advertising & Marketing Assoc/San Leandro, CA	415-352-3640
Vigon, Larry/Los Angeles, CA	213-394-6502
Visual Resources Inc/Los Angeles, CA	213-851-6688
Voltec Associates/Los Angeles, CA	213-467-2106

WYZ

Walton, Brenda/Sacramento, CA	916-456-5833
Webster, Ken/Orinda, CA	415-954-2516
Weideman and Associates/North Hollywood, CA	818-769-8488
Wertman, Chuck/San Francisco, CA	415-433-4452
West End Studios/San Francisco, CA	415-434-0380
West, Suzanne Design/Palo Alto, CA	415-324-8068
White + Assoc/Los Angeles, CA	213-380-6319
Whitely, Mitchell Assoc/San Francisco, CA	415-398-2920
Wilkins & Peterson Graphic Design/Seattle, WA	206-624-1695
Willardson + Assoc/Glendale, CA	818-242-5688
Williams & Ziller Design/San Francisco, CA	415-621-0330
Williams, Leslie/Norwalk, CA	213-864-4135
Williamson & Assoc Inc/Los Angeles, CA	213-836-0143
Winters, Clyde Design/San Francisco, CA	415-391-5643
Woo, Calvin Assoc/San Diego, CA	619-299-0431
Workshop West/Beverly Hills, CA	213-278-1370
Yamaguma & Assoc/San Jose, CA	408-279-0500
Yanez, Maurice & Assoc/Pasadena, CA	213-462-1309
Yee, Ray/Los Angeles, CA	213-465-2514
Young & Roehr Adv/Portland, OR	503-297-4501
Yuguchi Krogstad/Los Angeles, CA	213-383-6915
Zamparelli & Assoc/Pasadena, CA	818-799-4370
Zolotow, Milton/Westwood, CA	213-453-4885

GRAPHIC DESIGNERS

PRODUCTION/SUPPORT SERVICES

LABS & RETOUCHERS

NEW YORK CITY

Accu-Color Group Inc/103 Fifth Ave	212-989-8235
ACS Studios/2 West 46th St	212-575-9250
Adams Photoprint Co Inc/60 E 42nd St	212-697-4980
Alchemy Color Ltd/125 W 45th St	212-997-1944
American Blue Print Co Inc/7 E 47th St	212-751-2240
American Photo Print Co/285 Madison Ave	212-532-2424
American Photo Print Co/350 Fifth Ave	212-736-2885
Andy's Place/17 E 48th St	212-371-1362
Apco-Apeda Photo Co/250 W 54th St	212-586-5755
Appel, Albert/119 W 23rd St	212-989-6585
Arkin-Medo/30 E 33rd St	212-685-1969
ASAP Photolab/40 E 49th St	212-832-1223
AT & S Retouching/230 E 44th St	212-986-0977
Atlantic Blue Print Co/575 Madison Ave	212-755-3388
Authenticolor Labs Inc/227 E 45th St	212-867-7905
Avekta Productions Inc/164 Madison Ave	212-686-4550
AZO Color Labs/149 Madison Ave	212-982-6610
Bebell Color Labs/416 W 45th St	212-245-8900
Bell-Tait, Carolyn/10 W 33rd St	212-947-9449
Bellis, Dave/15 E 55th St	212-753-3740
Benjamin, Bernard/1763 Second Ave	212-722-7773
Berger, Jack/41 W 53rd St	212-245-5705
Berkey K & L/222 E 44th St	212-661-5600
Bishop Retouching/236 E 36th St	212-889-3525
Blae, Ken Studios/1501 Broadway	212-869-3488
Bluestone Photoprint Co Inc/19 W 34th St	212-564-1516
Bonaventura Studio/307 E 44th St #1612	212-687-9208
Broderson, Charles Backdrops/873 Broadway #612	212-925-9392
Brunel, Jean Inc/11 Jay St	212-226-3009
C & C Productions/445 E 80th St	212-472-3700
Cacchione & Sheehan/1 West 37th St	212-869-2233
Carlson & Forino Studios/230 E 44th St	212-697-7044
Cavalluzzo, Dan/49 W 45th St	212-921-5954
Certified Color Service/2812 41st Ave	212-392-6065
Chapman, Edwin W/20 E 46th St	212-697-0872
Chroma Copy/423 West 55th St	212-399-2420
Chrome Print/104 E 25th St	212-228-0840
CitiChrome Lab/158 W 29th St	212-695-0935
Clayman, Andrew/334 Bowery #6F	212-674-4906
Colmer, Brian-The Final touch/310 E 46th St	212-682-3012
Coln, Stewart/563 Eleventh Ave	212-868-1440
Color Design Studio/19 W 21st St	212-255-8103
Color Masters Inc/143 E 27th St	212-889-7464
Color Perfect Inc/200 Park Ave S	212-777-1210
Color Pro Labs/40 W 37th St	212-563-5599
Color Unlimited Inc/443 Park Ave S	212-889-2440
Color Vision Photo Finishers/642 9th Avenue	212-757-2787
Color Wheel Inc/227 E 45th St	212-697-2434
Colorama Labs/40 W 37th St	212-279-1950
Colorite Film Processing/115 E 31st St	212-532-2116
Colotone Litho Seperator/555 Fifth Ave	212-557-5564
Columbia Blue & Photoprint Co/14 E 39th St	212-532-9424
Commerce Photo Print Co/415 Lexington Ave	212-986-2068
Compo Photocolor/18 E 48th St	212-758-1690
Copy-Line Corp/40 W 37th St	212-563-3535
Copycolor/8 W 30th St	212-725-8252
Copytone Inc/8 W 45th St	212-575-0235
Corona Color Studios Inc/10 W 33rd St	212-239-4990
Cortese, Phyllis/306 E 52nd St	212-421-4664
Crandall, Robert Assoc/306 E 45th St	212-661-4710
Creative Color Inc/25 W 45th St	212-582-3841
The Creative Color Print Lab Inc/25 W 45th St	212-582-6237
Crowell, Joyce/333 E 30th St	212-683-3055
Crown Photo/370 W 35th St	212-279-1950
Dai Nippon Printing/1633 Broadway	212-397-1880

The Darkroom Inc/222 E 46th St	212-687-8920
Davis-Ganes/15 E 40th St	212-687-6537
Diamond Art Studio/11 E 36th St	212-685-6622
Diamond, Richard/50 E 42nd St	212-697-4720
Diana Studio/301 W 53rd St	212-757-0445
Dimension Color Labs Inc/1040 Ave of Amer	212-354-5918
DiPierro-Turiel/210 E 47th St	212-752-2260
Drop Everything/20 W 20th St	212-242-2735
Duggal Color Projects Inc/9 W 20th St	212-924-6363
Dzurella, Paul Studio/15 W 38th St	212-840-8623
Ecay, Thom/49 W 45th St	212-840-6277
Edstan Productions/240 Madison Ave	212-686-3666
Egelston Retouching Services/333 Fifth Ave 3rd Fl	212-213-9095
Evans-Avedisian DiStefano Inc/29 W 38th St	212-697-4240
Filmstat/520 Fifth Ave	212-840-1676
Fine-Art Color Lab Inc/221 Park Ave S	212-674-7640
Finley Photographics Inc/488 Madison Ave	212-688-3025
Flax, Sam Inc/111 Eighth Ave	212-620-3000
Fodale Studio/247 E 50th St	212-755-0150
Forway Studios Inc/441 Lexington Ave	212-661-0260
Four Colors Photo Lab Inc/10 E 39th St	212-889-3399
Foursome Color Litho/30 Irving Pl	212-475-9219
Frenchys Color Lab/10 E 38th St	212-889-7787
Frey, Louis Co Inc/90 West St	212-791-0500
Friedman, Estelle Retouchers/160 E 38th St	212-532-0084
Fromia, John A/799 Broadway	212-473-7930
FUJI FILM /350 FIFTH AVE, NEW YORK, NY (INSIDE BACK COVER)	
Gayde, Richard Assoc Inc/515 Madison Ave	212-421-4088
Gilbert Studio/210 E 36th St	212-683-3472
Giraldi, Bob Prodctns/581 Sixth Ave	212-691-9200
Goodman, Irwin Inc/1156 Avenue of the Americas	212-944-6337
Graphic Images Ltd/151 W 46th St	212-869-8370
Gray, George Studios/230 E 44th St	212-661-0276
Greller, Fred/325 E 64th St	212-535-6240
Grubb, Louis D/155 Riverside Dr	212-873-2561
GW Color Lab/36 E 23rd St	212-677-3800
H-Y Photo Service/16 E 52nd St	212-371-3018
Hadar, Eric Studio/10 E 39th St	212-889-2092
Hudson Reproductions Inc/76 Ninth Ave	212-989-3400
J & R Color Lab/29 W 38th St	212-869-9870
J M W Studio Inc/230 E 44th St	212-986-9155
Jaeger, Elliot/49 W 45th St	212-840-6278
Jellybean Photographics Inc/99 Madison Ave 14th Fl	212-679-4888
JFC Color Labs Inc/443 Park Ave S	212-889-0727
Katz, David Studio/6 E 39th St	212-889-5038
Kaye Graphics Inc/151 Lexington Ave	212-889-8240
KG Studios Inc/56 W 45th St	212-840-7930
Kurahara, Joan/611 Broadway	212-505-8589
LaFerla, Sandro/108 W 25th St	212-620-0693
Langen & Wind Color Lab/265 Madison Ave	212-686-1818
Larson Color Lab/123 Fifth Ave	212-674-0610
Lieberman, Ken Laboratories/13 W 36th St	212-564-3800
Loy-Taubman Inc/34 E 30th St	212-685-6871
Lucas, Bob/10 E 38th St	212-725-2090
Lukon Art Service Ltd/56 W 45th St 3rd Fl	212-575-0474
Mann & Greene Color Inc/320 E 39th St	212-481-6868
Manna Color Labs Inc/42 W 15th St	212-691-8360
Marshall, Henry/6 E 39th St	212-686-1060
Martin, Tulio G Studio/140 W 57th St	212-245-6489
Martin/Arnold Color Systems/150 Fifth Ave #429	212-675-7270
Mayer, Kurt Color Labs Inc/1170 Broadway	212-532-3738
McCurdy & Cardinale Color Lab/65 W 36th St	212-695-5140
McWilliams, Clyde/151 West 46th St	212-221-3644
Media Universal Inc/116 W 32nd St	212-695-7454
Medina Studios Inc/141 E 44th St	212-867-3113
Miller, Norm & Steve/17 E 48th St	212-752-4830
Modernage Photo Services/312 E 46th St	212-661-9190
Moser, Klaus T Ltd/127 E 15th St	212-475-0038
Motal Custom Darkrooms/25 W 45th St 3rd Fl	212-757-7874
Murray Hill Photo Print Inc/32 W 39th St	212-921-4175
My Lab Inc/117 E 30th St	212-686-8684

Please send us your additions and updates.

My Own Color Lab/45 W 45th St	212-391-8638
National Reprographics Co/110 W 32nd St	212-736-5674
New York Camera/131 W 35th St	212-564-4398
New York Film Works Inc/928 Broadway	212-475-5700
New York Flash Rental/156 Fifth Ave	212-741-1165
Olden Camera/1265 Broadway	212-725-1234
Ornaal Color Photos/24 W 25th St	212-675-3850
Paccione, E S Inc/150 E 56th St	212-755-0965
Palevitz, Bob/333 E 30th St	212-684-6026
Pastore dePamphilis Rampone/145 E 32nd St	212-889-2221
Pergament Color/305 E 47th St	212-751-5367
Photo Retouch Inc/160 E 38th St	212-532-0084
Photographics Unlimited/43 W 22nd St	212-255-9678
Photographic Color Specialists Inc./10-36 47th Rd	718-786-4770
Photorama/239 W 39th St	212-354-5280
PIC Color Corp/25 W 45th St	212-575-5600
Portogallo Photo Services/72 W 45th St	212-840-2636
Positive Color Inc/405 Lexington	212-687-9600
Precision Chromes Inc/310 Madison Ave	212-687-5990
Preferred Photographic Co/165 W 46th St	212-757-0237
Procil Adstat Co Inc/7 W 45th St	212-819-0155
Prussack, Phil/155 E 55th St	212-755-2470
Quality Color Lab/305 E 46th St	212-753-2200
R & V Studio/32 W 39th St	212-944-9590
Rahum Supply Co/1165 Broadway	212-685-4784
Rainbow Graphics & Chrome Services/49 W 45th St	212-869-3232
Ram Retouching/380 Madison Ave	212-599-0985
Ramer, Joe Assoc/509 Madison Ave	212-751-0894
Rasulo Graphics Service/36 E 31st St	212-686-2861
Regal Velox/25 W 43rd St	212-840-0330
Reiter Dulberg/157 W 54th St	212-582-6871
Renaissance Retouching/136 W 46th St	212-575-5618
Reproduction Color Specialists/9 E 38th St	212-683-0833
Retouchers Gallery/211 E 53rd St	212-751-9203
Retouching Inc/9 E 38th St	212-683-4188
Retouching Pius/125 W 45th St	212-764-5959
Rio Enterprises/240 E 58th St	212-758-9300
Rivera and Schiff Assoc Inc/21 W 38th St	212-354-2977
Robotti, Thomas/5 W 46th St	212-840-0215
Rogers Color Lab Corp/165 Madison Ave	212-683-6400
Russo Photo Service/432 W 45th St	212-247-3817
Sa-Kura Retouching/123 W 44th St	212-764-5944
San Photo-Art Service/165 W 29th St	212-594-0850
Sang Color Inc/19 W 34th St	212-594-4205
Scala Fine Arts Publishers Inc/65 Bleecker St	212-673-4988
Schiavone, Joe/301 W 53rd St #4E	212-757-0660
Scope Assoc/11 E 22nd St	212-674-4190
Scott Screen Prints/228 E 45th St	212-697-8923
Scott, Diane Assoc/339 E 58th St	212-355-4616
Sharkey, Dick The Studio/301 W 53rd St	212-265-1036
Sharron Photographic Labs/260 W 36th St	212-239-4980
Simmons-Beal Inc/3 E 40th St	212-532-6261
Slide by Slide/445 E 80th St	212-879-5091
Slide Shop Inc/220 E 23rd St	212-725-5200
Spano/Roccanova Retouching Inc/16 W 46th St	212-840-7450
Spector, Hy Studios/56 W 45th St	212-221-3656
Spectrum Creative Retouchers Inc/230 E 44th St	212-687-3359
Stanley, Joseph/211 W 58th St	212-246-1258
Stewart Color Labs Inc/563 Eleventh Ave	212-868-1440
Studio 55/39 W 38th St	212-840-0920
Studio Chrome Lab Inc/36 W 25th St	212-989-6767
Studio Macbeth Inc/130 W 42nd St	212-921-8922
Studio X/20 W 20th St	212-989-9233
Sunlight Graphics/401 5th Ave	212-683-4452
Super Photo Color Services/165 Madison Ave	212-686-9510
Sutton Studio/112 E 17th St	212-777-0301
T R P Slavin Colour Services/920 Broadway	212-674-5700
Tanksley, John Studios Inc/210 E 47th St	212-752-1150
Tartaro Color Lab/29 W 38th St	212-840-1640
Todd Photoprint Inc/1600 Broadway	212-245-2440
Trio Studio/18 E 48th St	212-752-4875
Truglio, Frank & Assoc/835 Third Ave	212-371-7635

Twenty/Twenty Photographers Place/20 W 20th St	212-675-2020
Ultimate Image/443 Park Ave S 7th Fl	212-683-4838
Van Chromes Corp/311 W 43rd St	212-582-0505
Venezia, Don Retouching/488 Madison Ave	212-688-7649
Verilen Reproductions/3 E 40th St	212-686-7774
Vidachrome Inc/25 W 39th St 6th Fl	212-391-8124
Vogue Wright Studios/423 West 55th St	212-977-3400
Wagner Photoprint Co/121 W 50th St	212-245-4796
Ward, Jack Color Service/220 E 23rd St	212-725-5200
Way Color Inc/420 Lexington Ave	212-687-5610
Weber, Martin J Studio/171 Madison Ave	212-532-2695
Weiman & Lester Inc/21 E 40th St	212-679-1180
Welbeck Studios Inc/39 W 38th St	212-869-1660
Wind, Gerry & Assoc/265 Madison Ave	212-686-1818
Winter, Jerry Studio/333 E 45th St	212-490-0876
Wolf, Bill/212 E 47th St	212-697-6215
Wolsk, Bernard/509 Madison Ave	212-751-7727
Zazula, Hy Assoc/2 W 46th St	212-819-0444

NORTHEAST

Able Art Service/8 Winter St, Boston, MA	617-482-4558
Adams & Abbott Inc/46 Summer St, Boston, MA	617-542-1621
Alfie Custom Color/155 N Dean St, Englewood, NJ	201-569-2028
Alves Photo Service/14 Storrs Ave, Braintree, MA	617-843-5555
Artography Labs/2419 St Paul St, Baltimore, MD	301-467-5575
Asman Custom Photo Service Inc/926 Pennsylvania Ave SE, Washington, DC	202-547-7713
Assoc Photo Labs/1820 Gilford, Montreal, QU	514-523-1139
Blakeslee Lane Studio/916 N Charles St, Baltimore, MD	301-727-8800
Blow-Up/2441 Maryland Ave, Baltimore, MD	301-467-3636
Bonaventure Color Labs/425 Guy St, Montreal, QU	514-989-1919
Boris Color Lab/35 Landsdowne St, Boston, MA	617-437-1152
Boston Photo Service/112 State St, Boston, MA	617-523-0508
Calverts Inc/938 Highland Ave, Needham Hts, MA	617-444-8000
Campbell Photo & Printing/1328 'I' St NW, Washington, DC	202-347-9800
Central Color/1 Prospect Ave, White Plains, NY	914-681-0218
Color Film Corp/440 Summer St, Boston, MA	617-426-5655
Colorama/420 Valley Brook Ave, Lyndhurst, NJ	201-933-5660
Colorlab/5708 Arundel Ave, Rockville, MD	301-770-2128
Colortek/111 Beach St, Boston, MA	617-451-0894
Colotone Litho Seperator/260 Branford Rd/Box 97, North Branford, CT	203-481-6190
Complete Photo Service/703 Mt Auburn St, Cambridge, MA	617-864-5954
The Darkroom/443 Broadway, Saratoga Springs, NY	518-587-6465
The Darkroom Inc/232 First Ave, Pittsburgh, PA	412-261-6056
Delbert, Christian/19 Linell Circle, Billerica, MA	617-273-3138
Dunigan, John V/62 Minnehaha Blvd, PO Box 70, Oakland, NJ	201-337-6656
Dunlop Custom Photolab Service/2321 4th St NE, Washington, DC	202-526-5000
Durkin, Joseph/25 Huntington, Boston, MA	617-267-0437
Eastman Kodak/343 State St, Rochester, NY	716-724-4688
EPD Photo Service/67 Fulton Ave, Hempstead, NY	516-486-5300
Five-Thousand K/281 Summer St, Boston, MA	617-542-5995
Foto Fidelity Inc/35 Leon St, Boston, MA	617-267-6487
G F I Printing & Photo Co/2 Highland St, Port Chester, NY	914-937-2823
Gould, David/76 Coronado St, Atlantic Beach, NY	516-371-2413
Gourdon, Claude Photo Lab/60 Sir Louis VI, St Lambert, QU	514-671-4604
Graphic Accent/446 Main St PO Box 243, Wilmington, MA	617-658-7602
Iderstine, Van/148 State Hwy 10, E Hanover, NJ	201-887-7879
Image Inc/1919 Pennsylvania Ave, Washington, DC	202-833-1550
Industrial Color Lab/P O Box 563, Framingham, MA	617-872-3280
JTM Photo Labs Inc/125 Rt 110, Huntington Station, NY	516-549-0010
K E W Color Labs/112 Main St, Norwalk, CT	203-853-7888
Leonardo Printing Corp/529 E 3rd St, Mount Vernon, NY	914-664-7890
Light-Works Inc/77 College St, Burlington, VT	802-658-6815
Meyers, Tony/W 70 Century Rd, Paramus, NJ	201-265-6000
Modern Mass Media/Box 950, Chatham, NJ	201-635-6000
Moore's Photo Laboratory/1107 Main St, Charleston, WV	304-357-4541
Muggeo, Sam/63 Hedgebrook Lane, Stamford, CT	212-972-0398
Musy, Mark/PO Box 755, Buckingham, PA	215-794-8851
National Color Labs Inc/306 W 1st Ave, Roselle, NJ	201-241-1010

PRODUCTION/SUPPORT SERVICES CONT'D.

Please send us your additions and updates.

National Photo Service/1475 Bergen Blvd, Fort Lee, NJ	212-860-2324
Northeast Color Research/40 Cameron Ave, Somerville, MA	617-666-1161
Ogunquit Photo School/PO Box 568, Ogunquit, ME	207-646-7055
Photo Dynamics/PO Box 731, 70 Jackson Dr, Cranford, NJ	201-272-8880
Photo Publishers/1899 'L' St NW, Washington, DC	202-833-1234
Photo-Colortura/PO Box 1749, Boston, MA	617-522-5132
Regester Photo Service/50 Kane St, Baltimore, MD	301-633-7600
Retouching Graphics Inc/205 Roosevelt Ave, Massapequa Park, NY	516-541-2960
Riter, Warren/2291 Penfield, Pittsford, NY	716-381-4368
Rothman, Henry/6927 N 19th St, Philadelphia, PA	215-424-6927
Select Photo Service/881 Montee de Liesse, Montreal, QU	514-735-2509
Snyder, Jeffrey/915 E Street NW, Washington, DC	202-347-5777
Spaulding Co Inc/301 Columbus, Boston, MA	617-262-1935
Sterling Photo Processing/345 Main Ave, Norwalk, CT	203-847-9145
Stone Reprographics/44 Brattle St, Cambridge, MA	617-495-0200
Subtractive Technology/338-B Newbury St, Boston, MA	617-437-1887
Superior Photo Retouching Service/1955 Mass Ave, Cambridge, MA	617-661-9094
Technical Photography Inc/1275 Bloomfield Ave, Fairfield, NJ	201-227-4646
Trama, Gene/571 South Ave, Rochester, NY	716-232-6122
Universal Color Lab/810 Salaberry, Chomeday, QU	514-384-2251
Van Vort, Donald D/71 Capital Hts Rd, Oyster Bay, NY	516-922-5234
Visual Horizons/180 Metropark, Rochester, NY	716-424-5300
Von Eiff, Damon/7649 Old Georgeton Std 9, Bethesda, MD	301-951-8887
Weinstock, Bernie/162 Boylston, Boston, MA	617-423-4481
Wilson, Paul/25 Huntington Ave, Boston, MA	617-437-1236
Zoom Photo Lab/45 St Jacques, Montreal, QU	514-288-5444

SOUTHEAST

AAA Blue Print Co/3649 Piedmont Rd, Atlanta, GA	404-261-1580
Advance Color Processing Inc/1807 Ponce de Leon Blvd, Miami, FL	305-443-7323
Allen Photo/3808 Wilson Blvd, Arlington, VA	703-524-7121
Associated Photographers/19 SW 6th St, Miami, FL	305-373-4774
Atlanta Blue Print/1052 W Peachtree St N E, Atlanta, GA	404-873-5911
B & W Processing/6808 Hanging Moss, Orlando, FL	305-677-8078
Barral, Yolanda/100 Florida Blvd, Miami, FL	305-261-4767
Berkey Film Processing/1200 N Dixie Hwy, Hollywood, FL	305-927-8411
Bristow Photo Service/2018 Wilson St, Hollywood, FL	305-920-1377
Chromatics/625 Fogg St, Nashville, TN	615-254-0063
Clark Studio/6700 Sharon Rd, Charlotte, NC	704-552-1021
Color Copy Center/5745 Columbia Cir, W Palm Beach, FL	305-842-9500
Color Copy Inc/925 Gervais St, Columbia, SC	803-256-0225
Color Image-Atlanta/478 Armour Circle, Atlanta, GA	404-876-0209
The Color Lab/111 NE 21st St, Miami, FL	305-576-3207
Colorcraft of Columbia/331 Sunset Shopping Center, Columbia, SC	803-252-0600
Customlab/508 Armour Cr, Atlanta, GA	404-875-0289
Dixie Color Lab/520 Highland S, Memphis, TN	901-458-1818
E-Six Lab/53 14th St NE, Atlanta, GA	404-885-1293
Eagle Photographics/3612 Swann Ave, Tampa, FL	813-870-2495
Florida Color Lab/PO Box 10907, Tampa, FL	813-877-8658
Florida Photo Inc/781 NE 125th St, N Miami, FL	305-891-6616
Fordyce, R B Photography/4873 NW 36th St, Miami, FL	305-885-3406
Gables Blueprint Co/4075 Ponce De Leone Blvd, Coral Gables, FL	305-443-7146
General Color Corporation/604 Brevard Ave, Cocoa Beach, FL	305-631-1602
Infinite Color/2 East Glebe Rd, Alexandria, VA	703-549-2242
Inter-American Photo/8157 NW 60th St, Miami, FL	305-592-3833
Janousek & Kuehl/3300 NE Expressway #1-I, Atlanta, GA	404-458-8989
Klickovich, Robert Retouching/1638 Eastern Pkwy, Louisville, KY	502-459-0295
Laser Color Labs/Fairfield Dr, W Palm Beach, FL	305-848-5121
Litho Color Plate/7887 N W 55th St, Miami, FL	305-592-1605
Mid-South Color Laboratories/496 Emmet, Jackson, TN	901-422-6691
Northside Blueprint Co/5141 New Peachtree Rd, Atlanta, GA	404-458-8411
Par Excellence/2900 Youree Dr, Shreveport, LA	318-869-2533
Photo-Pros/635 A Pressley Rd, Charlotte, NC	704-525-0551
Plunkett Graphics/1052 W Peachtree St, Atlanta, GA	404-873-5976
A Printers Film Service/904-D Norwalk, Greensboro, NC	919-852-1275

Remington Models & Talent/2480 E Commercial Blvd PH, Ft Lauderdale, FL	305-566-5420
Rich, Bob Photo/12495 NE 6th Ave, Miami, FL	305-893-6137
Rothor Color Labs/1251 King St, Jacksonville, FL	904-388-7717
S & S Pro Color Inc/2801 S MacDill Ave, Tampa, FL	813-831-1811
Sheffield & Board/18 E Main St, Richmond, VA	804-649-8870
Smith's Studio/2420 Wake Forest Rd, Raleigh, NC	919-834-6491
Spectrum Custom Color Lab/302 E Davis Blvd, Tampa, FL	813-251-0338
Studio Masters Inc/1398 NE 125th St, N Miami, FL	305-893-3500
Supreme Color Inc/71 NW 29th St, Miami, FL	305-573-2934
Taffae, Syd/3550 N Bayhomes Dr, Miami, FL	305-667-5252
Thomson Photo Lab Inc/4210 Ponce De Leon Blvd, Coral Gables, FL	305-443-0669
Viva-Color Labs/121 Linden Ave NE, Atlanta, GA	404-881-1313
Williamson Photography Inc/9511 Colonial Dr, Miami, FL	305-255-6400
World Color Inc/1281 US #1 North, Ormond Beach, FL	904-677-1332

MIDWEST

A-1 Photo Service/105 W Madison St #907, Chicago, IL	312-346-2248
Absolute Color Slides/197 Dundas E, Toronto 15A 124, ON	416-868-0413
AC Color Lab Inc/2160 Payne Ave, Cleveland, OH	216-621-4575
Ad Photo/2056 E 4th St, Cleveland, OH	216-621-9360
Advantage Printers/1307 S Wabash, Chicago, IL	312-663-0933
Airbrush Arts/1235 Glenview Rd, Glenview, IL	312-998-8345
Amato Photo Color/818 S 75th St, Omaha, NE	402-393-8380
Anderson Graphics/521 N 8th St, Milwaukee, WI	414-276-4445
Anro Color/1819 9th St, Rockford, IL	815-962-0884
Arrow Photo Copy/523 S Plymouth St, Chicago, IL	312-427-9515
Artstreet/111 E Chestnut St, Chicago, IL	312-664-3049
Astra Photo Service/6 E Lake, Chicago, IL	312-372-4366
Astro Color Labs/61 W Erie St, Chicago, IL	312-280-5500
Benjamin Film Labs/287 Richmond St, Toronto, ON	416-863-1166
BGM Color Labs/497 King St E, Toronto, ON	416-947-1325
Boulevard Photo/333 N Michigan Ave, Chicago, IL	312-263-3508
Brookfield Photo Service/9146 Broadway, Brookfield, IL	312-485-1718
Buffalo Photo Co/60 W Superior, Chicago, IL	312-787-6476
Carriage Barn Studio/2360 Riverside Dr, Beloit, WI	608-365-2405
Chroma Studios/2300 Maryland Ln, Columbus, OH	614-471-1191
Chromatics Ltd/4507 N Kedzie Ave, Chicago, IL	312-478-3850
Cockrell, Ray/1737 McGee, Kansas City, MO	816-471-5959
Color Central/612 N Michigan Ave, Chicago, IL	312-321-1696
Color Corp of Canada/1198 Eglinton W, Toronto, ON	416-783-0320
Color Darkroom Corp/3320 W Vliet St, Milwaukee, WI	414-344-3377
Color Detroit Inc/310 Livernois, Ferndale, MI	313-546-1800
Color Graphics Inc/5809 W Divison St, Chicago, IL	312-261-4143
Color International Labs/593 N York St, Elmhurst, IL	312-279-6632
The Color Market/3177 MacArthur Blvd, Northbrook, IL	312-564-3770
Color Perfect Inc/24 Custer St, Detroit, MI	313-872-5115
Color Service Inc/325 W Huron St, Chicago, IL	312-664-5225
Color Studio Labs/1553 Dupont, Toronto, ON	416-531-1177
Color Systems/5719 N Milwaukee Ave, Chicago, IL	312-763-6664
Color Technique Inc/57 W Grand Ave, Chicago, IL	312-337-5051
Color West Ltd/1901 W Cermak Rd, Broadview, IL	312-345-1110
Coloron Corp/360 E Grand Ave, Chicago, IL	312-265-6766
Colorprints Inc/410 N Michigan Ave, Chicago, IL	312-467-6930
Commercial Colorlab Service/41 So Stolp, Aurora, IL	312-892-9330
Copy-Matics, Div Lith-O-Lux/6324 W Fond du Lac Ave, Milwaukee, WI	414-462-2250
Corley D & S Ltd/3610 Nashua Dr #7, Mississaugua, ON	416-675-3511
Custom Color Processing Lab/1300 Rand Rd, Des Plaines, IL	312-297-6333
Cutler-Graves/535 N Michigan Ave, Chicago, IL	312-828-9310
D-Max Colorgraphics/1662 Headlands Dr, Fenton, MO	314-343-3570
Diamond Graphics/6324 W Fond du Lac Ave, Milwaukee, WI	414-462-2250
Drake, Brady Copy Center/413 N 10th St, St Louis, MO	314-421-1311
Draper St Photolab/1300 W Draper St, Chicago, IL	312-975-7200
Duncan, Virgil Studios/4725 E State Blvd, Ft Wayne, IN	219-483-6011
Dzuroff Studios/1020 Huron Rd E, Cleveland, OH	216-696-0120
Eastman Kodak Co/1712 S Prairie Ave, Chicago, IL	312-922-9691
Emulsion Stripping Ltd/4 N Eighth Ave, Maywood, IL	312-344-8100
Fotis Photo/25 E Hubbard St, Chicago, IL	312-337-7300
The Foto Lab Inc/160 E Illinois St, Chicago, IL	312-321-0900

PRODUCTION/SUPPORT SERVICES CONT'D.

Please send us your additions and updates.

Foto-Comm Corporation/215 W Superior, Chicago, IL	312-943-0450
Fromex/188 W Washington, Chicago, IL	312-853-0067
Gallery Color Lab/620 W Richmond St, Toronto, ON	416-367-9770
Gamma Photo Lab Inc/314 W Superior St, Chicago, IL	312-337-0022
Graphic Lab Inc/124 E Third St, Dayton, OH	513-461-3774
Graphic Spectrum/523 S Plymouth Ct, Chicago, IL	312-427-9515
Greenhow, Ralph/333 N Michigan Ave, Chicago, IL	312-782-6833
Grignon Studios/1300 W Altgeld, Chicago, IL	312-975-7200
Grossman Knowling Co/7350 John C Lodge, Detroit, MI	313-832-2360
Harlem Photo Service/6706 Northwest Hwy, Chicago, IL	312-763-5860
Hill, Vince Studio/119 W Hubbard, Chicago, IL	312-644-6690
Imperial Color Inc/618 W Jackson Blvd, Chicago, IL	312-454-1570
J D H Inc/1729 Superior Ave, Cleveland, OH	216-771-0346
Jahn & Ollier Engraving/817 W Washington Blvd, Chicago, IL	312-666-7080
Janusz, Robert E Studios/1020 Huron Rd, Cleveland, OH	216-621-9845
John, Harvey Studio/823 N 2nd St, Milwaukee, WI	414-271-7170
Jones & Morris Ltd/24 Carlaw Ave, Toronto, ON	416-465-5466
K & S Photographics/180 N Wabash Ave, Chicago, IL	312-207-1212
K & S Photographics/1155 Handley Industrial Ct, St Louis, MO	314-962-7050
Kai-Hsi Studio/160 E Illinois St, Chicago, IL	312-642-9853
Kier Photo Service/1627 E 40th St, Cleveland, OH	216-431-4670
Kitzerow Studios/203 N Wabash, Chicago, IL	312-332-1224
Kluegel, Art/630 Fieldston Ter, St Louis, MO	314-961-2023
Kolorstat Studios/415 N Dearborn St, Chicago, IL	312-644-3729
Kremer Photo Print/228 S Wabash, Chicago, IL	312-922-3297
LaDriere Studios/1565 W Woodward Ave, Bloomfield Hills, MI	313-644-3932
Lagasca, Dick & Others/203 N Wabash Ave, Chicago, IL	312-263-1389
Langen & Wind Color Service Inc/2871 E Grand Blvd, Detroit, MI	313-871-5722
Lim, Luis Retouching/405 N Wabash, Chicago, IL	312-645-0746
Lubeck, Larry & Assoc/405 N Wabash Ave, Chicago, IL	312-726-5580
Merrill-David Inc/3420 Prospect Ave, Cleveland, OH	216-391-0988
Meteor Photo Company/1099 Chicago Rd, Troy, MI	313-583-3090
Midwest Litho Arts/5300 B McDermott Dr, Berkeley, IL	312-449-2442
Multiprint Co Inc/153 W Ohio St, Chicago, IL	312-644-7910
Munder Color/2771 Galilee Ave, Zion, IL	312-764-4435
National Photo Service/114 W Illinois St, Chicago, IL	312-644-5211
NCL Graphics/575 Bennett Rd, Elk Grove Village, IL	312-593-2610
Noral Color Corp/5560 N Northwest Hwy, Chicago, IL	312-775-0991
Norman Sigele Studios/270 Merchandise Mart, Chicago, IL	312-642-1757
O'Brien, Tom & Assoc/924 Terminal Rd, Lansing, MI	517-321-0188
O'Connor-Roe Inc/111 E Wacker, Chicago, IL	312-856-1668
O'Donnell Studio Inc/333 W Lake St, Chicago, IL	312-346-2470
P-A Photocenter Inc/310 W Washington St, Chicago, IL	312-641-6343
Pallas Photo Labs/319 W Erie St, Chicago, IL	312-787-4600
Pallas Photo Labs/207 E Buffalo, Milwaukee, WI	414-272-2525
Parkway Photo Lab/57 W Grand Ave, Chicago, IL	312-467-1711
Photocopy Inc/104 E Mason St, Milwaukee, WI	414-272-1255
Photographic Specialties Inc/225 Border Ave N, Minneapolis, MN	612-332-6303
Photomatic Corp/59 E Illinois St, Chicago, IL	312-527-2929
Precision Photo Lab/5787 N Webster St, Dayton, OH	513-898-7450
Procolor/909 Hennepin Ave, Minneapolis, MN	612-332-7721
Proctor, Jack/2050 Dain Tower, Minneapolis, MN	612-338-7777
Professional Photo Colour Service/126 W Kinzie, Chicago, IL	312-644-0888
Quantity Photo Co/119 W Hubbard St, Chicago, IL	312-644-8288
Race Frog Stats/207 E Michigan Ave, Milwaukee, WI	414-276-7828
Rahe, Bob/220 Findlay St, Cincinnati, OH	513-241-9060
Rees, John/640 N LaSalle, Chicago, IL	312-337-5785
Reichart, Jim Studio/2301 W Mill Rd, Milwaukee, WI	414-228-9089
Reliable Photo Service/415 N Dearborn, Chicago, IL	312-644-3723
Repro Inc/912 W Washington Blvd, Chicago, IL	312-666-3800
The Retouching Co/360 N Michigan Ave, Chicago, IL	312-263-7445
Rhoden Photo & Press Service/7833 S Cottage Grove, Chicago, IL	312-488-4815
Robb Ltd/362 W Erie, Chicago, IL	312-943-2664
Robin Color Lab/2106 Central Parkway, Cincinnati, OH	513-381-5116
Ross-Ehlert/225 W Illinois, Chicago, IL	312-644-0244
Schellhorn Photo Techniques/3916 N Elston Ave, Chicago, IL	312-267-5141
Scott Studio & Labs/26 N Hillside Ave, Hillsdale, IL	312-449-3800
SE Graphics Ltd/795 E Kings St, Hamilton, ON	416-545-8484
Sladek, Dean/8748 Hollyspring Trail, Chagrin Falls, OH	216-543-5420
Speedy Stat Service/566 W Adams, Chicago, IL	312-939-3397
Standard Studios Inc/3270 Merchandise Mart, Chicago, IL	312-944-5300
The Stat Center/666 Euclid Ave #817, Clevland, OH	216-861-5467
Superior Bulk Film/442 N Wells St, Chicago, IL	312-644-4448
Thorstad, Gordy Retouching Inc/119 No 4th St #311, Minneapolis, MN	612-338-2597
Transparency Duplicating Service/847 W Jackson Blvd, Chicago, IL	312-733-4464
Transparency Processing Service/324 W Richmond St, Toronto, ON	416-593-0434
UC Color Lab/3936 N Pulaski Rd, Chicago, IL	312-545-9641
Uhlir, Louis J/2509 Kingston Rd, Cleveland Hts, OH	216-932-4837
Wichita Color Lab/231 Ohio, Wichita, KS	316-265-2598
Williams, Warren E & Assoc/233 E Wacker Dr, Chicago, IL	312-565-2689
Winnipeg Photo Ltd/1468 Victoria Park Ave, Toronto, ON	416-755-7779
Witkowski Art Studio/52098 N Central Ave, South Bend, IN	219-272-9771
Wood, Bruce/185 N Wabash, Chicago, IL	312-782-4287
Yancy, Helen/421 Valentine St, Dearborn Heights, MI	312-278-9345

SOUTHWEST

A-1 Blue Print Co Inc/2220 W Alabama, Houston, TX	713-526-3111
Alamo Photolabs/3814 Broadway, San Antonio, TX	512-828-9079
Alied & WBS/6305 N O'Connor #111, Irving, TX	214-869-0100
Baster, Ray Enterprises/246 E Watkins, Phoenix, AZ	602-258-6850
The Black & White Lab/4930 Maple Ave, Dallas, TX	214-528-4200
Casey Color Inc/2115 S Harvard Ave, Tulsa, OK	918-744-5004
Century Copi-Technics Inc/710 N St Paul St, Dallas, TX	214-741-3191
Collins Color Lab/2714 McKinney Ave, Dallas, TX	214-824-5333
Color Mark Laboratories/2202 E McDowell Rd, Phoenix, AZ	602-273-1253
The Color Place/4201 San Felipe, Houston, TX	713-629-7080
The Color Place/1330 Conant St, Dallas, TX	214-631-7174
The Color Place/2927 Morton St, Fort Worth, TX	817-335-3515
Commercial Color Corporation/1621 Oaklawn St, Dallas, TX	214-744-2610
Custom Photographic Labs/601 W ML King Blvd, Austin, TX	512-474-1177
Dallas Printing Co/3103 Greenwood St, Dallas, TX	214-826-3331
Five-P Photographic Processing/2122 E Governor's Circle, Houston, TX	713-688-4488
Floyd & Lloyd Burns Industrial Artist/3223 Alabama Courts, Houston, TX	713-622-8255
H & H Blueprint & Supply Co/5042 N 8th St, Phoenix, AZ	602-279-5701
Hall Photo/6 Greenway Plaza, Houston, TX	713-961-3454
Hot Flash Photographics/5933 Bellaire Blvd #114, Houston, TX	713-666-9510
Hunter, Marilyn Art Svc/8415 Gladwood, Dallas, TX	214-341-4664
Kolor Print Inc/PO Box 747, Little Rock, AR	501-375-5581
Magna Professional Color Lab/2601 N 32nd St, Phoenix, AZ	602-955-0700
Master Printing Co Inc/220 Creath St, Jonesboro, AR	501-932-4491
Meisel Photochrome Corp/9645 Wedge Chapel, Dallas, TX	214-350-6666
NPL/1926 W Gray, Houston, TX	713-527-9300
Optifab Inc/1550 W Van Buren St, Phoenix, AZ	602-254-7171
The Photo Company/124 W McDowell Rd, Phoenix, AZ	602-254-5138
PhotoGraphics/1700 S Congress, Austin, TX	512-447-0963
Pounds/909 Congress, Austin, TX	512-472-6926
Pounds Photo Lab Inc/2507 Manor Way, Dallas, TX	214-350-5671
Pro Photo Lab Inc/2700 N Portland, Oklahoma City, OK	405-942-3743
PSI Film Lab Inc/3011 Diamond Park Dr, Dallas, TX	214-631-5670
Raphaele/Digital Transparencies Inc/616 Hawthorne, Houston, TX	713-524-2211
River City Silver/906 Basse Rd, San Antonio, TX	512-734-2020
Spectro Photo Labs Inc/4519 Maple, Dallas, TX	214-522-1981
Steffan Studio/1905 Skillman, Dallas, TX	214-827-6128
Texas World Entrtnmnt/8133 Chadbourne Rd, Dallas, TX	214-351-6103
Total Color Inc/1324 Inwood Rd, Dallas, TX	214-634-1484
True Color Photo Inc/710 W Sheridan Ave, Oklahoma City, OK	405-232-6441

ROCKY MOUNTAIN

Cies/Sexton Photo Lab/275 S Hazel Ct, Denver, CO	303-935-3535
Pallas Photo Labs/700 Kalamath, Denver, CO	303-893-0101
Rezac, R Retouching/7832 Sundance Trail, Parker, CO	303-841-0222

PRODUCTION/SUPPORT SERVICES

Please send us your additions and updates.

WEST COAST

A & I Color Lab/933 N Highland, Los Angeles, CA	213-464-8361
ABC Color Corp/3020 Glendale Blvd, Los Angeles, CA	213-662-2125
Action Photo Service/251 Keany, San Francisco, CA	415-543-1777
Alan's Custom Lab/1545 Wilcox, Hollywood, CA	213-461-1975
Aristo Art Studio/636 N La Brea, Los Angeles, CA	213-939-0101
Art Craft Custom Lab/1900 Westwood Blvd, Los Angeles, CA	213-475-2986
Atkinson-Stedco Color Film Svc/7610 Melrose Ave, Los Angeles, CA	213-655-1255
Bakes, Bill Inc/265 29th St, Oakland, CA	415-832-7685
Black & White Color Reproductions/38 Mason, San Francisco, CA	415-989-3070
Bogle Graphic Photo/1117 S Olive, Los Angeles, CA	213-749-7461
Boston Media Productions/330 Townsend St #112, San Francisco, CA	415-495-6662
Chrome Graphics/449 N Huntley Dr, Los Angeles, CA	213-657-5055
Chromeworks Color Processing/185 Berry, San Francisco, CA	415-957-9481
Coletti, John/333 Kearny #703, San Francisco, CA	415-421-3848
Color Lab Inc/742 Cahuenga Blvd, Los Angeles, CA	213-466-3551
Colorscope/250 Glendale Blvd, Los Angeles, CA	213-250-5555
Colortek/10425 Venice Blvd, Los angeles, CA	213-870-5579
Complete Negative Service/6007 Waring Ave, Hollywood, CA	213-463-7753
CPS Lab/1759 Las Palmas, Los Angeles, CA	213-464-0215
Cre-Art Photo Labs Inc/6920 Melrose Ave, Hollywood, CA	213-937-3390
Croxton, Stewart Inc/8736 Melrose, Los Angeles, CA	213-652-9720
Custom Graphics/15162 Goldenwest Circle, Westminster, CA	714-893-7517
Custom Photo Lab/123 Powell St, San Francisco, CA	415-956-2374
The Darkroom Custom B&W Lab/897-2B Independence Ave, Mountain View, CA	415-969-2955
Faulkner Color Lab/1200 Folsom St, San Francisco, CA	415-861-2800
Focus Foto Finishers/138 S La Brea Ave, Los Angeles, CA	213-934-0013
Frosh, R L & Sons Scenic Studio/4114 Sunset Blvd, Los Angeles, CA	213-662-1134
G P Color Lab/215 S Oxford Ave, Los Angeles, CA	213-386-7901
Gamma Photographic Labs/555 Howard St, San Francisco, CA	415-495-8833
Gibbons Color Lab/606 N Almont Dr, Los Angeles, CA	213-275-6806
Giese, Axel Assoc/544 Starlight Crest Dr, La Canada, CA	213-790-8768
Glusha, Laura/1053 Colorado Blvd #F, Los Angeles, CA	213-255-1997
Good Stats Inc/1616 N Cahuenga Blvd, Hollywood, CA	213-469-3501
Graphic Center/7386 Beverly, Los Angeles, CA	213-938-3773
Graphic Process Co/979 N LaBrea, Los Angeles, CA	213-850-6222
Graphicolor/8134 W Third, Los Angeles, CA	213-653-1768
Hollywood Photo Reproduction/6413 Willoughby Ave, Hollywood, CA	213-469-5421
Imperial Color Lab/365 Howard St, San Francisco, CA	415-777-4020
Ivey-Seright/424 8th Ave North, Seattle, WA	206-623-8113
Jacobs, Ed/937 S Spaulding, Los Angeles, CA	213-935-1064
Jacobs, Robert Retouching/6010 Wilshire Blvd #505, Los Angeles, CA	213-931-3751
Johnston, Chuck/1111 Wilshire, Los Angeles, CA	213-482-3362
Kawahara, George/250 Columbus, San Francisco, CA	415-543-1637
Kimbo Color Laboratory Inc/179 Stewart, San Francisco, CA	415-288-4100
Kinney, Paul Productions/818 19th St, Sacramento, CA	916-447-8868
Landry, Carol/8148-L Ronson Rd, San Diego, CA	619-560-1778
Laursen Color Lab/1641 Reynolds, Irvine, CA	714-261-1500
Lee Film Processing/8584 Venice Blvd, Los Angeles, CA	213-559-0296
M P S Photo Services/17406 Mt Cliffwood Cir, Fountain Valley, CA	714-540-9515
M S Color Labs/740 Cahuenga Blvd, Los Angeles, CA	213-461-4591
Maddocks, J H/4766 Melrose Ave, Los Angeles, CA	213-660-1321
Marin Color Lab/41 Belvedere St, San Rafael, CA	415-456-8093
Mark III Colorprints/7401 Melrose Ave, Los Angeles, CA	213-653-0433
MC Photographics/PO Box 1515, Springfield, OR	503-741-2289
Metz Air Art/2817 E Lincoln Ave, Anaheim, CA	714-630-3071
Modern Photo Studio/5625 N Figueroa, Los Angeles, CA	213-255-1527
Modernage/470 E Third St, Los Angeles, CA	213-628-8194
Newell Color Lab/630 Third St, San Francisco, CA	415-974-6870
Olson, Bob Photo Blow-Up Lab/7775 Beverly Blvd, Los Angeles, CA	213-931-6643
Ostoin, Larry/22943 B Nadine Cr, Torrance, CA	213-530-1121
Pacific Production & Location/424 Nahua St, Honolulu, HI	808-924-2513
Paragon Photo/7301 Melrose Ave, Los Angeles, CA	213-933-5865
Personal Color Lab/1552 Gower, Los Angeles, CA	213-467-0721
Petron Corp/5443 Fountain Ave, Los Angeles, CA	213-461-4626
Pevehouse, Jerry Studio/3409 Tweedy Blvd, South Gate, CA	213-564-1336
Photoking Lab/6612 W Sunset Blvd, Los Angeles, CA	213-466-2977
Prisma Color Inc/5619 Washington Blvd, Los Angeles, CA	213-728-7151
Professional Color Labs/96 Jessie, San Francisco, CA	415-397-5057
Quantity Photos Inc/5432 Hollywood Blvd, Los Angeles, CA	213-467-6178
Rapid Color Inc/1236 S Central Ave, Glendale, CA	213-245-9211
Remos, Nona/4053 Eighth Ave, San Diego, CA	619-692-4044
Repro Color Inc/3100 Riverside Dr, Los Angeles, CA	213-664-1951
Retouching Chemicals/5478 Wilshire Blvd, Los Angeles, CA	213-935-9452
Revilo Color/4650 W Washington Blvd, Los Angeles, CA	213-936-8681
Reynolds, Carol Retouching/1428 N Fuller Ave, Hollywood, CA	213-874-7083
RGB Lab Inc/816 N Highland, Los Angeles, CA	213-469-1959
Ro-Ed Color Lab/707 N Stanley Ave, Los Angeles, CA	213-651-5050
Roller, S J/6881 Alta Loma Terrace, Los Angeles, CA	213-876-5654
Ross, Deborah Design/10806 Ventura Blvd #3, Studio City, CA	818-985-5205
Rudy Jo Color Lab Inc/130 N La Brea, Los Angeles, CA	213-937-3804
Schaeffer Photo Rapid Lab/6677 Sunset Blvd, Hollywood, CA	213-466-3343
Schroeder, Mark/70 Broadway, San Francisco, CA	415-421-3691
Snyder, Len/238 Hall Dr, Orinda, CA	415-254-8687
Staidle, Ted & Assocs/544 N Larchmont Blvd, Los Angeles, CA	213-462-7433
Stat House/8126 Beverly Blvd, Los Angeles, CA	213-653-8200
Still Photo Lab/1216 N LaBrea, Los Angeles, CA	213-465-6106
Studio Photo Service/733 N LaBrea Ave, Hollywood, CA	213-935-1223
Technicolor Inc/1738 No Neville, Orange, CA	714-998-3424
Thomas Reproductions/1147 Mission St, San Francisco, CA	415-431-8900
Timars/918 N Formosa, Los Angeles, CA	213-876-0175
Tom's Chroma Lab/514 No LaBrea, Los Angeles, CA	213-933-5637
Trans Tesseract/715 N San Antonio Rd, Los Altos, CA	415-949-2185
Tri Color Camera/1761 N Vermont Ave, Los Angeles, CA	213-664-2952
Universal Color Labs/1076 S La Cienega Blvd, Los Angeles, CA	213-652-2863
Vloeberghs, Jerome/333 Kearny St, San Francisco, CA	415-982-1287
Waters Art Studio/1820 E Garry St #207, Santa Ana, CA	
Wild Studio/1311 N Wilcox Ave, Hollywood, CA	213-463-8369
Williams, Alan & Assoc Inc/8032 W Third St, Los Angeles, CA	213-653-2243
Wolf Color Lab/6416 Selma, Los Angeles, CA	213-463-0766
Zammit, Paul/5478 Wilshire Blvd #300, Los Angeles, CA	213-933-8563
Ziba Photographics/591 Howard St, San Francisco, CA	415-543-6221

LIGHTING

NEW YORK CITY

Altman Stage Lighting Co Inc/57 Alexander	212-569-7777
Artistic Neon by Gasper/75-49 61st St	718-821-1550
Balcar Lighting Systems/15 E 30th St	212-889-5080
Barbizon Electric Co Inc/426 W 55th St	212-586-1620
Bernhard Link Theatrical Inc/104 W 17th St	212-929-6786
Big Apple Cine Service/49-01 25th Ave	718-626-5210
Big Apple Lights Corp/533 Canal St	212-226-0925
Camera Mart/456 W 55th St	212-757-6977
Electra Displays/122 W 27th St	212-924-1022
F&B/Ceco Lighting & Grip Rental/315 W 43rd St	212-974-4640
Feature Systems Inc/512 W 36th St	212-736-0447
Ferco/707 11th Ave	212-245-4800
Filmtrucks, Inc/450 W 37th St	212-868-7065
Fiorentino, Imero Assoc Inc/44 West 63rd St	212-246-0600
Four Star Stage Lighting Inc/585 Gerard Ave	212-993-0471
Kliegl Bros Universal/32-32 48th Ave	718-786-7474
Lee Lighting America Ltd/534 W 25th St	212-924-5476
Litelab Theatrical & Disco Equip/76 Ninth Ave	212-675-4357
Lowel Light Mfg Inc/475 10th St	212-949-0950
Luminere/160 W 86th St	212-724-0583
Metro-Lites Inc/750 Tenth Ave	212-757-1220
Movie Light Ltd/460 W 24th St	212-989-2318

New York Flash/156 Fifth Ave	212-741-1165
Paris Film Productions Ltd/213-23 99th Ave	718-740-2020
Photo-Tekniques/119 Fifth Ave	212-254-2545
Production Arts Lighting/636 Eleventh Ave	212-489-0312
Ross, Charles Inc/333 W 52nd St	212-246-5470
Stage Lighting Discount Corp/346 W 44th St	212-489-1370
Stroblite Co Inc/10 E 23rd St	212-677-9220
Tekno Inc/15 E 30th St	212-887-5080
Times Square Stage Lighting Co/318 W 47th St	212-541-5045
Vadar Ltd/150 Fifth Ave	212-989-9120

NORTHEAST

Barbizon Light of New England/3 Draper St, Woburn, MA	617-935-3920
Blake, Ben Films/104 W Concord St, Boston, MA	617-266-8181
Bogen/PO Box 448, Engelwood, NJ	201-568-7771
Capron Lighting & Sound/278 West St, Needham, MA	617-444-8850
Cestare, Thomas Inc/188 Herricks Rd, Mineola, NY	516-742-5550
Cody, Stuart Inc/300 Putnam Ave, Cambridge, MA	617-661-4540
Dyna-Lite Inc/140 Market St, Kenilworth, NJ	201-245-7222
Film Associates/419 Boylston St 209, Boston, MA	617-266-0892
Filmarts/38 Newbury St, Boston, MA	617-266-7468
Lighting Products, GTE Sylvania/Lighting Center, Danvers, MA	617-777-1900
Limelight Productions/Yale Hill, Stockbridge, MA	413-298-3771
Lycian Stage Lighting/P O Box 68, Sugar Loaf, NY	914-469-2285
Martorano, Salvatore Inc/9 West First St, Freeport, NY	516-379-8097
McManus Enterprises/111 Union Ave, Bala Cynwyd, PA	215-664-8600
Norton Assoc/53 Henry St, Cambridge, MA	617-876-3771
Packaged Lighting Systems/29-41 Grant, PO Box 285, Walden, NY	914-778-3515
Penrose Productions/4 Sandalwood Dr, Livingston, NJ	201-992-4264
R & R Lighting Co/813 Silver Spring Ave, Silver Spring, MD	301-589-4997
Reinhard, Charles Lighting Consultant/39 Ocean Ave, Massapequa, NY	516-799-1615

SOUTHEAST

Kupersmith, Tony/320 N Highland Ave NE, Atlanta, GA	404-577-5319

MIDWEST

Duncan, Victor Inc/32380 Howard St, Madison Heights, MI	313-589-1900
Film Corps/3101 Hennepin Ave, Minneapolis, MN	612-338-2522
Frost, Jack/234 Piquette, Detroit, MI	313-873-8030
Grand Stage Lighting Co/630 W Lake, Chicago, IL	312-332-5611
Midwest Cine Service/304 W 79th Terr, Kansas City, MO	816-333-0022
Midwest Stage Lighting/2104 Central, Evanston, IL	312-328-3966
Studio Lighting/1345 W Argyle St, Chicago, IL	312-989-8808

SOUTHWEST

ABC Theatrical Rental & Sales/825 N 7th St, Phoenix, AZ	602-258-5265
Astro Audio-Visual/1336 W Clay, Houston, TX	713-528-7119
Chase Lights/1942 Beech St, Amarillo, TX	806-381-0575
Dallas Stage Lighting & Equipment Co/2813 Florence, Dallas, TX	214-827-9380
Duncan, Victor Inc/2659 Fondren Dr, Dallas, TX	214-369-1165
FPS Inc/11250 Pagemill Rd, Dallas, TX	214-340-8545
Gable, Pee Wee Inc/PO Box 11264, Phoenix, AZ	602-242-7660
MFC-The Texas Outfit/5915 Star Ln, Houston, TX	713-781-7703
Southwest Film & TV Lighting/904 Koerner Ln, Austin, TX	512-385-3483

ROCKY MOUNTAIN

Rocky Mountain Cine Support/1332 S Cherokee, Denver, CO	303-795-9713

WEST COAST

Aguilar Lighting Works/3230 Laurel Canyon Blvd, Studio City, CA	213-766-6564
American Mobile Power Co/3218 W Burbank Blvd, Burbank, CA	213-845-5474
Astro Generator Rentals/2835 Bedford St, Los Angeles, CA	213-838-3958
B S Rental Co/18857 Addison St, North Hollywood, CA	213-761-1733
B S Rental Co/1082 La Cresta Dr, Thousand Oaks, CA	805-495-8606
Backstage Studio Equipment/5554 Fairview Pl, Agoura, CA	213-889-9816
Casper's Camera Cars/8415 Lankershim Blvd, Sun Valley, CA	213-767-5207
Castex Rentals/591 N Bronson Ave, Los Angeles, CA	213-462-1468
Ceco, F&B of CA Inc/7051 Santa Monica Blvd, Hollywood, CA	213-466-9361
Cine Turkey/2624 Reppert Ct, Los Angeles, CA	213-654-6495
Cine-Dyne Inc/9401 Wilshire Blvd #830, Beverly Hills, CA	213-622-7016
Cine-Pro/1037 N Sycamore Ave, Hollywood, CA	213-461-4794
Cinemobile Systems Inc/11166 Gault St, North Hollywood, CA	213-764-9900
Cineworks-Cinerents/5724 Santa Monica Blvd, Hollywood, CA	213-464-0296
Cool Light Co Inc/5723 Auckland Ave, North Hollywood, CA	213-761-6116
Denker, Foster Co/1605 Las Flores Ave, San Marino, CA	213-799-8656
Fiorentino, Imero Assoc Inc/6430 Sunset Blvd, Hollywood, CA	213-467-4020
Great American Market/PO Box 178, Woodlands Hill, CA	213-883-8182
Grosso & Grosso/7502 Wheatland Ave, Sun Valley, CA	213-875-1160
Hollywood Mobile Systems/7021 Hayvenhurst St, Van Nuys, CA	213-782-6558
Independent Studio Services/11907 Wicks St, Sun Valley, CA	213-764-0840
Kalani Studio Lighting/129-49 Killion St, Van Nuys, CA	213-762-5991
Key Lite/333 S Front St, Burbank, CA	213-848-5483
Leoinetti Cine Rentals/5609 Sunset Blvd, Hollywood, CA	213-469-2987
Mobile Power House/3820 Rhodes Ave, Studio City, CA	213-766-2163
Mole Richardson/937 N Sycamore Ave, Hollywood, CA	213-851-0111
Pattim Service/10625 Chandler, Hollywood, CA	213-766-5266
Picture Package Inc/22236 Cass Ave, Woodland Hills, CA	213-703-7168
Producer's Studio/650 N Bronson St, Los Angeles, CA	213-466-3111
Production Systems Inc/5759 Santa Monica Blvd, Hollywood, CA	213-469-2704
RNI Equipment Co/7272 Bellaire Ave, North Hollywood, CA	213-875-2656
Skirpan Lighting Control Co/1100 W Chestnut St, Burbank, CA	213-840-7000
Tech Camera/6370 Santa Monica Blvd, Hollywood, CA	213-466-3238
Wallace Lighting/6970 Varna Ave, Van Nuys, CA	213-764-1047
Young Generations/8517 Geyser Ave, Northridge, CA	213-873-5135

STUDIO RENTALS

NEW YORK CITY

3G Stages Inc/236 W 61st St	212-247-3130
The 95th St Studio/206 E 95th St	212-831-1946
American Museum of the Moving Image/31-12 36th St	718-784-4520
Antonio/Stephen Ad Photo/45 E 20th St	212-674-2350
Boken Inc/513 W 54th St	212-581-5507
C & C Visual/12 W 27th St 7th Fl	212-684-3830
Camera Mart Inc/456 W 55th St	212-757-6977
Cine Studio/241 W 54th St	212-581-1916
Codalight Rental Studios/151 W 19th St	212-206-9333
Contact Studios/165 W 47th St	212-354-6400
Control Film Service/321 W 44th St	212-245-1574
DeFilippo/207 E 37th St	212-986-5444
Duggal Color Projects/9 W 20th St	212-242-7000
Farkas Films Inc/385 Third Ave	212-679-8212
Gruszczynski Studio/821 Broadway	212-673-1243
Horvath & Assoc Studios/95 Chambers	212-741-0300
Matrix Studios Inc/727 Eleventh Ave	212-265-8500
Mothers Sound Stages/210 E 5th St	212-260-2050
National Video Industries/15 W 17th St	212-691-1300
New York Flash Rental/156 Fifth Ave	212-741-1165
Ninth Floor Studio/1200 Broadway	212-679-5537
North American Video/423 E 90th St	212-369-2553
North Light Studios/122 W 26th St	212-989-5498
Osonitsch, Robert/112 Fourth Ave	212-533-1920
PDN Studio/167 Third Ave	212-677-8418
Phoenix State Ltd/537 W 59th St	212-581-7721
Photo-Tekniques/119 Fifth Ave	212-254-2545
Production Center/221 W 26th St	212-675-2211

Please send us your additions and updates.

Professional Photo Supply/141 W 20th St	212-924-1200
Reeves Teletape Corp/304 E 44th St	212-573-8888
Rotem Studio/259 W 30th St	212-947-9455
Schnoodle Studios/54 Bleecker St	212-431-7788
Silva-Cone Studios/260 W 36th St	212-279-0900
Stage 54 West/429 W 54th St	212-757-6977
Stages 1&2 West/460 W 54th St	212-757-6977
Studio 35/35 W 31st St	212-947-0898
Studio 39/144 E 39th St	212-685-1771
Studio Twenty/6 W 20th St	212-675-8067
Vagnoni, A Devlin Productions/150 W 55th St	212-582-5572
Yellowbox/47 E 34th St	212-532-4010

NORTHEAST

Allscope Inc/PO Box 4060, Princeton, NJ	609-799-4200
Bay State Film Productions Inc/35 Springfield St, Agawam, MA	413-786-4454
Century III/651 Beacon St, Boston, MA	617-267-6400
Color Leasing Studio/330 Rt 46 East, Fairfield, NJ	201-575-1118
D4 Film Studios Inc/109 Highland Ave, Needham, MA	617-444-0226
Penrose Productions/4 Sandalwood Dr, Livingston, NJ	201-992-4264
Pike Productions Inc/47 Galen St, Watertown, MA	617-924-5000
September Productions Inc/171 Newbury St, Boston, MA	617-262-6090
Television Productions & Services/55 Chapel St, Newton, MA	617-965-1626
Ultra Photo Works/468 Commercial Ave, Palisades Pk, NJ	201-592-7730
Videocom Inc/502 Sprague St, Dedham, MA	617-329-4080
WGGB-TV/PO Box 3633, Springfield, MA	413-785-1911
WLNE-TV/430 County St, New Bedford, MA	617-993-2651

SOUTHEAST

Enter Space/20 14th St NW, Atlanta, GA	404-885-1139
The Great Southern Stage/15221 NE 21st Ave, North Miami Beach, FL	305-947-0430
Williamson Photography Inc/9511 Colonial Dr, Miami, FL	305-255-6400

MIDWEST

Emerich Style & Design/PO Box 14523, Chicago, IL	312-871-4659
Gard, Ron/2600 N Racine, Chicago, IL	312-975-6523
Hanes, Jim/1930 N Orchard, Chicago, IL	312-944-6554
Lewis, Tom/2511 Brumley Dr, Flossmoor, IL	312-799-1156
The Production Center/151 Victor Ave, Highland Park, MI	313-868-6600
Rainey, Pat/4031 N Hamlin Ave, Chicago, IL	312-463-0281
Sosin, Bill/415 W Superior St, Chicago, IL	312-751-0974
Stratford Studios Inc/2857 E Grand Blvd, Detroit, MI	313-875-6617
Zawaki, Andy & Jake/1830 W Cermak, Chicago, IL	312-422-1546

SOUTHWEST

AIE Studios/3905 Braxton, Houston, TX	713-781-2110
Arizona Cine Equipment/2125 E 20th St, Tucson, AZ	602-623-8268
Hayes Productions Inc/710 S Bowie, San Antonio, TX	512-224-9565
MFC Film Productions Inc/5915 Star Ln, Houston, TX	713-781-7703
Pearlman Productions Inc/2506 South Blvd, Houston, TX	713-523-3601
Stokes, Bill Assoc/5642 Dyer, Dallas, TX	214-363-0161
Tecfilms Inc/2856 Fort Worth Ave, Dallas, TX	214-339-2217

WEST COAST

Blakeman, Bob Studios/710 S Santa Fe, Los Angeles, CA	213-624-6662
Carthay Studio/5907 W Pico Blvd, Los Angeles, CA	213-938-2101
Chris-Craft Video Tape/915 N LaBrea, Los Angeles, CA	213-850-2236
Cine-Rent West Inc/991 Tennessee St, San Francisco, CA	415-864-4644
Cine-Video/948 N Cahuenga Blvd, Los Angeles, CA	213-464-6200
Columbia Pictures/Columbia Plaza, Burbank, CA	818-954-6000
Design Arts Studios/1128 N Las Palmas, Hollywood, CA	213-464-9118
Disney, Walt Productions/500 S Buena Vista St, Burbank, CA	818-840-1000
Dominick/833 N LaBrea Ave, Los Angeles, CA	213-934-3033
Eliot, Josh Studio/706 W Pico Blvd, Los Angeles, CA	213-742-0367
Goldwyn, Samuel Studios/1041 N Formosa Ave, Los Angeles, CA	213-650-2500
Great American Cinema Co/10711 Wellworth Ave, Los Angeles, CA	213-475-0937
Hollywood National Studios/6605 Eleanor Ave, Hollywood, CA	213-467-6272
Hollywood Stage/6650 Santa Monica Blvd, Los Angeles, CA	213-466-4393
Kelley, Tom Studios/8525 Santa Monica Blvd, Los Angeles, CA	213-657-1780
Kings Point Corporation/9336 W Washington, Culver City, CA	213-836-5537
Lewin, Elyse/820 N Fairfax Ave, Los Angeles, CA	213-655-4214
Liles, Harry Productions Inc/1060 N Lillian Way, Los Angeles, CA	213-466-1612
MGM Studios/10202 W Washington, Culver City, CA	213-836-3000
MPI Studios/1714 N Wilton Pl, Los Angeles, CA	213-462-6342
Norwood, David/21 Laguna Ct, Manhattan Beach, CA	213-827-2020
Paramount/5555 Melrose, Los Angeles, CA	213-468-5000
Raleigh Studio/650 N Bronson Ave, Los Angeles, CA	213-466-7778
Solaris TV Studios/2525 Ocean Park Blvd, Santa Monica, CA	213-450-6227
Studio AV/1227 First Ave S, Seattle, WA	206-223-1007
Studio Center CBS/4024 Radford Ave, Studio City, CA	818-760-5000
Studio Resources/1915 University Ave, Palo Alto, CA	415-321-8763
Sunset/Gower Studio/1438 N Gower, Los Angeles, CA	213-467-1001
Superstage/5724 Santa Monica Blvd, Los Angeles, CA	213-464-0296
Team Production Co Inc/4133 Lankershim Blvd, North Hollywood, CA	818-506-5700
Television Center Studios/846 N Cahuenga Blvd, Los Angeles, CA	213-462-5111
Trans-American Video/1541 Vine St, Los Angeles, CA	213-466-2141
Twentieth Century Fox/10201 W Pico Blvd, Los Angeles, CA	213-277-2211
Universal City Studios/Universal Studios, Universal City, CA	213-985-4321
UPA Pictures/4440 Lakeside Dr, Burbank, CA	213-842-7171
The Videography Studios/8471 Universal Plaza, Universal City, CA	213-204-2000
Vine Street Video Center/1224 Vine St, Pasadena, CA	213-462-1099
Warner Brothers/4000 Warner Blvd, Burbank, CA	213-843-6000
Wolin/Semple Studio/520 N Western Ave, Los Angeles, CA	213-463-2109

ANIMATORS

NEW YORK CITY

Abacus Productions Inc/475 Fifth Ave	212-532-6677
ALZ Productions/11 Waverly Pl	212-473-7620
Ani-Live Film Service Inc/45 W 45th St	212-819-0700
Animated Productions Inc/1600 Broadway	212-265-2942
Animation Camera Workshop/49 W 24th St	212-807-6450
Animation Center Inc/15 W 46th St	212-869-0123
Animation Services Inc/221 W 57th St 11th Fl	212-333-5656
Animation Service Center/293 W 4th St	212-924-3937
Animex Inc/1540 Broadway	212-575-9494
Animus Films/15 W 44th St	212-391-8716
Avekta Productions Inc/164 Madison Ave	212-686-4550
Backle, RJ Prod/321 W 44th St	212-582-8270
Bakst, Edward/160 W 96th St	212-666-2579
Beckerman, Howard/45 W 45th St #300	212-869-0595
Blechman, R O/2 W 47th St	212-869-1630
Broadcast Arts Inc/632 Broadway	212-254-5910
Cel-Art Productions Inc/20 E 49th St	212-751-7515
Charisma Communications/32 E 57th St	212-832-3020
Charlex Inc/2 W 45th St	212-719-4600
Cinema Concepts/321 W 44th St	212-541-9220
Clark, Ian/229 E 96th St	212-289-0998
Computer Graphics Lab/405 Lexington Ave	212-557-5130
D & R Productions Inc/6 E 39th St	212-532-5303
Dale Cameragraphics Inc/12 W 27th St	212-696-9440
Darino Films/222 Park Ave S	212-228-4024
DaSilva, Raul/137 E 38th St	212-696-1657
Devlin Productions Inc/150 W 55th St	212-582-5572
Diamond & Diaferia/12 E 44th St	212-986-8500
Digital Effects Inc/321 W 44 St	212-581-7760
Dolphin Computer Animation/140 E 80th St	212-628-5930
Doros Animation Inc/475 Fifth Ave	212-684-5043

Elinor Bunin Productions Inc/30 E 60th St	212-688-0759
Fandango Productions Inc/15 W 38th St	212-382-1813
The Fantastic Animation Machine/12 E 46th St	212-697-2525
Feigenbaum Productions Inc/25 W 43rd St # 220	212-840-3744
Film Opticals/144 E 44th St	212-697-4744
Film Planning Assoc/38 E 20th	212-260-7140
Friedman, Harold Consortium/420 Lexington Ave	212-697-0858
Gati, John/881 Seventh Ave #832	212-582-9060
Granato Animation Photography/15 W 46th St	212-869-3231
Graphic Motion Group Ltd/16 W 46th St	212-354-4343
Greenberg, R Assoc/240 Madison Ave	212-689-7886
Grossman, Robert/19 Crosby St	212-925-1965
High-Res Solutions Inc/10 Park Ave #3E	212-684-1397
Howard Graphics/36 W 25th St	212-929-2121
I F Studios/15 W 38th St	212-697-6805
ICON Communications/717 Lexington Ave	212-688-5155
Image Factory Inc/18 E 53rd St	212-759-9363
International Production Center/514 W 57th St	212-582-6530
J C Productions/16 W 46th St	212-575-9611
Kim & Gifford Productions Inc/548 E 87th St	212-986-2826
Kimmelman, Phil & Assoc Inc/50 W 40th St	212-944-7766
Kurtz & Friends/130 E 18th St	212-777-3258
Leo Animation Camera Service/25 W 43rd St	212-997-1840
Lieberman, Jerry/76 Laight St	212-431-3452
Locomo Productions/875 West End Ave	212-222-4833
Marz Productions Inc/118 E 25th St	212-477-3900
Metropolis Graphics/28 E 4th St	212-677-0630
Motion Picker Studio/416 Ocean Ave	718-856-2763
Murphy, Neil/208 W 23rd St	212-691-5730
Musicvision, Inc/185 E 85th St	212-860-4420
New York Siggraph/451 W 54th St	212-582-9223
Omnibus Computer Gaphics/508 W 57th St	212-975-9050
Ovation Films/49 W 24th St	212-675-4700
A P A/230 W 10th St	212-929-9436
Paganelli, Albert/21 W 46th St	212-719-4105
Perpetual Animation/17 W 45th St	212-840-2888
Polestar Films & Assoc Arts/870 Seventh Ave	212-586-6333
Rankin/Bass Productions/1 E 53rd St	212-759-7721
Rembrandt Films/59 E 54th St	212-758-1024
Robinson, Keith Prod Inc/200 E 21st St	212-533-9078
Seeger, Hal/45 W 45th St	212-575-8900
Shadow Light Prod, Inc/12 W 27th St 7th Fl	212-689-7511
Singer, Rebecca Studio Inc/111 W 57th St	212-944-0466
Stanart Studios/1650 Broadway	212-586-0445
Stark, Philip/312 E 90th St	212-777-8070
Sunflower Films/15 W 46th St	212-869-0123
Telemated Motion Pictures/PO Box 176	212-475-8050
Today Video, Inc/45 W 45th St	212-391-1020
Triology Design/25 W 45th St	212-382-3592
Videart Inc/39 W 38th St	212-840-2163
Video Works/24 W 40th St	212-869-2500
Weiss, Frank Studio/66 E 7th St	212-477-1032
World Effects Inc/20 E 46th St	212-687-7070
Zanders Animation Parlour/18 E 41st St	212-725-1331

NORTHEAST

The Animators/247 Ft Pitt Blvd, Pittsburgh, PA	412-391-2550
Aviation Simulations International Inc/Box 358, Huntington, NY	516-271-6476
Comm Corps Inc/711 4th St NW, Washington, DC	202-638-6550
Consolidated Visual Center/2529 Kenilworth Ave, Tuxedo, MD	301-772-7300
Felix, Luisa/180 12th St, Jersey City, NJ	201-653-1500
Hughes, Gary Inc/PO Box, Cabin John, MD	301-229-1100
Penpoint Prod Svc/331 Newbury St, Boston, MA	617-266-1331
Pilgrim Film Service/2504 50th Ave, Hyattsville, MD	301-773-7072
Symmetry T/A/13813 Willoughby Road, Upper Marlboro, MD	301-627-5050
Synthavision-Magi/3 Westchester Plaza, Elmsford, NY	212-733-1300
West End Film Inc/2121 Newport Pl NW, Washington, DC	202-331-8078

SOUTHEAST

Bajus-Jones Film Corp/401 W Peachtree St #1720, Atlanta, GA	404-221-0700
Cinetron Computer Systems Inc/6700 IH 85 North, Norcross, GA	404-448-9463

MIDWEST

AGS & R Studios/425 N Michigan Ave, Chicago, IL	312-836-4500
Associated Audio-Visual Corp/2821 Central St, Evanston, IL	312-866-6780
Bajus-Jones Film Corp/203 N Wabash, Chicago, IL	312-332-6041
The Beach Productions Ltd/1960 N Seminary, Chicago, IL	312-281-4500
Boyer Studio/1324 Greenleaf, Evanston, IL	312-491-6363
Coast Prod/505 N Lake Shore Dr, Chicago, IL	312-222-1857
Filmack Studios Inc/1327 S Wabash, Chicago, IL	312-427-3395
Freese & Friends Inc/1429 N Wells, Chicago, IL	312-642-4475
Goldsholl Assoc/420 Frontage Rd, Northfield, IL	312-446-8300
Goodrich Animation/405 N Wabash, Chicago, IL	312-329-1344
Kayem Animation Services/100 E Ohio, Chicago, IL	312-664-7733
Kinetics/444 N Wabash, Chicago, IL	312-644-2767
Optimation Inc/9055 N 51st St, Brown Deer, WI	414-355-4500
Pilot Prod/1819 Ridge Ave, Evanston, IL	312-328-3700
Quicksilver Assoc Inc/16 W Ontario, Chicago, IL	312-943-7622
Ritter Waxberg & Assoc/200 E Ontario, Chicago, IL	312-664-3934
Simott & Associates/676 N La Salle, Chicago, IL	312-440-1875

SOUTHWEST

Graphic Art Studio/5550 S Lewis Ave, Tulsa, OK	918-743-3915
Media Visions Inc/2716 Bissonnet #408, Houston, TX	713-521-0626

ROCKY MOUNTAIN

Phillips, Stan & Assoc/865 Delaware, Denver, CO	303-595-9911

WEST COAST

Abel, Bob & Assoc/953 N Highland Ave, Los Angeles, CA	213-462-8100
Animation Filmakers Corp/7000 Romaine St, Hollywood, CA	213-851-5526
Animedia Productions Inc/10200 Riverside Dr, North Hollywood, CA	213-851-4777
Bass, Saul/Herb Yeager/7039 Sunset Blvd, Hollywood, CA	213-466-9701
Bosustow Entertainment/1649 11th St, Santa Monica, CA	213-394-0218
Cinema Research Corp/6860 Lexington Ave, Hollywood, CA	213-461-3235
Clampett, Bob Prod/729 Seward St, Hollywood, CA	213-466-0264
Cornerstone Productions/5915 Cantelope Ave, Van Nuys, CA	213-994-0007
Court Productions/1030 N Cole, Hollywood, CA	213-467-5900
Craig, Fred Productions/932 S Pine, San Gabriel, CA	213-287-6479
Creative Film Arts/7026 Santa Monica Blvd, Hollywood, CA	213-466-5111
DePatie-Freleng Enterprises/16400 Ventura Blvd #312, Encino, CA	818-906-3375
Duck Soup Productions Inc/1026 Montana Ave, Santa Monica, CA	213-451-0771
Energy Productions/846 N Cahuenga Blvd, Los Angeles, CA	213-462-3310
Excelsior Animated Moving Pictures/749 N LaBrea, Hollywood, CA	213-938-2335
Filmcore/849 N Seward, Hollywood, CA	213-464-7303
Filmfair/10900 Ventura Blvd, Studio City, CA	213-877-3191
Gallerie International Films Ltd/11320 W Magnolia Blvd, Hollywood, CA	213-760-2040
Hanna-Barbera/3400 W Cahuenga, Hollywood, CA	213-466-1371
Jacques, Jean-Guy & Assoc/633 N LaBrea Ave, Hollywood, CA	213-936-7177
Kurtz & Friends/2312 W Olive Ave, Burbank, CA	213-461-8188
Littlejohn, William Prod Inc/23425 Malibu Colony Dr, Malibu, CA	213-456-8620
Lumeni Productions/1727 N Ivar, Hollywood, CA	213-462-2110
Marks Communication/5550 Wilshire Blvd, Los Angeles, CA	213-464-6302
Melendez, Bill Prod Inc/439 N Larchmont Blvd, Los Angeles, CA	213-463-4101
Murakami Wolf Swenson Films Inc/1463 Tamarind Ave, Hollywood, CA	213-462-6474
New Hollywood Inc/1302 N Cahuenga Blvd, Hollywood, CA	213-466-3686
Pantomime Pictures Inc/12144 Riverside Dr, North	

Please send us your additions and updates.

Hollywood, CA	818-980-5555
Pegboard Productions/1310 N Cahuenga Blvd, Hollywood, CA	818-353-4991
Quartet Films Inc/5631 Hollywood Blvd, Hollywood, CA	213-464-9225
R & B EFX/1802 Victory Blvd, Glendale, CA	818-956-8406
Raintree Productions Ltd/666 N Robertson Blvd, Hollywood, CA	213-652-8330
S & A Graphics/3350 Barham Blvd, Los Angeles, CA	213-874-2301
Spungbuggy Works Inc/8506 Sunset Blvd, Hollywood, CA	213-657-8070
Sullivan & Associates/3377 Barham Blvd, Los Angeles, CA	213-874-2301
Sunwest Productions Inc/1021 N McCadden Pl, Hollywood, CA	213-461-2957
Title House/738 Cahuenga Blvd, Los Angeles, CA	213-469-8171
Triplane Film & Graphics Inc/328 1/2 N Sycamore Ave, Los Angeles, CA	213-937-1320
U P A Pictures Inc/875 Century Park East, Los Angeles, CA	213-556-3800
Williams, Richard Animation/5631 Hollywood Blvd, Los Angeles, CA	213-461-4344

MODELS & TALENT

NEW YORK CITY

Abrams Artists/420 Madison Ave	212-935-8980
Act 48 Mgt Inc/1501 Broadway #1713	212-354-4250
Adams, Bret/448 W 44th St	212-246-0428
Agency for Performing Arts/888 Seventh Ave	212-582-1500
Agents for the Arts/1650 Broadway	212-247-3220
Alexander, Willard/660 Madison Ave	212-751-7070
Amato, Michael Theatrical Entrps/1650 Broadway	212-247-4456
Ambrose Co/1466 Broadway	212-921-0230
American Intl Talent/166 W 125th St	212-663-4626
American Talent Inc/888 Seventh Ave	212-977-2300
Anderson, Beverly/1472 Broadway	212-944-7773
Associated Booking/1995 Broadway	212-874-2400
Associated Talent Agency/41 E 11th St	212-674-4242
Astor, Richard/1697 Broadway	212-581-1970
Avantege Model Management/205 E 42nd St #1303	212-687-9890
Baldwin Scully Inc/501 Fifth Ave	212-922-1330
Barbizon Agency/3 E 54th St	212-371-3617
Barbizon Agency of Rego Park/95-20 63rd	718-275-2100
Barry Agency/165 W 46th St	212-869-9310
Bauman & Hiller/250 W 57th St	212-757-0098
Beilin, Peter/230 Park Ave	212-949-9119
Big Beauties Unlimited/159 Madison Ave	212-685-1270
Bloom, J Michael/400 Madison Ave	212-832-6900
Brifit Models/236 E 46th St 4th Fl	212-949-6262
Buchwald, Don & Assoc Inc/10 E 44th St	212-867-1070
Cataldi, Richard Agency/180 Seventh Ave	212-741-7450
Celebrity Lookalikes/235 E 31st St	212-532-7676
Click Model Management/881 Seventh Ave #1013	212-245-4306
Coleman-Rosenberg/667 Madison Ave	212-838-0734
Columbia Artists/165 W 57th St	212-397-6900
Cunningham, W D/919 Third Ave	212-832-2700
Deacy, Jane Inc/300 E 75th St	212-752-4865
DeVore, Ophelia/1697 Broadway	212-586-2144
Diamond Artists/119 W 57th St	212-247-3025
DMI Talent Assoc/250 W 57th St	212-246-4650
Dolan, Gloria Management Ltd/850 Seventh Ave	212-696-1850
Draper, Stephen Agency/37 W 57th St	212-421-5780
Eisen, Dulcina Assoc/154 E 61st St	212-355-6617
Elite Model Management Corp/150 E 58th St	212-935-4500
Faces Model Management/567 Third Ave	212-661-1515
Fields, Marje/165 W 46th St	212-764-5740
Ford Models Inc/344 E 59th St	212-753-6500
Foster Fell Agency/26 W 38th St	212-944-8520
Funny Face/440 E 62nd St	212-752-6090
Gage Group Inc/1650 Broadway	212-541-5250
Greco, Maria & Assoc/888 Eighth Ave	212-757-0681
Hadley, Peggy Ent/250 W 57th St	212-246-2166
Harth, Ellen Inc/149 Madison Ave	212-686-5600

Hartig, Michael Agency Ltd/114 E 28th St	212-684-0010
Henderson-Hogan/200 W 57th St	212-765-5190
Henry, June/175 Fifth Ave	212-475-5130
Hesseltine Baker Assocs/165 W 46th St	212-921-4460
Hunt, Diana Management/44 W 44th St	212-391-4971
Hutto Management Inc/405 W 23rd St	212-807-1234
HV Models/305 Madison Ave	212-751-3005
International Model Agency/232 Madison Ave	212-686-9053
International Creative Management/40 W 57th St	212-556-5600
International Legends/40 E 34th St	212-684-4600
Jacobsen-Wilder Inc/419 Park Ave So	212-686-6100
Jan J Agency/224 E 46th St	212-490-1875
Jordan, Joe Talent Agency/200 W 57th St	212-582-9003
Kahn, Jerry Inc/853 Seventh Ave	212-245-7317
Kay Models/328 E 61st St	212-308-9560
Kennedy Artists/237 W 11th St	212-675-3944
Kid, Bonnie Agency/25 W 36th St	212-563-2141
King, Archer/1440 Broadway	212-764-3905
Kirk, Roseanne/161 W 54th St	212-888-6711
KMA Associates/303 W 42nd St #606	212-581-4610
Kolmar-Luth Entertainment Inc/1501 Broadway #201	212-730-9500
Kroll, Lucy/390 West End Ave	212-877-0556
L B H Assoc/1 Lincoln Plaza	212-787-2609
L'Image Model Management Inc/114 E 32nd St	212-725-2424
The Lantz Office/888 Seventh Ave	212-586-0200
Larner, Lionel Ltd/850 Seventh Ave	212-246-3105
Leach, Dennis/160 Fifth Ave	212-691-3450
Leaverton, Gary Inc/1650 Broadway	212-541-9640
Leigh, Sanford Entrprs Ltd/440 E 62nd St	212-752-4450
Leighton, Jan/205 W 57th St	212-757-5242
Lenny, Jack Assoc/140 W 58th St #1B	212-582-0270
Lewis, Lester Assoc/110 W 40th St	212-921-8370
M E W Company/370 Lexington Ave	212-889-7272
Mannequin Fashion Models Inc/40 E 34th St	212-684-5432
Martinelli Attractions/888 Eighth Ave	212-586-0963
Matama Talent & Models/30 W 90th St	212-580-2236
McDearmon, Harold/45 W 139th St	212-283-1005
McDermott, Marge/216 E 39th St	212-889-1583
McDonald/ Richards/235 Park Ave S	212-475-5401
MMG Ent/Marcia's Kids/250 W 57th St	212-246-4360
Models Models Inc/37 E 28th St #506	212-889-8233
Models Service Agency/1457 Broadway	212-944-8896
Models Talent Int'l/1140 Broadway	212-684-3343
Morris, William Agency/1350 Sixth Ave	212-586-5100
New York Production Studio/250 W 57th St	212-765-3433
Nolan, Philip/184 Fifth Ave	212-243-8900
Oppenheim-Christie/565 Fifth Ave	212-661-4330
Oscard, Fifi/19 W 44th St #1500	212-764-1100
Ostertag, Barna Agency/501 Fifth Ave	212-697-6339
Our Agency/19 W 34th St #700	212-736-9582
Packwood, Harry Talent Ltd/250 W 57th St	212-586-8900
Palmer, Dorothy/250 W 57th St	212-765-4280
Perkins Models/1697 Broadway	212-582-9511
Petite Model Management/123 E 54th St #9A	212-759-9304
Pfeffer & Roelfs Inc/850 Seventh Ave	212-315-2230
Plus Models/49 W 37th St	212-997-1785
PlusModel Model Management Ltd/49 W 37th St	212-997-1785
Powers, James Inc/12 E 41st St	212-686-9066
Prelly People & Co/296 Fifth Ave	212-714-2060
Premier Talent Assoc/3 E 54th St	212-758-4900
Prestige Models/80 W 40th St	212-382-1700
Rogers, Wallace Inc/160 E 56th St	212-755-1464
Roos, Gilla Ltd/555 Madison Ave	212-758-5480
Rosen, Lewis Maxwell/1650 Broadway	212-582-6762
Rubenstein, Bernard/215 Park Ave So	212-460-9800
Ryan, Charles Agency/200 W 57th St	212-245-2225
Sanders, Honey Agency Ltd/229 W 42nd St	212-947-5555
Schuller, William Agency/1276 Fifth Ave	212-532-6005
Silver, Monty Agency/200 W 57th St	212-765-4040
Smith, Friedman/850 Seventh Ave	212-581-4490
The Starkman Agency/1501 Broadway	212-921-9191
Stars/360 E 65th St #17H	212-988-1400

STE Representation/888 Seventh Ave	212-246-1030
Stein, Lillian/1501 Broadway	212-840-8299
Stewart Artists Corp/215 E 81st St	212-249-5540
Stroud Management/119 W 57th St	212-688-0226
Summa/38 W 32nd St	212-947-6155
Szold Models/644 Broadway	212-777-4998
Talent Reps Inc/20 E 53rd St	212-752-1835
Tatinas Models & Fitters Assoc/1328 Broadway	212-947-5797
Theater Now Inc/1515 Broadway	212-840-4400
Thomas, Michael Agency/22 E 60th St	212-755-2616
Total Look/404 Riverside Dr	212-662-1029
Tranum Robertson Hughes Inc/2 Dag Hammarskjold Plaza	212-371-7500
Triad Artists/888 Seventh Ave	212-489-8100
Troy, Gloria/1790 Broadway	212-582-0260
Universal Attractions/218 W 57th St	212-582-7575
Universal Talent/505 5th Ave	212-661-3896
Van Der Veer People Inc/225 E 59th St #A	212-688-2880
Waters, Bob Agency/510 Madison Ave	212-593-0543
Wilhelmina Models/9 E 37th St	212-532-6800
Witt, Peter Assoc Inc/215 E 79th St	212-861-3120
Wright, Ann Assoc/136 E 57th St	212-832-0110
Zoli/146 E 56th St	212-758-5959

NORTHEAST

Cameo Models/392 Boylston St, Boston, MA	617-536-6004
Carnegie Talent Agency/300 Northern Blvd, Great Neck, NY	516-487-2260
Conover, Joyce Agency/33 Gallowae, Westfield, NJ	201-232-0908
Copley 7 Models & Talent/29 Newbury St, Boston, MA	617-267-4444
The Ford Model Shop/176 Newbury St, Boston, MA	617-266-6939
Hart Model Agency/137 Newbury St, Boston, MA	617-262-1740
Johnston Model Agency/32 Field Point Rd, Greenwich, CT	203-622-1137
National Talent Assoc/40 Railroad Ave, Valley Stream, NY	516-825-8707
Rocco, Joseph Agency/Public Ledger Bldg, Philadelphia, PA	215-923-8790
Somers, Jo/29 Newbury St, Boston, MA	617-267-4444

SOUTHEAST

Act 1 Casting Agency/1460 Brickell Ave, Miami, FL	305-371-1371
The Agency South/1501 Sunset Dr, Coral Gables, FL	305-667-6746
Amaro Agency/1617 Smith St, Orange Park, FL	904-264-0771
Artists Representatives of New Orleans/1012 Philip, New Orleans, LA	504-524-4683
Atlanta Models & Talent Inc/3030 Peachtree Rd NW, Atlanta, GA	404-261-9627
Birmingham Models & Talent/1023 20th St, Birmingham, AL	205-252-8533
Brown, Bob Marionettes/1415 S Queen St, Arlington, VA	703-920-1040
Brown, Jay Theatrical Agency Inc/221 W Waters Ave, Tampa, FL	813-933-2456
Bruce Enterprises/1022 16th Ave S, Nashville, TN	615-255-5711
Burns, Dot Model & Talent Agcy/478 Severn St, Tampa, FL	813-251-5882
Byrd, Russ Assoc/9450 Koger Blvd, St Petersburg, FL	813-586-1504
Carolina Talent/1347 Harding Pl, Charlotte, NC	704-332-3218
Cassandra Models Agency/635 N Hyer St, Orlando, FL	305-423-7872
The Casting Directors Inc/1524 NE 147th St, North Miami, FL	305-944-8559
Central Casting of FL/PO Box 7154, Ft Lauderdale, FL	305-379-7526
Chez Agency/922 W Peachtree St, Atlanta, GA	404-873-1215
Dassinger, Peter International Modeling/1018 Royal, New Orleans, LA	504-525-8382
A del Corral Model & Talent Agency/5830 Argonne Blvd, New Orleans, LA	504-482-8963
Directions Talent Agency/400-C State St Station, Greensboro, NC	919-373-0955
Dodd, Barbara Studios/3508 Central Ave, Nashville, TN	615-385-0740
Faces, Ltd/2915 Frankfort Ave, Louisville, KY	502-893-8840
Falcon, Travis Modeling Agency/17070 Collins Ave, Miami, FL	305-947-7957
Flair Models/PO Box 373, Nashville, TN	615-361-3737
Florida Talent Agency/2631 E Oakland Pk, Ft Lauderdale, FL	305-565-3552
House of Talent of Cain & Sons/996 Lindridge Dr NE, Atlanta, GA	404-261-5543
Irene Marie Models/3212 S Federal Hwy, Ft Lauderdale, FL	305-522-3262
Jo-Susan Modeling & Finishing School/3415 West End Ave, Nashville, TN	615-383-5850
Lewis, Millie Modeling School/10 Calendar Ct #A, Forest Acres, SC	803-782-7338
Lewis, Millie Modeling School/880 S Pleasantburg Dr, Greenville, SC	803-271-4402
Mar Bea Talent Agency/923 Crandon Blvd, Key Biscayne, FL	305-361-1144
Marilyns Modeling Agency/3800 W Wendover, Greensboro, NC	919-292-5950
McQuerter, James/4518 S Cortez, Tampa, FL	813-839-8335
Parker, Sarah/425 S Olive Ave, West Palm Beach, FL	305-659-2833
Polan, Marian Talent Agency/PO Box 7154, Ft Lauderdale, FL	305-525-8351
Pommier, Michele/7520 Red Rd, Miami, FL	305-667-8710
Powers, John Robert School/828 SE 4th St, Fort Lauderdale, FL	305-467-2838
Professional Models Guild & Workshop/210 Providence Rd, Charlotte, NC	704-377-9299
Remington Models & Talent/2480 E Commercial Blvd PH, Ft Lauderdale, FL	305-944-6608
Rose, Sheila/8218 NW 8th St, Plantation, FL	305-473-9747
Serendipity/3130 Maples Dr NE #19, Atlanta, GA	404-237-4040
Signature Talent Inc/PO Box 221086, Charlotte, NC	704-542-0034
Sovereign Model & Talent/11111 Biscayne Blvd, Miami, FL	305-899-0280
Spivia, Ed/PO Box 38097, Atlanta, GA	404-292-6240
Stevens, Patricia Modeling Agency/3312 Piedmont Rd, Atlanta, GA	404-261-3330
Talent & Model Land, Inc/1501 12th Ave S, Nashville, TN	615-385-2723
Talent Enterprises Inc/3338 N Federal Way, Ft Lauderdale, FL	305-949-6099
The Talent Shop Inc/3210 Peachtree Rd NE, Atlanta, GA	404-261-0770
Theatrics Etcetera/PO Box 11862, Memphis, TN	901-278-7454
Thompson, Jan Agency/1708 Scott Ave, Charlotte, NC	704-377-5987
Top Billing Inc/PO Box 121089, Nashville, TN	615-327-1133
Tracey Agency Inc/PO Box 12405, Richmond, VA	804-358-4004

MIDWEST

A-Plus Talent Agency Corp/666 N Lakeshore Dr, Chicago, IL	312-642-8151
Advertisers Casting Service/15 Kercheval Ave, Grosse Point Farms, MI	313-881-1135
Affiliated Talent & Casting Service/28860 Southfield Rd #100, Southfield, MI	313-559-3110
Arlene Willson Agency/9205 W Center St, Milwaukee, WI	414-259-1611
Creative Casting Inc/430 Oak Grove, Minneapolis, MN	612-871-7866
David & Lee Model Management/70 W Hubbard, Chicago, IL	312-661-0500
Gem Enterprises/5100 Eden Ave, Minneapolis, MN	612-927-8000
Hamilton, Shirley Inc/620 N Michigan Ave, Chicago, IL	312-644-0300
Lee, David Models/70 W Hubbard, Chicago, IL	312-661-0500
Limelight Assoc Inc/3460 Davis Lane, Cincinnati, OH	513-631-8276
Marx, Dick & Assoc Inc/101 E Ontario St, Chicago, IL	312-440-7300
The Model Shop/415 N State St, Chicago, IL	312-822-9663
Monza Talent Agency/1001 Westport Rd, Kansas City, MO	816-931-0222
Moore, Eleanor Agency/1610 W Lake St, Minneapolis, MN	612-827-3823
National Talent Assoc/3525 Patterson Ave, Chicago, IL	312-539-8575
New Faces Models & Talent Inc/310 Groveland Ave, Minneapolis, MN	612-871-6000
Pastiche Models Inc/161 Ottawa NW #300K, Grand Rapids, MI	616-451-2181
Powers, John Robert/5900 Roche Dr, Columbus, OH	614-846-1047
Schucart, Norman Ent/1417 Green Bay Rd, Highland Park, IL	312-433-1113
Sharkey Career Schools Inc/1299-H Lyons Rd Governours Sq, Centerville, OH	513-434-4461
SR Talent Pool/206 S 44th St, Omaha, NE	402-553-1164
Station 12-Producers Express/1759 Woodgrove Ln, Bloomfield Hills, MI	313-855-1188
Talent & Residuals Inc/303 E Ohio St, Chicago, IL	312-943-7500
Talent Phone Productions/612 N Michagan Ave, Chicago, IL	312-664-5757
Verblen, Carol Casting Svc/2408 N Burling, Chicago, IL	312-348-0047
White House Studios/9167 Robinson, Kansas City, MO	913-341-8036

SOUTHWEST

Aaron, Vicki/2017 Butterfield, Grand Prairie, TX	214-641-8539
Accent Inc/6051 N Brookline, Oklahoma City, OK	405-843-1303

PRODUCTION/SUPPORT SERVICES CONT'D.

Please send us your additions and updates.

Actors Clearinghouse/501 N IH 35, Austin, TX	512-476-3412
ARCA/ Freelance Talent/PO Box 5686, Little Rock, AR	501-224-1111
Ball, Bobby Agency/808 E Osborn, Phoenix, AZ	602-264-5007
Barbizon School & Agency/1647-A W Bethany Home Rd, Phoenix, AZ	602-249-2950
Blair, Tanya Agency/3000 Carlisle St, Dallas, TX	214-748-8353
Creme de la Creme/5643 N Pennsylvania, Oklahoma City, OK	405-721-5316
Dawson, Kim Agency/PO Box 585060, Dallas, TX	214-638-2414
Ferguson Modeling Agency/1100 W 34th St, Little Rock, AR	501-375-3519
Flair-Career Fashion & Modeling/11200 Menaul Rd, Albuquerque, NM	505-296-5571
Fosi's Talent Agency/2777 N Campbell Ave #209, Tucson, AZ	602-795-3534
Fullerton, Jo Ann/923 W Britton Rd, Oklahoma City, OK	405-848-4839
Hall, K Agency/503 W 15th St, Austin, TX	512-476-7523
Harrison-Gers Modeling Agency/1707 Wilshire Blvd NW, Oklahoma City, OK	405-840-4515
Kyle & Mathews/5250 Gulfton #3-A, Houston, TX	
The Mad Hatter/7349 Ashcroft Rd, Houston, TX	713-995-9090
Mannequin Modeling Agency/204 E Oakview, San Antonio, TX	512-231-4540
Melancon, Joseph Studios/2934 Elm, Dallas, TX	214-742-2982
Models and Talent of Tulsa/4528 S Sheridan Rd, Tulsa, OK	918-664-5340
Models of Houston Placement Agency/7676 Woodway, Houston, TX	713-789-4973
New Faces Inc/5108-B N 7th St, Phoenix, AZ	602-279-3200
Norton Agency/3900 Lemon Ave, Dallas, TX	214-528-9960
Plaza Three Talent Agency/4343 N 16th St, Phoenix, AZ	602-264-9703
Powers, John Robert Agency/3005 S University Dr, Fort Worth, TX	817-923-7305
Shaw, Ben Modeling Studios/4801 Woodway, Houston, TX	713-850-0413
Southern Arizona Casting Co/2777 N Campbell Ave #209, Tucson, AZ	602-795-3534
Strawn, Libby/3612 Foxcroft Rd, Little Rock, AR	501-227-5874
The Texas Cowgirls Inc/4300 N Central #109C, Dallas, TX	214-696-4176
Wyse, Joy Agency/2600 Stemmons, Dallas, TX	214-638-8999

ROCKY MOUNTAIN

Aspen/Vannoy Talent/PO Box 8124, Aspen, CO	303-771-7500
Colorado Springs/Vannoy Talent/223 N Wahsatch, Colorado Springs, CO	303-636-2400
Denver/ Vannoy Talent/7400 E Caley Ave, Engelwood, CO	303-771-6555
Illinois Talent/2664 S Krameria, Denver, CO	303-757-8675
Mack, Jess Agency/111 Las Vegas Blvd S, Las Vegas, NV	702-382-2193
Morris, Bobby Agency/1629 E Sahara Ave, Las Vegas, NV	702-733-7575
Universal Models/953 E Sahara, Las Vegas, NV	702-732-2499

WEST COAST

Adrian, William Agency/520 S Lake Ave, Pasadena, CA	213-681-5750
Anthony's , Tom Precision Driving/1231 N Harper, Hollywood, CA	213-462-2301
Artists Management Agency/2232 Fifth Ave, San Diego, CA	619-233-6655
Barbizon Modeling & Talent Agy/15477 Ventura Blvd, Sherman Oaks, CA	213-995-8238
Barbizon School of Modeling/452 Fashion Valley East, San Diego, CA	714-296-6366
Blanchard, Nina/1717 N Highland Ave, Hollywood, CA	213-462-7274
Brebner Agency/185 Berry St, San Francisco, CA	415-495-6700
Celebrity Look-Alikes/9000 Sunset Blvd #407, W Hollywood, CA	213-273-5566
Character Actors/935 NW 19th Ave, Portland, OR	503-223-1931
Commercials Unlimited/7461 Beverly Blvd, Los Angeles, CA	213-937-2220
Crosby, Mary Talent Agency/2130 Fourth Ave, San Diego, CA	714-234-7911
Cunningham, William D/261 S Robertson, Beverly Hills, CA	213-855-0200
Demeter and Reed Ltd/70 Zoe #200, San Francisco, CA	415-777-1337
Drake, Bob/3878-A Fredonia Dr, Hollywood, CA	213-851-4404
Franklin, Bob Broadcast Talent/10325 NE Hancock, Portland, OR	503-253-1655
Frazer-Nicklin Agency/4300 Stevens Creek Blvd, San Jose, CA	408-554-1055
Garrick, Dale Intern'l Agency/8831 Sunset Blvd, Los Angeles, CA	213-657-2661

Grimme Agency/207 Powell St, San Francisco, CA	415-392-9175
Hansen, Carolyn Agency/1516 6th Ave, Seattle, WA	206-622-4700
International Creative Management/8899 Beverly Blvd, Los Angeles, CA	213-550-4000
Kelman, Toni Agency/8961 Sunset Blvd, Los Angeles, CA	213-851-8822
L'Agence Models/100 N Winchester Blvd #370, San Jose, CA	408-985-2993
Leonetti, Ltd/6526 Sunset Blvd, Los Angeles, CA	213-462-2345
Liebes School of Modeling Inc/45 Willow Lane, Sausalito, CA	415-331-5383
Longenecker, Robert Agency/11500 Olympic Blvd, Los Angeles, CA	213-477-0039
Media Talent Center/4315 NE Tillamook, Portland, OR	503-281-2020
Model Management Inc/1400 Castro St, San Francisco, CA	415-282-8855
Neuman, Allan/825 W 16th St, Newport Beach, CA	714-548-8800
Pacific Artists, Ltd/515 N La Cienaga, Los Angeles, CA	213-657-5990
Playboy Model Agency/8560 Sunset Blvd, Los Angeles, CA	213-659-4080
Powers, John Robert/1610 6th Ave, Seattle, WA	206-624-2495
Remington Models & Talent/924 Westwood Blvd #545, Los Angeles, CA	213-552-3012
Schwartz, Don Agency/8721 Sunset Blvd, Los Angeles, CA	213-657-8910
Seattle Models Guild/1610 6th Ave, Seattle, WA	206-622-1406
Shaw, Glen Agency/3330 Barham Blvd, Los Angeles, CA	213-851-6262
Smith, Ron's Celebrity Look-Alikes/9000 Sunset Blvd, Hollywood, CA	213-273-5566
Sohbi's Talent Agency/1750 Kalakaua Ave #116, Honolulu, HI	808-946-6614
Stern, Charles Agency/9220 Sunset Blvd, Los Angeles, CA	213-273-6890
Studio Seven/261 E Rowland Ave, Covina, CA	213-331-6351
Stunts Unlimited/3518 Cahuenga Blvd W, Los Angeles, CA	213-874-0050
Tanner, Herb & Assoc/6640 W Sunset Blvd, Los Angeles, CA	213-466-6191
TOPS Talent Agency/404 Piikoi St, Honolulu, HI	808-537-6647
Wormser Heldford & Joseph/1717 N Highland #414, Los Angeles, CA	213-466-9111

CASTING

NEW YORK CITY

BCI Casting/1500 Broadway	212-221-1583
Brinker, Jane/51 W 16th St	212-924-3322
Brown, Deborah Casting/250 W 57th St	212-581-0404
Burton, Kate/271 Madison Ave	212-243-6114
C & C Productions/445 E 80th St	212-472-3700
Carter, Kit & Assoc/160 W 95th St	212-864-3147
Cast Away Casting Service/14 Sutton Pl S	212-755-0960
Central Casting Corp of NY/200 W 54th St	212-582-4933
Cereghetti Casting/119 W 57th St	212-307-6081
Claire Casting/118 E 28th St	212-889-8844
Complete Casting/240 W 44th St	212-382-3835
Contemporary Casting Ltd/41 E 57th St	212-838-1818
Davidson/Frank Photo-Stylists/209 W 86th St #701	212-799-2651
Deron, Johnny/30-63 32nd St	718-728-5326
DeSeta, Donna Casting/424 W 33rd St	212-239-0988
Digiaimo, Lou/PO Box 5296 FDR Sta	212-691-6073
Fay, Sylvia/71 Park Ave	212-889-2626
Feuer & Ritzer Casting Assoc/1650 Broadway	212-765-5580
Greco, Maria Casting/888 Eighth Ave	212-757-0681
Herman & Lipson Casting, Inc/114 E 25th St	212-777-7070
Howard, Stewart Assoc/215 Park Ave So	212-477-2323
Hughes/Moss Assoc/311 W 42nd St	212-307-6690
Iredale/ Burton Ltd/271 Madison Ave	212-889-7722
Jacobs, Judith/336 E 81st St	212-744-3758
Johnson/Liff/1501 Broadway	212-391-2680
Kressel, Lynn Casting/111 W 57th St	212-581-6990
L 2 Casting, Inc/4 W 83rd St	212-496-9444
McCorkle-Sturtevant Casting Ltd/240 W 44th St	212-888-9160
Navarro-Bertoni Casting Ltd/25 Central Park West	212-765-4251
Reed/Sweeney/Reed Inc/1780 Broadway	212-265-8541
Reiner, Mark Contemporary Casting/16 W 46th St	212-838-1818
Schneider Studio/119 W 57th St	212-265-1223
Shapiro, Barbara Casting/111 W 57th St	212-582-8228

PRODUCTION/SUPPORT SERVICES

Shulman/Pasciuto, Inc/1457 Broadway #308	212-944-6420
Silver, Stan/108 E 16th St	212-477-5900
Todd, Joy/250 W 57th St	212-765-1212
Weber, Joy Casting/250 W 57th St #1925	212-245-5220
Wollin, Marji/233 E 69th St	212-472-2528
Woodman, Elizabeth Roberts/222 E 44th St	212-972-1900

NORTHEAST

Baker, Ann Casting/6 Wheeler Rd, Newton, MA	617-964-3038
Booking Agent Lic/860 Floral Ave, Union, NJ	201-353-1595
Central Casting/623 Pennsylvania Ave SE, Washington, DC	202-547-6300
Dilworth, Francis/496 Kinderkamack Rd, Oradell, NJ	201-265-4020
Holt/Belajac & Assoc Inc/The Bigelow #1924, Pittsburgh, PA	412-391-1005
Lawrence, Joanna Agency/82 Patrick Rd, Westport, CT	203-226-7239
Panache/3214 N St NW, Washington, DC	202-333-4240

SOUTHEAST

Central Casting/PO Box 7154, Ft Lauderdale, FL	305-379-7526
DiPrima, Barbara Casting/2951 So Bayshore Dr, Coconut Grove, FL	305-445-7630
Elite Artists, Inc/785 Crossover, Memphis, TN	901-761-1046
Manning, Maureen/1283 Cedar Hts Dr, Stone Mt, GA	404-296-1520
Taylor Royal Casting/2308 South Rd, Baltimore, MD	301-466-5959

MIDWEST

Station 12 Producers Express Inc/1759 Woodgrove Ln, Bloomfield Hills, MI	313-855-1188

SOUTHWEST

Abramson, Shirley/321 Valley Cove, Garland, TX	214-272-3400
Austin Actors Clearinghouse/501 North 1H 35, Austin, TX	512-476-3412
Blair, Tanya Agency/Artists Managers/3000 Carlisle #101, Dallas, TX	214-748-8353
Chason, Gary & Assoc/5645 Hillcroft St, Houston, TX	713-789-4003
Greer, Lucy & Assoc Casting/600 Shadywood Ln, Richardson, TX	214-231-2086
Jr Black Acad of Arts & Letters/723 S Peak St, Dallas, Tx	214-526-1237
KD Studio/2600 Stemons #147, Dallas, TX	214-638-0484
Kegley, Liz/Shari Rhodes/2021 Southgate, Houston, TX	713-522-5066
Kegley, Liz/Shari Rhodes/5737 Everglade, Dallas, TX	214-475-2353
Kent, Rody/5338 Vanderbilt Ave, Dallas, TX	214-827-3418
New Visions/Box 14 Whipple Station, Prescott, AZ	602-445-3382
Schermerhorn, Jo Ann/PO Box 2672, Conroe, TX	409-273-2569

ROCKY MOUNTAIN

Aspen/Vannoy Talent/PO Box 8124, Aspen, CO	303-771-7500
Colorado Springs/Vannoy Talent/223 N Wahsatch, Colorado Springs, CO	303-636-2400
Denver/ Vannoy Talent/7400 E Caley Ave, Engelwood, CO	303-771-6555

WEST COAST

Abrams-Rubaloff & Associates/9012 Beverly Blvd, Los Angeles, CA	213-273-5711
Associated Talent International/9744 Wilshire Blvd, Los Angeles, CA	213-271-4662
BCI Casting/5134 Valley, Los Angeles, CA	213-222-0366
Celebrity Look-Alikes/9000 Sunset Blvd #407, West Hollywood, CA	213-273-5566
Commercials Unlimited/7461 Beverly Blvd, Los Angeles, CA	213-937-2220
Creative Artists Agency Inc/1888 Century Park E, Los Angeles, CA	213-277-4545
Cunningham, William & Assocs/261 S Robertson Blvd, Beverly Hills, CA	213-855-0200
Davis, Mary Webb/515 N LaCienega, Los Angeles, CA	213-652-6850

Garrick, Dale Internat'l Agency/8831 Sunset Blvd #402, Los Angeles, CA	213-657-2661
Hecht, Beverly Agency/8949 Sunset Blvd #203, Los Angeles, CA	213-278-3544
Kelman, Toni Agency/8961 Sunset Blvd, Los Angeles, CA	213-851-8822
Leonetti, Caroline Ltd/6526 Sunset Blvd, Los Angeles, CA	213-462-2345
Lien, Michael Casting/7461 Beverly Blvd, Los Angeles, CA	213-550-7381
Loo, Bessi Agency/8235 Santa Monica, W Hollywood, CA	213-650-1300
Mangum, John Agency/8831 Sunset Blvd, Los Angeles, CA	213-659-7230
Morris, William Agency/151 El Camino Dr, Beverly Hills, CA	213-274-7451
Pacific Artists Limited/515 N LaCienega Blvd, Los Angeles, CA	213-657-5990
REB-Sunset International/6912 Hollywood Blvd, Hollywood, CA	213-464-4440
Rose, Jack/6430 Sunset Blvd #1203, Los Angeles, CA	213-463-7300
Schaeffer, Peggy Agency/10850 Riverside Dr, North Hollywood, CA	818-985-5547
Schwartz, Don & Assoc/8721 Sunset Blvd, Los Angeles, CA	213-657-8910
Stern, Charles H Agency/9220 Sunset Blvd, Los Angeles, CA	213-273-6890
Sutton Barth & Venari/8322 Beverly Blvd, Los Angeles, CA	213-653-8322
Tannen, Herb & Assoc/6640 Sunset Blvd #203, Los Angeles, CA	213-466-6191
Wilhelmina/West/1800 Centyry Park E #504, Century City, CA	213-553-9525
Wormser Heldford & Joseph/1717 N Highland #414, Hollywood, CA	213-466-9111
Wright, Ann Assoc/8422 Melrose Place, Los Angeles, CA	213-655-5040

ANIMALS

NEW YORK CITY

All Tame Animals/37 W 57th St	212-752-5885
Animals for Advertising/310 W 55th St	212-245-2590
Berloni Theatrical Animals/314 W 57th St Box 37	212-974-0922
Canine Academy of Ivan Kovach/3725 Lyme Ave	718-682-6770
Captain Haggertys Theatrical Dogs/1748 First Ave	212-410-7400
Chateau Theatrical Animals/608 W 48th St	212-246-0520
Claremont Riding Academy/175 W 89th St	212-724-5100
Dawn Animal Agency/160 W 46th St	212-575-9396
Mr Lucky Dog Training School Inc/27 Crescent St Brooklyn NY	718-827-2792

NORTHEAST

American Driving Society/PO Box 1852, Lakeville, CT	203-435-0307
Animal Actors Inc/Box 221, RD 3, Washington, NJ	201-689-7539
Davis, Greg/Box 159T, RD 2, Greenville, NY	518-966-8229
Long Island Game Farm & Zoo/Chapman Blvd, Manorville, NY	516-727-7443
Parrots of the World/239 Sunrise Hwy, Rockville Center, NY	212-343-4141

SOUTHEAST

Dog Training by Bob Maida/7605 Old Centerville Rd, Manassas, VA	713-631-2125
Studio Animal Rentals/170 W 64th St, Hialeah, FL	305-558-4160

MIDWEST

Plainsmen Zoo/Rt 4, Box 151, Elgin, IL	312-697-0062

SOUTHWEST

Bettis, Ann J/Rt 1-A Box 21-B, Dripping Springs, TX	512-264-1952
Dallas Zoo in Marsalis Park/621 E Clarendon, Dallas, TX	214-946-5155
Estes, Bob Rodeos/PO Box 962, Baird, TX	915-854-1037
Fort Worth Zoological Park/2727 Zoological Park Dr., Fort Worth, TX	817-870-7050
International Wildlife Park/601 Wildlife Parkway, Grand Prairie, TX	214-263-2203
Newsom's Varmints N' Things/13015 Kaltenbrun, Houston, TX	713-931-0676
Scott, Kelly Buggy & Wagon Rentals/Box 442, Bandera, TX	512-796-3737

PRODUCTION/SUPPORT SERVICES CONT'D.

Please send us your additions and updates.

Taylor, Peggy Talent Inc/6311 N O'Connor 3 Dallas Comm, Irving, TX	214-869-1515
Y O Ranch/Dept AS, Mountain Home, TX	512-640-3222

ROCKY MOUNTAIN

Denver/ Vannoy Talent/7400 E Caley Ave, Engelwood, CO	303-771-6555

WEST COAST

American Animal Enterprises/PO Box 337, Littlerock, CA	805-944-3011
The American Mongrel/PO Box 2406, Lancaster, CA	805-942-7550
Animal Action/PO Box 824, Arleta, CA	818-767-3003
Animal Actors of Hollywood/864 Carlisle Rd, Thousand Oaks, CA	805-495-2122
Birds and Animals/25191 Riverdell Dr, El Toro, CA	714-830-7845
The Blair Bunch/7561 Woodman Pl, Van Nuys, CA	213-994-1136
Casa De Pets/11814 Ventura Blvd, Studio City, CA	818-761-3651
Di Sesso's, Moe Trained Wildlife/24233 Old Road, Newhall, CA	805-255-7969
Frank Inn Inc/12265 Branford St, Sun Valley, CA	818-896-8188
Gentle Jungle/3815 W Olive Ave, Burbank, CA	818-841-5300
Griffin, Gus/11281 Sheldon St, Sun Valley, CA	818-767-6647
Martin, Steve Working Wildlife/PO Box 65, Acton, CA	805-268-0788
Pyramid Bird/1407 W Magnolia, Burbank, CA	818-843-5505
Schumacher Animal Rentals/14453 Cavette Pl, Baldwin Park, CA	818-338-4614
The Stansbury Company/9304 Santa Monica Blvd, Beverly Hills, CA	213-273-1138
Weatherwax, Robert/16133 Soledad Canyon Rd, Canyon Country, CA	805-252-6907

HAIR & MAKE-UP

NEW YORK CITY

Abrams, Ron/126 W 75th St	212-580-0705
Baeder, D & Sehven, A/135 E 26th St	212-532-4571
Barba, Olga/201 E 16th St	212-420-8611
Barron, Lynn/135 E 26th St	212-532-4571
Beauty Booking/130 W 57th St	212-977-7157
Blake, Marion/130 W 57th St	212-977-7157
Boles, Brad/	212-724-2800
Boushelle/444 E 82nd St	212-861-7225
Braithwaite, Jordan/130 W 57th St	212-977-7157
Hammond, Claire/440 E 57th St	212-838-0712
Imre, Edith Beauty Salon/8 W 56th St	212-758-0233
Jenrette, Pamela/300 Mercer St	212-673-4748
Keller, Bruce Clyde/422 E 58th St	212-593-3816
Lane, Judy/444 E 82nd St	212-861-7225
Multiple Artists/42 E 23 St	212-473-8020
Narvaez, Robin/360 E 55th St	212-371-6378
Richardson, John Ltd/119 E 64th St	212-772-1874
Stessin, Warren Scott/	212-243-3319
Tamblyn, Thom Inc/240 E 27th St	212-683-4514
Weithorn, Rochelle/431 E 73rd St	212-472-8668

NORTHEAST

E-Fex/623 Pennsylvania Ave SE, Washington, DC	202-543-1241

SOUTHEAST

Irene Marie Models/3212 S Federal Hwy, Ft Lauderdale, FL	305-522-3262
Parker, Julie Hill/PO Box 19033, Jacksonville, FL	904-724-8483

MIDWEST

Adams, Jerry Hair Salon/1123 W Webster, Chicago, IL	312-327-1130
Alderman, Frederic/Rt 2 Box 205, Mundelein, IL	312-438-2925

Bobak, Ilona/300 N State, Chicago, IL	312-321-1679
Camylle/112 E Oak, Chicago, IL	312-943-1120
Cheveux/908 W Armitage, Chicago, IL	312-935-5212
Collins Chicago, Inc/67 E Oak, Chicago, IL	312-266-6662
Emerich, Bill/PO Box 14523, Chicago, IL	312-871-4659
International Guild of Make-Up/6970 N Sheridan, Chicago, IL	312-761-8500
Okains Costume & Theater/2713 W Jefferson, Joliet, IL	815-741-9303
Simmons, Sid Inc/2 E Oak, Chicago, IL	312-943-2333

SOUTHWEST

Dawson, Kim Agency/PO Box 585060, Dallas, TX	214-638-2414

ROCKY MOUNTAIN

DeRose, Mary Fran/7350 Grant Pl, Arvada, CO	303-422-2152

WEST COAST

Andre, Maurice/9426 Santa Monica Blvd, Beverly Hills, CA	213-274-4562
Antovniov/11908 Ventura Blvd, Studio City, CA	818-763-0671
Armando's/607 No Huntley Dr, W Hollywood, CA	213-657-5160
Bourget, Lorraine/559 Muskingum Pl, Pacific Palisades, CA	213-454-3739
Cassandre 2000/18386 Ventura Blvd, Tarzana, CA	818-881-8400
Cloutier Inc/704 N Gardner, Los Angeles, CA	213-655-1263
Craig, Kenneth/13211 Ventura Blvd, Studio City, CA	818-995-8717
Design Pool/11936 Darlington Ave #303, Los Angeles, CA	213-826-1551
Francisco/PO Box 49995, Los Angeles, CA	213-826-3591
Frier, George CA	213-393-0576
Gavilan/139 S Kings Rd, Los Angeles, CA	213-655-4452
Geiger, Pamela CA	213-274-5737
Hamilton, Bryan J/909 N Westbourne Dr, Los Angeles, CA	213-654-9006
Hirst, William/15130 Ventura Blvd, Sherman Oaks, CA	818-501-0993
HMS/1541 Harvard St #A, Santa Monica, CA	213-828-2080
Johns, Arthur/8661 Sunset Blvd, Hollywood, CA	213-855-9306
Ray, David Frank/15 Wave Crest, Venice, CA	213-392-5640
Samuel, Martin/6138 W 6th, Los Angeles, CA	213-930-0794
Serena, Eric/840 N Larabee, Bldg 4, W Hollywood, CA	213-652-4267
Studio Seven/261 E Rowland Ave, Covina, CA	213-331-6351
Total You Salon/1647 Los Angeles Ave, Simi, CA	805-526-4189
Towsend, Jeanne/433 N Camden Dr, Beverly Hills, CA	213-851-7044
Welsh, Franklyn/704 N LaCienega Blvd, Los Angeles, CA	213-656-8195

HAIR

NEW YORK CITY

Albert-Carter/Hotel St Moritz	212-688-2045
Benjamin Salon/104 Washington Pl	212-255-3330
Caruso, Julius/22 E 62nd St	212-751-6240
Daines, David Salon Hair Styling/833 Madison Ave	212-535-1563
George V Hair Stylist/501 Fifth Ave	212-687-9097
Moda 700/700 Madison Ave	212-935-9188
Monsieur Marc Inc/22 E 65th St	212-861-0700
Peter's Beauty Home/149 W 57th St	212-247-2934
Pierro, John/130 W 57th St	212-977-7157

NORTHEAST

Brocklebank, Tom/249 Emily Ave, Elmont, NY	516-775-5356

SOUTHEAST

Yellow Strawberry/107 E Las Olas Blvd, Ft Lauderdale, FL	305-463-4343

MIDWEST

Rodriguez, Ann/1123 W Webster, Chicago, IL	312-327-1130

PRODUCTION/SUPPORT SERVICES

SOUTHWEST

Southern Hair Designs/3563 Far West Blvd, Austin, TX	512-346-1734

ROCKY MOUNTAIN

City Lights Hair Designs/2845 Wyandote, Denver, CO	303-458-0131
Zee for Hair/316 E Hopkins, Aspen, CO	303-925-4434

WEST COAST

Anatra, M Haircutters/530 No LaCienega, Los Angeles, CA	213-657-1495
Barronson Hair/11908 Ventura, Studio City, CA	818-763-4337
Beck, Shirley CA	213-763-2930
Edwards, Allen/455 N Rodeo Dr, Beverly Hills, CA	213-274-8575
Ely, Shannon/616 Victoria, Venice, CA	213-392-5832
Fisher, Jim/c/o Rumours, 9014 Melrose, Los Angeles, CA	213-550-5946
Francisco/PO Box 49995, Los Angeles, CA	213-826-3591
Grieve, Ginger CA	818-347-2947
Gurasich, Lynda CA	818-981-6719
The Hair Conspiracy/11923 Ventura Blvd, Studio City, CA	818-985-1126
Hjerpe, Warren/9018 Beverly Blvd, Los Angeles, CA	213-550-5946
HMS/1541 Harvard St #A, Santa Monica, CA	213-828-2080
Iverson, Betty CA	213-462-2301
John, Michael Salon/414 N Camden Dr, Beverly Hills, CA	213-278-8333
Kemp, Lola CA	213-293-8710
Lorenz, Barbara CA	213-657-0028
Malone, John CA	213-246-1649
Menage a Trois/8822 Burton Way, Beverly Hills, CA	213-278-4431
Miller, Patty CA	818-843-5208
Morrissey, Jimie CA	213-657-4318
Payne, Allen CA	213-395-5259
Phillips, Marilyn CA	213-923-6996
Sami/1230 N Horn Ave #525, Los Angeles, CA	213-652-5816
Sassoon, Vidal Inc/2049 Century Park E #3800, Los Angeles, CA	213-553-6100
Trainoff, Linda CA	818-769-0373
Vecchio, Faith CA	818-345-6152

MAKE-UP

NEW YORK CITY

Adams, Richard/130 W 57th St	212-977-7157
Armand/147 W 35th St	212-947-2186
Bertoli, Michele/264 Fifth Ave	212-684-2480
Bonzignor's Cosmetics/110 Fulton	212-267-1108
Lawrence, Rose/444 E 82nd St	212-861-7225
Make-Up Center Ltd/150 W 55th St	212-977-9494
Richardson, John Ltd/119 E 64th St	212-772-1874
Ross, Rose Cosmetics/16 W 55th St	212-586-2590
Sartin, Janet of Park Ave Ltd/480 Park Ave	212-751-5858
Stage Light Cosmetics Ltd/630 Ninth Ave	212-757-4851
Suzanne de Paris/509 Madison Ave	212-838-4024

NORTHEAST

Damaskos-Zilber, Zoe/78 Waltham St #4, Boston, MA	617-628-6583
Douglas, Rodney N/473 Avon Ave #3, Newark, NJ	201-375-2979
Fiorina, Frank/2400 Hudson Terr #5A, Fort Lee, NJ	212-242-3900
Gilmore, Robert Assoc Inc/990 Washington St, Dedham, MA	617-329-6633
Meth, Miriam/96 Greenwood Ln, White Plains, NY	212-787-5400
Minassian, Amie/62-75 Austin St, Rego Park, NY	212-446-8048
Phillipe, Louise Miller/22 Chestnut Pl, Brookline, MA	617-566-3608
Phillipe, Robert/22 Chestnut Pl, Brookline, MA	617-566-3608
Rothman, Ginger/1915 Lyttonsville Rd, Silver Spring, MD	703-241-4556
Something Special/1601 Walter Reed Dr S, Arlington, VA	703-892-0551
Zack, Sandra/94 Orient Ave, East Boston, MA	617-567-7581

SOUTHEAST

Star Styled of Miami/475 NW 42nd Ave, Miami, FL	305-541-2424
Star Styled of Tampa/4235 Henderson Blvd, Tampa, FL	813-872-8706

SOUTHWEST

ABC Theatrical Rental & Sales/825 N 7th St, Phoenix, AZ	602-258-5265
Chelsea Cutters/One Chelsea Pl, Houston, TX	713-529-4813
Copeland, Tom/502 West Grady, Austin, TX	512-835-0208
Corey, Irene/4147 Herschel Ave, Dallas, TX	214-528-4836
Dobes, Pat/1826 Nocturne, Houston, TX	713-465-8102
Ingram, Marilyn Wyrick/10545 Chesterton Drive, Dallas, TX	214-349-2113
Stamm, Louis M/721 Edgehill Dr, Hurst, TX	817-268-5037

ROCKY MOUNTAIN

Moen, Brenda CO	303-871-9506

WEST COAST

Astier, Guy/11936 Darlington Ave #303, Los Angeles, CA	213-826-1551
Blackman, Charles F/12751 Addison, N Hollywood, CA	818-761-2177
Blackman, Gloria/12751 Addison, N Hollwyood, CA	818-761-2177
Case, Tom/5150 Woodley, Encino, CA	818-788-5268
Cooper, David/3616 Effie, Los Angeles, CA	213-660-7326
Cosmetic Connection/9484 Dayton Way, Beverly Hills, CA	213-550-6242
D'Ifray, T J/468 N Bedford Dr, Beverly Hills, CA	213-274-6776
Dawn, Wes/11113 Hortense St, N Hollywood, CA	818-761-7517
Fradkin, Joanne c/o Pigments/8822 Burton Way, Beverly Hills, CA	213-858-7038
Francisco/PO Box 49995, Los Angeles, CA	213-826-3591
Freed, Gordon CA	818-360-9473
Geike, Ziggy CA	818-789-1465
Henrriksen, Ole/8601 W Sunset Blvd, Los Angeles, CA	213-854-7700
Howell, Deborah/291 S Martel Ave, Los Angeles, CA	213-655-1263
Koelle, c/o Pigments/8822 Burton Way, Beverly Hills, CA	213-668-1690
Kruse, Lee C CA	818-894-5408
Laurent, c/o Menage a Trois/8822 Burton Way, Beverly Hills, CA	213-278-4430
Logan, Kathryn CA	818-988-7038
Malone, John E CA	818-247-5160
Manges, Delanie (Dee) CA	818-763-3311
Maniscalco, Ann S CA	818-894-5408
Menage a Trois/8822 Burton Way, Beverly Hills, CA	213-278-4431
Minch, Michelle/339 S Detroit St, Los Angeles, CA	213-484-9648
Natasha/4221 1/2 Avocado St, Los Angeles, CA	213-663-1477
Nielsen, Jim CA	213-461-2168
Nye, Dana CA	213-477-0443
Odessa/1448 1/2 N Fuller Ave, W Hollywood, CA	213-876-5779
Palmieri, Dante CA	213-396-6020
Penelope	213-654-6747
Pigments/8822 Burton Way, Beverly Hills, CA	213-858-7038
Romero, Bob/5030 Stern Ave, Sherman Oaks, CA	818-891-3338
Rumours/9014 Melrose, W Hollywood, CA	213-550-5946
Sanders, Nadia CA	213-465-2009
Shulman, Sheryl Leigh CA	818-760-0101
Sidell, Bob	818-360-0794
Striepke, Danny/4800 #C Villa Marina, Marina Del Rey, CA	213-823-5957
Tuttle, William	213-454-2355
Tyler, Diane	415-381-5067
Warren, Dodie	818-763-3172
Westmore, Michael	818-763-3158
Westmore, Monty	818-762-2094
Winston, Stan	818-886-0630
Wolf, Barbara CA	213-466-4660

Please send us your additions and updates.

STYLISTS

NEW YORK CITY

Baldassano, Irene/16 W 16th St	212-255-8567
Bandiero, Paul/PO Box 121 FDR Station	212-586-3700
Batteau, Sharon/130 W 57th St	212-977-7157
Beauty Bookings/130 W 57th St	212-977-7157
Benner, Dyne (Food)/311 E 60th St	212-688-7571
Berman, Benicia/399 E 72nd St	212-737-9627
Bromberg, Florence/350 Third Ave	212-255-4033
Cheverton, Linda/150 9th Avenue	212-691-0881
Chin, Fay/67 Vestry St	212-219-8770
Cohen, Susan/233 E 54th St	212-755-3157
D'Arcy, Timothy/43 W 85th St	212-580-8804
Davidson/Frank Photo-Stylists/209 W 86th St #701	212-799-2651
DeJesu, Joanna (Food)/101 W 23rd St	212-255-3895
Eller, Ann/7816 Third Ave	718-238-5454
Final Touch/55-11 13th Ave	718-435-6800
Galante, Kathy/9 W 31st St	212-239-0412
George, Georgia A/404 E 55th St	212-759-4131
Goldberg, Hal/11 Fifth Ave	212-982-7588
Greene, Jan/200 E 17th St	212-233-8989
Herman, Joan/15 W 84th St	212-724-3287
Joffe, Carole Reiff/233 E 34th St	212-725-4928
Klein, Mary Ellen/330 E 33rd St	212-683-6351
Lakin, Gaye/345 E 81st St	212-861-1892
Levin, Laurie/55 Perry St	212-242-2611
Lopes, Sandra/444 E 82nd St	212-249-8706
Magidson, Peggy/182 Amity St	212-508-7604
McCabe, Christine/200 W 79th St	212-799-4121
Meshejian, Zabel/125 Washington Pl	212-242-2459
Meyers, Pat/436 W 20th St	212-620-0069
Minch, Deborah Lee/175 W 87th St	212-873-7915
Nagle, Patsy/242 E 38th St	212-682-0364
Orefice, Jeanette/	718-643-8266
Ouellette, Dawn/336 E 30th St	212-799-9190
Peacock, Linda/118 W 88th St	212-580-1422
Reilly, Veronica/60 Gramercy Park N	212-840-1234
Sampson, Linda/431 W Broadway	212-925-6821
Scherman, Joan/450 W 24th St	212-620-0475
Schoenberg, Marv/878 West End Ave #10A	212-663-1418
Seymour, Celeste/130 E 75th St	212-744-3545
Sheffy, Nina/838 West End Ave	212-662-0709
Slote, Ina/7 Park Ave	212-679-4584
Smith, Rose/400 E 56th St #19D	212-758-8711
Specht, Meredith/166 E 61st St	212-832-0750
Weithorn, Rochelle/431 E 73rd St	212-472-8668
West, Susan/59 E 7th St	212-982-8228

NORTHEAST

Bailey Designs/110 Williams St, Malden, MA	617-321-4448
Baldwin, Katherine/109 Commonwealth Ave, Boston, MA	617-267-0508
E-Fex/623 Pennsylvania Ave SE, Washington, DC	202-543-1241
Gold, Judy/40 Sulgrave Rd, Scarsdale, NY	914-723-5036
Maggio, Marlene - Aura Prdtns/Brook Hill Ln Ste 5E, Rochester, NY	716-381-8053
Rosemary's Cakes Inc/299 Rutland Ave, Teaneck, NJ	201-833-2417
Rothman, Ginger/1915 Lyttonsville Rd, Silver Spring, MD	703-241-4556
Rubin, L A/359 Harvard St #2, Cambridge, MA	617-576-1808

SOUTHEAST

Foodworks/1541 Colonial Ter, Arlington, VA	703-524-2606
Gaffney, Janet D/464 W Wesley N W, Atlanta, GA	404-355-7556
Kupersmith, Tony/320 N Highland Ave NE, Atlanta, GA	404-577-5319
Parker, Julie Hill/PO Box 19033, Jacksonville, FL	904-724-8483
Polvay, Marina Assoc/9250 NE 10th Ct, Miami Shores, FL	305-759-4375

Torres, Martha/927 Third St, New Orleans, LA	504-895-6570

MIDWEST

Alan, Jean/1032 W Altgeld, Chicago, IL	312-929-9768
Carlson, Susan/255 Linden Park Pl, Highland Park, IL	312-433-2466
Carter, Karen/3323 N Kenmore, Chicago, IL	312-935-2901
Chevaux Ltd/908 W Armitage, Chicago, IL	312-935-5212
Emruh Style Design/714 W Fullerton, Chicago, IL	312-871-4659
Erickson, Emily/2954 No Racine, Chicago, IL	312-281-4899
Heller, Nancy/1142 W Diversey, Chicago, IL	312-549-4486
Lapin, Kathy Santis/925 Spring Hill Dr, Northbrook, IL	312-272-7487
Mary, Wendy/719 W Wrightwood, Chicago, IL	312-871-5476
Pace, Leslie/6342 N Sheridan, Chicago, IL	312-761-2480
Perry, Lee Ann/1615 No Clybourne, Chicago, IL	312-649-1815
Pohn, Carol/2259 N Wayne, Chicago, IL	312-348-0751
Rabert, Bonnie/2230 W Pratt, Chicago, IL	312-743-7755
Sager, Sue/875 N Michigan, Chicago, IL	312-642-3789
Seeker, Christopher/100 E Walton #21D, Chicago, IL	312-944-4311
Shaver, Betsy/3714 N Racine, Chicago, IL	312-327-5615
Style Vasilak and Nebel/314 W Institute Pl, Chicago, IL	312-280-8516
Weber-Mack, Kathleen/2119 Lincoln, Evanston, IL	312-869-7794

SOUTHWEST

Bishop, Cindy/6101 Charlotte, Houston, TX	713-666-7224
Janet-Nelson/PO Box 143, Tempe, AZ	602-968-3771
Taylor, John Michael/2 Dallas Commun Complex #, Irving, TX	214-823-1333
Thomas, Jan/5651 East Side Ave, Dallas, TX	214-823-1955

ROCKY MOUNTAIN

DeRose, Mary Fran/7350 Grant Pl, Arvada, CO	303-422-2152

WEST COAST

Akimbo Prod/801 Westbourne, W Hollywood, CA	213-657-4657
Alaimo, Doris/8800 Wonderland Ave, Los Angeles, CA	213-851-7044
Allen, Jamie R/, Los Angeles, CA	213-655-9351
Altbaum, Patti/244-CS Lasky Dr, Beverly Hills, CA	213-553-6269
Azzara, Marilyn/3165 Ellington Drive, Los Angeles, CA	213-851-0531
Castaldi, Debbie/10518 Wilshire Blvd #25, Los Angeles, CA	213-475-4312
Chinamoon/642 S Burnside Ave #6, Los Angeles, CA	213-937-8251
Corwin-Hankin, Aleka/1936 Cerro Gordo, Los Angeles, CA	213-665-7953
Craig, Kenneth/13211 Ventura Blvd, Studio City, CA	818-995-8717
Davis, Rommie/4414 La Venta Dr, West Lake Village, CA	818-906-1455
Design Pool/11936 Darlington Ave #303, Los Angeles, CA	213-826-1551
Frank, Tobi/1269 N Hayworth, Los Angeles, CA	213-552-7921
Gaffin, Lauri/1123-12th St, Santa Monica, CA	213-451-2045
Governor, Judy/963 North Point, San Francisco, CA	415-861-5733
Graham, Victory/24 Ave 26, Venice, CA	213-934-0990
Granas, Marilyn/200 N Almont Dr, Beverly Hills, CA	213-278-3773
Griswald, Sandra/963 North Point, San Francisco, CA	415-775-4272
Hamilton, Bryan J/1269 N Hayworth, Los Angeles, CA	213-654-9006
Hewett, Julie/7551 Melrose Ave, Los Angeles, CA	213-651-5172
Hirsch, Lauren/858 Devon, Los Angeles, CA	213-271-7052
HMS/1541 Harvard St #A, Santa Monica, CA	213-828-2080
Howell, Deborah/219 S Martel Ave, Los Angeles, CA	213-655-1263
James, Elizabeth/5320 Bellingham Ave, N Hollywood, CA	213-761-5718
Kimball, Lynnda/133 S Peck Dr, Beverly Hills, CA	213-461-6303
King, Max/308 N Sycamore Ave, Los Angeles, CA	213-938-0108
Lawson, Karen/6836 Lexington Ave, Hollywood, CA	213-464-5770
Lynch, Jody/19130 Pacific Coast Hwy, Malibu, CA	213-456-2383
Material Eyes/501 Pacific Ave, San Francisco, CA	415-362-8143
Miller, Freyda/1412 Warner Ave, Los Angeles, CA	213-474-5034
Minot, Abby/53 Canyon Rd, Berkeley, CA	415-841-9600
Moore, Francie/842 1/2 N Orange Dr, Los Angeles, CA	213-462-5404
Morrow, Suzanne/26333 Silver Spur, Palos Verdes, CA	213-378-2909
Neal, Robin Lynn/3105 Durand, Hollywood, CA	213-465-6037
Olsen, Eileen/1619 N Beverly Dr, Beverly Hills, CA	213-273-4496
Parshall, Mary Ann/19850 Pacific Coast Hwy, Malibu, CA	213-456-8303
Prindle, Judy Peck/6057 Melrose Ave, Los Angeles, CA	213-650-0962

Russo, Leslie/377 10th, Santa Monica, CA	213-395-8461
Shatsy/9008 Harratt St, Hollywood, CA	213-275-2413
Skinner, Jeanette/1622 Moulton Pkwy #A, Tustin, CA	714-730-5793
Skinner, Randy/920 S Wooster St, Los Angeles, CA	213-659-2936
Skuro, Bryna/134-B San Vicente Blvd, Santa Monica, CA	213-394-2430
Sloane, Hilary/6351 Ranchito, Van Nuys, CA	213-855-1010
Surkin, Helen/2100 N Beachwood Dr, Los Angeles, CA	213-464-6847
Thomas, Lisa/9029 Rangely Ave, W Hollywood, CA	213-858-6903
Townsend, Jeanne/433 N Camden Dr, Beverly Hills, CA	213-851-7044
Tucker, Joan/1402 N Fuller St, Los Angeles, CA	213-876-3417
Tyre, Susan/, CA, 213-877-3884	
Valade/ CA, 213-659-7621	
Weinberg & James Foodstyle/3888 Woodcliff Rd, Sherman Oaks, CA	213-274-2383
Weiss, Sheri/2170 N Beverly Glen, Los Angeles, CA	213-470-1650

COSTUMES

NEW YORK CITY

Academy Clothes Inc/1703 Broadway	212-765-1440
AM Costume Wear/135-18 Northern Blvd	718-358-8108
Austin Ltd/140 E 55th St	212-752-7903
Capezio Dance Theater Shop/755 Seventh Ave	212-245-2130
Chenko Studio/167 W 46th St	212-944-0215
David's Outfitters Inc/36 W 20th St	212-691-7388
Eaves-Brookes Costume/21-07 41st Ave	718-729-1010
G Bank's Theatrical & Custom/320 W 48th St	212-586-6476
Grace Costumes Inc/254 W 54th St	212-586-0260
Herbert Danceware Co/902 Broadway	212-677-7606
Ian's Boutique Inc/1151-A Second Ave	212-838-3969
Karinska/16 W 61st St	212-247-3341
Kulyk/72 E 7th St	212-674-0414
Lane Costume Co/234 Fifth Ave	212-684-4721
Martin, Alice Manougian/239 E 58th St	212-688-0117
Meyer, Jimmy & Co/428 W 44th St	212-765-8079
Michael-Jon Costumes Inc/39 W 19th St	212-741-3440
Mincou, Christine/405 E 63rd St	212-838-3881
Purcell, Elizabeth/105 Sullivan St	212-925-1962
Rubie's Costume Co/1 Rubie Plaza	718-846-1008
Sampler Vintage Clothes/455 W 43rd St	212-757-8168
Stivanello Costume Co Inc/66-38 Clinton Ave	718-651-7715
Tint, Francine/1 University Pl	212-475-3366
Universal Costume Co Inc/1540 Broadway	212-575-8570
Weiss & Mahoney Inc/142 Fifth Ave	212-675-1915
Winston, Mary Ellen/11 E 68th St	212-879-0766
Ynocencio, Jo/302 E 88th St	212-348-5332

NORTHEAST

At-A-Glance Rentals/712 Main, Boonton, NJ	201-335-1488
Baldwin, Katharine/109 Commonwealth Ave, Boston, MA	617-267-0508
Barris, Alfred Wig Maker/10 E Sirtsink Dr, Pt Washington, NY	516-883-9061
Costume Armour Inc/Shore Rd Box 325, Cornwall on Hudson, NY	914-534-9120
Douglas, Rodney N/473 Avon Ave #3, Newark, NJ	201-375-2979
House of Costumes Ltd/166 Jericho Tpk, Mineola, NY	516-294-0170
Penrose Productions/4 Sandalwood Dr, Livingston, NJ	201-992-4264
Westchester Costume Rentals/540 Nepperhan Ave, Yonkers, NY	914-963-1333

SOUTHEAST

ABC Costume/185 NE 59th St, Miami, FL	305-757-3492
Atlantic Costume Co/2089 Monroe Dr, Atlanta, GA	404-874-7511
Carol, Lee Inc/2145 NW 2nd Ave, Miami, FL	305-573-1759
Fun Stop Shop/1601 Biscyne Blvd Omni Int F27, Miami, FL	305-358-2003
Goddard, Lynn Prod Svcs/712 Pelican Ave, New Orleans, LA	504-367-0348
Poinciana Sales/2252 W Flagler St, Miami, FL	305-642-3441
Star Styled/475 NW 42nd Ave, Miami, FL	305-649-3030

MIDWEST

Advance Theatrical Co/1900 N Narragansett, Chicago, IL	312-889-7700
Backstage Enterprises/1525 Ellinwood, Des Plaines, IL	312-692-6159
Be Something Studio/5533 N Forest Glen, Chicago, IL	312-685-6717
Broadway Costumes Inc/932 W Washington, Chicago, IL	312-829-6400
Brune, Paul/6330 N Indian Rd, Chicago, IL	312-763-1117
Center Stage/Fox Valley Shopping Cntr, Aurora, IL	312-851-9191
Chicago Costume Co Inc/1120 W Fullerton, Chicago, IL	312-528-1264
Ennis, Susan/2961 N Lincoln Ave, Chicago, IL	312-525-7483
Kaufman Costumes/5117 N Western, Chicago, IL	312-561-7529
Magical Mystery Tour, Ltd/6010 Dempster, Morton Grove, IL	312-966-5090
Okains Costume & Theater/2713 W Jefferson, Joliet, IL	815-741-9303
Stechman's Creations/1920 Koehler, Des Plaines, IL	312-827-9045
Taylor, Corinna/1700B W Granville, Chicago, IL	312-472-6550
Toy Gallery/1640 N Wells, Chicago, IL	312-944-4323

SOUTHWEST

A & J Costume Rental, Dsgn & Const/304 White Oaks Dr, Austin, TX	512-836-2733
ABC Theatrical Rental & Sales/825 N 7th St, Phoenix, AZ	602-258-5265
Abel, Joyce/Rt 1 Box 165, San Marcos, TX	512-392-5659
Campioni, Frederick/1920 Broken Oak, San Antonio, TX	512-342-7780
Corey, Irene/4147 Herschel Ave, Dallas, TX	214-528-4836
Incredible Productions/3327 Wylie Dr, Dallas, TX	214-350-3633
Lucy Greer & Assoc. Casting/600 Shadywood Ln, Richardson, TX	214-231-2086
Moreau, Suzanne/1007-B West 22nd St, Austin, TX	512-477-1532
Nicholson, Christine/c/o Lola Sprouse, Carrollton, TX	214-245-0926
Old Time Teenies Vintage Clothing/1126 W 6th St, Austin, TX	512-477-2022
Second Childhood/900 W 18th St, Austin, TX	512-472-9696
Starline Costume Products/1286 Bandera Rd, San Antonio, TX	512-435-3535
Thomas, Joan S/6904 Spanky Branch Court, Dallas, TX	214-931-1900
Welch, Virginia/3707 Manchaca Rd #138, Austin, TX	512-447-1240

ROCKY MOUNTAIN

And Sew On-Jila/2017 Broadway, Boulder, CO	303-442-0130
Raggedy Ann Clothing & Costume/1213 E Evans Ave, Denver, CO	303-733-7937

WEST COAST

Aardvark/7579 Melrose Ave, Los Angeles, CA	213-655-6769
Adele's of Hollywood/5059 Hollywood Blvd, Hollywood, CA	213-663-2231
American Costume Corp/12980 Raymer, N Hollywood, CA	818-764-2239
Auntie Mame/1102 S La Cienaga Blvd, Los Angeles, CA	213-652-8430
Boserup House of Canes/1636 Westwood Blvd, W Los Angeles, CA	213-474-2577
The Burbank Studios Wardrobe Dept/4000 Warner Blvd, Burbank, CA	818-954-1218
California Surplus Mart/6263 Santa Monica Blvd, Los Angeles, CA	213-465-5525
Capezio Dancewear/1777 Vine St, Hollywood, CA	213-465-3744
CBS Wardrobe Dept/7800 Beverly Blvd, Los Angeles, CA	213-852-2345
Courtney, Elizabeth/8636 Melrose Ave, Los Angeles, CA	213-657-4361
Crystal Palace (Sales)/8457 Melrose Ave, Hollywood, CA	818-761-1870
Design Studio/6685-7 Sunset Blvd, Hollywood, CA	213-469-3661
E C 2 Costumes/431 S Fairfax, Los Angeles, CA	213-934-1131
Fantasy Costume/4310 San Fernando Rd, Glendale, CA	213-245-7367
International Costume Co/1269 Sartori, Torrance, CA	213-320-6392
Kings Western Wear/6455 Van Nuys Blvd, Van Nuys, CA	818-785-2586
Krofft Entertainment/7200 Vineland Ave, Sun Valley, CA	213-875-0324
LA Uniform Exchange/5239 Melrose Ave, Los Angeles, CA	213-469-3965
MGM/UA Studios Wardrobe Dept/10202 W Washington Blvd, Culver City, CA	213-558-5600
Military Antiques & War Museum/208 Santa Monica Ave, Santa Monica, CA	213-393-1180
Minot, Abby/53 Canyon Rd, Berkeley, CA	415-841-9600

Please send us your additions and updates.

Nudies Rodeo Tailor/5015 Lanskershim Blvd, N Hollywood, CA	818-762-3105
Palace Costume/835 N Fairfax, Los Angeles, CA	213-651-5458
Paramount Studios Wardrobe Dept/5555 Melrose Ave, Hollywood, CA	213-468-5288
Peabodys/1102 1/2 S La Cienega Blvd, Los Angeles, CA	213-352-3810
Piller's, Jerry/8163 Santa Monica Blvd, Hollywood, CA	213-654-3038
Tuxedo Center/7360 Sunset Blvd, Los Angeles, CA	213-874-4200
Valu Shoe Mart/5637 Santa Monica Blvd, Los Angeles, CA	213-469-8560
Western Costume Co/5335 Melrose Ave, Los Angeles, CA	213-469-1451

PROPS

NEW YORK CITY

Abet Rent-A-Fur/307 Seventh Ave	212-989-5757
Abstracta Structures Inc/347 Fifth Ave	212-532-3710
Ace Galleries/91 University Pl	212-991-4536
Adirondack Direct/219 E 42nd St	212-687-8555
Alice's Antiques/552 Columbus Ave	212-874-3400
Alpha-Pavia Bookbinding Co Inc/55 W 21st St	212-929-5430
Archer Surgical Supplies Inc/544 W 27th St	212-695-5553
Artisan's Studio/232 Atlantic Ave	718-855-2796
Artistic Neon by Gasper/75-49 61st St	718-821-1550
Arts & Crafters/175 Johnson St	718-875-8151
Arts & Flowers/234 W 56th St	212-247-7610
Associated Theatrical Designer/220 W 71st St	212-362-2648
Austin Display/139 W 19th St	212-924-6261
Baird, Bill Marionettes/41 Union Square	212-989-9840
Baker, Alex/30 W 69th St	212-799-2069
Bill's Flower Mart/816 Ave of the Americas	212-889-8154
Brandon Memorabilia/222 E 51st St	212-691-9776
Breitrose, Mark/156 Fifth Ave	212-242-7825
Brooklyn Model Works/60 Washington Ave	718-834-1944
California Artificial Flower Co/225 Fifth Ave	212-679-7774
Carroll Musical Instrument Svc/351 W 41st St	212-868-4120
Chateau Stables Inc/608 W 48th St	212-246-0520
Churchill/Winchester Furn Rental/44 E 32nd St	212-535-3400
Cooper Film Cars/132 Perry St	212-929-3909
Cycle Service Center Inc/74 Sixth Ave	212-925-5900
Doherty Studios/252 W 46th St	212-840-6219
Eclectic Properties Inc/204 W 84th St	212-799-8963
Encore Studio/410 W 47th St	212-246-5237
Florenco Foliage Systems Inc/30-28 Starr Ave	718-729-6600
Furs, Valerie/150 W 30th St	212-947-2020
Golden Equipment Co Inc/422 Madison Ave	212-838-3776
Gordon Novelty Co/933 Broadway	212-254-8616
Gossard & Assocs Inc/801 E 134th St	212-665-9194
Gothic Color Co Inc/727 Washington St	212-929-7493
Guccione/333 W 39th St	212-279-3602
Harra, John Wood & Supply Co/39 W 19th St, 11th Fl	212-741-0290
Harrison/Erickson/95 Fifth Ave	212-929-5700
Jeffers, Kathy-Modelmaking/106 E 19th St 12th Fl	212-475-1756
Joyce, Robert Studio Ltd/321 W 44th St #404	212-586-5041
Kaplan, Howard/35 E 10th St	212-674-1000
Karpen, Ben/212 E 51st St	212-755-3450
Kempler, George J/160 Fifth Ave	212-989-1180
Kenmore Furniture Co Inc/156 E 33rd St	212-683-1888
Mallie, Dale & Co/35-30 38th St	718-706-1234
The Manhattan Model Shop/40 Great Jones St	212-473-6312
Manhattan Model Shop/40 Great Jones St	212-473-6312
Maniatis, Michael Inc/48 W 22nd St	212-620-0398
Manwaring Studio/232 Atlantic Ave	718-855-2796
Marc Modell Associates/430 W 54th St	212-541-9676
Mason's Tennis Mart/911 Seventh Ave	212-757-5374
Matty's Studio Sales/543 W 35th St	212-757-6246
McConnell & Borow Inc/10 E 23rd St	212-254-1486
Mendez, Raymond A/220 W 98th St #12B	212-864-4689
Messmore & Damon Inc/530 W 28th St	212-594-8070
Metro Scenery Studio Inc/215-31 99th Ave	718-464-6328

Modern Miltex Corp/280 E 134th St	212-585-6000
Morozko, Bruce/41 White St	212-226-8832
Movie Cars/825 Madison Ave	212-288-6000
Newell Art Galleries Inc/425 E 53rd St	212-758-1970
Nostalgia Alley Antiques/547 W 27th St	212-695-6578
Novel Pinball Co/593 Tenth Ave	212-736-3868
The Place for Antiques/993 Second Ave	212-475-6596
Plant Specialists Inc/524 W 34th St	212-279-1500
Plastic Works /2107 Broadway @ 73rd	212-362-1000
Plexability Ltd/200 Lexington Ave	212-679-7826
Porter-Rayvid/155 Attorney	212-460-5050
Portobello Road Antiques Ltd/370 Columbus Ave	212-724-2300
The Prop House Inc/76 Ninth Ave	212-691-9099
The Prop Shop/26 College Pl	718-522-4606
Props and Displays/132 W 18th St	212-620-3840
Props for Today/15 W 20th St	212-206-0330
Ray Beauty Supply Co Inc/721 Eighth Ave	212-757-0175
Ridge, John Russell/531 Hudson St	212-929-3410
Say It In Neon/434 Hudson St	212-691-7977
Simon's Dir of Theatrical Mat/27 W 24th St	212-255-2872
Smith & Watson/305 E 63rd St	212-355-5615
Smith, David/	212-730-1188
Solco Plumbing Suplies & Bathtubs/209 W 18th St	212-243-2569
Special Effects/40 W 39th St	212-869-8636
Starbuck Studio - Acrylic props/162 W 21st St	212-807-7299
State Supply Equipment Co Inc/68 Thomas St	212-233-0474
Theater Technology Inc/37 W 20th St	212-929-5380
Times Square Theatrical & Studio/318 W 47th St	212-245-4155
Uncle Sam's Umbrella/161 W 57th St	212-582-1976
Whole Art Inc/259 W 30th St	212-868-0978
Wizardworks/67 Atlantic Ave	718-349-5252
Zakarian, Robert Prop Shop Inc/26 College Pl	718-522-4606
Zeller, Gary & Assoc/Special Effects/40 W 39th St	212-869-8636

NORTHEAST

Antique Bicycle Props Service/113 Woodland Ave, Montvale, NJ	201-391-8780
Atlas Scenic Studios Ltd/46 Brokfield Ave, Bridgeport, CT	203-334-2130
Baily Designs/110 Williams St, Malden, MA	617-321-4448
Baldwin, Katherine/109 Commonwealth Ave, Boston, MA	617-267-0508
Bestek Theatrical Productions/218 Hoffman, Babylon, NY	516-225-0707
Cadillac Convertible Owners/, Thiells, NY	914-947-1109
Dewart, Tim Assoc/83 Old Standley St, Beverly, MA	617-922-9229
Geiger, Ed/12 Church St, Middletown, NJ	201-671-1707
Hart Scenic Studio/35-41 Dempsey Ave, Edgewater, NJ	212-947-7264
L I Auto Museum/Museum Square, South Hampton, NY	516-283-1880
Master & Talent Inc/1139 Foam Place, Far Rockaway, NY	516-239-7719
Model Sonics/272 Ave F, Bayonne, NJ	201-436-6721
Newbery, Tomas/Ridge Rd, Glen Cove, NY	516-759-0880
Pennington Inc/72 Edmund St, Edison, NJ	201-985-9090
Rindner, Jack N Assoc/112 Water St, Tinton Falls, NJ	201-542-3548
Stewart, Chas H Co/6 Clarendon Ave, Sommerville, MA	617-625-2407

SOUTHEAST

Alderman Company/325 Model Farm Rd, High Point, NC	919-889-6121
Arawak Marine/PO Box 7362, St Thomas, VI	809-775-1858
Charisma Prod Services/PO Box 19033, Jacksonville, FL	904-724-8483
Crigler, MB/Smooth As Glass Prod Svcs/607 Bass St, Nashville, TN	615-254-6061
Dangar, Jack/3640 Ridge Rd, Smyrna, GA	404-434-3640
Dunwright Productions/15281 NE 21st Ave, N Miami Beach, FL	305-944-2464
Enter Space/20 14th St NW, Atlanta, GA	404-885-1139
Kupersmith, Tony/320 N Highland Ave NE, Atlanta, GA	404-577-5319
Manning, Maureen/1283 Cedar Heights Dr, Stone Mountain, GA	404-296-1520
Miller, Lee/Rte 1, Box 98, Lumpkin, GA	912-838-4959
Player, Joanne/3403 Orchard St, Hapeville, GA	404-767-5542
S C Educational TV/2712 Millwood Ave, Columbia, SC	803-758-7284
Smith, Roscoe/15 Baltimore Pl NW, Atlanta, GA	404-252-3540
Sugar Creek Studio Inc/16 Young St, Atlanta, GA	404-522-3270

Please send us your additions and updates.

Sunshine Scenic Studios/1370 4th St, Sarasota, FL	813-366-8848
Winslow, Geoffrey C/1027 North Ave, Atlanta, GA	404-522-1669

MIDWEST

Advance Theatrical/125 N Wabash, Chicago, IL	312-889-7700
Becker Studios Inc/2824 W Taylor, Chicago, IL	312-722-4040
Bregstone Assoc/440 S Wabash, Chicago, IL	312-939-5130
Cadillac Plastic/1924 N Paulina, Chicago, IL	312-342-9200
Carpenter, Brent Studio/314 W Institute Pl, Chicago, IL	312-787-1774
Center Stage/Fox Valley Shopping Cntr, Aurora, IL	312-851-9191
Chanco Ltd/3131 West Grand Ave, Chicago, IL	312-638-0363
Chicago Scenic Studios Inc/2217 W Belmont Ave, Chicago, IL	312-477-8362
The Emporium/1551 N Wells, Chicago, IL	312-337-7126
Hartman Furniture & Carpet Co/220 W Kinzie, Chicago, IL	312-664-2800
Hollywood Stage Lighting/5850 N Broadway, Chicago, IL	312-869-3340
House of Drane/410 N Ashland Ave, Chicago, IL	312-829-8686
Merrick Models Ltd/1426 W Fullerton, Chicago, IL	312-281-7787
The Model Shop/415 N State St, Chicago, IL	312-822-9663
Okains Costume & Theater/2713 W Jefferson, Joliet, IL	815-741-9303
Scroungers Inc/351 Lyndale Ave S, Minneapolis, MN	612-823-2340
Starr, Steve Studios/2654 N Clark St, Chicago, IL	312-525-6530
Studio Specialties/409 W Huron, Chicago, IL	312-337-5131
White House Studios/9167 Robinson, Kansas City, MO	913-341-8036

SOUTHWEST

Creative Video Productions/5933 Bellaire Blvd #110, Houston, TX	713-661-0478
Desert Wren Designs, Inc/7340 Scottsdale Mall, Scottsdale, AZ	602-941-5056
Doerr, Dean/11321 Greystone, Oklahoma City, OK	405-751-0313
Eats/PO Box 52, Tempe, AZ	602-966-7459
Janet-Nelson/PO Box 143, Tempe, AZ	602-968-3771
Marty, Jack/2225 South First, Garland, TX	214-840-8708
Melancon, Joseph Studios/2934 Elm, Dallas, TX	214-742-2982
Southern Importers/4825 San Jacinto, Houston, TX	713-524-8236
Young Film Productions/PO Box 50105, Tucson, AZ	602-623-5961

WEST COAST

A & A Special Effects/7021 Havenhurst St, Van Nuys, CA	818-782-6558
Abbe Rents/600 S Normandie, Los Angeles, CA	213-384-5292
Aldik Artificial Flowers Co/7651 Sepulveda Blvd, Van Nuys, CA	213-988-5970
Allen, Walter Plant Rentals/5500 Melrose Ave, Hollywood, CA	213-469-3621
Altbaum, Patti/244-CS Lasky Dr, Beverly Hills, CA	213-553-6269
Anabel's Diversified Services/PO Box 532, Pacific Palisades, CA	213-454-1566
Antiquarian Traders/8483 Melrose Ave, Los Angeles, CA	213-658-6394
Arnelle Sales Co Prop House/7926 Beverly Blvd, Los Angeles, CA	213-930-2900
Asia Plant Rentals/1215 225th St, Torrance, CA	818-775-1811
Astrovision, Inc/7240 Valjean Ave, Van Nuys, CA	818-989-5222
Backings, c/o 20th Century Fox/10201 W Pico Blvd, Los Angeles, CA	213-277-0522
Baronian Manufacturing Co/1865 Farm Bureau Rd, Concord, CA	415-671-7199
Barris Kustom Inc/10811 Riverside Dr, N Hollywood, CA	213-877-2352
Barton Surrey Svc/518 Fairview Ave, Arcadia, CA	818-447-6693
Beverly Hills Fountain Center/7856 Santa Monica Blvd, Hollywood, CA	
Bischoff's/449 S San Fernando Blvd, Burbank, CA	213-843-7561
Boserup House of Canes/1636 Westwood Blvd, W Los Angeles, CA	213-474-2577
Brown, Mel Furniture/5840 S Figueroa St, Los Angeles, CA	213-778-4444
Buccaneer Cruises/Berth 76W-33 Ports O'Call, San Pedro, CA	213-548-1085
The Burbank Studios Prop Dept/4000 Warner Blvd, Burbank, CA	818-954-6000
Cinema Float/447 N Newport Blvd, Newport Beach, CA	714-675-8888
Cinema Mercantile Co/5857 Santa Monica Blvd, Hollywood, CA	213-466-8201
Cinema Props Co/5840 Santa Monica Blvd, Hollywood, CA	213-466-8201
City Lights/404 S Figueroa, Los Angeles, CA	213-680-9876
Colors of the Wind/2900 Main St, Santa Monica, CA	213-399-8044
Corham Artifical Flowers/11800 Olympic Blvd, Los Angeles, CA	213-479-1166
Custom Neon/3804 Beverly Blvd, Los Angeles, CA	213-386-7945
D'Andrea Glass Etchings/3671 Tacoma Ave, Los Angeles, CA	213-223-7940
Decorative Paper Productions/1818 W 6th St, Los Angeles, CA	213-484-1080
Deutsch Inc/426 S Robertson Blvd, Los Angeles, CA	213-273-4949
Ellis Mercantile Co/169 N LaBrea Ave, Los Angeles, CA	213-933-7334
Featherock Inc/20219 Bohama St, Chatsworth, CA	818-882-3888
First Street Furniture Store/1123 N Bronson Ave, Los Angeles, CA	213-462-6306
Flower Fashions/9960 Santa Monica Blvd, Beverly Hills, CA	213-272-6063
Games Unlimited/8924 Lindblade, Los Angeles, CA	213-836-8920
Golden West Billiard Supply/21260 Deering Court, Canoga Park, CA	213-877-4100
Grand American Fare/3008 Main St, Santa Monica, CA	213-450-4900
Haltzman Office Furniture/1417 S Figueroa, Los Angeles, CA	213-749-7021
The Hand Prop Room/5700 Venice Blvd, Los Angeles, CA	213-931-1534
Hawaii Design Create/1750 Kalakaua Ave #116, Honolulu, HI	808-235-2262
The High Wheelers Inc/109 S Hidalgo, Alhambra, CA	213-576-8648
Hollywood Toys/6562 Hollywood Blvd, Los Angeles, CA	213-465-3119
House of Props Inc/1117 N Gower St, Hollywood, CA	213-463-3166
Hume, Alex R/1527 W Magnolia, Burbank, CA	213-849-1614
Independent Studio Svcs/11907 Wicks St, Sun Valley, CA	213-764-0840
Iwasaki Images/19330 Van Ness Ave, Torrance, CA	213-533-5986
Jackson Shrub Supply/9500 Columbus Ave, Sepulveda, CA	213-893-6939
Johnson, Ray M Studio/5555 Sunset Blvd, Hollywood, CA	213-465-4108
Krofft Enterprise/1040 Las Palmas, Hollywood, CA	213-467-3125
Laughing Cat Design Co/723 1/2 N La Cienega Blvd, Los Angeles, CA	213-854-0135
Living Interiors/7273 Santa Monica Blvd, Los Angeles, CA	213-874-7815
Macduff Flying Circus/5527 Saigon St, Lancaster, CA	805-942-5406
Malibu Florists/21337 Pacific Coast Hwy, Malibu, CA	213-456-2014
Marvin, Lennie Entrprs Ltd/1105 N Hollywood Way, Burbank, CA	818-841-5882
McDermott, Kate/1114 S Point View, Los Angeles, CA	213-935-4101
MGM Studios Prop Dept/10202 W Washington Blvd, Culver City, CA	213-836-3000
Modelmakers/216 Townsend St, San Francisco, CA	415-495-5111
Mole-Richardson/937 N Sycamore Ave, Hollywood, CA	213-851-0111
Moskatels/733 S San Julian St, Los Angeles, CA	213-627-1631
Motion Picture Marine/616 Venice Blvd, Marina del Rey, CA	213-822-1100
Music Center/5616 Santa Monica Blvd, Hollywood, CA	213-469-8143
Omega Cinema Props/5857 Santa Monica Blvd, Los Angeles, CA	213-466-8201
Omega Studio Rentals/5757 Santa Monica Blvd, Hollywood, CA	213-466-8201
Pacific Palisades Florists/15244 Sunset Blvd, Pacific Palisades, CA	213-454-0337
Paramount Studios Prop Dept/5555 Melrose Ave, Los Angeles, CA	213-468-5000
Photo Productions/400 Montgomery St, San Francisco, CA	415-392-5985
The Plantation/38 Arena St, El Segundo, CA	213-322-7877
Post, Don Studios/8211 Lankershim Blvd, N Hollywood, CA	818-768-0811
Producers Studio/650 N Bronson Ave, Los Angeles, CA	213-466-7778
Professional Scenery Inc/7311 Radford Ave, N Hollywood, CA	213-875-1910
Prop City/9336 W Washington, Culver City, CA	213-559-7022
Prop Service West/918 N Orange Dr, Los Angeles, CA	213-461-3371
Rent-A-Mink/6738 Sunset Blvd, Hollywood, CA	213-467-7879
Roschu/6514 Santa Monica Blvd, Hollywood, CA	213-469-2749
Rouzer, Danny Studio/7022 Melrose Ave, Hollywood, CA	213-936-2494
Scale Model Co/4613 W Rosecrans Ave, Los Angeles, CA	213-679-1436
School Days Equipment Co/973 N Main St, Los Angeles, CA	213-223-3474
Silvestri Studios/1733 W Cordova St, Los Angeles, CA	213-735-1481
Snakes/6100 Laurel Canyon Blvd, North Hollywood, CA	213-985-7777
Special Effects Unlimited/752 N Cahuenga Blvd, Hollywood, CA	213-466-3361
Spellman Desk Co/6159 Santa Monica Blvd, Hollywood, CA	213-467-0628
Stage Right/Box 2265, Canyon Country, CA	805-251-4342
Star Sporting Goods/1645 N Highland Ave, Hollywood, CA	213-469-3531
Studio Specialties/3013 Gilroy St, Los Angeles, CA	213-480-3101

Please send us your additions and updates.

Stunts Unlimited/3518 Cahuenga Blvd W, Los Angeles, CA	213-874-0050
Surf, Val/4807 Whitsett, N Hollywood, CA	818-769-6977
Transparent Productions/3410 S Lacienaga Blvd, Los Angeles, CA	213-938-3821
Tri-Tronex Inc/2921 W Alameda Ave, Burbank, CA	213-849-6115
Tropizon Plant Rentals/1401 Pebble Vale, Monterey Park, CA	213-269-2010
UPA Pictures/4440 Lakeside Dr, Burbank, CA	213-556-3800
Western Costume Company/5335 Melrose Ave, Hollywood, CA	213-469-1451
Wizards Inc/8333 Lahui, Northridge, CA	818-368-8974

LOCATIONS

NEW YORK CITY

Act Travel/310 Madison Ave	212-697-9550
Ayoub, Jimmy/132 E 16th St	212-598-4467
C & C Productions/445 E 80th St	212-472-3700
Carmichael-Moore, Bob Inc/PO Box 5	212-255-0465
Dancerschool/400 Lafayette St	212-260-0453
Davidson/Frank Photo-Stylists/209 W 86th St #701	212-799-2651
Howell, T J Interiors/301 E 38th St	212-532-6267
Juckes, Geoff/295 Bennett Ave	212-567-5676
Kopro, Ken/206 E 6th St	212-677-1798
Leach, Ed Inc/160 Fifth Ave	212-691-3450
Location Connection/31 E 31st St	212-684-1888
Location Locators/225 E 63rd St	212-832-1866
Loft Locations/50 White St	212-966-6408
Marks, Arthur/140 E 40th St	212-685-2761
Myriad Communications, Inc/208 W 30th St	212-564-4340
NY State Film Commission/230 Park Ave #834	212-309-0540
The Perfect Place Ltd/182 Amity St	718-570-6252
Ruekberg, Brad/3211 Ave I #5H	718-377-3506
Terrestris/409 E 60th St	212-758-8181
This Must Be The Place/2119 Albermarle Terrace	718-282-3454
Unger, Captain Howard/80 Beach Rd	718-639-3578
Wolfson, Paula/227 W 10th St	212-741-3048

NORTHEAST

C-M Associates/268 New Mark, Rockville, MD	301-340-7070
Cinemagraphics/100 Massachusetts Ave, Boston, MA	617-266-2200
Connecticut State Travel Office/210 Washington St, Hartford, CT	203-566-3383
Cooper Productions/175 Walnut St, Brookline, MA	617-738-7278
Delaware State Travel Service/99 Kings Highway, Dover, DE	302-736-4254
Dobush, Jim/148 W Mountain, Ridgefield, CT	203-431-3718
E-Fex/623 Pennsylvania Ave SE, Washington, DC	202-543-1241
Film Services of WV Library Comm/1900 Washington St E, Charleston, WV	304-348-3977
Florentine Films, Inc/25 Main St, Northampton, MA	413-584-0816
Forma, Belle/433 Claflin Ave, Mamaroneck, NY	914-698-2598
Gilmore, Robert Assoc Inc/990 Washington St, Dedham, MA	617-329-6633
Girl/Scout Locations/One Hillside Ave, Port Washington, NY	516-883-8409
Great Locations/97 Windsor Road, Tenafly, NJ	201-567-1455
Hackerman, Nancy Prod Inc/6 East Eager St, Baltimore, MD	301-685-2727
Hampton Locations/109 Hill Street, South Hampton, NY	516-283-2160
The Hermitage/PO Box 4, Yorktown Heights, NY	914-632-5315
Jurgielewicz, Annie/PO Box 422, Cambridge, MA	617-628-1141
Krause, Janet L/43 Linnaean St #26, Cambridge, MA	617-492-3223
Lewis, Jay/87 Ripley St, Newton Center, MA	617-332-1516
Location Scouting Service/153 Sidney St, Oyster Bay, NY	516-922-1759
Location Unlimited/24 Briarcliff, Tenafly, NJ	201-567-2809
The Location Hunter/16 Iselin Terr, Larchmont, NY	914-834-2181
Maine State Development Office/193 State St, Augusta, ME	207-289-2656
Maryland Film Commission/45 Talvert, Annapolis, MD	301-269-3577
Massachusetts State Film Bureau/100 Cambridge St, Boston, MA	617-727-3330
McGlynn, Jack/34 Buffum St, Salem, MA	617-745-8764

Nassau Farmer's Market/600 Hicksville Rd, Bethpage, NY	516-931-2046
New Hampshire Vacation Travel/PO Box 856, Concord, NH	603-271-2666
NJ State Motion Pic Dev/Gateway One, Newark, NJ	201-648-6279
Nozik, Michael/9 Cutler Ave, Cambridge, MA	617-783-4315
Pennington Inc/72 Edmund St, Edison, NJ	201-985-9090
Pennsylvania Film Bureau/461 Forum Bldg, Harrisburg, PA	717-787-5333
Penrose Productions/4 Sandalwood Dr, Livingston, NJ	201-992-4264
PhotoSonics/1116 N Hudson St, Arlington, VA	703-522-1116
Proteus Location Services/9217 Baltimore Blvd, College Park, MD	301-441-2928
Rhode Island State Tourist Division/7 Jackson Walkway, Providence, RI	401-277-2601
Strawberries Finders Service/Buck County, Reigelsville, PA	215-346-8000
Terry, Karen/131 Boxwood Dr, Kings Park, NY	516-724-3964
Upstate Production Services, Inc/277 Alexander St #510, Rochester, NY	716-546-5417
Verange, Joe - Century III/545 Boylston St, Boston, MA	617-267-9800
Vermont State Travel Division/134 State, Montpelier, VT	802-828-3236
Washington DC Public Space Committee/415 12th St, N W Washington, DC	202-629-4084

SOUTHEAST

Alabama State Film Commission/340 North Hull St, Montgomery, AL	800-633-5898
Baker, Sherry/1823 Indiana Ave, Atlanta, GA	404-373-6666
Bruns, Ken & Gayle/7810 SW 48th Court, Miami, FL	305-666-2928
Charisma Prod Services/PO Box 19033, Jacksonville, FL	904-724-8483
Crigler, MB/Smooth As Glass Prod Svcs/607 Bass St, Nashville, TN	615-254-6061
Dangar, Jack/3640 Ridge Rd, Smyrna, GA	404-434-3640
Darracott, David/1324 Briarcliff Rd #5, Atlanta, GA	404-872-0219
Fl State Motion Picture/TV Svcs/107 W Gaines St, Tallahassee, FL	904-487-1100
Georgia State Film Office/PO Box 1776, Atlanta, GA	404-656-3591
Harris, George/2875 Mabry Lane NE, Atlanta, GA	404-231-0116
Irene Marie/3212 S Federal Hwy, Ft Lauderdale, FL	305-522-3262
Kentucky Film Comm/Berry Hill Mansion/Louisville, Frankfort, KY	502-564-3456
Kupersmith, Tony/320 N Highland Ave NE, Atlanta, GA	404-577-5319
McDonald, Stew/6905 N Coolidge Ave, Tampa, FL	813-886-3773
Miller, Lee/Rte 1, Box 98, Lumpkin, GA	912-838-4959
Mississippi State Film Commission/PO Box 849, Jackson, MS	601-359-3449
Natchez Film Comm/Liberty Pk Hwy, Hwy 16, Natchez, MS	601-446-6345
North Carolina Film Comm/430 N Salisbury St, Raleigh, NC	919-733-9900
Player, Joanne/3403 Orchard St, Hapeville, GA	404-767-5542
Reel Wheels/2267 NE 164th St, Miami, FL	305-947-9304
Remington Models & Talent/2480 E Commercial Blvd PH, Ft Lauderdale, FL	305-566-5420
Rose, Sheila/8218 NW 8th St, Plantation, FL	305-473-9747
South Florida Location Finders/7621 SW 59th Court, S Miami, FL	305-445-0739
Tennessee Film Comm/James Polk Off Bldg, Nashville, TN	615-741-3456
TN State Econ & Comm Dev/1007 Andrew Jackson Bldg, Nashville, TN	615-741-1888
USVI Film Promotion Office/, St Thomas, VI	809-774-1331
Virginia Division of Tourism/202 North 9th St, Richmond, VA	804-786-2051

MIDWEST

A-Stock Photo Finder/1030 N State St, Chicago, IL	312-645-0611
Illinois State Film Office/100 W Randolph #3-400, Chicago, IL	312-793-3600
Indiana State Tourism Development/1 N Capital, Indianapolis, IN	317-232-8860
Iowa State Development Commission/600 E Court Ave #A, Des Moines, IA	515-281-3251
Kansas State Dept-Econ Div/503 Kansas Ave, Topeka, KS	913-296-3481
Location Services Film & Video/417 S 3rd St, Minneapolis, MN	612-338-3359
Manya Nogg Co/9773 Lafayette Plaza, Omaha, NB	402-397-8887
Michigan State Travel Bureau/PO Box 30226, Lansing, MI	517-373-0670
Minnesota State Tourism Division/419 N Robert, St Paul, MN	612-296-5029

Missouri State Tourism Commission/301 W High St, Jefferson City, MO	314-751-3051
ND State Business & Industrial/Liberty Memorial Bldg, Bismarck, ND	701-224-2810
Ohio Film Bureau/30 E Broad St, Columbus, OH	614-466-2284
Station 12 Producers Express/1759 Woodgrove Ln, Southfield, MI	313-569-7707
Stock Market/4211 Flora Place, St Louis, MO	314-773-2298

SOUTHWEST

Alamo Village/PO Box 528, Brackettville, TX	512-563-2580
Arkansas State Dept of Economics/#1 Capital Mall, Little Rock, AR	501-371-1121
Blair, Tanya Agency/3000 Carlisle, Dallas, TX	214-748-8353
Cinema America/Box 56566, Houston, TX	713-780-8819
Dawson, Kim Agency/PO Box 585060, Dallas, TX	214-638-2414
Duncan, S Wade/PO Box 140273, Dallas, TX	214-828-1367
El Paso Film Liaison/5 Civic Center Plaza, El Paso, TX	915-544-3650
Epic Film Productions/1203 W 44th St, Austin, TX	512-452-9461
Fashion Consultants/262 Camelot Center, Richardson, TX	214-234-4006
Flach, Bob/3513 Norma, Garland, TX	214-272-8431
Fowlkes, Rebecca W/412 Canterbury Hill, San Antonio, TX	512-826-4142
Grapevine Productions/3214-A Hemlock Avenue, Austin, TX	512-472-0894
Greenblatt, Linda/6722 Waggoner, Dallas, TX	214-691-6552
Griffin, Gary Productions/12667 Memorial Dr #4, Houston, TX	713-465-9017
Kessel, Mark/3631 Granada, Dallas, TX	214-526-0415
MacLean, John/10017 Woodgrove, Dallas, TX	214-343-0181
Maloy, Buz/Rt 1 Box 155, Kyle, TX	512-398-3148
Maloy, John W/718 W 35th St, Austin, TX	512-453-9660
McLaughlin, Ed M/3512 Rashti Court, Ft Worth, TX	817-927-2310
Murray Getz Commer & Indust Phot/2310 Genessee, Houston, TX	713-526-4451
Nichols, Beverly & Skipper Richardson/6043 Vanderbilt Ave, Dallas, TX	214-349-3171
OK State Tourism-Rec Dept/500 Will Rogers Bldg, Oklahoma City, OK	405-521-3981
Oklahoma Film Comm/500 Will Rogers Bldg, Oklahoma City, OK	405-521-3525
Putman, Eva M/202 Dover, Richardson, TX	214-783-9616
Ranchland - Circle R/Rt 3, Box 229, Roanoke, TX	817-430-1561
Ray, Al/2304 Houston Street, San Angelo, TX	915-949-2716
Ray, Rudolph/2231 Freeland Avenue, San Angelo, TX	915-949-6784
Reinninger, Laurence H/501 North IH 35, Austin, TX	512-478-8593
San Antonio Zoo & Aquar/3903 N St Marys, San Antonio, TX	512-734-7184
Senn, Loyd C/PO Box 6060, Lubbock, TX	806-792-2000
Summers, Judy/1504 Harvard, Houston, TX	713-661-1440
Taylor, Peggy Talent/6311 N O'Connor 3 Dallas Comm, Irving, TX	214-869-1515
TBK Talent Enterprises/5255 McCullough, San Antonio, TX	512-822-0508
Texas Film Commission/PO Box 12428 Capitol Station, Austin, TX	512-475-3785
Texas Pacific Film Video, Inc/501 North IH 35, Austin, TX	512-478-8585
Texas World Entrtnmnt/8133 Chadbourne Road, Dallas, TX	214-358-0857
Tucson Film Comm/Ofc of Mayor Box 27370, Tucson, AZ	602-791-4000
Wild West Stunt Company/Box T-789, Stephenville, TX	817-965-4342
Young Film Productions/PO Box 50105, Tucson, AZ	602-623-5961
Zimmerman and Associates, Inc/411 Bonham, San Antonio, TX	512-225-6708
Zuniga, Tony/2616 North Flores #2, San Antonio, TX	512-227-9660

ROCKY MOUNTAIN

Montana Film Office/1424 Ninth Ave, Helena, MT	406-449-2654
Wyoming Film Comm/IH 25 & College Dr #51, Cheyenne, WY	307-777-7851

WEST COAST

California Film Office/6922 Hollywood Blvd, Hollywood, CA	213-736-2465
Daniels, Karil, Point of View Prod/2477 Folsom St, San Francisco, CA	415-821-0435
Design Art Studios/1128 N Las Palmas, Hollywood, CA	213-464-9118
Excor Travel/1750 Kalakaua Ave #116, Honolulu, HI	808-946-6614

Film Permits Unlimited/8058 Allott Ave, Van Nuys, CA	213-997-6197
Herod, Thomas Jr/PO Box 2534, Hollywood, CA	213-353-0911
Juckes, Geoff/3185 Durand Dr, Hollywood, CA	213-465-6604
The Location Co/8646 Wilshire Blvd, Beverly Hills, CA	213-855-7075
Location Enterprises Inc/6725 Sunset Blvd, Los Angeles, CA	213-469-3141
Mindseye/767 Northpoint, San Francisco, CA	415-441-4578
Minot, Abby/53 Canyon Rd, Berkeley, CA	415-841-9600
Newhall Ranch/23823 Valencia, Valencia, CA	818-362-1515
Pacific Production & Location Svc/424 Nahua St, Honolulu, HI	808-926-6188
San Francisco Conv/Visitors Bur/1390 Market St #260, San Francisco, CA	415-626-5500

SETS

NEW YORK CITY

Abstracta Structures/347 Fifth Ave	212-532-3710
Alcamo Marble Works/541 W 22nd St	212-255-5224
Baker, Alex/30 W 69th St	212-799-2069
Coulson, Len/717 Lexington Ave	212-688-5155
Dynamic Interiors/760 McDonald Ave	718-435-6326
Golden Office Interiors/574 Fifth Ave	212-719-5150
LaFerla, Sandro/108 W 25th St	212-620-0693
Lincoln Scenic Studio/560 W 34th St	212-244-2700
Moroxko, Bruce/41 White St	212-226-8832
Oliphant, Sarah/38 Cooper Square	212-741-1233
Plexability Ltd/200 Lexington Ave	212-679-7826
Set Shop/3 W 20 St	212-929-4845
Siciliano, Frank/125 Fifth Ave	212-620-4075
Stage Scenery/155 Attorney St	212-460-5050
Theater Technology Inc/37 W 20th St	212-929-5380
Variety Scenic Studio/25-19 Borden Ave	718-392-4747
Yurkiw, Mark/568 Broadway	212-243-0928

NORTHEAST

The Focarino Studio/31 Deep Six Dr, East Hampton, NY	516-324-7637
Foothills Theater Company/PO Box 236, Worcester, MA	617-754-0546
Penrose Productions/4 Sandalwood Dr, Livingston, NJ	201-992-4264
Trapp, Patricia/42 Stanton Rd, Brookline, MA	617-734-9321
Videocom, Inc/502 Sprague St, Dedham, MA	617-329-4080
White Oak Design/PO Box 1164, Marblehead, MA	617-426-7171

SOUTHEAST

Crigler, MB/Smooth As Glass Prod Svcs/607 Bass St, Nashville, TN	615-254-6061
Enter Space/20 14th St NW, Atlanta, GA	404-885-1139
The Great Southern Stage/15221 NE 21 Ave, N Miami Beach, FL	305-947-0430
Kupersmith, Tony/320 N Highland Ave NE, Atlanta, GA	404-577-5319
Sugar Creek Scenic Studio, Inc/465 Bishop St, Atlanta, GA	404-351-9404

MIDWEST

Becker Studio/2824 W Taylor, Chicago, IL	312-722-4040
Centerwood Cabinets/3700 Main St NE, Blaine, MN	612-786-2094
Chicago Scenic Studios Inc/213 N Morgan, Chicago, IL	312-942-1483
Dimension Works/4130 W Belmont, Chicago, IL	312-545-2233
Douglas Design/2165 Lakeside Ave, Cleveland, OH	216-621-2558
Grand Stage Lighting Co/630 W Lake, Chicago, IL	312-332-5611
Morrison, Tamara/1225 Morse, Chicago, IL	312-864-0954

SOUTHWEST

Country Roads/701 Ave B, Del Rio, TX	512-775-7991
Crabb, Ken/3066 Ponder Pl, Dallas, TX	214-352-0581
Dallas Stage Lighting & Equipment/1818 Chestnut, Dallas, TX	214-428-1818
Dallas Stage Scenery Co, Inc/3917 Willow St, Dallas, TX	214-821-0002

PRODUCTION/SUPPORT SERVICES CONT'D.

Please send us your additions and updates.

Dunn, Glenn E/7412 Sherwood Rd, Austin, TX	512-441-0377
Edleson, Louis/6568 Lake Circle, Dallas, TX	214-823-7180
Eschberger, Jerry/6401 South Meadows, Austin, TX	512-447-4795
Freeman Design & Display Co/2233 Irving Blvd, Dallas, TX	214-638-8800
H & H Special Effects/2919 Chisholm Trail, San Antonio, TX	512-826-8214
Houston Stage Equipment/2301 Dumble, Houston, TX	713-926-4441
Reed, Bill Decorations/333 First Ave, Dallas, TX	214-823-3154
Texas Scenic Co Inc/5423 Jackwood Dr, San Antonio, TX	512-684-0091
Texas Set Design/3103 Oak Lane, Dallas, TX	214-426-5511

ROCKY MOUNTAIN

Love, Elisa/1035 Walnut, Boulder, CO	303-442-4877

WEST COAST

Grosh, R L & Sons Scenic Studio/4144 Sunset Blvd, Los Angeles, CA	213-662-1134
Act Design & Execution/PO Box 5054, Sherman Oaks, CA	818-788-4219
American Scenery/18555 Eddy St, Northridge, CA	818-886-1585
Backings, J C/10201 W Pico Blvd, Los Angeles, CA	213-277-0522
Carthay Set Services/5176 Santa Monica Blvd, Hollywood, CA	213-469-5618
Carthay Studio/5907 W Pico, Los Angeles, CA	213-938-2101
CBS Special Effects/7800 Beverly Blvd, Los Angeles, CA	213-852-2345
Cloutier Inc/704 N Gardner, Los Angeles, CA	213-655-1263
Erecter Set Inc/1150 S LaBrea, Hollywood, CA	213-938-4762
Grosh, RL & Sons/4144 Sunset Blvd, Los Angeles, CA	213-662-1134
Hawaii Design Create/1750 Kalakaua Ave #116, Honolulu, HI	808-235-2262
Hollywood Scenery/6605 Elenor Ave, Hollywood, CA	213-467-6272
Hollywood Stage/6650 Santa Monica Blvd, Los Angeles, CA	213-466-4393
Krofft Entrprs/1040 Las Palmas, Hollywood, CA	213-467-3125
Pacific Studios/8315 Melrose Ave, Los Angeles, CA	213-653-3093
Producers Studio/650 N Bronson Ave, Los Angeles, CA	213-466-3111
RJ Show Time/1011 Gower St, Hollywood, CA	213-467-2127
Shafton Inc/5500 Cleon Ave, N Hollywood, CA	818-985-5025
Superstage/5724 Santa Monica Blvd, Los Angeles, CA	213-464-0296
Triangle Scenery/1215 Bates Ave, Los Angeles, CA	213-661-1262

INDEX
Photographers

INDEX

continued on next page

INDEX
Photographers

continued from previous page